Issues in
Monetary
Economics

PROCEEDINGS OF THE 1972
MONEY STUDY GROUP CONFERENCE

EDITED BY

H. G. JOHNSON

AND

A. R. NOBAY

OXFORD UNIVERSITY PRESS

1974

Oxford University Press, Ely House, London W.1

GLASGOW NEW YORK TORONTO MELBOURNE WELLINGTON
CAPE TOWN IBADAN NAIROBI DAR ES SALAAM LUSAKA ADDIS ABABA
DELHI BOMBAY CALCUTTA MADRAS KARACHI LAHORE DACCA
KUALA LUMPUR SINGAPORE HONG KONG TOKYO

CASEBOUND ISBN 0 19 877021 9
PAPERBACK ISBN 0 19 877022 7

© OXFORD UNIVERSITY PRESS 1974

PRINTED IN GREAT BRITAIN
BY WILLIAM CLOWES & SONS, LIMITED
LONDON, BECCLES AND COLCHESTER

PREFACE

THE Money Study Group was formed in 1969 with the dual objectives of bringing together people in the United Kingdom concerned with the understanding of and research into the British monetary system, whether as academic scholars, bank economists, or officials of the Bank of England and the Treasury, and promoting research into monetary economics in the United Kingdom. The Group subscribes to no particular school of monetary doctrine; its membership includes Keynesians, monetarists, empiricists, and institutionalists.

The main activities of the Group to date have been directly or indirectly concerned with the organization of seminars and conferences on a wide range of monetary issues. In all, three conferences were held during the Group's first three years of activity. The first of these, meeting in Hove in November 1969, commemorated the tenth anniversary of the publication of the Radcliffe Report—the conference papers surveyed subsequent developments in the monetary field, both in institutions and policy and in empirical and theoretical work. The second conference, held in Sheffield in September 1970, again centred on issues directly in the field of monetary economics, whilst the third conference, held in London in February 1971, concentrated on the problems raised by the current inflation. The Group's seminars, held regularly at the London School of Economics, and financed by a grant from the Social Science Research Council, provide an important regular forum where research papers are presented to an audience of mainly academic scholars from various universities in the United Kingdom. On two occasions the Group has organized special seminars: in June 1971 to discuss the Bank of England's then consultative document on competition and credit control, which has since been implemented, and the Oxford seminar in honour of Sir John Hicks, held in July 1972. In addition to publishing the proceedings of the conferences and seminars, the Group has gathered together a comprehensive and hitherto unavailable volume of readings in British monetary economics.[1]

---

[1] The relevant publications are: D. Croome and H. G. Johnson (eds.), *Money in Britain* (Oxford, 1970); G. Clayton, J. C. Gilbert, and R. Sedgwick (eds.), *Monetary Theory and Monetary Policy in the 1970s* (Oxford, 1971); H. G.

This volume contains the proceedings of a major conference organized by the Money Study Group at Bournemouth in February 1972 and is designed to focus discussion on topics and research work in progress that previous conferences and seminars had suggested would warrant further attention. The papers centred around four major issues in monetary economics: money in an international economy, recent developments in monetary theory, money and economic activity, and recent developments in British monetary policy.

An important gap in the literature, as viewed from the standpoint of current issues of theory and policy, is the absence of a good treatment of international monetary aspects of and constraints on the conduct of monetary policy in open economies. We invited papers on the efficacy of monetary policy under fixed exchange rates by Swoboda, optimum currency areas and European monetary integrations by Pearce, and the control of international liquidity and the Euro-dollar market by Hirsch.

Two main developments in monetary theory were singled out for attention—the post-Patinkin developments in the theory of transactions costs, payment periods, and employment (Barro and Santomero) and the Tobin–Markowitz portfolio-balance approach to liquidity preference theory (Flemming).

At the Sheffield conference a considerable amount of lively discussion centred around the role of money in economic activity. The proliferation of large-scale economy-wide models and other econometric work offered an opportunity to evaluate the interaction between money and the real sector. Fisher and Sheppard provided an extensive survey of U.S. econometric studies. Sectoral micro-analysis with macro-econometric results for the U.S. were provided by Brechling in a study of neo-classical investment behaviour and the role of monetary policy, and by Wood in a study of commercial Bank loan and investment behaviour. Feige presented a survey of U.S. studies which have estimated demand functions for demand deposits utilizing pooled temporal cross-section data to draw conclusions concerning the degree of substitution between liquid assets. Three studies relating to the U.K. economy were

Johnson and A. R. Nobay (eds.), *The Current Inflation* (London, 1971); the September 1971 issue of the *Bankers' Magazine* (Competition and Credit Control Seminar); H. G. Johnson *et al.* (eds.), *Readings in British Monetary Economics* (Oxford, 1972), and the February 1973 issue of *Economica* (Sir John Hicks Seminar).

presented: a model of the U.K. monetary authorities' behaviour by Nobay reporting on research being undertaken at Southampton, a paper on the Sheffield research into financial intermediation in the U.K. by Clayton *et al.*, and research at the Bank of England on the term structures of debt and interest rates by White.

As mentioned earlier, there has been a revival of monetary policy and a re-evaluation of the techniques of monetary policy in the U.K., following the Bank of England's June 1971 document on competition and credit control. These developments were the subject of a special seminar convened at that time, and the session on domestic monetary policy provided a timely opportunity to carry out a further appraisal of the new measures. The paper by Artis considered policy in the 1970s in the light of the new measures, Harrington explained the implications of the role of competition for credit control, and Lomax provided a banker's view on the reforms.

Partly in view of his great influence on monetary theory, we wished to honour Don Patinkin. For this purpose, we invited him to give the first Sir Dennis Robertson lecture. We have named this honorific lecture after one whom we consider to have been the most subtle and undervalued of Keynes's contemporaries in the field of monetary economics. We also wished, in a period of hectic change in U.S. monetary policy, to provide our participants with a fresh and current view of developments there—hence we invited A. J. Meigs. These two events of the conference are collected in the Introductory section of the volume.

The sections of this volume are introduced by the Chairmen of the conference sessions, who were asked to go beyond the usual responsibilities of chairmen in placing the papers for their sessions in the perspective of the session fields. We wish to thank them, the conference contributors, and the official discussants. We should also like to thank the participants, whether on the official programme or not, for penetrating discussion from the floor that made the Conference an exceptionally lively and useful one. We regret that space limitations preclude us from following the useful practices of some conferences in either providing summaries of the floor discussions or inviting written versions of the unofficial discussants' comments; but the revised versions of the programme papers have benefited from the points made in the discussions.

We should like to thank the Committee of London Clearing Bankers for the financial support that made a conference on such a scale possible. One of the objectives of the Money Study Group, as noted above, has been to bring together monetary economists from all sectors of the British economy, and we are gratified that this endeavour has won the confidence of the financial community.

Finally, our grateful thanks are due to Phyl Barratt and Lois Rodgers for patient administrative and secretarial assistance.

H. G. JOHNSON
(*London School of Economics
and University of Chicago*)

A. R. NOBAY
(*University of Southampton
and Queen's University, Ontario*)

CONTENTS

I

SPECIAL GUEST LECTURES

Don Patinkin
A. James Meigs

KEYNESIAN MONETARY THEORY AND THE CAMBRIDGE SCHOOL*

DON PATINKIN
(*Hebrew University of Jerusalem*)

I AM indeed honoured to be invited here this evening in order to present the Sir Dennis Robertson lecture. I still remember with pleasure my first—and, unfortunately for me, only—meeting with Robertson some twenty years ago, as well as the discussions we continued to carry on by correspondence in subsequent years. And I find it particularly appropriate that my subject for this lecture deals with the very school of which Robertson himself was such an illustrious member.

Let me, then, turn to my subject. The monetarist revival of the last decade and more has been accompanied—especially in recent years—by a renewed interest in the nature of the quantity theory before Keynes. In this connection it seems to me that present-day adherents of this theory have claimed too much for it—and correspondingly too little for the Keynesian theory.[1]

The exaggerated claims for the quantity theory have expressed themselves in the attempt (especially by Milton Friedman) to present Keynes's monetary theory not as a new theory, but as a variation on the Cambridge cash-balance theory. It is this contention that I shall here examine—and, on the basis of this examination,

* I am very grateful to Stanley Fischer for helpful comments on an earlier draft. I am also indebted to Lord Robbins for illuminating discussions of various points dealt with here.

I wish to thank Allan Drazen and Akiva Offenbacher for their assistance. I am also indebted to the Central Research Fund of the Hebrew University of Jerusalem, and to the Israel Academy of Sciences and Humanities for research grants to cover the costs of technical assistance.

The reader is asked to keep in mind that this paper was delivered as the opening address of a conference—and to excuse accordingly various facetious remarks. A version of the paper has been previously published in the journal of the Banco Nationale De Lavoro.

[1] In what follows, I shall make free use of Patinkin (1969, 1972a, and 1972b).

reject. And lest I be misunderstood (though there is really no reason that I should), I should like to emphasize at the outset that this examination should not be interpreted as a criticism of the Cambridge school. For I would certainly consider it unjustified to criticize these economists for not having fully understood and integrated into their thinking what we have succeeded in learning only in the course of the subsequent development of Keynesian monetary theory. My criticism is only of those who make exaggerated claims for the Cambridge economists.

Before embarking on this examination, I would like to say a few words about my general approach to doctrinal history—which is certainly not an unusual one. This approach can be succinctly summarized by the statement that isolated passages do not a theory make. Instead, one of our major concerns in the study of the history of theory is the determination of the extent to which ideas expressed at various points in a work are integrated into—and hence really part of—its main theoretical framework. And this accordingly will be my major concern this evening.

Another point that I should clarify at the outset is my use of the terms 'quantity theory' and 'Keynesian theory'. By the first of these I mean—quite pragmatically—the monetary theory expounded at the end of the nineteenth century and through the late 1920s by Irving Fisher in the U.S. and by the Cambridge school (Marshall, Pigou, Robertson, Lavington—and the younger Keynes) in this country.

By 'Keynesian monetary theory' I mean the one developed in the *General Theory* and the literature to which it gave rise—though I should note that the aspect of the theory that is my primary concern here (namely, the treatment of money from the viewpoint of the choice of an optimum portfolio) is in some respects more precisely developed in Keynes's *Treatise on Money* and Hicks's 'Suggestion for Simplifying the Theory of Money'.[2] In so far as the later development is concerned, I have in mind in particular the work of James Tobin and his colleagues. And in a small voice I add: and Milton Friedman too. A small voice—because I do not want right at the beginning of this Conference to run the risk of setting off a violent argument. Nor do I want to offend the man who is really responsible for my being here this evening; for surely you

[2] Keynes (1930, i, pp. 36, 140–6, 248–57); Hicks (1935). Shackle (1967, pp. 222–7), however, claims that there are important differences between these two treatments.

would not have brought me all the way from Israel to speak on this antiquarian subject in a conference devoted to such currently pressing matters as European monetary integration, commercial bank behaviour, and U.K. monetary policy in the 1970s, were it not for the reawakened interest in the doctrinal history of the quantity theory that has been sparked in recent years by Friedman's repeated and provocative assertions about its alleged nature.

By the foregoing definition of the quantity theory, I obviously do not mean to imply that Fisher and the Cambridge school are coterminous with the quantity theory. Indeed, at the same time that they were doing their work, Léon Walras in Switzerland was developing his version of the quantity theory in terms of the *encaisse désirée*. And Knut Wicksell in Sweden (whom I continue to regard—by virtue of his own repeated declarations—as a quantity theorist) was making his invaluable contribution to our understanding of the way the quantity theory manifests itself through the interest-rate mechanism in an economy with a banking system.

But since neither Walras nor Wicksell had the sense to write in English, the sad fact—that at the time prompted the gentle chiding of Myrdal (1939 (1933), p. 8) about 'the attractive Anglo-Saxon kind of unnecessary originality'—the sad fact is that Wicksell's work, for instance, did not become known in this country until the mid-1920s. Furthermore—if I make the proper inference from Keynes's *Treatise* (i, pp. 186–8, 196–9, and especially p. 199, footnote 2)—the development of Keynes's thinking even then was not influenced by Wicksell. For this reason the work of Walras and Wicksell has no bearing on the question that concerns us, namely the relationship of Keynesian monetary theory as here defined to the quantity theory that Keynes knew and, indeed, at one time helped to develop.

I would like to emphasize one further point: what interests me now is monetary theory, not monetary policy. These represent two different spheres of discourse. And whatever the relationship between the two, it is clearly not a one-to-one correspondence: different policy recommendations can emanate from the same conceptual theoretical framework; and different frameworks can lead to the same policy recommendation.

Some of the clearest examples of this can be taken from the monetary field itself. Thus those of us who studied at Chicago under Henry Simons did not need the conceptual framework of the *General Theory* to advocate vigorously government deficits to combat depressions; for quite independently of Keynes—and, indeed, before the *General Theory*—Simons taught this to his students on the basis of the conceptual framework embodied in Fisher's $MV = PT$. Indeed, Simons taught us not to suffer patiently those conventional souls who continued to preach the righteous orthodoxy of a balanced budget even in the face of mass unemployment.

I might digress for a moment to note that Simons was far from being a voice in the wilderness at that time in the U.S.—and that there were then also similar voices here in England. Thus in a most remarkable passage in a work systematically based on the quantity theory, Pigou (1933, p. 213) made the distinction that only Keynesians are supposed to make between the efficacy of monetary policy in countering expansionary forces in the economy by raising the bank rate sufficiently and the limitations to which monetary policy is subject in countering 'a contraction in aggregate money income'. For though it is 'always possible for the Central Bank, by open market operations, to force out money into balances held by the public . . . there may be *no* positive rate of money interest that will avail to get this money used'. (A 'liquidity trap' at zero interest!) In such circumstances, Pigou continued, a purely monetary policy is 'bound to fail. If, however, at the same time that the banking system keeps money cheap, the government adopts a policy of public works, the risk of failure is greatly reduced.'[3]

Thus both quantity theorists and Keynesians—each from their own conceptual framework—advocated policies of combating unemployment by public-works expenditures and/or deficit financing. Conversely—and once again I must speak in a small voice— the common conceptual framework of most monetary theorists today—Friedman as well as Tobin—is (as I shall argue this evening) the Keynesian one; but this has clearly not precluded the emergence from this framework of quite different policy recommendations, based both on different political philosophies and on different interpretations of the empirical findings.

(As an aside, I might quite frankly note that what generates in me a great deal of scepticism about the state of our discipline is the

---

[3] Italics in original.

Actually, this passage is not as Keynesian as it sounds; for Pigou presents his argument in the Wicksellian terms of the effect of such public-works expenditure on the difference between the actual bank rate and the 'proper' one. At the same time, he does recognize that a decrease in public-works expenditures 'directly contracts to [the?] real demand for labour' (Pigou, 1933, pp. 213–14, especially footnote 1).

high positive correlation between the policy views of a researcher (or, what is worse, of his thesis director) and his empirical findings. I will begin to believe in economics as a science when out of Yale there comes an empirical Ph.D. thesis demonstrating the supremacy of monetary policy in some historical episode—and out of Chicago, one demonstrating the supremacy of fiscal policy.)

In any event, the examples of Simons, Pigou, and others have led me to suspect that the real Keynesian Revolution took place not in the sphere of economic policy (where changes were already occurring in the early 1930s), but in that of economic theory. I suspect that the real change wrought by Keynes's *General Theory* was in the conceptual framework from which we viewed the problems of employment, interest, and money. But that is a question that I shall defer for discussion on another occasion.[4]

I. On the meaning of a new theory

Let me return to our main question. Consider the familiar representation of the Keynesian model in terms of a simultaneous analysis of the markets for commodities and money. I think that everyone would agree that the conceptual framework of effective demand that Keynes developed to analyse equilibrium in the commodity market was indeed a new one (leaving aside the case of Kalecki and perhaps one or two other possible precursors). The question is whether the same can be said for the conceptual framework of liquidity preference that Keynes developed to analyse equilibrium in the money market. In order to answer that question, we must first clarify what we mean by a 'new theory'.

Those of us who live in Jerusalem need not be reminded of the words of a wise man of our city—many, many centuries ago—that there is nothing new under the sun. Clearly, every theory advanced at one point in time has some antecedents in earlier theories. Nevertheless, there are stages in the development of a science where, by consensus, a 'new' theory is said to develop. And one of the major questions discussed by philosophers and historians of science are the characteristics which justify calling a theory 'new'.[5] Some

---

[4] I might, however, note that I find support for the foregoing view in Winch's study (1969) of English economic thought and policy in the 1920s and early 1930s, and in Davis's corresponding study (1971) for the U.S.A. See also Hutchison (1953, ch. 24, 1968 Appendix).

[5] Cf. Kuhn (1970); see also Joseph Agassi (1968) and Stigler (1955).

related questions that I have already alluded to are the difference between 'the asides' referring to an idea in the antecedent theories, as compared with its 'systematic development' in the 'new theory'; and the difference between 'mentioning an idea in passing' or 'as an aside', as compared with 'integrating it into one's thinking'.

By their very nature, questions of this type are not susceptible of hard-and-fast answers. The general type of answer that has on occasion been given—and that I would like to give here—is that a theory is 'new' if it deals in a different manner with one of the central concepts of the science. Similarly, it is 'new' if it stimulates concentrated research along hitherto neglected directions.

Now, that does not take us very far, for it has merely replaced the mystery of 'new' by that of 'central' and 'neglected'. Still I think it can help us on the question now at issue.

Before turning to this issue, I would like to illustrate these distinctions in terms of another recent episode in the history of economic theory—the development of Friedman's permanent-income hypothesis. As we all know, the essence of this theory is that the individual's current consumption depends not on his current (or 'measured') income, but on his wealth or its surrogate, permanent income.

Now, in a sense this theory can be said to be incorporated already in Fisher's 1907 analysis, in his *Rate of Interest*,[6] of the individual maximizing his utility over two periods subject to the present value of his income stream. And, indeed, by his generous references to Fisher, Friedman (1957, p. 7) even encourages us to think in this way.

Even more to the point is Hicks's detailed and systematic 1939 discussion in his *Value and Capital* of the meaning of income—to which Friedman also refers (1957, p. 10, footnote 4); for in this discussion Hicks addressed himself directly to the question of the proper measure of an individual's income during a given period of time—and explains why, in a non-stationary economy, 'we should not regard the whole of his current receipts as income' (1939, p. 172). Instead, Hicks went on to explain, 'the calculation of income consists in finding some sort of *standard* stream of values whose present capitalized value equals the present value of the stream of receipts which is actually in prospect' (ibid., p. 184, italics in original).

But despite these discussions, the earlier Keynesian literature—

[6] This analysis is essentially repeated in Fisher's later *Theory of Interest* (1930).

and the related econometric studies in particular—all analysed consumption as a function of current income—with no one (not even—to the best of my knowledge—Hicks) criticizing this procedure. And even after the post-war failure to predict consumption correctly[7] led to the introduction of additional variables into these functions—including lagged income, and even lagged consumption—there was no full understanding of what this meant. Thus, for example, Klein and Goldberger (1955, p. 8) explained their introduction of lagged consumption into the function in terms of their contention that 'consumer behavior tends to be repetitive to some extent'.

Now 'all' that Friedman did was to infer from Fisher's analysis that the proper measure of income for use in the consumption function is an estimate of permanent income provided by an average of income over several periods of time. (Friedman's rationalization of this procedure is far more sophisticated—as is also the average he uses—but for our present purposes we can look at it in this oversimplified way.) But this 'simple suggestion'—as well as some related ones—sufficed to bring about a revolution in the way economists viewed the process of consumption, and to stimulate accordingly concentrated empirical research along hitherto neglected directions. Consumption has never been the same since.

This episode illustrates, better than any other that I can think of, one of the fundamental facts of the history of ideas: namely, that in general the full implications of a set of ideas are not immediately seen. Indeed, as frequently noted, if they were, then all mathematics would be a tautology; for its theorems are implicit in the assumptions made.

I think that all of us must be aware of these aspects of *la condition humaine*. I am sure all of us will empathize with my colleague Nissan Liviatan, who in one of our recent departmental seminars quietly answered the criticism that something he said was a tautology with the words 'Whether or not something is a tautology depends on how fast you think.'

Similarly, I am sure that all of us have had the experience of saying in the course of our work on a certain problem: 'Now why didn't I see that before?' If we are fortunate, we say this at some

[7] The role of these failures in generating the new theories of consumption can well be interpreted in terms of Kuhn's emphasis on the general feeling of dissatisfaction ('crisis in the scientific community') that leads to the development of a new theory (Kuhn, 1970, chs. 7–8).

later stage of the work when we indeed achieve that 'moment of truth' that enables us to see the deeper meaning of what we have done. And if we are less fortunate, we say it only after someone else has pointed it out.

II. The novelty of Keynesian monetary theory: stocks and flows

This is the viewpoint from which I approach the question of the novelty of Keynesian monetary theory.

To begin with, I think that we are all agreed that one of the central distinctions of economic theory is that between stocks and flows. Correspondingly, what I would consider to be one of the hallmarks of Keynesian monetary theory is the sharp distinction it draws between the two sets of decisions an individual has to make: the decision as to the forms in which to hold his stock of wealth at a given instant of time, and particularly the amount to be held in money; and the decision as to the rate at which to add to this wealth over time—i.e. the decision as to the flows of savings and investment.

The Keynesian approach has led to the development of the theory of the demand for money as part of a general theory of the choice of an optimum portfolio of assets. Correspondingly, the emphasis of this theory is on the optimal relationship between the stock of money and the stocks of other assets, as influenced primarily by the alternative rates of return available on these assets. Other determinants of this demand are the total wealth of the individual (which defines the wealth restraint that must be satisfied by the portfolio of assets) and the flow of income (which is the major determinant of the transactions demand for money).[8]

All agree that this conceptual framework is quite different from that of Fisher. The question is whether it is also different from that of the Cambridge school. (I might incidentally note that the sharp contrast that is traditionally drawn between the 'mechanical' Fisher and the 'behaviouristic' Cambridge economists is, in my opinion, largely a Cantabridgian tale; but the discussion of that question too must be deferred to another occasion.) Let me, then,

---

[8] This approach has received its most formal development at the hands of James Tobin (1955, 1963, 1969) and, more recently, Duncan Foley and Miguel Sidrauski (1971). The individual in this development is conceived as making his optimizing decisions while being subject to a wealth (stock) restraint as well as an income (flow) restraint.

See also Gurley and Shaw (1960).

contrast the foregoing conceptual framework with that of the Cambridge school—and with that of Keynes of the *Tract on Monetary Reform* in particular.

There is no doubt that Keynes of the *General Theory* is at one with Keynes of the *Tract* (1923, pp. 78–9) in taking as his point of departure the individual's demand for money holdings. Thus in his exposition of the *Tract* (which he explicitly bases on Marshall (1923) and Pigou (1917–18)) Keynes wrote that the demand for real 'purchasing power' in the form of money holdings depends

partly on the wealth of the community, partly on its habits. Its habits are fixed by its estimation of the extra convenience of having more cash in hand as compared with the advantages to be got from spending the cash or investing it. The point of equilibrium is reached where the estimated advantages of keeping more cash in hand compared with those of spending or investing it about balance. The matter cannot be summed up better than in the words of Dr. Marshall [1923, p. 78].

And here Keynes quotes at length from Marshall's well-known discussion in his *Money, Credit and Commerce* (1923, pp. 44–5)—which goes back to much earlier statements—about 'the fraction of their income which people find it worth while to keep in the form of currency', as well as Marshall's example of an economy whose inhabitants 'find it just worth their while to keep by them on the average ready-purchasing power to the extent of a tenth part of their annual income, together with a fiftieth part of their property'.[9] Keynes also notes, when referring to Marshall's discussion of the antecedents of this approach in the writings of Petty and others, that 'in modern conditions the normal proportion of the circulation [of money] to this national income seems to be somewhere between a tenth and a fifteenth' (Keynes, 1923, p. 79, footnote 1).

Actually, the clearest statement of the Cambridge approach—though one that Keynes does not cite, possibly because he was restricting himself to the writings of his teachers, as distinct from his contemporaries—is that of Lavington,[10] who also based himself on Marshall. After discussing 'the general principle on which an

[9] These passages are cited at length and further discussed in the Appendix below.

[10] Frederick Lavington (1881–1927) began his university studies (at Cambridge) relatively late (in 1908) after eleven years' service in a bank. He began his academic career at Cambridge in 1918, after a further period in administrative work. This late start—as well as his illness and early death—undoubtedly helps explain why his role in the development of Cambridge monetary thought was less than it otherwise would have been. But I suspect that an at least

individual distributes his resources among their various uses',
Lavington wrote:

Resources devoted to consumption supply an income of immediate
satisfaction; those held as a stock of currency yield a return of convenience and security; those devoted to investment in the narrower
sense of the term yield a return in the form of interest. In so far therefore as his judgement gives effect to his self-interest, the quantity of
resources which he holds in the form of money will be such that the
unit of resources which is just and only just worth while holding in this
form yields him a return of convenience and security equal to the yield
of satisfaction derived from the marginal unit spent on consumables, and
equal also to the net rate of interest (1921, p. 30; the reference to
Marshall is on p. 27).

I might note that no such passage appears in the first (1922) edition of Dennis Robertson's celebrated little volume on *Money* in
the Cambridge Economic Handbooks series—though there is one
in the third (1928) and later editions.

At first sight, these passages seem to indicate that the conceptual
approach of the Cambridge school did not differ much from that
of the later Keynesian monetary theory. What I shall, however,
now show is that this is not the case: First of all, there are some
substantive differences in the description of the optimum portfolio—
though less so with respect to Lavington than the others. Secondly—
and more important—the Cambridge economists did not recognize
the full implications of the optimum-portfolio approach to monetary
theory; they did not really integrate it into their thinking. In
particular, as I shall show in the next section, they failed to take
account of the implications of this approach at the appropriate
points in their discussions.

By my first point I mean that Cambridge monetary theory did
not draw the sharp and basic distinction Keynesian theory draws
between stocks and flows—and sometimes it even indiscriminately
interchanged 'wealth' and 'income'. Thus, it is not clear from the
foregoing passages whether the Cambridge economists conceived
of the individual as holding a quantity of money that is optimum

---

equally important factor was Lavington's self-effacing outlook on his own
work as reflected in his favourite saying that 'It's all in Marshall, if you'll
only take the trouble to dig it out.'

Cf. the obituaries of Lavington by H[arold] W[right] and C. R. F[ay] in
Economic Journal, xxxvii (1927), 503–5. (I am indebted to Lord Robbins for
the identification of Harold Wright, and for the information that Wright was
the author of the Cambridge Economic Handbook, *Population* (1923).)

with reference to his stocks of other assets, or optimum with reference to his income, or optimum with reference to some combination of the two.

In order to prevent any misunderstanding, I must emphasize that in actual fact the individual's holdings of money should be optimum with respect to both his wealth and his income. This, after all, is the view implicit in Keynes's liquidity-preference function $L_1(Y) + L_2(r)$—and explicit in the presentation of the demand for money by Tobin (1955, p. 208; 1969) and Foley and Sidrauski (1971, pp. 30-1). My point is, however, that some Cambridge economists (Pigou, Robertson, and possibly Lavington) expressed the demand for money as a function of income—without referring at all to wealth; and that even those who did refer to both wealth and income (Marshall and Keynes of the *Tract*) did so in a way that does not reveal awareness of the basically different roles these magnitudes play in determining the demand for money: namely, that tangible wealth is the variable that constitutes the total budget restraint on the holding of assets, including money—so that an increase in wealth generally results in increased holdings of all assets; whereas income is one of the relevant variables explaining the (transactions) demand for money in a portfolio of a given size—so that an increase in income increases the demand for money, at the expense of other assets.

In order to make this criticism more concrete, consider the basic passages from Marshall's *Money, Credit and Commerce* that Keynes cites in the *Tract* as an expression of his position too (above, p. 11). At one and the same time these consecutive passages present a theory of people's demand for money as a 'fraction of their income' and as 'a tenth part of their annual income, together with a fiftieth part of their property.' It is inconceivable to me that Marshall and Keynes of that time could have understood the full implications of the distinction between stocks and flows (and of the corresponding distinction between wealth and income), and yet that Marshall could have juxtaposed two such different descriptions of the demand for money—and that, even more so, Keynes could have cited them without comment.[11]

As further evidence on this point, consider Marshall's statement

[11] For further discussion of this point, see the Appendix below.

This failure of neoclassical economists to distinguish sharply between wealth and income may be related to the corresponding absence of a sharp distinction in the writings of the classical economists (and of Smith and Ricardo in particular), for whom capital (i.e. wealth) was last year's crop carried over to the current year.

that the 'relation between the volume of this currency and the general level of prices may be changed permanently by changes in . . . population and wealth, which change the aggregate income' (1923, p. 45). Marshall is clearly assuming here that an increase in wealth increases the demand for money only by first increasing the subsequent flow of income, and hence the transaction needs for money; there is no awareness here of the possibility that an increase in wealth may directly increase the demand for money as one of the assets in which form this wealth is held. In brief, if in modern monetary theory we sometimes use income as a proxy for wealth, here Marshall is using wealth as a proxy for income.

Significantly enough, my criticism on this point would seem to be related to one that Keynes of the *Treatise* makes of the Cambridge school, including explicitly Keynes of the *Tract*: namely, that the Cambridge equation $P = kR/M$—in which R represents 'the current income of the community'—can explain the demand for income (or demand) deposits, which are held for transactions needs; however, contends Keynes, it does not explain the demand for savings (or time) deposits. This demand, too, can be said to depend on the 'resources' of the individuals; 'but resources in this connection ought not be interpreted, as it is interpreted by Professor Pigou, as being identical with current *income*' (1930, i, pp. 231–2, italics in original).

I wish I could go on to say that Keynes explicitly states here that 'resources' in this connection should be interpreted as wealth. Unfortunately for me, he does not; but that this is what he meant is, I think, quite clear from Keynes's analysis earlier in the *Treatise* of the holding of saving deposits, in which he explicitly relates these holdings to the individual's total wealth, and not to the 'current increment' to this wealth (1930, i, pp. 140–1).

I must admit that Keynes's criticism here does not apply to Lavington, who explicitly stated that that part of the demand for money that is held as a contingency reserve changes 'in some measure independently of the volume of payments' (1921, p. 33). On the other hand, Lavington—unlike Keynes of the *Treatise*—does not relate this contingency reserve to the individual's wealth; nor does he relate its magnitude to the price of the securities that can be held as an alternative (Keynes, 1930, i, pp. 141–3). Instead, Lavington speaks only in general terms of the magnitude of this reserve being 'regulated largely by the general level of confidence' (1921, p. 33). It is also significant that Lavington himself considers his description of the demand for money as a contingency reserve to be 'rather different from (though not inconsistent with) that laid down by the Quantity theory' (1921, p. 32). Finally, it is significant that though Robertson ((1933) 1940, pp. 92–3)) defends the Cambridge equation against Keynes's criticisms here, he (Robertson), too, makes no mention of Lavington in this context.[12]

III. The novelty of Keynesian monetary theory: the recognition of the implications of the optimum-portfolio approach

The preceding discussion has explicated the distinction between Keynes and the Cambridge school that is reflected in their respective treatments of stocks and flows. A related distinction manifests itself in the already-noted fact that despite its description of an optimum portfolio, the Cambridge school did not realize the full implications of the portfolio approach to monetary theory. Conversely, it is the systematic application of this approach that is the hallmark of Keynesian monetary theory.

This distinction reflects itself, first of all, in the way these two approaches analyse the effects of a monetary increase on the economy. Keynesian theory analyses the initial impact of this increase on the balance sheet of the individual: it emphasizes that in order to persuade the public to hold a portfolio with such an increased stock of money, the rates of return on the other assets in this portfolio must fall. That is, stock equilibrium can be achieved now only at lower rates of return on these other assets. This decline in interest and other rates of return then increases the demand for the flow of consumption and (primarily) investment goods, thus disturbing the equilibrium in the commodity-flow markets, and thus causing an increase in output and/or prices (depending on the state of unemployment).

In brief, Keynesian theory analyses the impact of a monetary increase in terms of the substitution effects that it generates. I am sure that it will come as no surprise to anyone if I say that Keynesian economics is to be criticized for this concentration on the substitution effects, to the exclusion of the possible wealth—or real-balance— effect. For though there are indeed cases in which monetary changes do not generate a wealth effect (namely, some open-market operations),[13] there are other cases (namely, monetary changes generated by deficit financing) in which it does.

[12] For further details, see Appendix below.
[13] Cf. Patinkin (1965), ch. XII:4, especially p. 294, footnote 23.

On the other hand, I cannot think of a case in which a monetary change generates only a wealth effect, and not a substitution effect. And it is the fact that the Cambridge school nevertheless frequently analysed a monetary change precisely in this way that distinguishes it so sharply from the later Keynesian economics.

Ironically enough, this distinction is clearest from a passage by Keynes himself in the *Tract* that reads as follows: 'When people find themselves with more cash than they require..., they get rid of the surplus by buying goods or investments, or by leaving it for a bank to employ, or, possibly, by increasing their hoarded reserves' (1923, pp. 75–6; see also 1911). Thus Keynes here conceives of the individual as directly using his 'cash surplus' to increase his 'hoarded reserves', and makes no mention whatsoever of the variation in interest required to induce him to do so.[14] In this way Keynes fails to realize the full implications of his own description (cited above) of 'equilibrium [as being] reached where the estimated advantages of keeping more cash in hand compared with those of spending or investing it about balance' (1923, p. 78). He does not recognize the fact (that he was later to emphasize so systematically in the *General Theory*) that the monetary increase will disturb the foregoing balance at the margin—and that the individual's holdings of money and other assets can accordingly be in equilibrium once again only at a lower rate of interest.

The lack of appropriate references in the Cambridge literature to the dependence of the demand for money on interest is of great significance in the present discussion, not because such a dependence is necessarily of empirical importance, but because the recognition of such a dependence seems to me to constitute a critical and unambiguous indicator of whether the Cambridge economists really understood the analytical apparatus they described. Let me then provide some additional instances in which their writings fail to indicate such a recognition.

Thus, despite what I have said above, Cambridge economists did indeed assign an important role to changes in the rate of interest in their analysis of the effects of a monetary increase. But the

[14] I am indebted to Dr. Luigi Ceriani, editor of the Banco Nazionale del Lavoro: *Quarterly Review*, for pointing out an error in my original discussion of this passage. In that discussion I interpreted 'investments' as 'investment goods'—whereas it should have been clear from Keynes's use of 'investments' in other parts of the *Tract* (1923, pp. 5–7, 13 *et passim*) that what he meant by the term is *financial* investment—that is, the purchase of securities of various kinds.

way in which they discussed this role is itself evidence of how different their conceptual framework really was from that of the Keynesians. In particular, Marshall, Pigou, the younger Keynes, and other quantity theorists all analysed the effects of a monetary increase that reflected itself in the first instance in an increase in bank reserves. Indeed, this was the major case they considered. They argued that the resulting excess reserves would lead to an increased desire on the part of banks to make loans, hence to a decrease in the rate of interest[15] (Wicksell's 'money rate' or 'bank rate', though the Cambridge economists did not describe it in these terms), hence to increased borrowings, hence to increased demand for goods by the borrowers, and hence to a rise in prices.

Now, the interesting aspect of this description of the adjustment process is that none of these Cambridge economists even alluded to the fact—implicit in their analyses of the demand for money cited above—that the changes in the rate of interest would affect not only the amount of the public's borrowing, but also the quantity of money it chooses to hold.

A similar picture emerges when we consider the instances— unfortunately, few—in which Cambridge economists supplemented their theoretical monetary analysis with empirical observations.

Thus Pigou (1929, pp. 163–72) tried to apply to British data for the period 1878–1914 the same techniques used by Carl Snyder (1924) in his study of the equation of exchange for the U.S. Pigou concludes from the data that the higher price level of 1914 as compared with 1878 was the result of a higher velocity of circulation at that time (1914). Now, what is interesting about Pigou's discussion is that he does refer to the possibility that velocity is increased by an increasing price level (by Pigou's data (ibid., p. 592)—though he does not explicitly refer to them—prices had been *falling* before 1878, and had remained *constant* in the period 1912–14, which could have explained part of the higher velocity in the latter period). On the other hand, Pigou does not refer to the possible effect of changes in the rate of interest on velocity (though it must be conceded that the yield on consols in 1914 (3·3 per cent) was only slightly higher than in 1878 (3·2 per cent)) (*British Historical Statistics*, p. 455). Thus the evidence here is ambiguous.

[15] This can be interpreted as reflecting the optimum-portfolio adjustment of the banks; but the Cambridge economists did not present such an interpretation—nor should they be expected to have done so. Once again, however, Lavington (1921, pp. 30–1) is something of an exception; see Appendix below.

The situation with reference to Keynes is clearer. In his *Tract* (pp. 83–4) Keynes compares the data for prices and money supply in October 1920 with those for October 1922—and concludes that his k (which, of course, equals the Cambridge KT in the equation $M = KPT$) had increased significantly during this period. Now, Keynes does mention (though as the effect of the increase in k, and not as its cause) the sharp (33 per cent) decline in the price level during this period. On the other hand, he does not cite as a possible explanatory factor the fact that the yield on consols fell from 5·3 per cent in 1920 to 4·4 per cent in 1922—or that the maximum rate on three-month bills fell from 6·5 per cent in 1920 to 2·7 per cent in 1922. Of course, one might say that in accordance with Fisher's distinction between nominal and real rate of interest, this decline in nominal interest reflected in part the fact—which Keynes did mention—that the price level was declining. But it would be carrying things too far to try to explain away in this way Keynes's failure even to mention the rate of interest in this context.

Furthermore, in his immediately following discussion about the ways to stabilize k' (i.e. the real value of the demand for current deposits), Keynes states that 'a tendency of k' to increase may be somewhat counteracted by lowering the bank-rate, because easy lending diminishes the advantage of keeping a margin for contingencies in cash' (*ibid.*, p. 85). Now this sentence can be interpreted as reflecting the effect on the demand for money of the more ready availability of money substitutes like easy credit facilities. But however it is interpreted it will not yield a reaffirmation of the contention that, *ceteris paribus*, lowering the rate of interest causes an increase in k—and hence in the real amount of money demanded.

I might note that Pigou and Keynes are representative of what seems to have been a systematic tendency of quantity theorists to explain observed variations in the velocity of circulation in terms, not of the rate of interest, but of variations in the rate of change of prices (Patinkin, 1972a). Keynes's procedure on this score is particularly enigmatic; for in his description of the post-World War I inflations in his *Tract on Monetary Reform* (pp. 45 ff.), he provides a precise analysis of the influence of a high rate of increase of prices in causing the public to develop 'economizing habits' with reference to its demand for money; yet in his systematic presentation of the Cambridge demand for money (ibid., pp. 78 ff.) he does not mention this factor at all, but does analyse the influence of the rate of interest. In this discrepancy, too, I see additional evidence of the failure of the Cambridge economists to integrate the different elements of their monetary theory into their thinking.

A similar difference characterizes Pigou's analysis of the trade cycle (1929). Changes in the velocity of circulation play an important role in this analysis—but they are never related to the concurrent changes taking place (according to Pigou) in the rate of interest. Instead, the changes in velocity are attributed solely to the anticipation of price changes—and to changes in 'confidence'. A similar statement holds for Lavington's analysis (1922). As an aside, I might also note that the emphasis that both these writers placed on 'confidence' makes it clear that—in contrast with the 'modern quantity theory'—they did not think of velocity—and hence the demand for money—as a stable function of stipulated economic variables.

I would like to conclude this examination of the Cambridge literature with another indication of its failure to realize the full implication of its conceptual framework. It seems to me that if an economist has a full understanding of the portfolio approach to monetary theory, then one of the natural questions he will be led to ask is about the effects on the rates of returns of the various assets of a shift in tastes with reference to the forms in which individuals wish to hold their assets (of which Keynes's shift in liquidity preference is the archetype). It should be emphasized that such a shift will affect the rate of interest (and rates of return in general) even under conditions of full employment and perfectly flexible prices.[16] Correspondingly, the complete absence from the Cambridge literature of an analysis of such a shift in taste—in contrast with the attention paid to the effects of a shift in tastes with respect to the desired level of K—is to me clear evidence that the Cambridge quantity theorists did not really approach monetary problems from the viewpoint of an optimally composed portfolio of assets.

IV. Concluding remarks

My conclusion from the evidence presented here is that the conceptual framework of the Cambridge school was not really the Keynesian one described in the opening section of this paper: namely, a framework that conceives of the individual as deciding on the amount of his money holdings as a component of a portfolio of assets that is optimally composed with reference to the alternative rates of return available on these assets. A framework

[16] See Patinkin (1965), ch. X:4.

that (in contrast with the Cambridge school) distinguishes between the initial *stock* (or balance-sheet) adjustments generated by a monetary change, and the subsequent effect on the demand for *flows* of commodities of the changes in rates in interest generated by these adjustments.

One indication of this fact is the failure of the Cambridge school to analyse the effects on the equilibrium rate of interest of a shift in the tastes of the individual with reference to the desired asset-composition of his portfolio. Another indication is that despite the fact that the Cambridge school referred to the influence of the rate of interest on the demand for money, it did not really integrate this influence into its thinking: it did not call it into use in explaining observed variations of the velocity of circulation; nor did it cite it as a factor in its theoretical explanations of variations of the velocity of circulation over the trade cycle.

It is because of these differences from the Cambridge school that the Keynesian theory of liquidity preference can properly be considered only as a 'new theory'—one that makes it impossible for us today to approach monetary problems without taking account of these factors.[17]

I would like to end with some personal reminiscences that I hope will support this interpretation of the Cambridge school—though I am sure that for some it will merely be an indication of my prejudices.

There is some effrontery in claiming that though scholars described a certain analytical apparatus, they did not really understand its full implications. I dare nevertheless to advance this contention not only because of what I feel to be the convincing evidence presented here, but also on the basis of my own recollections of how I, too, failed at one time to see these implications. For though my studies of economics at Chicago began some years after the appearance of the *General Theory*, I was educated in the analytical spirit of the quantity theory that prevailed there. Hence, even though we also studied the *General Theory*, I know that I did not think then in terms of the sharp Keynesian distinction between stock and flow equilibrium. I know that my instinctive way of thinking of monetary influences at that time was directly from the increase in the stock of money to the increase in the demand for the flow of commodities—without the aid of any intervening portfolio-adjustment substitution

[17] It is for these reasons that I cannot accept the contrary conclusions of Eshag (1963), pp. 62–8.

effects. I know that I thought of a change in the velocity of circulation solely in terms of a change in tastes as to the desired proportion between the stock of money and the flow of expenditure on current commodities; not in terms of the consequence of a change in tastes as to the desired proportion between the stock of money and the stocks of other assets in a portfolio of a given size.

Knowing these things about the workings of my own mind, I hope that I will not be considered presumptuous if I interpret the detailed evidence from the writings of the Cambridge economists that I have here presented as evidence that they too were subject to a similar failure to see what is so clear to us today—as a result of the changes wrought by Keynesian monetary theory.

Appendix

The passages from Marshall's *Money, Credit and Commerce* (1923, pp. 44–5) referred to in the text are reproduced here, together with the relevant footnote:

To give definiteness to this notion, let us suppose that the inhabitants of a country, taken one with another (and including therefore all varieties of character and of occupation) find it just worth their while to keep by them on the average ready purchasing power to the extent of a tenth part of their annual income, together with a fiftieth part of their property; then the aggregate value of the currency of the country will tend to be equal to the sum of these amounts. . . .

Thus the position is this. In every state of society there is some fraction of their income which people find it worth while to keep in the form of currency; it may be a fifth, or a tenth, or a twentieth. A large command of resources in the form of currency renders their business easy and smooth, and puts them at an advantage in bargaining; but, on the other hand, it locks up in a barren form resources that might yield an income of gratification if invested, say, in extra furniture; or a money income if invested in extra machinery or cattle. . . . But, whatever the state of society, there is a certain volume of their resources which people of different classes, taken one with another, care to keep in the form of currency; and, if everything else remains the same, then there is this direct relation between the volume of currency and the level of prices, that, if one is increased by ten per cent., the other also will be increased by ten per cent. Of course, the less the proportion of their resources which people care to keep in the form of currency, the lower will be the aggregate value of the currency, that is, the higher will prices be with a given volume of currency.

This relation between the volume of the currency and the general level of prices may be changed permanently by changes in, first, population and wealth, which change the aggregate income; secondly, by the growth of credit agencies, which substitute other means of payment for currency; thirdly, by changes in the methods of transport, production, and business generally, which affect the number of hands through which commodities pass in the processes of making and dealing, and it may be temporarily modified by fluctuations of general commercial confidence and activity.*

* The above statement is reproduced from my answers to Questions 11,759–11,761 put by the Indian Currency Committee in 1899. In fact a considerable part of the present discussion of the problems of money and credit may be found in my answers to Questions 11,757–11,850 put by that Committee: and my answers to Questions 9623–10,014 and 10,121–10,126 put by the Gold and Silver Commission in 1887–8.

In his memoir on Marshall, Keynes (1924, pp. 27–8) states:

We must regret still more Marshall's postponement of the publication of his *Theory of Money* until extreme old age, when time had deprived his ideas of freshness and his exposition of sting and strength.

... his theories were not expounded in a systematic form until the appearance of *Money, Credit and Commerce* in 1923. By this date nearly all his main ideas had found expression in the works of others. He had passed his eightieth year; his strength was no longer equal to much more than piecing together earlier fragments; and its jejune treatment, carefully avoiding difficulties and complications, yields the mere shadow of what he had had it in him to bring forth twenty or (better) thirty years earlier.

It does not take any expertise in textual criticism to see how the passage cited here from *Money, Credit and Commerce* reflects such 'piecing together'. In particular, the first paragraph of this passage—in which the demand for money is expressed as 'a tenth part of their annual income, together with a fiftieth part of their property'—clearly presents a different theory of the demand for money than does the second paragraph—which refers only to the 'fraction of their income which people find it worth while to keep in the form of currency'. This difference is a reflection of the fact that the second and third[1] paragraphs in the passage cited essentially reproduce Marshall's 1899 testimony before the Indian

[1] The reader is reminded of the discussion in the text above emphasizing that the allusion in this paragraph to the influences of changes in wealth on the demand for money visualizes this effect not as a direct one, but as an indirect one exerted through the influence on this demand of the increase in income generated by the increase in wealth.

Currency Committee (1926, pp. 267–9) to which he refers in the first sentence of the footnote he attached to this passage. And this testimony essentially goes back to an unpublished manuscript that Marshall wrote around 1871.[2]

On the other hand, the first paragraph in this passage does not appear in any of Marshall's various testimonies as reprinted in *Official Papers*; nor, to the best of my knowledge, does it appear in any of his published works; nor, finally, does it appear in the unpublished manuscript for 1871 just mentioned. Thus it may have been written at the time Marshall was preparing his *Money, Credit and Commerce*.

In view of the circumstances under which Marshall wrote his *Money, Credit and Commerce* (as described by Keynes), it may be that one should not attach too much importance to the fact that Marshall described the demand for money in two different ways. But this cannot explain why Keynes in his *Tract* (1923, pp. 78–9) cites the foregoing passages from *Money, Credit and Commerce* at length—and makes no comment that would indicate his realization of the fact that from the stock-flow viewpoint there are indeed two different descriptions here.

In addition to the foregoing passages that he cites from Marshall, Keynes also describes this demand repeatedly (1923, pp. 76, 78 *et passim*) by the statement that the demand of individuals for money 'depends partly on their wealth, partly on their habits.' As the reader can verify, this statement does not appear in the above-cited passages from *Money, Credit and Commerce*. It does, however, appear in one of the memoranda that Marshall submitted in 1887 to the Gold and Silver Commission in which he states that 'the volume of the business in each country which requires the use of coin [is] determined by each country's wealth and habits' (1926, p. 177).

In this material we also find another example of the failure of Marshall to distinguish sharply between wealth and income in this context:

Assuming the habits of business to remain unchanged, the amount of coin which a person finds it convenient to carry about, taking one with another, depends upon his general *wealth*. A shopkeeper with an *in-*

---

[2] See pp. 13–14 of this manuscript, which is to be found in the Marshall Library of Economics in Cambridge (see Bibliography below). I am indebted to the Senior Assistant Librarian of the Library and to Professor Robin Matthews for providing me with a Xerox of the manuscript.

This manuscript is referred to by Keynes in his memorial essay on Marshall (1924, p. 28).

come of £1,000 a year would be likely to use a great deal more gold than an architect with the same *income*, but if prices rose generally so that the money income of each increased 10 per cent, and the expenditure of each in every direction increased also 10 per cent, then (their habits of business remaining unchanged) each of them would, I believe, keep 10 per cent more money in his purse. (1926, p. 43, italics added.)

The passages cited in the text above from Pigou's 'Value of Money' (1917–18, pp. 164–7) are the following—where once again the relevant footnote has been reproduced:

There is thus constituted at any given moment a definite demand schedule for titles to legal-tender money. Let R be the total resources, expressed in terms of wheat, that are enjoyed by the community (other than its bankers) whose position is being investigated; k the proportion of these resources that it chooses to keep in the form of titles to legal tender; M the number of units of legal tender, and P the value, or price, per unit of these titles in terms of wheat. Then the demand schedule just described is represented by the equation $P = kR/M$. When k and R are taken as constant, this is, of course, the equation of a rectangular hyperbola.

... consider the variable k. When the aggregate wheat value of the community's resources is given, the quantity of wheat value kept in the form of titles to legal tender is determined by the *proportion* of his resources that the average man chooses to keep in that form. This proportion depends upon the convenience obtained and the risk avoided through the possession of such titles, by the loss of real income involved through the diversion to this use of resources that might have been devoted to the production of future commodities, and by the satisfaction that might be obtained by consuming resources immediately and not investing them at all. These three uses, the production of convenience and security, the production of commodities, and direct consumption, are rival to one another. For our present purpose, the use of immediate consumption need not be particularly considered. Its presence mitigates, but never does more than mitigate, the effect of the principal causes with which we have to deal. Practically, the critical question for a business man—and the same class of question has to be asked by everybody—is, as Professor Carver well observes: 'will it pay better to have one more dollar in his cash drawer and one less on his shelves, or will it pay better to have one less dollar in his cash drawer and one more on his shelves.'*

* *American Economic Association Papers* (1905), 131.

Incidentally, I think that this was the first appearance in print of the Cambridge equation.

In view of Lavington's distinctive contributions to the Cambridge school, I should like to cite at length from Chapter 6 of his *English Capital Market* (1921):

In a modern community each person with resources at his disposal needs some means by which he can employ these resources in order to obtain goods from other parties, to pay his dues to the State and to meet more uncertain demands to which he may be exposed. . . . Each therefore will find it convenient to hold a part of his resources in the form of a stock of something which, being generally acceptable and easily transferable, serves as general purchasing power and may be readily passed from hand to hand as a means of making payments.

He will of course have to forego interest upon the resources which he invests in this particular form of a stock of money, but he will obtain instead facilities for making payments, which may be expressed as a return of convenience and security. His stock yields him an income of convenience, for it reduces the cost and trouble of effecting his current payments; and it yields him an income of security, for it reduces his risks of not being able readily to make payments arising from contingencies which he cannot fully foresee. The investment of resources in the form of a stock of money which facilitates the making of payments is then in no way peculiar; it corresponds to the investment by a merchant in the office furniture which facilitates the dispatch of business, to the investment of the farmer in agricultural implements which facilitate the cultivation of his land, and indeed to investment generally.

Such being the *nature* of an individual's demand for money, we have now to consider the causes governing its *amount*. In order to do so, let us first state the general principle on which an individual distributes his resources among their various uses, and then pass on to consider the causes determining the amount which he invests in this particular use— money.

This general principle is familiar enough. As a person extends the application of resources in any particular use, the yield from each successive unit of resources so applied satisfies a less and less urgent need. Accordingly he presses their employment in each use up to that point where in his judgment the marginal yield is equal all round; for if this yield differed as between any two uses it would pay him to transfer resources from one to the other. Resources devoted to consumption supply an income of immediate satisfaction; those held as a stock of currency yield a return of convenience and security; those devoted to investment in the narrower sense of the term yield a return in the form of interest. In so far therefore as his judgment gives effect to his self-interest, the quantity of resources which he holds in the form of money will be such that the unit of resources which is just and only just worth while holding in this form yields him a return of convenience and security equal to the yield of satisfaction derived from the marginal unit spent on consumables, and equal also to the net rate of interest.

This distinction between the yield of convenience and security brings out the consideration that the stock of money held by a business man serves not only to effect his current payments but also as a first line of defence against the uncertain events of the future. . . .

If we arrange a business man's investments in order of their marketability, we may regard his resources as distributed among a series of uses ranging from his stock of the supremely acceptable thing, money, up to his investments in the permanent plant from which he draws his main money income. This arrangement conveniently illustrates the essential similarity between the distribution of resources by a business man and the distribution effected by a bank, where the two main considerations, the need to meet current and contingent demands and the need to earn a profit, are shown in clearer contrast. . . .

Even in normal circumstances, therefore, the size of the stock of money held by a business man depends partly on the volume of his current transactions, partly on his individual business outlook. . . .

These considerations lead to a definition of the demand for money rather different from (though not inconsistent with) that laid down by the Quantity theory. In that theory the demand for money during the year is taken to be the aggregate of goods (and services) exchanged against money during that period. . . . Can this total, the volume of payments to be effected, be properly regarded as forming the demand for money? This question must be answered in the light of the considerations which have just been noticed. . . .

. . . In order to carry through his payments quickly and conveniently each person holds a part of his resources in the form of a stock of money. The size of that part of this stock which he holds to carry through current transactions depends directly upon the volume of his payments; . . . But the size of that part of this stock which he holds as a first line of defence against emergencies depends less directly upon the volume of his payments; it depends upon his *estimate* of contingent payments, and consequently varies with his state of mind, or, more concretely, with the business outlook. . . . It seems reasonable, therefore, to regard this latter part of the aggregate money stock as a reserve whose size is regulated largely by the general level of confidence—a reservoir from which money flows into active circulation when times are good, and into which money flows from active circulation when times are bad. . . . Accordingly it seems that theory is brought into closer relation with the facts when we recognize that part of the demand for money arises from the need to make provision against contingent payments, and that this part of the demand fluctuates in response to changes in the general condition of confidence in some measure independently of the volume of payments. (1921, pp. 29–33, italics in original.)

In its clear distinction between the two incentives for holding money—and in its explicit statement that that part held as a contingency reserve changes 'in some measure independently of the volume of payment'—this striking passage is, to the best of my knowledge, unique in the Cambridge literature. I find it accordingly significant that Lavington himself considers this description of the demand for money to be 'rather different from (though not inconsistent with) that laid down by the Quantity theory'.

As noted in the text, there is no discussion of the relative advantages of holding different assets in the first (1922) edition of Robertson's book on Money. In the third (1928) and later editions, however, Robertson wrote that

> ... taking the country as a whole at any given time, we can express its demand for money—that is, the real value of its money supply—as a proportion of its real national income . . .
> On what then does the magnitude of this proportion depend? It depends on the one hand, as has been said, on the convenience and sense of security derived from the possession of a pool of money, and on the other, on the strength of the alternative attractions of increased consumption, or lucrative investment in trade capital or in Government or industrial stocks, against which these advantages have to be weighed up. Thus the magnitude of the demand for money, like that of the demand for bread, turns out to be the result of a process of individual weighing-up of competing advantages *at the margin* . . . (1928, pp. 38–9, italics in original; the same passage appears on pp. 36–7 of the 1948 edition.)

Keynes's criticism in the *Treatise* of Pigou's presentation of the Cambridge equation, $P = k\,R/M$ (cited above), is as follows:

> the introduction of the factor R, the current income of the community, suggests that variation in this is one of the two or three most important direct influences on the demand for cash resources. In the case of the income-deposits this seems to me to be true. But the significance of R is much diminished when we are dealing, not with the income-deposits in isolation, but with the total deposits. Indeed the chief inconvenience of the 'Cambridge' Quantity Equation really lies in its applying to the total deposits considerations which are primarily relevant only to the income-deposits, and in its tackling the problem as though the same sort of considerations which govern the income-deposits also govern the total deposits [i.e. income-deposits *plus* savings deposits—or in U.S. terminology, demand deposits *plus* time deposits] . . .
> The prominence given to k, namely the proportion of the bank-deposits to the community's *income*, is misleading when it is extended beyond the income-deposits. The emphasis which this method lays

on the point that the amount of real balances held is determined by the comparative advantages of holding resources in cash and in alternative forms, so that a change in k will be attributable to a change in these comparative advantages, is useful and instructive. But 'resources' in this connection ought not to be interpreted, as it is interpreted by Prof. Pigou, as being identical with current *income*. (1930, i, pp. 231–2, italics in original.)

I might note that even though Robertson defends the Cambridge equation against Keynes's criticisms here, he does not question Keynes's interpretation of Pigou's term 'resources' as 'income'. Robertson's not very convincing answer to Keynes is as follows:

It is of course true (as is recognized in Marshall's own illustration of the 'Cambridge' theory) that many people will have other quantities than their income in mind (for instance, their capital or their business turnover) in deciding upon their monetary requirements. But from the fact that their money stock is not exclusively *determined* as a proportion of their income, it does not follow that it cannot usefully be *expressed* as such a proportion; still less that the real value of the whole community's total money stock cannot usefully be expressed (as in the equation $M/P = KR$) in terms of the constituents of real income or output. For the whole of M is *potentially* expendable against output, and if in any period of time more or less of it were to be so expended than was previously the case, P would alter. It is of the utmost importance that under certain conditions money which has been imprisoned in what Mr. Keynes calls the 'savings deposits' and 'business deposits' may seep out, raise the aggregate of incomes and 'income deposits,' and drive up P. Such a change is represented in the 'Cambridge' approach by a diminution of K: it would not be represented by any change in a symbol which stood for the proportion borne to R by the real value of 'income deposits' alone. ((1933) 1940, pp. 92–3, italics in original.)

I presume that what Robertson had in mind in his reference to 'Marshall's own illustration of the "Cambridge" theory' is Marshall's discussion in the first paragraph of the citation from *Money, Credit and Commerce* (1923, p. 44) that is cited at the beginning of this Appendix. In any event, as already noted in the text, it is puzzling that Robertson does not refer here to the far more substantive discussion in Lavington (1921, pp. 32–3) cited above in this Appendix (last three paragraphs of the passage cited).

REFERENCES

AGASSI, Joseph (1968). 'The Novelty of Popper's Philosophy of Science', *International Philosophical Quarterly* (Sept.), pp. 442–63.

DAVIS, J. Ronnie (1971). *The New Economics and the Old Economists* (Ames, Iowa: Iowa State University Press).

ESHAG, Eprime (1963). *From Marshall to Keynes* (Oxford: Blackwell).

F[AY], C. R. (1927). '[Obituary of] Frederick Lavington', *Economic Journal*, pp. 503–5.

FISHER, Irving (1907). *The Rate of Interest* (New York: Macmillan).

—— (1930). *The Theory of Interest* (New York: Macmillan).

FRIEDMAN, Milton (1957). *A Theory of the Consumption Function* (N.B.E.R.: Gen. Ser. No. 63) (Princeton, N.J.: Princeton University Press).

FOLEY, D. K., and SIDRAUSKI, M. (1971). *Monetary and Fiscal Policy in a Growing Economy* (New York: Macmillan).

GURLEY, John G., and SHAW, Edward S. (1960). *Money in a Theory of Finance* (Washington, D.C.: The Brookings Institution).

HICKS, J. R. (1935). 'A Suggestion for Simplifying the Theory of Money', *Economica*, pp. 1–19; reprinted in Lutz, F. A., and Mints, L. W. (eds.), *Readings in Monetary Theory* (London: Allen and Unwin, 1952), pp. 13–32.

—— (1939). *Value and Capital* (Oxford: Clarendon Press).

HUTCHISON, T. W. (1953). *A Review of Economic Doctrines 1870–1929* (Oxford: Clarendon).

—— (1968). *Economics and Economic Policy in Britain 1946–66* (London: Allen and Unwin).

KEYNES, J. M. (1911). 'Review of I. Fisher's "The Purchasing Power of Money"', *Economic Journal*, pp. 393–8.

—— (1923). *Tract on Monetary Reform* (London: Macmillan).

—— (1924). 'Alfred Marshall, 1842–1924', *Economic Journal* as reprinted in Pigou, A. C. (ed.), *Memorials of Alfred Marshall* (New York: Kelley and Millman, 1956), pp. 1–65.

—— (1930). *A Treatise on Money* (London: Macmillan).

—— (1936). *The General Theory of Employment, Interest and Money* (New York: Harcourt, Brace).

KLEIN, L. R., and GOLDBERGER, A. S. (1955). *An Econometric Model of the United States 1929–1952* (Amsterdam: North-Holland).

KUHN, Thomas S. (1970). *The Structure of Scientific Revolutions* (2nd edn.) (International Encyclopedia of Unified Science, vol. 2, No. 2), (Chicago: University of Chicago Press).

LAVINGTON, F. (1921). *The English Capital Market* (London: Methuen).

—— (1922). *The Trade Cycle* (London: King).

MARSHALL, Alfred (*c.* 1871). Unpublished Manuscript; Marshall Red Box 2 (Money and Banking, Exchanges), Item 6, in the Marshall Library of Economics, Cambridge.

—— (1923). *Money, Credit and Commerce* (London: Macmillan).

—— (1926). *Official Papers* (London: Macmillan).

MITCHELL, B. R., and DEANE, P. (1962). *Abstract of British Historical Statistics* (Cambridge: Cambridge University Press).

MYRDAL, Gunnar (1939). *Monetary Equilibrium* (Glasgow: William Hodge (trans. from the German work of 1933)).

PATINKIN, Don (1965). *Money, Interest, and Prices* (2nd edn., New York: Harper and Row).

—— (1969). 'The Chicago Tradition, the Quantity Theory, and Friedman', *Journal of Money, Credit and Banking* (Feb.), pp. 46–70.

—— (1972a). 'On the Short-Run Non-Neutrality of Money in the Quantity Theory', Banca Nazionale del Lavoro, *Quarterly Review* (Mar.), pp. 3–22.

—— (1972b). 'Friedman on the Quantity Theory and Keynesian Economics', *J.P.E.* (Sept./Oct.), pp. 883–905.

PIGOU, A. C. (1917–18). 'The Value of Money', *Q.J.E.*, as reprinted in Lutz, F. A. and Mints, L. W. (eds.), *Readings in Monetary Theory* (London: Allen and Unwin, 1952).

—— (1929). *Industrial Fluctuations* (2nd edn., London: Macmillan).

—— (1933). *The Theory of Unemployment* (London: Macmillan).

ROBERTSON, D. H. (1922). *Money* (New York: Harcourt, Brace; 3rd edn., London: Nisbet, and Cambridge: Cambridge University Press, 1928; 4th edn., London: Pitman, 1948).

—— (1940). 'A Note on the Theory of Money', in *Essays in Monetary Theory* (London: Staples Press), reprinted from *Economica* (1933).

SHACKLE, G. L. S. (1967). *The Years of High Theory* (Cambridge: C.U.P.).

SNYDER, Carl (1924). 'New Measures in the Equation of Exchange', *American Economic Review* (Dec.), pp. 699–713.

STIGLER, George J. (1955). 'The Nature and Role of Originality in Scientific Progress', *Economica* (Nov.), as reprinted in *Essays in the History of Economics* (Chicago and London: University of Chicago Press, 1965), pp. 1–15.

TOBIN, James (1955). 'A Dynamic Aggregative Model', *J.P.E.* (Apr.).

—— (1963). 'An Essay on Principles of Debt Management', in *Fiscal and Debt Management Policies* (Commission on Money and Credit) (Englewood Cliffs, N.J.: Prentice-Hall), pp. 143–218.

—— (1969). 'A General Equilibrium Approach to Monetary Theory', *Journal of Money, Credit and Banking* (Feb.), pp. 15–29.

WINCH, Donald (1969). *Economics and Policy* (London: Hodder and Stoughton).

WRIGHT, Harold (1923). *Population* (New York: Harcourt, Brace).

W[RIGHT], H[arold] (1927). '[Obituary of] Frederick Lavington', *Economic Journal*, pp. 503–5.

THE NIXON ADMINISTRATION AND THE FEDERAL RESERVE: A FLAWED EXPERIMENT IN MONETARY POLICY?

A. JAMES MEIGS
(*Argus Research Corporation*)

WHEN President Nixon came into office in 1969 his economic advisers gave monetary policy, and the money supply in particular, far more weight in their statements and plans than had their predecessors of the Kennedy–Johnson administrations. Although they were not card-carrying monetarists, the Nixon advisers could fairly be accused of being somewhat Friedmanesque. Furthermore, Milton Friedman himself was believed to be an unofficial White House adviser, as his fiscalist counterpart, Paul Samuelson, had been in the early days of the Kennedy regime. The adoption of monetarism provided the Nixon advisers with a strategy that was a clear alternative to that of the Democrats. Expansive fiscalism had provided a strategy for the Kennedy advisers in 1961 that was a clear alternative to the restrictive fiscalism of the Eisenhower advisers.

Holding growth of the money supply to a slower and less variable rate than it had followed in the preceding four years was one of the key parts of the Republican strategy for gradually slowing inflation with minimum cost in unemployment. The second main element in the plan was a determination to hold Federal expenditures within the revenues that would be generated by the tax system when the economy was at full employment. Reliance on free-market adjustment of wages and prices was the third main element of the new strategy; there were to be no guideposts or other measures for exerting direct influence on wage and price decisions.

President Nixon summed up the strategy in his first Economic Report to the Congress: '. . . we must achieve a steadier and more evenhanded management of our economic policies. Business and labor cannot plan, and consumers and homebuyers cannot effectively manage their affairs, when Government alternates between keeping first the accelerator and then the brake pedal to the floor'.[1]

During the first three years of the Nixon administration, however, events departed widely from the plan:

—U.S. money-supply growth gyrated more widely than at any time since World War II.

—The economy slid into a recession in late 1969 from which it has not yet fully recovered.

—Inflation was more persistent than expected.

—Unemployment was higher at the end of the three years than it was at the beginning.

—Interest rates and stock prices fluctuated over extraordinarily wide ranges.

—The balance-of-payments deficit swelled to a flood.

—The dollar was devalued.

—The Federal budget went deeply into deficit.

—Direct controls over wages and prices were imposed in August of last year.

One could easily conclude from this woeful catalogue that the Nixon experiment with relying on monetary policy for subduing inflation was a disastrous mistake. Consequently, the monetary assault on the citadels of political influence and intellectual prestige must have been decisively repulsed. Harry Johnson had predicted such a fate for monetarism in his provocative and prophetic lecture to the American Economic Association in December 1970:

. . . I believe [he said] the Keynesians are right in their view that inflation is a far less serious social problem than mass unemployment. Either we will vanquish inflation at relatively little cost, or we will get used to it. The odds at present are that we will accept it as a necessary price of solving other pressing domestic issues—this seems to be the current view of the present [Nixon] Administration—and in that case monetarism will again be reduced to attempting to convince the public of the importance of the problem it is equipped to solve before it can start arguing about the scientific superiority of its proposed solution to the problem.[2]

[1] Richard M. Nixon, *Economic Report of the President*, together with *The Annual Report of the Council of Economic Advisers*, Feb. 1970 (Washington, D.C.: U.S. Government Printing Office, 1970), p. 10.

[2] Harry G. Johnson, 'The Keynesian Revolution and the Monetarist Counter-Revolution', *American Economic Review*, lxi, No. 2 (May 1971), 12.

President Nixon appeared to observe the Johnsonian dichotomy between a theory to serve those who are concerned about inflation and a theory for those who are concerned about unemployment in early 1971 when he said, 'I am now a Keynesian'. Even Milton Friedman was interpreted as losing faith in monetary policy last December when he said prices had taken longer to respond to monetary restraint than he had predicted in 1969.[3]

When we look back on this period later on we may well decide that the most novel aspect of the Nixon economic policy—as carried out rather than as originally planned—was the forceful use of fiscal policy. Herbert Stein can say, as he did before the Joint Economic Committee this month, 'We are running the biggest deficit ever, except for World War II'.[4] This has put the economic advisers of the opposition party at a psychological disadvantage, for the current Republican deficit is a far larger one than any the Democratic advisers have yet been able to sell to a President. President Kennedy dismayed his advisers by being a fiscal conservative with little taste for increasing expenditures or deficits. The large deficits of the Johnson Administration were deplored by fiscalists, including some of the President's own advisers, because those deficits came at the wrong time.

Monetary policy, I am sorry to say, was not novel at all. Although they were widely believed to be following a strange new course prescribed by the monetarists, the operations of the Federal Reserve in 1969, 1970, and 1971 actually obeyed doctrines and reflexes that had been fixed in the 1920s. The results could hardly be pleasing to monetarists, Keynesians, the Nixon administration, or, indeed, the monetary authorities themselves.

Since the early 1920s, the Federal Reserve has concentrated most of its attention on interest rates, credit-availability, and other money-market conditions in its day-by-day open-market operations. It usually, but not always, tries to minimize short-run fluctuations in interest rates and other symptoms of 'disorderly markets' while letting the money supply wander as it will. As late as mid-1969, Sherman Maisel, a member of the Board of Governors, could say without fear of being contradicted, '. . . the Fed has not attempted

---

[3] Milton Friedman, *Have Monetary Policies Failed?* paper delivered at annual meeting of the American Economic Association, Dec. 1971.
[4] *Wall Street Journal*, 9 Feb. 1972.

to control, within very wide limits, the growth of the narrowly defined money supply in any week or month'.[5]

By 1969, monetarists had collected mountains of evidence to show that the Federal Reserve's time-hallowed operating procedures have caused unintended fluctuations in money-supply growth that have in turn caused unemployment or price inflation during the administrations of Presidents Coolidge, Hoover, Roosevelt, Truman, Eisenhower, Kennedy, and Johnson. President Nixon's advisers had considered much of this evidence. Without departing from their belief that fiscal policy matters too, they stated a moderate view about the uses and limitations of monetary policy in their first *Economic Report* in February 1970: 'Prudence . . . suggests the desirability of not allowing monetary policy to stray widely from the steady posture that is likely on the average to be consistent with long-term economic growth, even though forecasts at particular times may seem to call for a sharp variation in one direction or another.'[6]

Moreover, they said, there was abundant evidence that the steadiness of monetary policy cannot be measured by steadiness of interest rates. Better results might be obtained 'by concentrating more on the steadiness of the main monetary aggregates, such as the supply of money, of money plus time deposits, and of total bank credit'.[7]

Paul McCracken pointed out that it takes time for changes in policies to work and that instant results could not be expected. 'This is a difficult matter for impatient people,' he said, 'and Americans have never been criticized for excessive patience.'[8] Unfortunately, some of the most impatient Americans were in the Federal Reserve System at the time.

As 1969 began, the System was just recovering from its embarrassing over-reaction to the fears of 'fiscal overkill' that seized Washington when the Revenue and Expenditure Control Act of 1968 was passed. Furthermore, some Federal Reserve people were troubled by the thought that if they had stuck to their guns a little longer in

---

[5] Sherman J. Maisel, 'Controlling Monetary Aggregates', *Controlling Monetary Aggregates*, Proceedings of the Monetary Conference held on Nantucket Island, 8–10 June 1969 (Boston: Federal Reserve Bank of Boston), p. 61.
[6] CEA, *Annual Report*, Feb. 1970, p. 68.   [7] Ibid.
[8] Paul W. McCracken, 'The Game Plan for Economic Policy', American Statistical Association, *1969 Proceedings of the Business and Economic Statistics Section*, p. 298.

1966 or had not been so concerned about recession and high interest rates in 1967 they could have beaten back inflation before it became so well entrenched. William McChesney Martin, who had been expected to step down so that Dr. Arthur Burns could take over, decided to serve another year as Chairman of the Board of Governors to lead one last battle.

The Council of Economic Advisers said later that it was difficult to tell at the time what rate of growth in the money supply would achieve Chairman Martin's intention to 'disinflate without deflating'. But it certainly was necessary for the money supply to grow more slowly than the 7·1 per cent increase of 1968.[9]

Some spectators on the sidelines urged a policy of monetary gradualism. The First National City Bank *Monthly Economic Letter* said in January 1969, for example:

Just as the inflationary implications of money supply growth should not have been overlooked in 1967 and 1968, the restrictiveness of an abrupt reduction in monetary growth should not be underestimated in 1969. In the past, sharp reductions in the rate of growth of the money supply have been followed by economic recessions. It would appear prudent, therefore, to move to a less expensive monetary policy gradually.[10]

Milton Friedman recommended that money-supply growth be slowed down in small steps at intervals of several months to minimize the risk of recession.[11]

The Federal Reserve, however, did not seem to heed either the Council of Economic Advisers or the nagging monetarists. Its 1969 campaign was much like the one of 1966. It featured a determined effort to restrict bank business loans by reducing the supplies of funds to those banks that specialize in lending to large businesses. Regulation Q—the ceiling on rates banks can pay for time deposits—became the 'cutting edge' of policy, as it had been in 1966. Again it caused severe distortions and repercussions in U.S. money markets and the Euro-dollar market. The methods chosen by the Federal Reserve for curbing inflation, therefore, imposed some adjustment costs on other countries.

As in 1966, furthermore, money-supply growth soon fell to a much lower rate than monetarists considered safe. In late May, Milton Friedman sounded a warning in his *Newsweek* column: '*It would*

[9] CEA, *Annual Report*, Feb. 1970, p. 33.
[10] First National City Bank, 'A Turn in Monetary Policy', *Monthly Economic Letter*, Jan. 1969, p. 6.
[11] Milton Friedman, 'The Inflationary Fed', *Newsweek*, 20 Jan. 1969.

be a major blunder for the Fed to step still harder on the monetary brakes. That would risk turning orderly restraint into a severe economic contraction. If anything, the Fed has already gone too far.' [12] Revised figures soon indicated that money-supply growth had actually been higher than the rate on which the monetarists' early warnings were based, although it was sharply lower than the 1968 rate. From the middle of the second quarter, however, money-supply growth was held virtually to zero. By September, monetarists were convinced that there would be a substantial slowdown in business activity and a rise in unemployment in late 1969 and early 1970. Consumer spending had already responded to the slowing in monetary expansion.

Notwithstanding the fact that control of the money supply had become a central part of the Administration's economic strategy, high Federal Reserve spokesmen launched scathing criticisms of monetarism in general and Milton Friedman in particular throughout 1969 and into January, 1970.[13] One line of argument in these massively documented replies to the monetarists was that the System cannot, or does not, control the money supply. Another was that the monetarists had not proved that money-supply changes cause business fluctuations. This was argued with all the zeal of a Dairy Institute responding to charges that milk-drinking is injurious to health. The third line of argument, often combined with either or both of the others, was that anyone who recommended less

---

[12] Milton Friedman, 'Money and Inflation', *Newsweek*, 26 May 1969.

[13] Among the most effective defenders of the Federal Reserve in this period were: Alan R. Holmes, 'Operational Constraints on the Stabilization of Money Supply Growth', in *Controlling Monetary Aggregates*; Sherman J. Maisel, 'Controlling Monetary Aggregates', ibid., pp. 152–74 and pp. 65–77; Richard G. Davis, 'How Much Does Money Matter? A Look at Some Recent Evidence', Federal Reserve Bank of New York, *Monthly Review*, June 1969, pp. 119–31; J. Dewey Daane, 'New Frontiers for the Monetarists', remarks before the Northern New England School of Banking, Dartmouth College, 8 Sept. 1969; Andrew J. Brimmer, 'United States Money Policy in 1969', a paper presented at the Sixteenth Annual Bankers' Forum, Georgetown University, 4 Oct. 1969; Alfred Hayes, 'Inflation: A Test of Stabilization Policy', an address before the forty-second annual midwinter meeting of the New York State Bankers Association, 26 Jan. 1970 (reprinted in Federal Reserve Bank of New York, *Monthly Review*, Feb. 1970, pp. 19–24); George W. Mitchell, 'A New Look at Monetary Policy Instruments', remarks at the Conference of University Professors, Milwaukee, Wisc., 10 Sep. 1969, 'Bank Lending Practices and Change in the Monetary Environment', remarks at the Robert Morris Associates Conference, San Juan, Puerto Rico, 27 Oct. 1969, 'New Standards for Credit and Monetary Policy', delivered before the *Business Week* Conference on Money and the Corporation, 8 Dec. 1969.

restraint in 1969 was not sufficiently concerned about the danger of inflation. This last argument was ironic in view of the common belief that monetarists are concerned only with curing inflation.

Before the Fed's campaign for winning the hearts and minds of the American people died down, the recession of 1969–70 had begun. At its first meeting in 1970, the Federal Open Market Committee decided to seek moderate expansion of the monetary aggregates and to give lower priority to the control of interest rates. This was a revolutionary step. When word of it leaked to the outside world, monetarists were overjoyed, because they saw the change as the beginning of a fruitful experiment. After Dr. Arthur Burns became Chairman of the Board of Governors in February 1970, the System settled down to applying the new strategy of controlling the money supply.

The System had not adopted a Friedman-type constant-growth rule for the money supply, although some of the dealers and other participants in the money markets feared that this might be so. Financial institutions were disturbed about what they viewed as arbitrary changes in the rules of the money-market game that might cause interest rates to fluctuate more widely than in the past. While criticizing the excessive variability of past monetary policies, Chairman Burns was careful to stress that monetary policy must be ready to adapt quickly to unanticipated developments in the economy and in financial markets. Hopeful monetarists may have paid too much attention to the first part of the Chairman's position and not enough to the second.

Nor was the new policy an anti-recession policy at first. Although the Open Market Committee staff had virtually forecast a recession at the final meeting in 1969, the January–February turn was meant to be only a slight reduction in the degree of restraint. There was an understandable reluctance to concede the possibility of recession, in view of the strong statements made in refuting the monetarists' recession forecasts just a few weeks earlier. Furthermore inflationary pressures still appeared to be very strong.

According to Andrew Brimmer, a member of the Board of Governors, the highwater mark of monetarist influence in the Federal Reserve came at the 10 March 1970 meeting of the Open Market Committee.[14] The policy directive adopted that day said: 'To

[14] Andrew F. Brimmer, *The Political Economy of Money: Evolution and Impact of Monetarism in the Federal Reserve System*, paper presented at the annual meeting of the American Economic Association, 27 Dec. 1971.

implement this policy, the Committee desires to see moderate growth in money and bank credit over the months ahead. System open market operations until the next meeting of the Committee shall be conducted with a view to maintaining money market conditions consistent with that objective.'[15] Money and bank credit shared top billing as targets in the first sentence of the directive. The second sentence could be interpreted as requiring the Manager of the Open Market Account to buy or sell enough securities to keep short-term interest rates and other measures of money market conditions at levels that would induce the public and the banking system to expand bank credit and money at the moderate rates desired by the Committee.

Estimates of what those rates might be were smoked out of the Chairman by Senator William Proxmire, of the Joint Economic Committee, a few days later. In a letter to the Senator, Chairman Burns said that if the 1970 economic projections of the Council of Economic Advisers turned out to be an accurate description of the economy's course, 'the monetary variables could gradually return to a more normal growth rate—say, 3–4 percent for the narrowly defined money supply and perhaps 6–8 percent for total bank credit'.[16] This was a felicitous statement because in 1968 the Joint Economic Committee had asked the Fed to keep monetary growth rates between 2 per cent and 6 per cent.

Dr. Burns did not say, however, that these growth rates were necessary for achievement of the Council's goal-forecast nor did he believe they were the only ones consistent with that forecast. Furthermore, changes in conditions could be imagined that would call for unusual monetary stimulus or continued monetary restraint. 'Monetary policy is by nature one of the most adaptable instruments of economic stabilization [he said], and it is my intention to do everything within my power to keep it flexible and responsively attuned to unexpected variations in the performance of the economy as they occur or come into prospect.'

Some of those unexpected variations came into prospect almost immediately: a postal strike in April, the Cambodia incursion in May, plunging stock prices, student riots, the wreck of the Penn

[15] Record of Policy Actions of the Federal Open Market Committee, meeting held on 10 Mar. 1970.

[16] Letter of Arthur Burns, Chairman of the Board of Governors of the Federal Reserve System, to Senator William Proxmire, Chairman of the Joint Economic Committee, 17 Mar. 1970, *Congressional Record-Senate*, S4299.

Central Railroad in June, and fears of a liquidity crisis kept the Federal Reserve busy acting as a traditional central banker. For a time, holding money-supply growth to a moderate rate was considered to be less important than the task of calming fears of breakdown in the financial markets. Nevertheless, the Federal Reserve could no longer be casual about large increases in money supply. After growing at a 7·2 per cent annual rate from the first quarter to the second, the narrowly-defined money supply grew at a 5·3 per cent rate for the third quarter and a 3·8 per cent rate in the fourth.

Although monetarists might criticize the Federal Reserve's methods of controlling the money supply, they generally considered the Fed's 1970 performance the best in many years. And they believed the performance would improve. Unfortunately, however, the recession became an acute embarrassment to the Administration. After Republican candidates fared poorly in the November elections there was intense speculation in the press about Administration pressure on the Federal Reserve to give up the fight against inflation and to swing into restoring full employment before the 1972 elections.

The President's January 1971 Budget Message did not indicate the expected swing to a more expansionary fiscal policy, but it did contain a 'policy forecast' of a $1,065 billion GNP for 1971. Many economists outside the government believed this GNP goal could not be achieved without much more expansive fiscal and monetary policies. Monetarists did not, and could not, offer the Administration a prescription for quickly and easily returning the economy to high employment without risking a reacceleration of inflation; they doubted that anyone knew how to do that. Moreover, there was the compelling recent experience of 1966–7 to cite in advising against a departure from the moderate approach of the Administration's original game plan.

The one monetarist who could vote where it really mattered was Darryl Francis, President of the Federal Reserve Bank of St. Louis. At the 12 January meeting of the Open Market Committee he dissented from the Committee decision 'to promote accommodative conditions in credit markets' and argued for a growth rate of about 5 per cent for narrowly defined money supply.[17] This was about the average rate over the second half of 1970. The rest of the committee

[17] FOMC Policy Record, meeting of 12 Jan. 1971.

appeared to prefer a rate of 7·5 per cent, in order to compensate for a shortfall from the growth rate that had been expected in the fourth quarter.

When Paul McCracken, Chairman of the Council of Economic Advisers, faced the Joint Economic Committee in February, he was asked how much money-supply growth would be required for the GNP to reach the $1,065 billion target. He said that the Council's review of 1952–70 experience indicated that the desired 9 per cent increase in GNP might be realized with a 6 per cent increase in money supply, although 1967–9 experience suggested that an increase of 7·2 per cent might be needed.[18]

A sceptical Senator Hubert Humphrey said to him:

The fact is that your evidence reveals that with less than a 6 percent money supply you are not going to get anyplace, and the fact of the matter is you say so. But then you say you need a 7·2 percent money supply increase . . ., and now we look at the solid facts and find out Mr. Federal Reserve actually is giving us less than 4 percent.

What assurance do you have, Mr. McCracken, that the Federal Reserve is going to come up with a 7 percent increase? What assurance do you have that they would maintain it at 6 percent?[19]

The Council of Economic Advisers had no such assurance and Dr. Burns did not offer it when he took his turn on the stand. He observed that rates of increase above the 5 to 6 per cent range had intensified inflationary pressures in the past, if continued for a long period. Furthermore, increases of income velocity had at times permitted strong cyclical recoveries of production and employment to occur with modest increases in money supply. He assured the Committee that the Federal Reserve would 'continue to supply the money and credit needed for healthy economic expansion', but would not 'become the architects of a new wave of inflation'.[20]

A few weeks later, Chairman Burns told the Senate Banking, Housing and Urban Affairs Committee that balance-of-payments considerations reinforced the need for prudence in monetary policy. 'Caution in the monetary sphere is required [he said], lest a fresh wave of inflationary forces be released. Such a development could do incalculable damage to the structure of international confidence

[18] Joint Economic Committee, Hearings on the President's 1971 Economic Report, Feb. 1971, Part 1, p. 7.
[19] JEC Hearings on 1971 Economic Report, Part 1, p. 30.
[20] Statement of Arthur Burns to JEC Hearings, 19 Feb. 1971.

and economic cooperation that has been built up over the past quarter century.'[21]

Despite the conservative tenor of Dr. Burns's statements in February and March, the money supply rocketed upward at a 12 per cent annual rate from the first quarter to the second quarter. The proximate cause of this monetary explosion appeared to be a Federal Reserve attempt to push long-term interest rates down, or to moderate their rise. As Dr. Burns explained it later, 'In view of the delicate state of the economic recovery, which was just getting underway, it seemed desirable to prevent the possible adverse effects of sharply higher interest rates on expenditure plans and public psychology.'[22]

Unfortunately for the international monetary system, currency speculators and many sober businessmen who would never dream of calling themselves speculators believed what they had been reading in the American press about unemployment, elections, and 'benign neglect' of the balance of payments. The sudden rise in U.S. money supply confirmed their fears that political pressure would force the Federal Reserve to give up the fight against inflation. Although an international monetary crisis might eventually have come in any case, I believe the monetary explosion in the United States precipitated the one of last year. The international monetary crisis in turn contributed mightily to the so-called confidence crisis in the United States that called forth President Nixon's New Economic Policy of wage-price controls, fiscal stimulants, and devaluation of the dollar.

It occurred to very few people at the time that the upsurge in U.S. money supply in the first half of 1971 might be an accident. Now that the Policy Record of the Open Market Committee for that period is available, we can see that the growth in the money supply greatly exceeded the Committee's expectations. Furthermore, the Committee's directives for the meetings of 11 May, 8 June, 29 June, and 27 July all said, 'The Committee seeks to moderate growth in monetary aggregates over the months ahead', or words to that effect.[23]

[21] Statement of Arthur Burns before the Senate Banking, Housing and Urban Affairs Committee, 10 Mar. 1971.

[22] Statement of Arthur Burns before the Joint Economic Committee, 23 July 1971.

[23] FOMC Policy Record, Meeting of 11 May, 8 June, 19 June, and 27 July 1971.

A perhaps even more bizarre accident occurred in the second half of the year. After the New Economic Policy was announced, the money supply abruptly stopped growing. This halt in money-supply growth was neither intended nor expected by the Open Market Committee, according to the Committee's own Policy Record. Inasmuch as the Administration's policy was avowedly expansionary at the time, the half in money-supply growth also seemed inconsistent with what the rest of the Government was attempting to do.

No matter how the monetary authorities may rationalize the strange behaviour of the money supply after the fact, it is clear that they would have preferred it to behave differently in 1971, that is, closer to the moderate-growth plan. Monetarism appears to have had more influence on Federal Reserve intentions last year than on Federal Reserve execution. There is reason to expect execution to improve.

The main source of the difference between intentions and results, it seems to me, is the so-called 'money-market-conditions' strategy used in conducting open-market operations. In effect, the Fed tries to peg the price of credit—'money-market-conditions'—at a level that will induce the banking system and the public to expand the money supply at the desired rate. But if the peg is set at the wrong level, or if demand conditions change during the operating period, the money supply will grow faster, or slower, than the Committee's desired rate.

In practice, an unexpected rise of interest rates will tend to increase the growth rate of the money supply until the Committee, or the Manager of the Open Market Account, adjusts the peg. Falling rates tend to reduce the growth rate of the money supply until the peg is adjusted. For considerable periods, the Committee may lag in adjusting the peg, like a gunner who fails to lead a moving target.

The current situation bears an eerie resemblance to early 1960. In March of that year, Arthur Burns warned Richard Nixon, who was then making his first try for the Presidency, that a recession was imminent. They tried to get fiscal and monetary policy action to counter the threat but were not successful. Federal Reserve people had become concerned about the fact that the money supply had been declining since the previous July. Although the Open Market Committee voted to ease monetary policy on 1 March, the money supply continued to contract for four more months—until well after the 1960–1 recession had begun.

At the 22 March meeting of the Open Market Committee, Delos C. Johns, President of the Federal Reserve Bank of St. Louis, attributed the discrepancy between intentions and results to the way the Committee's instruction was expressed:

> The time had come, in his opinion, for the Committee to subordinate its consideration of net borrowed reserves and other money market pressures to objectives expressed in terms of total bank reserves or the money supply. He did not mean to say that the Committee thereby would have adopted a system that would assure the avoidance of mistakes, but the use of such a technique would help to avoid doing things to total reserves and money that the Committee did not intend.[24]

Today, almost exactly twelve years later, consideration of net borrowed reserves and other money market pressures is still causing System operations to do things to total reserves and money supply that the Committee does not intend. In 1960, a fall of interest rates brought on by the approach of recession caused the money supply to contract. In early 1972, a fall of interest rates, apparently brought on by central-bank purchases of U.S. Treasury securities, has made it difficult for the Federal Reserve to make the money supply grow.

The swings in money-supply growth during 1969, 1970, and 1971 were wider than the Federal Reserve intended them to be. The extreme changes can only be viewed as accidents. But they were nevertheless damaging to the prospects for restoring stability and high employment in the United States and in much of the rest of the world, as I shall argue in a moment. Furthermore, the monetary policies recommended by the Administration in the published reports of the Council of Economic Advisers were better, in my opinion, than the policies that were actually carried out by the Federal Reserve.

The monetarist prescription of steady, moderate growth in the money supply was not tried except for a few months in 1970. William Wolman, my colleague at Argus, argues that the growing influence of monetarism on the monetary authorities may actually have had perverse effects; it may have increased their confidence that policy errors can be quickly repaired by changes in the growth rate of the money supply. Last year, however, public disillusionment with the idea that changes in monetary policy can quickly curb inflation or stimulate rises in output and employment discredited both

[24] Minutes of the Federal Open Market Committee, National Archives of the United States Microfilm Publications, Microcopy No. 591, Roll No. 15, 12 Jan.–24 May 1960. Meeting of 22 Mar. 1960.

monetary policy and monetarism. I need not remind this company, however, that one of the first verses in the Monetarist Credo is: 'The lags in effects of money-supply changes are variable and long.'

The 1969–72 experiment in U.S. monetary policy was indeed flawed in some important respects. Nevertheless, we can draw some useful implications from it. One of the first—a short-run implication—is that the accidental deceleration in money-supply growth since last July has raised the risk that the recovery from the 1969–70 recession could be aborted, as was the recovery from the 1957–8 recession in 1960. I do not believe that will happen, but there is a possibility that GNP growth will fall short of the Council of Economic Advisers' forecast in the first half.

There are signs that the monetary authorities are keenly aware of the danger and that they are going to make the money supply grow again. Given the complaints from their fellow central bankers in other countries about low interest rates in the United States, they are in an uncomfortable position. However, they really have no choice now but to bite the bullet and do what is required to facilitate domestic recovery. A disappointing recovery, or a new recession, in the United States this year would have worse consequences for the international monetary system than would be a brief period of low rates in the New York money market. The only way to get rates up, furthermore, is through increasing U.S. income and output.

For the long run, I believe this experience powerfully reinforces the arguments for a steady-growth monetary rule. And it reinforces the need for improving the Federal Reserve's methods for controlling the money supply. The United States needs steadier, more predictable economic policies in order to reduce the uncertainty that has been inhibiting growth of output and employment and to restore public confidence in the economy and the government. We simply do not yet know enough to predict the results of fine-tuning operations, whether in money policy or fiscal policy. And the imposition of direct wage-price-credit controls in order to make up for alleged deficiencies in the response of the economy to monetary and fiscal policies only makes matters worse.

To me, the most interesting lesson of the past three years is that the United States can no longer enjoy the luxury of a forceful, discretionary monetary policy; the world is now too closely knit for that. Nor can it afford to coddle domestic money markets with attempts to iron out short-run fluctuations of interest rates; in suppressing ripples, the Federal Reserve generates waves that spread abroad. The frequent alternations between excessive restraint and hyper-expansiveness in U.S. monetary policies have been deeply disturbing to the rest of the world. And the United States itself is not immune from inconvenient effects of lagged feedbacks of its policies through the international monetary system. The extra-ordinary effects of exchange-rate speculation on U.S. short-term interest rates in 1971 and early 1972 are but one example of these strange and unexpected feedback effects.

The greatest contribution the United States could make toward achieving world monetary equilibrium, I believe, would be to re-nounce all attempts to influence the level or term-structure of interest rates and to adopt a policy of keeping the money supply growing at a moderate, steady rate. These recommendations should apply whether the world continues to maintain a fixed-exchange-rate system or moves to floating rates. Not until the United States settles down can we hope to establish a stable monetary framework for the world economy.

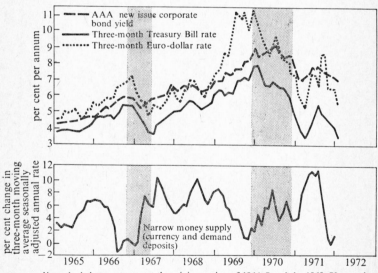

Note: shaded areas represent the mini-recession of 1966–7 and the 1969–70 recession
Sources: Federal Reserve Board; Dept. of the Treasury; First National City Bank
© Argus Research Corporation

CHART I.1. *Money Supply Changes Related to Interest-Rate Movements*

II

MONEY IN AN INTERNATIONAL ECONOMY

Introduced by HARRY G. JOHNSON

ALEXANDER K. SWOBODA
I. F. PEARCE
FRED HIRSCH

Discussion papers
(*a*) J. H. WILLIAMSON
(*b*) G. L. REUBER

MONEY IN AN INTERNATIONAL ECONOMY

INTRODUCTION

HARRY G. JOHNSON
(London School of Economics and Political Science and University of Chicago)

THE international monetary system has been both the scene of considerable disturbance in recent years and the inspiration of much interesting new work, at the theoretical level, or in some cases the refurbishing of pre-existing knowledge and application of it to new problems.

At the highest level of theory, there has been increasing questioning of the Keynesian model of balance-of-payments determination and theory of economic policy for an open economy, represented most notably by James Meade's classic work on internal and external balance. This model involves the assumptions that the authorities can use fiscal and monetary policy to control aggregate demand and the exchange rate to control the division of domestic and foreign expenditure among domestic and foreign goods and so control the balance of payments. By contrast, the emerging 'monetarist' approach, reverting to Hume's price–specie–flow mechanism, assumes the mobility of goods and capital among countries, and stresses the self-correcting nature of international reserve flows and the limitations this places on national autonomy in the use of fiscal and monetary policies. The difference is important in two practical contexts: first, the new approach suggests that it is not the quantity of money but the volume of domestic credit and/or the amount of the country's international reserves over which the central bank has control in the longer run; second, the new approach suggests that inflation is an international monetary problem, and not a series of national problems that can be fought by domestic fiscal and monetary policy, within a fixed exchange rate system. The new approach is represented in this session by the first paper, on 'Monetary Policy under Fixed Exchange Rates: Effectiveness, the

Speed of Adjustment, and Proper Use' by Professor Alexander Swoboda.

On a more directly policy-oriented level, the internal contortions of the European Community in its efforts to make a community of itself have led to agreement to establish a common European currency—to which this country is committed also—while international monetary experts concerned about the propagation of inflation from the United States to Europe through the fixed exchange-rate system have seen advantages in a European currency of international stature that would fluctuate in value against the dollar. The two concerns have produced a revival of interest in the theory of optimum currency areas, which had apparently reached a dead end by the time of the Chicago Conference on International Monetary Problems of 1966. The subject being of concern now to policy makers and economists in this country, a British literature on it has begun to emerge, including recently what may be described to this audience as 'The Williamson-Magnifico Report'. We are happy to have, as author of our second paper, an original and internationally reputed economist who has not yet been heard from on the European common currency issue. Professor Ivor Pearce's paper is on 'Some Aspects of European Monetary Integration'.

As already mentioned, the monetarist position regards the recent inflation everywhere in the Western world as an international monetary problem. A properly understood Keynesian approach to the system as a whole would produce the same conclusion, even though Keynesianism applied on an implicit closed-economy basis takes domestic inflation to be a national problem controllable by domestic economic policies. If inflation is an international problem, both the monetarist and the sophisticated Keynesian positions would suggest that its control requires management of the volume and growth of international reserves. But here we encounter a problem familiar from domestic monetary debates: monetary control will become more difficult—and some go so far as to argue impossible— if financial intermediation of one kind or another can manufacture close substitutes for money as conventionally defined and controlled (whether intermediaries can in fact do so is of course a subject of continuing debate). In the international field it appears that recently close substitutes for international liquidity have been manufactured in a large scale, through the Euro-dollar market, thus posing serious problems for rational centralized management of international liquidity as envisaged in the establishment of the plan for the issue of Special Drawing Rights at the International Monetary Fund. We have been fortunate to obtain, as author of our third paper in this session, Fred Hirsch, whom many of you will remember from his earlier days as a financial journalist here, and whose paper is on 'Control of International Liquidity and the Euro-dollar Market'.

MONETARY POLICY UNDER FIXED EXCHANGE RATES: EFFECTIVENESS, THE SPEED OF ADJUSTMENT, AND PROPER USE*

ALEXANDER K. SWOBODA

(*Graduate Institute of International Studies, Geneva*)

SOME, though far from total, agreement has begun to emerge as to the role and effects of monetary policy in a closed economy. At least major issues have been delineated and the battle joined in terms of fairly well-defined analytical frameworks. The impact of changes in the stock of money (or its rate of change) on prices, output, and interest rates has been discussed at the theoretical level and investigated empirically. Much dispute remains as to the lag-structure of response to monetary disturbances, as to the division into output and price effects, and as to proper monetary targets and policy indicators. Nevertheless, most economists would agree that monetary policy can be used as a counter-cyclical device, and that the stock of money (or its rate of growth) can, in some average sense over the medium run, be controlled, however difficult it may be to exercise such control in the very short run and however poorly monetary authorities have actually performed in this respect.

Discussion of monetary policy in the open economy, on the other hand, has proceeded at a higher level of abstraction (or over-simplification) and empirical work has remained scarce. The reason is close at hand: with some notable exceptions, recent developments in monetary theory and policy analysis have been, largely, the work of U.S.-based or U.S.-trained economists and, from an American vantage point (especially a Middle-Western one and before the

* This paper is a revised version of my 'Monetary Policy in the Open Economy: Some Analytical Notes', presented at the Second Konstanz Seminar on Monetary Theory and Policy held in June 1971. I am indebted to the participants (in particular to Karl Brunner and Leonall Anderson) for their incisive discussion and to Harry G. Johnson for his helpful comments. A version of the paper has previously been published in *Economica* (May 1973).

so-called 'dollar' crises), what more natural simplifying assumption than that of the closed economy? Yet, in recent years, under the pressure of events and following the rediscovery of Hume and Ricardo and the work of, among others, Meade, Alexander, Tsiang, Johnson, and Mundell, the analysis of monetary policy in the open economy has made much progress, at least on a theoretical plane. The focus and conclusions of that work, especially that of Mundell, have been rather different from those of analyses dealing with the closed economy: the monetary balance-of-payments adjustment mechanism, the role of capital mobility and of the size of countries are emphasized; severe limits to the use (and controllability) of the money stock as a counter-cyclical device are found and one asks not only whether monetary policy can, but also whether it should, be used for anti-cyclical purposes.

This paper attempts a brief summary of the analytical conclusions reached as to the effectiveness and proper use of monetary policy in an open economy under fixed exchange rates. Its usefulness, if any, should lie in clarification of some implicit assumptions and conclusions that have perhaps received insufficient attention in the literature. Much confusion and controversy can be avoided by precise specification of definitions and assumptions on the one hand, and by explicit delineation of the exact aims and limits of a particular piece of analysis or conclusion, on the other hand.

The first section below discusses the proposition that the money supply is an endogenous variable in an open economy under fixed exchange rates in terms of comparative statics analysis. The second section focuses on the determinants of the length of time required to regain equilibrium after a monetary disturbance. The third deals with the proper use of monetary policy under fixed exchange rates, while some concluding remarks are offered in Section IV.

I. The effectiveness of monetary policy

In a fundamental sense, monetary policy can have no lasting impact on the income level of a small open economy under fixed exchange rates. It is important to understand the meaning and limitations of this proposition as well as the assumptions required to make it hold.

First, monetary policy must be defined as an exogenous once-and-for-all change in the domestic assets of the consolidated banking system (or of the domestic source component of the base) and *not* as an exogenous change in the money supply or the rate of interest (as the point of the analysis is to show that these two variables are endogenous and not exogenous). Second, an economy will be said to be small if it cannot influence foreign interest rates, income levels, and so forth. Third, by lasting influence is meant a permanent change in income after the economy has adjusted fully to the change in the domestic assets of the banking system (i.e. the proposition is stated in terms of full-equilibrium comparative statics). Fourth, by fixed exchange rates is meant that the spot rate is rigidly fixed by the exchange-stabilization operations of the government. For simplicity, assume that the spot rates, and all other variables, are expected to remain at current levels so that the forward rate coincides with the spot exchange rate.[1]

Given these definitions, we need only three assumptions to prove the proposition stated at the beginning of this section, namely, (1) that the economic system is stable, (2) that an increase in the money supply, from equilibrium, tends to create a balance-of-payments deficit, and (3) that the associated reserve loss tends to reduce the money supply.[2] For, suppose now that we start from a position of full equilibrium in the economy; let the monetary authorities increase the domestic assets of the consolidated banking system; for a given stock of foreign-exchange reserves the money supply increases and a balance-of-payments deficit emerges (by assumption 2); reserves fall and the money supply contracts (by assumption 3); as long as the money supply has not returned to its initial value there must be a balance-of-payments deficit and a further contraction of the money stock; final equilibrium will occur when the system has returned to its initial equilibrium position, as it will under assumption 1. In the final equilibrium, the money supply is returned to its initial level, as are all real variables and prices. Only the composition of the consolidated banking system's assets has changed, the increase in domestic assets being matched by an equal decrease in foreign reserves.[3]

[1] This assumption is not strictly necessary to the proof of the proposition stated at the beginning of this section. If we assume that the system is stable and that people learn, the full equilibrium to which the system eventually converges will not be affected. However, some assumptions result in an unstable model.

[2] Under most 'reasonable' dynamic postulates, if the third assumption is satisfied, then satisfaction of the second becomes a necessary condition for stability of the system, i.e. for satisfaction of the first. This interdependence is merely noted here but plays a fundamental role in the analysis of Section III, below.

[3] This assumes, of course, that the composition of the banking system's assets does not *per se* affect the public's behaviour.

Note that this conclusion has been reached independently of any specific assumptions as to the existence of capital movements, the responsiveness of the latter to interest-rate changes, the ratio of traded to non-traded goods, or the extent to which transitional changes take the form of real output or price variations. These factors will affect the path of adjustment (and their role in this context will be discussed in the next section) but not the final equilibrium. That this should be so is readily explained. Our assumptions imply that the money supply in an open economy and under fixed exchange rates is an endogenous variable, that, other things equal, there is only one money stock compatible with payments equilibrium, and that the monetary mechanism of adjustment works properly, i.e. that it will ensure that the money stock converges to its equilibrium value. In an important sense, our conclusion is nothing but the small-country counterpart of the Ricardian 'natural distribution of specie'.

Before proceeding to remove the small-country assumption, it will be useful to illustrate the above general proposition in the specific context in which it was originally put by Mundell and amplified by the present writer.[4] Figure II.1 represents the combinations

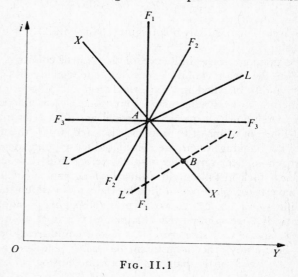

Fig. II.1

[4] See R. A. Mundell [9], as reprinted in [11], and A. K. Swoboda [14], from which Fig. II.1 is reproduced with minor changes.

of interest rate and income level that equate the supply of domestic output with the demand (the sum of domestic spending and the balance of trade) along XX, the demand for money with the supply along LL, and for which the trade balance is equal but opposite in sign to the capital account, leaving the balance of payments in equilibrium, along the curves FF. These last three curves correspond to various degrees of capital mobility (defined as the interest sensitivity of capital inflows), ranging from capital immobility along F_1F_1 to perfect capital mobility along F_3F_3. Two interpretations can be given to variations in 'income': changes in real output with prices constant or changes in domestic prices (foreign prices assumed constant) with real output constant.[5] An increase in the domestic assets of the banking system temporarily pushes LL out and to the right to, say, $L'L'$. A payments deficit emerges and the money supply contracts until LL is re-established. That is, an integral component of this type of model, in addition to the excess demand functions for money, domestic output, and foreign exchange, is the equation that ensures endogeneity of the money supply, an equation of the form:

$$\frac{\mathrm{d}M}{\mathrm{d}t} = h(F), \quad (h' > 0)$$

where F is the excess supply of foreign exchange and M the domestic money supply.

Before turning to the influence of the size of countries on this conclusion, the meaning of the expression 'endogeneity of the money stock' should be clarified and contrasted with that of 'controllability of the money stock'. Endogeneity of an economic variable is always defined in relation to a particular model and to a relevant length of run. Thus, in terms of the models discussed so far, the domestic assets of the banking system are considered to be policy-determined and exogenous over any relevant time period and endogeneity of the money stock in full equilibrium (the long run after all adjustments have taken place) is implied by the way in which the model is specific to the monetary mechanism of payments adjustment. Alternatively, one could treat changes in the stock of money as exogenous in the very short run (that is, one could treat the impact effect—before any other adjustment has taken place—of a change in domestic assets of the banking system on the stock of money as

---

[5] For the variable price case see, in particular, R. A. Mundell [10] also reprinted in [11].

exogenous in the very short run), the *rate* of change of the money stock as endogenous in the intermediate run (defined by reference to an ongoing balance-of-payments adjustment process), and the equilibrium money stock as endogenous to the system in the long run (defined by reference to complete adjustment in all markets).[6] Endogeneity, however, should not be confused with 'uncontrollability'. In buffer stock analysis, the quantity and price of coffee bought and sold are endogenous variables, yet they may or may not be 'controllable' depending on the buffer stock's inventories of coffee and money relative to the flow of private excess demands or supplies. In the present context, controllability of the money stock will depend (a) on limits set to the decumulation or accumulation of foreign-exchange reserves by the availability of foreign-exchange reserves on the one hand and that of domestic assets on the other hand, and (b) on the speed of adjustment of the system to a discrepancy between the actual and equilibrium money stock. This topic will be pursued further in Section II below.

The conclusion that monetary policy affects only the composition of the banking system's assets is of course valid only for the definition of monetary policy adopted here, namely, a once-and-for-all change in the stock of domestic assets of the consolidated banking system. This definition rules out systematic neutralization operations by the monetary authorities, that is, the creation of a *flow* of domestic assets equal in size but opposite in sign to the flow of foreign-exchange reserves. The above conclusion as to the ineffectiveness of monetary policy in terms of the full-equilibrium values of real variables depends also crucially on the 'small-country' assumption.

Define the effectiveness of monetary policy as the change in domestic income or interest rate that results from a one 'dollar' change in the domestic assets of the banking system. It is possible to show that the effectiveness of monetary policy thus defined is directly proportional to the relative size of the country undertaking the open-market operation. This proportion has been advanced by Mundell for the case of perfect capital mobility within a 'Keynesian' framework.[7] We will show that it is a fact quite general and that it follows from the proposition that, under fixed exchange rates, the final impact on all variables, except the distribution of the world's reserves, of an increase in the domestic assets of country A, is the

---

[6] This three-fold classification follows on a suggestion made by Karl Brunner at the Konstanz meeting.

[7] See [11], appendix to ch. 18.

same as that of an equivalent increase in domestic assets in any other country. That is, the final outcome is entirely determined, with the exception noted above, by the impact of the increase in domestic assets on the 'world money supply'—the sum of the money stocks in the hands of the publics of various countries.

In terms of a two-country model, we can write:

$$M_w = M_1 + M_2 = D_1 + D_2 + R_1 + R_2$$
$$= D_1 + D_2 + R_1 + (R_w - R_1) = D_1 + D_2 + R_w, \quad (1)$$

where M refers to money supply, D to the domestic assets of the consolidated banking system, R to foreign exchange reserves, the subscripts 1, 2, and w refer to country 1, country 2, and the world, respectively, and where world reserves R_w are assumed to be given. The proof of our statement is particularly simple if we can assume that each country is specialized in the production of one good, that full employment prevails in both countries, and that the income elasticity of the demand for money is unity in both countries. This case is illustrated in Fig. II.2. TT shows those combinations of the money prices of the two goods which keep the balance of trade in equilibrium (this line goes through the origin and stays fixed as long as 'real' forces do not change the equilibrium terms of trade). KK shows those combinations of the two money price levels that would keep the world money supply equal to the sum of the demands for money in the two countries. A movement along KK

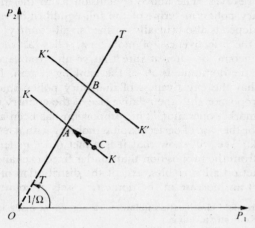

Fig. II.2

corresponds to a redistribution of the world money supply between the two countries. For a given world money supply, the distribution of specie is unique; suppose we take money away from the residents of country 2 to give it to those of country 1 and let prices vary so that we are at C. At that point there would be an excess demand for the goods of country 2 (a trade surplus for country 2) and money would flow from 1 to 2 until equilibrium is re-established at A. Suppose now that the central bank in country 1 increases the domestic assets of its banking system. By equation (1) this increases the world money supply and KK shifts up to $K'K'$. Country 1 experiences a temporary balance-of-payments deficit until the world money supply is redistributed and prices adjusted to make B the new equilibrium point. Note that the final equilibrium would also be at B had country 2 engineered the money supply increase.

It is now a simple matter to prove that the impact of a given change in the money supply of country 1 is proportional to the size of that country. Briefly, the quantity equation for the two countries is given by equations (2) and (3) below, and trade equilibrium requires (4):

$$P_1 Y_1 = M_1 V_1, \tag{2}$$

$$P_2 Y_2 = M_2 V_2, \tag{3}$$

$$\frac{P_1}{P_2} = \Omega, \tag{4}$$

where V_1 and V_2 are income velocities of circulation, Y_1 and Y_2 are real income levels, and Ω is a constant. Substituting and carrying out log differentiation yields:

$$\begin{aligned} \mathrm{d}\log P_1 + \mathrm{d}\log Y_1 &- \mathrm{d}\log P_2 - \mathrm{d}\log Y_2 \\ &= \mathrm{d}\log M_1 + \mathrm{d}\log V_1 - \mathrm{d}\log M_2 - \mathrm{d}\log V_2 = 0 \end{aligned} \tag{5}$$

Noting the Y_1, Y_2, V_1, and V_2 are assumed constant (we assumed unit income elasticity of the demand for money), (5) yields:

$$\mathrm{d}\log M_1 = \mathrm{d}\log M_2;$$

the increase in the world money supply is distributed proportionately to existing money stocks, the latter being obviously related to the size of countries (and exactly related if $V_1 = V_2$). For instance suppose that, initially the money stock of country 1 is \$10 and that of country 2 is \$90. Now let country 1 increase the money supply by \$1; in the final equilibrium the money supply of country 1

will have increased by $0·10, the other $0·90 spilling out to country 2 to increase the latter's money stock. Money prices will have increased by only 1 per cent even though the stock of money was *initially* increased by 10 per cent in country 1.

Much the same type of result can be obtained in a 'Keynesian world' where each country's economy is represented by the type of model depicted in Fig. II.1 above. The bare bones of such a model are given in Fig. II.3.[8] Income levels replace prices on the abcissa

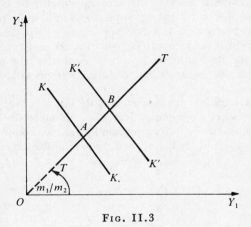

FIG. II.3

and ordinate, and the slope of the balance-of-payments equilibrium schedule TT is equal to m_1/m_2, the ratio of marginal propensities to import. Assuming that the income elasticity of the demand for imports is unity in both countries and that the capital account is initially balanced, an increase in the world money supply (whatever its origin) again shifts the KK curve to $K'K'$ and changes income levels in the two countries in the same proportion. If we now assume that the income and the interest elasticities of the demand for money are the same in the two countries, the increase in the world money supply is again distributed among the two countries in proportion to their income levels (and initial money stocks) as the system moves from A to B. This result is independent of the degree of capital mobility since, as Rudiger Dornbusch and the present writer have shown, the shift in KK is independent of the degree of capital

[8] A complete analysis of this model can be found in A. K. Swoboda and R. Dornbusch [16].

mobility and the equilibrium interest-rate differential is invariant with respect to changes in the world money supply.[9]

To summarize, the effectiveness of monetary policy, defined as the full-equilibrium impact on domestic money income of a one-dollar open-market operation is directly proportional to the size of the home country relative to that of the rest of the world, this effectiveness tending to zero as the country becomes very small in relative terms.

So far, the analysis has been carried out under the assumption of stationary expectations and once-and-for-all changes in the money supply. As has been shown by Mundell, similar results hold in terms of the comparative dynamics of equilibrium growth and inflationary paths.[10] Neglecting stock adjustments, assuming for simplicity that all goods are perfect substitutes in the world economy and that the money-income elasticity of the demand for money is unity, the equilibrium percentage rate of growth of the money supply is equal to the sum of the percentage rates of growth of output and prices. Any attempt at increasing (decreasing) the rate of monetary expansion above (below) its equilibrium level through changes in the rate of domestic credit expansion results only in a balance-of-payments deficit (surplus) in the small open economy. Equilibrium in the balance of payments (no change in the stock of reserves) requires a rate of domestic credit expansion,

$$\frac{1}{D}\frac{\mathrm{d}D}{\mathrm{d}t}, \quad \text{equal to} \quad \frac{M}{D}\left(\frac{1}{P}\frac{\mathrm{d}P}{\mathrm{d}t} + \frac{1}{Y}\frac{\mathrm{d}Y}{\mathrm{d}t}\right),$$

with symbols defined as before. Note that in this type of model, inflation in the small country is always of the imported type, except in the very short run. Prices of goods and services are determined in the international market and domestic monetary policy has but a negligible influence on international prices. Note that the inflation (or deflation) is imported through goods arbitrage; capital movements are neither necessary nor sufficient for the process to take place. They will, however, in practice, influence the speed of adjustment to inflationary or non-inflationary equilibrium, the subject to which we now turn.

---

[9] Ibid.
[10] The most important contribution is R. A. Mundell [12], ch. 15. See also Mundell [11], ch. 9; R. Komiya [5]; H. G. Johnson [3], and a forthcoming paper by A. Laffer.

II. The speed of adjustment

The discussion so far has been concerned with full-equilibrium comparative statics and once-and-for-all changes in the domestic source component of the monetary base. For practical purposes, it is important to ask how long it will take for full equilibrium to be re-established after an initial monetary disturbance and whether and to what extent disequilibrium policies can be effected. In terms of Fig. II.1 the questions we want to ask are: (a) how long will it take to restore the initial equilibrium after a shift of LL to, say, $L'L'$; (b) how feasible is it, and what is required, to keep the money supply at a level consistent with maintenance of the system at a point such as B. To answer these questions satisfactorily would require, at the analytical level, building a complete dynamic model of the adjustment process and, empirically, determining the value of the parameters that enter the analytical model. Our approach below will be a much more modest one; we will discuss, intuitively and separately, the probable influence of two factors—the degree of capital mobility and the proportion of traded to non-traded goods —on the speed of adjustment of the system. We will also consider briefly the role of exchange-rate margins. The analysis is non-rigorous and subject to all the usual caveats about implicit dynamics.

One possible procedure to obtain partial answers to these questions is as follows: suppose that somehow the system temporarily settles at point B in Fig. II.1 then ask how the magnitude of the disequilibrium at B (in a flow per unit of time sense) is affected by the two factors mentioned above. Presumably, the larger the disequilibrium at B, the more speedily, other things equal, would the (stable) system tend to return to equilibrium and the harder would policies have to be applied to maintain it at B.[11] One way of analysing this issue is to ask what policies are required to turn the temporary disequilibrium point B into a 'quasi-equilibrium' point.

Consider point B: the demand for domestic output is equal to the supply, and the demand for domestic money by residents is equal to the supply, but there is a balance-of-payments deficit. Other things equal, there would be a tendency for the money supply to decline

[11] This statement is approximate rather than exact, since the length of time required to reach equilibrium after a temporary disturbance depends not only on the speeds of adjustment in various markets but also on whether the approach to equilibrium is direct or cyclical.

as the monetary authorities intervene in the foreign-exchange market to prevent a depreciation of the home currency. However, the authorities can keep the money supply at the level implied by $L'L'$ by neutralizing the monetary effects of reserve losses.[12] Denoting the base by B, the money multiplier (assumed constant) by m, foreign-exchange reserves by R, and the domestic securities held by the central bank by D^*, we have:

$$M = mB = m(R + D^*), \qquad (6)$$

$$\frac{1}{M}\frac{\mathrm{d}M}{\mathrm{d}t} = \frac{1}{B}\left(\frac{\mathrm{d}R}{\mathrm{d}t} + \frac{\mathrm{d}D^*}{\mathrm{d}t}\right). \qquad (7)$$

Thus, keeping the money supply constant requires

$$\frac{\mathrm{d}D^*}{\mathrm{d}t} = -\frac{\mathrm{d}R}{\mathrm{d}t}. \qquad (8)$$

In words, the monetary authorities must increase (decrease) the domestic source component of the base by the same amount as the foreign source component decreases (increases), namely, by an amount equal to the balance of payments deficit (surplus), $\mathrm{d}R/\mathrm{d}t$. Thus, the extent of the balance-of-payments disequilibrium at B determines the rate of neutralization operations required to keep the system in a state of quasi-equilibrium and, in the absence of neutralization, will help determine the time interval needed to restore full equilibrium.

In this context, consider, first, the role of capital mobility, defined for simplicity as the interest-rate responsiveness of international flows of capital.[13] In the simple framework of Fig. II.1, the

[12] It may seem, at first, that treating points like B as quasi-equilibria violates Walras's law. For, how can there be a disequilibrium in the foreign-exchange market when both the money and goods markets are in equilibrium? The answer is that a *flow* excess supply of securities by the public matches their flow excess demand for foreign exchange. The authorities prevent these disequilibria from affecting the goods and money markets by absorbing the flow excess supply of securities at the existing rate of interest through their neutralization operations and supplying the foreign exchange at the existing exchange rate through their exchange-stabilization operations.

[13] Conceptually, it would be preferable to treat capital movements as a result of a stock adjustment process. The flow approach could be considered as a special short-run version of the stock-adjustment one, the interest sensitivity of flows depending, in part, on the speed at which portfolios are adjusted.

balance-of-payments disequilibrium at a quasi-equilibrium point
like B is given by expression (9) below:

$$\frac{\mathrm{d}R}{\mathrm{d}t} = \left\{ \frac{mE_i - (s + m)K_i}{-(s + m)L_i - L_yE_i} \right\} \cdot (M - M^*) < 0, \qquad (9)$$

where s and m are the marginal propensities to save and import,
respectively, E is domestic expenditure, L the demand for money,
K net capital imports, Y money income, i the rate of interest, M
and M^* are, respectively, the actual and full-equilibrium stocks of
money, and subscripted variables denote partial derivatives with
respect to the subscript.[14] Obviously, the higher the interest responsiveness of capital flows, K_i, the larger the payments disequilibrium
created by a discrepancy between the actual and full-equilibrium
money stock. In the limit, the payments disequilibrium tends to
infinity as capital mobility becomes perfect $(K_i \to \infty)$. This is the
case where neutralization becomes impossible and self-contradictory
as it would require open-market operations to be undertaken at an
infinite rate; this is inconsistent with positive and finite reserve
stocks—a deficit country would rapidly lose all its reserves, a surplus country accumulate the world's entire stock of reserves. To
summarize, the higher the degree of capital mobility the less scope
for the disequilibrium effects of monetary policy and the larger
the rate of neutralization operations required to maintain a given
quasi-equilibrium stock of money.[15]

Consider, next, the role of non-traded goods. To focus on the
point at issue, imagine that there are only three goods in the system, traded or international goods, non-traded or domestic goods,
and money; assume that the three goods are substitutes. Assume
further that the foreign-currency price—and hence the domestic-
currency price at a given exchange rate—of international goods is
fixed or exogenously determined. From equilibrium, let the monetary
authorities increase the money supply; the impact effect is to create
an excess supply of money and an excess demand for both domestic
and international goods. The excess demand for foreign goods is
reflected in an excess demand for foreign exchange and the money

---

[14] For a derivation and further explanation see A. K. Swoboda [14].

[15] If the stock-adjustment view of capital movements is adopted, the required extent of neutralization policies becomes independent of the degree of
capital mobility in the long run; after the stock adjustment has been completed, the neutralization rate depends only on the trade disequilibrium
associated with the quasi-equilibrium point B.

supply will tend to decrease as the authorities sell foreign exchange to stabilize the exchange rate. In the end, full equilibrium will be re-established when the money supply has returned to its original level, with international prices and domestic prices unchanged. However, there will have been a transitory increase in domestic goods prices. The length of time it will take for the system to return to equilibrium will depend partly on the size of the impact effect on the excess demand for foreign exchange and hence on the balance of payments and the rate of change of the money supply. To the extent that part of the excess supply of money is absorbed by a rise in the prices of domestic goods, the excess demand (per unit of time) for international goods will be smaller than it otherwise would be (by Walras's law). Therefore, other things equal, we would expect the rapidity with which the system adjusts to a monetary disturbance to be directly related to the ratio of traded to non-traded goods, even though the final equilibrium is not.

The same type of reasoning can be applied to the analysis of the role of non-traded goods in the transmission of 'imported inflation'. We will show that, contrary to a sometimes expressed belief, the presence of non-traded goods does not affect the full transmission of inflation in the long run and in the absence of neutralization policies; it does, however, affect the 'length of the short run' and the rate at which neutralization operations need to be carried out to maintain the domestic below the international rate of inflation.

These points are illustrated in Fig. II.4, which is based on a diagram used by R. A. Mundell to analyse the effects of devaluation (an issue with which we are not concerned here).[16] The curve DD shows those combinations of domestic goods prices, P_D, and international goods prices, P_I, that equate the demand and supply of non-traded goods, II those combinations of P_I and P_D that leave the excess demand for international goods equal to zero, and MM those combinations of the two prices that equate the demand for money with the existing stock. The three curves are drawn on the assumption that the three goods are substitutes; in addition, assume that the real excess demand functions are homogeneous of degree zero in the two money prices and the nominal quantity of money. Initial equilibrium is at Q. Suppose now that the price of international goods rises in the rest of the world; the domestic-currency price of international goods must rise in the same proportion, say from P_I to P_I^*, if the rate of exchange is fixed and if goods arbitrage

[16] See R. A. Mundell [12], ch. 9.

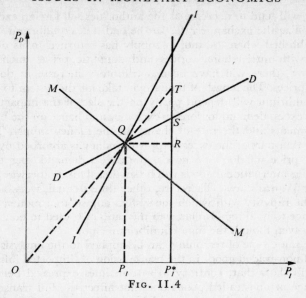

FIG. II.4

takes place. Before the price of domestic goods changes, the impact effect of the rise in foreign prices is to move the commodity prices to point R; there is now an excess demand for money and domestic goods and an excess supply of foreign goods. The price of domestic goods begins to rise, and the country experiences a balance-of-payments surplus that shifts the MN curve up and to the right pulling the DD and II curves in its wake. Final equilibrium is established at T; by the homogeneity postulate the money prices and the money supply will all have increased by $P_I P_I^*/OP_I$.[17]

The movement to T, however, will tend to be slower with non-traded goods present in the system. For, as domestic goods prices rise, part of the initial excess supply of money will be eliminated and the deficit per unit of time be lower. Similarly, keeping the money supply at its initial level involves a lower rate of sterilization

[17] It may be interesting to note that Mundell shows that a devaluation of $P_I P_I^*/OP_I$ leads to a final equilibrium at T. Thus we have shown that an $x\%$ devaluation is equivalent in its effects to an $x\%$ 'exogenous' increase in foreign prices, a point that is consistent with a proposition developed by E. A. Kuska [6] in an analysis of devaluation based on a Patinkin-type disaggregated model. Kuska shows that an $x\%$ devaluation is equivalent to a $(100x/100 - x)\%$ increase in foreign money stocks. With due attention paid to the definition of percentage changes, the two propositions are equivalent.

operations when non-traded goods are present. As foreign prices rise and the money supply is kept constant, domestic goods prices rise until the market for domestic goods is cleared, i.e. the system moves to point S. At S, the flow excess supply of international goods is equal to the payments surplus and to the rate of sterilization operations required to keep MM fixed. Define an aggregate price index by $P = aP_D + (1 - a)P_I$, where the quantity weights are, respectively, the shares of domestic and international goods in total expenditure. Sterilization policies keep the percentage increase in P below the percentage increase in P_I by preventing P_D from rising in the same proportion. The higher the share of non-traded goods in total expenditure, the less P will increase for given increases in total expenditure, the less P will increase for given increases in P_I and lesser increases in P_D (such as those involved in moving to point S). The greater the elasticity of substitution between traded and non-traded goods, the closer the percentage increase in P_D will be to that in P_I (the closer point S will lie to point T) and the less successful will a sterilization policy be in moderating the rise in the price index P.

The analysis above was carried out in terms of a once-and-for-all increase in international goods prices. It could easily be recast in terms of rates of increase of international goods prices, domestic goods prices, and money supply, care being taken to allow for the stock effects on the demand for real balances owing to changes in the expected rate of inflation.

Finally, we have assumed so far that the spot rate of exchange was perfectly fixed and expected to remain so, and that there was no difference between the spot and forward rates. This is clearly an 'unrealistic' assumption and an inappropriate one in certain circumstances. In the real world, the spot rate is allowed to fluctuate, albeit within narrow intervention limits, and the forward rate is not systematically pegged. Complete discussion of the complications introduced by this flexibility is impossible here. Suffice it to say that exchange-rate margins make it possible for the system to behave somewhat like a flexible-rate system as long as the margins are not reached. For instance, an increase in the money supply would lead to a permanent increase in prices or income (with fixed money wages and money illusion) as the home currency depreciates, that is, as long as the price of foreign exchange does not rise to the upper intervention point; moreover, the higher the degree of capital mobility, the greater the effectiveness of monetary policy under flexible exchange rates.[18] The flexibility of *forward* rates gives some additional scope for the use of monetary policy even in the face of a high degree of capital mobility and pegged spot rates. For, if it is the flow of arbitrage capital that is in perfectly elastic supply with respect to the *covered* interest-rate differential, it is still possible to create a divergence between domestic and foreign interest rates by affecting the premium or discount on forward exchange. However, the scope for affecting premia on forward exchange is severely limited as long as confidence in the parity is maintained; for the speculative supply or demand for forward exchange will tend to become perfectly elastic at the exchange-rate margins.

The main strands of the argument up to this point can be summarized by four propositions. (1) The full-equilibrium effect on incomes, prices, and interest rates of a once-and-for-all change in the domestic assets of the banking system of an open economy is directly proportional to the economic size of the country relative to the rest of the world. A corollary of this proposition is that the effectiveness of monetary policy thus defined tends to zero as the country becomes smaller and smaller. (2) This conclusion is independent of the degree of capital mobility and the proportion of traded to non-traded goods. (3) In the short run, however, it is possible for a country to affect its price and income level by maintaining the money stock at a given level through neutralization policy, that is, by combining a money-*stock* policy with a *flow*-neutralization policy—where the flow of open-market sales (purchases) equals the balance-of-payments surplus (deficit) implied by the maintenance of the money supply below (above) its full-equilibrium value. This possibility is not available when capital is perfectly mobile or there are no non-traded goods as the required rate of neutralization policy would rapidly become infinite. (4) In the long run, however, the maintenance of quasi-equilibrium positions is incompatible with fixed exchange rates; the limits are reached in theory when only domestic assets back the money supply in case of a deficit, and when only foreign assets back the money supply in case of a surplus. As the ratio of domestic to foreign assets is usually larger than 1, this means that a quasi-equilibrium involving a surplus can, potentially, be maintained for a longer lapse of time than one involving a deficit.[19]

---

[18] See R. A. Mundell [11], chs. 17 and 18, and E. Sohmen [13].

[19] This statement is subject to at least two qualifications. First, in practice, the limits are reached faster than in theory as speculation as to exchange-rate

The effects of monetary and neutralization policy under fixed exchange rates have now been outlined. It remains to try to define the appropriate use of monetary policy in an open economy.[20]

III. The appropriate use of monetary policy

There are, we have argued, severe limits to the effectiveness of monetary policy as a counter-cyclical device under fixed exchange rates except in the short run. However, within the limits set by the available stock of reserves and the openness of the economy as measured by its relative size, the degree of capital mobility, and the ratio of traded to non-traded goods, monetary policy coupled with neutralization of reserve flows can still be used to stabilize income and prices in the short run. Under what circumstances is it 'appropriate' to use the monetary instrument in such a fashion under fixed exchange rates?

The answer, I would argue, is 'in those cases where the balance of payments takes care of itself in the long run'. There are two principal cases where this statement would apply.

First, suppose that the initial position is one of internal and external balance; then introduce cyclical variations in the balance of payments, deficits alternating with surpluses but averaging out to zero over a finite time period. In that case it may be appropriate to maintain the money supply at its long-run 'average' equilibrium level, neutralizing temporary reserve changes through open-market operations. A prerequisite for the success of such a policy is that the reserve stock be large enough relative to disturbances to finance temporary deficits without causing anticipations of devaluation. Moreover, this policy will succeed in stabilizing income and prices

---

changes sets in. Second, as payments imbalances are usually defined, the foreign-exchange assets that are accumulated (decumulated) in the case of a surplus (deficit) are those of the monetary authorities; the ratio of domestic to foreign-exchange assets of the monetary authorities is quite low in several open economies; in this case the scope for neutralization of a surplus through traditional open-market operations will be limited. A substitute for open-market operations is to induce commercial banks to absorb into their portfolios the foreign-exchange assets that would otherwise flow to the central bank; this is one of the goals of the German Bundesbank's policy of offering commercial banks special swap rates.

[20] In what follows, I abstract, however, from the problem of the proper use of monetary policy by the centre or nth country of the system.

only if the payments disturbances originate predominantly in the capital account, that is, if in Fig. II.1 the curve *FF* shifts while the *XX* curve stays put. If this is not the case, stabilizing the money supply will not suffice to stabilize prices and income.[21]

Second, consider disequilibrium situations where the monetary-policy requirements of internal and external balance coincide, that is, situations where inflation is coupled with a deficit or where deflation is accompanied by a payments surplus. In these cases, directing monetary policy towards internal balance will also relieve the existing payments disequilibrium.

On the other hand, the attempt to use monetary policy as a counter-cyclical device in so-called dilemma cases, unless these reverse themselves fairly rapidly, is incompatible with a regime of fixed exchange rates. For, suppose that deflation is accompanied by a deficit, using monetary policy (coupled with neutralization operations) to restore full employment will eventually lead to exhaustion of foreign-exchange reserves and vice versa for the case where a payments surplus is coupled with inflation. These are, of course, the dilemma cases emphasized in Meade's classic work.[22]

The preceding remarks should not be interpreted to mean that there is no important role for monetary policy in the open economy under fixed exchange rates. For, though monetary policy is rarely appropriate as a counter-cyclical device and taken by itself, unless the level of reserves is of no concern, it does represent a very powerful instrument of balance-of-payments policy. In terms of full-equilibrium comparative statics a \$1 open-market sale of securities increases the stock of foreign-exchange reserves by \$1 $(M_w - M_1)/M_w$ under the assumptions listed in Section I above. As M_1 becomes very small relative to M_w, the reserve gain tends to equality with the open-market sale.

This suggests that some other instrument be used for internal balance, leaving monetary policy to take care of residual payments imbalances. This is precisely the purpose of Mundell's well-known monetary-fiscal policy-mix analysis which consists of two separate (though related) propositions:[23] (1) that fiscal and monetary policy have different impacts on internal and external balance and

---

[21] A case can also be made for the use of monetary policy to stabilize income and prices, when disturbances originate in finite shifts in the public's portfolio preferences.

[22] See J. E. Meade [7].

[23] See R. A. Mundell [8], reprinted in [11].

hence represent two separate instruments with the help of which it is possible to achieve simultaneously internal and external balance, a comparative-statics proposition or possibility theorem; (2) that, in a decentralized system of policy responses, *assigning* monetary policy to external balance and fiscal policy to internal balance leads to convergence to the desired position of simultaneous internal and external balance while the reverse assignment of instruments to targets does not, a proposition in economic dynamics.

Whereas the first of these propositions suggests that to achieve internal and external balance simultaneously it is sufficient to find those values of the monetary and fiscal instruments that will do so and set these instruments accordingly, the second proposition asserts that in a system of decentralized response—or more fundamentally in a system of limited information—the proper use of monetary policy under fixed exchange rates is for external balance. The fundamental basis for this assignment of the monetary instrument resides in the automatic monetary mechanism of payments adjustment. As a matter of fact, it can be shown that stability of the open economy requires as a necessary condition that an increase in the money supply, from equilibrium, leads to a deterioration of the balance of payments. It turns out that fulfilment of that condition is necessary and sufficient to ensure stability of the assignment of monetary policy to the balance of payments and of fiscal policy to internal balance.[24]

To conclude this section, a few remarks on the interpretation of the expression 'appropriate' or 'proper' use of monetary policy are in order. The normative content of these expressions is limited even though, I would argue, important. The appropriateness of the particular recommendations discussed above is conditional on certain maintained hypotheses and restricted to a narrow concept of 'appropriateness'. The principal maintained hypothesis is that a fixed-exchange regime prevails and that no alternative system is available. Appropriateness basically means (a) 'possible' in terms of a fixed-target framework limited to fairly narrow definitions of internal and external balance, and (b) convergent under a system of decentralized decision-making under limited information. In addition, trying monetary policy to the balance of payments is seen to be the only governing principle for monetary policy consistent with maintenance of a fixed exchange-rate system in the long run.

[24] This point is demonstrated and related to the problem of limited information in A. K. Swoboda [15].

These conclusions are quite consistent with (a) a stock-adjustment view of capital movements—the latter implying simply that reconciliation of internal and external balance through manipulation of the capital account is possible only in the short run but would imply ever-widening interest-rate differentials in the long run, and (b) with the argument first advanced by Johnson and pursued by Williamson that the composition of the balance of payments that results from application of the policy may, or even is likely to, run counter to the dictates of the welfare considerations implied by maximization of a social welfare function over time.[25] In the context of the policy-mix model, this last consideration implies that a third instrument be found to make the composition of the balance of payments consistent with the steady-state composition of the balance of payments that maximizes world welfare over time.

IV. Concluding remarks

The main thrust of my analysis has been to argue that monetary policy is an appropriate instrument of anti-cyclical policy under fixed exchange rates in a small open economy in anything but the short run. That is, systematic use of monetary policy to stabilize incomes and prices is, save under exceptional circumstances, incompatible with the proper functioning of a system of fixed exchange rates. This argument does not require that the stock of money be uncontrollable; except under extreme circumstances (such as perfect mobility of capital), some measure of control over the stock of money can be retained in the short run; rather, the issue concerns the use to which the remaining measure of control should be put. The simultaneous pursuit of internal and external balance requires the use of at least two instruments of economic policy, say, fiscal and monetary policy, and the assignment of instruments to targets is not a matter of indifference, the monetary instrument having a clear comparative advantage in affecting the balance of payments and the stock of reserves.

These are well-known conclusions; this paper has merely tried to make their basis quite explicit and to deal in more detail with the role of capital mobility and non-traded goods. Much further work needs to be done on these issues, notably, at an empirical level, on the role of size, capital mobility, forward markets, and non-traded

[25] See Harry G. Johnson [4] and John H. Williamson [17].

goods.[26] Finally, new issues for analysis and policy arise in an inflationary world where all goods are close substitutes; for, in such a world, fiscal policy of the counter-cyclical variety loses much of *its* power to affect income and price levels in small countries and the issues of control of the over-all inflationary process, and the role of large and reserve-issuing countries therein, becomes of paramount importance.

REFERENCES

[1] BRAINARD, W. 'Uncertainty and the Effectiveness of Policy', *American Economic Review*, vol. lvii, No. 2, May 1967, pp. 411–25.

[2] COURCHENE, Thomas J. 'The Price–Specie–Flow Mechanism and the Gold-Exchange Standard: Some Exploratory Empiricism Relating to the Endogeneity of Country Money Balances', in H. G. Johnson, A. K. Swoboda (eds.), *The Economics of Common Currencies* (London: George Allen & Unwin, 1973).

[3] JOHNSON, H. G. 'The Monetary Approach to Balance-of-Payments Theory', in M. B. Connolly and A. K. Swoboda (eds.), *International Trade and Money* (London: George Allen & Unwin, 1973).

[4] —— 'Theoretical Problems of the International Monetary System', in *Further Essays in Monetary Economics* (London: George Allen & Unwin, 1973).

[5] KOMIYA, R. 'Economic Growth and the Balance of Payments: A Monetary Approach', *J.P.E.*, vol. 77, No. 1, Jan.–Feb. 1969, pp. 153–70.

[6] KUSKA, E. A. 'The Theory of Devaluation', *Economica*, vol. 39, No. 155, Aug. 1972, pp. 309–15.

[7] MEADE, J. E. *The Balance of Payments* (London: Oxford University Press, 1951).

[8] MUNDELL, R. A. 'The Appropriate Use of Monetary and Fiscal Policy under Fixed Exchange Rates', *I.M.F. Staff Papers*, vol. 9, No. 1, Mar. 1962.

[9] —— 'The International Disequilibrium System', *Kyklos*, vol. 14, 1961, pp. 153–70.

[10] —— 'The Monetary Dynamics of International Adjustment under Fixed and Flexible Exchange Rates', *Q.J.E.*, vol. lxxiv, No. 2, May 1960, pp. 227–57.

[11] —— *International Economics* (New York: Macmillan, 1968).

[12] —— *Monetary Theory: Inflation, Interest, and Growth in the World Economy* (Pacific Palisades: Goodyear, 1971).

[26] For some interesting empirical work on the issue of controllability and endogeneity of the money stock, see Thomas J. Courchene [2] and Manfred Willms [18].

[13] SOHMEN, E. *Flexible Exchange Rates*, revised edn. (Chicago: University of Chicago Press, 1969).

[14] SWOBODA, A. K. 'Equilibrium, Quasi-Equilibrium, and Macro-Economic Policy under Fixed Exchange Rates', *Q.J.E.*, vol. 86, 1972, pp. 162–71.

[15] —— 'On Limited Information and the Assignment Problem' (paper presented at the Paris–Dauphine Conference on 'Stabilization Policies in Interdependent Economies', Mar. 1971), in E. Claassen and P. Salin (eds.), *Stabilization Policies in Interdependent Economies* (Amsterdam: North-Holland, 1972).

[16] —— and DORNBUSCH, R. 'International Adjustment, Policy, and Monetary Equilibrium in a Two-Country Model', in Connolly and Swoboda (eds.), op. cit.

[17] WILLIAMSON, John H. 'On the Normative Theory of Balance-of-Payments Adjustment', in G. Clayton, J. C. Gilbert, and R. Sedgwick (eds.), *Monetary Theory and Policy in the 1970s* (Oxford: Oxford University Press, 1971).

[18] WILLMS, Manfred. 'Controlling Money in an Open Economy: The German Case', *F.R.B. of St. Louis Review*, vol. 53, No. 4, Apr. 1971.

SOME ASPECTS OF
EUROPEAN MONETARY INTEGRATION

I. F. PEARCE
(*University of Southampton*)

Towards the end of 1971 the government of the United Kingdom committed itself, or perhaps one should say almost committed itself, to entry into the European Economic Community. As the rules of the Community provide that the rules should from time to time be changed, the full implications of this commitment are by definition unspecified. Except for the privilege of a seat upon the board of management, our position might well be compared to that of a shareholder in the celebrated joint-stock company set up in 1719 'for a purpose so secret that it could not be revealed even to the subscribers of capital'.

One likely change in the rules can, however, be foreseen. We have it on the authority of the Werner Commission that there is every intention that member states will, eventually, be required to abolish their national currency and accordingly to abandon local control of the quantity of money and credit. This obviously implies the removal of the possibility of making home industry immediately more competitive, if required, by devaluation of the currency relative to the currencies of other regions. It should be noted especially that this is a proposal to 'abandon', to 'abolish', or to 'remove' an instrument of policy. It is a proposal, therefore, which should be treated with infinite suspicion. At least we should suppose it to be guilty until proved innocent.

It is not the purpose of this paper to offer a definitive account of the pros and cons of a common currency. Rather it is designed only to draw attention to one or two points which are much less frequently referred to than some others. It is not impossible that a policy which on the surface looks like a desirable simplification may in practice call for structural changes and dislocation of such magnitude that the cost would far outweigh the gains. Since an invitation is here extended to count the cost of monetary integration, it is obviously proper to mention the gains, so as a first step we attempt this.

Gains from a common currency

The most obvious advantage of a common currency is perhaps best summed up in the attitude of the apocryphal traveller abroad who is supposed to wonder why it is that foreigners do not use sensible money like the British. There are costs involved in diversification of units in which value is measured. Again there are obvious economies of scale to be gained in standardizing instruments of credit and in the management of financial institutions, although the exact point at which economies of scale become diseconomies owing to communication difficulties is not at all clear. At the very least, a common currency would allow us to escape a certain amount of arithmetic.

Speculative capital movements might be reduced considerably, certainly those which are generated by rumours of currency depreciation. On the other hand, more centralized financial institutions could lead to even greater speculative capital movements between common currency areas as a counterweight to the reduction between member states. The larger the area where currency is at risk, the larger the holding of funds likely to be affected.

Again it is argued that a common currency would remove the risk attached to foreign currency dealing. If a country devalues, all foreigners holding the devalued money suffer a loss. This injustice would be avoided if devaluation were impossible. But once more it is difficult to see the force of this unless the whole world used a common currency; for the larger the devaluing area the more holders of its currency there are likely to be.

The Werner Commission itself seem to take the view that one of the most important means of maintaining balanced international payments is via capital movements designed to take advantage of interest-rate differentials between countries. The Commission clearly believes that a common currency would facilitate these movements by removing an element of risk. The rise in the rate of interest required to encourage a movement of capital discourages investment, however, so that one suspects that balance-of-payment adjustments may be brought about as much by changes in the level of employment as by capital transfers if this mechanism is relied upon.

It is sometimes said also that a common currency would encourage trade and lead to a welfare gain accordingly. In so far as trading costs are reduced and trading risks mitigated this may be marginally true, but to look for large-scale gains on this account would seem to involve some wishful thinking. The suggestion, for example, that transactions are a function of frequency of contacts, obeying a cube rule, and that a common money is like a common language, comes close to presupposing that businessmen cannot do sums (which may be true) or that if they cannot they have insufficient wit to employ accountants who can (which is certainly not true).

We turn now to another quasi-argument for a common currency which is deserving of a separate heading.

They do it, why not us?

Whenever doubts are expressed about the feasibility of a common currency someone is sure to say, 'Look at the United States of America' or 'Look at Ireland and the U.K.' 'If U.S.A. can have a common currency why should a common currency be impossible for Europe?' This looks like a very respectable empirical argument until one puts the boot on the other foot. There is equally good evidence to support a contrary view. There have been eight major currency revaluations in Europe in twelve years and at the time of writing a partial abandonment of fixed parities. All of these adjustments occurred in spite of the authorities' declared intention to maintain fixed rates and against the obvious wishes of government. Devaluations certainly did not take place as part of a planned policy to change rates so as to achieve some desired end.

In the face of these facts it is difficult to avoid the conclusion that there must be something about the European case which is very different from North America. Europe and America have different institutions, different histories, and they have different problems. To recommend the abolition of European currencies in order to gain economies of scale is rather like recommending that we cut the tails off all monkeys to avoid the need to distinguish them from chimpanzees, thereby gaining economies in the use of language. It is like arguing that any monkey must be able to manage without a tail because chimpanzees do so without any obvious ill effect. But no one would dispute the monkey's loss of efficiency and welfare. Indeed, for all we know, a chimpanzee might be able to make good use of a tail himself if he had one.

This may be a good point at which to refer briefly to the more standard argument for the retention of national currencies, so that we may fairly present the opposing view. The introduction of a common currency does not automatically unify the structure of economic institutions, including trade unions, nor does it magically endow participating countries with a common background of experience. Hence it does not unify attitudes to full employment, inflation, or productivity and growth. Again, if there are impediments to the free movement of factors of production between regions, technical change and/or changes in demand call for changes in the real terms of trade, i.e. in relative commodity prices. Employment policy, varying pressures for increased wages, and ordinary market forces combine to generate differing rates of change in the general level of prices between countries. Exchange-rate depreciation provides a ready means of adjusting these disparities without undue disturbance. It would seem to be foolish to abolish such a convenient instrument of policy.

Representing the opposite view I now quote Professor Robert Mundell.[1] 'It is sometimes argued that a fixed exchange system cannot work because there is no adjustment mechanism. The argument is sheer nonsense. First no-one would deny that there is a highly effective exchange mechanism operating between the different districts of the Federal Reserve System. But who could deny that Canada ... has had an adjustment mechanism from 1962 to 1968?' ... (They do it why not us!) ... 'Under a fixed (exchange) rate the *quantity* of money is used to achieve balance of payments equilibrium while the *price* of money is fixed to achieve stability; under a flexible rate the price of money is used to achieve balance of payments equilibrium while the quantity of money is used to achieve price stability. An extra degree of freedom is achieved only if one or other target is given up.'

This argument of Professor Mundell's purports to show that one does not after all throw away an instrument of policy by imposing fixed exchange rates (a common currency). But this is only because he sets a new target over and above those which would be considered sufficient by advocates of occasional exchange-rate adjustment; exchange-rate adjustment is an *alternative* method of balancing international payments when the general level of prices get out of line. If exchange-rate adjustment does the job then we do not need to keep the general level of prices in line. Yet Mundell imposes this as a target to be attained by controlling the quantity of money.

[1] 'Towards a better International Monetary System', *Journal of Money, Credit and Banking*, Aug. 1969.

It is true of course that we may wish, as a target, to moderate the rate of inflation and that fiscal and monetary policy may play a part in this. But this is a very different thing from setting a target which requires the maintenance of a particular ratio of the general level of prices with those of the rest of the world, particularly when that ratio will naturally change under the influence of growth and technological change.

If it were true, as Mundell implies, that control of the quantity of money is an effective instrument both in the discouragement of inflation and in balancing the balance of payments, no one would wish to argue for flexible exchange rates. Mundell says it can be such an instrument and quotes North American experience. Others say it cannot and quote European experience. The truth is probably that for some areas one mechanism will work, whilst other areas require both. It all depends whether we are talking of a monkey or a chimpanzee.

The new quantity theorists have their arguments which are interesting and important. Some economists, however, would explain the correlation between the general level of prices and the quantity of money the other way round, by saying that the general level of prices determines the quantity of money. Pressure to increase some money wage rates combined with fierce resistance to reductions in others may force up the general level of prices. If sufficient money is not forthcoming to finance increased prices then the development of new forms of credit or credit-creating institutions is induced; or fears of unemployment may force governments to act to increase the quantity of money whether they like it or not. The truth probably lies somewhere in between. Control of the money supply may go some way towards maintaining price stability but not the whole way. Conversely, inflationary pressures of one kind or another will inhibit the power of governments to control the money supply. The strength of these forces probably varies from country to country. North America is a chimpanzee which manages quite well without a tail. Europe needs its tail.

The analogy of the monkey and the chimpanzee may be pursued still further. The monkey could have evolved its tail because of its way of life, or it could have chosen its way of life because it was blessed with a tail. Whichever way it was, it would prefer not to have it cut off. Similarly national institutions, attitudes, and expectations in Europe may have grown up because currency depreciation is possible, or currency depreciation may have been made necessary by national attitudes. No doubt if one cut off the European tail, attitudes and expectations would adapt. But at what cost? The point is not whether this or that method of adjustment is *possible*, but which method of adjustment is *socially desirable*.

It is more than probable that when, in the past, the quantity and price of money were simultaneously determined more by the relationship between money and gold than by government policy and when gold was a *de facto* common currency, balance-of-payments equilibrium was achieved more by changes in the level of employment than by changes in the general level of prices. To reimpose the same sort of rigidity with a common currency may be to reimpose the same 'solution' to the balance-of-payments problem.

Exchange-rate adjustment as an equilibrium-hastening policy

At an earlier point it was explained that the main purpose of this paper is to introduce one or two less familiar arguments against a common currency rather than to present a definitive account of the pros and cons. The stage is now set for this.

The quantity-of-money mechanism for adjusting the balance of payments is essentially one which is supposed to ensure that no country will consume more than the value of its product. Once we have this, market forces may be relied on to adjust prices so as to equate supply and demand for all of the various commodities involved and the correct real terms of trade will emerge.

Looked at this way, we see that there is much more to balance-of-payments adjustment than simply keeping the general level of prices in line with other countries. Reference to market forces reminds us that in order to maintain balanced payments in the face of growth and technical change we require continuous changes in relative prices. This ordinarily means changes in the relative prices of traded and non-traded goods as well as in the real terms of trade. When relative prices change, the very meaning of the general level of prices becomes ambiguous. Conversely, some price changes are called for even when the general level of prices, suitably defined, remains constant. The point I now make is that it is frequently easier and much less socially disruptive to bring about these changes by currency depreciation than by leaving everything to market forces.

Consider, for example, two countries in a trading relationship with balanced payments and full employment. Suppose now that in country 1 there is a technological advance which increases production, for given resources, in the commodity exported and that this is unmatched by any corresponding change in country 2. Output and incomes go up in country 1 increasing the demand for imports with no corresponding increase in demand for exports. To put matters right, prices must rise in country 2 or fall in country 1. Alternatively, country 1 might devalue its currency, leaving money prices constant in both countries. Which is easier and more convenient? The adjustment via devaluation will take place as quickly as the consumer can adjust to new prices. Left to ordinary market forces, however, the problem of adjustment could be much more complicated.

The immediate impact of the technological change postulated must be an increase in unsold stocks in country 1 and the opposite in country 2. Unemployment will appear in country 1. If an attempt is made to get rid of this by running a budget deficit or by increasing the quantity of money, then an imbalance of payments will occur. Reserves will flow from country 1 to country 2. There should be a rise in prices in country 2 which will raise the price of imports in country 1. This should switch demand to country 1's commodity and full employment will return without the aid of further budget deficits or further increases in the money supply. This is a long and complicated path with transitory unemployment by the way. Moreover it is just one account of what might happen, full of possibilities for things to go wrong.

Government policy is, or should be, of two kinds. Some policies, for example, taxation, are designed to affect the character of the final market equilibrium. That is, some policies seek to change the fundamental structure of the economy because it is believed that one pattern of production and consumption is better than another. Other policies, however, are equilibrium-hastening policies intended not to affect the final 'real' situation but to cause the equilibrium pattern of prices and production to emerge as quickly as possible with as little disruption as possible during the transition period. If current money prices *in disequilibrium* are closer to what would be equilibrium prices after devaluation than they are to those prices necessary for equilibrium without devaluation, then we may reach equilibrium quicker and with less toil and trouble by devaluation.

Nor is this all. It is misleading to say, as we sometimes do, that market forces will adjust everything as long as wages and prices are fully flexible. We say this not because we believe full employment, balanced payments, and the rest follow immediately, once we have the right prices, but because we believe that prices will not change in the direction necessary for equilibrium *until* people are willing to accept equilibrium rewards and produce equilibrium quantities of goods. Inflexible prices are a symptom of corresponding production rigidities, not a cause. What is needed is not only flexible prices and wages but also flexible supplies of goods and flexible locations of industry and/or mobility of factors of production. All of these things are assumed when we talk of the market-equilibrium process. And the fact is that the market-equilibrating process in this sense frequently does not work and is widely recognized not to work. Indeed, the whole theory of international trade exists precisely because we recognize that labour and other factors of production are not sufficiently mobile across national boundaries. Nor is there any reason to suppose they would become so if a common currency were introduced.

Whether a group of regions form an optimal currency area or not is a question of how well certain kinds of market-equilibrating forces operate within that region. And it may be that some measure of the efficiency of market forces is given by the extent to which it has proved necessary to develop alternatives. Monetary arrangements which permit countries from time to time to change exchange rates may have evolved because the failure of market forces has demonstrated the need for some other mechanism. Or, alternatively, the fact that parities can be changed may have allowed different regions to develop their institutions separately so as to inhibit the 'proper' operation of market forces.

The point we wish to make in this section is simply this. There is a sharp distinction between regions within which factors of production are mobile and location of industry is flexible, and larger areas composed of separate countries with different languages and customs which inhibit the operation of market forces in the wider sense. In the one, adjustment takes place by changing the structure and location of industry. In the other, the adjustment is effected by allowing prices to accommodate themselves to the more rigid structure. It does not matter whether the differences arise because of differing institutional arrangements or whether the differing institutional arrangements generated the differences. The differences are there, are real, and will not be removed simply by the imposition of a common currency. Adjustable exchange rates are needed precisely because they constitute a valuable instrument for smoothing the path to equilibrium wherever the real underlying rigidities in the market processes, which we identify with international trade, are present. The remainder of this paper considers a selection of market-adjustment difficulties which might be the consequence of abolition of present institutional arrangements.

Wage formation under a common currency

Most of what follows derives from a crucial assumed consequence of the abolition of national currencies. It is a fact that money wage rates in various industries are greatly influenced by the activities of trade unions. They must also be influenced by the forces of supply and demand. It may well be that the conflict between these two pressures together with downward stickiness goes some way towards an explanation of the rise in the general level of prices which is a persistent feature of almost any money economy. One obvious consequence of the abolition of national currencies would seem to be to add a third pressure, the influence of which might be totally disruptive. We explain this as follows.

Given that factors of production are not mobile across national boundaries, it is easy to show that ordinary market forces do not necessarily operate to equate either the real or money rewards of those factors on either side of the border. It is to be expected that a labourer in (say) the agricultural industry in France would not be paid a wage in France equivalent to the sterling wage of his U.K. counterpart. The reason for this is that, although their product goes to satisfy a common world demand, techniques of production tend to differ because of differing supplies of capital and labour within the separate regions.

On the other hand, as long as French labour is paid in francs and U.K. labour is paid in sterling, and as long as commodity prices in the two countries are expressed in different currencies, it is not at all easy to observe differences in *real* wages. Furthermore, as long as France remains France and the U.K. remains the U.K., the arguments for *expecting* or *thinking it right* that real wages should be the same are not strong. An integrated Europe with a common currency would be in a very different situation. As soon as a common currency is imposed, differences in real wages between the national groups become obvious. It is impossible to believe that trade unions would miss the opportunity afforded and it is impossible to believe that employers' arguments (if they could think of any) for maintaining national differentials would be acceptable.

With a national currency different from all others, trade union negotiators appeal to *national* cost of living changes and seek to maintain or improve differentials with *other* trades than their own or are concerned with their own industry's capacity to pay. It is easy to imagine in these circumstances that the forces of supply and demand are dominant. A strong trade union may demand and get higher wages but this simply means that competitive forces will now direct capital to those industries with the stronger union, and hence the higher wages, precisely because they have high wages. The marginal productivity rule remains. High wages tend to be associated with a high value of the marginal product, whether the high capital labour ratio justifying high wages is a consequence of high wages or the cause. We do not deny the influence of trade union activity in forming wage rates in a national economy. We claim only a reasonable correlation between high productivity and high wages. Coal miners are poorly paid relatively because they are part of a declining industry. A rise in wage rates brings about a faster decline and so on.

In an integrated Europe we are likely to have more than one level of productivity, simply because of differing techniques of production owing to different patterns of national resources or other causes. The pressures will be to equate all *money* wages throughout the whole common currency area with those of the group with the highest productivity, industry by industry. Eventually productivity must adjust. But it must adjust without factor mobility, or at least with a much inhibited factor mobility. The social dislocation involved could be considerable. It is not difficult to show that whole industries may have to disappear. In the next section we give examples.

Before proceeding to examples, however, we repeat two essential points. If real wages in various industries were the same in every country in the integrated area *before* the imposition of a common currency there would be no problem. Our argument rests, therefore on the likelihood that real wages among trading countries with separate national currencies will ordinarily be different. The question at once arises 'Are they in the case of the European Community?' There would be little point in continuing if it was possible to say at once that there is no difference in the real wage for various classes of labour throughout Western Europe. Unfortunately this issue is not as easily settled as one might think at first sight. Table

II.1 in the Appendix presents figures selected from the results of an I.L.O. survey of October 1970. It presents hourly wage rates (estimated) in U.K. pence by class of labour for some of the member countries or applicants for membership of the E.E.C. Percentage differences between the highest and lowest range from 29 to 230, averaging 69 per cent. But we do not wish to make too much of this. Wage rates converted at going rates of exchange do not necessarily measure the real wage. Exchange rates are determined so as to equalize world prices of the relatively few commodities which enter into world trade, whereas all prices enter into the cost of living. Furthermore, the term 'wage rate' is highly ambiguous. On the other hand, if a common currency were imposed and exchange rates fixed roughly in accord with those currently operative, trade unions which looked no further than official statistics would find themselves facing a set of figures not unlike those of Table II.1.

Table II.2 offers an alternative approach. Some of the difficulties of comparison are removed (at the cost of introducing a new set) if we look at *relative* factor prices calculated using uncorrected national currencies. Table II.2 shows, for each country, the difference between the wage rate for each class of labour and the wage for unskilled labour in the construction industry, expressed as a percentage of the wage for unskilled labour in construction. If relative wage rates were the same in every country, the figures in Table II.2 would read the same across rows. Frequently they are not even of the same sign. We conclude that there is no immediate evidence to support the hypothesis that real wages are everywhere the same in Europe. One might even say that such evidence as we have does not contradict the hypothesis that they are different.

We do not now wish to claim that the introduction of a common currency would immediately equalize the numbers across the rows of Table II.1. We do suggest however that there might very well be considerable pressure in this direction. We examine the possible consequences of this pressure by supposing that the equalization must be complete before the pressure is removed.

The case of external economies of scale

Consider the extremely simple yet devastating case where there are two countries, each producing with two factors of production and trading two commodities under conditions where, for both commodities in both countries, some external economies of scale are present. We assume that the external economies are small enough not to outweigh the usual factor-mix conditions which ordinarily lead to convexity of production possibility sets. Accordingly there need not be specialization in production. Production of both commodities occurs in both countries and, since both goods enter into trade, relative commodity prices must be the same. Indeed, it is very simple to construct a case where relative factor prices are the same also. If one country is small, however, so that it gains few economies of scale, the real rewards of both factors must be lower than is the case in the larger region.

This does not mean there can be no trade. Low productivity in the small country is offset by low factor rewards so that world commodity prices are the same whatever the country of origin. Commodity prices must of course be the same for all traded commodities, provided they are expressed in a common currency.

Suppose that we now imposed a common currency, so that wage rates also are expressed in say £ sterling in both countries. It must now be obvious to both unions and employers that workers in the small country are lower paid and indeed worse off than those in the larger country where prices are the same. Moreover, the circumstances of the currency union must be expected to be such that workers have been invited to consider themselves part of a new larger political grouping which they have joined precisely so that they would enjoy certain 'gains' in welfare. Ordinary notions of justice would demand 'equal pay for equal work'. With separate countries and separate currencies the lower standard of living of the small country would not have been so obvious. Currency conversions are complicated. More important still, a different country is a different country and one does not *expect as of right* necessarily to have the same standard of living. With union, however, both these stabilizing factors disappear.

Clearly, if money wages rates do rise in the small country, it will no longer be profitable to produce either commodity unless profit rates fall. Of course, it might be possible to raise the productivity of labour to the level of that in the foreign country by massive investment of capital. But who would be willing to invest in a region where profit rates are already low? Moreover, raising capital intensity will tend to reduce the marginal product of capital, as it raises the product of labour, thus reducing the rates of interest still further.

It might now be objected that we do not necessarily need to invest more capital to raise the productivity of labour. If resources are shifted away from production of whichever commodity is manufactured capital-intensively, then capital intensity rises in both industries simultaneously even though no new capital is created. There are two difficulties with this. First, such a move will reduce the profitability of capital where it is already unprofitable. Second, and more important, there is no guarantee that the increased product can be sold, even at home, unless the change reduces price below that of the large country in the commodity now specialized in. Of course there will be economies of scale not previously realized by the terms of the problem; but it is easy to imagine a case where these economies are insufficient to make production profitable at any level attainable with the limited resources of the small country. What may emerge is a gigantic depressed area comprising the whole of what was originally a small viable country.

The Werner Commission looks forward (perhaps for different reasons) to the possible appearance of depressed areas in the E.E.C. when monetary union becomes a fact. It proposes that this problem be dealt with by appropriate regional policies, whatever that might mean. It is as well to understand, therefore, that the model above identifies a situation where the only possible 'regional policy' is one which offers a permanent subsidy to all producers in the area, whatever they choose to manufacture, or, of course, the equivalent of a subsidy in some other form. This subsidy has to be permanent for obvious reasons. The area identified by immobility of factors across boundaries began with a disadvantage of size. Integration with the larger area achieved precisely nothing except a stimulation of the aspirations of the local population and perhaps a more general recognition of the small country's depressed status. Since no economic advantage can be gained by the union, that depressed status can be alleviated only with a permanent subsidy.

More important still is the need to recognize that if the subsidy is not forthcoming after monetary union, the new state of the area is likely to be infinitely worse than its first. What had previously been simply a poor area now suffers 100 per cent unemployment. The only alternative to a subsidy is to depopulate the region together with its capital, lock, stock, and barrel.

We have now to draw attention to the fact that the kind of difficulty we have been looking at does not in any way rest upon the presence of increasing returns to scale, although for convenience it was presented initially in this context. The real problem is too few degrees of freedom. We turn, therefore, to the constant returns to scale case where we can proceed more formally.

The constant returns to scale case

The theme of these sections is that monetary union will lead to special difficulties whenever it is imposed upon two or more trading countries where factor prices are not equalized between those countries as a consequence of trade. It is as well to remind ourselves therefore what these cases are.

In Fig. II.5 axes measure units of capital and labour. AB is an arbitrary line, say the 45° line making $OA = OB$. The point 11 therefore may be taken to be the ratio of capital to labour used in country 1 to produce commodity one. 21 is the corresponding ratio

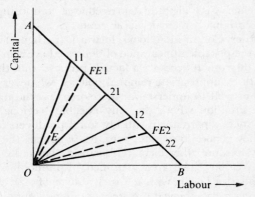

Fig. II.5

for commodity two in country 1 and so on for 12 and 22. $FE1$ is the ratio of total quantities of capital and labour (factor endowment) in country 1 and $FE2$ is the factor-endowment ratio for country 2. The actual quantities produced of each commodity serve as weights to input ratios in such a way that the factor-endowment proportion must be a weighted average of the factor-input ratios used in manufacture. In other words, $FE1$ must lie *between* 11 and 21 and $FE2$ must lie between 12 and 22. For factor prices to be equal in both countries, on the usual assumptions the same techniques of production must be in use, i.e. 11 must coincide with 12 and 21 with 22. If Fig. II.5 represents a before-trade position it is easy to construct cases where the opening-up of trade will cause factor prices (1) to approach equality, either rising in one country and falling in the other, or vice versa, or (2) to rise in both countries, or (3) to fall in both countries. The points 11, 21, 12, 22 will move along AB in the same direction up or down, or 11 and 12 will approach one another and 21 and 22 will approach one another. If, however, 11 reaches $FE1$ before it attains coincidence with 12 the movement will cease, since 11 reaching $FE1$ implies that country 1 produces only commodity one. No further movement is possible. In all cases *except* the cases where 11 and 12 and 21 and 22 become coincident, factor prices will remain unequal after trade, even though commodity prices *are* equal when expressed in the same currency.

As an example let us imagine that after trade is established factor prices began to move towards one another but that eventually country 2 is forced to specialize in commodity two. 22 becomes coincident with $FE2$. Suppose, however, that country 1 is not forced to specialize and that accordingly 11 and 21 remain on opposite sides of $FE1$ as drawn. If a common currency is now imposed, the prices of goods will be the same in both countries but wage rates will be lower in country 2 and interest rates higher because commodity 2 is produced labour-intensively.

Suppose now that labour in country 2 demands and succeeds in attaining the same money wage rate as equivalent workers in country 1. Evidently producers in country 2 are now priced out of the market. They must either go out of business or pay lower profits. Currency depreciation as a palliative is ruled out. The only way to allow any production at all is to change the technique of production of commodity two to a level of capital intensity equal to that in country 1. Since no more capital is available, first because it is immobile across boundaries, and second because, even if it were mobile, the reduced rate of profit in country 2 may not be sufficiently attractive, the only possibility remaining is to lay off labour measured by the distance between E and $FE2$. Unemployment will naturally occur in country 2, since at the high wage level it is profitable to dismiss labour even if it means reduced production. The only possible equilibrium position is at E.

Nor will it ever be possible to reintroduce the production of commodity one without still further unemployment. This is easily seen by recalling that the total *employed* factor ratio in country 1 is measured by OE. To be profitable at the new high wage rate, commodity one must be produced with a technique equal to that in country 1. But for the production-weighted average to be equal to the employed-factor ratio OE we require zero production of good one. And, if unemployment is to be reduced, E must move to the right, which is impossible if production of either good is to be profitable. Still more unemployment is necessary if both goods are to be produced.

As in the increasing returns to scale case, the only solution is a permanent production subsidy or migration of labour abroad.

The general case—more goods and factors

It is natural now to wonder whether in the real world in which we live, where there are many kinds of commodities, some traded and some not traded, and many kinds of factors, some mobile and some not mobile, there might not be additional degrees of freedom which allow the system to adjust to a new institutional environment more readily than seems to be the case in the theoretical world we have studied so far. The answer is no. Indeed it is worse than no, for we shall see that the more complicated the world the more numerous are the adjustments which have to be made.

The easiest way to test this proposition is to choose a model with a very high level of generality and examine its properties on various assumptions. It is sufficient to consider as before just two countries, but we shall now allow any number of commodities (say n) and any number of factors (say m). Factors may be mobile across boundaries or not mobile, as the case may be. Commodities may be traded or not suitable for trading (e.g. services). We proceed by setting out in equation form the conditions for equilibrium in international trade with an explanatory comment on each equation. The number of equations will be compared with the number of unknowns so as to identify degrees of freedom. For convenience we suppose that a common currency has been imposed, so that prices of goods are the same in both countries. In the first instance we imagine that all commodities are traded and that all factors of production are immobile across national boundaries. Classes of equations are numbered for easy reference and the number of equations in each class stated. Side by side with the equations the unknowns are listed for ease of comparison. The model is presented on the next page.

Equations (i) are production functions stating that production s_i is dependent on inputs A_{ij} of the jth factor into the ith product. There are $2n$ of these equations as long as all n products are in production in both of two countries. Equations (ii) state that for each commodity and factor the price p_j of the factor j is equal to the value of its marginal product in the ith use, q_i being the market price of the ith commodity. Since trade equalizes market prices between countries, and since all prices are expressed in a common

Equation class	No. of equations in class	Class of variables	No. of variables in class
(i) $s_i = s_i(A_{i1} \ldots A_{im})$	$2n$	s_i	$2n$
(ii) $p_j = q_i \dfrac{\partial s_i}{\partial A_{ij}}$	$2mxn$	A_{ij}	$2mxn$
(iii) $A_j = \sum_i A_{ij}$	$2m$	p_j	$2m$
(iv) $s_i + s_i' = x_i + x_i'$	n	q_i	n
(v) $x_i = x_i(q_1 \ldots q_n y)$	$2n$	x_i	$2n$
(vi) $y = \bar{y}$	$1\big\}$	y	2
(vii) $y' = \sum q_i' s_i'$	1		

currency, we need distinguish only n prices q_i. There are $2m$ factor prices, however, since trade does not equalize factor prices. Equations (iii) are the full-employment equations stating that total factor usage for each of the m factors equals factor endowment in each country. Equations (iv) state that world supply for each commodity equals world demand $(x_i + x_i')$. x_i is the amount demanded of the ith commodity, and primes are used to distinguish country 1 and country 2. There are $2n$ demand equations (v), y being aggregate money spending. (vi) says that country 1's money spending is given by $\bar{y}$. This numeraire-type equation is necessary to ensure that absolute prices are determined by the equation system. The well-known homogeneity conditions present would otherwise allow determination only of *relative* prices. (vii) states that country 2's aggregate spending is equal to the value of its product. Note that from these (vii) equations we may easily deduce that the balance of payments *must* be balanced and that country 1's aggregate spending also is equal to the value of its product. The system, as it is, is just determined and implies all the properties ordinarily associated with a trading equilibrium.

If now, on top of what we have, we add what we fear may be the consequence of full monetary union, the system becomes over-determined. What we fear is that for some factors the price p_j (which may be a wage rate) in country 1 will be forced into equality with the corresponding rate p_j' in country 2. We have an *additional* set of equations

$$p_j = p_j'$$

for each j affected to add to the system (i)–(vii). It is *impossible* in general that all these equations should be satisfied simultaneously.

Of course if it should happen that the system (i)–(vii) yields $p_j = p'_j$ of its own accord—that is, if the unconstrained solution satisfies this condition—then adding the new constraints does nothing. If, on the other hand, factor prices are *not* equalized by trade then we are in trouble. Assuming that the equality $p_j = p'_j$ is attained, then something must give way. At least one of the equations (i)–(vii) must be abandoned for each factor price which is equalized. The problem is which equations will it be.

It cannot be (i), since production functions must be satisfied by the laws of physics. It cannot be (ii), since these are 'profitability' equations. If they are not satisfied, businessmen will find it profitable to do something else and equilibrium is destroyed. It cannot be (iv), since supply must equal demand. It cannot be (v) unless there is rationing in shops. (vi) is in any case an arbitrary numeraire condition which must be imposed. (vii) is necessary to the assumed balance-of-payments equilibrium. It is (vii) which is abandoned when a permanent unrequited subsidy is passed from one country to another. This could, of course, be a solution to the problem as already noted.

This leaves (iii), the full-employment equations, as the most likely candidates for the chop. Migration of factors is a possibility. In place of two of the equations (iii) namely

$$A_j = \sum_i A_{ij} \quad \text{and} \quad A'_i = \sum_i A'_{ij},$$

we might write just one equation

$$A_j + A'_j = \sum_i A_{ij} + \sum_i A'_{ij},$$

which says that there is full employment in the two countries together but does not specify in which country the employment opportunity exists. If there is factor mobility for each factor where price p_j has to be equated with p'_j then the system is again determinate with over-all full employment. Conversely, if there is factor mobility then p_j and p'_j will be expected to be equal *ipso facto*, a fact which justifies an earlier statement that the presence of mobile factors does not get rid of the problem as long as there exists even one immobile factor, where prices will tend to equality as a consequence of monetary union alone.

If there is immobility of any factor, or if mobility is not complete, then there must be permanent and intractable unemployment unless (vii) is relaxed and a permanent subsidy is paid by one country to another. The problem remains exactly as we saw it in earlier examples.

We now note that it makes no difference if specialization is forced on any country. Suppose, for example, the ith good is not produced in country 1 after trade is established. We have then to drop the equation for s_i in (i). But by the same token we lose the unknown s_i, so that the balance of equations and unknowns remains unaffected.

Non-traded goods

In this section we observe first that the presence of non-traded goods gives no extra degrees of freedom. If the jth good is non-traded it is true that we have an additional unknown, for it is no longer to be expected that $q_j = q_j'$. Both have to be determined by the equation system. But the fact that j is non-traded gives us an extra equation, since equation (iv) for the jth good now breaks up into two equations, namely $x_j = s_j$ and $x_j' = s_j'$. Monetary union, as before, promises to create intractable unemployment just as effectively where non-traded goods are important.

Next we note another serious consequence. It does not matter whether unemployment appears, or whether migration of factors takes place, or whether a permanent subsidy is offered by one country to another as the chosen 'solution' to the stress set up by monetary union. Any of these 'policies' must involve much more than just the unemployment, or just the subsidy, or just the migration of factors. What we are doing in effect is introducing a new equation $p_j = p_j'$ and eliminating some other one, say one of (iii) or (vii). Whatever happens, the new equilibrium will have *changed every variable in the system*. In general, every price will have changed, even those of non-traded goods. At the same time the production and supply patterns as well as the trading patterns of both countries will be affected, perhaps catastrophically. There will be disruptive movements of resources, and consequent reconstruction of capital structure, which may be large or small—nobody knows—and to what purpose? It could mean that whole industries would disappear or it could mean that very little adjustment is needed at all. Everything depends on the magnitude of numbers that we do not know. The monkey may get along without its tail very well, or it may take years and much misery to adapt, or it may not adapt at all. It is incumbent therefore upon anyone who proposes to set off these changes to show at least that there is reason to believe that the gains will be worth the disruption. And this in the present state of knowledge is not possible. We have to take a step in the dark and, this being the case, it is proper that everyone should understand that it *is* a step in the dark. It may then, be that it would come to be understood that sudden sharp changes in policy like monetary union are best avoided. If structural changes have to be faced, it is better that policies which generate them should be applied little by little rather than all at once.

Factor mobility

We now recall that the introduction and encouragement of factor mobility across national boundaries is one possible way to meet the stresses which might be set up by monetary union. It is instructive to look at this proposition the other way round. If factors did become mobile, many economists would suppose that this would lead at once to equal factor prices throughout the integrated area. What we have been looking at is a time reversal of this process. We imagined that monetary union would induce equal factor prices *before* any factor movement actually takes place, thereby inducing the factor movements to accommodate. Indeed, we have taken the even stronger view that factor movements will not take place at all and that unemployment and/or actual budget subsidies are the most likely consequences of monetary union. This is because we see nothing in monetary union *per se* likely to remove the forces inhibiting factor movements, for example, language, customs, laws, traditions, family groupings, etc.

The Werner Commission appears to believe the contrary. It relies heavily upon factor movements, not to remove regional unemployment of the structural kind we have been investigating but to remove regional unemployment generated as a result of loss of a local budgetary mechanism. In this it appears excessively optimistic; for simple observation of Northern Ireland, South Italy, or Appalachia in U.S.A. proves how thoroughly intractable the local unemployment problem can be, even when the language and most other of the more obvious barriers to factor mobility are not present. Moreover, the Commission ruefully comments upon the lack of capital mobility so far noted throughout the Common Market, even though one would have expected capital to be more mobile than most factors.

But it is not really the purpose of this section to comment upon the Commission's hopes. We have drawn attention to the symmetry between factor movements which equate rewards and the factor movements necessary to accommodate to previously equated rewards in order to speculate on the stability of the migration process in the almost impossible event that it should occur.

Spontaneous labour migration would be expected to take place from regions of low wage rates to regions of high wage rates. This, according to the most naïve version of the laws of supply and demand, will reduce wage rates where they are high and increase them where they are low. But this is far from obvious. The migration of labour not only increases the supply of labour, it also increases the demand for labour. It increases the demand for labour, since each newly arrived labourer spends his income on goods which require labour for their production. More than this, if the migration of labour truly does change wage rates as the naïve theory says it does, then it must *ipso facto* change commodity prices and hence the real terms of trade. This leads to a shift in real demand from one trading area to another. Only a very brave prophet would be prepared to predict that the resulting adjustment in the demand for labour in the host region would always be less than the increased supply. And indeed it is easy to construct hypothetical cases where the migration of labour from a low wage area to a high wage area results in still higher wages where they were already high and still lower wages where they were low. Nor does there seem to be anything odd or unusual about such examples.

The moral of all this is clear. If the migration of labour sometimes fails to equate wages, can we be sure that the equalization of wages triggered off by a monetary union would generate the right sort of migration? We cannot be sure. Grandiose economic schemes sometimes sound rational and politically attractive. But with our presently poor statistical information and in the absence of an agreed and tested model of gigantic proportions, capable of investigating the ramifications of any policy in very considerable detail, it is impossible to foresee more than a very few of consequences of even the simplest proposal. Each generation invents a new economic muddle. There are signs that the new Europe will not disappoint us in this respect.

Appendix
TABLE II.1

Hourly Wage Rates in Local Currency less Hourly Wage Rates for Unskilled Labour in Construction as a Percentage of Unskilled Labour in Construction

		Holland	Belgium	Italy	U.K.	Ireland	Germany[a]	Difference between min. and max.
Coal	Coal hewers	+46	+84	—	+30	—	+25	59
Bakery	Bakers	+17	+16	—	+28	—	+6	22
Textiles	Weavers	−19	—	−10	+7	−18	+6	26
	Labourers	−12	—	−20	+3	−23	−13	26
Furniture	Cabinet-makers	+20	+30	−9	+14	+13	+10	39
	French polishers	+21	+30	−18	+14	+13	−13	48
Printing	Hand compositors	+20	+20	+35	+36	+28	+40	20
	Machine compositors	+25	+25	+55	+40	+30	+40	30
Chemicals	Unskilled labour	+13	−15	−27	−12	+9	+1	40
Machinery mfg.	Fitters	+22	+7	−13	+8	+20	+16	35
	Pattern makers	+22	+7	−4	+23	+20	+11	26
	Unskilled labour	−4	−15	−25	−14	−8	−8	21
Construction	Bricklayers	+16	+5	+21	+17	+16	+22	17
	Carpenters	+16	+21	+21	+17	+16	+22	6
	Painters	+23	+21	+21	+17	+16	+22	7
	Electricians	+25	+25	+21	+37	+12	+22	25
	Unskilled labour	0	0	0	0	0	0	0
Electric power	Fitters	+31	+36	+61	+29	+46	+16	45
	Labourers	+15	+15	+13	+2	—	−6	21
Transport	Railway porters	+22	−16	−15	+7	−7	—	38
	Truck drivers	+8	−20	−15	+10	−4	−34	42
Parks and gardens	Labourers	+15	−20	—	−3	−14	−27	42
Agriculture	Male day labourers	+44	−4	—	+11	−32	+52	76

SOURCE: Derived from I.L.O. statistics.

a Calculated on earnings not wages rates.

TABLE II.2

Hourly Wage Rates in Selected Trades by Country—U.K. pence

		Holland	France	Belgium	Italy	U.K.	Ireland	Germany	% Difference between lowest and highest
Coal	Coal hewers	57	55	84	—	47	—	61	80
Bakery	Bakers	46		53	—	47	50	59	29
Textiles	Weavers	32		—	31	40	35	42	36
	Labourers	34		—	28	37	34	42	50
Furniture	Cabinet-makers	47		59	31	43	49	53	90
	French polishers	47		59	28	43	49	59	111
Printing	Hand compositors	47		55	47	51	56	65	38
	Machine compositors	49		58	54	53	57	78	59
Chemicals	Unskilled labour	44		39	28	33	47	52	86
Machinery mfg.	Fitters	48	51	49	30	41	53	51	70
	Pattern makers	48	55	49	33	46	53	59	78
	Unskilled labour	38		39	26	33	40	45	73
Construction	Bricklayers	45		48	42	44	50	69	64
	Carpenters	45		56	42	44	50	69	64
	Painters	48		56	42	44	50	69	64
	Electricians	49		58	35	53	49	61	45
	Unskilled labour	39		46	56	38	44		31
Electric power	Fitters	51		63	39	49	64	62	31
	Labourers	45		52	29	38	—	53	36
Transport	Railway porters	48		38	29	40	40	—	38
	Truck drivers	42		37	—	41	42	43	48
Parks and gardens	Labourers	45		37	—	36	38	47	27
Agriculture	Male day labourers	56		44	—	42	30	99	230

SOURCE: Adapted from results of I.L.O. survey Oct. 1970 and F.A.O. Annual Report. Conversions made at 1970 exchange rates.

CONTROL OF
INTERNATIONAL LIQUIDITY AND
THE EURO-DOLLAR MARKET*

F

RED

 H

IRSCH

(*Nuffield College, Oxford*)

T

HIS

 paper discusses the connection between the Euro-currency
markets (and especially the Euro-dollar market) [1] and the control
of international liquidity at the official level. The subject has been
only glanced upon in academic discussion of the Euro-dollar market. In non-academic quarters—where most discussion concerning
the Euro-markets has begun—views taken of the connection between
Euro-markets and 'high' international finance have sometimes been
strongly held, but over the past decade they have swung almost a
full 180 degrees, as I shall presently suggest. I do not consider the
connection to be one of central importance or interest, but rather
as one facet of the more general problem concerning control of
international liquidity. Consideration of the Euro-dollar connection
is useful mainly for the sidelights it throws on that more general
problem.

The paper is in four parts. Section I sets out the background to
the form in which the question has been put. Section II discusses
some general effects of the Euro-dollar market on the demand for
and supply of international liquidity, and examines the influence
of central bank participation in the market in this context. Section
III considers the main factors involved in the recent growth of
official reserves held in the Euro-markets. Section IV draws together
the implications of the above for regulation of international liquidity.

* At the time this paper was prepared the author was on the staff of the International Monetary Fund; he alone is responsible for the views expressed.

[1] The term 'Euro-dollar' is not used in the text as a synonym for all Euro-
currencies; however, since the analysis is primarily in terms of Euro-dollars,
I have retained the narrower term in the title. The term Euro-currency
market is used to cover bank deposits (excluding inter-bank deposits in so far
as the data allow) held as money market investments in currencies other than
that of the country in which the bank is located.

I

The Euro-markets in dollars and some other currencies, which became a distinctive feature of international money markets from about the late 1950s, represented a spontaneous response of market institutions to banking and credit needs that were otherwise unmet or frustrated by official or self-imposed restrictions on the banking industry. This much is common ground. The implications of this commercial development for monetary authorities—national or international—has naturally been much more controversial. In the early days of the Euro-dollar market, its enthusiasts, including a small minority of academics, saw this development of private sector liquidity, in response to market demand, not only as contributing to the micro-efficiency of banking services, but also as an effective solvent of the emerging tensions then being felt in the international financial system at the macro or official level. In this view, development of the Euro-dollar market and other private capital markets, perhaps supported by parallel development of intercentral-bank credit facilities which would equally be in *ad hoc* response to evolving needs, would be a more feasible and perhaps also a more effective remedy for these tensions than major reliance on deliberate, institutionalized reform in the official sector, whether through new arrangements affecting the holding of reserves or through new arrangements for regulation of exchange rates. Outside academic quarters, such a view was quite common until the mid-1960s.[2]

This view was subsequently transmuted along with the rapid development of events in the international monetary system, and of official thinking in their wake. The need for institutional changes at the official level became generally recognized in the second half of the 1960s, and found partial expression in the establishment in 1969 of the Special Drawing Rights facility. The SDR mechanism provides an international instrument for supplementing existing

[2] The most prominent exponent of this view, and one of the few who committed himself on the record, was Sir George Bolton (see 'A Banker's World', in Richard Fry (ed.), *Speeches and Writings of Sir George Bolton*, London: Hutchinson, 1970). In the academic community, qualified support for this approach was expressed by Kindleberger in various writings, in his emphasis on the potential contribution of integration of private financial markets, including the Euro-dollar market, and on the limited role of official measures as supportive to private financial integration. See Charles P. Kindleberger, *Europe and the Dollar* (The M.I.T. Press, 1966), pp. 84–8; and Émile Despres, Charles P. Kindleberger, and Walter Salant, 'The Dollar and World Liquidity', *The Economist*, 5 Feb. 1966.

forms of official reserves, but does not, in its existing form, provide other means of regulating total reserves. In 1970 and 1971, the first years of SDR allocations, the estimates of needed growth in total reserves on which these allocations had been based were greatly exceeded as a result of increases in unprecedented magnitude in foreign exchange reserves, preponderantly claims in U.S. dollars. A substantial though minority proportion of these unwelcome and unintended increases in foreign exchange reserves were in the form of official claims held in the Euro-dollar market (Table II.3 and Chart II.1).

It should be recalled that in the spring of 1971, the United States had not yet acknowledged that its balance of payments was in fundamental disequilibrium, and much attention was devoted to the role of cyclical and special influences in the U.S. over-all deficit, and, more broadly, in the acquisition of dollars by foreign central banks. In this context, emphasis was given to the role of the Euro-dollar market not only as a channel for flows of short-term capital from the United States to other countries, but beyond this, as an independent source of the dollars that foreign central banks were acquiring in unwelcome amounts. The very rapid expansion of the Euro-dollar market, which appeared to be proceeding at an almost constant compound rate (Chart II.2), was now widely seen as an independent source for the creation of international reserves, creating 'foreign-grown' dollars that were adding in an uncontrollable way to the flow of external liquidity which European central banks had to absorb or somehow deter. The active role of the Euro-dollar market in reserve creation was attributed in particular to the use by central banks of the market as a repository for external reserves, which had notably increased and become widely publicized, although such use had been an important part of the market from its beginnings.[3]

[3] Professor Fritz Machlup ventured the judgement that 'perhaps more than one half of all Euro-dollars now in existence have been "made in Europe"' ('The Magicians and their Rabbits', *Morgan Guaranty Survey*, May 1971, p. 10). Dr. Otmar Emminger, Vice-President of the Deutsche Bundesbank, wrote at about the same time: 'Of the enormous increase in world reserves in 1970—by far the largest ever recorded in any one year—an amount of $5 to $6 billion is estimated to have been due to reserve creation via the Eurodollar market, largely by way of Central Banks and the BIS redepositing reserves with this market. It is doubtful whether this is an appropriate and stable foundation for such massive reserve creation.' ('Short-Term Capital Flows—A Threat to International Equilibrium', *Euromoney*, May 1971, p. 8.)

These preoccupations suggested the conclusion that control of the Euro-market in dollars and other currencies, or at the least of the participation of central banks therein, was a necessary (and in some views, a major) condition for preventing uncontrolled gyrations in the level of international liquidity. Such gyrations would be clearly incompatible with the evolution of the global reserve system toward a greater degree of international regulation, a goal that now commanded widespread support. Thus, at the time this paper was commissioned, in the summer of 1971, the pendulum of thinking about the Euro-dollar market in banking and some official quarters had swung, in effect, to the opposite of its earlier extreme. Far from being seen as making improved official regulation of international liquidity less necessary, as it was by some in the early 1960s, the Euro-dollar market was now seen as in danger of making a needed regulation impossible.

I have expressed these different concerns in a deliberately polarized way in order to focus attention on the change in thinking that has occurred in the connection between Euro-currency liquidity and official liquidity. As in other aspects of the Euro-currency market, notably its role in promoting flows of short-term capital whether in an equilibrating or in a disequilibrating direction, there is an undoubted tendency to attribute to this particular institutional portion of the money market effects that lie behind institutional forms and that have a more general source.

II

This section discusses the effect of the Euro-dollar market on the demand for and supply of international liquidity. International liquidity is defined for this purpose in the now-accepted official usage, as resources readily available to monetary authorities for the financing of balance of payments deficits. Presently, official reserves consist of monetary authorities' holdings of gold; Special Drawing Rights; Reserve Positions in the Fund (i.e. drawing facilities on the I.M.F. freely available to meet any balance of payments need); and official holdings of foreign exchange.[4] Also considered part of

---

[4] Holdings of foreign exchange, where they constitute claims on a reserve centre, are a negative element in the liquidity position of that centre: and will therefore not add correspondingly to liquidity of the world as a whole. The extent of the allowance to be made on this count may be low in the early stages of reserve currency expansion, but substantial at a later stage, as the reserve centre may then be sensitive to deterioration in its net reserve position.

international liquidity, but not of freely available reserves, are bilateral credit lines with central banks and treasury agencies (swaps), and the remaining drawing facilities on the I.M.F. which are subject to negotiation about policies to be pursued by the drawing country.

An alternative concept, sometimes used in academic discussion, focuses on liquid holdings of foreign exchange in the hands of commercial banks and perhaps other private-sector institutions, on the ground that it is these balances—and not official reserves—that are used in the financing of international transactions and that therefore give a more meaningful index of the adequacy of international transactions balances.[5] However, the influence exerted by international liquidity on actions taken by governments in matters such as exchange rates and trade restrictions (see page 112) is dependent on the liquidity available to the official sector, in relation to calls made on such liquidity; and while such calls will be affected by the amount and growth of private external liquidity, this latter effect may vary not only in force but also in direction according to the associated circumstances. Thus, a generalized increase in private balances which reflects increased cross-investment between national money markets for arbitrage and speculative purposes, if it is in a direction that intensifies rather than offsets imbalances in other payments, will increase the size of imbalances to be financed, perhaps by more than the increase in the supply of private balances. There seems little doubt that the very rapid recent expansion in recorded commercial bank holdings of foreign exchange (in the three years 1967–70 the combined holdings of deposit money banks of industrial countries more than doubled, to over $50 billion)[6] has been associated with money market investment rather than with additional international trade financing (though trade financing may have been involved). This variability in the relationship between private and official external liquidity, together with major deficiencies in data on the former (e.g. the varying and generally

Where the reserve currency is inconvertible into other reserve assets, as is presently the U.S. dollar, the influences become more complex, and may extend to the effective liquidity of the holders.

[5] H. Robert Heller, 'The Transactions Demand for International Means of Payments', *J.P.E.*, vol. 76, No. 1 (Jan.–Feb. 1968), p. 142. See also Klaus Friedrich, 'The Euro-Dollar System and International Liquidity', *Journal of Money, Credit and Banking*, Aug. 1970.

[6] *International Financial Statistics*, Mar. 1972, p. 25.

incomplete allowance made for liabilities), make it preferable to regard private balances as a factor influencing demand for international liquidity, in the official concept, rather than as part of the supply of liquidity in a wider concept.

Balances held in the Euro-dollar market are in the form of interest-bearing deposits of varying maturity, for the most part three months or less. Such balances may be indirectly available for the financing of transactions; and existence of these balances, as of other time deposits, enables their holders to economize in their holdings of demand deposits. These demand deposits are held with banks in the United States; and the portion of U.S. demand deposits which constitutes cash reserves of Euro-banks becomes high-powered reserve money, which may support a larger total of lending to final borrowers by Euro-banks. The Euro-dollar market can therefore be regarded as increasing the velocity of money (narrowly defined) and, to the extent that the market has added to total dollar balances through internal generation of additional deposits, as increasing the quantity of money plus quasi-money. In assessing the amount of internal deposit generation, allowance has to be made for the effect of such deposit creation in reducing the level of Euro-dollar interest rates, thereby encouraging some outflow of funds that originated outside the market.

In these respects, the Euro-dollar market, in a widely accepted view, performs the function of a financial intermediary between the U.S. money market and banking system *vis-à-vis* the non-banking sector and the securities market, including holders of dollar assets and borrowers of dollar funds who are located outside the United States. In addition, the market performs a different, geographical intermediary function between money markets in the United States and the rest of the world (Canada, Japan, and Singapore as well as Western Europe) in so far as dollar deposits with banks located in these centres are regarded by their holders in some sense as a half-way house between investment in the U.S. money market and investment in local money markets denominated in local currency. Thus, a given differential in interest rates (or in the equivalent in prospective capital gains) between the U.S. market and local markets in domestic currency will induce a larger shift of funds, with the Euro-dollar market acting both as an intermediary between the domestic markets, and as a way station conducting lending business of its own. By making dollar balances more attractive for private foreign holders, the market may also increase private external balances at the expense of official balances; though this influence will be offset in so far as Euro-dollar credits are used as substitutes for funds that would otherwise have been obtained from the United States.

These broad influences exerted by the Euro-dollar market will have the following effects on demand[7] for and supply of international liquidity as defined above:

(a) Increases in private external balances that tend to reduce dollar balances held in official reserves of countries other than the United States will (i) correspondingly reduce the supply of international liquidity, but will also (ii) reduce the demand in so far as the private balances are used to finance international transactions that would otherwise have led to calls on official foreign-exchange balances, and (iii) to the extent of (i), will improve the U.S. balance on official settlements and its net reserve position. The first of these influences tends to lessen the degree of ease in international liquidity, the second and third influences tend to increase ease. The net impact will not necessarily be positive, as Clendenning infers,[8] if private balances are used for additional arbitrage and investment purposes (discussed below) rather (or more) than for trade financing.

(b) To the extent that the Euro-dollar market increases the volume of externally held dollar balances through internal deposit expansion, the market will provide additional funds available for financing of international transactions, in part by 'freeing' demand deposits held in the United States for this purpose. If such trade finance replaces funds that would have been provided by local (i.e. non-U.S.) banks, which in turn would have drawn the foreign exchange from their central banks, the effect is to reduce calls on official holdings of foreign exchange, and thereby to reduce demand for international liquidity. If, on the other hand, the trade finance would otherwise have been drawn from sources in the United States, the effect on reserves outside the United States will be neutral. The U.S. balance of payments on the 'liquidity' basis would then improve as a result of the reduced outflow of private capital. Since

[7] References to the 'demand' for reserves are in the standard usage of a demand function by monetary authorities, which will shift in response to various factors (e.g. the degree of flexibility in exchange rates) influencing the degree to which a given amount of reserves can achieve a given policy objective.

[8] E. Wayne Clendenning, *The Euro-dollar Market* (Oxford: Clarendon Press, 1970), pp. 160–1.

the expansion in Euro-dollar deposits would also tend to reduce Euro-dollar interest rates, unless the additional Euro-dollar deposits were themselves used for trade financing, there would tend to be a further improvement in the U.S. liquidity balance.

(c) By increasing the sensitivity of domestic balances to interest-rate differentials or speculative opportunities prevailing in international markets (including the domestically located Euro-dollar market), the Euro-dollar market will induce additional flows of short-term funds. Such flows will be a substitute for reserve flows when these arbitrage and speculative flows are in the opposite direction of other net flows (and are equilibrating in this sense). By contrast, where arbitrage and speculative flows exacerbate imbalance in other payments flows, they will increase official reserve movements, and thereby add to demand for reserves. Thus, where requirements of domestic stabilization coincide with requirements of external stabilization (the inflation–deficit and recession–surplus case), the Euro-dollar market tends to strengthen the force of monetary policy in correcting or overcorrecting the payments imbalance, though in the interests of domestic stabilization, the domestic influence of inflows and outflows of funds may need to be offset. Where, however, domestic and external requirements are in conflict (the inflation–surplus and the recession–deficit cases), the Euro-dollar market will tend to heighten the policy conflict. Unless it is assumed that exchange-rate adjustment will be used for all cases of policy conflict (which may not be appropriate for cyclical disturbances), the effect will be to increase demand for reserves in situations in which reserves are most needed, and to reduce demand for reserves in situations in which they are barely needed: which must increase the trend demand for reserves. It should be emphasized that the net effect of the Euro-dollar market in increasing the potential demand for reserves as a result of increased flows of disequilibrating capital will be considerably smaller than the amount of such flows that takes place through the Euro-markets, since some portion and probably a substantial portion of these movements replaces flows that would otherwise take place directly between domestic money markets.

To sum up on the influence of the Euro-dollar market on demand for official international liquidity, the influences under (a), (b), and (c) together seem at least as likely to increase such demand as to reduce it: and to have a clear tendency to do so in conditions of conflict between domestic and external requirements for monetary policy, thereby tending on balance to reduce the degree of global liquidity ease.

(d) The Euro-dollar market may also influence international liquidity preponderantly from the supply side; and this is a clear-cut influence tending to increase liquidity. This will result from the depositing of dollar balances in the Euro-dollar market by central banks, which in turn provides a basis for further, internal genera-tion of Euro-dollar flows. Official deposits in the market have been regarded as a particularly powerful source of reserve creation, and one least amenable to control, on the ground that the two elements of central bank depositing and of deposit multiplication in the Euro-dollar market are mutually reinforcing.

The extent of deposit multiplication in the Euro-dollar market is limited by three factors:

(a) the size of Euro-banks' reserve ratios (believed to be low, making for a high multiplier);

(b) the length of the chain of interbank deposits (frequently high, reducing the multiplier); and

(c) the size of the leakage of funds from the holdings of non-banks out of the Euro-dollar system into either (i) deposits with banks in the United States, or (ii) deposits in domestic currency outside the United States.[9] This leakage has also been believed to be high, and together with (b), this has limited the multiplier to a size for which there are no good estimates, but which is certainly far lower than the deposit multiplier in domestic banking systems (despite the absence of minimum reserve requirements in the Euro-dollar system).

Now the leakage through (c) (ii) operates through the sale of dollars against domestic currency to the domestic central bank; and if the central bank redeposits these or equivalent dollars in the Euro-market, this will have the effect of closing the leakage through this channel. Hence the concern, which was widely expressed in 1971, that such redeposits greatly increase the deposit-creating and reserve-creating capacity of the Euro-dollar market.

However, while such flows undoubtedly exert some additional expansionary force, they remain subject to a variety of checks which in usual conditions will exert a fairly powerful restraint on the multiplicative impact. Thus, the normal restrictive influences exerted by (b) and (c) (i) (i.e. by the length of the bank redepositing

[9] For a systematic exposition of these processes, see Friedrich, op. cit.

chain and leakages to the United States) will still apply. The latter influence is indeed likely to be reinforced by the effect of official deposits in the Euro-market in reducing interest rates in that market; which in turn will encourage flows to the United States from the market, or discourage flows from the United States to the market. Admittedly, the same downward influence on Euro-dollar rates will in itself increase the attraction of borrowing in Euro-dollars for corporations in Europe, as an alternative to borrowing in domestic currency, and it is such action that would involve 'recycling' of dollars to European central banks, and a further round of expansion if these dollars were also deposited in the Euro-market. But these transactions under (c) (ii), unlike others in the above categorization, must involve some participants in the Euro-market, whether banks or final borrowers, in an uncovered exchange position: long of domestic currency and short of dollars.

In conditions of neutral exchange-rate expectations, considerations of portfolio balance will place strict limits on the extent to which these participants are willing to increase an open exchange position; and coverage in the forward market, unless forward cover is provided by the authorities at an invariant price, will induce other private parties to undo the effects of the initial transactions (i.e. to borrow domestic currency and hold dollars), so that the inducement for arbitrage between Euro-dollars and domestic currency will tend to narrow and eventually disappear.[10]

In conditions of heavy one-way exchange speculation, however, where the predominant sentiment is for a coming appreciation of domestic currency, the force of this usual equilibrating 'portfolio' influence will be blunted, and may become overwhelmed. In these conditions also, other restraining influences such as the length of the redepositing chain may also be reduced, as the inducement to acquire a long position in the potentially appreciating currency gains cumulative and probably self-generating force.

In these speculative conditions, therefore, the image of a 'carousel' of funds from Euro-market to central bank and back to Euro-market, round and round, is a realistic representation. It is no accident that the image of the carousel made its first appearance in the D-mark speculation of May 1969, when the Deutsche Bundesbank stopped recycling dollars to its own commercial banks which it found itself buying back the same day. In spring 1971, when speculation on

[10] The connection between 'recycling' of Euro-dollars and open exchange positions was first pointed out to me by J. Marcus Fleming.

revaluation of the deutsche mark and some other currencies again became prevalent, corresponding inducements re-emerged for the acquisition of short positions in Euro-dollars. And while little public mention of speculative activity was made during 1970, it is significant that German enterprises increased their net external liabilities in foreign currency by $0·6 billion in that year, adding a further $0·7 billion in the first six months of 1971.[11]

The connection between autonomous expansion of the Euro-dollar market and acquisition of net or uncovered currency positions by the private sector has been given inadequate attention in the literature. In analysis such as that by Friedman [12] in which no central role was given to participation by European central banks, this omission was not logically crucial, at least to the extent that dollar credits were assumed to be used outside the United States to pre-finance accruing dollar receipts without conversion into domestic currency. In the process of generation of Euro-dollars through the actions of European central banks, the role of the currency position of the private sector does seem crucial, yet has been hardly mentioned in most discussion on the subject.[13]

The process of generation of Euro-dollars via round-trip flows from the domestic central bank and back must mean that some commercial bank or private corporation is acquiring domestic currency against a dollar liability. In a Mundellian world of eternally fixed exchange rates, in which the 'moneyness' of the U.S. dollar was scarcely less outside the United States than within it, this imbalance of currency liabilities and assets would be of little consequence. In the real world in which exchange rates may and do move, acquisition of net positions in domestic currency vis-à-vis foreign currency is subject to inherent limitations. In conditions of neutral exchange-rate expectations, the limitation will be imposed by movement of various market interest and arbitrage rates in response to portfolio pressures. In conditions of one-way expectations of a change in official currency pegs, a limitation will be imposed sooner or later by the unwillingness or inability of monetary

[11] Deutsche Bundesbank, *Statistical Supplement*, Ser. 3, Nov. 1971, Table 17.

[12] Milton Friedman, 'The Euro-Dollar Market: Some First Principles', *Morgan Guaranty Survey*, Oct. 1969.

[13] Including the extensive discussion by Fritz Machlup: see especially 'The Magicians and their Rabbits', *Morgan Guaranty Survey*, May 1971; and 'The Euro-Dollar System and its Control', American Enterprise Institute, Conference on International Monetary Problems, 22–3 Sept. 1971, Washington, D.C.

authorities to acquire net currency positions the 'wrong' way. However, in these latter conditions of one-way speculation, the limitation will be in suspense until the requisite action is taken by the monetary authorities. But in conditions of underlying exchange speculation, the Euro-dollar market is only one of the vehicles through which speculation or hedging can be undertaken, or through which foreign-exchange reserves can be created and destroyed in exceptional amounts: thus, as indicated in Section IV, stronger effects in this sphere can be exerted through acquisition of official balances in a potentially appreciating currency, where this acts as a secondary reserve currency.

The significance of central bank deposits for autonomous expansion of the Euro-dollar market was therefore exaggerated by the speculative conditions of 1969 and 1971. In a world in which exchange rates can vary, the fact that the Federal Reserve is the only central bank able to create dollars remains a limitation on aggregate creation of dollars, in the Euro-dollar market too.

This is not to deny that such deposits have a special significance because of their potential role in reducing a leakage from the Euro-market. The following section looks more closely at their recent development.

III

Foreign-exchange balances held by monetary authorities with commercial banks in Euro-markets are included in the data on foreign-exchange assets of the respective countries, and in the global reserve data; but do not constitute official liabilities of the reserve centres in whose currency the balances are expressed. Consequently, a rough measure of exchange reserves held in Euro-markets has sometimes been taken to be the difference between reported foreign-exchange assets and the official liabilities of the United States and the United Kingdom, the two leading reserve centres. This approach will overstate official holdings in the Euro-markets to the extent that reserves are held in national markets in currencies other than U.S. dollars and sterling; the most important such currency is now the deutsche mark, with official holdings in Germany of $1·5 billion at the end of 1970. However, the 'residual' approach will understate the amount of official Euro-currency holdings to the extent that there is a normal negative item in the residual, arising from the fact that the data on U.S. and U.K. currency liabilities are more comprehensive than the data on official foreign-exchange holdings shown in I.F.S. (e.g. the liabilities include holdings of non-metropolitan territories such as Hong Kong, which are not included in the foreign-exchange asset totals). In 1971, direct information of official holdings of Euro-dollars became available for a large sample of 51 countries reporting to the I.M.F.; this information, for the years 1964 through 1970, is shown in Table II.4. Table II.3, which classifies the main sources of reserve growth since 1961 according to reserve components, shows the remaining residual of unidentified sources (line 4f).

Identified official holdings of Euro-dollars rose in 1970 from $3·4 billion to $8·9 billion; and increases in unidentified holdings of Euro-dollars, as well as of official holdings of other Euro-currencies and particularly deutsche mark, are likely to have been the main influence in the increase of about $1·5 billion in the residual item. Thus, total reserves in Euro-currencies may have increased by $7 billion in 1970, or by almost as much as the increase in foreign-exchange holdings in national markets in the year, which was itself of exceptional magnitude.[14]

The expansion of official holdings in the Euro-currency markets in 1970 and the early months of 1971 was clearly of exceptional size, both as a component of the total increase in Euro-currency deposits, and as a component of the total increase in foreign-exchange reserves. A number of factors were involved.

(a) The marked decline in U.S. interest rates in 1970–1 increased the attractiveness of short-term investment in the Euro-dollar market, especially for central banks, which through their exemption from the Regulation Q ceiling had during the tight-money phase of 1969 enjoyed higher rates on their investments in the United States than were available in the Euro-market.

(b) Central banks in 1970–1 acquired dollars in unprecedented amounts at a time in which concern about a possible depreciation of the dollar *vis-à-vis* other currencies and perhaps other reserve assets had also reached new heights. Since the practical possibility of converting the dollars into gold or SDRs was limited, this made

[14] From a different set of data, which is in line with the broad magnitudes discussed above, Mr. Milton Gilbert of the Bank for International Settlements has estimated total placement of official funds in Euro-markets from early 1970 to April 1971 at roughly $10 billion (Statement before the Subcommittee on International Exchange and Payments of the Joint Economic Committee, U.S. Congress, 22 June 1971).

central banks particularly anxious to maximize interest return on their dollar balances; a number of central banks may also have turned to the Euro-dollar market in an attempt to minimize the reduction in their interest return.

(c) As Gilbert has pointed out, a shift in the relative composition of reserve holdings from dollars to deutsche mark will also have tended to increase the Euro-currency component, since this accounts for a larger portion of deutsche mark reserves than of total dollar reserves. As noted earlier, the data also show an increase in direct DM holdings.

The proportion of total deposits in the Euro-dollar market accounted for by official deposits rose to about one-fifth as a result of the sharp increase in official deposits in 1970. Similar proportions had been shown for earlier years, 1965 and 1966, without drawing critical attention, although the absolute magnitudes involved were of course much smaller.[15] The earlier official participation in the Euro-currency markets had not obtruded against collective objectives in the field of international liquidity. Indeed, in 1965 and 1966, deposits and placements under swap by and through the Bank for International Settlements in the Euro-currency markets had helped to offset a tightening of the market which had been unwelcome to a number of monetary authorities, and this activity was seen by some analysts as the beginning of 'open-market operations' in the Euro-currency markets.[16]

Open-market operations on the restrictive side proved institutionally more difficult to set in motion. After it became evident in early spring of 1971 that official operations in the Euro-dollar market were in a 'pro-cyclical' direction, certain restraining actions were taken. In an attempt to reduce the interest differential between Euro-dollars and short-term rates in European currencies, the U.S. Treasury and other official U.S. agencies placed substantial issues with U.S. banks in the Euro-dollar market. More directly, the leading central banks represented in the BIS agreed, in June 1971, that they would for the time being not place additional funds in the

[15] Bank for International Settlements, *37th Annual Report* (Basle 1967), p. 142. The coverage of dollars made available to the market by official institutions differs in some respects from the data in Table II.4.

[16] Charles P. Kindleberger, 'The Euro-Dollar and the Internationalization of United States Monetary Policy', Banca Nazionale del Lavoro, *Quarterly Review*, Mar. 1969, p. 13. The operations are described in Charles A. Coombs, 'Treasury and Federal Reserve Foreign Exchange Operations', F.R.B. of New York, *Monthly Review*, Mar. 1966, Mar. 1967, and Mar. 1968.

Euro-currency market and would withdraw funds 'when such action was prudent in the light of market conditions'. However, the significance of this latter action was limited by the fact that the countries concerned, while they had played the largest part in the expansion in identified official holdings of Euro-dollars in 1970, accounted for less than half of the total official Euro-dollar holdings (Table II.4). (No comparable breakdown is available for other Euro-currencies.) At a time that foreign-exchange holdings in many non-industrial countries, including groups such as the oil-producing countries, are expanding rapidly, an agreement of this character among the larger countries is not sufficient to regulate total reserve holdings in Euro-currency markets.

The recent currency realignment might be expected to have two broad effects in this field.

(a) To the extent that the one-way speculation on an appreciation of currencies against the dollar is ended, the special influence noted at the end of Section II tending to attract Euro-dollar deposits into central banks should cease to operate, or be reversed along with reversal of speculative influences; this should in itself tend to reduce deposit creation in the Euro-dollar market.

(b) The expected eventual improvement in the U.S. balance of payments would reduce the flow of dollars to the market emanating from the United States.

Thus, both these factors, as well as the administrative restraints referred to above, would tend to counter the expansionary influences on the Euro-dollar market of 1970–1. There should also be less immediate inducement for an expansion in holdings of 'non-traditional' reserve currencies, both in national markets and in Euro-markets, in the expectation of early appreciation of such currencies; on the other hand, diversion of foreign-exchange reserves toward holdings in such currencies might continue in so far as reserve managers respond to past experience, which is extrapolated to long-term expectations.

IV

This section attempts to set the problem of regulating reserve holdings through the Euro-dollar market in the context of regulating official liquidity as a whole. For the purpose of this discussion, it is assumed that such regulation is desired and necessary in order to fulfil certain broad objectives of the international monetary system. Thus, it is assumed that a given movement in global liquidity is considered necessary or helpful to achieve a desired influence on factors such as avoidance of restrictions on trade and payments; maintenance of a given broad balance between currency devaluations and revaluations; and perhaps also objectives in the field of foreign aid and influence on domestic monetary and economic policies.[17]

International liquidity, in the concept mentioned in Section II, has six main components—gold, SDRs, Reserve Positions in the Fund, and foreign exchange, which are freely available reserves; and credit tranche positions in the I.M.F. and central bank swaps, which comprise conditional liquidity. These components may be ranked in rough order of their amenability to collective official control.

(1) *Special Drawing Rights*, made available under annual allocations,[18] are in principle fully under control, though in practice allocations are likely to be easier to implement than cancellations.

(2) *Credit tranche positions* in the Fund are also under administrative control,[19] through adjustments in Fund quotas, with somewhat less flexibility than adjustments in the SDR allocations.

(3) Credit lines available through central bank and treasury *swaps* are adjustable with minimum formality, but this full bilateral control involves weak collective control.

(4) *Gold* reserves are nowadays subject to only small vagaries, as a result of (a) cessation of official intervention in private gold markets, and (b) limitation of the offtake of new gold production to such amounts as South Africa chooses to absorb in its own reserves when its over-all payments balance is in surplus, or such amounts

---

[17] The effect of changes in international liquidity is discussed from a number of standpoints in I.M.F., *International Reserves—Needs and Availability* (Washington, D.C., 1970), containing papers and proceedings of a seminar on this topic. See in particular Richard N. Cooper, 'International Liquidity and Balance of Payments Adjustment' (pp. 125–45) and the background papers by the Fund staff.

[18] Decisions on allocations are made for 'basic periods' which are five years, unless the Fund decides otherwise (as it did in making the first basic period three years); but allocations can be changed within a basic period in the event of 'unexpected major developments' (I.M.F. Articles of Agreement, Article XXIV).

[19] In the economic sense: both allocations of SDRs and increases in Fund quotas require approval by weighted vote of the I.M.F. Board of Governors, and in some countries, parliamentary legislation.

as it chooses to sell to the I.M.F. or other monetary authorities from current production when the price in the free market is below the official parity.[20] Gold reserves of national monetary authorities may vary as a result of transactions with international monetary institutions, against reserve claims on them, but this has no effect on total reserves.

(5) *Reserve Positions in the Fund* represent in part, as referred to above, the exchange of reserves held in national hands for Fund positions (predominantly through gold subscriptions to quota increases), and to this extent do not affect on the level of global reserves; they also represent use of members' currencies in Fund drawings, and to this extent, Reserve Positions in the Fund rise and fall with other members' use of Fund credit. Such creation and destruction of reserves through the Fund's General Account is subject to substantial variation—in the two years to November 1971 there was a fall in the outstanding total from $3·8 billion to $1·3 billion; but such fluctuations, like fluctuations in foreign exchange claims derived from other countries' drawings on swaps,[21] will often parallel corresponding fluctuations in demand for reserves, as evidenced by drawings on credit facilities.[22]

(6) The most mercurial component of international liquidity is *foreign exchange*. This component may be divided for the present purpose into four sub-categories:

(i) Foreign exchange claims that are the counterpart of the credit extended under swaps (Table II.3, line 4e). Such claims are subject to considerable variation, but, as indicated above, this will often be parallel to variations in demand for reserves.

(ii) Official claims on the United States, forming the largest portion of foreign-exchange reserves (Table II.3, line 4a (i) and Chart II.1). Fluctuations in these balances have become increasingly geared to fluctuations in the U.S. balance of payments on official settlements, as the ability of foreign monetary authorities to convert dollars into gold or other reserve assets held by the United States was limited first in a practical way, and then,

[20] I.M.F. Executive Board Decision No. 2914-(69/127), adopted 30 Dec. 1969, cited in I.M.F. *Annual Report 1970*, pp. 184–9.

[21] Swap claims are normally counted as a part of foreign exchange reserves, as mentioned under (6) (i).

[22] J. Marcus Fleming, 'The Bearing of the Supply of Other Reserves on the Need for Special Drawing Rights', in I.M.F., *International Reserves—Needs and Availability*, pp. 322–7.

CHART II.1. *Main Reserve Sources and Their Variation*

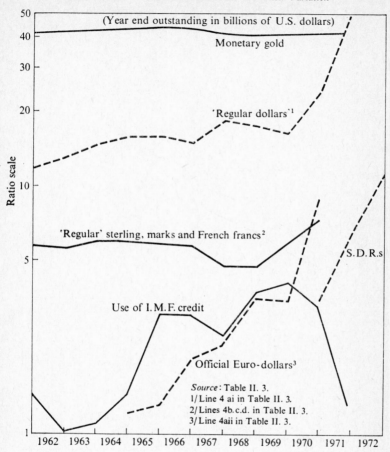

after August 1971, formally terminated 'for the time being'. The upsurge in foreign official dollar holdings in 1970 and 1971 reflected the combination of an underlying deficit aggravated by (and in the past the cause of) large outflows of short-term capital. Since the financing of short-term capital flows through accumulation of reserve currency does not entail specific provisions for reversal, such as apply to use of I.M.F. credit or central bank swaps, less presumption exists that they are associated with a

CHART II.2. *Estimated Size of the Euro-currency Market (Outstanding amount of foreign currency credits channelled through reporting European banks)* (In billions of U.S. dollars)

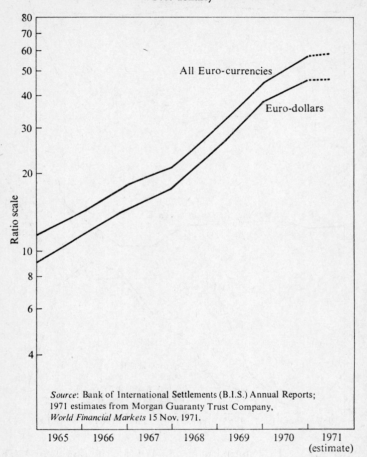

Source: Bank of International Settlements (B.I.S.) Annual Reports; 1971 estimates from Morgan Guaranty Trust Company, *World Financial Markets* 15 Nov. 1971.

reversible imbalance, and hence there is less justification for regarding such increases in official dollar balances as implying a parallel increase in demand for reserves. Collective official control over this reserve component has been weak in the past, and in the nature of a last resort, through the international pressure exerted on the United States to adjust.

(iii) Official claims on other reserve centres; the largest secondary reserve centre is still the United Kingdom, but Germany is increasingly important. The recent increase in claims on these centres has had a multiple expansionary effect as all the main centres concerned—the United Kingdom, Germany, and France —have kept increments in their own reserves in dollars (by contrast with the earlier London practice of maintaining only small working balances in dollars). Thus, increased holdings of these currencies has put an extra layer on the reserve currency pyramid. In the case of sterling, international arrangements, associated with the Basle Agreement, now provide assurance against sudden *reductions* in official reserve holdings; but these arrangements do not correspondingly check expansion in such holdings, and indeed promote such expansion (particularly through the provisions for exchange guarantees and minimum sterling proportions).[23] The German authorities have on a number of occasions emphasized their desire to prevent the development of the deutsche mark as a reserve currency. They have from time to time forbidden payment of interest on foreign-held balances in deutsche mark and have imposed differentially high reserve requirements in respect of such balances. These restrictions account in part for the relatively high proportion of reserves in deutsche mark held in the Euro-markets.

(iv) Official reserves are held in the Euro-currency markets in the magnitudes outlined in Section III. For the reasons discussed earlier in this paper, a switch in the holding of dollar reserves from the United States to the Euro-dollar market will in normal circumstances almost certainly exert a smaller expansionary effect on global reserves than a switch of the same reserves to domestic currency deposits in another reserve centre.

Inferences for regulation of international liquidity

(1) Regulation of reserve holdings in Euro-currency markets, e.g. by co-operative agreement among monetary authorities to stabilize or reduce such holdings, would not by itself be sufficient to regulate total foreign exchange reserves. If undertaken in isolation, such regulation would very probably tend to increase inducements for

---

[23] The U.K. authorities have, however, indicated, in the context of entry into the E.E.C., their intention to 'stabilize' the official sterling balances and to envisage 'an orderly and gradual run down' after accession to the E.E.C. (H.M.S.O., Cmnd. 4715).

reserve managers to diversify holdings to new, potentially appreciating currencies; such diversification would often involve larger fluctuations both for global reserves and for reserve holdings of individual countries than diversification of reserves from holdings in national money markets to holdings in Euro-markets in the same currency.

(2) While the recent growth in reserve holdings in Euro-markets may have added somewhat to the extent of total reserve growth, it was in part induced by the exceptional growth attributable to expansion of the supply of reserve currencies from their national sources; the growth of reserve holdings in Euro-markets at times obscures the role of this latter influence in the statistical data.

(3) This recent experience confirms that, as is now widely recognized,[24] collective control over the course of international liquidity requires collective control over the accumulation (and decumulation) of currency balances in reserve holdings. The central element in such control would have to be reduction or regulation in the use of reserve currencies for the financing of payments imbalances, measured on official settlements. This would imply the obligation (and not merely the right) of holders of accruing reserve currencies to convert them into a primary reserve asset such as Special Drawing Rights. In principle, such regulation might not need to cover the location of foreign-exchange holdings; in practice, the holding of exchange reserves outside the national money markets could be troublesome on two counts, causing erratic fluctuations in officially-measured imbalances of reserve centres, and beyond this, perhaps contributing to generation of additional deposit balances in the Euro-markets. To the extent that regulation of the amount of currency balances to be retained in official reserves limited such holdings to needed working balances, the scope for reserve holdings in Euro-markets would in any case be small.

(4) It is sometimes suggested that fluctuations in reserves held in Euro-currencies could be avoided or lessened by controls imposed on those Euro-markets. Such controls are also sometimes seen as helping to reinforce attempts made by some national authorities to curb reserve holdings in their currencies, since such attempted discouragements have been reduced in their effectiveness by the availability of Euro-markets exempt from the regulations of the domestic reserve centre. However, to curb these markets by inter-

[24] And as reflected in the main speeches at the 1971 Annual Meeting of the I.M.F., particularly that by the Chancellor of the Exchequer.

nationalization of controls would be far less efficacious for the regulation of reserve holdings, and would require a far greater task of supervision, than would be involved in self-imposed regulations or restraints adopted by monetary authorities in their capacity as reserve holders. This is not only because of the much smaller numbers involved—a hundred or so reserve holders, against many thousand commercial bank bidders or potential bidders for Euro-currencies. More important, the costs to individual countries of curbing their Euro-currency business would in many cases appear substantial; and, for one or more countries, the gains of holding out and capturing the business driven away from regulated markets would exceed the apparent benefits to them from collective reserve creation. By contrast, the sacrifice to the individual country involved in a collective agreement on the form and location of reserve holdings would be limited to the differential in interest return and in other reserve characteristics (a differential that could itself be adjusted through regulation of the interest rate on the international reserve asset), and there would be no special pay-off for non-participants. Free rider problems could be mitigated by binding actual and potential benefits from the collective reserve scheme in a single package with the commitments on reserve holdings.

Official controls on Euro-currency operations have hitherto been imposed sporadically, and have then usually been limited to regulating either access of domestic borrowers and lenders to Euro-markets, or the net (as distinct from gross) positions of Euro-banks themselves. Control on a more comprehensive basis may be called for on a variety of grounds. In my personal view, these include the desirability of even-handedness in regulation of competing banking systems; avoidance of differential advantage to multi-national and other large corporations *vis-à-vis* firms that lack access to the international money market; avoidance of an undesired degree of integration with the international money market, such as may inhibit pursuit of national cyclical or social policies that are legitimate economic and political objectives; and protection against fiscal evasion. This paper has not touched on these issues. It has suggested that in control of international liquidity, control of the Euro-currency markets is second order.

TABLE II.3

Sources of Reserve Growth, 1961–1971[a]

(In billions of U.S. dollars)

Annual changes in	1961	1962	1963	1964	1965	1966	1967	1968	1969	1970	Jan.–Sep. 1971
1. Gold Reserves											
Monetary gold	0·6	0·4	0·8	0·7	0·2	—	−1·6	−0·7	0·1	0·3	−0·1
Gold transactions by I.M.F. and other international institutions (sales +)	0·2	—	0·1	−0·1	0·8	−0·9	0·2	0·1	0·1	−2·1	−0·9
Countries' gold reserves	0·8	0·4	0·9	0·6	1·0	−0·9	−1·4	−0·6	0·2	−1·9	−1·0
2. Special Drawing Rights											
Allocation of SDRs	—	—	—	—	—	—	—	—	—	3·4	2·9
I.M.F. holdings of SDRs (increase −)	—	—	—	—	—	—	—	—	—	−0·3	−0·2
Countries' SDR holdings	—	—	—	—	—	—	—	—	—	3·1	2·8
3. Reserve Positions in I.M.F.											
Use of I.M.F. credit	1·0	−0·4	0·1	0·3	1·6	—	−0·5	1·2	0·3	−0·8	−1·9
I.M.F. gold transactions (inflow +)[b]	−0·4	0·1	0·1	−0·1	−0·3	1·0	—	−0·4	—	1·6	0·3
I.M.F. transactions in SDRs (inflow +)	—	—	—	—	—	—	—	—	—	0·3	0·2
I.M.F. surplus (increase −)	−0·1	−0·1	−0·1	—	−0·1	−0·1	−0·1	−0·1	−0·1	−0·1	—
Reserve positions in I.M.F.	0·6	−0·4	0·1	0·2	1·2	1·0	−0·6	0·7	0·2	1·0	−1·4
4. Foreign Exchange Holdings											
a. U.S. dollars											
U.S. deficit on official settlements[c]	1·3	2·7	2·0	1·6	1·3	−0·3	3·4	−1·6	−2·7	10·7[d]	23·9[d]
U.S. reserve assets (including foreign exchange) used in											

						...	3·3	...	-0·7	-1·5	7·7	21·7
(ii) Identified official holdings of Euro-dollars[g]	...	...	...	...	0·1	0·7	...	1·2	-0·1	5·5	...
b. Official sterling holdings of overseas sterling area	0·2	...	0·4	0·1	-0·1	-0·2	0·3	-0·2	0·9	0·5	1·2
c. Official deutsche mark holdings[h]	...	...	...	...	...	...	...	...	0·3	0·9	...
d. Official French franc holdings[i]	—	-0·1	—	-0·1	—	0·1	—	-0·1	-0·1	0·1	...
e. Foreign exchange claims arising from swap credits and related assistance[j]	—	—	—	0·4	-0·3	0·7	0·9	1·2	-0·1	-2·2	...
f. Unidentified Euro-currencies and residual[k]	-0·4	-0·5	0·2	-0·6	-0·4	-0·1	-1·3	0·1	1·7	1·6	...
Countries' holdings of foreign exchange	0·5	0·5	2·2	1·2	-0·6	0·1	2·2	1·5	1·1	14·1	24·8
Total Reserve Growth	2·0	0·6	3·3	2·1	1·6	0·2	0·2	1·5	1·5	16·2	25·2

SOURCES: *International Financial Statistics*; Deutsche Bundesbank, *Monthly Bulletin*; I.M.F., *1971 Annual Report*; Bank of England, *Quarterly Bulletin*, Dec. 1971.

[a] Adjusted reserves. See footnote 1, p. 18 of *1971 Annual Report*.

[b] Including gold subscriptions and effect of I.M.F. gold deposits and gold investments.

[c] Unlike the other components of reserve growth listed above, the deficit is already in a flow dimension and therefore is not expressed as a change from the previous year.

[d] Before allocation of SDR 0.9 billion.

[e] Includes claims on the United States denominated in the claimant's own currency, i.e. Roosa bonds.

[f] Excludes $0·4 billion in respect of reduction in I.M.F. gold investment.

[g] Fund staff estimates based on information supplied by 51 countries.

[h] Estimates of deutsche mark claims of monetary authorities on Deutsche Bundesbank and German commercial banks, derived from Deutsche Bundesbank, *Monthly Bulletin*, Dec. 1970 and May 1971.

[i] Comprises foreign exchange holdings of the Malagasy Republic, Mali, and of common central banks of Equatorial Africa and West Africa, plus Fund staff estimates.

[j] See footnote 4 on p. 20 of *1971 Annual Report*.

[k] Includes asymmetries arising from the fact that data on U.S. and U.K. currency liabilities are more comprehensive than data on official exchange holdings shown in *International Financial Statistics*.

TABLE II.4

Estimated Official Holdings of Euro-Currencies, 1964–1970

(In billions of U.S. dollars)

	1964	1965	1966	1967	1968	1969	1970
Identified official holdings of Euro-dollars [a]							
Ten industrial countries [b]	0·4	0·5	1·0	0·9	1·7	1·0	4·1
Other industrial countries [c]	0·2	0·2	0·3	0·5	0·5	0·5	0·8
Total, industrial countries	0·7	0·8	1·3	1·4	2·1	1·5	4·9
More developed areas	0·2	0·2	0·3	0·3	0·4	0·4	1·3
Less developed areas	0·2	0·3	0·4	0·7	0·9	1·5	2·7
Total, primary producing countries	0·4	0·5	0·6	0·9	1·3	1·9	4·0
Total, 51 countries	1·1	1·2	1·9	2·3	3·4	3·4	8·9
Unidentified official holdings of Euro-currencies and residual sources of reserves [d]	1·7	1·2	1·0	−0·4	−0·5	1·0	2·4

SOURCES: I.M.F., *1971 Annual Report.*

[a] Fund staff estimates based on information supplied by 51 countries.

[b] Belgium, Canada, France, Germany, Japan, Italy, the Netherlands, Sweden, Switzerland, and the United Kingdom.

[c] Austria, Denmark, and Norway.

[d] Includes asymmetries in data on reserves and liabilities: see footnote [k] of Table II.3.

Discussion Papers

(a) J. H. WILLIAMSON
(*University of Warwick*)

ON first reading the paper of Mr. Hirsch I was puzzled by his choice of a topic of apparently limited importance. The mystery was, however, resolved by our Chairman this morning. He drew an analogy between the initial theoretical work on financial intermediation in the domestic context and the recent writing on the Euro-dollar market, and he pointed out that later work on domestic intermediation had refuted the fears that monetary policy would be seriously undermined. Mr. Hirsch had therefore been invited to examine whether the intermediation of the Euro-dollar market was capable of leading to a loss of control over the volume of international liquidity, or whether the fears of this are as exaggerated in the international as they proved to be in the domestic context. In response, Hirsch has provided the definitive analysis of the effects of the Euro-dollar market on both the demand for and the supply of international reserves; he has concluded that the topic is of only limited importance and that most of the fears are exaggerated. It is valuable to have had this established.

The paper by Professor Swoboda is concerned with the theorem that in the long run a fixed exchange-rate system deprives a country of the freedom to determine its monetary policy independently of the monetary policy of the rest of the world. This has been familiar since Polak's basic paper in 1957, and what Swoboda has contributed is a useful tidying-up of the assumptions that are sufficient to establish the theorem's validity. He is ambiguous about his attitude to the normative significance of the theorem: he acknowledges some of the criticisms that have been levelled at a policy of subordinating monetary policy to the balance of payments, but nevertheless concludes that 'monetary policy is an inappropriate instrument of anti-cyclical policy', albeit qualifying this by 'under fixed exchange rates . . . in anything but the short run'. My own view is that the theorem is totally devoid of normative significance;

i.e. that central bankers should not refrain from using monetary policy for domestic stabilization purposes. The most fundamental reason for this is one to which Professor Reuber also makes allusion, namely that exchange rates are not immortally fixed and analysis should ask whether they should be rather than producing formulae for preserving fixity irrespective of the cost. The secondary reason is that an objective of avoiding parity changes is best pursued by adopting long-run policies aimed at an appropriate reserve target, while in the short run reserves should be treated as a *constraint* on monetary policy and not as a *target*.

I come now to Professor Pearce's paper. I have never been a great devotee of analogies, so I propose to by-pass the monkeys and chimpanzees and proceed to the heart of the paper, which is the following:

Theorem: If factors are immobile between regions but are guaranteed the same remuneration in each, factors will not all be fully employed unless either

(a) the conditions of the Factor Price Equalization Theorem are satisfied; or

(b) a permanent production subsidy is transferred between regions.

This theorem seems to me to pose three questions:

(1) Is the theorem correct?

(2) What is the theorem's relationship to the more frequently expressed worry that differential cost trends will lead to regional problems within a monetary union?

(3) Will monetary union actually lead to an equalization of factor remuneration? If so, will either (a) or (b) prevent the feared unemployment materializing?

On the first of these questions, Pearce has proved that the theorem is valid in a neo-classical world with a unique equilibrium. One might, of course, reflect that convincing sufficient conditions for uniqueness have never been established. It is interesting to note that Pearce's own evidence (Table II.1) shows that 'labourers' receive significantly different wages in different industries, contrary to neo-classical assumptions. It is obvious that different wage rates for the same type of labour in different industries virtually guarantee non-uniqueness. In that case there is a potential welfare gain from the enforced equalization of factor remunerations in the same industry in different countries; for, with wage rates determined by 'sociological accidents' and differing between countries, countries could be exporting products that were intensive in cheap factors even where productivity was relatively low—whereas common wage rates would ensure that the pattern of specialization was determined by efficiency. But this line of argument does not, so far as I can see, refute Pearce's contention that wage equalization could cause unemployment; it merely serves to point out the possible existence of welfare gains that are overlooked by over-conventional models.

My second question concerned the relationship of the theorem to the fear of differential cost trends that has appeared so prominently in the recent writing of, among others, Harry Johnson, and the Federal Trust Report on European Monetary Integration. Is the theorem a generalization? or is it orthogonal, in the sense that both could hold simultaneously? or is it an alternative? To pose the question is enough to make the answer clear. If Pearce is right, relative costs would be determined by the equalization of wages and would not cumulatively diverge: the two theories are therefore alternatives.

The final question concerns whether factor remuneration actually would be equalized. I do not pretent to know the answer. It is obviously an empirical question, to which Tables II.3 and II.4 do not begin to give an empirical answer: for that one would require equivalent data on wage differentials between intra-national regions. But let us assume that Pearce is right in believing that monetary unification would lead to equal factor prices throughout the union. The question then is whether unemployment would be avoided by either (a) or (b). I would agree with Pearce in being reluctant to rely on the conditions of the Factor Price Equalization Theorem being satisfied. That implies that one would have to rely on fiscal transfers to avoid unemployment. Consider the proposal for a regionally-differentiated payroll tax/subsidy—a proposal which is analytically equivalent to a series of regional depreciations with the terms-of-trade costs neutralized. Provided Pearce is right in thinking that cost divergences would not be cumulative, there will presumably exist a set of tax and subsidy rates that would restore full employment. The vital question is whether the monetary union covers an area with sufficient political and social cohesion to support income transfers of the necessary size. If the answer is yes, an egalitarian will prefer the combination of monetary union and transfer to monetary autarchy.

The above analysis leads me to offer my own definition of an optimum currency area. I suggest that it is the largest of:

(a) the area that already has a single currency (on Fleming's[1] argument that it is impractical to break up currency areas);

(b) the area within which the problem of differential cost trends has been mastered and social cohesion is adequate to support the transfers needed for full employment.

Will Europe be an optimum currency area in this sense in 1980? I do not claim to know. Let me add that such agnosticism is completely compatible with the Federal Trust approach of limited integration in the short run and full union only after the necessary preconditions are satisfied.

[1] J. M. Fleming, 'On Exchange Rate Unification', *Economic Journal*, Sept. 1971.

Discussion Papers

(b) G. L. REUBER
(University of Western Ontario)

ALTHOUGH these three papers deal with different aspects of money in an international economy, all reflect the central phenomenon of a close and growing integration of international markets for goods, services, and assets and are concerned with the consequences of this phenomenon for the achievement of domestic economic objectives. The other common feature is the postulate of a fixed price at which the money issued by one country exchanges for that issued by another. Within this framework, three questions are explored:

(1) What are the implications of such a world for the use of monetary policy? Swoboda's question.

(2) What are the implications of eliminating domestic control over the money supply altogether and joining a common currency area? Pearce's question.

(3) Assuming that nations maintain control of their domestic money supply, what determines the total stock of international resources available in the world and how might this control be improved? Hirsch's question.

The lucid analysis presented by each author contributes significantly to an understanding of these complex and important issues.

As Swoboda acknowledges, the conclusions he establishes are now pretty well recognized; he has attempted to make the theory more explicit and to deal in detail with the role of capital movements and non-traded goods. What one misses in the discussion is any insight into the process whereby the economy moves to a new equilibrium position because of a change in the money supply and any empirical feeling for the relationships that are described. As a consequence, one remains in the dark about the mechanism of adjustment. Nor is one very clear about how much practical significance to attribute to the theoretical relationship that is emphasized—a relationship derived from a series of assumptions that one may view as highly restrictive.

Within this context it may be interesting to make a few references to Canadian experience. Canada is a small country in Swoboda's terms and its capital market is, of course, very highly integrated with that in the U.S. and, to a lesser degree, with those in Europe as well.[1] The evidence suggests that the scope for using monetary policy to influence domestic activity in Canada is severely limited under fixed exchange rates. This is mainly because of the large and rapid response in the capital account to changes in domestic monetary policy. The evidence for the period 1952–61 suggests, for example, that the effectiveness of monetary policy in terms of its impact on interest rates was reduced on the order of one-third because of the direct effect of capital flows. And it was reduced substantially more if one allows, in addition, for the indirect effect occurring because expectations about interest rates in Canada are considerably influenced by interest rates in the United States. As far as lags are concerned, the Canadian evidence suggests that capital flows respond very rapidly, virtually all of the adjustment occurring within the same quarter as a given change in monetary policy. Moreover, if exchange-rate adjustments are precluded, the impact of a given change in monetary policy, in the short run and over an extended time period, is substantially greater on the capital account than on the current account.

Reference to the current-account effects of a change in monetary policy brings one to the distinction Swoboda draws between traded and non-traded goods and his reference to the response lags in the non-traded sector. Although this distinction may be of some interest, it leaves the status of non-traded-but-potentially-tradeable goods ambiguous. Moreover, adjustment lags are likely to occur for many items included in the traded category as well as for those included in the non-traded category. For these reasons it may be preferable to think in more conventional terms about the lagged expenditure effects on the current-account balance arising from a change in monetary policy. Canadian evidence for the 1952–61 period sug-

[1] For a more detailed discussion and references to other work see Richard E. Caves and Grant L. Reuber, *Capital Transfers and Economic Policy: Canada, 1951–1962* (Cambridge, Mass.: Harvard University Press, 1970); 'International Capital Markets and Canadian Economic Policy Under Flexible and Fixed Exchange Rates, 1952–69', Conference on United States–Canadian Economic Relations, Sept. 1971, Federal Reserve Bank of Boston (forthcoming).

gests that such expenditure effects are relatively small and that the adjustment process via the current account is long drawn out.

Pearce's paper takes us a step further than Swoboda's by assuming not only *permanently* fixed exchange rates but also a common money supply determined in some undefined way for a group of countries— a common currency area for the E.E.C. This amounts to foreclosing or severely restricting the use by any member, at its own initiative, of the conventional arsenal of stabilization policy instruments— monetary, exchange-rate, and debt-management policies, as well as fiscal policy to some degree. In these circumstances we have largely left the muddy ground of international monetary economics and find ourselves knee-deep in the quagmire of the economics of federalism—a quagmire well-known in Canada for its hazards.

How one sees the prospect of a common currency area depends in part on one's perspective. Two questions in particular arise: Is one concerned with the welfare of one particular member of the area or with the area as a whole? Is one concerned with the long-term consequences, abstracting from the transitional adjustment process, or with the short-run adjustments arising from joining a union? Pearce focuses mainly on the consequences for one member, rather than for the area as a whole. This leaves open the question of how the picture he portrays would change if one allowed not only for direct effects but also for any indirect effects accruing to a particular country because of the costs and benefits accruing to the area as a whole. The paper focuses on such long-run effects as the possible reduction in transactions costs and risk as well as on the adjustment process entailing price, income, and employment effects and factor movements. The range of policies to be considered in this context include such measures as transfer payments to achieve a desirable distribution of income, adjustment assistance to promote the transition and cushion its impact on particular sectors, and the removal of institutional and other impediments restricting the efficiency of the money and credit system. Over the long term at least, it is doubtful whether the 'currency illusion', which Pearce suggests at present reduces the difficulties that governments face with respect to wage demands, is of much significance.

It is useful to distinguish these issues from the related but separable questions concerned with stabilization policy—be it from the standpoint of one particular country or for the area as a whole. If one interprets the evidence available as suggesting that short-run stabilization policies, as practised in most countries since World War II, have either been ineffective or have been as likely to make things worse rather than better, one may conclude that the constraints placed on short-run stabilization policies by monetary union are unimportant or possibly even helpful. If, on the other hand, one reads this evidence as suggesting that national stabilization policies afford opportunities to cope more effectively with exogenous disturbances and to attain a price-change/employment experience that is better than it would otherwise be, one is left with several subsidiary questions. Can such policies be run more effectively by the union as a whole than by individual countries? Even if they can be, how closely do the preferences and empirical relationships for the union as a whole, to which a collective policy presumably will be geared, coincide with the preferences and empirical relationships for any one country? If there are wide disparities, are the indirect benefits from the effects of stabilization policy via other members of the union likely to compensate for the direct costs of forgoing preferable policies seen solely from a national standpoint? And if the answer is no, are the costs to the member country emanating from its loss of control over stabilization policy less than the net long-run welfare gains resulting from monetary union?

In order to pursue these questions very far it is necessary to have a fairly clear notion of the terms of the monetary union as well as the other policy arrangements linking members of the union. It is also necessary to make a variety of empirical and other judgements about the economies included in the union. I agree with Pearce that lessons drawn from U.S. experience are not very persuasive. Canadian experience may be more relevant if only because the country is less homogeneous—economically, politically, and socially —and Provincial Governments are substantially more powerful relative to the Federal Government. Anyone familiar with Canadian experience will be aware of the difficult and acrimonious relations that have frequently arisen between the Federal and Provincial Governments. Some of these difficulties have centred on policies for income redistribution. Some of the discussion has reflected concern about the depopulation of less prosperous areas. And some of the controversy has focused on the timing and effects of stabilization policies pursued from the centre which, in terms of the conditions found in particular provinces, seemed highly inappropriate. For example, not only have unemployment rates been much higher on average in the Atlantic Provinces than in Ontario but also they have fluctuated considerably more in response to variations in economic activity. This has led to various suggestions for regional monetary and fiscal policies.

Given the functioning monetary systems found at present among members of the E.E.C., one may share Pearce's scepticism about the net advantages of adopting a monetary union even if one does not agree with all of his analysis. Monetary union by itself will not reduce the number of governments found within the E.E.C. nor the range of economic difficulties that arise: the main effect may be to restrict what these governments can do to alleviate the problems that confront them.

A common currency area is one way of attempting to gain control over the money stock available to a group of countries. Leaving aside the unrealistic prospect of such an area encompassing the whole world, Hirsch directs our attention to the issue of effectively controlling the total stock of internationally accepted monies in the world, given fixed exchange rates and the propensity of competitive international markets to develop new institutional arrangements to economize on the cost of holding money and to take advantage of the most profitable investment outlets available. The most dramatic development of this kind during the past decade has been the Euro-currency market. While this development may have increased the amount of international liquidity available in the world, Hirsch suggests that it has not been the major factor. He also suggests that the instability in the supply of international liquidity arising from the Euro-currency market has in large part reflected exchange-rate speculation. It is further pointed out that an agreement among the leading central banks of Europe not to invest resources in Euro-currencies is not a sufficient condition to control the total supply of liquidity; what is required to achieve such control is collective control over changes in the stock of currency balances in reserve holdings.

The main questions that arise to my mind are not with the historical and technical aspects of the analysis—which are excellent— nor with the inferences drawn, but rather with some of the underlying assumptions. The restrictive nature of these assumptions is fully recognized in the paper, leaving one nonetheless in some doubt about the significance of the issues reviewed. Three questions in particular might be raised in this context.

The first relates to the trade-off, if any, between the efficiency gains to the international community from greater capital market integration and the gains that might accrue from greater control over the total supply of international liquidity. The answer depends partly on the type of controls one foresees. Much of the present discussion assumes a non-price system of controls in which market adjustments via interest and exchange-rate changes are given low priority in comparison with administrative arrangements which inhibit the market mechanism. These arrangements conceivably could limit the efficiency of the international capital market quite significantly.

A second question concerns the concept of control. One may argue that the volume of international liquidity now is under a considerable measure of control and that the problem really arises because this control is largely exercised by the U.S. which, understandably, gears the rate at which it creates dollars more closely to domestic than to international considerations. Thus the issue is not only to find reserve assets that provide preferable alternatives to dollars but also to find sufficient agreement among countries to make it feasible to run an effective international monetary policy on a collective basis.

Thirdly, even if the *nominal* money supply could be more effectively controlled, there is the further question of how much control could be gained over the *real* quantity of international money in the long run since the public can alter the price level to achieve the real quantity of money that it wants.

Finally—and this applies to all three of the papers presented—discussion of money in an international economy is seriously bridled if it sticks exclusively to the highly restrictive assumption of fixed exchange rates made throughout these papers. Whether one allows for exchange-rate adjustments on a flexible or a sliding or an adjustable peg basis, it is important to recognize that exchange-rate changes *do* occur not infrequently. Allowance for exchange-rate adjustments makes a major difference to the analysis. Some of the issues raised in this session either would disappear or would be transformed if the authors had been prepared to modify their assumptions to give some recognition to the possibility of changes in exchange rates.

III

RECENT DEVELOPMENTS IN MONETARY THEORY
Introduced by FRANK BRECHLING

J. S. FLEMMING
ROBERT J. BARRO *and*
ANTHONY M. SANTOMERO

Discussion Papers
(*a*) K. BORCH
(*b*) EDGAR L. FEIGE

RECENT DEVELOPMENTS IN
MONETARY THEORY

INTRODUCTION

FRANK BRECHLING

(Northwestern University and University of Essex)

IN recent decades the great debates on the macro-economic role of money in capitalist societies have dominated the literature and attracted a great deal of limelight. By contrast, the less glamorous, but possibly more important, developments in the micro-economic theory of money have proceeded with less of a fanfare but with thoughtful scholarship. The two papers, which are under discussion in the present session, represent a significant contribution in this area.

The micro-economic theory of money is concerned essentially with the determination of the demand for and supply of money by individual households, firms, and financial institutions. The individual decision units are assumed explicitly to maximize some objective (for instance, utility or profits) under certain constraints and their optimum holdings of money are examined. Since, however, money is usually held in relation to some other variables, these models of micro-economic behaviour have other rich implications. A number of different strands of the micro-economic theory of money can be distinguished.

The first set of theories is based on the Markowitz–Tobin approach in which individual asset-holders face uncertain returns on assets and take current portfolio decisions. If they are risk-averse they will typically hold some money and the amount will normally be an inverse function of the rate of interest. John Flemming's paper is a contribution in this area. Although these theories incorporate uncertainty explicitly, they are usually static in the sense that they need not involve planning or movement through time.

By contrast, the second set of theories, which are based on the Baumol–Tobin approach to the transactions demand for money, involves time explicitly and necessarily because the demand for money depends on the frequency with which money payments are made. A change in the stock of money is assumed to have an adjustment cost (a brokerage charge) and the average cost of adjustment is smaller for large than for small adjustments. Such a cost leads to non-continuous adjustments in the stock of money and thus to an optimal average level of money holdings. In Barro and Santomero's paper these notions are developed for the theory of the firm and the labour market. The frequency with which wage payments are made is an essential prediction of their model. Knowledge of the frequency with which money payments are made seems necessary for our understanding of the micro- and macro-dynamic role of money in the economy. Hence, this type of approach promises to be fruitful.

Both the portfolio and the adjustment-cost approaches have already led to important micro-economic theories of monetary behaviour. Moreover, as the two papers before us show, additional interesting results and helpful insights seem to await discovery.

PORTFOLIO CHOICE AND LIQUIDITY PREFERENCE: A CONTINUOUS-TIME TREATMENT*

J. S. FLEMMING
(Nuffield College, Oxford)

IN two articles in 1969 Borch [3] and Feldstein [7] criticized the analytical basis of Tobin's original contribution 'Liquidity Preference as Behaviour Towards Risk' [21]. Tobin's reply only partly rebutted their attack: he admitted the need for 'a more general and less vulnerable approach' (than his own) which would 'yield the kind of comparative-static results that economists are interested in' [23, p. 14]. Borch and Feldstein did not claim to provide such an alternative approach. The purpose of this paper is to argue that the reformulation of the problem in continuous time provides an opportunity for the relatively rigorous development of results at once both interesting and fairly general. In the process I hope to present Merton's continuous time portfolio analysis [15] in a form more accessible to those who, like the author, are intimidated by the terminology of stochastic processes and integrals. It will also be shown that continuous trading enables one to construct 'log-normal' portfolios from 'log-normal' assets—an issue which arose in the exchange between Feldstein and Tobin.

Throughout the paper attention is focused on the rather special case in which investment opportunities are stationary and consumption preferences also isoelastic. These assumptions enormously simplify the arguments—and the results: the approach, however, is by no means restricted to this case.[1]

* I am grateful for discussion at various stages with Karl Borch, Avinash Dixit, Martin Feldstein, Louis Gevers, Peter Hammond, Jeremy Hardie, John Helliwell, Robert Merton, Dick Meyer, Jim Mirrlees, and Michio Morishima. These discussions uncovered errors, none of which are attributable to the earlier discussants.

[1] Though this case simplifies partial analysis of the type employed in this paper it presents serious difficulties in a general equilibrium context which

The basic model is developed in Section I, the simple two-asset case of Tobin's original contribution is examined in Section II, while Section III pursues the more general Slutsky analysis of the demand for many risky assets following the example of Bierwag and Grove [2], Royama and Hamada [18], and Morishima [16].

I

The potential advantage of a continuous-time approach to the analysis of risk-taking is implicit in Pratt's 1964 result that, in the limit as the risks become negligible in magnitude, so they can be adequately described by means and variances [17].[2] A continuous-time model is the limiting case as the period for which the investor is committed to particular holdings tends to zero: it thus follows the logic of the common justification of mean-variance analysis as a first approximation. Unfortunately the 'first approximation' argument provides very weak foundations for rigorous theorizing in a context such as discrete time, which precludes infinitesimal risks: the status of Tobin's results is ambiguous for this reason—how is one to interpret an 'approximate result'? Is the analysis really capable of being better than suggestive?

I know of no two-parameter discrete-time analysis of risk-taking which is not open to very serious objections: the quadratic utility function implies negative marginal utility of wealth above a certain level; normally distributed asset prices imply a non-zero probability that they will be negative;[3] Arrow's elegant technique [1] is applicable only to two assets—moreover one of them is usually assumed to be riskless.[4] It therefore seems well while exploring the continuous-time case. This is not to suggest that it is entirely unobjectionable: the mere existence of transaction costs in security markets is sufficient to undermine the realism of the associated continuous-trading assumption. Nevertheless, I hope to show that it is a fruitful case to study, and, in as much as the other available models do

---

are referred to in [10] where I have also examined the consequences of non-stationary opportunities and preferences.

[2] Restated by Samuelson in [19].

[3] See Feldstein [7] for reasons for restricting discussion to the normality assumption as an alternative to quadratic utility in this context.

[4] Stiglitz [20] relaxes the riskless-asset assumption but only to the extent of substituting the requirement that the riskiness of the two assets can be ranked according to a rather restrictive criterion.

not appeal directly to trading costs to justify discrete-time analysis, it is also the purest available case.

It is important throughout the analysis to remember that the continuous-time model can only be treated—or understood—as the limit of a discrete model. We therefore start by deriving some well-known results in a way that enables us to establish some useful notational conventions. Consider an asset which has a serially independent[5] random return $\tilde{r}(h)$ with mean mh and finite[6] variance vh proportional to the holding period h.[7] An investor who put all his initial wealth (W_0) into this asset would, in continuous time, have wealth at time t given by:

$$\tilde{W}_t = W_0 \lim_{h \to 0} \prod_{s=0}^{t/h} (1 + \tilde{r}_s(h)). \tag{1}$$

Provided that the distribution of $\tilde{r}(h)$ is continuous (with probability one) it can be shown,[8] by reference to the Central Limit Theorem, that $\tilde{W}_t$ is lognormally distributed; we need only derive the parameters of the distribution in terms of m and v.[9]

The assumption that asset prices are continuously distributed is strong, but not, perhaps, unreasonable: it amounts to ruling out jumps in prices. For our purposes one must consider the likelihood of such jumps in the absence of transactions costs. There are two types of reason for there not to be jumps; that information arrives in such small amounts that the 'state of information' is effectively continuous; and secondly that the process of information diffusion through the relevant market population is such that price changes consequential even upon discrete information changes are suitably continuous—this last assumption is the more plausible the more numerous and the more risk-averse are market agents.

[5] This requirement is basically the random-walk hypothesis the evidence for which is considered in [4].

[6] I thus rule out the distributions considered by Mandelbrot [12] and Fama [6].

[7] Higher moments disappear in the limit being less than proportional to h. Brownian motion and Wiener processes conform to these requirements.

[8] See for instance [8] ch. VI and [5] ch. VIII. The version of this paper presented to the Conference was deficient at this point, in as much as no reference was made to the necessary continuity assumption. I am grateful to Professor Borch for presenting a counter-example to the proposition then put forward and to Professor Mirrlees for suggesting the solution here adopted.

[9] As Professor Borch pointed out, the lognormal is a three-parameter distribution, but where asset prices are concerned the third parameter (the lower limit to the range of the variate) is naturally set equal to zero.

Taking logs of (1) we obtain

$$\log{(\tilde{W}_t)} = \log{(W_0)} + \lim_{h \to 0} \sum_{s=1}^{t/h} \log{\{1 + \tilde{r}_s(h)\}} \tag{2}$$

$$= \log{(W_0)} + \lim_{h \to 0} \sum_{s=1}^{t/h} [\tilde{r}_s(h) - \tfrac{1}{2}\{\tilde{r}_s(h)\}^2 \ldots] \tag{3}$$

whence, given the independence of $\tilde{r}_s(h)$,

$$\mathrm{E}(\log{(\tilde{W}_t)}) = \log{(W_0)} + \lim_{h \to 0} (t/h)\{mh - \tfrac{1}{2}vh + 0(h^2)\} \tag{4}$$

$$= \log{(W_0)} + t(m - v/2). \tag{5}$$

From (3) and (4)
$\mathrm{Var}(\log{(\tilde{W}_t)})$

$$= \mathrm{E}\left[\lim_{h \to 0} \sum_{s=1}^{t/h} \{(\tilde{r}_s(h) - mh) - \tfrac{1}{2}((\tilde{r}_s(h))^2 - vh) + 0(h^2)\}^2\right] \tag{6}$$

$$= \mathrm{E}\left[\lim_{h \to 0} \sum_{s=1}^{t/h} \{(\tilde{r}_s(h))^2 + 0(h^2)\}\right] \tag{7}$$

$$= tv. \tag{8}$$

Thus $(m - v/2)$ and v are respectively the mean and variance, per unit time, of the logarithm of wealth: m itself is related to the logarithm of expected wealth as can be seen by taking expectations of (1) to get

$$\mathrm{E}(\tilde{W}_t) = W_0 \lim_{h \to 0} (1 + mh)^{t/h}, \tag{9}$$

whence

$$\log{(\mathrm{E}(\tilde{W}_t))} = \log{(W_0)} + \lim_{h \to 0} (t/h) \log{(1 + mh)} \tag{10}$$

$$= \log{(W_0)} + tm. \tag{11}$$

We would usually write a lognormally distributed random variable not in terms of the limit used in (1), but directly as

$$Y = e^{\tilde{\rho}} \quad \text{where} \quad \tilde{\rho} = N(\mu, \sigma^2); \tag{12}$$

whence

$$\mathrm{E}(\log{(\tilde{Y})}) = \mu \quad \text{and} \quad \mathrm{Var}(\log{(\tilde{Y})}) = \sigma^2 \tag{13}$$

while

$$\log{(\mathrm{E}(\tilde{Y}))} = \mu + \sigma^2/2. \tag{14}$$

Thus the μ of equation (13) corresponds to the $(m - v/2)$ of equation (5) and $\bar{\rho}$ to $(\bar{r} - v/2)$.

We referred above to the fact that independent and identically distributed multiplicative increments generate a lognormal distribution provided that the sample functions of the process are continuous (with probability one). If individual assets meet these conditions, so also will a portfolio of such assets, provided that the share of wealth held in any one asset is constant over the relevant interval,[10] for then the portfolio structure at each point of time is independent of previous performance, thus ensuring both the independence and identical distribution of successive increments.

We can therefore simply substitute $\sum_i x_{is}\bar{r}_{is}(h)$ for $\bar{r}_s(h)$, where $x_{is}(\geq 0)$ is the proportion of wealth held in the ith asset at time s.[11] We then have the portfolio mean return

$$m_s = \sum_i x_{is}m_{is} = \sum_i x_{is}(\mu_{is} + v_{is}/2) = \mu_s + v_s/2 \qquad (15)$$

with variance

$$v_s = \sum_i \sum_j x_{is}x_{js}v_{ijs} = \sigma_s^2 \qquad (16)$$

where

$$\mu_s = \sum_i x_{is}(\mu_{is} + v_{is}/2) - \sum_i \sum_j x_{is}x_{js}v_{ijs}/2 \qquad (17)$$

and the v_{ij}'s are the covariances.

In [7] Feldstein used a lognormally distributed asset (and logarithmic utility) to construct a counter-example to Tobin's assertions that two-parameter distributions are associated with convex indifference curves in the space of the mean and standard deviation of wealth [21]. In his reply [23] Tobin appealed to the fact that a

[10] Since this paper was prepared, this proposition has been demonstrated more rigorously by R. C. Merton. 'Optimum Consumption and Portfolio Rules in a Continuous Time Model', *Journal of Economic Theory*, Dec. 1971, pp. 373–413, especially pp. 384–5 Theorem II (2).

[11] Throughout the paper it will be assumed that short sales are not allowed; this is not because the non-negativity constraint solves any analytical problem—quite the contrary—but because it does not seem to me adequate simply to drop the non-negativity constraint on asset holdings. Up to a point my short position may be as 'good' as the stock itself, but eventually my liabilities have to take on the characteristics of the assets which secure them. Thus, while a strong case can be made for admitting short sales, it cannot be done without a whole host of complications which are best left aside for the present. For a criticism of this constraint see Hester [11].

fixed-holding (not a fixed-value-share) portfolio of lognormal assets will not itself be lognormally distributed, being the simple sum of its constituents. In fact we will see that our own analysis establishes convex indifference curves for risk-averse investors—but in the space of the mean and standard deviation of *returns* $(m, \sqrt{v})$—thus re-establishing Tobin's proposition that 'Risk averters are diversifiers' [21, p. 76].

These indifference curves are more easily derived in terms of the expected rate of change of wealth, μ, than the rate of change of expected wealth, m (see (5), (11), (13)). However, the indifference curves relate only to the aggregate portfolio mean μ, and this can be transformed to the m's more appropriate to the analysis of portfolio structure by the equation $m = \mu + v/2$.

Consider first the Tobin-type problem of maximizing the expected utility of terminal wealth, utility being a direct isoelastic function of wealth.

$$\operatorname*{Max}_{x} \mathrm{E}_0(U(\tilde{W}_t)) \tag{18}$$

where

$$U(W) = (1/\gamma)W^\gamma \tag{19}$$

and

$$\tilde{W}_t = W_0\, \mathrm{e}^{\tilde{\rho}(t)} \tag{20}$$

where

$$\tilde{\rho}(t) = N(\mu t, vt) \tag{21}$$

whence

$$\mathrm{E}_0(U(\tilde{W}_t)) = (1/\gamma)W_0^\gamma\, \mathrm{e}^{\gamma(\mu + \gamma v/2)t} \tag{22}$$

since the variance of $\gamma\tilde{\rho}$ is $\gamma^2 v$. Thus

$$k = \mu + \gamma v/2 \tag{23}$$

defines an indifference curve in $\mu - v$ space; or, substituting $(m - v/2)$ for μ we have, in $m - v$ space,

$$k = m - (1 - \gamma)v/2. \tag{24}$$

Confronting these [indifference curves with the investment-opportunity locus defined by equations (15) and (16), for constant value share portfolios, yields identical results, in terms of the appropriately defined mean (m) and standard deviation $(\sigma, \sqrt{v})$ of the portfolio rate of return, as does the conventional model [10, 11, 20] in terms of the mean and standard deviation of W_t itself. Figure III.1 shows the two curves both in m–σ and m–v space.

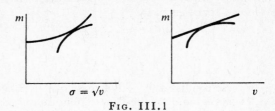

FIG. III.1

In the preceding analysis—as in most of the literature—utility is postulated to be a direct function of wealth: wealth is treated as an end in itself, not merely as a means to the end—consumption. One of the major virtues of Merton's continuous-time analysis [15] is its integration of consumption and portfolio choice. In fact, with an infinite horizon and isoelastic utility, the indirect-utility function reduces to the direct one used above—however, it has the advantage of justifying the constant-value share restriction considered above. The stationarity of the whole problem, when utility is isoelastic and investment opportunities themselves are stationary, ensures the optimality of constant portfolio composition and also the policy of consuming at a rate proportional to wealth ($C_t = cW_t$).[12] In this case our problem can be written:

$$\phi(W_0) = \underset{x,\,c}{\text{Max}} \int_0^\infty e^{-\alpha t} U(c\tilde{W}_t)\, dt, \qquad (25)$$

where α is the rate of pure time preference and,

$$U(C) = (1/\gamma)C^\gamma \qquad (26)$$

while

$$\tilde{W}_t = W_0\, e^{\tilde{p}(t) - ct} \qquad (27)$$

whence

$$\phi(W) = \underset{x,\,c}{\text{Max}}\,(c^\gamma/\gamma) W_0^\gamma \int_0^\infty e^{-\{(\alpha + \gamma c) - \gamma(\mu + \gamma v/2)\}t}\, dt. \qquad (28)$$

The explicit solution of this problem is straightforward, but is left

[12] For a more formal derivation of similar results under these conditions see Flemming [9].

to the footnote below;[13] for our purposes it is sufficient to notice that ϕ depends on α, γ, c, and $(\mu + \gamma v/2)$, and since c depends on the others, of which α and γ are fixed independently of the portfolio choice, ϕ must vary with $(\mu + \gamma v/2)$. Thus we again have indifference curves in m–v space given by,

$$k = m - (1 - \gamma)v/2. \tag{29}$$

II

We can apply these results to the simple case of one risky and one riskless asset, 'Consols' and 'money', as Tobin described them in [21].

Noticing that $(1 - \gamma)$ is the Pratt–Arrow relative risk-aversion measure

$$R = \frac{-CU_{cc}}{U_c} = 1 - \gamma, \tag{30}$$

we can rewrite the indifference curves (24) and (29) as

$$k = m - Rv/2 \tag{31}$$

while in the general two-asset case

$$\left. \begin{array}{l} m = x_1 m_1 + (1 - x_1)m_2, \\ v = x_1^2 v_{11} + 2x_1(1 - x_1)v_{12} + (1 - x_1)^2 v_{22}. \end{array} \right\} \tag{32}$$

Differentiating (32) by x_1 enables us to derive

$$\frac{\mathrm{d}m}{\mathrm{d}v} = \frac{m_1 - m_2}{2\{x_1(v_{11} - 2v_{12} + v_{22}) + (v_{12} - v_{22})\}} \tag{33}$$

along the opportunity set, while from (31) the indifference curves have slope

$$\frac{\mathrm{d}m}{\mathrm{d}v} = \frac{R}{2}, \tag{34}$$

whence at a maximum

$$x_1 = \frac{m_1 - m_2 + R(v_{22} - v_{12})}{R(v_{11} - 2v_{12} + v_{22})}. \tag{35}$$

[13] Integrating (28) and differentiating the result with respect to c yields the following first-order condition for a maximum,

$$c = \{\alpha - \gamma(\mu + \gamma v/2)\}(1 - \gamma)^{-1},$$

whence substitution into the integral of (28) gives,

$$\phi(W_0) = \underset{x}{\mathrm{Max}} \; (1/\gamma) W_0^\gamma [(1 - \gamma)/\{\alpha - \gamma(\mu + \gamma v/2)\}]^{(1-\gamma)}.$$

If the first asset is riskless $v_{11} = v_{12} = 0$ in which case

$$x_1 = \frac{m_1 - m_2 + Rv_{22}}{Rv_{22}} \tag{36}$$

and

$$x_2 = \frac{m_2 - m_1}{Rv_{22}}. \tag{37}$$

Thus demand for risky assets is an increasing function of their yield and diminishes with their riskiness; these results are unambiguous—unlike Tobin's—because there is no 'income effect' operating (this point is pursued further below in Section III).

From (37) two significant conclusions can be drawn: first, the condition for a positive demand for 'money' $(x_2 < 1)$ is that

$$Rv_{22} > m_2 - m_1, \tag{38}$$

or in terms of μ,

$$Rv_{22} > \mu_2 + v_{22}/2 - \mu_1, \quad \text{i.e.} \quad (R - \tfrac{1}{2})v_{22} > \mu_2 - \mu_1. \tag{39}$$

Feldstein [7] derived a similar condition [p. 9]; however, he considered the Bernoulli logarithmic utility function for which $R = 1$ and concluded that 'the risk averter may well be a plunger'. However, $R = 1$ is a very low value for the elasticity of marginal utility; in other contexts $R = 3$ would not be considered at all extreme.

Secondly the elasticity of the (proportionate) demand for 'Consols', x_2, with respect to m_2 is

$$m_2/(m_2 - m_1). \tag{40}$$

In Tobin's case $m_1 = 0$ so that this elasticity is independent of m_2, being constant at unity. This result appears to conflict with his conclusion that the 'demand for consols is less elastic at high interest rates than at low' [21, p. 79]. In fact in terms of μ_2 the opposite result holds: the elasticity is

$$\frac{\mu_2}{\mu_2 + v_{22}/2 - \mu_1} \tag{41}$$

which, with $\mu_1 = 0$, increases with μ_2. The interest elasticity of demand for money is, of course, negative but its absolute value also increases with m_2; this unKeynesian result reflects the linearity of the demand functions (36) and (37). The absolute value of the interest elasticities, of the demands, become infinite as x_1 and x_2 respectively go to zero.

III

An important class of more general results derivable from the analysis of Section I relates to the demand functions for individual risky assets. From (31) we have indifference curves

where now
$$k = m - Rv/2$$
$$m = \sum_i m_i x_i \quad \text{and} \quad v = \sum_i \sum_j x_i x_j v_{ij}. \tag{42}$$

Consider the effect on the demand for the ith asset (Wx_i) of a change in m_j or v_{jk}: at the initial values x^0 this would change the utility index k. These changes would in general set up 'income-', 'wealth-' or, as Morishima rightly prefers to call them, 'want pattern-' effects by changing R, which is an exogenous parameter only in the stationary isoelastic case. Thus we have a case of some interest in which we can legitimately ignore any effects other than simple substitution. Moreover, given the linearity of the objective function in m and v, the structure of asset substitution is determined simply by the variance–covariance matrix of the uncertain returns $\|v_{ij}\|$. The following analysis requires that this matrix be positive definite which implies that all variances v_{ii} be strictly positive—there is *no* riskless asset.

We can write the portfolio problem in this case as

subject to
$$\text{Max } k = \sum_i x_i m_i - R \sum_i \sum_j x_i x_j \, v_{ij}/2$$
$$\sum_i x_i = 1, \qquad x_i \geq 0. \tag{43}$$

If we assume that all the assets enter the optimal portfolio positively so that the inequality constraints are not binding, we can form a Lagrangean and derive the $n + 1$ first-order conditions:

$$-m_i = -R \sum_i \sum_j x_j v_{ij} - \lambda$$
$$-1 = -\sum_i x_i \tag{44}$$

or, in matrix notation,

$$
\begin{bmatrix} -m_i \\ \vdots \\ -m_n \\ -1 \end{bmatrix} = H \begin{bmatrix} Rx_1 \\ \vdots \\ Rx_n \\ \lambda \end{bmatrix} \quad \text{where} \quad H = \begin{bmatrix} -v_{11} & \cdots & -v_{1n} & -1 \\ \vdots & \ddots & \vdots & \vdots \\ -v_{n1} & \cdots & -v_{nn} & -1 \\ -1 & \cdots & -1 & 0 \end{bmatrix}
$$

$$(45)$$

whence

$$
\begin{bmatrix} Rx_1 \\ \vdots \\ Rx_n \\ \lambda \end{bmatrix} = H^{-1} \begin{bmatrix} -m_1 \\ \vdots \\ -m_n \\ -1 \end{bmatrix}.
\tag{46}
$$

Differentiating (44) totally while holding v_{ij} constant yields

$$
\left.
\begin{aligned}
-\mathrm{d}m_i &= -R \sum_j \mathrm{d}x_j v_{ij} - \mathrm{d}\lambda \\
0 &= - \sum_j \mathrm{d}x_j,
\end{aligned}
\right\}
\tag{47}
$$

i.e.

$$
\begin{bmatrix} -\mathrm{d}m_1 \\ \vdots \\ -\mathrm{d}m_n \\ 0 \end{bmatrix} = H \begin{bmatrix} R\,\mathrm{d}x_1 \\ \vdots \\ R\,\mathrm{d}x_j \\ \mathrm{d}\lambda \end{bmatrix},
\tag{48}
$$

whence

$$
\begin{bmatrix} R\,\mathrm{d}x_1 \\ \vdots \\ R\,\mathrm{d}x_n \\ \mathrm{d}\lambda \end{bmatrix} = H^{-1} \begin{bmatrix} -\mathrm{d}m_1 \\ \vdots \\ -\mathrm{d}m_n \\ 0 \end{bmatrix}.
\tag{49}
$$

From (49) it follows directly that

$$
\frac{R\,\partial x_j}{\partial m_i} = -\frac{D_{ij}}{D},
\tag{50}
$$

where D is the determinant of H, and D_{ij} is the cofactor of the (ij)th element of H. If (46) is to represent the maximal solution of (42) the bordered principal minors of H must alternate in sign so that

$$
\frac{D_{ii}}{D} < 0.
\tag{51}
$$

Thus given $R > 0$—i.e. positive risk-aversion—we can deduce

$$\frac{\partial x_i}{\partial m_i} > 0$$

the demand for an asset increases with the mean return m_i ($= \mu_i + v_{ii}/2$). This result is more secure than Tobin's, since in his framework Tobin could not eliminate 'income effects' and in particular the perverse income effects associated with negative marginal utility under a quadratic function.

To examine the effects of changes in the matrix $\|v_{ij}\|$ we differentiate (44), holding m_i constant to obtain

$$\left.\begin{aligned} 0 &= -R \sum_j dx_j\, v_{ij} - R \sum_j x_j\, dv_{ij} - d\lambda \\ 0 &= -\sum_j dx_j, \end{aligned}\right\} \tag{52}$$

or

$$H \begin{bmatrix} -R\,dx_1 \\ \vdots \\ -R\,dx_n \\ -d\lambda \end{bmatrix} = \begin{bmatrix} dv_{11} & \cdots & dv_{1n} & -1 \\ \vdots & \ddots & \vdots & -1 \\ dv_{n1} & \cdots & dv_{nn} & -1 \\ -1 & & -1 & 0 \end{bmatrix} \begin{bmatrix} -Rx_1 \\ \vdots \\ -Rx_n \\ 0 \end{bmatrix}. \tag{53}$$

Since

$$v_{ij} = v_{ji}, \qquad dv_{ij} = dv_{ji}$$

thus from (53) we obtain

$$R \frac{\partial x_k}{\partial v_{ij}} = R \left[x_i \frac{D_j k}{D} + x_j \frac{D_{ik}}{D} \right] \quad (i \neq j) \tag{54}$$

and

$$\frac{\partial x_k}{\partial v_{ii}} = x_i \frac{D_{ik}}{D}; \tag{55}$$

in particular we thus have

$$\frac{\partial x_i}{\partial v_{ii}} = x_i \frac{D_{ii}}{D} < 0 \tag{56}$$

the demand for an asset decreases with its own variance v_{ii}.[14] Equation (56) also indicates the usual result that $\partial x_i / \partial v_{ii}$ vanishes as x_i tends to zero.

[14] Note that this result refers to changes in v_{ii} while m_i is constant; the results would be different if μ_i ($= m_i - v_{ii}/2$) were held constant. The preceding results on $\partial x_i / \partial m_i$ hold also for $\partial x_i / \partial \mu_i$ since, given v_{ii}, $\partial \mu_i = \partial m_i$.

REFERENCES

[1] ARROW, K. J., *Aspects of the Theory of Risk-Bearing*. Helsinki, 1965.

[2] BIERWAG, G. O., and GROVE, M. A., 'Slutsky Equation for Assets', *J.P.E.*, 1968, pp. 114–27.

[3] BORCH, K., 'A Note on Uncertainty and Indifference Curves', *Rev. Econ. Stud.*, vol. xxxvi (1), No. 105, Jan. 1969, pp. 1–4.

[4] COOTNER, P. H. (ed.), *The Random Character of Stock Market Prices*. Cambridge, Mass., 1964.

[5] DOOB, J. L., *Stochastic Processes*. New York, 1953.

[6] FAMA, E. F., 'The Behaviour of Stock Market Prices', *Journal of Business*, 1965, p. 34.

[7] FELDSTEIN, M. S., 'Mean Variance Analysis in the Theory of Liquidity Preference and Portfolio Selection', *Rev. Econ. Stud.*, vol. xxxvi (1), No. 105, Jan. 1969, pp. 5–12.

[8] Feller, W., *An Introduction to Probability Theory and its Applications*. New York, 1966.

[9] FLEMMING, J. S., 'The Utility of Wealth and the Utility of Windfalls', *Rev. Econ. Stud.*, vol. xxxvi (1), Jan. 1969, pp. 55–66.

[10] —— 'Portfolio Choice and Taxation in Continuous-Time' (mimeo), July 1971.

[11] HESTER, D. D., 'Efficient Portfolios with Short Sales and Major Holdings', in Hester and Tobin (eds.), *Risk Aversion and Portfolio Choice*, Cowles Foundation Monograph 19, 1967.

[12] MANDELBROT, B., 'The Variation of Certain Speculative Prices', *Journal of Business*, 1963, p. 343.

[13] MARKOWITZ, H., 'Portfolio Selections', *Journal of Finance*, 1952, pp. 77–91.

[14] —— *Portfolio Selection*, Cowles Foundation Monograph 18, 1959.

[15] MERTON, R., 'Lifetime Portfolio Selection Under Uncertainty: The Continuous Case', *Rev. Econ. Stats.*, Aug. 1969, pp. 247–57.

[16] MORISHIMA, M., 'A Two-Parametric "Revealed Preference" Type Theory of Portfolio Selection' (mimeo), 1971.

[17] PRATT, J., 'Risk Aversion in the Small and the Large', *Econometrica*, Jan.–Apr. 1964, pp. 122–36.

[18] ROYAMA, S. and HAMADA, K., 'Substitution and Complementarity in the Choice of Risky Assets', in Hester and Tobin (eds.), *Risk Aversion and Portfolio Choice*, Cowles Foundation Monograph 19, 1967.

[19] SAMUELSON, P. A., 'The Fundamental Approximation Theorem of Portfolio Analysis in Terms of Means, Variances and Higher Movements', *Rev. Econ. Stud.*, vol. xxxvi (4), Oct. 1970, pp. 537–42.

[20] STIGLITZ, J. E., 'The Effects of Income Wealth and Capital Gains Taxation on Risk-Taking', *Q.J.E.*, 83 (3), 1969, pp. 263–83.

[21] Tobin, J., 'Liquidity Preference as Behaviour Towards Risk', *Rev. Econ. Stud.*, Feb. 1958.

[22] —— 'The Theory of Portfolio Selection', in Hahn and Brechling (eds.), *Theory of Interest Rates*, 1965.

[23] —— 'Comment on Borch and Feldstein', *Rev. Econ. Stud.*, vol. xxxvi (1), No. 105, Jan. 1969, pp. 13–14.

TRANSACTIONS COSTS, PAYMENT PERIODS, AND EMPLOYMENT*

ROBERT J. BARRO
(*University of Chicago*)

ANTHONY M. SANTOMERO
(*University of Pennsylvania*)

THIS paper develops a model for determining employment and output when transactions costs exist for paying wages and for paying dividends to stockholders. Section I considers the household formulation of labour supply when wage payments are made at discrete intervals, rather than in a continuous fashion synchronized with the rendering of labour services. Section II formulates the firm's labour demand and output supply when wage and dividend transactions are costly. An important element in the firm's calculus is the determination of payment frequencies for the two types of costly transactions. Section III utilizes the supply-and-demand analyses from Sections I and II to obtain the labour-market-clearing condition for determining the real wage and the quantities of employment and output. The effects of changes in transactions technology on the levels of real wage, employment, and output are examined. Section IV discusses possibilities for extending the model by adding transactions costs for commodity purchases and for capital market exchanges. The extended framework would determine real wages, prices, and discount rates in a general equilibrium model with transactions costs.

I. Behaviour of working households

Working households supply a homogeneous type of labour service as a function of wage offers from firms. The households evaluate wage offers by considering two characteristics: first, the conventional

* National Science Foundation Grant G.S.-3246 supported this research.

real wage, w (goods per manhour), and, second, the period of wage payment, T_w (years per payment), which is assumed to represent a deferral of payment beyond the (average) time at which services are rendered.[1] Acting as 'price' takers with respect to both w and T_w, households formulate a labour supply function which can be written in general form as

$$\ell^s = \ell^s(w, T_w). \tag{1}$$

The wage package, (w, T_w), represents an offer to pay the discrete amount, $w\ell T_w$, at interval T_w in exchange for the flow of labour services ℓ (manhours per year). It is assumed that ℓ refers to a constant continuous flow of labour services, and that the first wage payment is deferred by time T_w from the onset of work.

Assuming that working households possess a positive discount rate, they view wage offers as less favourable the longer the payment period, for a given explicit real wage w. Further, in evaluating wage offers, households are willing to trade-off reductions in w at a certain rate for reductions in T_w. Assuming a constant real discount rate r_w,[2] the explicit trade-off is determined from a present-value calculation involving w, T_w and the amount of employment ℓ. A useful way to express the trade-off is to derive the non-deferred real wage w^*, which provides the same present value (for any value of ℓ) as the wage package, (w, T_w). This effective real wage rate can be determined as [3]

$$w^* \approx w(1 - \tfrac{1}{2}r_w T_w). \tag{2}$$

In equation (2) the effective wage is determined by subtracting the amount, $\tfrac{1}{2}wr_w T_w$, from the explicit wage. This determination of w^* may be explained as follows. Given an amount of employment ℓ, the wage offer, (w, T_w), implies that $w\ell T_w$ is the amount of each discrete wage payment. Since services are rendered at the continuous rate ℓ, and since payments are deferred at interval T_w, the average amount of wage payment owed by firms to employees is $\tfrac{1}{2}w\ell T_w$. Hence, $(\tfrac{1}{2}w\ell T_w)r_w T_w$[4] is the 'interest' loss (as evaluated

[1] It is assumed throughout this paper that wage payments are deferred, rather than advanced. Some considerations which influence the decision to defer or advance this type of payment are discussed in Barro (1970, p. 1235).

[2] The analysis may be readily extended to allow r_w to vary with T_w, etc.

[3] The exact formula is $w^* = (r_w T_w \, e^{-r_w T_w}/1 - e^{-r_w T_w})$. The approximation for w^* as given in equation (2) follows if $r_w T_w \ll 1$.

[4] This calculation neglects any compounding of interest loss over the interval T_w. The implicit assumption which allows this approximation is $r_w T_w \ll 1$. See n. 3, above.

by workers) on one wage payment, due to the payment deferral. Expressed as a rate per amount of employment (i.e. dividing by ℓT_w), the interest loss implies a reduction of $\frac{1}{2}wr_wT_w$ from the explicit real wage, as indicated in equation (2).

Since the only feature of (w, T_w) packages which is relevant to workers is the combination $w(1 - \frac{1}{2}r_wT_w)$, the labour supply function of equation (1) can be specialized to

$$\ell^s = \ell^s(w^*) = \ell^s\{w(1 - \tfrac{1}{2}r_wT_w)\}. \tag{3}$$

The direction of effect of w^* on ℓ^s is ambiguous, since a positive substitution effect (favouring goods over leisure) is offset by a negative wealth effect. However, it is assumed in the analysis of Section III that the net effect of w^* on ℓ^s is positive within the relevant range of w^*.

Based on the above analysis of a representative unit's behaviour and the assumption that households are identical in their set of wage offers and in their discount rates, equation (3) is assumed to describe the aggregate labour-supply function of working households.

II. Behaviour of firms

Firms produce a homogeneous output flow y (goods per year), using labour services as the sole factor input. The production function is

$$y = F(\ell_p), \tag{4}$$

where ℓ_p denotes the manhours per year of labour services used in production. Both y and ℓ_p are treated as continuous variables. The marginal product of production labour is assumed to be positive and decreasing; hence, the derivative conditions $F_{\ell_p} > 0, F_{\ell_p\ell_p} < 0$.

Firms engage in two types of costly transactions in this model—wage payments and dividend payments—both of which are assumed to occur in the form of money.[5] The two types of transactions are costly in the sense of requiring positive inputs of labour services. For simplicity, the labour requirements are assumed to be solely lump-sum—that is, dependent only on the number of transactions of each type which occur. Assuming that the wage and dividend

---

[5] All transactions in this model are assumed to involve 'money'—the general medium of exchange. The (nominal) quantity of money is implicitly regarded as exogenous and constant. Implications of changes in the quantity of money would be an interesting extension of the analysis. See Section IV, below.

pay periods set by the firm are T_w and T_d, the (average) labour input per time expended on transactions is [6]

$$\ell_\tau = \frac{\beta_w}{T_w} + \frac{\beta_d}{T_d}, \tag{5}$$

where β_w and β_d are the (constant) amounts of labour input per transaction required for the two types of transactions.[7] Hence, lower values of β_w and β_d signify a more efficient transactions technology. Transactions involved with sales of output (for money) are assumed to be costless, and output and sales are assumed to be perfectly synchronized.[8]

Given total labour input ℓ, equations (5) and (4) imply the production function

$$y = F\left(\ell - \frac{\beta_w}{T_w} - \frac{\beta_d}{T_d}\right). \tag{6}$$

Hence, y increases with increases in ℓ, T_w, and T_d, and falls with increases in β_w and β_d.

The objective of firms is to maximize the present value of dividends, as calculated by their shareholders. In carrying out this present-value calculation, firms assume that the shareholders apply a constant real discount rate r_d to deferred dividend payments. Further, firms are assumed to obtain a constant real rate of return r_f on any (interim) funds that they hold.[9] The possibility of (short-term) borrowing by firms is omitted—hence, interim fund holdings are constrained to be non-negative in this model.

In carrying out the above maximization, firms are assumed to act as perfect competitors in the goods and labour markets. In the

---

[6] For simplicity, ℓ_τ is treated as a continuous variable which is comparable in dimension to ℓ_p.

[7] This set-up implies, in particular, that transactions costs for wage payments depend only on T_w, and not on the total amount of payment or on the number of employees. One possible modification is to assume $\beta_w = \beta_w(\ell)$, with $d\beta_w/d\ell > 0$. See n. 13, below.

[8] This assumption is made for analytical convenience in order to examine the effects of transactions costs in a relatively simple framework. Extensions of the model to include transactions costs for commodity sales and also for financial asset exchanges would be useful. These types of transactions costs have been included in Santomero (1971) and in Feige and Parkin (1971).

[9] If other stores of value were unavailable, r_f would be the real rate of return on money. The current model abstracts from the existence of financial assets with different rates of return and from the presence of transactions costs for exchanges between financial assets. See Section IV, below.

present context this assumption implies that each firm acts as a price-taker with respect to output price and also with respect to the effective real wage rate, $w^* = w(1 - \frac{1}{2}r_w T_w)$. Given the constraint of meeting this competitive wage package, the firm chooses output, employment, the explicit real wage rate, and the two pay periods, T_w and T_d, subject to the production function as given by equation (6).

The direct calculation of the present value of dividend payments involves a summation of discounted, discrete payments which are made at interval T_d. Further, each discrete payment involves a summation of accumulated (continuous) sales, less accumulated (discrete) wage payments, plus earnings at rate r_f on average interim fund holdings of the firm. Maximizing this present-value expression can be shown to correspond to maximizing a certain 'effective' profit flow. This effective profit flow is constructed in two steps below.

First, consider the uniform profit flow $\hat{\pi}$ which can be maintained for a given value of T_w (and for given values of y and ℓ) when $T_d = 0$ is chosen. The flow $\hat{\pi}$ is determined by cumulating at interest rate r_f over a time interval T_w the excess of y over $\hat{\pi}$, and then equating this expression to the lump-sum wage payment, $w\ell T_w$, which occurs after a time T_w. That is,

$$\int_0^{T_w} (y - \hat{\pi})\, e^{r_f(T_w - t)}\, \mathrm{d}t = w\ell T_w.$$

Using the approximation, $e^{r_f T_w} \approx 1 + r_f T_w + \frac{1}{2}(r_f T_w)^2$, which holds when $r_f T_w \ll 1$, the solution for $\hat{\pi}$ is [10]

$$\hat{\pi} \approx y - \frac{w\ell}{1 + \frac{1}{2}r_f T_w} = y - \left(\frac{w^*\ell}{(1 + \frac{1}{2}r_f T_w)(1 - \frac{1}{2}r_w T_w)} \right),$$

where the expression for w^* in equation (2) has been substituted. Assuming $r_f T_w \ll 1$ and $r_w T_w \ll 1$, $\hat{\pi}$ can be further approximated as

$$\hat{\pi} \approx y - w^*\ell\{1 + \frac{1}{2}(r_w - r_f) T_w\}. \tag{7}$$

At $T_d = 0$, $\hat{\pi}$ represents the continuous flow of dividend payments from the firm to its stockholders. If $T_w = 0$ is also chosen (so that wage payments, dividends payments, and sales are perfectly synchronized flows), then $\hat{\pi} = y - w^*\ell$. When $T_w > 0$, an average

<hr/>

[10] The exact formula for $\hat{\pi}$ is (using the expression for w^* from n. 3)

$$\hat{\pi} = y - w^*\ell\left[\frac{r_f}{r_w} \frac{(e^{r_w T_w} - 1)}{(e^{r_f T_w} - 1)} \right].$$

debt from the firm to its workers of (approximately) size $\frac{1}{2}w^*\ell T_w$ is created. Firms earn interest on this average holding at rate r_f, but they must also compensate workers at rate r_w (by appropriate changes in the explicit real wage) in order to maintain the competitive wage package w^*. If $r_w > r_f$, there is a net interest cost associated with $T_w > 0$, as measured by the term, $-\frac{1}{2}w^*\ell(r_w - r_f)T_w$, in equation (7).

When $T_d > 0$, dividend payments are also deferred, and an average 'debt' from the firm to its stockholders of size $\frac{1}{2}\hat{\pi}T_d$ is created. Since deferred payment is discounted by stockholders at rate r_d, and since the firm earns interest at rate r_f on its interim fund holdings, the interest cost per time associated with this debt is $\frac{1}{2}\hat{\pi}T_d(r_d - r_f)$. The cost is positive if $r_d > r_f$. The effective profit flow which the firm seeks to maximize (thereby maximizing the present value of dividend payments as viewed by its shareholders) is determined by subtracting this interest cost from the $\hat{\pi}$ expression which is given in equation (7).[11] Denoting the effective profit flow by π^*, the result is[12]

$$\pi^* \approx \hat{\pi}\{1 - \tfrac{1}{2}(r_d - r_f)T_d\}$$
$$\approx [y - w^*\ell\{1 + \tfrac{1}{2}(r_w - r_f)T_w\}]\{1 - \tfrac{1}{2}(r_d - r_f)T_d\}. \quad (8)$$

The essential trade-off which determines the optimal pay periods involves a weighing of interest costs against transactions costs. From equations (5) and (6), increases in T_w and T_d reduce the amount of labour needed for transactions, and, therefore, raise output for a given amount of total employment. On the other hand, equation (8) shows that if $r_w > r_f$ and $r_d > r_f$, increases in the pay periods

---

[11] If $r_d > r_f$ (and borrowing at a rate below r_d is excluded), all accumulated profits are optimally paid out as dividends at interval T_d. The simultaneous presence of retained earnings and dividends could be explained by specifying the firm's rate of return r_f as a declining function of the amount of 'investment'. If the initial return is above r_d and the final return (that is, the return corresponding to the retention of all accumulated profits) is below r_d, some interior division of accumulated profits between retained earnings and dividends would be optimal. However, a full treatment would require an inter-temporal specification of rate of return on investment as a function of the cumulated amount of past investment, and as a function of other variables which may change over time. The optimal division between retained earnings and dividends would also be affected by different tax treatment of capital gains and dividend income.

[12] The exact formula for π^*, using the expression for $\hat{\pi}$ from n. 10 is

$$\pi^* = \left[y - w^*\ell\left\{\frac{r_f}{r_w}\frac{(e^{r_w T_w} - 1)}{(e^{r_f T_w} - 1)}\right\}\right]\left\{\frac{r_d}{r_f}\frac{(e^{r_f T_d} - 1)}{(e^{r_d T_d} - 1)}\right\}.$$

also imply higher interest costs. The optimal pay periods are determined such that marginal reductions in transactions costs just balance marginal increases in interest costs. However, if either $r_w \leq r_f$ or $r_d \leq r_f$ applies (and if these rates do not change with changes in T_w or T_d), an increase in the associated pay period (T_w or T_d) has a negative effect on interest costs. Since transactions costs invariably fall when the pay periods are lengthened, the associated pay period will be set at infinity in this case. Essentially, if $r_f \geq r_w$, firms can always profitably overcompensate workers for further delays in wage payment. Therefore, $T_w = \infty$ in this case. Similarly, if $r_f \geq r_d$, firms can always profitably overcompensate stockholders for further delays in dividend payments; hence, $T_d = \infty$ in this case. However, if r_w and r_d were positive functions of T_w and T_d, finite periods would be determined even if $r_f \geq r_w$ or $r_f \geq r_d$ applied over some ranges of T_w and T_d. In the subsequent analysis the discount rates are assumed to be constant, but they are assumed to satisfy the conditions $r_w > r_f$ and $r_d > r_f$. When these conditions are satisfied, the optimizing firm will choose finite pay periods.

Choosing y, ℓ, w, T_w, and T_d so as to maximize π^* as given in equation (8), subject to the production condition as given in equation (6) and subject to a given value of w^*, leads to the following first-order equations for the firm:

$$F_{\ell_p} = w^*\{1 + \tfrac{1}{2}(r_w - r_f)T_w\} \approx w(1 - \tfrac{1}{2}r_f T_w), \tag{9}$$

$$T_w = \left\{\frac{2F_{\ell_p}\beta_w}{w^*\ell(r_w - r_f)}\right\}^{1/2} = \left[\frac{2w^*\beta_w\{1 + \tfrac{1}{2}(r_w - r_f)T_w\}}{w^*\ell(r_w - r_f)}\right]^{1/2}, \tag{10}$$

$$T_d = \left[\frac{2F_{\ell_p}\beta_d\{1 - \tfrac{1}{2}(r_d - r_f)T_d\}}{\hat{\pi}(r_d - r_f)}\right]^{1/2}$$

$$= \left[\frac{2w^*\beta_d\{1 + \tfrac{1}{2}(r_w - r_f)T_w\}\{1 - \tfrac{1}{2}(r_d - r_f)T_d\}}{\hat{\pi}(r_d - r_f)}\right]^{1/2}. \tag{11}$$

In equations (9)–(11), F_{ℓ_p} is the marginal product of production labour and $\hat{\pi}$ is the (non-deferred) profit flow as defined in equation (7). Dividing equation (10) by equation (11) yields

$$\frac{T_w}{T_d} = \left[\left(\frac{r_d - r_f}{r_w - r_f}\right)\left(\frac{\beta_w/w^*\ell}{\beta_d/\hat{\pi}}\right)\right] \frac{1}{\{1 - \tfrac{1}{2}(r_d - r_f)T_d\}}\right]^{1/2}. \tag{12}$$

Equation (9) indicates that the firm should employ labour for production up to the point of equality between the marginal product of production labour and the discounted explicit real wage, $w(1 - \frac{1}{2}r_f T_w)$. Hence, the marginal product is set below the explicit real wage, but above the effective real wage, $w^* \approx w(1 - \frac{1}{2}r_w T_w)$, as long as $r_w > r_f$.[13]

Equation (10) determines T_w as a positive function of the ratio of transactions cost to transactions volume, $F_{\ell_p}\beta_w/w^*\ell$, and as an inverse function of the discount rate differential, $(r_w - r_f)$. The existence of a positive differential, $(r_w - r_f) > 0$, is the essential motivating force for making wage transactions at positive frequency (i.e. for choosing $T_w < \infty$). The higher the differential, the greater the pay-off in terms of reduced interest costs for more frequent payments; hence, the negative relationship between T_w and $(r_w - r_f)$, for a given value of $F_{\ell_p}\beta_w/w^*\ell$.

Similarly, in equation (11), T_d depends positively on the ratio, $[F_{\ell_p}\beta_d\{1 - \frac{1}{2}(r_d - r_f)T_d\}]/\hat{\pi}$, and inversely on $(r_d - r_f)$.

Equation (12) indicates that the ratio of periods, T_w/T_d, depends on the relative discount-rate differentials and on the relative values of the transactions cost–transactions volume ratios. In particular, T_d will be large relative to T_w if the shareholder's discount rate is much closer than the worker's discount rate to the firm's rate of return on interim fund holdings.

Equations (6) and (9)–(11) determine the representative firm's output supply, labour demand, and optimal pay periods as functions of the effective real wage, w^*, and as functions of the exogenous transactions costs and discount rates, $(\beta_w, \beta_d, r_w - r_f, r_d - r_f)$. Regarding labour demand, the firm's total demand ℓ^d is divided between labour demanded for transactions purposes, $\ell_\tau^d = \beta_w/T_w + \beta_d/T_d$, and labour demanded for production purposes, $\ell_p^d = \ell^d - \ell_\tau^d$. The dependence of the two components of labour demand on w^* and on the parameters, $(\beta_w, \beta_d, r_w - r_f, r_d - r_f)$, is implicitly determined from equations (6) and (9)–(11). The resulting demand functions can be written in the following functional forms:

$$\frac{\beta_w}{T_w} + \frac{\beta_d}{T_d} = \ell_\tau^d = \ell_\tau^d\,(w^*; \beta_w, \beta_d, r_w - r_f, r_d - r_f), \qquad (13)$$
$$\qquad\qquad\qquad\quad (-)\ \ (+)\ (+)\qquad (+)\qquad\quad (+)$$

[13] If variations in ℓ change the lump-sum transactions charge β_w, the optimal condition is

$$F_{lp} = \frac{w^*\{1 + \frac{1}{2}(r_w - r_f)T_w\}}{1 - (1/T_w)(d\beta_w/d\ell)}.$$

Therefore, if the transactions charge increases with ℓ, the firm sets a higher value of F_{lp}, and, correspondingly, a lower value of ℓ_p for a given value of w^*.

$$\ell_p^d = \ell_p^d \, (w^*; \beta_w, \beta_d, r_w - r_f, r_d - r_f), \qquad (14)$$
$$(-) \quad (-) \, (\approx 0) \quad (-) \qquad (\approx 0)$$

$$\ell_\tau^d + \ell_p^d = \ell^d = \ell^d \, (w^*; \beta_w, \beta_d, r_w - r_f, r_d - r_f). \qquad (15)$$
$$(-) \quad (?) \, (+) \quad (?) \qquad (+)$$

The sign below each argument in the above functions denotes the partial derivative of the dependent variable with respect to that argument. Formally, these partials can be determined from total differentiation of the system described by equations (6) and (9)–(11). The signs as indicated in equations (13)–(15) emerge from this calculation, assuming the approximations $(r_w - r_f)T_w \ll 1$ and $(r_d - r_f)T_d \ll 1$. These conditions guarantee that, within the relevant range, the amount of resources devoted to transactions remains small relative to the amount devoted to production—that is, $\ell_\tau^d = \beta_w/T_w + \beta_d/T_d \ll \ell_\tau^d$ applies. The calculations leading to equations (13)–(15) are straightforward, but entail a considerable amount of algebraic manipulation. However, the final results can be readily interpreted in a non-rigorous manner.

An increase in w^* reduces ℓ_p^d in accordance with equation (9). Since ℓ is reduced, T_w increases from equation (10) and, hence, β_w/T_w falls. The increase in w^* and implied fall in $\hat{\pi}$ both tend to raise T_d; hence, β_d/T_d also falls. Therefore, $\ell_\tau^d = \beta_w/T_w + \beta_d/T_d$ falls in response to a rise in w^*. The negative effect of w^* on ℓ^d is the sum of the negative effects on ℓ_p^d and on ℓ_τ^d.

Increases in β_w or β_d raise ℓ_τ^d directly. These direct effects are offset —but only partially—by the positive relation between the pay periods and the β's which is described in equations (10) and (11). On net, ℓ_τ^d is positively related to both β_w and β_d. The increase in T_w produced by the rise in β_w also implies that the marginal product of production labour in equation (9) must be equated to a higher discounted real wage (given w^*). Hence, ℓ_p^d falls when β_w rises. The net effect of β_w on ℓ^d involves offsetting movements toward transactions labour and away from production labour. The sign of the net effect is ambiguous and depends on certain characteristics of the production function.[14] The effect of β_d on ℓ^d follows the positive effect on ℓ_τ^d, since the effect of β_d on ℓ_p^d is of a smaller order of magnitude. In effect, an increase in β_d makes the transferring of profit more expensive, but, at least on the first order, does not affect the quantity of

---

[14] Ignoring second-order terms, the effect of β_w on ℓ^d follows the sign of $|F_{lplp}| - F_{lp}/\ell_p$. This term cannot be positive for all values of ℓ_p since it would imply $y \to -\infty$ as $\ell_p \to 0$. However, within the relevant range of ℓ_p, the term could be either positive or negative.

production labour which maximizes profit. Hence, an increase in β_d increases transactions labour at the expense of profit, but not at the expense of production labour.

Increases in $(r_w - r_f)$ or $(r_d - r_f)$ reduce the associated pay period as indicated in equations (10) and (11). Hence, ℓ_τ^d is positively related to both discount-rate differentials. An increase in $(r_w - r_f)$ also has the effect of reducing ℓ_p^d, in accordance with equation (9). As in the case of β_w, the net effect of $(r_w - r_f)$ on ℓ^d is ambiguous. (The relevant characteristic of the production function for determining the sign of the net effect is again the one described in footnote 14.) The impact of $(r_d - r_f)$ on ℓ^d is positive, since the effect of $(r_d - r_f)$ on ℓ_p^d is negligible.

The determination of ℓ_p^d in equation (14) also implies the supply of output function for the firm

$$F(\ell_p^d) = y^s = y^s(w^*; \beta_w, \beta_d, r_w - r_f, r_d - r_f). \qquad (16)$$
$$\quad\; (-)\quad (-)\,(\approx 0)\qquad (-)\qquad (\approx 0)$$

Based on the above analysis of a representative unit's behaviour and the assumption that firms are identical in production conditions, transactions technology (β_w and β_d), and discount rates,[15] and that they face the same competitive labour market which determines the single effective wage package w^* for homogeneous labour input, equations (13)–(16) are assumed to represent the aggregate labour demand and output supply of firms.

III. Labour market analysis

The analysis of household labour supply from Section I and the analysis of firm labour demand from Section II are brought together in Fig. III.2. The ℓ^s curve is shown as upward-sloping *versus* w^*. The positive effect of w^* on l^s reflects the assumption that, within the relevant range, the substitution effect of an increase in w^* outweighs the income effect. The labour demand curve ℓ^d, which is downward-sloping *versus* w^*, is the sum of the two components, $\ell_\tau^d + \ell_p^d$, which are each shown separately as downward-sloping *versus* w^*. The labour demand curves all represent partial effects of changes in w^* for a given set of parameters, ($\beta_w, \beta_d, r_w - r_f,$

[15] If firms differ in any of these characteristics, they will generally also differ in their choices of optimal pay periods. Therefore, given the constraint that w^* must be uniform across firms (because labour is homogeneous and is purchased under competitive conditions), 'competitive' firms can vary in their explicit real wage rates.

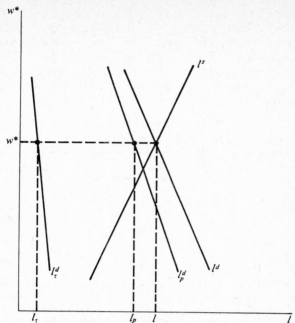

FIG. III.2. The Labour Market

$r_d - r_f$). For a given set of these parameters, w^* and ℓ are determined to clear the labour market; that is, by the condition

$$\ell^s(w^*) = \ell^d(w^*; \beta_w, \beta_d, r_w - r_f, r_d - r_f) = \ell. \qquad (17)$$

Output is then determined by the condition [16]

$$y = y^s(w^*; \beta_w, \beta_d, r_w - r_f, r_d - r_f) = F(\ell_p^d). \qquad (18)$$

Since w^*, ℓ, and y are determined from equations (17) and (18) for a given set of parameters, $(\beta_w, \beta_d, r_w - r_f, r_d - r_f)$, comparative-statics analysis can be applied to determine the impact of shifts

[16] The commodity price level is assumed to adjust to obtain $y^d = y^s$, where y^s is determined as a function of the w^* value which satisfies equation (17). The analysis would be more complicated if adjustments in the price level, given w^*, affected the labour-market-clearing condition. For example, this interaction between the commodity and labour markets would arise if there were a real balance term in the ℓ^s function, as is true in Barro and Grossman (1973, ch. 1).

in the elements of this vector of parameters on the market-clearing values of w^*, ℓ, and y (and on the associated values of T_w, T_d, ℓ_τ, ℓ_p, and π^*). The impact of shifts in the four elements of the vector $(\beta_w, \beta_d, r_w - r_f, r_d - r_f)$, are summarized in Table III.1. We analyse in detail, below, the effect of shifts in β_w and β_d, which can be viewed as exogenous changes in the technology of conducting transactions.

TABLE III.I

Effects of Exogenous Disturbances

	β_w	β_d	$(r_w - r_f)$	$(r_d - r_f)$
T_w	+	−*	−	−*
T_d	+*	+	+*	−
ℓ_τ	+	+	+	+
l_p	−	−	−	−
ℓ	?	+	?	+
y	−	−	−	−
w^*	?	+	?	+
π^*	−	−	−	−

Note: The sign in each position signifies the effect of a shift in the vertical variable on the associated horizontal variable. An asterisk indicates that the effect is of smaller order than the effect of a shift in the other β or discount-rate variable.

Consider first an increase in β_w. From equations (13)–(15), there is an exogenous increase in ℓ_τ^d and an exogenous decrease in ℓ_p^d. The net effect on ℓ^d is ambiguous. In terms of the graph in Fig. III.2, ℓ_τ^d shifts to the right, ℓ_p^d to the left, and the direction of movement in ℓ^d is uncertain. Given the ambiguous movement in the ℓ^d curve, the effects on ℓ and w^* are ambiguous, as indicated in Table III.1. However, ℓ_τ unambiguously increases and ℓ_p unambiguously decreases. Since y^s depends only on ℓ_p, production must fall in this case. The owners of the firms are clearly worse off because of the increase in β_w, since π^* unambiguously falls as shown in Table III.1. However, the net effect on the welfare position of workers is uncertain, since the net movement in w^* depends on offsetting movements toward transactions labour and away from production labour.

Consider now an increase in β_d with β_w fixed. From equation (13), the ℓ_τ^d curve again shifts to the right, but the effect on the ℓ_p^d curve is negligible. Therefore, ℓ^d unambiguously shifts rightward in this case. Given the upward-sloping ℓ^s curve, ℓ and w^* both increase. Since the ℓ_p^d curve has not shifted, there will be a lower value of ℓ_p corresponding to the higher value of w^*. Hence, ℓ_p and y respond negatively to the increase in β_d, even though total employment increases in this case. The shareholders are worse off with the increase in β_d, since π^* falls, but workers are actually better off (because of the initial movement toward transactions labour) as reflected by the increase in w^*.

IV. Extensions of the model

The discussion of Section III involves partial equilibrium analysis since the focus is on the clearing of the labour market while the equilibration of the commodity and capital markets is abstracted from. The former abstraction was made possible by the assumption that the equilibration of the commodity market (through movements in the price level) could be accomplished without any repercussions on the labour market. The latter abstraction was made possible by taking the discount-rate differentials to be exogenous. The extension of the model to a general equilibrium setting which includes the commodity and capital markets would be very useful.

The extension to include the commodity market would involve some consideration of the effect of transactions costs for commodity purchases on the supply and demand for commodities. In this type of extended framework one could explore the impact of changes in these types of transactions costs, and one could also examine the interaction between the commodity and labour markets.

Because the existence of differentials between the various discount rates is crucial for payment-period determination—that is, crucial for motivating transactions at positive frequency—it would be extremely interesting to extend the model to a determination of these discount rates by incorporating a capital market. Imperfections in the capital market—that is, transactions costs associated with exchanges on this market—would have to be a central part of this extension of the model.

REFERENCES

BARRO, R. J. (1970). 'Inflation, the Payments Period, and the Demand for Money', *J.P.E.*, 78 (Nov.–Dec.), pp. 1228–63.

BARRO, R. J., and GROSSMAN, H. I. (1973). *Money, Employment, and Inflation*, ch. 1, forthcoming.

FEIGE, E., and PARKIN, M. (1971). 'The Optimal Quantity of Money, Bonds, Commodity Inventories, and Capital', *American Economic Review* 61 (June), pp. 335–49.

SANTOMERO, A. M. (1971). 'Optimal Transactions Behavior and the Demand for Money', Ph.D. Dissertation, Brown University.

Discussion Papers

(a) K. Borch
(Norwegian School of Economics and Business Administration)

JOHN FLEMMING's paper is written to help economists who are intimidated by stochastic processes. This is a worthwhile objective, but one should bear in mind that it is very easy to mislead this group of economists.

I have some difficulties in following the author when he goes to the limit in Section I. I would prefer to write his formula (1) as follows:

$$U_t = Y(t_1) + Y(t_2 - t_1) + \cdots + Y(t_n - t_{n-1}) + Y(t - t_n),$$

where

$$U_t = \log W_t \quad \text{and} \quad Y(t_i - t_{i-1}) = \log\{1 + r(t_i - t_{i-1})\}.$$

This should lead us to think of *infinitely divisible distributions*, rather than of the Central Limit Theorem.

The author seems to conclude that U_t must be normally distributed if this expression holds for an arbitrary partition of the interval $(0, t)$. This is obviously not correct. For the benefit of those who are easily intimidated, I shall give a counter-example.

Let the variate Y_i have the gamma density

$$\frac{e^{-y} y^{h_i - 1}}{\Gamma(h_i)}$$

and hence mean and variance equal to h_i. The variate $Y_t = \sum Y_i$ will then have the gamma density

$$\frac{e^{-y} y^{t-1}}{\Gamma(t)},$$

where $t = \sum h_i$.

If the Y_i are normally distributed, so is of course Y_t. The author seems to make this assumption in his comments on equations (15)–(17), so it is possible that I may have misunderstood him. On the whole I find it difficult to sort out the assumption actually made by the author. My interpretation of his model is the following:

The rate of return r of an asset is a variate with a lognormal distribution over the interval $(-1, \infty)$. If the whole initial wealth $W_0 = 1$ is invested in this asset, final wealth will be $1 + r$, i.e. a variate with a lognormal distribution over the interval $(0, \infty)$.

Let now r_1 and r_2 be the rates of return on two assets. By placing the fractions x and $(1-x)$ of the initial wealth in the two assets, we obtain a portfolio which will give the final wealth

$$W = x(1 + r_1) + (1 - x)(1 + r_2) = 1 + xr_1 + (1 - x)r_2.$$

The variate W will in general not have a lognormal distribution.

As $\log U = x \log (1 + r_1) + (1 - x) \log (1 + r_2)$ obviously is normally distributed, the variate

$$U = (1 + r_1)^x (1 + r_2)^{1-x}$$

will have a lognormal distribution over $(0, \infty)$.

In a purely formal manner we can write

$$(1 + r_1)^x (1 + r_2)^{1-x}$$
$$= 1 + xr_1 + (1 - x)r_2 - x\frac{(1 - x)}{2} (r_1 - r_2)^2 + \cdots$$

This might raise some hopes that a portfolio of lognormally distributed assets should have a distribution which at least is approximately lognormal. Such hopes will, however, be in vain. The expansion above does not even converge.

I am unable to see how any portfolio-management policy—even in continuous time—can lead to a final wealth with a lognormal distribution. I can, therefore, not express any strong interest in the ndifference curves which the author presents on Fig. III.1.

I am among those economists who are intimidated by lengthy elementary mathematical manipulations. Let me, therefore, indicate how these can be avoided. The general lognormal distribution has the density

$$f(x) = \frac{1}{s(x - a)\sqrt{2\pi}} \exp\left[-\frac{1}{2}\left\{\frac{\log (x - a) - m}{s}\right\}^2\right] \quad (x > a).$$

The moments are given by

$$M_n = \int_a^\infty (x - a)^n f(x) \, dx = \exp (nm + \tfrac{1}{2}n^2s^2).$$

This expression can be found in some textbooks, and is given as an exercise in others. The integral exists also for non-integral values of n, and hence it gives the expected utility assigned to a lognormal variate, if the utility function is $u(x) = x^\alpha$.

We find

$$U = \int (x - a)^\alpha f(x) \, \mathrm{d}x = e^{\alpha m + 1/2\alpha^2 s^2} = (M_1^{2-\alpha} M_2^{1/2\alpha - 1/2})^\alpha.$$

From this we can derive indifference curves in an EV-plane, and we can, as the author does, derive the equivalents of the Slutsky conditions in demand analysis. I do not think these mathematical exercises have any economic significance. The underlying utility function is arbitrary, although fairly reasonable. The probability distribution does not have the divisibility properties which seem essential in portfolio analysis.

In his introduction Flemming notes that Feldstein and I do not claim that we have provided an alternative to the mean-variance approach to portfolio analysis. This is correct, but I have on several occasions claimed that no *simple* alternative exists. Investment in the real world is not a simple two-dimensional affair. It cannot be analysed with the simple tools which we use only when teaching elementary economics to first-year students.

The paper by Barro and Santomero deals with transactions costs. We all agree that these costs are important, but for many of us this is just lip-service. When we write respectable papers, trying to derive significant results, we often feel free to ignore transactions costs. I have sinned in this respect myself. I have published several papers explaining how the activities of insurance companies lead to an optimal distribution of the risks in our society. In these papers I have conveniently 'assumed away' the transactions costs, although more than 30 per cent of the insurance premiums paid by the public are used to cover just such costs. I cannot even claim good faith, since a number of my good friends in the insurance world seem to live very well on transactions costs, and they don't mind if these costs are overlooked in economic analysis.

Barro and Santomero should certainly be commended for having taken up the long-neglected question of transactions costs. Their approach may seem rather pedestrian, and the problem of determining the optimal frequency of wage-payments cannot be considered as exciting. In fact, the authors virtually derive the classical square-root formula in the theory of inventory management. In this theory one considers the expression

$$cT + \frac{s}{2T}$$

where $T =$ number of times per year that new stock is ordered,
 $c =$ cost of placing an order,
 $s =$ storage cost per unit.

The problem is to determine the value of T which maximizes this expression, and the solution is

$$T = \sqrt{\frac{s}{2c}}.$$

This problem was popular some thirty years ago, when professors had to convince businessmen that advanced mathematics was useful in practice.

There are, however, a number of interesting suggestions contained in this simple problem. The businessman, who seeks the optimal inventory policy, may be confronted with a production engineer, who wants to produce in optimal batch sizes. The two must reach some compromise, and it seems interesting to study both how they arrive at this and whether the resulting compromise in some sense represents a social optimum. The paper opens the door to a number of interesting problems of this kind. The authors work with a simple model, but I have no objections to this. It is a sound approach to study all aspects of a simple model before developing more general, and possibly more realistic, models.

Discussion Papers

(b) Edgar L. Feige
(University of Wisconsin)

Not since Irving Fisher, who suggested that velocity had something to do with transactions periods, has anybody seriously looked into the very interesting question of what determines transactions periods. We observe them to change over time, however, and I think Barro's contribution has been to specify an interesting model which determines these transactions periods consistently with profit-maximizing behaviour. I think the model is interesting in itself, but I want to comment on the conclusion regarding the optimal quantity of money, which is, I think, incorrect. Barro concluded that we should pay zero interest on money, as a consequence of maximizing social utility via the profits function. What should surely be maximized is real income; but, given his definition of income which is specified as a function of transactions periods, in order to maximize income the transactions period must go to infinity. To get the transactions period to infinity also requires that the rate of return on money be equal to the rate of return on equities, which is the usual result one gets from both the neo-classical and the Baumol–Tobin extensions of inventory theory. Now the reason one gets the 'correct' result (that the interest paid on money is equal to the rate on equities), together with an infinite transactions period, is that Barro has left out the other side of the economy. He has wages and dividends being paid out and incurring transactions costs, but money is not 'consumed', which is why those transactions do not yield social utility. The reason that money has to be paid out is, of course, that people need it to buy goods and services. They consume continuously, but if they were to purchase continuously and there were any commodity market transactions costs, that would be very expensive; so they hold inventories. There is a cost of holding inventories (call it alpha). If you maximize total social income minus the real cost of all transactions and inventories (including the carrying cost), so that people use the dividends and wages paid to go to the store and accumulate inventories, you find that the rate of interest on dividends must be equal to the rate of interest on money less alpha, which can be thought of as the net rate of return on capital. This confirms the Feige/Parkin result, and specifies the producers' sector, which is missing from the model.

IV

MONEY, FINANCIAL MARKETS, AND ECONOMIC ACTIVITY

Introduced by DAVID LAIDLER and
MICHAEL PARKIN

G. R. FISHER *and* D. K. SHEPPARD
EDGAR L. FEIGE
A. R. NOBAY
G. CLAYTON, J. C. DODDS,
J. L. FORD, *and* D. GHOSH
W. R. WHITE *and* J. P. BURMAN
J. H. WOOD
FRANK BRECHLING

Discussion Papers
(*a*) ALAN WALTERS
(*b*) MICHAEL J. HAMBURGER
(*c*) DAVID LAIDLER
(*d*) P. K. TRIVEDI
(*e*) R. J. O'BRIEN
(*f*) KARL BORCH

Rejoinders
G. R. FISHER *and* D. K. SHEPPARD
EDGAR L. FEIGE

MONEY, FINANCIAL MARKETS, AND ECONOMIC ACTIVITY

INTRODUCTION

DAVID LAIDLER
(*University of Manchester*)
MICHAEL PARKIN
(*University of Manchester*)[1]

THE papers in this section deal with various aspects of the effects of monetary policy on the level of economic activity. The general problem area is, of course, one of the oldest in economics, going back at least as far as the writings of David Hume. However, the contemporary debate, the distinguishing characteristic of which is its heavy empirical content, did not begin in earnest until the early 1960s.[2] In the last decade an enormous amount of empirical work has been done, mainly for the United States but also, and recently in increasing volume, for many other countries, including the United Kingdom.

Two substantive questions have dominated this work. They are:

(i) what are the channels through which monetary and real phenomena interact?

(ii) what are the characteristics of the time lags involved in that interaction?

In addition, there has been a good deal of discussion about which econometric techniques are most appropriate for tackling these questions. There is broad agreement, in qualitative, if not quantitative terms, about the answer to the first question. A change in the

---

[1] The papers in this section are taken from four sessions of the Conference, two introduced by the authors and the other two by Frank Brechling and Marcus Miller. We have drawn on notes provided by them in writing this general introduction.

[2] For a vivid reminder of this, contrast the style and content of the Radcliffe Report (1959) with that of the first empirical paper in the current debate, Friedman and Meiselman (1963).

quantity of money changes the implicit yield on money balances, changes the structure of the non-bank public's desired portfolios of both financial and real assets, thus ultimately changing the demand for currently produced goods and services. Within this broad frame-work, differences of opinion arise over two related issues. The first concerns the range of assets between which substitutions take place and the second concerns the size of the substitution effects involved. At the 'Keynesian' extreme are those who regard changes in the quantity of money as primarily affecting the prices of financial assets, and through these changes, the demand for a narrow sub-set of real assets purchased mainly by the business sector. This group also believes that substitution effects are large between various financial assets but small between financial and real assets. On this view, 'causation' runs from a change in the money supply through small changes in bond and equity prices, to small changes in business-sector investment spending.

At the 'monetarist' extreme of the debate are those who regard the whole range of financial and real assets (including current con-sumption)[3] as being affected by monetary changes. This group also believes that the substitution effects between financial assets and real assets are large and important. On this view, a change in the money supply changes all asset prices, leads to strong and direct substitution effects between money and real assets, and hence to significant changes in current expenditure flows.

There is much less disagreement on the question of time lags. The view is widely taken that this is essentially an empirical matter and, on the basis of present knowledge, it is hard to deny that the lags in question are 'long and variable' and only imperfectly under-stood.[4]

Broadly speaking, two types of procedure have been used to investigate empirically the operation of monetary policy. One is to build complete macro-economic models; the other is to study particu-lar individual behaviour equations, the properties of which bear directly, though incompletely, on the questions posed. Investigations using complete models are usefully divided into two sub-classes: those that are highly aggregative (typically one or two equations) reduced-form models and those that rely on relatively disaggregative structural-equation systems. Typical of the first approach is the so

---

[3] Consumption itself is a flow, so the relevant asset is the present value of con-sumption. Note also that consumer durable goods represent stock of assets.

[4] One of us has surveyed the problem elsewhere. Cf. Laidler (1971).

called Friedman and Meiselman debate.[5] Structural econometric models were, of course, pioneered by such workers as Tinbergen (1939) and Klein and Goldberger (1955) but, from the point of view of the present discussion, the work of Goldfeld (1966) and the same author's contributions to the Brookings Model (1969), de Leeuw (1965 and 1969) and the work of Helliwell *et al.* on the Canadian RDX models are more relevant.

Relevant studies of individual behaviour equations have dealt with the investment demand and consumption functions, the demand and supply of money functions, not to mention the term structure of interest rates. The interest elasticities and time-lag structures of these relationships have been of particular interest.

Questions concerning the behaviour of the monetary authorities have attracted a good deal of attention recently. It is often argued that the 'monetarist' view of the transmission mechanism only gets support from empirical evidence because the monetary authorities respond passively to conditions in the real sector of the economy. Causation, it is argued, runs in the opposite direction to that posited by the 'monetarist'. The specification of 'reaction functions' for the monetary authority is a potentially powerful way of dealing with this issue because it is possible, at least in principle, to identify separately the authorities' reactions and the structure of the economy which is generating the data to which they are reacting. There is also an important statistical reason why attempts should be made to construct models of the authorities' behaviour: simultaneous equations bias. If the data which are used for estimating the parameters of the economic system are generated by the simultaneous interactions of the authorities and the rest of the economy, then estimation procedures which allow for this should give consistent estimates of the parameters, not only of the authorities' reaction functions, but also of the private-sector behaviour equations.

The papers presented in this section deal with all the questions raised above and encompass all the alternative methodological approaches. The first two are surveys. Fisher and Sheppard survey the bulk of the empirical literature available on the transmission mechanism for the United States. They also discuss the methodological questions involved in the choice between structural macro-models and highly aggregated single-equation studies. They suggest that many of the complete macro-models studied have had a built-in

[5] See for example Friedman and Meiselman, Ando and Modigliani, DePrano and Mayer (1965), Hester (1964).

bias towards minimizing the apparent effects of money on real variables.

Feige surveys the literature (again for the U.S.A.) on the demand for money function. The conclusion which emerges very forcefully from this study is that the interest elasticity of demand for money is low, but significantly non-zero. This, of course, is in line with all other studies but is particularly significant since Feige has concentrated on those parts of the literature which have looked at substitution effects between money and what all would agree are 'near money' assets. Even here the substitution effects are small. These findings, of course, lend support, but not conclusive support, to the 'monetarist' interpretation of the transmission mechanism.

Nobay investigates the reactions of the U.K. monetary authorities to changes in the variables which they seek to control. The only other work on this problem for the U.K. is contained in papers by Fisher (1968) and Pissarides (1972). Nobay's paper makes important advances over these earlier studies in two ways. First, his statistical procedures are more sophisticated and, we would judge, superior to those used in earlier studies. Second, and more important, he has tried to approach the problem in more detail, paying due attention to the problem of the frequency of policy changes and the sequential nature of decisions made inside a large Central Bank Treasury machine.

The three papers by Clayton et al., White, and Wood deal with various aspects of the behaviour of financial markets, White dealing with the term structure of interest rates, Wood with Commercial Bank behaviour, and Clayton et al. with the demand and supply of a large number of financial assets in the context of a partial equilibrium sub-system of the financial sector.

Finally Brechling's paper on investment behaviour represents a contribution to the study of the last link in the transmission mechanism, that between monetary variables and expenditure on real goods.[6] Earlier work by Jorgenson (1963), which led many of us to the conclusion that interest rates do significantly affect investment, is criticized by Brechling. He finds that, when a rigorous specification of the investment function is deduced from explicit inter-temporal choice theory, ambiguities and problems arise which leave us unable to state any confidently held conclusions on this question. However,

---

[6] Brechling's paper as printed in this volume differs considerably from the version read at the Conference. Hence no discussants' comments on the paper appear here.

if Brechling's paper leaves us with a problem, it also provides an impressive example of the kind of research strategy that is increasingly dominating work in this area and will undoubtedly become more widely used in future.

REFERENCES

ANDO, A., and MODIGLIANI, F. (1965). 'The Relative Stability of Monetary Velocity and the Investment Multiplier', *American Economic Review* 55 (Sept.), pp. 693–728.

ARTIS, M. J., and NOBAY, A. R. (1969). 'Two Aspects of the Monetary Debate', *National Institute Economic Review* (Aug.), pp. 33–51.

COMMITTEE ON THE WORKING OF THE MONETARY SYSTEM (Radcliffe Committee) (1959). *Report*, Cmnd. 827 (London: H.M.S.O.).

DE LEEUW, F. (1965). 'A Model of Financial Behaviour' in J. S. Duesenberry, G. Fromm, L. R. Klein, and E. Kuh (eds.), *The Brookings Quarterly Econometric Model of the U.S.* (Amsterdam: North-Holland).

—— (1969). 'A Condensed Model of Financial Behaviour' in J. S. Duesenberry, G. Fromm, L. R. Klein, and E. Kuh (eds.), *The Brookings Model: Some Further Results* (Amsterdam: North-Holland).

DEPRANO, M. and MAYER, T. (1965). 'Tests of the Relative Importance of Autonomous Expenditure and Money', *American Economic Review* 55 (Sept.), pp. 729–52.

FISHER, D. (1968). 'The Demand for Money in Britain: Quarterly Results 1951 to 1967', *Manchester School* 36 (Dec.), pp. 329–44.

FRIEDMAN, M., and MEISELMAN, D. (1963). 'The Relative Stability of Monetary Velocity and the Investment Multiplier in the United States 1897–1958', in *Stabilisation Policies* (Washington, D.C.: Commission on Money and Credit).

—— —— (1965). 'Reply to Ando and Modigliani and to DePrano and Mayer', *American Economic Review* 55 (Sept.), pp. 754–85.

GOLDFELD, S. M. (1966). *Commercial Bank Behaviour and Economic Activity* (Amsterdam: North-Holland).

—— (1969). 'An Extension of the Monetary Sector' in J. S. Duesenberry, G. Fromm, L. R. Klein, and E. Kuh (eds.), *The Brookings Model: Some Further Results* (Amsterdam: North-Holland).

HESTER, D. (1964). 'Keynes and the Quantity Theory: Comment on Friedman and Meiselman, C. M. C. Paper', *Rev. Econ. Stats.* 46 (Nov.), pp. 364–86.

JORGENSON, D. W. (1963). 'Capital Theory and Investment Behaviour' *American Economic Review* (Papers and Proceedings, May), reprinted in L. R. Klein and R. A. Gordon (eds.), *Readings in Business Cycles* (London: Allen and Unwin, 1966), ch. 20, pp. 367–78.

KLEIN, L. R., and GOLDBERGER, A. S. (1955). *An Econometric Model of the U.S. 1929–52* (Amsterdam: North-Holland).

LAIDLER, D. E. W. (1971). 'The Influence of Money on Economic Activity—A Survey of Some Current Problems' in G. Clayton, J. Gilbert, and R. Sedgwick (eds.), *Monetary Theory and Monetary Policy in the 1970s* (Oxford: Oxford University Press), pp. 75–135.

PISSARIDES, C. A. (1972). 'A Model of British Macroeconomic Policy, 1955–69', in *Manchester School* 40, No. 3 (Sept.), pp. 245–61.

TINBERGEN, J. (1939). *Statistical Testing of Business Cycle Theories II: Business Cycles in the U.S.A. 1919–32* (Geneva: League of Nations).

INTERRELATIONSHIPS BETWEEN REAL AND MONETARY VARIABLES: SOME EVIDENCE FROM RECENT U.S. EMPIRICAL STUDIES*

G. R. FISHER *and* D. K. SHEPPARD

(*University of Southampton and University of Birmingham respectively*)

I. Introduction

THE last decade has seen a remarkable growth in the quantity and quality of econometric research in the field of monetary economics,

* This paper is a revised version of a paper read to the Money Study Group Conference held in Bournemouth, 21–5 February 1972. We are grateful to Alan Walters, the official discussant of the paper, for drawing our attention to some ambiguities in the original paper and for his comments. We have attempted to clarify the ambiguities in this version of the paper.

The paper is based on a study prepared by the authors for the Organisation for Economic Co-operation and Development (O.E.C.D.) which will be published in full by O.E.C.D. under the title: *A Survey of Econometric Evidence on the Impact of Monetary Policy in the United States.* The invitation to undertake the study arose in the case of G. R. Fisher from his involvement in the project entitled 'An Econometric Model of the U.K. and Its Trading Partners', which is financed in part by a grant from the Social Science Research Council (U.K.) to the University of Southampton.

We are grateful to Niels Thygesen, Head of the Monetary Division, O.E.C.D., for encouragement and advice, and to A. R. Nobay for giving so freely of his time to advise, criticize, and comment on our work. For general comments we are indebted to D. C. Rowan, G. McKenzie, and C. Goodhart; for specific comments, on Section V, we are indebted to J. L. Jordan and, on Section IV, to F. G. Adams and R. L. Teigen. We are also grateful to M. J. Hamburger for correcting some mistakes in an earlier draft of Section V. We thank A. Chesher for making available a descriptive account of the work of the St. Louis school. Finally, we are deeply indebted to Pravin Trivedi for advice and for allowing us to make use of an unpublished report on some of the U.S models discussed in Section IV. We suggested that Trivedi might like to join us as a third author to prepare this paper, but he declined. Whether this is the result of prudence or modesty we cannot say.

For the arduous task of preparing and typing the paper for publication, we are most grateful to Miss H. Roddie and Mrs. F. Kilmister. Naturally, we accept full responsibility for the paper as it now stands.

principally in the United States. The major contribution by Friedman and Meiselman [49] initiated empirical support for the theoretical views of the 'New Monetarists' in their controversy with the Keynesian school, and this stimulated further empirical research on both sides. In terms of economic theory in a comparative static context, Teigen [104] has shown the degree of correspondence between the quantity-theory approach to expenditure determination and the Keynesian income–expenditure approach, using the familiar Hicksian IS–LM analysis (see also Laidler [24, ch. 4]). But at an empirical level, a satisfactory comparative evaluation of the two theories has not emerged and we are led to ask: why? Is it that the strength of prior beliefs has worked against the acceptance of scientific results? Or is it that econometric methodology has once again revealed its inadequacies at distinguishing between alternative economic hypotheses? As we shall see, neither of these arguments is entirely satisfactory.

Both the monetarists and the Keynesians are agreed that in principle the measurement and appraisal of the full impact of monetary phenomena requires the formulation of a structure which provides an explicit and logically consistent account of the dynamics of monetary adjustment. In principle, then, both schools of thought regard economic structure as fundamental to a proper empirical assessment of a particular theory, and hence to a scientific resolution of theoretical differences between the two (see e.g. [104]). Unfortunately, the economic principles which are used to create this structure must be tempered by practical restraints in empirical studies. Gaps in the available data, for example, make the testable structure a shadowy replica of its theoretical counterpart and distort the empirical results.

For example, consider first the difference between the monetarist and the non-monetarist view as put forward in [49]. Here a distinction is drawn between the 'credit' and the 'monetary' effects of monetary policy. The credit view emphasizes the effects of monetary policy on a narrow, well-defined range of capital assets and on a correspondingly narrow range of associated expenditures. The central interest rate is one that summarizes the yields on this narrow class of assets. The monetary view, in contrast, emphasizes that the portfolio of assets held by firms and households contains a very large range of assets; associated with each asset is a yield and a stream of expenditures (which may be implicit or unobservable). It is by affecting the whole spectrum of these yields and expenditures, and consequently by affecting the proportions of corresponding assets in the portfolios of the economic micro-units, that monetary policy impinges on the economy.

Thus, while there is a general similarity of view, there is an essential qualitative difference between the two schools of thought, in terms of the range of assets and interest rates considered. The similarities naturally help explain the use of tools by one school that have been traditionally emphasized by the other. Keynesians have tended to use the IS–LM framework yet 'there is nothing inherent in the Keynesian system which is inconsistent with the introduction of a general portfolio adjustment mechanism' [104, p. 18]. On the other hand, Friedman (e.g. [50, 24, ch. 3]) has recently adopted what is essentially the IS–LM framework thus leaving himself open to the obvious monetarist criticism that he has neglected the general portfolio-adjustment mechanism, i.e. the very mechanism which he and other monetarists have traditionally emphasized (e.g. [24, pp. 58–72, ch. 4, and pp. 136–50]). More important in the present context, the qualitative difference between the two schools has important implications for an empirical appraisal of the two views.

In the specification of an econometric model it is necessary to compromise between the structure to be described and analysed, the objectives of the analysis (e.g. short-term forecasting or policy analysis), and the availability of data. With regard to the last mentioned, a model-builder is typically restrained to work within the Keynesian national income accounting framework. Given this, other data that are required must naturally conform with the same framework. For example, we would usually need to make use of representative 'market rates of interest' in expenditure functions. While such restraints are not a burden from a Keynesian (credit) viewpoint, they undoubtedly vitiate against the formulation of a structure which adequately represents the monetarist doctrine, for precisely the qualitative reasons which distinguish the latter from the former view. Recently, there has been a substantial shift in Keynesian thinking toward the introduction of a portfolio-adjustment mechanism. Nevertheless, a monetarist adjustment mechanism is required to be broader and more detailed, and it is difficult to visualize how it may be tested with the data that are normally available.

Given the data restrictions and a desire to test the power of the monetarist doctrine, it seems that only two avenues are open. Either we must embark on the mammoth task of collecting appropriate data, or we must by-pass the structure and seek an alternative approach to model-building. The latter course has received much attention. Thus attempts have been made to demonstrate the power of monetarist theory by examining the extent to which variations in, say, the money base succeed in explaining variations in GNP. (See e.g. [4, 5, 49].) Unfortunately, such a procedure—which has become known, somewhat inappropriately, as the reduced-form approach—essentially requires the structure, in particular all the over-identifying restrictions, to be cast aside. This means that a proper testing of the empirical validity of a theory is no longer possible; the economic structure is not specified and, therefore, it is no longer clear what causal interpretation may be given to the estimated coefficients. However powerful the results, a critic may with merit argue that only correlations have been observed.

We do not wish to imply that the above argument renders useless the results obtained from studies of the reduced-form type. Nor should it be taken to indicate our unswerving support for the empirical evidence derived from structural models of the whole economy, for these too encounter major practical difficulties. In addition, their formal elegance has not been matched by their predictive abilities and much needs to be done to improve design and estimating and testing procedures before such models can serve as efficient operational tools of economic management. The point we have been making is that practical restraints, rather than the strength of prior beliefs or the inadequacies of econometric methods, have been primarily responsible for the failure of empirical research to produce a scientific resolution of differences between the monetarists and the Keynesian school. These practical restraints, together with the natural growth in the quantity and quality of empirical research, have engendered an increasing commitment on each side to its own methodological approach. On the one hand, the monetarists have continued to emphasize small, reduced-form models which taken on trust the underlying transmission mechanism. On the other hand, the Keynesians, being unconvinced by the power of implicit reasoning yet stimulated by monetarist research, have developed their own thinking and practice in respect of portfolio-adjustment processes which they have sought to make explicit and to test within the framework of structural models. Empirical research, therefore, naturally falls into two broad groups: first, studies in the tradition of Friedman and Mieselman, which are discussed in Section V; second, a wider range of studies concerned with various aspects of the transmission mechanism and hence implicitly critical of reduced-form methodology. In view of its breadth, it will aid the discussion to consider this second group in three separate but related sections; namely, Sections II, III, and IV.

Research into the transmission mechanism has been concerned with the dynamics of monetary adjustment in respect of over-all aggregates and of particular sectors and behavioural groups. Studies of the spending behaviour of particular behavioural groups are discussed in Section II. The dynamics of adjustment in small-scale sector models and in respect of aggregate expenditures are discussed in Section III. In building large-scale econometric models, the sort of evidence provided by detailed studies of the kind described in these two sections will typically form the basis of an initial specification of the structure. Thus Section IV, where we turn to large-scale models which have a particular bearing on economy-wide problems of monetary adjustment, may be seen as a natural development of Sections II and III.

While Sections II–IV represent a line of research that is distinct from the reduced-form models of Section V, there is a notable link between them. In respect of small, economy-wide, aggregative models of the kind discussed in Section III, there have been attempts to relate the final forms of such models to the so-called reduced-form models of the St. Louis school. Thus in Sections III and V we pay some attention to a recent paper by Moroney and Mason [86] which, *inter alia*, attempts to provide a testable structure through which equations of the type used by Anderson and Jordan [5] may be given an acceptable economic interpretation.

Finally, we should like to emphasize three general points concerning the structure and content of the paper. First, our aim is not to debate issues of economic theory. It is to appraise some of the more interesting empirical evidence which seems to contribute to the development of economic theory. Our approach to theory, therefore, is essentially eclectic, and theoretical differences will be referred to only where they are relevant to econometric issues or to the interpretation of results.

Secondly, with regard to the balance of the discussion, the reader will learn that we devote the greatest number of pages to a discussion of large-scale econometric models in Section IV. This should not be interpreted as a prejudice against small-scale studies, in favour of large-scale models as *the* most important and rewarding area of research. On the contrary, we eventually conclude that, in some areas, large-scale models, involved as they must be in numerous technical difficulties, have very little to add to small-scale studies, where the technical problems are considerably smaller. The length of our discussion on large-scale models derives from (i) the fact that such models, being large, automatically require a lengthy discussion; (ii) the purpose of Section IV, which is both to survey the area and to summarize, appraise, and compare a whole range of literature on which large-scale models have been built, and (iii) our decision to consider the results of large models in terms of policy simulations, a practice we have not adopted elsewhere.

Thirdly, our comments relate only to the U.S. economy. This is a convenient restriction, but one which also reflects the fact that most of the outstanding empirical work in monetary economics in recent years has been done by American economists using U.S. data. In respect of other industrialized countries, e.g. the U.K. and other European economies, the U.S. is atypical because, quite apart from institutional and other differences, it is in the nature of a closed economy. Consequently, the studies reported in this paper should not be regarded as a substitute for corresponding research on those countries where the external sector plays a much more significant role. Empirical analyses of such economies, to be realistic, must necessarily be complicated by this additional feature.

II. Studies of the spending behaviour of particular behavioural groups

In this section we discuss five studies of spending behaviour which were published between August 1967 and May 1970. All these studies were conducted during or shortly after a period of severe monetary restraint. Most of them were designed to assess the impact of that restraint. Consequently, their findings should be useful in assessing the effects and the transmission mechanism of monetary measures on expenditures, during or shortly after a period of tight monetary policy.

McGouldrick and Peterson [82] were concerned to assess the impact of the severe monetary restraint of 1966 on large state and local government units, by a sample survey of over 1,000 large spending units. Evidently, tight monetary conditions in 1966 led directly to the abandonment of something like $1·3 billion or 20 per cent of new long-term debt offerings, and to the postponement of approximately $0·4 billion the following year. Nevertheless, in

1966 and 1967 this shortfall in financing had a very insubstantial impact on this sector's expenditure (1–1½ per cent total cutback), because large state and local government units had ample liquid reserves to cushion the effect of credit stringency, they had easy access to, and made use of, short-term borrowing, and their planned expenditures had long gestation periods: they were planned well before the tight money conditions became fully effective.

Phelps [92] considered state and local highway expenditure annually over the period 1951–66. Applying the capital stock-adjustment model developed in [46], Phelps found highway expenditure in constant prices to be closely correlated with authorizations of Federal aid, with real income per capita, and with the discrepancy between the actual and the expected level of the nominal interest rate on municipal bonds.

While Phelps interpreted her findings as showing that a rise in the actual above the expected interest rate could noticeably cut down the speed of adjustment of the actual capital stock to its desired level (she estimated this effect to have *reduced* highway expenditure by $221 million in 1966), she also pointed out why this adjustment effect tended to get outweighed (actual highway investment expenditure *increased* from $8·2 to $8·9 billion per annum from 1965 to 1966). Several reasons were advanced for this short-run insensitivity. There was a long delay between recognizing the need for a new road and actually commencing its construction. For example, origin and destination studies had to be completed and, if Federal aid was required, the project then had to be submitted to the Bureau of Public Roads for approval. Moreover, while an increase in the interest rate became effective by increasing bonded debt costs, in practice these costs were not especially important because, on average, only 18 per cent of highway expenditure was financed through bond issues. Finally, in 1966 the interest-rate net-cost effect was small compared with that induced by tight money conditions in 1953 or 1957, because of the recent expansion of the Inter-state Highway Aid Programme.

A year before [82] was published, Crockett, Friend, and Shavell [26] presented their findings on the determinants of large firms' plant and equipment expenditures in 1966. They found that the extraordinarily tight financial conditions in 1966 were relatively unimportant in determining the over-all cutback in planned investment (cf. [82]). Unanticipated *increases* in plans and equipment commitments were much more prevalent than unanticipated *decreases.* Changes in sales and in costs were decisive expansionary factors, and among those firms who failed to reach their investment targets, delays in delivery and in construction programmes were the most influential factors. Quantitatively, the increase in credit stringency was found to have curtailed investment in 1966 by $500 million out of a total of $75 billion, and in 1967 by $940 million. They concluded that the '. . . slow reaction is not unexpected in view of the greater formality and rigidity of the capital programmes of the largest firms, the long lead times for much of their equipment and perhaps the more advanced arrangements for financing' [26, p. 20].

Nevertheless, by comparing results from their 1966 survey with those in two earlier surveys conducted in 1949 and 1955 by the Department of Commerce, Crockett *et al.* demonstrated that financial factors had a much greater impact on the planned outlays of large corporations. In 1966, for instance, financial factors accounted for 11 per cent of the reduction in planned outlays, whereas in 1969 and 1955 they accounted for less than 1 per cent. They were also able to identify from the sample returns the channels through which changes in financial conditions were transmitted to large corporations. These were, in order of declining importance, (i) the rise in interest rates, (ii) the difficulty in obtaining loans from banks, and (iii) the decline in the stock market. However, the response to higher interest rates was not based on cost considerations; it was based on their influence on business expectations. Rising interest rates and falling equity prices were associated with a poor business outlook. Finally, while the impact of financial conditions on the plant and equipment expenditures of large corporations had been relatively small in 1966, the corresponding effect on the housing industry was both prompt and substantial. Housing starts fell from $27 billion in the first quarter of 1966 to $20·9 billion in the fourth quarter of 1967. Thus '. . . it appears that monetary policy impinges to a much greater extent on the housing market than on business investment . . .' [26, p. 26].

The two studies which round off this preliminary analysis are cross-section studies: one by Mueller and Lean [87] is concerned with the factors which determined how household savings balances were used; the other by Gelfand [53] is a study of the factors which influenced spending on private dwellings. The former provides some evidence on the importance of 'excess liquidity' in influencing households' spending decisions. In particular, it helps to assess whether the existence of certain types of household assets which are not a means of payment might influence the position of the budget constraint on certain spending decisions. The latter study is an interesting sequel, because it provides a verified rationalization as to why household holdings of readily encashable assets play a part in the adjustment process.

Mueller and Lean were concerned with the motives underlying savings deposit accumulations and the uses to which these savings were put. Two sample surveys were conducted, one in May 1964 and the other between October and November 1965. The second survey was used to determine how the initial sample of savers had behaved during the interim period.

Evidently, the motives which underlie the accumulation of savings balances were primarily connected with emergency considerations, then planned education expenses and, finally, retirement. The *provision* of funds for some expected short-term expenditure, such as house repairs, received a relatively small weight (10 per cent) in the formulation of savings plans. In contrast, accrued balances were often used to finance part of a major household durable expenditure. The variation in the savings balances showed that '. . . many families alternate between adding to their stock of durable goods and adding to their stock of financial assets' [87, p. 393].

Householders were found to regard withdrawals as temporary, even though 29 per cent of them had firm plans to finance outlays by a further withdrawal in the subsequent year. Those who made the most withdrawals were the largest savers from the households which had used their accounts for such a purpose in the previous year. Moreover, when a withdrawal was used to finance the purchase of a consumer durable, it was used to meet the down-payment commitment. Typically, this amount was a large proportion of the existing balance and caused the range in the size of savings balances to be much more variable than the corresponding range for checking account balances, despite the infrequency of use of the former. In summary: 'The major implication of this study is that funds for the most cyclically variable consumer transactions are drawn to a significant extent from savings accounts' [87, p. 421].

In [53], Gelfand considered the influence on realizable housing demand of changes in (a) credit terms (interest rates, down-payment requirements, and mortgage maturity periods) and (b) credit conditions (ratio of monthly carrying charges to family income, tenure status of the land, and accommodation preference status of the house selected for financing). The data were derived from a sample of approximately 1,500 home purchasers in Pennsylvania, and were analysed via computer simulations. First, a financing programme was constructed to show how home purchases would vary if either one or more of the credit terms or credit conditions were varied, it being assumed that these terms or conditions would act as a bottleneck to realizable housing commitments. Then various computer simulations were run. These related accumulated household assets to required down-payments, householders' earnings to mortgage carrying costs, and evaluated how responsive the sample would have been to an exogenously induced change in the financing programme. According to the results, '. . . the elimination of the down-payment requirement is the most effective single action that can be taken to spur potential housing demand' [53, p. 166]. It was also observed that downward movements in the interest rate had some effect, which was enhanced by an accompanying reduction in down-payments. A lengthening of the repayment period was less effective. Finally, the only changes in credit conditions which exerted substantial influence were measures which decreased the full cost of purchase, e.g. the sale of the leasehold of the land.

It is not unreasonable to assume that Gelfand's finding concerning the importance of the down-payment requirement would also apply to the purchase of durable goods. If this is the case, then Gelfand's results may be used to complement those of Mueller and Lean. It would then appear that in respect of large durable consumption commitments, the down-payment requirement plays an important role in the decision to purchase, and that the size and previous utilization of financial savings are, in turn, important in determining whether or not the down-payment will be met. Down-payment requirements are essentially a form of credit rationing, yet such rationing would appear to be less effective the larger the existing financial savings deposits, these being a substitute for borrowing. More specifically, the larger per capita savings balances are relative to the average financial gap on desired durable goods commitments, the more likely it is that these commitments will be fulfilled and vice versa, for any given level of per capita income.

The studies examined so far suggest that, in estimating realizable demand, financial factors should be considered as potentially important variables. They also suggest, however, that the potency of these variables differs considerably between the various spending groups, and with the type of good which is being purchased.

Explicitly, it seems that the larger state and local government entities and the larger private corporations' concurrent spending plans are relatively insensitive to changes in financial conditions in the short run. Their reaction is primarily to rearrange their asset–liability mix. Financial assets and financial liabilities are manipulated so as to reduce expected debt servicing costs and to obtain the necessary finance for their planned expenditure commitments. The demand decisions of households, however, are more dependent on financial market conditions, particularly when they are planning large consumer durable purchases. It seems that these demands will respond to a change in credit terms quite quickly, especially a change in the degree to which the full purchase price needs to be financed. The speed of reaction to a change in the size of this 'credit gap' would seem to depend on how adequate households view their holdings of readily encashable assets, particularly institutionally issued savings instruments, which have been shown to be an important source of finance for this purpose. Overall then, the evidence suggests that in as much as financial sector changes exert an influence, this first shows up as a change in the spending commitments of the household sector for new housing and car purchases. In contrast, the investment commitments of large corporations and of large state and local government units should be much less sensitive for quite a considerable period. A large component of what is often defined as autonomous expenditure is expected to be relatively insensitive to sudden changes in financial conditions. Nevertheless, as recent studies have shown, if the degree of financial stringency is long sustained, it may exert a significant impact on certain autonomous expenditures. For example, as shown in his 1971 study [91], Petersen found that state and local spending was significantly reduced by the tight credit conditions existing in the fiscal year 1970. Similarly, he found that the presence of interest-rate ceilings which induced credit rationing '. . . may have caused net spending cutbacks by state and local units in fiscal 1970 roughly double what they otherwise would have been' [91, p. 210].

III. Studies of the financial determinants of various forms of private expenditure

Several studies have attempted to identify the channels through which the monetary sector influences various forms of private expenditure. In these, we would anticipate careful consideration being given to the lag structure, yet this is not always the case. Indeed, the specifications put forward, the sophistication of the econometric evaluation, and the interpretation of the results varies considerably. Consequently, it is difficult to synthesize results.

For example, within a quarterly, dynamic, IS–LM framework, Tanner [102] estimates that the interest rate has a five times larger numerical effect on commodity demand than on the demand for money ($-8 \cdot 3$ compared with $-1 \cdot 7$). He then *argues* that this is consistent with a strong *indirect* monetary effect, but he makes no attempt to measure the impact of a shift in the IS schedule in response to a change in the money stock. Moreover, his argument breaks down when GNP minus taxes is replaced in the commodity-demand equation by disposable income, because the interest-rate coefficient then acquires a positive sign.

Another example is Cohen [25], where the effects of both the rate of interest *and* financial stocks are incorporated into various expenditure equations, but without due consideration of lag structures, on the ground that the major interest was to estimate current period effects. It seems likely that this exclusion will have biased the results. Nevertheless, Cohen's results in the household-sector studies do conform with [53] (that levels and changes in short-run interest rates are not much of a barrier to private housing expenditure), and with [87] (that financial savings balances may act as a substitute for credit, cf. [62]). In addition, only long-run interest rates were significant with the expected sign, a result which might really be attributed to a net worth effect via movements in, say, stock market prices (cf. [31]).

In respect of the non-financial corporate sector, Cohen concludes that his '. . . results offer strong support for the relative effectiveness of financial flows . . .' [25, p. 17] as the dominant financial sector influence on the corporate sector's current investment expenditure. But this conclusion is not really substantiated by the empirical results, especially in view of the absence of lags. Probably the latter causes the direct credit impact to be accentuated, a view supported by the evidence that financial institutions adjust their portfolios procyclically to demand pressures [95]. In this sense it is possible that their loan placements are demand determined, whereupon Cohen would seem to misinterpret the direction of causation.

Similarly, Cohen's perverse results for interest rates in respect of the corporate sector's current investment expenditure may also be explained by the absence of lags. Studies, for example, by Jorgenson and Stephenson [66] and by Evans [38] have shown that changes in nominal interest rates do exert the expected impact on real corporate investment plans, but that it takes a year or more for these effects to be recognized. In turn, it may be that Cohen's significant positive interest-rate coefficients simply reflect the Central Bank's attempts to stabilize the economy (see [57]). Cohen's conclusions and our interpretations, however, must remain unsupported conjectures until his data are re-examined so as to assess directly the role and effect of lagged variables.

The finding that investment spending is significantly affected by interest rates with lags which vary by industry has an interesting parallel in a study of consumer expenditure by Hamburger [58]. This paper applies a modified capital stock-adjustment model to quarterly data, 1953–64, and derives an optimal lag structure statistically. All variables are considered as quarterly changes and expenditure flows are seasonally adjusted, in constant prices. Essentially two expenditure equations are considered, one for durable consumption automobile expenditure and another for non-automobile durable consumption expenditure, using selected groups of explanatory variables in each case.

The results reveal that the long-term nominal rate of interest on bonds is a significant determinant of both forms of durable consumption expenditure, with a $4\frac{1}{2}$ or 6 quarter lag. The sizes of the coefficient of this interest rate is roughly four times as large for automobile expenditure as it is for other durables, with corresponding elasticities of -0.85 for the former and -0.17 for the latter. For automobile expenditures, the income elasticity outweighs the substitution elasticity (4.32 and -1.17 respectively). On the other hand, in respect of other durable expenditures, the price elasticity is slightly more important (1.65 and -1.81 respectively). These results conform with those of Suits [100] and Chow [20]. The rate of return on savings accounts has no significant effect on automobile expenditure, but for other durables it is significant with an implied elasticity of -0.40. Finally, the incorporation of the broadly defined money stock as an explanatory variable does not substantially influence the size or the significance of the interest-rate coefficients in either of the expenditure relationships.

Hamburger interprets his income-elasticity results and the importance of lagged income for automobiles as evidence that consumers take longer to make up their minds for these large expenditure commitments. The larger long-term interest-rate coefficient for automobile expenditure evidently reflects the greater importance of consumer credit in financing these purchases, compared with other durable goods, while the $4\frac{1}{2}$ quarter lag is interpreted as the time taken by the suppliers of consumer credit to adjust their charges to higher interest costs, an interpretation which is substantiated by earlier results. Evidently, then, consumer durable expenditure is determined by disposable income, relative prices, interest rates, and the stock of household savings, and Hamburger claims to have isolated '. . . a significant relationship between expenditures on durable goods and interest rates' [58, p. 1141]. He concludes that '. . . consumer behaviour is influenced not only by the supply, but also [by] the demand for loanable funds, in particular the demand for credit by other sectors of the economy' [58, p. 1145].

Hamburger's results and interpretations dovetail nicely with those of [87] on the utilization of savings balances, and with those of [25] on the importance of the asset side of financial institutions' balance sheets. The former found that households use their savings balances to finance the down-payment requirement, and the greater the increase in these balances, the more likely they would be used for such a purpose in the future. It was also found, however, that this utilization was negatively associated with the availability of consumer credit. What is more, once having run down their savings balances to make such a commitment, households then proceed to build them up once again to their old levels. In this respect, it is not surprising that the coefficients of lagged income and lagged savings balances in the automobile regressions are both positive. Increases in both of these variables would obviously help to satisfy the 'credit gap' engendered by the down-payment requirement; and, given the greater availability of consumer credit accorded to large durable expenditure commitments, it would then have been surprising if the nominal interest rate on savings accounts had received a significant negative coefficient in the automobile regression. For we know that savings balances are extensively drawn on for large durable consumer expenditures, whence savings institutions might have reacted to the loss of deposits by raising their rates. In this case, the rate on savings accounts would have a significant *positive* sign, given that appropriate lags were introduced.

With regard to other durables, the credit cost variable is smaller and has a longer lag and its coefficient is smaller than in the automobile expenditure regression. This may be explained by the more highly competitive consumer credit market for automobiles than for other durables. Moreover, to acquire other durable consumer goods which are not so well financed, householders presumably need to draw on their savings balances, in so far as disposable incomes are insufficient to meet relatively lumpy expenditure commitments. Thus for other durables we would anticipate a significant positive coefficient on savings balances and a significant negative coefficient on the rate of interest, results that were indeed obtained.

In summary, the interpretations put forward for Hamburger's results are sustained by other studies. Evidently movements in disposable income, in relative prices, and, to a lesser extent, in the stock of financial savings have a fairly prompt impact on real consumer durable commitments; and corresponding to recent studies of real investment determination, nominal interest rates play a significant role with a decisive lag.

We have emphasized above that in seeking to describe the dynamic adjustment paths by which the influence of monetary variables are transmitted to the real sector, much depends on the lag distribution that in practice is estimated. Early attempts to do this made use of the first-order Pascal distribution put forward and used by Koyck [78]. More recently, flexible lags have been used, and greater attention has been paid to a method put forward by Almon [1, 2]. We have some comments to make on some of the problems associated with this technique, but we delay making them until Section V. In respect of studies relevant to the topic of this section, we now turn to a paper by Branson and Klevorick [15] which makes use of the Almon technique in evaluating the role of consumer prices in the determination of real consumption expenditure.

Branson and Klevorick applied a variant of the life-cycle hypothesis in which the consumer goods price index was introduced as an additional explanatory variable, and all explanatory variables were permitted to take effect via contemporaneous and lagged values, up to a seven-quarter lag:

$$\ln c_t = b + \Sigma_i v_i \ln y_{t-i} + \Sigma_j q_j \ln w_{t-j} + \Sigma_k z_k \ln p_{t-k} + \varepsilon_t,$$

where ε is a residual error, c = real per capita consumption, y = real per capita labour income, w = real per capita consumer net worth, and p = consumer goods price index (1958 = 100). The subscripts refer to time periods, and b, v, q, and z are coefficients to be estimated. This model was fitted to seasonally adjusted, quarterly data 1955 (1)–1965 (4).

With respect to the price level, the estimates imply that real per capita consumption expenditure will rise with the level of the consumer price index with a lag of one and four quarters, given real per capita labour income and real per capita net worth. Several hypotheses could be advanced to interpret this result.

First, it could be argued that the result is essentially spurious, merely arising, in the tradition of Yule's nonsense correlations, because of the intervention of time, all variables having a positive trend over the period examined. However, similar results emerged when the model was refitted using deviations from trends.

Second, it could be argued that the price effect is more in the nature of an effect of price expectations, the distributed lag on observed prices being the statistical artifice for evaluating such expectations. The knowledge that prices have been rising induces additional consumption from the fear that the rise will continue.

A third possibility is that the coefficients of real incomes and of prices might have been inflated and the coefficients of real net worth deflated by biases induced by simultaneity. An attempt was made to test this view by application of instrumental variables. This test revealed only weak evidence of simultaneous equation bias. While the regression coefficients were (naturally) affected, the resulting changes were insignificant, both numerically and statistically.

A fourth argument relies on a change in the price–wage ratio leading to a redistribution of income from consumers to producers, which in turn produces a sharp increase in investment and then in income and output. To test this last-mentioned effect, Branson and Klevorick introduced into the consumption function the ratio of actual to potential real GNP. While this new variable received a positive coefficient, the sum of the price coefficient was raised, not reduced, and it was concluded that the original price effects were not spuriously picking up an income-redistribution effect.

Finally, the positive coefficients on the price variable were interpreted as evidence that consumers are affected by the phenomenon of money illusion in framing spending plans in real terms. If this is the case, the demand for commodities is not homogeneous of degree zero with respect to prices and money incomes. Moreover, if producers also suffer from money illusion in planning expenditures for their own 'households' (firms), then there would be an immediate rationalization for the use of nominal rather than real interest rates as explanatory variables in models of real income determination (e.g. [38, 58]). Further, Chow [21] found that changes in consumption and investment expenditures were positively related to lagged movements in the price index.

Quite clearly, if the money-illusion argument is correct, there are far-reaching and interesting implications for economic theory, for demand management, and for the construction of large macro-models (see Section IV). Cost increases induced by rises in factor prices may readily be passed on if consumers are, in turn, induced to respond by buying more in real terms as product prices rise. As we have already indicated, if this real positive price effect is to produce a sustained increase in consumption, then it must have an impact on supply as well, both to stimulate domestic production—which implies additional investment—and to raise imports. Not surprisingly, then, Branson and Klevorick suggest that 'greater attention should be paid to the link between the price–wage sector and the expenditure sector' ([15, p. 846], see also Section IV).

Branson and Klevorick also found that real per capita consumption responds quite quickly to a change in per capita net worth and somewhat more slowly to changes in per capita labour income and the consumer price index. This seems to conform with the results of other studies. Evidently, a change in household net worth exerts a fairly immediate over-all impact on per capita consumption, but its effect is fully realized after two quarters. Similarly, some of the quantity-theory studies of consumption determination have shown that the lagged impact of a change in the money stock does not continue to exert an effect after three quarters (see e.g. [5]). As shown in [87], this type of short-range impact of an increase in householders' net worth is precisely what one might expect if such a store of wealth is needed to bridge the financial gap on large consumer durable expenditures. Moreover, in [58], the money-stock effect in real terms was presumably not significant after two quarters, whereas the interest-rate effect was shown to be exerting its maximum impact only after four to six quarters had elapsed. It appears, therefore, that a change in the household sector's wealth holdings, *ceteris paribus*, will induce a fairly quick response in this sector's consumption expenditure.

Finally, the result, that both the current level and, with progressively declining weights, the past levels of net per capita labour income act as important determinants of real per capita consumption, is well supported by other empirical work, for example, the permanent-income hypothesis and the life-cycle hypothesis. The implied estimates of the marginal propensity to consume out of income (0·71) and out of net worth (0·024) are fairly similar to those derived by Ando and Modigliani [9] (0·70 and 0·06). Moreover, given that the current and lagged values of per capita income may be interpreted as a proxy for per capita human wealth, it is interesting to observe that the impact of per capita income declines rapidly. The immediate income elasticity of demand for consumption goods, given a change in the current period's labour income, is shown to be 0·274. Four quarters later, this impact has fallen to 0·039. This suggests that if a measure for the current period's human wealth had been used in the regression, instead of the current and lagged values of per capita labour income, its impact, like the impact of consumers' non-human wealth (w), would have been shown to exert its full force quite promptly. Such a prompt response to a change in the stock of consumer wealth or some part of it (money or money more broadly defined to include other forms of financial savings) has been observed in numerous empirical tests of consumers' behaviour.

Tanner's paper [102], referred to above, has recently been developed in more detail by Moroney and Mason [86], who tested a dynamic macro-model designed to estimate short-run responses of GNP to changes in selected fiscal and monetary policy instruments. Moroney and Mason, like Tanner, deal with expenditure relationships in current prices using seasonally adjusted quarterly data. The model treats GNP, consumption, gross investment, imports, disposable income, the demand for and supply of money, and the short- and long-term interest rates as endogenous variables. In treating the money supply as endogenous they hold, like [54, 95], that movements in the short-term rate of interest, by influencing portfolio behaviour, will exert a positive impact on the money stock. In addition, and unlike Tanner, they design their consumption function so that direct money-stock effects can be assessed along with disposable income and the lagged influence of the dependent variable. Indirect monetary effects, those induced by movements in the two-quarter lagged value of the long-term interest rate, are incorporated into their gross investment function. This rate of interest in turn is held to be influenced by the level of income, a proxy for the influence of the demand for loanable funds, and by the short-term interest rate which they represent as determined by an inverse form of a money demand function of the Hicksian LM variety. The model is estimated by three-stage least squares over the period 1953 (1)–1965 (4).

The structural estimates reveal that monetary variables play a significant role in the consumption and gross investment functions. The current level of the money stock (M) exerts a significant positive influence on consumption expenditure (C), whereas M_{t-1} does not.

According to Moroney and Mason, the significant coefficient for M_t reflects a liquidity effect and a money-stock effect induced by changing the implicit rate of discount on consumer durables, and consequently raising their present value. The failure of M_{t-1} to exert much influence is taken as evidence that the wealth effect of the level of this stock on consumer expenditure is not significant. However, this result could have arisen either from colinearity between M_t and M_{t-1} or because M is defined as the money stock plus adjusted demand deposits. By excluding time deposits, a progressively more dominant component of banking-sector liabilities, it would have been surprising if the money stock had yielded the expected wealth effects [54].

In the gross investment function, the two-quarter lagged level of the long-term interest rate exerts a negative and significant influence and direct monetary effects also exert an influence via $(C_{t-1} - C_{t-2})$. Finally, the money stock and the fiscal variables evidently have long-lasting effects, a result established by calculating appropriate dynamic impact multipliers.

Moroney and Mason believe that their structural estimates vindicate their endogenous treatment of the money supply. In this function, the level of the short-term interest rate has a significant positive coefficient; though the adjusted reserve base has a more decisive influence. Similarly, the estimated short- and long-term interest-rate equations reveal that both rates are closely correlated (which is interpreted as indicating that movements in the short rate induce movements in the long rate) and that each rate is associated with the level of aggregate economic activity in the expected direction. Taken together, these results suggest that movements in the money stock and the interest rates, though influenced by movements in the reserve base as determined by the monetary authority, are far from being easily prescribed by the authority's intervention in the market, because endogenously generated demand pressure exerts a potent influence.

Moroney and Mason establish, that an interim form equation for GNP is dynamically stable, whence they derive dynamic multipliers for government expenditure (G) and the (adjusted) monetary base B (see Section V). Clearly these multipliers are not independent of the sample period (which avoids the main impact of public expenditure for the Korean and Vietnam wars), or of the prior lag specification. Nevertheless, they yield interesting and potentially useful information.

The calculated multipliers suggest that G rather than B is the more suitable instrument for stabilization policy, a conclusion at variance with the policy implications of the St. Louis school (see Section V). The initial impact of a change in G is large, but it tapers off quickly after the first period. The impact of a change in B, however, rises for the first three quarters and then falls back slowly to about its first-period level only after another year has elapsed. Moreover, this positive impact is sustained at a higher level and for longer than the corresponding impact of G, the cumulative impact exceeding that of an equivalent dollar increase in G in all but the first quarter. Thus the results corroborate the '. . . important role of the money stock in determining the rate of aggregate economic activity' [86, p. 793]. They indicate, moreover, that changes in G have a more prompt influence and that '. . . its effects are dispersed much more quickly than those of monetary policy' [86, p. 810]. 'Thus careful management of the monetary base, which would seem to require avoiding erratic changes, appears to be a matter of the highest consequence for effective stabilization.' [86, p. 810.] As such, their conclusion is at variance with [102] and [5] which argue that monetary measures should be used as a stabilization tool.

Before we turn to examine some economy-wide, dynamic models of the U.S. in Section IV, let us attempt to summarize the position we have now reached.

There seem to be at least four channels through which the financial sector transmits its influence to the real sector: an interest-rate effect, a money-stock effect, a credit-availability effect, and a price effect. The empirical studies which have been designed to test these effects indicate that their over-all impact and their incidence over time depend on the type of expenditure commitment considered. The evidence suggests that money-stock effects and/or credit-availability effects exert a fairly prompt impact on household spending commitments; in other words, that the stock of household savings and the availability of consumer mortgage credit are arguments which should be considered in determining this sector's expenditure. In contrast, various other studies suggest that financial stock considerations do not have a direct impact on the corporate sector's spending decisions in the short run.

Evidently, corporate investment spending decisions are relatively insensitive to corporate-sector liquidity (as measured by retained earnings and depreciation allowances, or cash flow) [38, 64, 66]. In as much as this liquidity has an influence, it occurs with a substantial lag and is restricted to affecting just a few industries in the manufacturing sector of the economy. These findings concerning liquidity are supported by the cross-section results of [27]. Investment commitments in this sector, being well budgeted and well planned, take considerable time to become operational and hence are relatively inflexible. Consequently, the impact of extremely tight money market conditions in 1966 on business investment in 1966 and 1967 was very modest.

In contrast to the variable incidence of the money-stock or credit-availability effects, the evidence suggests that both planned corporate and realized consumer expenditures exhibit some sensitivity to interest-rate changes. Some studies (e.g. [38, 58, 66]) suggest that, in constant prices, this sensitivity is somewhat delayed; moreover, that other variables (such as capacity utilization [38] or disposable income and relative prices [58]) exert a more immediate, as well as a more decisive, influence. To be sure [102] and [25] suggest that the negative interest-rate effect on private expenditure commitments in current prices exerts its influence promptly. But these results, as we have indicated, are not very convincing in view of the specifications used. It therefore appears that in current prices as well as in constant prices lagged interest rates are more potent determinants of expenditure than are current rates.

While the evidence suggests that changes in the stock of money may exert a prompt if somewhat erratic effect on total expenditure, it is far from clear that short-run changes in the money stock may be determined with a great deal of precision by the U.S. monetary authorities. The variability of the reserve ratios for different kinds of monetary liabilities and Chetty's evidence [19] of the very high elasticity of substitution between interest-bearing liquid assets supports the finding that portfolio demand pressures modulate the authorities' efforts to produce a prescribed fluctuation on the monetary stock [54]. The same type of considerations apply to the Central bank's efforts to use open market operations to influence credit availability in the short run, though, to be sure, the presence of officially prescribed deposit and loan interest-rate ceilings may induce a very potent degree of credit rationing in the housing market, as the 1966 experience showed. Short-run stabilization objectives, then, may be difficult to achieve through money-stock regulation. Similarly, the control over real economic activity which may be exercised in a year or less by manipulating interest rates, also seems limited. The evidence suggests that, given a change in the money stock, it takes approximately seven months before the full interest-rate change has been achieved [17]. Thereafter, the time-response of economic activity to this change is shown not to commence for at least a further three to four quarters. The same type of considerations seem to apply to the role of the price level, and this variable seems particularly insensitive to monetary management (see Section IV).

In all then, it seems that the policy implications for financial management of the real sector's economic activity is in accord with Friedman's proposals. The financial sector should be regulated so that its effects fit in with long-term economic policy. In the meantime, however, continuing efforts should be made to appraise the short-run real sector impact of financial developments even though other policy tools, e.g. fiscal measures, seem to be more effective in curbing undesirable short-run fluctuations in over-all economic activity [86]. We return to this research in Section V and we examine more disaggregated macro-models in the next section.

Finally, the evidence relating to the price effect from [15] has been interpreted in a variety of ways. While we have followed Branson's and Klevorick's interpretation of money illusion, we are not entirely convinced by the evidence. Nevertheless, whatever the interpretation, we would certainly endorse their plea that greater attention should be paid to the link between prices and wages on the one hand and expenditures on the other.

IV. Some evidence from dynamic economy-wide econometric models

In Section III our attention has been focused primarily on single-equation time-series studies. The results of such studies are undoubtedly useful and informative, yet their interpretation is essentially confined to one of four classes of statistical or functional relationship:

(i) A single equation may simply represent an interesting statistical association between economic time-series in which there is no serious attempt to distinguish cause from effect. Such an equation is clearly of limited use in analysing policy, though it may be a convenient device for extrapolative forecasting.

(ii) A second interpretation is that a single equation describes a unilateral causal dependence in a well-defined recursive model or in a recursive block of an otherwise interdependent system. Provided there is no residual time dependence either between or within equations, such an equation would describe a link between cause and effect. The full implications of this link, however, cannot be revealed without a complete specification and appraisal of the entire system.

(iii) Another interpretation is that a single equation is one equation in the reduced form, or an intermediate form or the final form of an interdependent system. If this is the case, then the underlying theory from which the equation is derived cannot in general be tested without additional information; in any case, the mechanism through which a cause is transmitted to produce an effect is masked.

(iv) Finally, a single equation may represent one equation in an interdependent structure so that, in general, the explanatory variables will contain endogenous components. Of course, standard single-equation techniques will produce misleading results in these circumstances. Though these may be overcome, there still remain links with the rest of the system to be evaluated. Without these, the full implications of the equation within the system cannot be analysed.

We do not believe that the equations so far presented belong to type (i). Nor do we believe it would be fruitful to classify the previously presented equations into the remaining types described above. Our purpose in presenting the classification is to bring out the important property of single-equation studies, namely that they are restricted in their ability to portray the links between the financial sector, on the one hand, and the rest of an economy, on the other. A broader and a more detailed view of economic behaviour is necessary. We therefore turn in this section to an examination of the evidence from economy-wide, dynamic econometric models of the U.S.A.

We emphasize 'economy-wide' models because our intention is to examine how various econometric models attempt to portray the forces which determine the magnitude of important interest rates, rates of change of financial assets, etc., and how these variables, in turn, affect various broad economic aggregates such as consumption, investment, employment, and gross national income. We also emphasize 'dynamic' to bring out the implications for such broad economic aggregates of alternative plausible monetary policies, both in terms of their initial impact effects and of their short-run dynamic effects over a horizon of two–three years. A major reason for our interest in the results obtained from economy-wide dynamic models is the implications they have for stabilization policies. Consequently, it is natural to be concerned not only with the *initial impact effects* of alternative policies—that is with reduced-form coefficients of the policy instruments—but also with the *time path* of the effects and with the *speed of response* of the target variables to changes in monetary instruments. For these reasons the numerical estimates obtained by various investigators will be compared by reference to the results obtained from policy simulations carried out by them.

It is worth illustrating one aspect of the differences between small-scale studies and dynamic economy-wide models before proceeding further. As we have seen, some of the small-scale studies have attempted to evaluate the direct effects of, for example, money stocks, prices, and interest rates on particular expenditures (e.g. [15, 25, 58, 102]). Unfortunately, the interpretation of the results of these studies is limited, principally because the estimating equations are not capable on their own of capturing the full spectrum of causal links within the monetary sector and between it and the real sector, and hence the explanatory variables are not themselves independently determined. In the U.S. economy these causal links are very complicated. Consequently they are very difficult to formulate and very time-consuming to evaluate. Moreover, since a quick, approximate evaluation is often required in practice, there is a natural temptation to look for short-cuts, for example, to search for indicators of monetary policy. Briefly, an indicator of monetary policy is a variable which yields information on the effects of monetary-policy actions on present and future values of goal variables. Among Keynesians, the tendency has been to regard rates of interest as indicators, while monetarists, on the other hand, have tended to be quantity watchers. A question that then arises is: are these variables reliable indicators and, if so, which is the more reliable? (See [111].) One approach to this question is to evaluate directly the net effects of the indicators on particular goal variables, an approach which is essentially similar to that adopted in some of the small-scale studies we have examined in the previous sections. But large-scale models are, of course, capable of being applied to precisely the same exercise, but in so doing they concentrate on the specified causal links embodied in their structures. The place and role of money stocks is then very important, for in the small-scale models, for example [25, 58, 102], money stocks have been built in directly, this being necessitated by the limited scale of these studies. In many of the large models discussed in this section, the channels of monetary policy used essentially direct the stock effects via the rate of interest. To the extent that these large-scale model structures are satisfactory, it is then natural to regard the small-scale results as being more in line with the reduced-form results discussed in Section IV, even though, as we have noted, they contribute directly and indirectly to the specifications used in the large-scale work.

Before an econometric model can be said to represent the behaviour it purports to describe it is obvious that it should be tested against 'the facts'. The tests to be applied depend in part on the applications for which the model is intended. But it is not a simple matter to decide whether a whole system is satisfactory or to detect which part or parts of it are inadequate. The tendency, therefore, has been to examine sequentially various pieces of evidence and from these to make a judgement as to the over-all capacity of the model to perform its intended task satisfactorily. For example, if the primary concern is with a simulation analysis of alternative monetary policies, there are three classes of test that might be performed on the model, before embarking on the analysis. These are:

   (a) standard statistical tests of significance;
   (b) dynamic simulations;
   (c) genuine forecasts.

Of these, (a) and (b) test a model against known information, while (c) applies the model to an unobserved situation. If a model establishes a good record by these tests, particularly dynamic simulations extending beyond the sample period, greater confidence can be placed in its ability to represent real world behaviour. For example, it is of considerable interest to know how an economy would have behaved in the past if, with the benefit of hindsight, a more appropriate—or just a different—policy had been followed. The effects of such different policies may be studied by means of policy simulations. Policy simulations, and (a), (b), and (c), above are clearly described in [23] and [52].

In respect of various possible tests, the reader should bear in mind that it is as important—perhaps more important—to test the statistical characteristics of the equation errors as it is to test the economic specification embedded in the structural form. As we have indicated, much of what we will have to say is concerned with the dynamic properties of various models. The hope is that the dynamic properties of the system will be captured in the economic specification. In practice this is seldom completely possible, in which case the errors themselves may have their own dynamic structure and be amenable to systematic analysis. The important point here is not so much the implications for estimation, though these are of course important; rather that the dynamic error structure is part of the dynamic structure of the econometric model being investigated, indeed that part which either cannot be or has not been explicitly incorporated into the economic specification. It may, in practice, capture an important component of economic behaviour and failure to take it into account will engender an incorrect picture of the full dynamic characteristics of the entire model. For example, consider, in standard notation, the over-identified dynamic system in M endogenous variables y and K exogenous variables x, with zero mean error vector ε, t representing time period in the usual way:

$$y(t) = Ay(t) + By(t-1) + Cx(t) + Dx(t-1) + \varepsilon(t) \qquad (1)$$

where $\varepsilon(t)$ obeys the first-order stationary autoregressive process

$$\varepsilon(t) = R\varepsilon(t-1) + u(t), \qquad (2)$$

$u(t)$ being serially independent and the capital letters denoting suitably behaved matrices of appropriate order. If $\char`\^$ denotes estimated value, then a one-period forecast would be:

$$\hat{y}(t+1) = (I - \hat{A})^{-1}\hat{B}y(t) + (I - \hat{A})^{-1}\hat{C}\hat{x}(t+1) \\ + (I - \hat{A})^{-1}\hat{D}x(t) + (I - \hat{A})^{-1}\hat{R}\hat{\varepsilon}(t). \qquad (3)$$

In this case, we can take account of the memory embedded in the error vector by (2), using the estimate $\hat{\varepsilon}(t)$. But we can go no further in this case, for with a two-period forecast $\hat{\varepsilon}(t+1)$ would be required, and this is unknown at time t. With policy simulations, therefore, we cannot capture the full dynamic characteristics of the model, since the future path of y is unknown and hence the last term in (3) cannot be evaluated at each stage. Thus in so far as errors in practice are serially dependent, policy simulations necessarily suffer from the inherent drawback that the stochastic part of the model cannot be taken into account via estimated residuals.

The point just made is not a piece of econometric pedantry. There are three reasons for making this assertion, and a growing body of empirical evidence to back it up. First, dynamic models, in single or simultaneous form, must inevitably depend on the evaluation of various distributed lags. We know from distributed lag theory that a given lag distribution typically *induces* serial dependence in the error structure, so we have reason to suspect it will appear (see e.g. [56]). Consider, then, evidence that it does indeed appear in practice with distributed lag models: e.g. in inventory behaviour, Trivedi [106]; in investment behaviour, Bischoff [12]; in dividend behaviour, Feldstein [44] and Fisher [45]; and, finally, the simulation results of Hendry and Trivedi [61], and of Evans *et al.* [42]. Note also that the estimates and the inferences are typically different, depending on whether or not account is taken of serial correlation in such models, particularly [12].

Second, there is the question of dynamic stability. Nearly all large-scale econometric models contain non-linearities, and one purpose of simulations performed on them is to evaluate whether or not they are dynamically stable. Unfortunately, it is not a simple matter to evaluate whether the whole model is stable, given that the estimated economic structure is stable. It is quite possible for a stable economic structure to be stochastically unstable and vice versa (see [88]). Since, however, we cannot make use of the stochastic components for policy simulations, we should in practice be very cautious in our interpretation of the results they produce. It follows that, prior to simulation, great care and attention should be devoted to testing the structure, including a full appraisal of the error-generating processes. This is seldom done at the level of sophistication required. Indeed, usually only 'standard' linear tests are applied and it is rare that over-identifying restrictions are even put to test. If serial correlation is present but not allowed for, then standard errors will not be correctly calculated. However, we need not go to this level of sophistication, because even when R^2's and t-ratios apply, they are notoriously ineffective at discriminating between alternative economic hypotheses.

One way round the difficulty of being unable to make use of residuals in simulations is to estimate the variance–covariance structure of the errors and then to make use of this to generate 'proxy' stochastic elements in a stochastic simulation. Suppose, for example, that $(I - A)^{-1}\varepsilon(t) \sim N(O, \Sigma)$, then we may construct pseudo-errors by random selection from $N(O, \hat{\Sigma})$, where $\hat{\Sigma}$ is the estimate of the variance–covariance matrix Σ. These may then be used in a simulation of the reduced form. An example of this type of simulation is [90]. Obviously such an approach permits a stochastic evaluation of the dynamic properties of the model. Nevertheless, such simulations are seldom attempted and when they are it is typically at a late stage in the development of a model (e.g. [42]).

The third reason for concern with serial dependence in the errors derives from the fact that observations are inherited and are not, in general, collected for time intervals which correspond with the decision period on which behaviour is based. There are no very strong reasons to suppose, for example, that a quarter of a year is fundamental to the taking of decisions throughout the economy, and we are naturally drawn to make approximations which we hope will come as close as we can to reality with the data available. This is another argument which underlies the use of distributed lags (and of course simultaneity). In so far as the approximation is not entirely successful we would expect serially dependent errors to emerge. Alternatively, a better approximation may be achieved by setting up the model in continuous time and seeking to estimate a discrete approximation to such a model. While this approach has been considered (e.g. [11, 94]), it has not been widely applied and none of the models included here belongs to this type.

As we have indicated above, we have chosen to comment on the estimates obtained from various policy simulations. Because the discussion is biased toward those studies which are more complete in this respect, the range of models examined is quite narrow. Nevertheless, some reference is made to a wider class of models where we believe this to be relevant and helpful.

An alternative to concentrating on policy simulations would have been to examine single equations or blocks of equations relating to the financial sector or to the non-financial sector. Such an examination would attempt to arrive at conclusions regarding the effectiveness of monetary policy by considering individual coefficients, their sampling properties, and how these are linked through the system to affect variables in the real sector. Alternatively, we could simulate the behaviour of a block of endogenous variables by regarding as exogenous all variables not explained within the block. Neither of these two alternatives seems particularly attractive. We have already explained the weakness of standard (single-equation) test statistics. In addition, we would add that the tracing of effects from one variable or equation to the rest of the system is cumbersome to evaluate and, in any case, is more conveniently and more effectively handled by simulations. The second approach just mentioned, while being more illuminating than the first, also leaves much to be desired. For example, a set of simulation runs might be made using a block of investment equations in which prices and wages are treated as exogenous. Such a simulation might be misleading precisely because the effects of the policy on prices and wages are ignored.

In the models we have examined, we have paid greater attention to those which we believe to have well-defined, coherent structures, and those in which the structure plays a central role. On the whole, we have disregarded reduced-form models in this section. Of course, making use of various structural models does not in itself imply approval of all of their features. Indeed we turn below to a critical survey of the literature we have used. Before doing this, we remind the reader of the view expressed in the opening paragraphs of this paper. Namely, that economy-wide econometric models which are concerned to evaluate the influence of the monetary sector on real economic activity are inevitably biased toward a Keynesian viewpoint. Because of this, we now turn to an examination of the alternative ways in which various econometricians have attempted to formulate the interdependence between real and monetary variables. In doing so, we shall focus largely on the latest available version of the FRB–MIT model. We do this for two reasons. First, the work on this model was undertaken with the specific intention of specifying fully the different channels of monetary policy within the framework of a large econometric model, a task which has been only partly attempted in earlier models. Second, the FRB–MIT model, in spite of its demerits, attempts to deal with this task in a more comprehensive fashion than hitherto. It facilitates, therefore, an understanding of other models in so far as these share some of its features.

The three main channels represented in the FRB–MIT model (see [31]) are:

(i) the cost of capital which affects investment and the consumption of durables;

(ii) rates of return on bonds, which affect the wealth position of households;

(iii) credit rationing, which mainly affects the housing market.

The cost of capital

The idea that financial variables affect investment expenditures by changing the price of capital goods is based on the work of Jorgenson.[1]

---

[1] Of course, the approach used by Jorgenson has been called into question in the paper by Brechling in this volume.

Jorgenson has argued that since the producing firms own their capital stock, they must charge to themselves an accounting price for the services of their own capital stock. Call this the implicit rental price of the services of the capital stock. Several factors determine the implicit rental price of equipment. These include the tax structure, an appropriate rate of interest, and expected capital gains. A firm with a neo-classical production function which attempts to maximize its net worth will equate the marginal product of capital to the cost of capital. The equilibrium stock of capital in this case can be shown to be a function of output and the rental price of capital. The nature of the functional relationship depends on the form of the production function. While this explains the manner in which financial factors influence *desired* capital stock through the cost of capital, it does not tell us with what speed *actual* investment responds to changes in the desired stock of capital. Nor does the theory say whether the speed of response to changes in output is faster or slower than the response of actual investment to changes in the cost of capital. Here econometric practice cannot really be divorced from economic theory.

Following Eisner and Nadiri [36] and Bischoff [12], the FRB–MIT model assumes that the 'putty–clay' hypothesis applies, i.e. new capital can be moulded into any shape (putty) but, once installed, it is not malleable (clay). This implies that changes in the real rental price, leading to a change in the equilibrium stock of capital, would be affected to a large extent only as the older capital wears out. In the case of increases in output, the additional capital would be desired without a long lag. It is desirable, therefore, to specify an investment function in which the distributed lag response to output is different from that to the rental price of capital. The FRB–MIT model employs a flexible Almon distributed lag model [1, 2] to embody the putty–clay hypothesis (see our remarks on the Almon technique in Section V).

The concept of the cost of capital is also used to explain investment in structures, although this variable is constructed somewhat differently in this case. But once again the industrial bond rate and the dividend–price ratio appear as determinants of the rental price of structures.

The cost of capital variable enters the determination of residential construction in an important way. Most U.S. econometric models give considerable weight to the financial determinants of residential construction by introducing the differential between the long-term and short-term interest rate in the demand for residential construction. The important point here is that the financial variables enter as determinants of the supply of funds to the housing market as well as in the function for housing starts. The demand side is dealt with in the FRB–MIT model by making the equilibrium stock of houses dependent on the implicit rental price of housing which, in turn, is determined by the mortgage rate and the corporate bond rate. Finally, housing starts themselves depend, through a distributed lag model, on the ratio of asset prices to housing construction costs and on credit rationing. Credit rationing is an important financial phenomenon which also affects investment; this is explained below.

It is worth noting that the purchase of consumer durables by households is in the nature of investment, since the acquisition of such a stock gives rise to a stream of services. Therefore, the effect of changes in the financial variables on the implicit rental price of the services of consumer durables may be included as an additional channel through which the effects of monetary policy are transmitted.

Credit rationing

The cost-of-capital argument outlined above could be regarded as a more detailed description of those considerations which are usually present, in varying degrees, in the expenditure functions of most econometric models. The same is not, however, true of the credit-rationing channel.

If the interest rate on commercial loans were such that the market is always cleared, then credit rationing would not exist. If, however, interest rates adjust only partly or sluggishly to changes in demand conditions, various non-price devices may be used to deal with potential borrowers. *A priori* reasoning would suggest that variations in the non-price terms might affect the expenditure plans of at least certain classes of borrowers. The FRB–MIT model is one of the few that explicitly introduces this channel of influence. Even in this case, the emphasis is on the way in which credit rationing affects new mortgage loans made by savings institutions. In the U.S., the flow of deposits to savings institutions is volatile. Moreover, government-regulated mortgage rates fail to adjust sufficiently quickly to clear the market. The combination of these factors ensures that credit rationing is an important determinant of new mortgages and, through this, of residential investment.

Credit rationing may be an important determinant of other forms of expenditure, in addition to residential investment. Unfortunately, because it is a disequilibrium phenomenon, it is not a straightforward concept to identify and measure, and this has perhaps deterred model-builders from including the concept explicitly in their models. Credit rationing does not appear to have been introduced in all of the models discussed here. In the case of the housing market in the FRB–MIT model, it is measured by the ratio of actual deposit flows of savings institutions to the deposit flows that might have been expected, the latter being measured by the average over the previous three years, adjusted for growth. Evidently various other indicators of credit rationing have been tested, without success, in the following sectors: the commercial loan market, investment in plant and equipment, and inventory investment: 'Further work on representing and testing for [credit] rationing effects might prove fruitful' [31].

The wealth effect

If households are assumed to hold bonds as well as other assets in their portfolios, variations in the value of both of these, brought about by changes in financial factors, will affect the net worth of households. Theories of consumption of the permanent-income or expected-income type would then suggest that changes in net worth will affect consumption. If such an influence is at all significant, then household consumption would be expected to vary in response to stock market fluctuations.

Although this influence has been specifically incorporated into the FBR–MIT model, it has been rather neglected in other econometric models. Indeed, very little evidence is available on the significance of the wealth effect on aggregate consumption behaviour in large-scale models.

Financial sectors of some econometric models

Econometric models, like biological organisms, develop, grow, and change their structures: they evolve. It can therefore be misleading to take a particular version of a model and subject it to critical appraisal, for what is criticized now may already be in the mind of the model-builder for incorporation into a new version. Nevertheless, a critical appraisal is called for, because we need a framework for discussing and interpreting the results obtained.

The models we have chosen for specific comment are listed below and Tables IV.1 and IV.2 summarize various features of these:

1. The Wharton Econometric Forecasting Unit Model (W–EFU) as described in Evans and Klein [41].

Tabular Summary of Eleven Quarterly Econometric Models of the United States

| | Complete Model — Estimation | | No. of eqns. | Financial Model | | | | | | | | | |
| | | | | No. of equations[a] | | | No. of endogenous variables[b] | | | No. of financial Endogenous: | | Exogenous variables |
	Period	Method[c]		B	I	T	S	R	IR	Assets[d]	Sectors[e]	
W-EFU	1948-64	OLS, 2SLS	76	2	0	2	0	0	2	0	0	2
S-M-8[f]	1950-64	OLS, 2SLS	61	15	5	20	13	0	7	6	6	7
A-G	1948-60	LI, 2SLS	50	17	12	29	22	3	4	6	2	9
OB	1948-60	OLS	359	15	4	19	15	0	4	6	6	9
CB	1948-60	OLS	177	5	3	8	5	0	3	3	2	8
Liu	1947-59	2SLS	34	6	0	6	3	0	3	3	2	3
Tgn	1953-64	2SLS, OLS	17	8	3	11	5	3	3	5	2	1
FRB-MIT:D-7			102	21	10	31	18	3	10	11	6	7
FRB-MIT:J-8	-1965	OLS	75	11	1	12	5	0	7	4	2	7
FRB-MIT:D-8			111	17	2	19	8	0	11	7	5	7
FRB-Ch			113	18	3	21	10	0	11	7	5	8

[a] B = Behavioural, I = Identities, T = Total.

[b] S = Stocks, R = Ratios, IR = Interest rates.

[c] OLS = Ordinary Least Squares; 2SLS = Two-Stage Least Squares; LI = Limited Information Maximum-likelihood.

[d] Endogenous assets classified as Currency and Reserves (C & R); Demand Deposits (DD); Time Deposits (TD); TD, Passbook; TD, Nonpassbook; Mutual Savings TD (MTD); Savings and Loan Savings (SLS); Life Insurance Savings (LIS); SLS + LIS; Commercial Loans (CL); Non-commercial loans and Investments (NCL + I); Loans and Private Investment (L + PI); Common Stock (CS); Mortgages (M); Government Debt (GD); Household Liquid Assets (HLA).

[e] Sectors having endogenous financial assets and liabilities, classified as Commercial Banks; Member Banks; Mutual Savings Banks; Savings and Loan Assocns.; Life Insurance; Savings and Loan plus Life Insurance; Non-bank Financial; Household; Non-financial Business; Non-bank Private.

[f] An annual model is described in Suits [101], but he also discusses a quarterly model.

2. The Evans Model (Evans), [39].
3. Suits's Michigan Model, 1968 version (S–M–8), [101].
4. The Ando–Goldfeld Model (A–G), [8].
5. The Original Brookings Model (OB), [29].
6. The Condensed Brookings Model (CB), [30] and [31].
7. The Liu Model (Liu), [80].
8. The Teigen Model (Tgn), [103].
9. The FRB–MIT Model, December 1967 version (FRB–MIT: D–7), [93].
10. The FRB–MIT Model, January 1968 version (FRB–MIT: J–8), [32].
11. The FRB–MIT Model, December 1968 version (FRB–MIT: D–8), [33].
12. The FRB–Chicago Model (FRB–Ch), [67].

Broadly speaking, the models fall into one of two categories: those in which the financial sector plays no essential part and/or is small relative to the whole model; and those in which the financial sector is large and detailed and dominates the whole structure, the real sector being comparatively small. We consider the first group first.

W–EFU is a quarterly model with a very small financial sector: only 2 of its 76 endogenous variables are financial, namely the (long-term) corporation bond rate and the (short-term) commercial paper rate. The commercial paper rate is determined by exogenous variables and the corporate bond rate is determined by its own lagged rate and the commercial paper rate. Thus these two variables, while correctly termed endogenous, are essentially exogenous to the rest of the system. In addition, there are two exogenous financial variables: the free reserve ratio and the discount rate.

The Evans model is similar to though smaller than W–EFU: it contains 50 endogenous variables, 31 stochastic equations, and 19 identities. As in W–EFU, the long-term rate on corporate bonds and the short-term rate on prime commercial paper of 4–6 months are both endogenous. The corporate bond rate is determined by its own lagged rate and the lagged short rate. The short rate is determined by its own lagged rate and the discount rate, which is one of three exogenous financial variables. Thus again the two interest rates are essentially exogenous to the rest of the system. The other two exogenous variables are the broadly defined money stock (including time deposits) and the interest on government debt. The last-mentioned variable merely appears in the definition of personal

TABLE IV.2

Endogenous Financial Variables and Exogenous Monetary Policy
Variables in Ten Quarterly Econometric Models of the United States

Model	Endogenous financial variables	Exogenous monetary policy variables
W–EFU	1. r(commercial paper) 2. r(corporation bonds)	1. Free reserve ratio 2. Discount rate
A–G	1. r(3-month TB) 2. r(10-year GB) 3. r(C & IL) cb 4. r(TD)cb 5. C 6, 7, 8. DD 9, 10, 11. TD 12, 13, 14. C & IL 15. Loan-deposit ratio 16, 17. Excess reserves 18, 19. Borrowing from FRB 20, 21. Holdings, SGS 22, 23. Holdings, LGS 24, 25. Holdings, MS 26. RR 27. Potential DD 28, 29. Change RRR	1, 2, 3. RRR for DD 4. Change supply MS 5. Change supply LGS 6. FR rediscount rate 7. Max. r(TD) 8. Change supply SGS 9. Unborrowed reserves & C
OB	1. C 2. Borrowed reserves 3. Excess reserves 4. RR 5. DD 6. r(TD) 7. TD 8. SLS + LIS 9, 10, 11, 12. Debt 13. r(TB) 14. r(T bond) 15, 16, 17, 18. GS 19. r(government debt)	1. C & unborrowed reserves 2. RRR for DD 3. RRR for TD 4. Discount rate 5. Max. r(TD) 6. FHLB loans 7. Treasury (DD) 8, 9. U.S. debt maturity structure
CB	1. Free reserves 2. RR 3. DD 4. r(TD) 5. TD 6. r(TB) 7. r(T bond) 8. Wealth	1. Unborrowed reserves 2, 3, 4, 5. as in OB 6. Treasury (DD) 7, 8. U.S. debt maturity structure
Liu	1. Business holdings: C, DD, and TD 2. Household holdings: C and DD	1. Discount rate 2. Ratio excess reserves to RR

TABLE IV.2—*continued*

Model	Endogenous financial variables	Exogenous monetary policy variables
Liu—*continued*	3. Household holdings: TD and Savings 4. r(prime commercial paper) 5. r(Moody's corporate bond yield) 6. Average r(TD + Savings)	3. Household holdings: U.S. Savings bonds
Tgn	1. DD, cb 2. TD, cb 3. C 4. C & IL of cb 5. r(TB) 6. r(LGS) 7. Unborrowed reserves, mb 8. Discount rate	1. RRR
FRB–MIT: D–7	1. C 2. Free reserves 3. Unborrowed reserves 4, 5. DD 6. Ratio DD to DD(mb) 7, 8. r(TD) 9, 10. TD 11. r(CD) 12, 13, 14. TD(mb) 15. MTD 16. r(MTD) 17. SLS 18. r(SLS) 19. LIS 20. r(CL) 21. r(commercial paper) 22. r(corp. bonds) 23, 24. CL 25. L + I(cb) 26. NCL + I(mb) 27. Ratio CL to CL(mb) 28. Ratio L + I(cb) to L + I(mb) 29. r(M) 30. M(cb) 31. r(TB)	1. C + unborrowed reserves 2. RRR(DD) 3. RRR(TD) 4. Discount rate 5. Max. r(TD) 6. Treasury (DD) 7. Treasury (TD)
FRB–MIT: J–8	1. C 2. Free reserves 3. DD 4. r(TD) 5. TD	1. Unborrowed reserves 2. RRR (DD) 3. RRR (TD) 4. Released reserves 5. Discount rate

TABLE IV.2—*continued*

Model	Endogenous financial variables	Exogenous monetary policy variables
FRB–MIT: J–8— *continued*	6. r(CL) 7. r(commercial paper) 8. r(corp. bonds) 9. CL 10. r(CS) 11. r(M) 12. r(TB)	6. Max. r(TD) 7. Treasury (DD)
FRB–MIT: D–8	1–12. as in FRB–MIT: J–8 13. r(MTD) 14. MTD 15. SLS 16. r(SLS) 17. r(industrial bonds) 18. Household holdings, CS 19. r(state and local)	As for FRB–MIT: J–8
FRB–Ch	1. C 2. Borrowed reserves 3. Excess reserves 4. Unborrowed reserves via OMO 5–21. Same as 3–19 of FRB–MIT: D–8	1. Total reserves 2. RRR(DD) 3. RRR(TD) 4. Released reserves 5. Released unborrowed reserves 6. Discount rate 7. Max. r(TD) 8. Treasury (DD)

C	= Currency	LGS	= Long-term government securities
C & IL	= Commercial and industrial loans	mb	= Member banks
cb	= Commercial banks	MS	= Municipal securities
CD	= Certificate of Deposit	OMO	= Open market operations
FHLB	= Federal Housing and Loan Board	r	= Rate on
FR	= Federal Reserve	RR	= Required reserves
FRB	= Federal Reserve Banks	RRR	= Required reserve ratio
GB	= Government bonds	SGS	= Short-term government securities
GS	= Government securities	TB	= Treasury bills
L + I	= Loans and investments	T bond	= Treasury bond

Other notation used in Table IV.2 is defined in the notes to Table IV.1.

income which then explains personal income taxes. Of course, other components of personal income are endogenous.

There is no cost of capital variable in any of the several investment functions, but the long-term interest rate enters the plant and

equipment investment function with a five-quarter lag. The investment function for residential construction contains as explanatory
variables the difference between the long- and the short-rate, lagged
three-quarters, and the lagged rate of change in the broadly defined
money stock. A money supply variable lagged two-quarters also
enters the demand for automobiles.

The Evans model contains no government debt variables other
than interest on government debt, mentioned above, or reserve
requirement ratio variables. Consequently the model is not capable
of simulating the effects of changes in either of these. But the discount
rate and the stock of money (though not necessarily with the same
definition as used in the model) would be regarded by many as most
important monetary instruments. Since both appear exogenously
with lags, it is certainly possible to simulate the model for the effects
of changes in each of them.

A change in the short-term interest rate brought about by a change
in the (exogenous) discount rate, will lead to a change in the long-
rate with a lag. The principle impact of this change would be on
plant and equipment investment. As far as residential construction is
concerned, the model implies that the long-run expenditure effects
of such a change are negligible because, in the long run, the long rate
will adjust to the short rate. The short-term effects, however, are
quite substantial.

W–EFU and Evans are, of course, models in the tradition of
those by Tinbergen [105], and Klein and Goldberger [77]. Indeed
Evans [39], for example, not only recognizes this explicitly but also
notes similarities of his model with OB and Liu, described below,
even though these models—especially OB—have more extensive
financial sectors. The Office of Business Economics (OBE) model
[79], though not referred to below, is also similar, at least in the
sense that it does not contain a well-developed financial sector: it has
4 financial equations (the short rate on commercial paper, the
corporate bond rate, a mortgage rate, and household liquid assets)
and two exogenous monetary policy variables (the excess reserve
ratio and the discount rate). S–M–8 is another model which shares a
similar philosophy to that of Evans and W–EFU, although it might
appear, at first sight, to have a much more comprehensive financial
sector. S–M–8, however, sidesteps a great deal of the monetary
mechanism by regarding the Treasury bill rate as an exogenous
monetary policy variable. This eliminates from the model the impact
of changes in required reserves against demand deposits, variations in

open-market operations, and changes at the discount window. Seven of the 20 financial equations are concerned with mortgages and several sectors are incompletely represented: e.g. mutual savings banks, and savings and loan associations.

A–G provides a contrast to W–EFU and Evans. The A–G model has a total of 29 behavioural equations out of which 12 are bank-behaviour equations, 14 are demand functions for financial assets, and 3 are structure-of-interest-rates equations (see Tables IV.1 and IV.2). Quite clearly A–G and models similar to it explain the inter-action between the financial and non-financial sectors much better than models like W–EFU, Evans, and the OBE model. For example, the demands for currency, for time deposits and demand deposits are all formulated as functions, *inter alia*, of the level of income; changes in the demand for commercial loans are partly determined by inventory investment. In turn, components of income are partly de-termined by financial factors. For example, real durable consumption expenditures depend partly on demand deposits plus currency. The theoretical case for specifying and estimating a model which includes a substantial financial sector which interacts with the real sector is quite sound. This is well recognized and is illustrated in Tables IV.1 and IV.2.

The 1965 version of the Brookings model (OB) has 9 exogenous financial variables. The model endogenizes long-term and short-term interest rates, and the stock of money is determined within the model by appropriate supply and demand functions. These features of OB are also shared, in varying degrees, by Liu, Tgn, and CB. The FRB–MIT models have financial sectors which are as well developed, if not better. There is no point in expanding on this point, since the Tables list the endogenous and exogenous variables of the financial sectors of these models.

In OB, financial factors play an important role in determining investment in plant and equipment, trade inventories and con-sumption. But there is much greater emphasis on the cost of capital channel of influence than on the credit rationing or wealth effects. For example, variables like expected capital gain do not enter the consumption functions. This comment applies even more to CB, which is used for policy simulation (see below) and in which various equations in OB are replaced by simpler versions. In Tgn and Liu, the rate of interest in the investment expenditure functions is the main source of interaction between the real and financial parts of the model.

Comments on the structures

It is convenient to classify our comments on the structures of the models described into those relating to economic structure and those which are concerned with econometric issues. We begin with the former.

The main comments concerning economic specification fall under four headings:

    (a) The choice of exogenous policy variable(s)
    (b) Sector balance sheets
    (c) The government budget restraint
    (d) Interactions between the financial and the price–wage sectors.

Those who construct financial models do not always agree on the variables which correspond most nearly to those that the monetary authorities can control. Consider, for example, the treatment of the variable to represent open-market operations. In A–G, OB, and FRB–MIT:D–7, the variable selected is currency plus unborrowed reserves, i.e. the stock of unborrowed, high-powered money. In CB, FRB–MIT:J–8, and FRB–MIT:D–8, it is somewhat broader: unborrowed reserves plus borrowed reserves. In Tgn, the exogenous instrument is the required reserve ratio, while unborrowed reserves of member banks plus currency outside banks is used to represent System open-market operations, which is endogenous. Another view, which none of the models described uses, is that the Federal Reserve might be undertaking open-market operations so as to offset any variation in member bank borrowing, i.e. so that the total stock of high-powered money, not the unborrowed stock, is exogenous. It is difficult to justify either the broader or the narrower definition given above, because the non-bank private sector can exchange currency for deposits at will, and this will affect reserves but leave unchanged currency plus reserves. While it is certainly true that there are a number of plausible variables to represent open-market operations, the use of slightly different definitions will lead, in general, to different results when the models are used for policy analysis.

It is of course possible to design a financial sub-model at various levels of sector detail. Nevertheless, a complete specification evidently requires at least three sectors: a government sector (to include the Federal Reserve System), a banking sector, and a non-bank-private sector. Whatever the number of sectors, there will be some inter-sectoral dependence represented by a set of balance sheets each showing, as assets, the claims of one sector on each of the others and, as liabilities, the claims of the others on the one. To be complete balance sheets, physical assets should be included as a separate item (sector), whereupon the balancing items will be each sector's net worth. If inter-sectoral flows are considered in this way and the model seeks to explain ex-post observations, because the balance sheets must balance, the portfolio behavioural equations must be functionally dependent. If, for example, the balancing item net worth is taken as given, the implication of this functional dependence is that at least one of each sector's asset-demand or liability-supply equations must depend on the same sector's net worth. Moreover, functional dependence also requires that if a particular explanatory variable appears in one asset-demand or one liability-supply equation of a sector, the same variable must also appear in at least a second equation for the same sector, for otherwise the balance sheet will not balance. These two requirements should hold, in principle, for every sector where behaviour is considered as endogenous.

A similar condition also applies to inter-sectoral claims, for the balance sheet of any one sector is not independent of all of the others. If all but one are satisfied, the remaining one must be as well.

To complete the picture, a fully specified financial sub-model should also contain, at least by implication, total market demand and supply equations relating, *inter alia*, quantities and yields for each asset considered as endogenous. For a fuller explanation see [23].

None of the models outlined above is complete in the sense just described. To be sure, each of the models, save for W–EFU and Evans, has a commercial bank sector and a non-bank private sector. There are other sector breakdowns that may be determined from Tables IV.1 and IV.2, including, in some, a household sector: two have five sectors and three have six sectors. Similarly, there are various breakdowns of financial assets. But only Tgn has an endogenous government sector (open-market operations and the discount rate are endogenous), and none has enough stock variables fully to represent the complete balance sheet of each sector that it sets out to include. In this sense, the models are not complete. Hence it is not possible to tell whether or not they are properly specified, since no check can be carried out on the various interrelations already described.

Probably a more important omission in the models discussed relates indirectly to the government budget restraint. There are good prior grounds for arguing that the amount and the maturity structure of Federal debt will play an important role in determining the term structure of interest rates. Consequently, we would expect the total stock of privately held U.S. government securities, save for that part of it which is institutionally prescribed, to appear as a policy variable. Evidently ([22, 23]), it *must* appear if the model is to be consistent with the government budget restraint. But neither the total stock of privately held U.S. government securities nor the budget restraint itself appears in any of the models cited. It is, however, the case that OB and FRB–MIT:D–8 have among their policy variables ratios that allow for the distribution of privately held government debt among short, medium, and long maturities, which, to be sure, affects the term structure of interest rates. Attempts have been made to defend recent versions of the MIT–FRB model against this criticism but, according to [23], the claim that the government budget restraint is implicit in these models is unwarranted. It has also been demonstrated ([22]) that an implication of this mis-specification is that the fiscal policy multiplier will be calculated incorrectly.

A major weakness of the leading econometric models discussed in this section is the specification of the price–wage equations: either these equations are relatively poorly specified or, in certain cases— especially in respect of the simulations, prices and wages are taken as given. It is sometimes argued that this weakness combined with other features of the models makes them unreliable instruments for measuring the effectiveness of monetary policy. The 'other features' the critics appear to have in mind are (i) the heavy emphasis on the cost of capital variable as a channel of influence, with the cost of capital being determined by a small set of market interest rates, and (ii) the inclusion of nominal rather than real rates of interest. Although the different strands of criticism are obviously related, it is convenient to deal with them separately.

The first criticism about the inadequate way in which the models take account of the interaction between monetary policy and price changes, on one hand, and price changes and spending decisions on the other, is closely related to the Friedman and Meiselman [49] discussion of the role of implicit yields in spending decisions. It is argued that individuals hold a variety of assets, including money, and corresponding to each asset there is an implicit yield. If, for example, by open-market operations the central authorities change the volume of cash balances held by individuals, then individuals will change the composition of their portfolios. If such changes take the form of increases in the values of those assets whose supply is fixed in the short run, the prices of these assets obviously rise, thus lowering their yields. Changes in the relative prices of assets will influence spending decisions, which in turn will affect the structure of relative prices in general. In such a framework there is a close interrelationship between price changes, changes in implicit yields, and expenditure decisions. To the extent that econometric models do not have well-specified price–wage equations and typically do not include implicit yields of assets, they cannot (it is argued) capture the full extent of the impact of monetary policies.

The above outline is of course based on the presumption that a logically consistent, dynamic model of the decision processes of individuals and their impact on relative prices exists. There is disagreement as to whether such a model has ever been put forward.

Another feature of econometric models, which has been a target of the Chicago school, is their use of nominal rather than real interest rates. The classical theory of interest rates is a theory of the real interest rate. The real rate of interest is defined as the nominal rate minus the rate of change in the price level, and it equals the pure rate of time preference. It equals the nominal rate only if the rate of change in prices is zero. According to theories of the real interest rate, interest is the pure yield of capital and 'a reward for abstaining from present consumption'. But the pure yield of capital is essentially a matter of long-run factors, such as productivity and thrift. In contrast, most econometric models treat the interest rate as a *monetary* phenomenon. Concerned as they usually are with the short run, they take the interest rate as determined in the money market. Such a view is, of course, in sharp contrast to a quantity theory view which, in one way or another, is forced to emphasize the 'realness' of the interest rate. According to this view, the interest rate relevant to many expenditure decisions is not the nominal rate but the real rate. This is because the nominal rate of interest will change with changes in the price level or, more correctly, with changes in expected prices. Let the equation $r = n - \dot{p}$ denote the proposition that the real rate is the difference between the nominal rate and the expected percentage change in the price level. Evidently, if expected price changes affect the demand for and supply of bonds and equities, they will influence the nominal rates but may still leave unchanged the real rate of interest. Now, if major investment decisions depend on actual or anticipated levels of the real rather than nominal rates of return, a model which relies on nominal rates only may perform very differently in a period of inflation from the one which uses real rates.

This is one point made by some quantity theorists. Note that a model which relies on the expected real rate variable will need equations which explain the way in which price expectations are generated. If the expected rate depends on current and past observed changes, then in the interests of completeness it will be necessary to include price–wage equations in the model. In this framework, therefore, properly specified price–wage equations are essential for high-lighting the role of monetary variables. With the exception of Liu, the models discussed here do not appear to have used real rates to any great extent.

We now turn to some general econometric comments on large-scale models, the purpose being to focus attention on major difficulties and to sound yet another note of caution before introducing simulation results. There are two broad areas on which we shall comment: first, the problems and difficulties relating to size and aggregation and, second, the meaning and the implications of 'good performance'.

In general, greater disaggregation in an econometric model does not necessarily yield more reliable information concerning the interaction of economic variables. With greater disaggregation comes a greater likelihood of mis-specification and greater difficulty in detecting it. Moreover, we would normally expect that the more disaggregated a model, the greater the difficulties in obtaining appropriate economic statistics. In so far as these must be constructed, we should expect a decrease in the reliability of the data on which estimates of the model are to be based. For this and other reasons, we might also anticipate increasing complexity in residual time-dependence, both within and between equations, especially in quarterly models; and with a large equation system such dependence is not only difficult to detect, it is also correspondingly problematic to take into account in estimation procedures. Finally, even without residual problems, greater disaggregation brings with it increased difficulties in systems estimation. It is perhaps worth noting here that small sector models typically increase the feasibility of detailed specification and estimation, and while the results may be more restricted, they are usually more precise.

If fairly complicated and detailed questions are asked of econometric models, it seems unlikely that small, simple models will yield answers to them, even though such models may have merit for some alternative purpose. For this reason we are sceptical of claims made on behalf of the four-equation Federal Reserve Bank of St. Louis reduced-form model [4] which has the rate of change of money stock as a major determinant of income. On the other hand, large econometric models pose major estimation and conceptual problems. Typically, they violate almost every tenet of econometric theory, and the methods used to work with them often do not have a complete formal justification. Consider the following examples: equations for inclusion in a model are usually selected on a single-equation basis, and sometimes on a block basis. While they may have satisfactory properties considered individually, they may not yield a model which shares such properties. Two investigators who provide two stable distributed lag equations which they put together, do not necessarily construct a stable two-equation system. Consider also a system of equations, some of which are well-specified and others not. If simulation and prediction using this system do not yield satisfactory results for a set of variables, it is by no means easy to identify what needs changing. The system may be amended on the basis of hunch or suspicion, but this may not always work. In a nutshell then, a system is much more than the sum of its parts, and assurance that the financial sector is well-specified does not necessarily increase confidence in the conclusions arrived at on the basis of systems results.

Every econometric model discussed here has some equations or sectors with which the model-builders themselves are not happy. For example, as indicated above, even CB and FRB–MIT:D–8 appear to have unsatisfactory price–wage equations.

If any of the present models were to be judged on the basis of their ability to track the economy over the sample period to which they refer by dynamic simulations and/or forecasts, they would all appear to fit quite well. With regard to forecasting, it is worth noting, in passing, that W–EFU and S–M–8 have had particularly good forecasting records, even though they have very small financial sectors. For the Federal Reserve Bank of St. Louis model [4], the authors have claimed a forecasting record for GNP no worse than that of W–EFU.

Two points are worth making in this context. First, it is difficult to assess the performance of econometric models in several different dimensions, since there are no standard measures of model performance. Model-building may be tackled in the spirit of a statistical inquiry. Model A might be judged to be superior to Model B, because its statistical properties are in some acceptable sense more desirable (even if only asymptotically) than those of Model B. But even this is not an unambiguous statement, since the weight attached to different statistical properties must be determined by the loss function which the users of the model have in mind. Typically, the users do not have an explicit loss function and they themselves would be at a loss in choosing between models of different size which are designed for different purposes. The second point is that there may well be a certain amount of independence between the various properties of the model. Desirable statistical properties, a good fit, a high level of disaggregation, etc. need not imply either a good forecasting performance or reliable simulation results. Conversely, very good forecasts (in the mean-square-error sense) of a limited number of variables may be made from models which shed no light on particular hypotheses which are interesting and important. A good forecasting record, while reassuring, is not in itself a particularly strong recommendation for appraising a model's policy simulations.

Policy simulations

Some of the models described above have been used for policy analysis of the following measures:

(1) A change in the discount rate.
(2) An increase or a decrease in the reserve base (unborrowed reserves or unborrowed reserves plus currency) brought about by open-market operations. For some models the monetary instrument chosen is the free reserve ratio.
(3) An increase or decrease in the required reserve ratio for demand deposits (RRR on DD) of the Federal Reserve member banks.
(4) A change in the required reserve ratio for time deposits (HRR on TD) of member banks.
(5) A change in the maximum rate of interest on time deposits.
(6) A change in the maturity composition of the Federal debt. For example, an increase by a specified percentage in the 0–5 year proportion of the Federal debt.
(7) A change in Treasury cash balances held at commercial banks.

In addition, a combination of any of the measures (1)–(7) could also be tried.

Obviously, it is not possible to simulate the behaviour of the economy for every one of these measures, simply because not all models contain the necessary exogenous variables. In the references we have consulted, a full set of simulation runs (1)–(7) is not available for any one of the models. A–G and CB report policy simulations for policy measures (1)–(4) above. For W–EFU there are simulation results for (1) and (2) only. For the FRB–MIT models we have simulation results for (2) only.

Even in those cases where similar simulation runs have been attempted, the comparisons between the outcomes are complicated by (a) differences in the choice of initial conditions, (b) differences in the comprehensiveness of results provided, and (c) the differences in the choice of units used. The importance of (a) lies in the non-linear nature of most of the models. The importance of (b) arises from the need to consider the impact of changes in monetary instruments not only on the real variables of the system, but also on other endogenous monetary variables, because the strength of monetary policy is mediated, in part, by the decisions of financial intermediaries. For these reasons the Tables set out below differ in their content.

The methodology of a typical policy simulation with a large non-linear model (i.e. a model with a large number of endogenous variables) is described in [52] and is followed in most of the simulations presented below. An exception seems to be the simulations carried out on A–G. Evidently in this case the period-to-period changes in a particular endogenous variable have been calculated. We should therefore anticipate the A–G simulations to be different in numerical characteristics from those of the other models.

With the exception of A–G, which simulates the behaviour of a linearized version of the model, all the large models report the results of simulation runs based on the original non-linear version. No simulation runs are available for Liu or Tgn or FRB–MIT:D–7.

Change in the money base

One way in which a change in the money supply can be brought about is through an increase in unborrowed reserves plus currency which is achieved by the purchase of government securities in open-market operations. An increase in unborrowed reserves leads to a reduction in the short-term interest rate which is expected to stimulate borrowing and eventually expenditure. Table IV.3 displays simulation results of an *increase* of $1 billion in unborrowed reserves *or* in unborrowed reserves plus currency.

Remembering that the time-paths generated by different models are not entirely comparable, we now look at the extent of agreement on the effects as brought out by different models. An exception is CB, which shows a reduction in GNP in the first quarter, followed by a steady increase up to the sixth quarter. After this, the time-path

TABLE IV.3

Policy Simulations of the Effects of Open-market Operations

Model: FRB–MIT:D–8.
Policy measure: Step increase of $1 billion in unborrowed reserves.
Initial conditions: 1963 (1).

Variable	Quarter							
	1	2	3	4	5	6	7	8
Real GNP (1958 $ bn.)	0·7	2·0	3·6	5·4	7·0	8·3	9·3	10·0
GNP deflator	0·0	0·0	0·1	0·1	0·2	0·3	0·4	0·6
Unemployment (%)	−0·1	−0·2	−0·3	−0·4	−0·5	−0·6	−0·6	−0·6

Model: CB.
Policy measure: Increase of $1 billion in unborrowed reserves.
Initial conditions: 1960 (2).

Variable	Quarter				
	1	2	3	4	5
Real GNP (1954 $ bn.)	−1·5	2·7	2·6	4·5	5·1
Total real investment	0·0	0·7	1·1	1·9	2·2
Total real consumption	−0·5	1·0	1·1	1·9	2·4
Treasury bill rate (%)	−1·48	−0·58	−0·42	−0·42	−0·39
Bond rate	−0·70	−0·11	−0·19	−0·23	−0·26
GNP price deflator	0·2	−0·4	−0·3	−0·5	−0·6
Unemployment (%)	0·0	0·0	−0·1	−0·2	−0·2

Variable	Quarter				
	6	7	8	9	10
Real GNP (1954 $ bn.)	11·6	8·9	8·9	7·9	8·6
Total real investment	5·6	3·2	3·2	3·3	3·2
Total real consumption	4·5	4·2	4·5	4·5	4·8
Treasury bill rate (%)	−0·50	−0·39	−0·40	−0·40	−0·38
Bond rate	−0·33	−0·29	−0·30	−0·31	−0·30
GNP price deflator	−1·2	−0·7	−0·7	−0·6	−0·5
Unemployment (%)	−0·4	−0·5	−0·5	−0·5	−0·5

Model: FRB–MIT:J–8.
Policy measure: Step increase of $1 billion in unborrowed reserves.
Initial conditions: 1963 (1).

Variable	Quarter							
	1	2	3	4	5	6	7	8
Real GNP	0·5	1·0	1·1	2·0	4·0	6·0	7·5	8·0
Real investment	0·0	0·02	0·6	1·0	1·5	2·0	2·5	2·7
Consumption	0·0	0·0	0·5	0·5	1·5	2·25	3·0	4·0
Treasury bill rate	−1·2	−0·6	−0·5	−0·5	−0·45	−0·4	−0·38	−0·35

TABLE IV.3—*continued*

Model: A–G.
Policy measure: Increase of $1 billion unborrowed reserves + currency.
Initial conditions: 1965 (1).

| Variable | Quarter | | | |
	1	2	3	4
GNP (current)	1·911	0·318	0·071	0·356
Investment	0·499	0·481	0·314	0·242
Consumption	0·942	0·113	−0·040	0·094
Treasury bill rate	−0·836	0·295	0·111	0·311
10-year bond rate	−0·305	0·065	0·007	0·081
GNP deflator (1958 = 100)	0·011	0·002	−0·002	−0·002
Employment (millions)	0·128	0·108	0·078	0·074

seems to be a little erratic. The FRB–MIT models show a steady increase until the eleventh quarter (not shown in the Table). The A–G results do not agree with those of any of the above models, as anticipated above.

All models agree that the initial impact on interest rates is to reduce both the Treasury bill rate and the government bond rate. This is followed by an increase above the lowest attained level, but after 8 quarters the level is still below the initial level. These results are not in complete agreement with [17] and [102], which indicate that the rate of interest rises above the initial level after a considerable lag.

Both CB and FRB–MIT:D–8 show consumption and investment increasing slowly at first and more rapidly after 2–3 quarters. Again the path traced out by A–G does not agree with the other results, for the reasons given above.

Of the three models concerned, only FRB–MIT:D–8 shows an appreciable increase in prices during the period of expansion. The results for A–G and CB (that, after an initial rise, prices fall during an expansionary period) do not seem credible.

When the FRB–MIT:D–8 model was simulated for the effects of a *decrease* in reserves, the effects on real GNP were found to be similar to those of an increase with the exception of the sign of the change. But prices were found to change less (sticky prices) and unemployment more.

Change in the discount rate

A change in the discount rate affects the reserve position of the member banks. An increase in the discount rate relative to the short-term interest rate discourages member banks from borrowing at the discount window and may affect short-term interest rates

directly. W–EFU and CB find that a reduction in the discount rate
leads to an increase in real investment, real consumption, real GNP,
and a reduction in unemployment. Once again, however, CB finds
falling prices (see Table IV.4).

One interesting result found in Table IV.4 is that after 20 quarters
or so relaxation in monetary policy has perverse results (cf. also [86]).
The Table shows that unemployment rises. In addition Evans [40]
has argued *that the rise in prices is much greater* than under fiscal
stabilization policy. Evans explains this surprising result by arguing
that the supply schedules for fixed investment and of residential
construction are inelastic in the short run. A rapid increase in
expenditure in these areas leads to a rapid bidding-up of the prices,
rather than an increase in output. This leads him to conclude that 'a
change in monetary policy that stimulates the economy has only
rapid growth to recommend it; there is a perverse long-run effect on
unemployment, a rapid price increase, and the largest decrease in the
balance of payments' [40, pp. 578–9].

Finally, the last part of Table IV.4 sets out the effects of an
increase in the discount rate by one percentage point. The results
appear to be rather similar (with the exception of the sign) to those
of a reduction in the discount rate.

Although the qualitative effects of an increase in unborrowed
reserves are similar to those of a reduction in the discount rate, there
are certain differences in their transmission mechanism. For the

TABLE IV.4

Policy Simulations of the Effects of Changes in the Discount Rate

Model: W–EFU.
Policy measure: Decrease in the discount rate by 1 percentage point.
Initial conditions: 1963 (1).

Variable	Quarter 1	2	3	4	5
Real GNP (1958 $ bn.)	0·0	0·0	0·36	3·32	4·35
Real investment	0·0	0·0	0·18	1·89	2·49
Prices (consumer)	0·0	0·0	0·0	0·02	0·06
Unemployment (%)	0·0	0·0	−0·02	−0·32	−0·39

Variable	Quarter 6	7	8	20	40
Real GNP (1958 $ bn.)	4·65	4·77	4·66	3·23	4·27
Real investment	2·94	3·20	3·36	2·65	2·60
Prices (consumer)	0·10	0·13	0·17	0·30	0·43
Unemployment (%)	−0·37	−0·32	−0·27	0·12	0·15

TABLE IV.4—*continued*

Model: CB.
Policy measure: Decrease in discount rate by 1 percentage point.
Initial conditions: 1960 (2).

Variable	1	2	3	Quarter 4	5	6	7	8
Real GNP	−0·60	0·70	1·5	2·9	4·0	7·5	8·5	9·2
Real investment	0·00	0·30	0·70	1·1	1·7	3·5	3·6	3·6
Consumption	−0·20	0·30	0·60	1·2	1·7	3·0	3·7	4·3
Treasury bill rate (per cent)	−0·62	−0·63	−0·61	−0·56	−0·53	−0·56	−0·53	−0·52
10-year bond rate	−0·29	−0·23	−0·23	−0·24	−0·26	−0·31	−0·33	−0·34
GNP price deflator (1954 = 100)	0·1	−0·1	−0·2	−0·4	−0·5	−0·8	−0·8	−0·8
Unemployment %)	0·1	0·0	0·0	−0·1	−0·2	−0·3	−0·4	−0·5

Model: A–G.
Policy measure: Increase in discount rate of 1 percentage point.
Initial conditions: 1965 (1).

Variable	1	Quarter 2	3	4
GNP (current)	0·267	−0·036	−0·183	−0·291
Investment	0·081	−0·013	−0·101	−0·168
Consumption	0·083	0·001	−0·040	−0·102
Treasury bill rate	0·489	−0·090	−0·103	−0·083
10-year bond rate	0·006	−0·032	−0·041	−0·040
GNP deflator (1958 = 100)	0·001	0·001	0·001	0·001
Employment (%)	0·018	0·010	−0·006	−0·023

TABLE IV.5

Policy Simulations of Changes in the Reserve Requirement Ratio on Time Deposits and Demand Deposits

Model: CB.
Policy measure: Reduction in reserve requirement ratio on time deposits of 1 percentage point.
Initial conditions: 1960 (2).

Variable	1	2	3	Quarter 4	5	6	7	8
Real GNP	−0·8	1·4	1·5	2·6	3·1	6·8	5·7	5·9
Real investment	0·0	0·4	0·7	1·0	1·4	3·3	2·1	2·2
Consumption	−0·3	0·5	0·6	1·1	1·4	2·7	2·6	2·9
Bill rate	−0·82	−0·38	−0·38	−0·30	−0·28	−0·36	−0·32	−0·32
Bond rate	−0·39	−0·09	−0·13	−0·15	−0·17	−0·22	−0·21	−0·22
Implicit GNP deflator	0·1	−0·2	−0·2	−0·3	−0·4	−0·7	−0·5	−0·5
Unemployment (%)	0·1	0·0	0·0	−0·1	−0·2	−0·3	−0·3	−0·3

TABLE IV.5—*continued*

Policy measure: Reduction in reserve requirement ratio on demand deposits of 1 percentage point.

Variable	1	2	3	Quarter 4	5	6	7	8
Real GNP	−1·4	2·5	2·5	4·4	4·9	11·1	8·8	8·9
Real investment	0·0	0·7	1·1	1·8	2·2	5·4	3·2	3·3
Consumption	−0·5	0·9	1·1	1·8	2·3	4·3	4·1	4·5
Bill rate	−1·39	−0·58	−0·49	−0·42	−0·41	−0·52	−0·41	−0·41
Bond rate	−0·66	−0·12	−0·19	−0·22	−0·26	−0·34	−0·29	−0·31
Implicit GNP deflator	0·2	0·0	−0·3	−0·5	−0·6	−1·2	−0·7	−0·7
Unemployment (%)	0·0	0·0	−0·1	−0·2	−0·2	−0·4	−0·5	−0·5

Model: A–G.
Policy measure: Increase in reserve requirement ratio on demand deposits of 1 percentage point.
Initial conditions: 1965 (1).

Variable	1	Quarter 2	3	4
GNP	−2·136	−0·356	−0·088	−0·418
Investment	−0·068	−0·252	−0·277	−0·365
Consumption	−0·157	−0·126	−0·002	−0·100
Treasury bill rate	0·978	−0·338	−0·132	−0·357
10-year bond rate	0·357	−0·074	−0·009	−0·092
GNP deflator	−0·012	−0·002	−0·088	−0·084
Employment (millions)	−0·143	−0·121	−0·088	−0·084

latter case the impact effect on the bill rate and the bond rate is smaller, as is the speed of decline in these rates. The effect on free reserves and deposits is also slightly higher.

Change in reserve requirement ratios

Table IV.5 displays the simulation results of changes in the money supply brought about by changes in the reserve requirement ratio (RRR). Only the CB and A–G models appear to have considered this.

The CB results show a 1 percentage reduction in RRR on demand deposits to have a much greater effect than the corresponding 1 percentage reduction on time deposits. The initial impact on both the bill rate and the bond rate (−1·39 and −0·66) is much sharper than in the case of time deposits (−0·82 and −0·39). The effects of both changes are qualitatively similar to those of a reduction in the discount rate. Once again, the reduction in the level of the GNP deflator does not seem reasonable.

Change in the maximum rate on time deposits

Effects of changes in the maximum rate payable on time deposits have been simulated by A–G and CB. In the A–G an increase in this rate leads to a shift away from demand deposits into time deposits, which leads to a fall in expenditure on consumer durables and in nominal GNP. The first of these results is also found in the case of CB.

Change in maturity composition of Federal debt

CB has considered the effect of 5 per cent increase in 0–5 year proportion of the Federal debt, and finds that its effect on the *difference* between the bill rate and the bond rate is in the desired direction. But the size of the change is so small that its effect on economic activity would be negligible.

TABLE IV.6

A: Change in National Income due to $1·0 Billion Increase in Monetary Policy Instrument[a]

Quarter	FRB–MIT: J–8	FRB–Ch	CB	A–G
1	0·7	1·2	−0·8	1·9
2	2·1	3·7	1·3	2·2
3	4·3	7·2	1·6	2·3
4	6·7	10·8	2·9	2·7

[a] Monetary instrument = unborrowed reserves in Brooking and FRB–MIT: J–8
= Total reserves in FRB–Ch
= Total reserves + currency in A–G.

B: Change in the Short-term Interest Rate (in basis points) due to Monetary Policy[b]

Quarter	FRB–MIT: J–8	FRB–Ch	CB	A–G
1	−114·7	−210·9	−148·1	−83·6
2	−27·3	−24·5	−57·6	−54·1
3	−43·9	−55·9	−47·9	−43·0
4	−39·0	−35·4	−41·5	−11·9

[b] $1 billion change in open-market instrument.

C: Changes in Money Stock due to Monetary Policy

Quarter	FRB–MIT: J–8	FRB–Ch	CB	A–G
1	4·7	9·1	3·2	1·8
2	6·0	10·0	3·6	2·8
3	7·0	10·5	4·1	3·7
4	8·0	11·1	4·6	4·0

Money stock = private time deposits + DD.   Policy action as in Table IV.3.

Finally, Table IV.6 provides certain summary comparisons based on various simulation runs, taken from [111]. This Table shows that in FRB–Ch monetary policy is more effective and more fast-acting than any other model. But part of the difference between the models is due to different definitions. The FRB–Ch has a broader definition of the monetary instrument than the other models.

All these models regard the discount rate and reserves as monetary instruments. But, of course, these could be regarded as endogenous variables, since changes in them are presumably determined by the size of some other variables which enter the policy-makers' objective function. Tgn does not regard Federal Reserve policy as exogenous (in the sense of being determined without reference to variables such as employment and interest rates). In [103] the author removes what he considers to be a source of inconsistency by relating Federal Reserve open-market and discount policy to variables representing the objectives of income and price stability, long-term and short-term interest rates. This model has a slightly different purpose from the others discussed, but simulations are not available.

Lags in monetary policy

The question of lags between changes in monetary variables and the effects of such changes on household and firm behaviour is obviously a crucial one. The well-known paper [8] on lags in monetary policy distinguishes between the 'inside' lag, the intermediate lag, and the 'outside' lag. The 'inside' lag is defined as the lag between recognition that a change in policy is desirable, and action by the Federal Reserve. The intermediate lag is that between the action by the Federal authorities and the emergence of changed conditions facing the banking system. Finally, the 'outside' lag measures the length of period elapsing between the changed financial conditions and their effects on the actual economic behaviour of the households and firms. This last lag obviously relates to expenditure on fixed and inventory investment, residential investment, and non-durable and durable consumption. With the exception of Tgn, which endogenizes the policy actions of the Federal Reserve, the econometric models discussed here do not do so and so do not shed any light on the 'inside' lag. They are, in general, more concerned with the joint effects of the intermediate and the 'outside' lags.

Comparison of the Effects of Monetary Policy in Four Econometric Models

A major question is whether the time lags involved are short or long. Friedman [47, 48] has argued that the lags involved are *long* and *variable*, of the order of eighteen months, thus making monetary policy an extremely dangerous tool of stabilization. The methods used by Friedman in arriving at this conclusion have been criticized quite widely. It is therefore of considerable interest to find out whether in fact the lags involved are long.

We are not entirely confident that large-scale econometric models have anything significant to add to what emerges from the single-equation studies of investment [1, 13, 28, 65], of consumer expendture [58], and of residential construction [81, 89, 97].

With respect to fixed investment, both Jorgenson and Stephenson [65], and Bischoff [13], in spite of their theoretical differences, find long lags in response to changes in financial determinants of investment in plant and equipment. For example, Jorgenson has reported a mean lag of 7 quarters between changes in the rental price of capital stock and investment in manufacturing. Bischoff's theoretical treatment is less restrictive than that of Jorgenson, in so far as the former argues that a putty–clay model is more appropriate. On theoretical grounds he argues that the investment response to changes in financial factors should be slow. He finds this to be so. His equations are also embodied in the FRB–MIT models which, like other econometric models discussed, show that the peak effect of a change in the rate of interest comes after several quarters. In CB and W–EFU a gradual response of investment to changes in financial variables is revealed. All these results appear to be fairly plausible given the long lags between the initiation of investment projects and the actual placing of orders, and also the long lags in the manufacture of many types of heavy capital equipment. The putty–clay hypothesis also seems more realistic than the putty–putty hypothesis, and the former suggests that the lagged response will be slow.

Not all econometric models have separate equations for plant and equipment, on one hand, and structures, on the other. FRB–MIT:D–8 model has such separate equations, and the lag between changes in the rental price of capital and changes in investment is similar to that between changes in output and changes in investment. The response to changes in financial factors is fairly quick, thus indicating that a putty–putty hypothesis for structures is not inappropriate.

Several econometric studies, including the FRB–MIT models, find that the interest rate affects housing starts, and state and local government expenditures, with a short lag, which suggests existence of exploitable effects for purposes of stabilization policy (cf. [91.

92]). Similar results are also found for consumer expenditure on durables (cf. [58]).

These results call for a few comments. First, the impression that emerges from them is one of long rather than short lags, especially in the models which are disaggregated. This finding is a little suspicious, because long lags and slow responses are reported even in those cases where a faster adjustment would be expected. Further, the estimation of long lags is based on the use of a sample period characterized by a narrow range of variation in monetary policy. Second, as we have indicated, there are many econometric problems associated with the calculation of lagged responses on the basis of time-series data collected at regular intervals. A major difficulty faced by econometricians is the problem of time aggregation which almost certainly biases the estimates of mean lags. (See e.g. [37, 85].) Third, large econometric models frequently resort to arbitrary treatment of individual blocks of equations which deserve more careful treatment. For instance, CB replaces Jorgenson's investment equations by very much simpler versions; the FRB–MIT models treat the price–wage block as exogenous; W–EFU excludes almost all bank-behaviour equations. It is hard to believe that this constitutes harmless simplification! More likely, it constitutes a mis-specification which affects model behaviour. Fourth, Friedman's contention that the lag in monetary policy is *variable* (and long) is largely untested. To test this, one would have to construct models in which the distributed lag weights are determined by values assumed by other variables, exogenous or endogenous. The theoretical arguments in favour of a variable distributed lag model are quite strong. At the level of single equations there is some evidence to show that variable distributed lag models are quite plausible (see e.g. [55]). But the estimation problems created by them in a large econometric model are such that (simpler) approximations are likely to be preferred. Finally, there is probably some truth in the criticism that the simulation results reflect the theoretical predilections of those who construct the model in the first place. In his discussion of Ando and Modigliani's paper [10], Meiselman remarks: '. . . I take exception to the Ando–Modigliani view about the channels through which money and monetary policy work—rather, their presumption that theirs is the only channel or temporal sequence for money and monetary policy to affect other variables in the economy. This clearly biases many results.' For this reason and what it implies for specification generally we cannot regard the conclusions of econometric models as entirely objective.

Monetary versus fiscal policy

A proper detailed discussion of the rival merits and demerits of monetary and fiscal policies is outside the scope of this paper. We only note that most of the models which aim at any disaggregation at all show that *both* fiscal *and* monetary policy measures make a significant contribution to the determination of major macro-aggregates, such as output and employment. The major difference appears to be in the channels of influence, the speed of response, and in the sectoral impact of different policies, rather than in the total effectiveness of one and the total impotence of the other. Indeed, we would argue that the focusing of attention on the effectiveness of one policy (say, monetary policy) with the other (fiscal policy) to be regarded as ineffective is entirely ill-directed, simply because the range of possible answers is unnecessarily constrained. In our view, the proper *approach* to an evaluation of the relative merits of monetary and fiscal policies is to seek to determine a combination of the two which would be most effective for the achievement of given policy objectives in particular circumstances, rather than to seek to determine a global rule as to which is the more effective in general. We can begin to do this with the aid of large-scale models, so long as proper account is taken of the government budget restraint. Such models render feasible the evaluation of interactions via the budget restraint, and clearly allow for joint, as well as separate, consideration of the two policies. The outcome of such an evaluation may eventually lead to the conclusion that one (monetary or fiscal) policy alone is indeed the most effective of all possible combinations available. But such an answer, in this case, is not constrained at the outset to be either one or the other of a dichotomy of choices.

V. Methodological issues in the St. Louis approach

We introduced this paper with a discussion of various econometric issues which emerge from the Keynesian–monetarist debate, and it became clear that structural models of the economy would naturally be biased toward a Keynesian viewpoint. This theme was developed in more detail in Section IV. In this section, we turn to the other side of the debate and examine a monetarist approach as exemplified by various pieces of research from the Federal Reserve Bank of St. Louis (FRB–St. L.) [3–7, 16, 18, 34, 43, 60, 63, 68–75, 83, 84, 98, 99, 110]. We shall not review this literature in detail but concentrate on important methodological issues.

Reduced to fundamentals, it would appear that the FRB–St. L. approach, as typified in the work of Anderson and Jordan [5], is based on two econometric heresies: disregard for structure and the spurning of disaggregation. Specifically, two steps are involved. First, instead of the usual practice of specifying the causal links by which fiscal and monetary instruments work their way, step by step from sector to sector, through the economy, the FRB–St. L formulation avoids the intermediate steps and goes directly from changes in policy to their final net cumulative effect on a scalar measure of economic activity, typically GNP. Second, while in the real world fiscal policy and monetary policy are vector-valued variables, the elements of which are the appropriate instruments, these two policy vectors are each formulated as real-valued variables. These real-valued variables are derived from the corresponding vectors either by selecting a 'typical' element, such as the quantity of money, or by a process of aggregation, as in the case of the budget surplus. An obvious cost of this approach is a loss of information, an obvious gain is simplicity. But simplicity has brought with it a widening of the potential audience capable of comprehending the challenge to Keynesian orthodoxy that the FRB–St. L results imply. In particular, that money is more important than fiscal policy in influencing the level of economic activity. We make this point not as a pejorative comment, but rather to emphasize an important product of the FRB–St. L work which is seldom explicitly recognized. Namely that, whatever its scientific merits, it has done much, like the work of Friedman and Meiselman [49] which preceded it, to reawaken interest in money and monetary policy both among practical men who have had an influence on economic policy, and among scientists who have wished to delve deeper into its scientific foundations and the validity of the inferences drawn from its empirical results.

As we indicated in Section I, the specifications used in the FRB–St. L work are examples of an approach to applied econometrics known as the *reduced-form approach*. However, the use of the term 'reduced form' in this context is misleading, and the reduced-form approach is not a well-defined concept. Some clarification must be made.

In the reduced-form approach a specified equation resembles a reduced-form equation, in the sense that an endogenous variable is expressed as a function of exogenous and predetermined variables alone (save for an error term). The Anderson–Jordan equations are postulated to contain no lagged endogenous variables, so that all the explanatory variables are exogenous. No structural form is specified or estimated. Thus, if a specified equation is known to be a proper reduced-form equation, we are still left ignorant of the precise interaction between endogenous and exogenous variables, first because only one endogenous variable is postulated, and second because we have no information on which variables appear in which structural equations.

The reduced-form approach, however, does not require the specification and estimation of equations which are *proper* reduced forms. The precise relation between the structure and a specified equation is, like the structure itself, a matter for conjecture. Consequently, it would be illogical to claim that the reduced-form approach avoids mis-specification of the structure, since the structure cannot be known without additional information.

Traditionally it is the structural form, not the reduced form, which has been the central focus in econometric model construction. The reason for this lies in the correspondence between the underlying economic theory of a model and its empirical structure, the reduced form being a convenient statistical artifice for estimation purposes. The case for the central role of theory—and hence of the structural form—is put convincingly by Frisch [51]. 'But no amount of statistical information . . . can by itself explain economic phenomena. If we are not to get lost in the overwhelming, bewildering mass of statistical data . . ., we need the guidance and help of a *powerful theoretical framework*. Without this, *no significant interpretation and co-ordination of our observations will be possible*.' (Our italics.)

Thus, in contradistinction from the reduced-form approach used by the FRB–St. L school, specification of a structure would *necessitate* the tracing-out of the channels through which monetary and fiscal policy are *assumed* to influence the economy. When estimated, this structure would yield a particular parametric description of the underlying theory and, more important, permit a testing of the theory against factual information. It is by such means that a coherent interpretation of statistical information emerges as the end-result of econometric inquiry.

On the other hand, it may be argued that a proper reduced form is merely a rearrangement of the corresponding structural form. Consequently, provided the former incorporates all of the structural-form information, the two forms must be capable of yielding precisely the same amount of statistical information. Why then is the structural form regarded as the more important?

In the case of a just-identifiable system, the two forms are capable of yielding the same amount of information, for there is a one-for-one correspondence between them. But in the more usual over-identifiable system, the reduced form can be and often is regarded as a re-written structure which is to be estimated *without imposing the 'extra' a priori restrictions*. In this case, there is no *uniquely* determinable statistical structure, even if the theoretical structure is known. Indeed, an unconstrained estimate of the reduced form yields a multiplicity of estimated structures which is perhaps a debating advantage, but hardly a scientific one.

In the FRB–St. L work, the specified equations are merely *asserted* to be reduced forms, and their lag structure is empirically specified, not specified *a priori*. If we accept the equations as genuine reduced forms and we assume they are derivable from an over-identifiable structure, then their coefficient estimates must in general be statistically inefficient and incapable of deriving a unique structure, because no over-identifying restrictions are imposed. In particular, it is possible for the estimated reduced form to be consistent with *no* acceptable structure. In view of the absence of prior restrictions to act as testable 'checks', it is not unreasonable to argue that an implied 'specification' of structure consistent with the estimated reduced form is more prone to errors than is the case when a structural approach is adopted at the outset. If you are unsure whence you have come, you are more likely to fail in determining your origin than if the origin is given at the outset.

Usually the case for the FRB–St. L equations is argued on less technical grounds, similar to the following. Because it is often the case that interest centres on one or two key variables, there is no need to estimate the entire structure. Moreover, because the economy is very complicated, an accurate evaluation of the structure is not really possible with the methods and statistical information currently available. A structural approach, therefore, might yield misleading results. On the other hand, it is argued, a direct evaluation of, for example, fiscal and monetary policy on GNP is certainly feasible and avoids some of the pitfalls of the structural approach. In addition, the results which emerge will be useful, particularly in policy analysis—and because of the simplicity—for forecasting (see [59]).

We can accept these points as general comments on the advantages of the reduced-form approach and some of the disadvantages of the structural approach to applied econometrics. But we also believe that when advantages are discussed, a careful analysis of corresponding disadvantages should also be undertaken. With regard to the FRB–St. L work, we have already noted several disadvantages. We believe that the most important of these is the inability to test underlying theory and hence an inability to provide a significant interpretation of the results. Thus, without an explicit structure, the FRB–St. L results have to remain interesting but as yet unexplained (and unexplainable) statistical correlations; bizarre results remain mysterious, without interpretation. Perhaps, for example, the results reflect the existence of an underlying structure whose parametric description yields reasonable though different results from those hitherto obtained. If this is the case, how may the interpretation be distinguished from the case when the same results reflect a new and as yet undiscovered set of processes by which monetary and fiscal policy affect the economy? Or, to put the matter more generally— and more bluntly, do the results emerge from a failure properly to specify a theoretical system or are they coincidental, or just plain spurious? [96] We hope to provide some clues to answer these questions in what follows below.

Attempts have been made to suggest a structure which will lead to equations of the form examined by Anderson and Jordan. One of these [86] has already been discussed in Section III. Another, which we shall use because of its simplicity, is given in [96]. The variables in this model are, in real terms: consumption (C), investment (I), total taxes received (T), GNP (Y), and government expenditure (G); M^D is the demand for, and M^S the supply of, money; r is the rate of interest. The model consists of the following equations:

$$C_t = c(Y_t - T_t) + C_0 + \varepsilon_{1t}$$
$$T_t = xY_t + A_t + \varepsilon_{2t}$$
$$I_t = vr_t + I_0 + \varepsilon_{3t}$$
$$Y_t = C_t + I_t + G_t$$
$$M_t^D = mr_t + kY_t^* + M_0 + \varepsilon_{4t}$$
$$M_t^D = M_t^S = M_t$$
$$Y_t^* \equiv Y_{t-1}$$

The first equation is the consumption function in which c is the marginal propensity to consume, C_0 autonomous consumption expenditure, and ε_{1t} a random error. The second equation describes the behaviour of tax receipts, A_t representing autonomous taxes and ε_{2t} another random error. Investment varies with the rate of interest and a third random error, and the national income identity is given the fourth equation. The demand for money depends on the rate of interest and expected income (Y^*). Expected income in quarter t is assumed equal to observed income at quarter $t - 1$.

It is assumed that G_t, M_t, and A_t are exogenous; the remaining variables are endogenous, and clearly Y_{t-1} is predetermined. The reduced form equation for Y_t is easily derived and converted into a corresponding equation in the first-difference of income, ΔY_t:

$$\Delta Y_t = \frac{v}{m\{1 - c(1 - x)\}} \Delta M_t - \frac{c}{1 - c(1 - x)} \Delta A_t$$

$$+ \frac{1}{1 - c(1 - x)} \Delta G_t - \frac{vk}{m\{1 - c(1 - x)\}} \Delta Y_{t-1}$$

$$+ \frac{1}{1 - c(1 - x)} \{\Delta \varepsilon_{3t} + (\Delta \varepsilon_{1t} - c\Delta \varepsilon_{2t}) - \frac{v}{m} \Delta \varepsilon_{4t}\}.$$

Note carefully that the error term in this equation is a moving average process of the first-differences of the structural errors, with parameters derived from the structural-form coefficients. We shall denote this error by u_t, and define $z = -vk/[m\{1 - c(1 - x)\}]$. Note also that in the reduced-form equation for ΔY_t there are four coefficients which are functions of five structural-form coefficients. Hence without further information we can only determine x, c, k, and v/m. Nevertheless, putting this matter aside, equations of the Anderson–Jordan type may be obtained by substitution for ΔY_{t-1}, then ΔY_{t-2} and so on; i.e. by moving from the reduced-form to an interim-form equation in ΔY_t:

$$\Delta Y_t = \frac{cm}{vk} \sum_{i=0}^{n-1} z^{i+1} \Delta A_{t-i} - \frac{1}{k} \sum_{i=0}^{n-1} z^{i+1} \Delta M_{t-i}$$

$$-\frac{m}{kv} \sum_{i=0}^{n-1} z^{i+1} \Delta G_{t-i} + z^n \Delta Y_{t-n} + \sum_{i=0}^{n-1} z^i u_{t-i}. \quad (4)$$

Clearly when $n = 4$ this last equation resembles the Anderson–Jordan model, but it includes the term in ΔY_{t-n} and, even if u_t is not serially correlated, $\sum z^i u_{t-1}$ will be, the form of time dependence being very complicated. In short, first-differencing this equation will not, in general, eliminate serial correlation, and Durbin–Watson statistics will not in general detect its presence.

If the system is stable $|z| < 1$. Consequently z^n can be made arbitrarily small by appropriate choice of n. If the original structural model had contained more lagged endogenous variables, these would have appeared in the reduced-form equation, in which case the interim form would be that much more complicated. Whether or not it would then be satisfactory to disregard these additional variables (as well as the term in ΔY_{t-n}) would depend on the sizes of the appropriate structural coefficients and how these were combined to form interim coefficients. As Smith has said [96, p. 780]: 'In terms of the Anderson–Jordan model the question is whether endogenous forces of the accelerator–multiplier type originating four periods back are still significantly affecting the economy. It seems highly probable to me that they would be.'

As we have already reported in Section III, the model of Moroney and Mason [86] leads to an interim-form equation in Y_t similar to that obtained from the simple illustrative model just described. In respect of scientific foundations, a major difference between Moroney's and Mason's equation and the equations of Anderson and Jordan is that the former is based on an explicitly tested structure whereas the latter is not. It is noteworthy that Moroney's and Mason's conclusions are not entirely in accord with those of Anderson and Jordan. Firstly, the former conclude that both fiscal *and* monetary policy are important to the determination of GNP, while the latter lay much greater stress on monetary policy. Secondly, in respect of stabilization policy, Anderson and Jordan argue for 'greater reliance being placed on monetary actions than on fiscal actions' [5, p. 22]. Moroney and Mason argue: 'Fiscal policymakers face comparatively few problems attributable to the cumulative effect of the flow of government spending during preceding quarters. Monetary policymakers, by contrast, face a more formidable task, because the monetary policy of the recent past seems to have a more consequential bearing on the present and future pace of the economy' [86, p. 810]. Because of this, 'it would seem more difficult to reverse the direction of influence [of monetary policy] on aggregate demand' [86, p. 811].

The implications of a model for stabilization policy naturally rest very heavily on the empirically evaluated lag structure, whether this is done indirectly via the structure or by directly estimating a final-form equation. In regard to the illustrative model discussed above, it seems unlikely that the simple lag structure put forward would be entirely satisfactory for empirical analysis. To the extent that it would be more complicated in the structure, it would, *pari passu*, be more complicated in the final form, both in terms of the variables included and in terms of the error structure. Anderson and Jordan use the Almon technique [1] to evaluate an empirical lag structure in respect of included variables, but they pay no attention to the possibility of a complex lag structure in the errors.

In applying the Almon technique to equations of the general form

$$y(t) = a \sum_{i=0}^{n} w(i)x(t - i) + u(t),$$

the $w(i)$ are approximated by a polynomial function of i in the interval $[0, n]$. It is then necessary to decide simultaneously what degree of polynomial (say, r, $r < n$) shall be used, what the value of n shall be, and what restrictions shall be placed on the end-points of the sequence $\{w(i)\}$. Unfortunately, for a small number of possible values of these, the number of estimating equations is uncomfortably large. Consequently, it is tempting to look for short-cuts. A popular short-cut is $w(-1) = w(n + 1) = 0$, but if this is empirically unjustified, it may lead to distorted estimates of the $w(i)$ and thereby to a possible distortion in policy recommendations. Trivedi [107] reports disturbing results in this connection, and notes that different lag structures may be consistent with similar values of the variation explained by the equation (e.g. R^2 or $\bar{R}^2$). Trivedi's results are not general, and it is possible for the chosen end-point restrictions to be innocuous in particular cases. Consequently, he recommends the application of appropriate statistical tests, a procedure not adopted by Anderson and Jordan.

Another piece of evidence concerning the Anderson–Jordan lag structure is [27], in which Davis applies a second-degree polynomial in place of the fourth degree used by the former. While this less-restricted form produces similar results, when Davis applies unconstrained least squares (which is even less restrictive), the lag structure changes considerably. Evidently either 29 per cent or 46 per cent of the ultimate effect of money on income can be attributed to the current quarter, the higher value being obtained when the unrestricted least-squares lag distribution is applied (see [27] and cf. [59]). This result could, of course, be explained in terms of co-linearity between successive observations of the explanatory variables. Davis also presents weak evidence to support the view that the lag structure varies with time. This could arise because of mis-specification of the estimating equation, a not unreasonable view considering, for example, the corresponding dynamic equation used by Moroney and Mason [86, p. 807] which, like (4), includes some lagged effects of income. If the appropriately lagged change in income were inserted into the Anderson–Jordan equations, their econometric evaluation would become much more difficult given, as seems likely, that the error structure itself is also time-dependent over more than one period. Such complexities are essentially hidden by the overt simplicity which the reduced-form approach adopts. Had a structural approach been adopted, the causes of aggregate economic fluctuations would have been decomposed into their interrelated parts, not considered as a complicated whole which is *seemingly* simple. Therefore, it would seem unwise to regard lags estimated by the Almon technique according to the Anderson–Jordan specifications as a firm basis for scientific conclusions or policy recommendations.

Perhaps the most econometrically novel methodological aspect of the FRB–St. L work arises from their use of β-coefficients in testing propositions concerning, for example, the relative strengths of monetary and fiscal policy on economic activity. β-coefficients or *path coefficients* play a role in *path analysis* which corresponds to the role played by regression coefficients in regression analysis. Path analysis was originally developed by the geneticist Sewall Wright (see e.g. [108, 109]) to examine problems of Mendelian inheritance under different systems of mating. This has been regarded by Duncan [35] as a *direct application* of path analysis to problems involving *axiomatic deductions*. Thus the mating schemes determine the paths of causation, it being taken as axiomatic that inheritance can only take place if mating has taken place. The estimated path coefficients provide an empirical measure of the 'strength' of inheritance which may then be compared with deduced theoretical values.

Path analysis has also received attention in *dependence analysis* in sociology where applications have been regarded as *indirect* [14]. In these cases, there are no practically obvious paths of causation like mating, and theoretical schemes of causal dependence must be assumed *a priori*. The empirical analysis then amounts to estimating the strengths of paths to account for observed correlations, the calculations being constrained by the chosen causal ordering of the variables. Clearly in such an application a powerful theory is ideally required. Since this is not always possible, it is important to have 'built-in' checks against mis-specification and misinterpretation. In path analysis such checks are possible because the analysis permits the strengths of potential paths of dependence to be revealed among those variables which are not, according to the theory, chosen for specific investigation. Such non-causal paths of dependence are distinguished from the causal paths by a different notation. For example in Fig. V.1 the variables x and y help determine z along with a residual item r, though x and y themselves happen to be correlated. The causal paths are indicated by straight lines with a single-headed arrow, the arrow going in the direction of causation. On the other hand, the non-causal, unanalysed path between x and y is indicated by a curved line with arrows pointing in both directions.

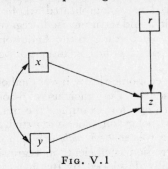

Fig. V.1

In applied economics the situation is much the same as in sociology, and economists are forced to work in terms of a causal scheme which is assumed and stated *a priori*. Hence the assertion: '. . . We need the guidance and help of a powerful theoretical framework' noted above. Moreover, it is well known in time-series analysis in economics that time itself can play the role of an intervening variable and lead to spurious, non-causal correlations. These two observations emphasize a need in the FRB–St. L work to guard against misspecification and misinterpretation. It is our view that Anderson and Jordan fail to do this adequately, and we now turn to the analysis on which this opinion is based.

To aid the exposition, we confine ourselves to a simple case and we shall not prove results rigorously. However, the argument can be made rigorous. It can also be extended to handle the more general case examined by Anderson and Jordan. Unfortunately, the statistics made available by Anderson and Jordan in [5] render application of this general model infeasible.

Consider the simple regression model in which the variables are all measured from their sample means:

$$y = b_1 x_1 + b_2 x_2 + u. \tag{5}$$

The x's are to be regarded as exogenous, y is endogenous, and u is the residual term. There are n observations and equation (5) represents a *fitted* equation. Let s denote sample standard deviation: s_0 refers to y, s_1 to x_1, s_2 to x_2, and s_u to the residual u. Then (5) may be rewritten as

$$\frac{y}{s_0} = \left(\frac{b_1 s_1}{s_0}\right) \frac{x_1}{s_1} + \left(\frac{b_2 s_2}{s_0}\right) \frac{x_2}{s_2} + \left(\frac{s_u}{s_0}\right) \frac{u}{s_u}. \tag{6}$$

We now let $Y = y/s_0$, $X_1 = x_1/s_1$, $X_2 = x_2/s_2$, and $u/s_u = U$. Moreover, p will denote a path (or β-) coefficient: p_{10} is the path coefficient from X_1 to Y; p_{20} is from X_2 to Y, and p_{u0} from U to Y, where $p_{i0} \equiv b_i s_i/s_0$ $(i = 1, 2)$, and $p_{u0} \equiv b_u s_u/s_0$ $(b_u \equiv 1)$. Equation (6) may now be rewritten:

$$Y = p_{10}X_1 + p_{20}X_2 + p_{u0}U. \tag{7}$$

Using (7), it is easy to show that:

$$R^2 = p_{10}^2 + p_{20}^2 + 2p_{10}p_{20}r_{12} = (1 - p_{u0}^2). \tag{8}$$

The interpretation of (8) is obvious: R^2 is the proportion of the sample variance of y explained by the regression (5), and this is equal to the sum of squares of the paths of X_1 and X_2 to Y plus $2p_{10}p_{20}r_{12}$ which is in the nature of an interaction term. Indeed it is also easy to show that

$$\left.\begin{array}{l} r_{10} = p_{10} + r_{12}p_{20}, \\ r_{20} = r_{21}p_{10} + p_{20}, \end{array}\right\} \tag{9}$$

where the r's are elementary correlation coefficients. Thus if there is no interaction, X_1 and X_2 will be orthogonal and $r_{12} = r_{21} = 0$. In this case, $p_{10} = r_{10}$ and $p_{20} = r_{20}$, and the whole of the effect of X_1 on Y goes *directly* from X_1 to Y without 'passing through' X_2; similarly the whole of the effect of X_2 on Y goes *directly* to Y without 'passing through' X_1. On the other hand, it is likely that there will be some correlation between X_1 and X_2, in which case the path coefficient p_{10} measures the *direct* effect of X_1 on Y, and the *indirect* effect is measured by $r_{12}p_{20} = r_{10} - p_{10}$. The indirect effect is that part of the variation in X_1 which is channelled through X_2 (r_{12}) and thence, by its path p_{20}, to Y. A corresponding interpretation may be given to the second equation in (9). One advantage of path coefficients, therefore, is that they readily allow direct and indirect paths to be quantitatively assessed, and this provides a complete description of the pattern of statistical dependence between the variables. What is taken as causal in the scheme, of course, still remains a matter for prior judgement. Nevertheless observed correlations may suggest a scheme of dependence that had not previously been thought to be reasonable.

One group of the Anderson–Jordan regressions follows the form

$$\Delta G^*(t) = \alpha + \sum_{i=0}^{3} \beta(i) \, \Delta M^*(t - i) + \sum_{i=0}^{3} \gamma(i) \, \Delta R^*(t - i)$$
$$+ \sum_{i=0}^{3} \lambda(i) \, \Delta E^*(t - i) + U^*(t) \quad (10)$$

in which G^* denotes GNP, M^* the narrowly defined money stock, and R^* and E^* are high employment receipts and expenditures respectively; α, β, γ, and λ are coefficients to be estimated, and U^* is the residual term. To proceed within the bounds of available statistics, we shall group the terms in ΔR^* and ΔE^* together into a composite term to be thought of as a change in the 'budget surplus', and we shall also group together the distributed lags on each of the terms. To do this, first rewrite (10) in path form

$$\Delta G(t) = \sum p_{MG}(i) \, \Delta M(t - i) + \sum p_{RG}(i) \, \Delta R(t - i)$$
$$+ \sum p_{EG}(i) \, \Delta E(t - i) + p_{UG} U(t), \quad (11)$$

the p's being path coefficients, and the variables without asterisks being corresponding standardized variables of those with asterisks. Then we may write for example

$$\sum p_{MG}(i) \, \Delta M(t - i) = p_{MG}\{\sum (p_{MG}(i)/p_{MG}) \, \Delta M(t - i)\},$$

where $p_{MG} = \sum p_{MG}(i)$. The term in braces is now denoted by ΔM. We may also define ΔR and ΔE in a corresponding way whereupon, since $p_{EG} < 0$,

$$p_{RG} \, \Delta R - |p_{EG}| \, \Delta E = |p_{EG}| \{(p_{RG}/|p_{EG}|) \, \Delta R - \Delta E\} = p_{FG} \, \Delta F,$$

the term in braces being denoted by ΔF and $|p_{EG}| \equiv p_{FG}$, F denoting the 'fiscal indicator'. Thus (11) becomes

$$\Delta G = p_{MG} \, \Delta M + p_{FG} \, \Delta F + p_{UG} U, \quad (12)$$

the time designations on $\Delta G(t)$ and $U(t)$ being dropped.

We now apply (12) to equation 1.4 of [5, Table II, p. 19], as an illustrative example. In this equation, $p_{MG} = 0\cdot91$ and $p_{FG} = 0\cdot21$. Perhaps the sign of the path coefficient p_{FG} is surprising, because we would normally expect an increase in the budget surplus to be deflationary and hence to be associated with a decline in G; i.e. we would expect ΔG and ΔF to be negatively associated, while the path coefficient is actually positive. However, p_{FG} represents the net outcome of direct and indirect effects, and negative association is confirmed since $r_{FG} \simeq -0.61$ (see below).

Since for the same equation $R^2 = 0.53$, applying equations (8) and (9) we have $P_{UG} \simeq 0.69$, $r_{MG} \simeq 0.72$, $r_{FG} \simeq -0.61$, and $r_{MF} \simeq -0.90$. These calculations allow us to draw up the scheme of dependence shown in Fig. V.2. Anderson and Jordan pay little attention to the negative correlation between ΔM and ΔF.

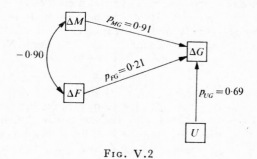

FIG. V.2

Since, however, a fiscal policy must imply a monetary policy, we might visualize the scheme of dependence somewhat differently. In particular, using our knowledge about the correlation between ΔM and ΔF, we could reinterpret the Anderson–Jordan scheme of dependence as shown in Fig. V.3. In Fig. V.3, the direct path effect of ΔF on ΔG is 0.21, but this is supplemented by an *indirect* path effect through ΔM which is $(-0.90)(0.91) \simeq -0.82$. In other words,

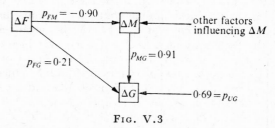

FIG. V.3

the net path effect of ΔF on ΔG is $-0.82 + 0.21 = -0.61$ ($= r_{FG}$). If, in addition, the influence of ΔF on ΔM is 'taken out' of the direct effect of ΔM on ΔG, the net effect of ΔM on ΔG is reduced from 0.91 to $0.91 + (-0.90)(0.21) \simeq 0.72$. This, of course, is still numerically greater than the net path effect of ΔF, but the two are nevertheless comparable. Indeed, the regression coefficients of $\Delta R^*(t - i)$ and $\Delta E^*(t - i)$ in [5] are not significant, and this is probably due to the high correlation between these variables and those which are represented by ΔM. The same close negative association would also account for the 'perverse' signs on the original regression coefficients.

In summary, then, it would appear that in at least one case, the Anderson–Jordan regressions and their path coefficients are open to objections and to reinterpretation. But note carefully that the new scheme proposed has in its present form no clear meaning. For if we adopt the revised scheme of causation the 'structural' equations would be

$$\Delta M = \alpha_0 + \alpha_1 \Delta F + u_1$$
$$\Delta G = \beta_0 + \beta_1 \Delta F + \beta_2 \Delta M + u_2,$$

and ΔF would then be the only exogenous variable in a causal chain of the Wold type. In such a case, however, it is obvious that the second equation is not identifiable,[1] for a linear combination of the two equations would yield an equation precisely of the form of the second. In any case, the reverse causation argument ([3, 34, 70, 83]) leads us to suspect simultaneity between ΔM and ΔG and, since ΔF is dependent on the level of unemployment compensation, there must also be a measure of interdependence between ΔF and ΔG. But the matter of interdependence would seem to be wider than this. We have already noted that the Anderson–Jordan equations are suspect because explanatory variables have been omitted from them. To the extent that this is the case and the excluded variables are positively correlated with the monetary variables, these excluded variables, given our earlier empirical finding that the monetary and fiscal variables are negatively correlated, may well be negatively correlated with the fiscal variables. Such excluded variables will then cause a correlation between the errors in the Anderson–Jordan equations and the explanatory variables ΔM and ΔF, thereby imparting an upward bias to the coefficient of ΔM and a downward bias to the coefficient of ΔF. We cannot, of course, be definitive on this matter without a more careful and detailed statistical inquiry.

In discussing the FRB–St. L work we have concentrated on methodological criticisms with particular regard to the research of Anderson and Jordan. This emphasis derives from the over-all aim

[1] Unless suitable restrictions are placed on the variance–covariance matrix of the u's.

of this paper, namely to appraise empirical research from the view-point of its contribution to the development of economic theory. Our view is that the use of the reduced-form approach essentially precludes the testing of theory and hence precludes empirical results from contributing significantly to the development of theory. In concentrating on this and other methodological points, we recognize that our argument may appear unbalanced, because it fails to recognize the contribution of the FRB–St. L research in other areas. For example, while limited in scope (see e.g. [76]), Anderson's and Jordan's equations and the model of Anderson and Carlson [4] undoubtedly provide useful forecasts. Also, there is the contribution to policy appraisal. Evidently, for example, the high-employment budget concept was chosen for empirical analysis precisely because the Council of Economic Advisors and the economic advisers of the Federal Open Market Committee have in the past relied, and continue to rely, heavily on this measure in their own deliberations. It is also worth re-emphasizing that in encouraging criticism by being susceptible to it, the FRB–St. L results have done much to stimulate others to seek alternative explanations for their observed correlations. Unfortunately, many critics have sought to contest the FRB–St. L propositions using the same reduced-form approach, thereby implicitly condoning its efficacy as a scientific method.

These brief comments, while stressing the imbalance in our argument, are also designed to provide substance to some cautionary points we feel must be made. The strong implication of the FRB–St. L results that the monetary sector matters is a point which we take, and their empirical support for this view certainly seems to be corroborated by the majority of studies we have reviewed. Nevertheless, it would seem that the monetary sector's effect should be scrutinized much more critically than is possible at present, using the methods designed hitherto by the St. Louis school. In our view, at the very least, expenditure magnitudes which the monetary stock is asserted to influence should be disaggregated, and it is surely arguable, even from a strong monetarist standpoint, that total private expenditure, not GNP, should be used as the dependent variable in the FRB–St. L tests. With respect to advancements in theory and in the practice of monetary policy, it now seems appropriate to undertake more detailed, precise research. Much more needs to be known about the channels of monetary effects and their separate influences and incidences over time on particular forms of private expenditure. It is on this type of research, detailed studies in depth of the role and influence

of the financial sector, on which the advancement of our understanding of the over-all impact of this sector now depends.

VI. Concluding remarks

Our aim in this paper has been to survey recent empirical evidence
concerning interrelationships between the real and monetary sectors
of the U.S. economy, particularly in respect of the contribution of
this evidence to the development of economic theory. In general, it
seems that in the U.S. economy, developments in the monetary sector have had a significant impact on the pace of economic activity
both in constant and in current prices. The channels through which
this impact seems to be directed are at least three: via interest rates,
directly via monetary stocks, and through credit availability. Evidence has also been presented which suggests that there may be a
price effect as well. In terms of the development of economic theory,
then, it is our view that U.S. empirical researchers have established
beyond reasonable doubt that the monetary sector matters in the
process of income, expenditure, and output determination.

We do not believe that it would be fruitful to go beyond this level
of generality at this stage, for two reasons. First, we have already been
more specific and adventurous in the main body of the paper and to
re-emphasize conclusions already reached would be to promote
them from the tentative to the definite. We have no wish to do this.
The majority of papers on which this survey is based reach tentative
conclusions and we are aware that we may have misinterpreted the
record. In any case, because of the large volume of literature involved, our reading has necessarily been restricted. Secondly, very few
of the results on which we have drawn are directly comparable.
Quite apart from the strength of *a priori* views, conflicting results are
likely to emerge as a result of differences in time periods examined,
differences in definitions of the data used, differences in the econometric methods applied, and differences in the structures (or other
equation forms) put forward for test.

On the other hand, the impressive amount of energy, imagination,
and intellectual application with which American economists have
endeavoured to obtain an empirically based understanding of the
operations and the impact of their own monetary sector certainly
merits the promulgation of a 'decisive view' in a survey of this kind.
Consequently, in the spirit of this paper, which has tended to concentrate on the econometric appraisal of empirical results, it is

incumbent upon us to make a number of specific comments. There are four of these and they are in the nature of cautionary comments or prescriptive suggestions for future research, rather than criticism or summary of the results on which the survey is based.

The first of these concerns disaggregation. Some of the variability in empirical results that we have observed reflects the special characteristics of different sectors and behavioural groups. This suggests that while a similar *form* of theoretical framework may be satisfactory for analysing a variety of sectors, the corresponding *parametric description* of a particular sector within this framework may be quite different from the description of other sectors, and that empirical results will in general vary, depending on the level of disaggregation achieved. This not only emphasizes the need for more intensive study of different sectors and behavioural groups, but also raises issues concerning the interpretation of the parameters in aggregative models. If the numerical values of the parameters of each sector are different, then the parameters of the corresponding aggregate model may be regarded as 'average' measures of the different sector parameters. It may therefore be more realistic to treat sector parameters as random variables, a possibility which has recently received renewed attention by Zellner [112]. We believe this to be a fruitful area for future research both at the theoretical and empirical level.

Our second point concerns the evaluation and interpretation of lag distributions in the structure and in other forms of a model. We have stressed throughout the paper the fundamental role of the structure for the interpretation of empirical results, and we have also remarked on the difficulties of estimating lag distributions in various forms of a model, particularly in the presence of time-dependent errors. To be consistent, the final form of a model should, in principle, be derived from the structure. On this last point we think it appropriate to make a cautionary comment.

When a final form is derived from a structure, its coefficients are typically treated as fixed numbers, not as random variables. In so doing, an unfortunate and improper element of precision is inadvertently introduced. A complete evaluation of a final form ought to include appropriate measures of the sampling variability of the coefficients. This is not an easy task and perhaps it is not even important if the object is merely to check that the underlying structure is dynamically stable. But when it comes to applying such a final form to stabilization policy, for example, the situation is somewhat different. This is because a direct estimate of the final form may yield very different coefficient estimates from those derived from the structure itself, yet the two sets may still be insignificantly different for one another, because of the large sampling variability involved. Moreover, the direct estimates may be more 'robust' in the sense that they are less prone to small errors in the structural coefficients which get compounded in deriving the final form. We cannot be definite on this matter, in view of the absence of empirical information. The point, however, does suggest that great caution should be exercised in applying final forms to policy analysis until we have more complete information concerning the sampling errors of final form coefficients and what these imply for the 'confidence intervals' of estimated dynamic adjustment paths.

In respect of equation errors, it seems likely that the derived final form errors may be so convoluted as to render infeasible a direct estimation of the final form. If this is the case, one wonders whether the final-form coefficients derived from the structure are of any practical value, for it would seem that the structure of the stochastic error in the final form then becomes the major source of 'systematic' variation in the dependent variable.

Our third concluding remark is addressed to the scale of econometric inquiry in the light of our apparent emphasis on large-scale models. We have stressed that, in some areas, we are not entirely confident that large-scale models have anything significant to add to what emerges from small-scale—typically single-equation—results. To a large extent, the scale of an inquiry must depend on the sort of questions to which the inquiry seeks to provide answers. Yet it does need stressing that large-scale models are very much restrained by the availability of consistent data and the availability of econometric methods to appraise them, particularly computational restraints. On the other hand, small-scale studies are much less restricted in these two respects. In particular, small-scale sector studies typically permit a more detailed, precise form of theory to be tested, since they are not restrained to be consistent with the other sectors which would comprise a larger-scale model. Further, the development of large-scale models must ultimately rest on detailed sector evidence, a point we have already stressed in respect of disaggregation. It is in this latter sense that small- and large-scale studies are complementary.

Finally, it also needs stressing that the policy simulations of large-scale models to which we have paid special attention are very much a product of the structure of the model on which the simulation is based. In this sense, such simulations are more a guide to the behaviour of the structure under 'stress' than they are a definitive guide to the behaviour of the real world in actuality. Further, the simulations we have examined are not only restricted by the structure used and the problems of its econometric appraisal, but they also exclude consideration of the stochastic components, namely those components which essentially distinguish a model in economic theory from its counterpart in econometric practice.

REFERENCES

[1] ALMON, S. (1965). 'The Distributed Lag Between Capital Appropriations and Expenditures', *Econometrica*.

[2] —— (1968). 'Lags Between Investment Decisions and Their Causes', *Rev. Econ. Stats.*

[3] ANDERSON, L. C. (1969). 'The Influence of Economic Activity on the Money Stock—Additional Evidence on the Reverse-Causation Argument', *F.R.B. St. Louis Review*.

[4] —— and CARLSON, K. M. (1970). 'A Monetarist Model for Economic Stabilization', *F.R.B. St. Louis Review*.

[5] —— and JORDAN, J. L. (1968). 'Monetary and Fiscal Actions: A Test of Their Relative Importance in Economic Stabilization', *F.R.B. St. Louis Review*.

[6] —— —— (1968). 'The Monetary Base—Explanation and Analytic Use', *F.R.B. St. Louis Review*.

[7] —— —— (1969). 'Monetary and Fiscal Actions: A Test of the Relative Importance in Economic Stabilization—Comment—Reply', *F.R.B. St. Louis Review*.

[8] ANDO, A., and GOLDFELD, S. M. (1968). 'An Econometric Model for Evaluating Stabilization Policies', in A. Ando, E. C. Brown, and A. F. Friedlaender (eds.), *Studies in Economic Stabilization* (Washington, D.C.: Brookings).

[9] —— and MODIGLIANI, F. (1963). 'The "Life-Cycle" Hypothesis of Saving: Aggregate Implications and Tests', *American Economic Review*.

[10] —— —— (1969). 'Econometric Analysis of Stabilization Policies', *American Economic Review*.

[11] BERGSTROM, A. R. (1967). *The Construction and Use of Economic Models* (London: E.U.P.).

[12] BISCHOFF, C. W. (1969). 'Hypothesis Testing and the Demand for Capital Goods', *Rev. Econ. Stats.*

[13] —— (1971). 'The Effect of Alternative Lag Distributions', in G. Fromm, *Tax Incentives and Capital Spending* (Washington, D.C.: Brookings).

[14] BOUDON, R. (1965). 'A Method of Linear Causal Analysis', *American Sociological Review*.

[15] BRANSON, W. H., and KLEVORICK, A. K. (1969). 'Money Illusion and the Aggregate Consumption Function', *American Economic Review*.

[16] BRUNNER, K. (1968). 'The Role of Money and Monetary Policy', *F.R.B. St. Louis Review*.

[17] CAGAN, P., and GANDOLFI, A. (1969). 'The Lag in Monetary Policy as Implied by the Time Patterns of Monetary Effects on Interest Rates', *American Economic Review* (Papers and Proceedings).

[18] CARLSON, K. (1967). 'Estimates of the High-Employment Budget 1947–67', *F.R.B. St. Louis Review*.

[19] CHETTY, V. K. (1969). 'On Measuring the Nearness of Near-Moneys', *American Economic Review*.

[20] CHOW, G. C. (1958). *Hearings on Administered Prices in the Automobile Industry* (Washington D.C.: U.S. Government Printing Office).

[21] —— (1967). 'Multiplier, Accelerator, and Liquidity Preference in the Determination of National Income in the U.S.', *Rev. Econ. Stats.*

[22] CHRIST, C. F. (1968). 'A Simple Macroeconomic Model with a Government Budget Restraint', *J.P.E.*

[23] —— (1971). 'Econometric Models of the Financial Sector', *Journal of Money, Credit and Banking*.

[24] CLAYTON, G., GILBERT, J. C., and SEDGWICK, R. (eds.), (1971). *Monetary Theory and Monetary Policy in the 1970s* (Oxford: O.U.P.).

[25] COHEN, J. (1968). 'Integrating the Real and Financial Via the Linkage of Financial Flows', *Journal of Finance*.

[26] CROCKETT, J., FRIEND, I., and SHAVELL, H. (1967). 'The Impact of Monetary Stringency on Business Investment', *Survey of Current Business*.

[27] DAVIS, R. G. (1969). 'How Much Does Money Matter? A Look at Some Recent Evidence', *F.R.B. of New York Review*.

[28] DE LEEUW, F. (1962). 'The Demand for Capital Goods by Manufacturers', *Econometrica*.

[29] —— (1965). 'A Model of Financial Behaviour', in J. S. Duesenberry, G. Fromm, L. R. Klein, and E. Kuh (eds.), *The Brookings Quarterly Economics Model of the U.S.* (Amsterdam: North-Holland).

[30] —— (1969). 'A Condensed Model of Financial Behaviour', in J. S. Duesenberry, G. Fromm, L. R. Klein, and E. Kuh (eds.), *The Brookings Model: Further Results* (Amsterdam: North-Holland).

[31] —— and GRAMLICH, E. (1969). 'The Channels of Monetary Policy', *Federal Reserve Bulletin*.

[32] —— —— (1968). 'The Federal Reserve–MIT Econometric Model', *Federal Reserve Bulletin*.

[33] —— —— (1969). 'The Channels of Monetary Policy: A Further Report on the Federal Reserve–MIT Model', *Journal of Finance*.

[34] —— and KALCHBRENNER, J. (1969). 'Monetary and Fiscal Actions: A Test of Their Relative Importance in Economic Stabilization—Comment', *F.R.B. St. Louis Review*.

[35] DUNCAN, O. D. (1966). 'Path Analysis: Sociological Examples', *American Journal of Sociology*.

[36] EISNER, R., and NADIRI, I. (1968). 'Investment Behaviour and Neo-classical Theory', *Rev. Econ. Stats*.

[37] ENGLE, R., and LIU, T. C. (1971). 'Effects of Aggregation over Time on the Dynamic Character of an Econometric Model', paper to the N.B.E.R. Conference on Simulation.

[38] EVANS, M. K. (1967). 'A Study of Industry Investment Decisions', *Rev. Econ. Stats*.

[39] —— (1967). 'Multiplier Analysis of a Post-war Quarterly U.S. Model and a Comparison with Several Other Models', *Rev. Econ. Studs*.

[40] —— (1969). *Macroeconomic Activity* (New York: Harper Row).

[41] —— and KLEIN, L. R. (1967). *The Wharton Econometric Forecasting Model* (Philadelphia: University of Pennsylvania).

[42] —— —— and SAITO, M. (1969). 'Short-run Production and Long-run Simulation of the Wharton Model', paper to the N.B.E.R. Conference on Research in Income and Wealth (mimeographed).

[43] FAND, D. I. (1970). 'Some Issues in Monetary Economics', *F.R.B. St. Louis Review*.

[44] FELDSTEIN, M. (1970). 'Corporate Taxation and Dividend Behaviour', *Rev. Econ. Studs*.

[45] FISHER, G. R. (1970). 'Quarterly Dividend Behaviour', chapter 6 of K. Hilton and D. F. Heathfield (eds.), *The Econometric Study of the U.K.* (London: Macmillan).

[46] FRIEDLAENDER, A. F. (1968). 'The Federal Highway Programme as a Public Works Tool', in A. Ando, E. C. Brown, and A. F. Friedlaender (eds.), *Studies in Economic Stabilization* (Washington D.C.: Brookings).

[47] FRIEDMAN, M. (1961). 'The Lag in Effect of Monetary Policy', *J.P.E.*

[48] —— (1963). 'Money and Business Cycles', *Rev. Econ. Stats*.

[49] —— and MEISELMAN, D. (1963). 'The Relative Stability of Monetary Velocity and the Investment Multiplier in the United

States 1897–1958', in *Stabilization Policies* (Washington D.C.: Commission on Money and Credit).

[50] FRIEDMAN, M. (1970). 'A Theoretical Framework for Monetary Analysis', *J.P.E.*

[51] FRISCH, R. (1933). Editorial, *Econometrica.*

[52] FROMM, G., and TAUBMAN, P. (1968). *Policy Simulations with an Econometric Model* (Washington D.C.: Brookings).

[53] GELFAND, J. E. (1970). 'Mortgage Credit and Lower-Middle Income Housing Demand', *Land Economics.*

[54] GRAMLEY, L. E., and CHASE, JR., S. B. (1965). 'Time Deposits in Monetary Analysis', *Federal Reserve Bulletin.*

[55] GREENBERG, E. (1964). 'A Stock Adjustment Investment Model', *Econometrica.*

[56] GRILICHES, Z. (1967). 'Distributed Lags: A Survey', *Econometrica.*

[57] GUTTENTAG, J. M. (1966). 'The Strategy of Open Market Operations', *Q.J.E.*

[58] HAMBURGER, M. J. (1967). 'Interest Rates and the Demand for Consumer Durable Goods', *American Economic Review.*

[59] —— (1971). 'The Lag in the Effect of Monetary Policy: A Survey of Recent Literature', *F.R.B. of New York Review.*

[60] HENDERSHOTT, P. H. (1970). 'Neutralization of the Money Stock', *F.R.B. St. Louis Review.*

[61] HENDRY, D. F., and TRIVEDI, P. K. (1972). 'Maximum Likelihood Estimation of Difference Equations with Moving Average Errors: A Simulation Study', *Rev. Econ. Studs.*

[62] JAFFEE, D. M. (1971). *Credit Rationing and the Commercial Loan Market* (New York: Wiley).

[63] JORDAN, J. L. (1969). 'Elements of Money Stock Determination', *F.R.B. St. Louis Review.*

[64] JORGENSON, D. W., and SIEBERT, C. D. (1968). 'A Comparison of Alternative Theories of Corporate Investment Behaviour', *American Economic Review.*

[65] —— and STEPHENSON, J. A. (1967). 'Investment Behaviour in U.S. Manufacturing 1947–60', *Econometrica.*

[66] —— —— (1967). 'The Time Structure of Investment Behaviour in U.S. Manufacturing, 1947–60', *Rev. Econ. Stats.*

[67] KAUFMAN, G. C., and LAURENT, R. D. (1969). 'Three Experiments with Simulating a Modified FRB–MIT Model', mimeographed paper, Federal Reserve Bank of Chicago.

[68] KERAN, M. W. (1969). 'Monetary and Fiscal Influences on Economic Activity: The Foreign Experience', *F.R.B. St. Louis Review.*

[69] —— (1969). 'Monetary and Fiscal Influences on Economic Activity—The Historical Evidence', *F.R.B. St. Louis Review.*

[70] —— (1969). 'The Influences of Economic Activity on the Money Stock—Comments on the St. Louis Position—A Reply', *F.R.B. St. Louis Review*.

[77] —— (1970). 'Economic Theory and Forecasting', *F.R.B. St. Louis Review*.

[72] —— (1970). 'Neutralization of the Money Stock—Comment', *F.R.B. St. Louis Review*.

[73] —— (1970). 'Selecting a Monetary Indicator—Evidence from the United States and Other Developed Countries', *F.R.B. St. Louis Review*.

[74] —— (1971). 'Expectations, Money and the Stock Market', *F.R.B. St. Louis Review*.

[75] —— and BABB, C. T. (1969). 'An Explanation of Federal Reserve Actions (1933–68)', *F.R.B. St. Louis Review*.

[76] KLEIN, L. R. (1968). *An Essay on the Theory of Economic Prediction* (Helsinki: The Academic Book Store).

[77] —— and GOLDBERGER, A. S. (1955). *An Econometric Model of the U.S. 1929–52* (Amsterdam: North-Holland).

[78] KOYCK, L. M. (1954). *Distributed Lags and Investment Analysis* (Amsterdam: North-Holland).

[79] LIEBENBERG, M., HIRSCH, A. A., and POPKIN, J. (1966). 'A Quarterly Econometric Model of the U.S.: A Progress Report', *Survey of Current Business*.

[80] LIU, T. C. (1963). 'An Exploratory Quarterly Model of Effective Demand in the Postwar U.S. Economy', *Econometrica*.

[81] MAISEL, S. J. (1965). 'Non-business Construction', in J. S. Duesenberry, G. Fromm, L. R. Klein, and E. Kuh (eds.), *The Brookings Quarterly Model of the U.S.* (Amsterdam: North-Holland).

[82] McGOULDRICK, P. F., and PETERSON, J. E. (1968). 'Monetary Restraint and Borrowing and Capital Spending of Large State and Local Governments in 1966', *Federal Reserve Bulletin*.

[83] MELICHAR, E. (1969). 'The Influence of Economic Activity on the Money Stock—Comments on the St. Louis Position', *F.R.B. St. Louis Review*.

[84] MELTZER, A. H. (1969). 'Controlling Money', *F.R.B. St. Louis Review*.

[85] MORIGUCHI, C. (1970). 'Aggregation over Time in Macroeconomic Relations', *International Economic Review*.

[86] MORONEY, J. R., and MASON, J. M. (1972). 'The Dynamic Impacts of Autonomous Expenditures and the Monetary Base on Aggregate Income', *Journal of Money, Credit and Banking*.

[87] MUELLER, E., and LEAN, J. (1967). 'The Savings Account as a Source of Financing Large Expenditures', *Journal of Finance*.

[88] MUKERJI, V. (1972). 'Non-linear Stochastic Models', unpublished paper.

[89] MUTH, R. F. (1960). 'The Demand for Non-farm Housing', in A. C. Harberger (ed.), *The Demand for Durable Goods* (Chicago: U.C.P.).

[90] NAGAR, A. L. (1969). 'Stochastic Simulation of the Brookings Econometric Model', in J. S. Duesenberry, G. Fromm, L. R. Klein, and E. Kuh (eds.), *The Brookings Model: Some Further Results* (Amsterdam: North-Holland).

[91] PETERSEN, J. E. (1971). 'Response of State and Local Governments to Varying Credit Conditions', *Federal Reserve Bulletin*.

[92] PHELPS, C. D. (1969). 'Real and Monetary Determinants of State and Local Highway Investment, 1951–66', *American Economic Review*.

[93] RASCHE, R. H., and SHAPIRO, H. T. (1968). 'The FRB–MIT Econometric Model Its Special Features', *American Economic Review* (Papers and Proceedings).

[94] SARGAN, J. D. (1973). 'Some Discrete Approximations to Continuous Time Stochastic Models', forthcoming.

[95] SHEARER, R. A. (1963). 'The Expansion of Bank Credit: An Alternative Approach', *Q.J.E.*

[96] SMITH, W. L. (1971). 'On Some Current Issues in Monetary Economics: An Interpretation', *Journal of Economic Literature*.

[97] SPARKS, G. R. (1967). 'An Econometric Analysis of the Role of Financial Intermediaries in Postwar Residential Building Cycles', in R. Ferber (ed.), *Determinants of Investment Behaviour* (Princeton: N.B.E.R.).

[98] SPENCER, R. W. (1969). 'The Relation Between Prices and Employment: Two Views', *F.R.B. St. Louis Review*.

[99] —— (1971). 'Population, The Labour Force, and Potential Output: Implications for the St. Louis Model', *F.R.B. St. Louis Review*.

[100] SUITS, D. B. (1958). 'The Demand for Automobiles', in *Report of the Sub-Committee on Antitrust and Monopoly* (Washington, D.C.).

[101] —— (1969). 'The Economic Outlook for 1969', in *The Economic Outlook for 1969* (Ann Arbor: The University of Michigan).

[102] TANNER, J. E. (1969). 'Lags in the Effects of Monetary Policy: A Statistical Investigation', *American Economic Review*.

[103] TEIGEN, R. L. (1969). 'An Aggregate Quarterly Model of the U.S. Monetary Sector, 1953–64', in K. Brunner, *Targets and Indicators of Monetary Policy* (San Francisco: Chandler).

[104] —— (1972). 'A Critical Look at Monetarist Economics', *F.R.B. of St. Louis Review*.

[105] TINBERGEN, J. (1939). *Statistical Testing of Business Cycle Theories II: Business Cycles in the U.S.A. 1919–32* (Geneva: League of Nations).

[106] TRIVEDI, P. K. (1970). 'Inventory Behaviour in U.K. Manufacturing 1956–67', *Rev. Econ. Studs*.

[107] —— (1970). 'A Note on the Application of Almon's Method of Calculating Distributed Lag Coefficients', *Metroeconomica*.

[108] WRIGHT, S. (1934). 'The Method of Path Coefficients', *Annals of Mathematical Statistics*.

[109] —— (1960). 'Path Coefficients and Path Regressions: Alternative or Complementary Concepts?', *Biometrics*.

[110] YOHE, W. P., and KARNOSKY, D. S. (1969). 'Interest Rates and Price Level Changes, 1952–69', *F.R.B. St. Louis Review*.

[111] ZECHER, R. (1970). 'Implications of Four Econometric Models for the Indicators Issue', *American Economic Review* (Papers and Proceedings).

[112] ZELLNER, A. (1972). 'On the Aggregation Problem: A New Approach to a Troublesome Problem', pp. 365–74 in K. A. Fox *et al.* (eds.), *Economic Models, Estimation and Risk Programming: Essays in Honour of Gerhard Tintner* (Berlin: Springer Verlag).

ALTERNATIVE TEMPORAL CROSS-SECTION SPECIFICATIONS OF THE DEMAND FOR DEMAND DEPOSITS

EDGAR L. FEIGE*

(*University of Wisconsin*)

OVER a decade has passed since Gurley and Shaw [5] alerted the economics profession to the importance of considering the implications of the growth of non-bank financial liabilities for monetary theory and policy. This period has produced agreement that one of the central empirical magnitudes which requires investigation is the degree of substitutability, and the stability of the substitution relationship between demand deposits and other liquid assets. Among the interrelated issues for which this magnitude has consequences are:

(1) The appropriate definition of money.
(2) The impact of the growth of financial intermediaries on the effectiveness of monetary policy.
(3) The effects of interest-rate competition on the profitability and net worth of financial intermediaries.
(4) The effects of interest-rate ceilings and prohibitions on the portfolio positions of financial intermediaries.
(5) Regulation policies concerning proposed mergers of financial institutions which are regarded as being in 'distinct lines of commerce'.
(6) The impact and wisdom of extending monetary authority controls to non-bank financial intermediaries.
(7) The incidence effects of monetary policy for different sectors of the economy, particularly the market for residential mortgages.

* The author wishes to acknowledge the excellent assistance of Robert Avery, Douglas Pearce, and P. A. V. B. Swamy. Dennis Aigner provided helpful comments.

Given the importance of the foregoing issues, I wish to inquire whether the cornucopia of empirical studies undertaken in the past decade has produced some consensus concerning the degree of substitution between liquid assets. Since a complete survey of these results is beyond the scope of this paper, I will restrict my overview to those studies which have estimated demand functions for demand deposits utilizing pooled temporal cross-section data. This limitation in scope necessarily excludes valuable evidence from time-series data, as well as evidence derived from the estimation of demand functions for other liquid assets. Therefore, a final evaluation of the empirical evidence must await a broader study. There is, however, sufficient richness in the temporal cross-section evidence to merit a separate investigation.

Economists, as a rule, have a poor track record for attempting exact replications of prior empirical studies. Indeed, product differentiation rather than replication seems to be the price of entry into most major journals. Fortunately, we have available attempted replications of empirical results dealing with estimates of substitution elasticities among liquid assets from temporal cross-section data. By limiting my overview to a particular class of studies, I hope to be able to discriminate between semantic product differentiation and substantive differences in empirical results. More importantly, since the studies reviewed, while basically similar, still exhibit variations in data bases, time periods, functional form, and estimation procedures, it is possible to examine the robustness of the results over different specifications and estimation procedures.

Section I reviews and evaluates the existing evidence on the degree of substitution between demand deposits, time deposits, mutual savings bank deposits, and savings and loan deposits, gleaned from studies which estimate the demand function for demand deposits from temporal cross-section data. This review suggests that while a remarkable degree of consensus emerges, the differential use of dummy variables in the model specifications appears to be an important factor in explaining substantive variations between studies. In Section II we construct a covariance model of the demand for demand deposits and test this model against a more restrictive specification in order empirically to determine the importance of dummy variable specifications. In Section III we elaborate and test a random coefficient model of the demand for demand deposits. This model, while more restrictive than the covariance model with respect to temporal dummy variables, allows a richer specification of variation in behaviour across states.

I. A review of the existing studies of the demand for demand deposits based on temporal cross-section data

During the post World War II period in the United States, theoretical developments and casual empirical observation coalesced to create the intellectual predisposition to the belief that the liabilities of non-bank financial intermediaries were close substitutes for commercial bank liabilities. At the theoretical level, the Gurley–Shaw thesis suggested that the effectiveness of monetary action does not depend simply on the elasticity of substitution between government debt and money, but rather on the degree of substitution between money and a broad spectrum of liquid assets including the liabilities of non-bank financial intermediaries. It was left to Tobin and Brainard [17] to develop rigorously a model which showed how the impact of a given monetary action depended critically upon the the degree of substitution between those intermediary liabilities which were directly controlled by the government and uncontrolled intermediary liabilities.

At the empirical level, the termination and reversal of the well-established secular decline in velocity,[1] coupled with the dramatic post-war growth in non-bank financial intermediary liabilities, reinforced the prevalent notion that demand deposits and other liquid assets were highly competitive. Substantive empirical work was expected to establish the extent to which substitution relationships were stable and predictable.

Given this intellectual climate, it was surprising to discover that systematic efforts to estimate the elasticities of substitution between demand deposits and other intermediary liabilities could not confirm the importance of the substitution relationships. The tension between the apparently overwhelming casual evidence of high substitutability, and the systematic evidence of the absence of strong substitution, led Laidler [10] in his excellent survey of the theoretical and empirical issues concerning the definition of money cautiously to conclude,

With the evidence we have at the moment, it is possible to come to only tentative conclusions about what set of assets the monetary authorities

[1] Selden [15].

should attempt to manipulate in carrying out monetary policy. . . . However, there does seem to have been some change over time, particularly since the second world war, in the assets to whose rate of return the demand for money however defined is most sensitive. The apparent importance of savings and loan associations in recent years is particularly noteworthy. These conclusions must, however, be treated with care, since they are contradicted by Feige's important study.

Since the process of 'disintermediation' and 'reintermediation' appears to be as dramatic in the 1970's[2] as it was in the earlier decades, I must share Laidler's scepticism concerning the failure of several attempts at finding economically significant elasticities of substitution between key liquid assets. The evidence from temporal cross-section studies of the demand for demand deposits indicates that the debate concerning the degree and stability of substitution relationships has not come to rest. At the one extreme are the findings of Feige [3], Hartley [6], and Kichline [9], which conclude,

demand deposits do not appear to be close substitutes for other liquid assets. (Feige [3], p. 43.)

demand deposits and time deposits in commercial banks are weak substitutes . . . demand deposits and savings and loan shares are strong complements. (Hartley [6], p. 80.)

the limited substitutability of demand deposits for income yielding depository type claims does not support Gurley and Shaw's contention that such deposits exhibit a high degree of substitutability. (Kichline [9], p. 29.)

At the other extreme is the temporal cross-section evidence of Lee [11], who concludes that, 'savings and loan shares are close substitutes for money. . . . The empirical evidence from the various data investigated unequivocally substantiates the substitution hypothesis of Gurley and Shaw.' (Lee [11], pp. 452 and 455.)

In order to attempt to reconcile these diametrically opposed viewpoints, I wish to consider the evidence in some detail and deal with several of the critiques which have been raised concerning the reliability of the temporal cross-section studies. The studies considered in this paper share many common elements. Almost all of these studies estimate a demand function for demand deposits using as arguments, income and the rates of return on demand deposits, commercial bank time deposits, savings and loan deposits,

[2] See Economic Report of the President [2].

and mutual savings deposits. With the exception of Lee's [11] study dealing with individual household survey data, all the studies use as the basic unit of observation area-wide holdings of demand deposits of individuals, corporations, and partnerships. The data span the period 1949–64.

Laidler [10] has levelled several criticisms against Feige's original study which deserve explicit attention, since the issues raised are common to all of the studies reported in this paper.

Laidler [10] correctly suggests that to the extent that different ownership classes exhibit different portfolio behaviour, demand deposits data which combine the holdings of individuals, partnerships, and corporations may represent too gross a measure. Unfortunately, no data are directly available by ownership classification, and attempts to correct this problem by use of ancillary ownership data have shown the estimates of substitution elasticities to be quite insensitive to ownership adjustments.[3]

The second problem raised by Laidler [10] is that the deposit data by states reflect the ownership of deposits by residents of all states. Thus, even if out-of-state ownership of deposits represented only a small fraction of the total, these deposits might be quite sensitive to rates of return in all states and thus represent a specification error in the temporal cross-section models. A casual test of this hypothesis can be carried out by examining the pattern of residuals between adjoining states where this type of cross-over is likely to be prevalent. My own investigation of residual patterns displayed no systematic cross-over effect. Moreover, to the extent that such an effect exists, it is likely to be captured in dummy variables which take account of centres of financial activity.

The final critique by Laidler [10] deals with the common usage of measuring the negative rate of return on demand deposits as the ratio of service charges to average deposit balances. Laidler ([10], p. 522) argues,

The ratio of bank charges to deposits may not remain a constant in the absence of changes in the interest rate on demand deposits. For a given volume of payments this ratio might be expected to rise as the quantity of demand deposits falls, for it should be related to the rate of deposit turnover. Bank charges are primarily bookkeeping charges and are related to the flow of payments made by check rather than to the stock of demand deposits in existence. If the volume of check payments is roughly related to the level of permanent income, one would

[3] See Feige [3], and Hartley [6].

expect a negative relationship to hold between the ratio of bank charges to deposits and the level of demand deposits held, given the level of permanent income, a relationship such as Feige finds. It would arise from variations in the rate of turnover implied by their being held in different ratios to permanent income. This relationship though would reflect the nature of bank charges and not the influence of the rate of return on demand deposits.

Laidler concludes that the demand deposit rate proxy measures the true return very inaccurately, but he cannot assess the effects of this inaccuracy on the elasticity estimates. Since the negative return on demand deposits is used in all the studies under consideration here, and is statistically significant for all studies, the rationale for its use requires further explication.

Demand deposits yield a flow of non-pecuniary services which are assumed to be roughly proportional to the stock of deposits held. Commercial banks charge the deposit holder for the services provided by means of a service charge. The service charge, taken as a percentage of the average deposit balance, is viewed as the negative pecuniary rate of return on demand deposits. An increase in the cost of holding cash balances can be viewed in two ways. An increase in costs can be seen as compensation to the bank for the provisions of additional services per dollar per unit of time. Alternatively, it may simply represent an increase in the per unit cost of services. In the former instance, the increased charge is simply an equalizing differential which represents the marginal cost of additional services per dollar of deposit. The marginal holder of deposits would presumably be indifferent between paying the extra cost of the incremental flow of services per dollar of deposit or retaining the original flow of services per dollar and avoiding the incremental cost. Thus, if increased service charges merely reflect an increase in the flow of non-pecuniary services per dollar of deposit, as suggested by Laidler, this increase is unlikely to affect the quantity of demand deposits demanded. Alternatively, if the increase in the cost of services is not offset by an increase in the flow of services per dollar of deposit, this represents to the holder of demand deposits a real increase in the cost of his deposits and will lead him to reduce his holdings of demand deposits and increase his holdings of some other income-yielding asset. Since the non-pecuniary services per dollar of deposit are not directly measurable, one must determine empirically the extent to which an increase in service charges is offset by an increase in service flow per dollar, by examining the relationship between service charges and the demand for demand deposits. If changes in service charges have no effect on the desired level of deposits, one can conclude that such changes merely represent equalizing differentials which are offset by an increased flow of services per dollar of deposit. Alternatively, if increased service charges are associated with a reduction in the demand for the stock of demand deposits, one can infer that the negative rate of return (or cost) of demand deposits has increased and thus induced individuals to shift out of demand deposits and into other assets.

The models and the evidence

The temporal cross-section models reviewed in this section can be characterized by the following model specification. Given N states and T time periods, y_{nt} represents an observation of the per capita level of demand deposits for the nth state and the tth time period. Let x_{jnt} represent an observation on the jth independent variable (of which there are K) for the nth state and the tth time period and z_{lnt} represent the lth dummy variable (of which there are D) for the nth state and tth time period.

The model we are concerned with is

$$y_{nt} = \alpha + \sum_{j=1}^{K} \beta_j x_{jnt} + \sum_{\ell=1}^{D} \gamma_\ell z_{\ell nt} + \varepsilon_{nt}, \tag{1}$$

where ε_{nt} is a random error term. In matrix notation the model can be written as

$$Y = [i \vdots X \vdots Z] \begin{pmatrix} \alpha \\ \vdots \\ \beta \\ \vdots \\ \gamma \end{pmatrix} + \varepsilon, \tag{2}$$

where

$$Y = \begin{bmatrix} y_{11} \\ \vdots \\ y_{1T} \\ \vdots \\ y_{N1} \\ \vdots \\ y_{NT} \end{bmatrix}, \qquad X = \begin{bmatrix} x_{111} & \cdots & x_{K11} \\ \vdots & & \vdots \\ x_{11T} & \cdots & x_{K1T} \\ \vdots & & \vdots \\ x_{1N1} & \cdots & x_{KN1} \\ \vdots & & \vdots \\ x_{1NT} & \cdots & x_{KNT} \end{bmatrix},$$

$$(NT \times 1) \qquad\qquad (NT \times K)$$

$$
Z = \begin{bmatrix} z_{111} & \cdots & z_{D11} \\ \vdots & & \vdots \\ z_{11T} & \cdots & z_{D1T} \\ \vdots & & \vdots \\ z_{1NT} & \cdots & z_{DN1} \\ \vdots & & \vdots \\ z_{1NT} & \cdots & z_{DNT} \end{bmatrix}, \qquad \varepsilon = \begin{bmatrix} \varepsilon_{11} \\ \vdots \\ \varepsilon_{1T} \\ \vdots \\ \varepsilon_{N1} \\ \vdots \\ \varepsilon_{NT} \end{bmatrix} \tag{3}
$$

$$(NT \times D) \qquad\qquad (NT \times 1)$$

and i is a $NT \times 1$ vector of ones, α is a scaler, β is a $K \times 1$ vector of behaviour coefficients, and γ is a $D \times 1$ vector of dummy variable coefficients. The X matrix contains observations on income and the rates of return on various liquid assets and the Z matrix includes regional dummy variables. Under some specifications considered below the dummy variables are entirely suppressed, and this specification is characterized by constraining the γ vector $= 0$.

In order to gauge the degree of consensus between different temporal cross-section estimates of the demand functions for demand deposits, Table IV.7 summarizes the critical elasticity estimates from different studies. Table IV.7 also indicates the estimation procedure employed, the time period under study, the functional form utilized, the unit of observation, and the type of dummy variable specification used. A more complete specification of the specific dummy variables used in each of the studies is included in Appendix A.

The first cross-sectional study which revealed weak substitutability between demand deposits and other liquid assets is Feige [T1–1]. After estimating separate demand functions for each year, Feige tested and could not reject the hypothesis that the coefficients were stable over the entire period 1949–59. The elasticities presented as [T1–1] reflect the pooled temporal cross-section estimates. Hartley [T1–2] successfully replicated Feige's results. The first empirical challenge to these surprising results appeared in Lee's [T1–3] recalculation of Feige's estimates. Lee argued that 'the strange results in Feige's study stem from an excessive use of dummy variables' (Lee [11]). Lee asserted that since the regional dummy variables were highly correlated with the included interest-rate variables, 'such high multicollinearity clearly indicates the spuriousness of Feige's regression estimates'. As Friedman and Schwartz [4] have subsequently pointed out,

Feige uses these variables to allow for special circumstances of particular states or regions, such as states that permit establishment of mutual

TABLE IV.7

Summary of Existing Pooled Temporal Cross-Section Evidence from Demand Functions for Demand Deposits[a]

Reference number	Author	Estimation procedure[b]	Time period	Functional form	Unit of observation	Dummy variable specification[c]	Elasticity estimates[d]				
							η_{rdd}	η_{rdt}	η_{rds}	η_{rdm}	η_{jy}
[TI-1]	Feige	OLS	1949–59	Linear	State	RD	0.31*	−0.10*	0.30*	0.04	0.92*
[TI-2]	Hartley (replication)	OLS	1949–59	Linear	State	RD	0.31*	−0.10*	0.30*	0.04	0.92*
[TI-3]	Lee	OLS	1949–59	Linear	State	ND	0.37*	0.02	−0.31*	−0.05*	1.36*
[TI-4]	Hartley (replication)	OLS	1949–59	Linear	State	ND	0.39*	−0.06	0.06	−0.05*	1.43*
[TI-5]	Hartley	OLS	1949–64	Linear	State	ND	0.34*	−0.19*	0.11	−0.06*	1.46*
[TI-6]	Hartley	REE	1949–64	Linear	State	RD	0.27*	−0.18*	0.32*	−0.02	0.97*
[TI-7]	Feige	REE	1949–53	Linear	State	RD	0.32*	−0.21*	0.01	0.13*	0.98*
[TI-8]	Feige	OLS	1954–8	Linear	State	RD	0.38*	−0.06	−0.19*	0.17*	0.94*
[TI-9]	Lee		1956–9	Linear	Household	RD	0.49*	0.40	−1.61*	—	N.A.
[TI-10]	Kichline	OLS	1965–6	Linear	SMSA[e]	RD	N.A.	0.001	−0.006	−0.005*	0.80*
[TI-11]	Cohen	OLS	1950–60	Log-linear	State	RD	0.22*	−0.34*	—	—	1.12*

[a] All elasticities are computed at the mean for linear functions.
[b] OLS denotes ordinary least squares; REE denotes restricted efficient estimation.
[c] RD denotes regional dummies, ND denotes no dummies.
[d] * denotes significance at the 5% level.
[e] SMSA denotes Standard Metropolitan Statistical Areas.

savings banks and those that do not and states that contain the main financial centers of each of four regions and those that do not. As evidence that the use of dummy variables is excessive, Lee cites multi-collinearity between them and other independent variables. This does suggest a real problem with the statistical stability of Feige's estimates. However, it certainly does not mean that if the special features Feige seeks to control are present, as they clearly are, correct results can be obtained by neglecting them, as Lee does in a regression using Feige's data (though not in one using Consumer Survey data).

The major effect of Lee's omission of the dummy variables was to produce an estimate of the elasticity of substitution of demand deposits for savings and loan shares of -0.31, which by conventional standards would not be regarded as 'strong substitutability'. More problematic, however, was the failure of Hartley's study [T1–4] to replicate Lee's results. Hartley, using the same data but omitting the dummy variables, found a non-significant cross elasticity of 0.06. When Hartley [T1–5] extended the data to include the period 1960–4, omitting dummy variables, he again found a non-significant positive cross elasticity for demand deposits and savings and loan shares. His final recalculation of Feige's original model, extended over the period 1949–64, again confirmed a complementarity relationship between demand deposits and savings and loan shares [T1–6].

The other elasticity estimates appear to be remarkably robust given different specifications for dummy variables and different time periods. The major exception appears in the higher income elasticity estimated when the dummy variables are suppressed.

The fact that Lee's critique collapses under both theoretical scrutiny and econometric attempts at replication leaves the original evidence of weak substitution largely intact. Lee's critique of the use of regional dummy variables does give rise to the suggestion that rather than an 'excessive use' of dummy variables, the prior studies might be criticized on the grounds of using too few dummy variables. If individual states, for example, had fixed but different intercepts, a richer specification would eliminate the implicit constraint that all these intercepts be equal. This richer specification is attempted in Section II.

Feige also attempted to estimate the demand function for demand deposits by taking account of the Slutsky condition which imposes a constraint on the substitution coefficients across demand equations. The restricted efficient estimates are reported for two sub-periods as [T1–7] and [T1–8], and suggest at best a weak substitution relationship between demand deposits, time deposits, and savings and loan shares.

The most dramatic evidence of a strong substitution relationship is found in Lee's study [T1–9] of individual households from household survey data. Lee estimates a cross elasticity of −1·6 between demand deposits and savings and loan shares. While a higher cross elasticity is to be expected for household data, Lee's results seem highly implausible. They suggest that a one percentage point rise in the cost of demand deposits will reduce per capita demand deposits by $660, and raise the total of time deposits and savings and loan deposits by $951.[4] One problem with Lee's study may arise from the fact that he assigns regional interest rates to individual households. He claims ([11], p. 449) that the regional rates for any single cross section 'do not exhibit variations which are large enough to yield meaningful estimates for the purpose of statistical inference'. Thus the large estimated effect may result from temporal variations in the rates. In this case his evidence might be considered better with other time-series studies. Unfortunately, a review of the extensive time-series literatures is beyond the scope of this study.

Kichline [9] has provided us with independent evidence [T1–10] which uses Standard Metropolitan Statistical Areas as the basic unit of analysis. His study uses announced interest rates rather than effective rates and he includes convenience cost variables which do not appear to have important effects. Kichline's estimates do not lend support to the substitution hypothesis.

The final study by Cohen [1] uses aggregate data rather than per capita data and does not include the rate of return on savings and loan association shares [T1–11]. Although his functional form is log-linear and his demand deposit holdings are reputedly for individuals, his evidence is broadly consistent with earlier studies, particularly when one notes that the rate of return on time deposits may also reflect some substitution between demand deposits and savings and loan shares.

---

[4] See Friedman–Schwartz [4]. Another study by Mueller and Osborne [13] based on the same survey data concludes that 'savers at large are not ready to be diverted from their present financial policies by moderate changes in yield patterns'. Only one family in twelve responded affirmatively to a question asking whether changes in saving account interest rates influence what they do with their savings.

When all the evidence presented in Table IV.7 is considered, one can conclude that with one notable exception [T1–9], the evidence appears to be remarkably consistent. The greatest consistency is found in the estimate of the own rate elasticity for demand deposits. Considering all of the studies, the estimated range for the elasticity is 0·22 to 0·49. When Lee's household survey study [T1–9] is eliminated, the range is reduced to 0·22 to 0·39. In all studies the rate is highly significant and obviously robust over different specifications.

The evidence for substitutability between demand deposits and time deposits is also remarkably consistent. If one excludes the household survey [T1–9] study and the non-replicated study by Lee [T1–3], there are six studies reporting statistically significant but low elasticities ranging from −0·10 to −0·34. Since Cohen's study may also reflect substitution from savings and loan shares, the range may be narrowed to −0·10 to −0·21. The remaining three studies show statistically non-significant elasticities ranging from −0·06 to 0·06. The evidence thus supports the contention of a low elasticity of substitution between demand deposits and time deposits.

The evidence for savings and loan shares is by far the most ambiguous. Putting aside Lee's household estimates and his non-replicated study, the range is from −0·19 to +0·32. Four studies indicate low and statistically non-significant elasticities, while three studies show significant complementarity and one significant substitutability. With the exception of Lee's household study, however, the weight of the evidence is counter-intuitive, suggesting little evidence for the substitution hypothesis and some confirming evidence for the surprising complementarity relationship.

The demand deposit substitution relationship with mutual savings bank deposits appears to be generally consistent with a weak substitution hypothesis. The complementarity result yielded by the restricted efficient estimates may stem from weight given to evidence from the demand functions for other liquid assets.

Finally, the income elasticities range from 0·80 to 1·46, but it appears that the suppression of dummy variables may be responsible for the higher income elasticity estimates. In order to examine this specific hypothesis and to get a clear test of the effects of a richer dummy variable specification, we turn to a covariance or error components model which allows for separate state and time effects.

II. Covariance and error components specifications of the demand for demand deposits

The review in the preceding section suggests the possibility that the relevant elasticity estimates may be sensitive to changes in the specification of the temporal cross-section model. In particular, it has become commonplace in temporal cross-section studies to incorporate dummy variables to account for time and state effects which are not readily attributable to identifiable causal variables.[5] For the case of estimating demand functions for demand deposits, it has already been argued that states which include major financial centres may attract a higher level of demand deposits than could be explained by the states' income or rates of returns. Similarly, state laws concerning mutual savings banking, branch banking, bank holding companies, etc. may have an independent effect on the quantity of demand deposits held in a particular state. Analogously, there may be temporal changes which have symmetrical effects on all geographic regions but differ over time. Thus, changes in federal regulations or policy and changes in general expectations may account for shifting levels of demand deposits over time. To the extent that such effects are present, a model which does not take account of them entails a specification error which can result in biased estimates of the remaining behavioural parameters. In order to test this hypothesis, we first estimate a demand function for demand deposits which suppresses all dummy effects.

The model estimated is similar to Hartley's study [T1–5]. The data base was updated to cover the period 1949–65 and the functional form was assumed to be log-linear. The log-linear form which assumes constant elasticities rather than constant coefficients was chosen after noting the robustness of the elasticity estimates over different time periods. Zarembka's independent investigation of the functional form of the demand function for money also supports the log-linear formulation.[6] All other variables are analogous to those used in the earlier studies with the sole exception that the time deposit interest rate is taken as a weighted average of the rates on commercial bank time deposits and mutual savings bank deposits. The estimated elasticities are presented in Table IV.8 [T2–1]. Not surprisingly, the elasticity estimates are roughly consistent with those obtained in Section I for models excluding dummy variables.

[5] See Wallace and Hussain [18], Hoch [8], and Mundlak [14].
[6] See Zarembka [19].

The cross elasticities are low and non-significant and the own elasticity is significant and falls within the expected range. As before, the income elasticity exceeds unity.

In order to allow for a richer specification which includes temporal and spatial effects, we turn to a covariance specification of the temporal cross-section model. Given N states and T time periods, the relationship connecting the observations on the dependent variable y_{nt}, with the K independent variables $x_{1nt} \ldots x_{Knt}$ is

$$y_{nt} = \alpha + U_n + V_t + \sum_{j=1}^{K} \beta_j x_{jnt} + \varepsilon_{nt}$$

$$(n = 1 \ldots N; t = 1 \ldots T) \quad (4)$$

where ε_{nt} is a random error with mean zero and variance σ^2. Letting

$$Y = \begin{bmatrix} y_{11} \\ \vdots \\ y_{1T} \\ \vdots \\ y_{N1} \\ \vdots \\ y_{NT} \end{bmatrix}, \quad \alpha = \begin{bmatrix} \alpha \\ \vdots \\ \alpha \\ \vdots \\ \alpha \\ \vdots \\ \alpha \end{bmatrix}, \quad U + V = \begin{bmatrix} U_1 + V_1 \\ \vdots \\ U_1 + V_T \\ \vdots \\ U_N + V_1 \\ \vdots \\ U_N + V_T \end{bmatrix},$$

$$X = \begin{bmatrix} X_{111} & \cdots & X_{K11} \\ \vdots & & \vdots \\ X_{11T} & \cdots & X_{K1T} \\ \vdots & & \vdots \\ X_{1N1} & \cdots & X_{KN1} \\ \vdots & & \vdots \\ X_{1NT} & & X_{KNT} \end{bmatrix}, \quad \beta = \begin{bmatrix} \beta_1 \\ \vdots \\ \beta_K \end{bmatrix}, \quad \varepsilon = \begin{bmatrix} \varepsilon_{11} \\ \vdots \\ \varepsilon_{1T} \\ \vdots \\ \varepsilon_{N1} \\ \vdots \\ \varepsilon_{NT} \end{bmatrix}$$

be a $TN \times 1$ vector, $TN \times 1$ vector, $TN \times 2$ matrix, $TN \times K$ matrix, $K \times 1$ vector, and $TN \times 1$ vector respectively, we have,

$$Y = \alpha + U + V + X\beta + \varepsilon. \quad (5)$$

The first model estimated in this section is simply (5) with the restriction that $U = V = 0$. The richer unconstrained model represented by (5) can be viewed as a covariance model which requires estimation of $N + T$ state and time intercepts. Alternatively, if U and V are regarded as random errors, (5) can be viewed as an error components model requiring the estimation of the means and variances of the time and state error components.[7] Since the major

---

[7] See Maddala [12].

focus of our interest is to estimate the β coefficients, it is computationally possible to 'sweep out' the state and time intercept terms by means of a covariance transformation. Letting I_T, I_{NT}, P_T, and P_{NT} be $T \times T$ and $NT \times NT$ identity matrices and $T \times T$ and $NT \times NT$ matrices of ones respectively, and defining

$$A = \begin{bmatrix} I_T^{11} & \cdots & I_T^{1N} \\ \vdots & \ddots & \\ I_T^{N1} & \cdots & I_T^{NN} \end{bmatrix}, \qquad B = \begin{bmatrix} P_T^{11} & & 0 \\ & \ddots & \\ 0 & & P_T^{NN} \end{bmatrix},$$

the transformation operator,

$$Q = \left[I_{NT} - \frac{1}{N} A - \frac{1}{N} B + \frac{1}{NT} P_{NT} \right]$$

can be applied to (5) to 'sweep out' the intercept terms since

$$QY = Q\alpha + Q(U + V) + QX\beta + Q\varepsilon$$

reduces to

$$QY = QX\beta + Q\varepsilon. \tag{6}$$

The effect of the covariance transformation operator is to transform the variables of the analysis into deviations from state and time means plus the grand mean. Ordinary least-square estimators applied to the transformed model (6) are unbiased and efficient. If (5) is viewed as an error components model, Wallace and Hussain [18] and Henderson [7] have shown that ordinary least-squares estimators are unbiased and asymptotically as efficient as the generalized least-squares estimators when the state and time effects dominate the residual error component. Since we have no *a priori* reason for choosing between the fixed intercept covariance model and the error components interpretation, we assume the covariance specification and estimate the appropriately transformed equation system by ordinary least squares.

The results of the covariance model estimates are presented in Table IV.8 as [T2–2]. As expected, the income elasticity is lower than that found in the more restrictive prior studies. The own elasticity is significant but lower than in previous estimates and the cross elasticity for time and mutual deposits is low and insignificant. The cross elasticity for savings and loan associations is $-0\cdot18$ and significant.

In order to test the appropriateness of the covariance specification against the more restrictive model estimated as [T2–1], we

Table IV.8

Covariance Model Estimates of the Demand for Demand Deposits

Reference number	Author	Estimation procedure	Time period	Functional form	Unit of observation	Dummy variable specification	Elasticity estimates			
							η_{rdd}	η_{rdtm}	η_{rds}	η_y
[T2–1]	Feige	OLS	1949–65	Log-linear	State	ND	0.36*	−0.04	−0.01	1.20*
[T2–2]	Feige	OLS	1949–65	Log-linear	State	T + SD	0.20*	0.03*	−0.18*	0.71*

Table IV.9

Random Coefficient Model Estimates

Reference number	Author	Estimation procedure	Time period	Functional form	Unit of observation	Dummy variable specification	Elasticity estimates			
							η_{rdd}	η_{rdtm}	η_{rds}	η_y
[T3–1]	Feige	GLS	1949–65	Log-linear	State	ND	0.37*	−0.07*	0.08*	1.20*
[T3–2]	Feige	WGLS	1949–65	Log-linear	State	Random coefficients	0.09*	−0.02	−0.21*	0.62*

can test the null hypothesis that $U = V = 0$. The hypothesis can be tested by

$$F = \frac{(e^{*\prime}e^* - e'e)/T + N + 1}{e'e/TN - T - N - 3}$$

where $e^{*\prime}e^*$ and $e'e$ are respectively the residual sum of squares for the constrained and unconstrained regressions. The F-statistic is distributed as F with $T + N + 1$ and $TN - T - N - 3$ degrees of freedom. The resulting F-statistic of 258·22 is highly significant, rejecting the hypothesis of zero time and state intercepts. The test suggests that Lee's [11] concern over an 'excessive use of dummy variables' is entirely unfounded, and that an appropriate temporal cross-section model must allow for separate state and time intercepts. Interestingly enough, however, the results of the covariance model are broadly consistent with earlier estimates.

III. A random coefficient specification of the demand function for demand deposits

While the covariance model presented in the preceding section is a considerably less restrictive specification than that of earlier models, it still assumes homoscedastic disturbances across states and identical slope coefficients over time and states. Feige [3] tested the stability of slope coefficients over time, but no comparable test has been performed to test stability of the coefficients over states. Updating of the temporal cross-section data to include a larger number of years makes this test possible.

The concern of this section is the relaxation of the assumptions of homoscedastic disturbances and fixed slope and intercept parameters over states.

Specification of heteroscedastic disturbances would be appropriate if different states were differentially affected by random temporal disturbances. For example, changes in monetary policy may result in larger shifts in deposits in states with sophisticated financial markets. In order to take account of this type of effect, consider a model for the nth state as,

$$y_n = X_n \beta_n + \varepsilon_n, \tag{7}$$

where y_n is a $T \times 1$ vector of dependent observations, X_n is a $T(K + 1)$ matrix of observations on the nth state, β_n is a $(K + 1) \times 1$ vector of coefficients, and ε_n is a $T \times 1$ vector of random disturbances, with each element distributed with mean zero and variance

σ_n^2. For simplicity, we shall no longer differentiate between the intercept and coefficient vector since they are treated symmetrically for the remainder of the paper. Thus, the first column of the observation matrix has unit elements, and the first element in the β vector is the state intercept. When the N states are pooled, and we impose the restriction,

$$\beta_n = \beta \quad \text{for } n = 1 \ldots N, \tag{8}$$

the model is identical to the constrained model estimated in the preceding section [T2–1] except that it allows for heteroscedastic disturbances.

This constrained model

$$y_n = X_n\beta + \varepsilon_n \tag{9}$$

can be estimated by means of the Aitken–Zellner generalized least-squares estimator, and the resulting elasticities are presented in Table IV.9 as [T3–1]. The estimated elasticities correspond closely with the estimates obtained by ordinary least squares for the homoscedastic model [T2–1].

Having allowed for heteroscedastic disturbances, we wish to examine the hypothesis that behaviour is consistent across states, that is, whether (8) is a valid restriction. Zellner [20] has shown that the estimated parameters $(\hat{\beta}_n)$ and error variances (s_n^2), derived from the N state models (7), can be combined with the generalized least-squares estimates $(\hat{\beta})$ of the pooled model (9), so that under hypothesis (8), the asymptotic distribution of

$$F = \frac{1}{(N-1)(K+1)} \sum_{n=1}^{N} \left\{ (\hat{\beta}_n - \beta)' \frac{X_n' X_n}{S_n^2} (\hat{\beta}_n - \beta) \right\}$$

is the F distribution with $(N-1)(K+1)$ and $(T-K-1)N$ degrees of freedom. The value of the calculated F-statistic was 208·61 which is well above the 5 per cent value of F with 240 and 588 degrees of freedom. We therefore cannot confirm the hypothesis of fixed and equal intercepts and slopes across states.

Rejection of hypothesis (8) suggests the specification of a less restrictive model which makes explicit allowance for inter-state variation. Swamy [16] has developed estimation procedures for a class of random coefficient models whose specification permits bounded variation across states. In particular, the random coefficient specification replaces the assumption (8) of fixed state intercepts and slopes, with the assumption that the β_n's in (7) are independently and identically distributed with

$$E\beta_n = \beta \tag{10}$$

$$E(\beta_n - \beta)(\beta_m - \beta)' = \Delta \quad \text{for } n = m$$
$$= 0 \quad \text{for } n \neq m$$

where Δ is a $(K + 1) \times (K + 1)$ variance–covariance matrix. Retaining the assumption of heteroscedastic error disturbances, the best linear unbiased estimator of β given the specifications in (7) and (10) is

$$\hat{\beta} = \sum_{n=1}^{N} W_n^* \hat{\beta}_n \tag{11}$$

where

$$W_n^* = \left[\sum_{n=1}^{N} \{\Delta + s_m^2 (X_m' X_m)^{-1}\}^{-1} \right]^{-1} \{\Delta + s_n^2 (X_n' X_n)^{-1}\}^{-1}$$

and $\hat{\beta}_n$ and s_n^2 are the ordinary least-squares estimates of the state parameters and error variances. Swamy has demonstrated that an unbiased estimator of Δ is

$$\hat{\Delta} = \frac{\sum_{n=1}^{N} \hat{\beta}_n \hat{\beta}_n' - (1/N) \sum_{n=1}^{N} \hat{\beta}_n \sum_{n=1}^{N} \hat{\beta}_n'}{N - 1} - \frac{1}{N} \sum_{n=1}^{N} s_n^2 (X_n' X_n)^{-1}. \tag{12}$$

The random coefficient model was estimated as outlined above and the results are reported in Table IV.9 as [T3–2]. The own elasticity is significant with the expected sign but considerably below the range found in other studies. The cross elasticity for time and mutual savings deposits conforms with that found in earlier studies and the savings and loan cross elasticity indicates a statistically significant elasticity of -0.21. The income elasticity is significant, but somewhat lower than that found in earlier studies.

The results for the random coefficient model must, however, be approached with some caution. The estimated variance–covariance matrix $\hat{\Delta}$ is formed as the difference between two matrices as shown in (12). While one would theoretically expect Δ to be positive semi-definite, Swamy has pointed out that 'in some numerical applications, $\hat{\Delta}$ will yield negative estimates for the variances of some coefficients'.[8] In our calculations, the variance of the time deposits

[8] Swamy [16], p. 170.

elasticity was found to be negative. This finding suggests that the data did not entirely meet the specifications and assumptions of the random coefficient model and thus the results cannot be regarded as conclusive. The estimates do, however, underline some of the findings based on the earlier covariance model.

Unfortunately, no formal test exists which allows a direct comparison between the appropriateness of the covariance specification *vis-à-vis* the random coefficient specification. The covariance model is less restrictive with respect to state slope specification. The common element of both models is the allowance of state intercept variation. Since the results are qualitatively similar, one might hazard the presumption that allowance for separate state intercepts is the critical specification requirement. When all the studies are reviewed, however, the only systematic effect of the inclusion of separate state intercept terms is to reduce the estimated income elasticity. No such systematic effects are observed for the interest-rate elasticities.

Summary and conclusions

We have reviewed the evidence on the demand function for demand deposits based on temporal cross-section data and have considered a rather rich menu of alternative model specifications. Tests of alternative model specifications led to the conclusion that an appropriate temporal cross-section specification must allow for the inclusion of separate state effects and possibly separate temporal effects.

Considering the differences in data bases, model specifications, and estimation procedures reviewed, one cannot help but be struck with the over-all robustness of the parameter estimates. With one notable and troublesome [T1–9] exception, the studies seem to support the following generalizations:

(1) The rate of return on demand deposits is an important argument of the demand function and the own elasticity appears to fall in the range 0·20 to 0·40.

(2) Demand deposits and commercial bank time deposits appear to be weak substitutes with a cross elasticity range of −0·20 to 0.

(3) Demand deposits and mutual savings bank deposits appear to be weak substitutes; however, one cannot exclude the possibility of a weak complementarity relationship. The range of the cross elasticity estimates is from −0·05 to +0·15.

(4) The relationship between demand deposits and savings and loan deposits remains somewhat ambiguous. At best the two assets exhibit weak substitutability; however, a complementarity relationship cannot be entirely ruled out. The estimated range for the cross elasticity is −0·20 to +0·30.

(5) The income elasticity of demand deposits for the post-war period appears to be less than unity. There is a strong systematic relationship between model specifications with respect to dummy variables and the estimated income elasticity. The more appropriately specified models which include separate spatial effects yielded income elasticities ranging between 0·65 and 0·95.

Since the evidence presented is limited to demand deposit estimates from the class of temporal cross-section models, the need remains for a systematic investigation of the consistency of the foregoing results with evidence culled from time-series studies and estimates of the demand functions for other liquid assets.

Appendix A

To facilitate comparisons across studies this appendix presents the following information on each study in the following order:

A. Title and source of the study.
B. Type and time period of the data.
C. Functional form of the regression equation.
D. Estimation technique.
E. Variables used in the regression from which the quoted elasticities were calculated.
F. Estimated demand function for demand deposits.
G. Table- and page-references for the elasticities reported and/or the regressions used to calculate the elasticities.

1. A. Edgar L. Feige, *The Demand for Liquid Assets: A Temporal Cross-Section Analysis* (Englewood Cliffs, N.J.: Prentice Hall, 1964).

   B. Pooled annual cross-section data by state, 1949–59.

   C. Linear functional form.

   D. Single-equation least-squares estimation.

   E. D Per capita commercial bank demand deposits (IPC);
      Y Permanent per capita personal income;

r_d Actual interest rate on commercial bank demand deposits (negative);

r_t Actual interest rate on commercial bank time deposits;

r_s Actual interest rate on savings and loan association shares;

r_m Actual interest rate on mutual savings bank deposits;

D_m Dummy variable for existence of mutual savings banks in a state;

I Survey estimate of ratio of individually held demand deposits to total demand deposits in commercial banks;

Cal Dummy variable (1 for California; 0 for all other states);

DC Dummy variable (1 for Washington, D.C.; 0 for all other states);

Ill Dummy variable (1 for Illinois; 0 for all other states);

NY Dummy variable (1 for New York; 0 for all other states);

W Dummy variable (1 for Western states excluding California; 0 for all other states);

S Dummy variable (1 for Southern states excluding Washington, D.C.; 0 for all other states);

C Dummy variable (1 for Central states excluding Illinois; 0 for all other states);

NE Dummy variable (1 for North-eastern states excluding New York; 0 for all other states).

F. $D = 0.365Y \quad +535r_d \quad -35r_t \quad +53r_s \quad +25r_m \quad -126D_m$
   $\quad (0.080) \quad (48) \quad\quad (13) \quad\quad (13) \quad\quad (15) \quad\quad (34)$

   $\quad +405I \quad +4\text{Cal} \quad +283\text{DC} \quad +151\text{Ill} \quad +734\text{NY}$
   $\quad (71) \quad\quad (57) \quad\quad (55) \quad\quad (48) \quad\quad (48)$

   $\quad +10\text{W} \quad -103\text{S} \quad +0.2\text{C} \quad -32\text{NE}$
   $\quad (43) \quad\quad (42) \quad\quad (43) \quad\quad (45)$

$\bar{R}^2 = 0.978$

G. Reported elasticities are one from Table 1, p. 25 and regression equation is from p. 24.

2. A. Philip B. Hartley, 'The Demand Function for Selected Liquid Assets: A Temporal Cross-Section Analysis', unpublished Ph.D. dissertation, University of Washington, 1966.

B. Pooled annual cross-section data by state, 1949–59.

C. Linear functional form.

D. Single-equation least-squares estimation.

E. Exactly the same variables used as Feige (Appendix, I.E).

F. $D = 0.365Y \quad +535r_d \quad -35r_t \quad +53r_s \quad +25r_m \quad -125D_m$

$\qquad (0.018) \quad (48) \quad\quad (13) \quad\quad (13) \quad\quad (15) \quad\quad (34)$

$\qquad +405I \quad +4\text{Cal} \quad +283\text{DC} \quad +151\text{Ill} \quad +734\text{NY}$

$\qquad (71) \quad\quad (57) \quad\quad (55) \quad\quad\quad (48) \quad\quad\quad (44)$

$\qquad +10\text{W} \quad -103\text{S} \quad +0.2\text{C} \quad -32\text{NE}$

$\qquad (43) \quad\quad (42) \quad\quad (43) \quad\quad (45)$

$\bar{R}^2 = 0.978$

G. Reported elasticities are from Table 4, p. 79 and regression equation is from Table 3, p. 78.

3. A. Tong Hun Lee, 'Substitutability of Non-Bank Intermediary Liabilities for Money: The Empirical Evidence', *Journal of Finance*, vol. 21, Sept. 1966, pp. 441–57.

B. Pooled annual cross-section data by state 1949–59.

C. Linear function form.

D. Single-equation least-squares estimation.

E. D Per capita commercial bank demand deposits (IPC);

$\quad Y$ Permanent per capita personal income;

$\quad r_d$ Actual interest rate on commercial bank demand deposits (negative);

$\quad r_t$ Actual interest rate on commercial bank time deposits;

$\quad r_s$ Actual interest rate on savings and loan association shares;

$\quad r_m$ Actual interest rate on mutual savings bank deposits.

F. The regression equation from which the reported elasticities were calculated was not given by Lee.

G. Reported elasticities are from Table 3, p. 454.

4. A. Hartley, op. cit.

B. Pooled annual cross-section data by state, 1949–59.

C. Linear functional form.

D. Single-equation least-squares estimation.

E. D Per capita commercial bank demand deposits (IPC);
    Y Permanent per capita personal income;
    r_d Actual interest rate on commercial bank demand deposits (negative);
    r_t Actual interest rate on commercial bank time deposits;
    r_s Actual interest rate on savings and loan association shares;
    r_m Actual interest rate on mutual savings bank deposits;
    I Survey estimate of ratio of individually held demand deposits to total demand deposits in commercial banks.

F. $D = 0 \cdot 566Y \quad +662r_d \quad -20r_t \quad +10r_s \quad -32r_m \quad +2I$
    $(0\cdot019) \quad (61) \quad (18) \quad (15) \quad (6) \quad (86)$

    $\bar{R}^2 = 0\cdot946$

G. Reported elasticities are from Table 44, p. 176 and the regression equation is from Table 41, p. 173.

5. A. Hartley, ibid.

   B. Pooled annual cross-section data by state, 1949–64.

   C. Linear functional form.

   D. Single-equation least-squares estimation.

   E. Exactly the same variables used as in the reference immediately above (Appendix, 4.E).

   F. $D = 0 \cdot 534Y \quad +485r_d \quad -54r_t \quad +19r_s \quad -35r_m \quad +30I$
       $(0\cdot015) \quad (39) \quad (12) \quad (13) \quad (4) \quad (60)$

       $\bar{R}^2 = 0\cdot949$

   G. Reported elasticities are from Table 44, p. 176 and the regression equation is from Table 41, p. 173.

6. A. Hartley, ibid.

   B. Pooled annual cross-section data by state, 1949–64.

   C. Linear functional form.

   D. Single-equation least-squares estimation.

   E. Exactly the same variables used as Feige (Appendix, 1.E).

F. $D = 0 \cdot 357Y \quad +388r_d \quad -51r_t \quad +54r_s \quad -12r_m \quad -54D_m$
$ (0 \cdot 015) \quad (32) \quad (10) \quad (11) \quad (9) \quad (24)$

$ +400I \quad -28\text{Cal} \quad +309\text{DC} \quad +118\text{Ill} \quad +720\text{NY}$
$ (60) \quad (45) \quad (44) \quad (38) \quad (36)$

$ +0 \cdot 2W \quad -99\text{S} \quad -18\text{C} \quad -31\text{NE}$
$ (34) \quad (33) \quad (33) \quad (35)$

$\bar{R}^2 = 0 \cdot 979$

G. Reported elasticities are from Table 4, p. 79 and the regression equation is from Table 3, p. 78.

7. A. Feige, op. cit.

B. Pooled annual cross-section data by state, 1949–53.

C. Linear functional form.

D. Restricted efficient estimation.

E. Exactly the same variables used as in Feige (Appendix, 1.E).

F. $D = 0 \cdot 420Y \quad +674r_d \quad -98r_t \quad +2r_s \quad +97r_m \quad -261D_m$
$ (0 \cdot 030) \quad (78) \quad (21) \quad (13) \quad (30) \quad (57)$

$ +431I \quad +192\text{Cal} \quad +366\text{DC} \quad +310\text{Ill} \quad +870\text{NY}$
$ (96) \quad (93) \quad (91) \quad (78) \quad (71)$

$ +169W \quad +68\text{S} \quad +171\text{C} \quad +151\text{NE}$
$ (71) \quad (65) \quad (68) \quad (74)$

G. Reported elasticities are from Table 2, p. 39 and the regression equation is from Table 19, p. 64.

8. A. Feige, ibid.

B. Pooled annual cross-section by state, 1954–8.

C. Linear functional form.

D. Restricted efficient estimation.

E. Exactly the same variables used as in Feige (Appendix, 1.E).

F. $D = 0 \cdot 355Y \quad +600r_d \quad +20r_t \quad -33r_s \quad +103r_m$
$ (0 \cdot 027) \quad (63) \quad (17) \quad (18) \quad (28)$

$ -301D_m \quad +448I \quad +255\text{Cal} \quad +519\text{DC} \quad +322\text{Ill}$
$ (66) \quad (101) \quad (98) \quad (91) \quad (82)$

$ +823\text{NY} \quad +202W \quad +93\text{S} \quad +184\text{C} \quad +110\text{NE}$
$ (76) \quad (76) \quad (71) \quad (73) \quad (76)$

G. Reported elasticities are from Table 2, p. 39 and the regression equation is from Table 19, p. 64.

9. Lee, op. cit.

B. Pooled cross-section data by household, 1956–9.

C. Linear function form.

D. Ordinary least-squares estimation.

E. D Commercial bank demand deposits per household;

   Y^d Disposable income per household;

   Y^k Income from household total assets;

   r_d Actual interest rate on demand deposits equal to the negative of the ratio of service charges to demand deposits;

   r_{tm} Weighted average of actual rates on commercial bank time deposits and mutual savings bank deposits-weights are deposit balances for state at the beginning of the year;

   r_s Actual interest rate on savings and loan association shares;

   P_c Consumer price index;

   A Age of household head;

   N Number of persons in household;

   $O_i, i = 1, 4$ Dummy variables for occupation of head of household;

   $C_i, i = 1, 3$ Dummy variables for size of city;

   R_c, R_s, R_w Regional dummies for north central, south, and west;

   T_{57}, T_{58}, T_{59} Dummy variables for year of survey.

F.
$$D = 0\cdot5632 \underset{(1\cdot083)}{} + \underset{(0\cdot0061)}{0\cdot1488Y_k} + \underset{(0\cdot0169)}{0\cdot3802Y_k} + \underset{(0\cdot2714)}{0\cdot6605r_d}$$

$$+ \underset{(0\cdot0703)}{0\cdot0882r_{tm}} - \underset{(0\cdot1047)}{0\cdot2272r_s} - \underset{(1\cdot073)}{0\cdot3564P_c} + \underset{(0\cdot0131)}{0\cdot0664A}$$

$$- \underset{(0\cdot0116)}{0\cdot828N} - \underset{(0\cdot0755)}{0\cdot2622O_1} + \underset{}{0\cdot3786O_2} - \underset{}{0\cdot1401O_3}$$

$$+ \underset{}{0\cdot8296O_4} - \underset{(0\cdot0525)}{0\cdot1350C_1} - \underset{(0\cdot0525)}{0\cdot0403C_2} - \underset{(0\cdot0466)}{0\cdot0253C_3}$$

$$+ \underset{(0\cdot0776)}{0\cdot2746R_c} + \underset{(0\cdot0751)}{0\cdot3580R_s} + \underset{(0\cdot1183)}{0\cdot5713R_w} - \underset{(0\cdot0542)}{0\cdot0699T_{57}}$$

$$-0.0072\,T_{58} \quad -0.0101\,T_{59}$$
$$(0.0838) \qquad (0.1047)$$

$$R^2 = 0.2383$$

G. Reported elasticities and the regression equation are from Table 2, p. 451.

10. A. James L. Kichline, 'Substitutability of Claims at Depository Institutions', unpublished paper presented at the Federal Reserve System Committee on Financial Analysis, Oct. 1968.

B. Pooled cross-section data by SMSA: 1 Dec. 1965; 1 Mar. 1966; 1 May 1966.

C. Linear functional form.

D. Ordinary least-squares estimation.

E. D Per capita demand deposits;

R_D Actual interest rate on commercial bank demand deposits equal to the ratio of service charges to average demand deposits but assumed constant over the sample period;

R_{P-D} Differential of the announced yield on passbook savings at commercial bank minus the yield on demand deposits;

R_{T-D} Differential of the announced yield on time deposits at commercial banks minus the yield on demand deposits;

R_{S-D} Differential of the announced yield on savings and loan association shares minus the yield on demand deposits;

MAD Dummy variable—coded 1 for mutual savings bank areas;

Y Permanent income per capita;

SO Savings and loan association offices per 100 square miles;

CO Commercial bank offices per 100 square miles;

NY Dummy variable for New York.

F. $D = -1.023 R_{P-D} \quad +0.205 R_{T-D} \quad -0.895 R_{S-D}$
     $(-1.732)^* \qquad (0.333) \qquad (-1.079)$

$$-97 \cdot 2MAD \quad +0 \cdot 235Y \quad -92 \cdot 6SO \quad -116 \cdot 1CO$$
$$(-2 \cdot 810) \quad (4 \cdot 803) \quad (-0 \cdot 771) \quad (-2 \cdot 105)$$
$$+1109 \cdot 1NY \quad +1075 \cdot 3$$
$$(10 \cdot 769) \quad (4 \cdot 719)$$

*t-statistic

$$\bar{R}^2 = 0 \cdot 563$$

G. Elasticities were calculated from the above regression equation, Table I, p. 8 with data supplied by Mr. Kichline.

11. A. Bruce C. Cohen, 'The Demand for Money by Ownership Category', *National Banking Review*, vol. 4, No. 3, Mar. 1967, pp. 317–36.

B. Pooled annual cross-section data by state, 1950–60—all data are in deviations from annual means.

C. Log-linear functional form.

D. Ordinary least-squares estimation.

E. DD_{ind} Demand deposits of individuals in real terms, state totals;

   SV Service charges as a per cent of demand deposits;

   R_t Actual interest rate on commercial bank time deposits;

   Y_p Permanent income;

   H_c Dummy variable for presence of holding company banking;

   M_s Dummy variable for presence of mutual savings banks.

F. $DD_{ind} = 0 \cdot 0045 \quad -0 \cdot 2188SV \quad -0 \cdot 3389R_t \quad +1 \cdot 1155Y_p$
         $(0 \cdot 0199) \quad (-3 \cdot 2403) \quad (-2 \cdot 2040) \quad (44 \cdot 749)$
           $+1 \cdot 9215H_c \quad -3 \cdot 7997M_s$
            $(2 \cdot 9301) \quad (-6 \cdot 9378)$

$$R^2 = 0 \cdot 8485$$

G. Reported elasticities are the coefficients of the log-linear regression equation from Table 3, p. 330.

REFERENCES

[1] COHEN, B. C., 'The Demand for Money by Ownership Category', *National Banking Review*, vol. 4, No. 3, Mar. 1967, pp. 317–36.

[2] *Economic Report of the President—Annual Report of the Council of Economic Advisers—1972* (Washington, D.C.: U.S. Government Printing Office, 1972).

[3] FEIGE, E. L., *The Demand for Liquid Assets: A Temporal Cross-Section Analysis* (Englewood Cliffs, N.J.: Prentice Hall, 1964).

[4] FRIEDMAN, M., and SCHWARTZ, A. J., *Monetary Statistics of the United States: Estimates, Sources, Methods* (New York: National Bureau of Economic Research, 1970).

[5] GURLEY, J. G., and SHAW, E. S., *Money in a Theory of Finance* (Washington, D.C.: Brookings Institution, 1960).

[6] HARTLEY, P. B., 'The Demand Function for Selected Liquid Assets: A Temporal Cross-Section Analysis', unpublished Ph.D. dissertation, University of Washington, 1966.

[7] HENDERSON, C. R., Jr., 'Comment on the Use of Error Components Models in Combining Cross Section with Time Series Data', *Econometrica*, vol. 39, No. 2, Mar. 1971, pp. 397–401.

[8] HOCH, I., 'Estimation of Production Function Parameters Combining Time-Series and Cross-Section Data', *Econometrica*, vol. 30, No. 1, Jan. 1962, pp. 34–53.

[9] KICHLINE, J. L., 'Substitutability of Claims at Depository Institutions', unpublished paper presented at the Federal Reserve System Committee on Financial Analysis, Oct. 1968.

[10] LAIDLER, D., 'The Definition of Money: Theoretical and Empirical Problems', *Journal of Money, Credit and Banking*, vol. I, No. 3, Aug. 1969, pp. 509–25.

[11] LEE, T. H., 'Substitutability of Non-Bank Intermediary Liabilities for Money: The Empirical Evidence', *Journal of Finance*, vol. 21, Sept. 1966, pp. 441–57.

[12] MADDALA, G. S., 'The Use of Variance Components Models in Pooling Cross Section and Time Series Data', *Econometrica*, vol. 39, No. 2, Mar. 1971, pp. 341–58.

[13] MUELLER and OSBORNE, 'Consumer Time and Savings Balance: Their Role in Family Liquidity', *American Economic Review*, May 1965, pp. 265–75.

[14] MUNDLAK, Y., 'Empirical Production Free of Management Bias', *Journal of Farm Economics*, vol. 43, No. 1, Feb. 1961, pp. 44–56.

[15] SELDEN, R. T., 'Monetary Velocity in the United States', in Milton Friedman (ed.), *Studies in the Quantity Theory of Money* (Chicago: University of Chicago Press, 1956).

[16] SWAMY, P. A. V. B., *Statistical Inference in Random Coefficient Regression Models* (New York: Springer-Verlag, 1971).

[17] TOBIN, J., and BRAINARD, W. C., 'Financial Intermediaries and Effectiveness of Monetary Controls', *American Economic Review*, vol. 53, May 1963, pp. 372–400.

[18] WALLACE, T. D., and HUSSAIN, A., 'The Use of Error Components

Models in Combining Cross Section with Time Series Data', *Econometrica*, vol. 37, No. 1, Jan. 1969, pp. 55–72.

[19] ZAREMBKA, P., 'Functional Form in the Demand for Money', *Journal of the American Statistical Association*, vol. 63, June 1968, pp. 502–11.

[20] ZELLNER, A., 'An Efficient Method of Estimating Seemly Un-related Regressions Tests for Aggression Bias', *Journal of the American Statistical Association*, vol. 57, 1962, pp. 348–68.

A MODEL OF THE UNITED KINGDOM MONETARY AUTHORITIES' BEHAVIOUR 1959–1969*

A. R. NOBAY
(University of Southampton)

I. Introduction

IT is conventional, in large-scale economy-wide models, to regard instruments of monetary policy as being exogenously determined. Such a treatment, however, by not explicitly recognizing that the setting of instruments by the authorities may be affected by the rest of the economic system, and so require joint estimation, results in inconsistent estimates of the parameters of the system. It is reasonable to assume that the authorities do not behave randomly when setting instruments of monetary policy. Therefore, it is desirable to incorporate into the monetary sectors of such systems, a set of relationships to explain the setting of the major instruments of monetary policy by the authorities.

There is, of course, one further advantage from treating instruments of policy as endogenous to such models—a considerable amount of interest and controversy centres around the behaviour of the monetary authorities and the perennial issues of the exogeneity/endogeneity of monetary aggregates in empirical studies of money and economic stabilization. An explicit examination of the behaviour of variables commonly regarded as monetary instruments may help to shed some light on these issues.

* I am grateful to Michael Artis, Harry Johnson, Marcus Miller, Michael Parkin, and David Rowan for comments and discussions, and to Alastair Morgan for research assistance. I am deeply indebted to Pravin Trivedi for extensive discussions and generous help in the computations reported, and to Gordon Fisher for encouragement and interest in this work.

The parameter estimates reported in this paper were obtained using the computer programmes FIML and ARTSLS, by D. F. Hendry (L.S.E.), converted for use on the Southampton ICL 1907 with slight changes by P. K. Trivedi. I am grateful to both Hendry and Trivedi for this generous help.

This paper reports on initial attempts to explain the behaviour of the U.K. monetary authorities in their setting of four conventionally accepted 'instruments' of monetary policy—the Bank's portfolio of government securities (the open-market instrument), Bank Rate (the administered short rate), Special Deposits and Advances Ceilings (quantitative restrictions and directives).

Whilst the paper falls into the general form of 'reaction function' studies, undertaken by Dewald and Johnson [6], and the important extensions of Wood [21], both conducted in the context of U.S. policy, it differs from these in three particular respects: (i) we attempt to explain the simultaneous setting of the four instruments noted above, in contrast to individual instrument setting; (ii) the explicit normative maximization, subject to constraints approach adopted by Wood is rejected in favour of a 'filtered preference' model, in an attempt to by-pass some of the difficulties raised by the former approach; and (iii) we extend the authorities' objectives to considering external equilibrium and debt management in addition to the conventional stabilization objectives. These issues are considered in Section II. In Section III we set out our own model of the authorities' behaviour, and present and interpret the econometric results for the specified structural equations.

II. Reaction functions—some outstanding issues

II.1. 'Instruments' of monetary policy examined

It will be useful to begin our analysis by stating and explaining the choice of policy instruments for consideration. We begin by defining the monetary base as follows:

$$B \equiv S_1 + C + A_D - G_D - O_D + Z_1 \qquad (1A)$$

		£ million
where S_1	≡ The Bank of England's security portfolio	3676·6
C	≡ Coin in circulation	337·0
A_D	≡ Discounts and advances	64·0
G_D	≡ Government deposits	13·6
O_D	≡ Other deposits	136·9
Z_1	≡ A balancing item which is small	4·7

Figures refer to the values of these magnitudes as at 21 January 1970.
The identity sets out the sources of legal tender, notes and coin, in the hands of the non-bank public and the commercial banks'

holding of notes, coin, and deposits at the Bank. The corresponding identity of the use of the base is as follows:

$$B \equiv R + S_2 + C_p^D \qquad (2A)$$

where $R \equiv$ Reserves of the commercial banks
$S_2 \equiv$ Special deposits
$C_p^D \equiv$ The non-bank public's holding of legal tender

The familiar reserve identity is derived from combining (1A) with (2A), yielding

$$R \equiv S_1 + C - S_2 - C_p^D - G_D - O_D + A_D + Z_1 \qquad (3A)$$

It is common to regard R as being determined by central banking action, as the authorities can determine S_1 and S_2 and A_D. In the U.K. context it would not be too incorrect to assume that the public's holdings of legal tender are continuously equal to their demand, which is a function primarily of variables determined in the real sector. In the present study, we have chosen to consider two of the components: S_1, the familiar open-market instrument, and S_2, sometimes described as a variable ratio instrument.

The monetary authorities have frequently over the period imposed quantitative restrictions on advances extended by the banks. These 'advances ceilings' may be interpreted as a quantitative instrument acting directly on the asset preferences of the commercial banks. In addition to considering advances ceilings, A^*, we also examine the setting of Bank Rate, RB, which together with S_1 is the traditional instrument of monetary policy.

The validity of the assumption that commercial bank reserves, advances ceilings, and Bank Rate have been controlled by the monetary authorities for the purposes of economic stabilization can of course be verified by examining the empirical results for the authorities' reaction function. We stress that these variables have been adopted as instruments in order to test whether the authorities in fact treated them as such.

II.2. The traditional framework of analysis

The traditional framework for postulating the behaviour of the monetary authorities may be briefly formulated as follows:

(a) The authorities have under their control a number of policy instruments such as Bank Rate, the Bank of England security portfolio, etc. The vector of instruments we denote by

Z, and the values of the instruments in any period t are chosen by the authorities.

(b) The Z_i instruments affect the vector of intermediate variables F_j, these being typically interest rates and financial quantities via a process of portfolio adjustment over time, or through institutional arrangements such as administered rates of interest.

(c) Monetary policy is seen to affect the ultimate targets Y_m via the relationship between them and the intermediate targets F_j. These will generally affect the real variables with a lag response which exceeds the observation period, which in our case is a quarter—i.e. Φ_{rj}, the response of the rth real variable to the jth financial variable exceeds one quarter. Thus, the current values of the real variables with respect to the monetary instruments and targets can be treated as being predetermined.

Systematic variations in monetary instruments by the authorities may be explained by (i) their preference functions relating to the target variables Y_m, (ii) given these preferences, their conditional forecast, at time t, of the target variables $t + \Phi$ periods ahead, together with the authorities' model of how the economy operates, i.e. their estimates of the transformation of U, the exogenous variables, and the Z_i^s into the Y_m.

This simple framework, however, presents us with three major problems. In the first place, the precise choice of a variable to be considered as an instrument is not an easy one to make, for whilst it is relatively easy to assign certain variables as instruments, it is not always clear that they possess the necessary characteristics of instruments of monetary policy. In the U.K., for instance, there has been a continuing controversy over whether the reserve base and consequently the money supply is an exogenous variable—some academic observers have explicitly assumed that this is the case, whereas others, including the central bank, have assiduously claimed that the base is neither an instrument, nor can it be used as one, given certain objectives and institutional arrangements. The second and related problem arises over the delineation of instruments and targets, and in particular the possibility of simultaneous setting of policy instruments, given the organization of policy-making in the economy. Finally, there is the problem of whether one proceeds to study the behaviour of the authorities on the basis of some utility maximization subject to constraints approach, or via some other less 'rigorous' but more pragmatic or *ad hoc* framework. These issues are considered below.

II.3. Choice of policy instruments

An instrument of monetary policy may be defined to possess ideally the characteristic of: being completely under the control of the authorities, relatively immune from exogenous influences, and, either directly or indirectly, via intermediate financial targets to affect the ultimate targets of the monetary authorities. The simplifying assumption that the authorities' preference function includes only variables such as employment, balance of payments and prices, and, further, that their model of the expected outcome of their target variables is derived from the latest available information pertaining to the target variables (suitably weighted perhaps) yields the following type of function, to explain the behaviour of the authorities with respect to the setting of their instruments.

$$Z_{i(t)} = Z(Y_{j(t-n)}, Y_j^*) \tag{1B}$$

where $i \neq j$, n is the information lag and Y^* refers to the long-run desired value of the targets.

The behaviour outlined above explicitly assumes that the instruments are exogenously determined, and react systematically to real variables alone. Consequently, if such a function were appropriate for our identity (3A), the base would become exogenous, and given the cash ratio constraint, a mechanical deposit supply function would be applicable. This is the implicit assumption made by Crouch [5] for instance, and explicitly introduced by Walters [20] to derive a money supply equation. More recently, Fisher [7] has attempted to study the behaviour of the U.K. authorities by reference exclusively to real variables.

However, there are grounds for suspecting that such a specification might not be an appropriate one. In the first place, the monetary authorities may, given the information lag on contemporaneous real variables, treat the F_j's or some subset F_m of these as indicators of the state of the economy. Secondly and more important, the monetary authorities may include some of the financial intermediate targets as objectives themselves, other than in pursuance of their stabilization objectives. Such behaviour arises, for instance, when the authorities pursue a policy of 'leaning into the wind' in order to facilitate their debt management objectives. It is, of course, irrelevant whether such behaviour is appropriate or not—the conduct of such a policy will result in the relevant 'instruments' ceasing to remain exogenous policy-determined variables as they will no longer be determined independently of the contemporaneous values of the financial variables. Thus, for instance, the reserve base would no longer be an exogenously set instrument which exclusively, or substantially, establishes the level of deposits in the economy. Instead, we would derive a short-period supply function for reserves, which *together* with the banks' demand for deposits and reserves would determine the level of deposits in the economy.

A considerable amount of discussion on monetary policy and the empirical work on monetary multipliers has centred round precisely this issue. It is desirable, therefore, to test both the alternative forms of the 'reaction function'. The form of the reaction function will determine whether variables commonly considered in the literature as instruments of policy are, or have been, treated as such—there is clearly a distinction between Bank Rate responding only to the authorities' stabilization objectives and a situation where, in addition, overseas rates have had a substantial impact on its determination. The empirical form of the reaction function, however, only indicates whether a variable has been treated as an instrument or not—it does not preclude the use of the variable as an instrument given an amended form of behaviour by the authorities. Thus, whereas the empirical results may indicate that in the past the authorities have not varied their security portfolio for economic stabilization objectives, a change in their behaviour with regard to debt management could rehabilitate that variable as an instrument. But it is then important to note that future behaviour of the demand for money will not necessarily be invariant to the new situation. Analogously, treating variables as instruments of policy in large-scale econometric models, when in fact they have not been so, will clearly yield biased and inconsistent estimates with consequent effects on policy simulation of the model.

Christ [3], in his recent survey of financial sectors of large-scale econometric models of the U.S., notes the variants of the exogenous monetary policy variables used in these models. Whilst the choice of variables varies considerably from model to model, there are two commonly used instruments—variables to represent open-market operations, and the required reserve ratio. As one would expect, there is no standard choice of the open-market variable, and neither is there generally any explicit or empirically founded reason for the choices made.[1] Consequently, the possibility exists that far from being exogenous policy instruments, the variables chosen may in

[1] For an example of the type of studies we have in mind see Wood [21], Keran [15].

effect be endogenous.[2] The effect of the choice of instrument is not insignificant in the simulations carried out—thus the Kaufman–Laurent [14] version of the FRB–MIT model, in choosing total reserves as the open-market variable in preference to unborrowed reserves, yields substantially different results for policy simulations. Should the open-market variable turn out not to have been treated as a policy instrument by the authorities, the required reserve ratio constraint simply explains the demand for reserves by the banks.

II.4. Interdependence of instruments setting

The concept of a reaction function for the monetary authorities was first proposed and applied empirically by G. L. Reuber. Since that study, there have been a number of papers which have examined the behaviour of the monetary authorities.[3] These have specifically chosen one instrument, sometimes considered in the context of indicators, for consideration—thus Dewald and Johnson examine the setting of the money supply, and alternatively free reserves as instruments of policy;[4] Wood examines only the free reserves; whilst Keran and Babb consider only the Federal Reserve holdings of government securities. In practice, of course, the authorities have an array of instruments at their disposal—in terms, for instance, of the balance sheet framework of the base, presented earlier, there are a number of components which qualify for study and interpretation as instruments of policy.

The proposition that instruments of policy themselves might interact with each other, i.e., that Z_i could be set with reference to the value assumed by Z_j has not been considered before.[5] The independent setting of instruments presupposes that the authorities can manipulate instruments and formulate plans in a highly centralized bureaucratic structure, where the policy instruments are not 'structurally' linked, such that an alteration in one instrument

[2] In terms of the statistical classification of the variables by the time dependence of the error structure with the 'explanatory' variables.

[3] See G. L. Reuber, 'The Objectives of Monetary Policy', Staff Study, Royal Commission on Banking and Finance (Ottawa, 1962), Dewald and Johnson [6], Wood [21], Harvilesky [10], Christian [4], Keran and Babb [16], and Fisher [7].

[4] In our terminology, these variables are the intermediate monetary targets. One recent exception which does consider the setting of six instruments of monetary policy is Fisher.

[5] Dewald and Johnson at one stage include the money supply, previously treated as an instrument in their free reserves equation, and note the distinct improvements in their results.

does not impinge upon the value of other instruments. In practice what is likely to occur is that the structure of policy-making will be hierarchical with a parallel structure controlling the links within the process of economic policy. Here the distinction between a target and an instrument is neither obvious nor unambiguous. Within the Bank of England, for instance, the role of the Government Broker, whilst hopefully not entirely unrelated to that of economic stabilization, is also one of managing the gilt-edged market with other objectives in mind, analogously to that of the Desk at the New York Federal Reserve Bank.[6] It is not unreasonable that the Broker, moved by the 'feel of the market' and other such apt day-to-day considerations will be influenced by Bank Rate and other instruments set by other officials within the Bank—such instruments to him are targets. There is one additional point to be noted: the individual instruments have varying degrees of flexibility with respect to the manipulation of their values. Whilst, for instance, the open-market variable S_1 can be altered on an hour-to-hour basis, the same is not true for Bank Rate, which amongst other effects is thought of as having a powerful 'announcement effect' on the economy. The authorities, whilst in theory able to alter their instruments at will, will in practice be faced with costs of doing so, and in these circumstances it is reasonable to expect them to consider values and movements in other instruments when considering changes in any one instrument.

In the present paper we consider the proposition that the 'instruments' of policy chosen, are set simultaneously, as well as following the conventional treatment of considering them as being determined independently of each other. The estimation techniques that are appropriate to the former case are methods of instrumental variables and other simultaneous estimation techniques, and it is of some interest to note that signs and significances of coefficients estimated alter with the method of estimation employed.

II.5. The constrained maximization framework

The approach adopted by Wood in his study of Federal Reserve behaviour was to derive a reduced-form equation following the

---

[6] Alan R. Holmes, Senior Vice-President of the Federal Reserve Bank of New York, notes the 'vital inter-relationships between interest rates and monetary aggregates that will ensue from any policy decision'. See Holmes [12]. See also 'Official Transactions in the Gilt Edged Market', *Bank of England Quarterly Bulletin*, June 1966, for the relationships between Bank Rate and the debt management as reflected in open-market operations.

Tinbergen–Theil framework of 'optimal' policy. This framework maximizes the authorities' utility or preference function, subject to constraints, these being the authorities' model of the interaction of *both* the instruments and the exogenous variables with the target variables. Thus, the reduced-form tests the normative hypothesis of how the authorities ought to behave, given their postulated preference function and model. Although such an approach is clearly attractive in the sense of presenting a rigorous analysis of the specified problem, it is nevertheless subject to a number of important drawbacks.

Whilst, in theory, it is possible to specify a preference function for the authorities on the basis of their public statements and articles, viz. the Radcliffe Report and the Bank of England quarterly bulletins, in practice such a task is somewhat difficult. As Anna Schwartz notes,[7] though many central banks state their goals in terms of growth, employment, price stability, and balance of payments, in practice they confine their operations to specific money market variables. Even when it is possible to identify the authorities' goals, the precise testing of the hypothesis is rendered statistically difficult by the fact that the authorities' objectives and ordering of them change from time to time. A number of the commonly adopted targets are mutually dependent—i.e. it is not always possible to achieve price stability and an employment goal at the same time, and the problem is further magnified by the inclusion of a balance-of-payments objective under fixed exchange rates.[8]

The preference function, of course, is maximized, subject to the constraint—the authorities' model. But the authorities themselves possess no explicit model of the economy—their conditional forecasts are based on a number of behavioural equations tempered by varying degrees of 'judgement' and eclecticism (see Worswick [22] for a cogent underwriting of this point). The certainty equivalence theorem requires that: (i) the relationship between the result variables and the rest of the model be such that they are linear and stochastic only by additive random disturbances, and (ii) the utility function is quadratic. Then, the optimal values of the instruments

---

[7] Anna Schwartz, 'Short-term Targets of Three Foreign Central Banks', in Karl Brunner (ed.), *Targets and Indicators of Monetary Policy*, 1969.

[8] Sure enough, a theoretical trade-off exists between the policy objectives as expressed via the minimization of the total quadratic loss function. However, when one objective assumes primary importance, say prices in a balance-of-payment crisis, unemployment assumes the role of the instrument, via the Keynesian Phillips curve.

are the same as if there were no uncertainty. These requirements are somewhat stringent. Note that the requirement that there exists no time dependence between the error vector and the instrument vector is a formal statistical requirement for the exogeneity of the independent variables.[9] This underlies the implications of the exogeneity of policy instruments assumptions noted earlier. Further, the condition of additive errors only holds in the 'certainty equivalence' case when all the uncertainty is ascribed to the impact of the exogenous variables on the target variables—no allowance is made for uncertainty to exist between the policy instruments and the targets—see Brainard [2] and Theil [19]. This requires that the monetary authorities, even if they manipulated their instruments exogenously, would need to have complete non-stochastic information about the relationships between the instruments and the targets. In practice, of course, policy-makers face a considerable amount of uncertainty about such relationships. An additional limitation of the utility maximization approach, first highlighted by Wood, is that it is not possible to identify between the parameters reflecting the authorities' preferences and their structural model, without independent knowledge of the structural parameters. Consequently, we are not strictly able to derive 'trade-offs' between the various objectives of the authorities, although it is possible to derive measures of the relative efficiencies of the various instruments.

In the following section we present an alternative framework, which incorporates the possibility of the authorities setting their instruments simultaneously, and by-passes the difficulties of explicitly setting out the authorities' preference function and their model. The model is applied to United Kingdom data, and estimated over the period 1959 to 1969.

III. An alternative formulation of the U.K. authorities' behaviour

III.1. The model detailed in this section has developed from our initial attempts to relate the setting of monetary policy instruments within the framework employed earlier by Reuber and by Dewald and Johnson. Such a model has recently been applied to United Kingdom data by Fisher. The preference function specified by

---

[9] For an extensive empirical study of stochastic specification of an economy-wide model, and the related econometric issues, see David F. Hendry [11].

Fisher, in including only real variables, and so excluding any reaction by the authorities to financial factors, yields a model where the authorities set their instruments exogenously. Our own initial attempt postulated a similar model,[10] as a preliminary to seeing whether the results indicated 'exogenous' setting of the instruments under consideration. The results for this model are presented in the Tables below. They indicate that such a model does not satisfactorily explain the authorities' behaviour, and is subject to two possible interpretations: (i) that the 'instruments' chosen have not been utilized by the authorities for stabilization purposes, and (ii) that the model is not satisfactorily specified and estimated.

III.2. In the previous section we raised three major reservations to the estimation of traditional reaction functions for the authorities. Specifically these were (a) that the authorities, in their pragmatism, might have objectives other than, and in addition to, their stabilization goals, (b) that the specification and estimation of the authorities' preference function and model is subject to substantial drawbacks, and (c) that the authorities may set their instruments simultaneously. These considerations lead us to specify a model which, where appropriate, postulates additional financial and debt management considerations and also introduces an element of simultaneity in

[10] The reduced-form equation is derived from the following simple model

$$Z_{i(t)} - Z_{i(t-1)} = \lambda\{Z_{it}^* - Z_{i(t-1)}\}$$

(the familiar partial adjustment model)   (i)

$$Z_t^* = \alpha_0 + \alpha_1 A_t^*$$ (ii)

where A^* refers to the authorities' desired level of bank advances, the dominant channel of monetary policy.

$$A_t^* = \beta_1 U_{(t+\Phi)}^* - \beta_2 P_{(t+\Phi)}^* + \beta_3 BP_{(t+\Phi)}^*$$ (the authorities' targets)   (iii)

where U, P, and BP refer to unemployment, prices, and the balance of payments, and Φ is the lag between the effect of monetary policy (A^*) and the targets, assumed for simplicity to be equal.

$$U_{t+\Phi}^* = U_{t-\delta} + \gamma_1(U^{**} - U_{t-\delta}); \qquad P_{t+\Phi}^* = (1 + \gamma_2);$$ (iv)
$$BP_{t+\Phi}^* = BP_{t-\delta} + \gamma_3(BP^{**} - BP_{t-\delta})$$

where the relationships specify the desired level of the targets to equal the latest information on the targets, δ being the information lag, and the discrepancy between this and their long-run targets, U^{**}, P^{**}, and BP^{**}.

Equations (i) through (iv) yields

$$Z_{i(t)} = (\alpha_0\lambda + \lambda\alpha_1\beta_1\gamma_1 U^{**} + \lambda\alpha_1\beta_3\gamma_3 BP^{**}) + \lambda\alpha_1\beta_1(1 - \gamma_1)U_{(t-\delta)}$$
$$- \lambda\alpha_1\beta_2(1 + \gamma_2)P_{t-\delta} + \lambda\alpha_1\beta_3(1 - \gamma_3)BP_{t-\delta} + (1 - \lambda)Z_{i(t-1)}$$
$$Z_{i(t)} = a_0 + a_1 U_{t-\delta} - a_2 P_{t-\delta} + a_3 BP_{t-\delta} + a_4 Z_{i(t-1)}.$$

the setting of the instruments. These, however, are not fundamental to the issue—they can easily be incorporated into the traditional framework, as does Wood in the appendix to his paper. We are still faced with the problem of specifying the authorities' utility function and, yet more formidable, their model of the economy. The approach adopted in this paper is to introduce a surrogate variable which both reflects the authorities implicit preferences with respect to their stabilization goals and subsumes their model of the domestic economy.

III.3. We begin by assuming (i) that the monetary authorities are a part of the total economic policy machinery. This aggregation of the authorities enables us to make the not unreasonable assumption that the utility function of the monetary authorities is identical to that of the rest of the machinery—that is, substantially the Treasury's. This will arise either, as all those in authority share the same objectives, or because the monetary authorities in a Keynesian policy-orientated situation merely adopt the Treasury's objectives, (ii) the model in the hands of the authorities (be they beliefs, and/or numerous 'relationships') is essentially devoid of explicit or substantial monetary influences, except via bank advances. It would be fair to assume, for instance, that the conclusions reached by the Radcliffe Report fundamentally reflected and influenced the views of the authorities on the effects of monetary factors on economic activity.

These two considerations lead us to the premise that the authorities' fiscal stance will reflect (a) their 'conditional' forecast of the economy, *including* the exogenous variables, and (b) their model transforming the fiscal instruments into the real targets, given their preference function, which may vary from time to time. We can now observe the movements of the monetary 'instruments' in response to the surrogate, without having to specify either the preference function or the authorities' model, as both are given in the surrogate.

The precise choice of the surrogate is a somewhat difficult one. The literature on public finance would suggest the use of full-employment receipts, expenditures, and surplus. In practice, as we experienced in an earlier paper, the construction of such measures is subject to a considerable amount of difficulty and variability, mainly because of the problems of measuring the necessary tax revenue functions. The surrogate we propose to use in this study is the measure of the (cumulative) impact of the 'first-round' effects on the G.D.P. of defined taxation changes.[11] As we noted elsewhere, this Government Fiscal Measure (henceforth ITC) corresponds rather well to a measure of those policy actions which are taken for granted in orthodox descriptions of British economic policy as being the effective tools of demand management.

III.4. *Some preliminaries*

In order to incorporate a simple dynamic structure to the model, the individual equations were initially specified in the partial-adjustment form. As is well known, the inclusion of the lagged dependent term amongst the regressors induces serial correlation of the residuals, which, although in principle can be handled, introduces considerable computational difficulties at the level of simultaneous estimation. On economic grounds we expect that the dynamic adjustments are shorter than the observation period, and equations which explained the variation in policy instrument equally well without the lagged term, on the basis of the standard error of equation and the Durbin–Watson statistic were preferred.

The Special Deposit variable refers to the money value of the call. This definition is adopted because we are attempting to explain the major components of the base. We assume that the authorities consider the money value to be the appropriate variable and thus set the ratio with reference to values assumed for deposit levels. The Advances Ceilings variable also is in money terms and is derived as follows: when no advances 'requests' were made the variable assumes the value of advances extended; 'requests' for 'restraint' are made with reference to proposed growth rates,[12] and these are applied to the actual advances level prior to the call for restraint.

---

[11] These are, broadly, all taxation changes with a principal direct or indirect effect on persons. Thus, the measure includes all changes on rates of purchase- and income-tax, S.E.T., and corporation tax, but excludes changes in investment grants, and any estimates of the impact of measures which affect both companies and persons (as, for example, in the case of corporation income-tax). The series is derived from the approach of Hopkins and Godley [13] and has been elaborated by Shepherd and Surrey [18]. See M. J. Artis, in Beckerman (ed.), *Labour's Economic Record* (Duckworth, 1972), for an extensive analysis of fiscal policy measures in the U.K.

[12] The growth rate for advances expansion is derived from R. G. Alford, 'Indicators of direct controls on the U.K. capital market, 1951–1957' (unpublished), and N.I.E.R. Reviews.

Specification of the model—the individual equations

III.5. *Bank of England security portfolio*

The Bank's security portfolio, in traditional analysis, when viewed as the open-market instrument, is the primary determinant of the level of deposits in the economy, and hence the money supply. However, as is well documented,[13] the Bank's security portfolio has been operated essentially as an instrument for debt management, and in particular for gilt-edged market 'stabilization', on the basis of the authorities' view of that market. The policy of 'leaning into the wind' is simply describable as the authorities' judgement of 'destabilizing' changes in interest rates on government securities and the appropriate measures via their security portfolio, to reverse the situation to acceptable levels of the rate. This policy is not easily quantifiable, as what precisely is regarded as destabilizing is derived from an intimate judgement of the situation—thus similar rates of change from the same level, may on different occasions be viewed quite differently.

Goodhart [8] suggests that 'a policy of leaning into the wind' still allows the authorities considerable freedom of action to pursue monetary policy. Thus, even within the context of a leaning into the wind policy, the authorities may vary their portfolio with reference to their stabilization objectives. It is important to note, however, that the security portfolio no longer remains a strictly exogenous policy instrument.[14] The variable used to test the proposition that the authorities manipulated the security portfolio for economic stabilization purposes is our surrogate, ITC described earlier.[15]

Leaving aside for a moment the authorities' economic stabilization objectives, the variables one might consider in explaining the security portfolio behaviour would be the changes in interest rates on government securities, and the outstanding marketable debt, on

[13] See Goodhart [8], *Bank of England Quarterly Bulletin*, June 1966, and Norton [17], all readily accessible in H. G. Johnson *et al.* (eds.), *Readings in British Monetary Economics*. We refer, of course, to policy before the Bank altered its tactics in the market. See *B.E.Q.B.*, Mar. 1969.

[14] An indication of the relative roles of economic stabilization and gilt-edged stabilization in the portfolio variation and hence the degree of exogeneity is provided by the beta coefficients of the equation.

[15] *A priori* we would expect this variable to be insignificantly different from zero, as the authorities have not attempted to control monetary aggregates, but liquidity, for stabilization purposes. However, it is possible that increases in the security portfolio are viewed as adding to the liquidity position of the public.

consideration of an 'even-keel' (to retain the nautical flavour) policy. This, however, would be inappropriate for the following reasons: when the interest rate becomes a proximate target variable, to the extent that this policy is pursued successfully, the interest rate will vary little (in some sense) compared to the instrument utilized to achieve the end. One would therefore not necessarily expect to find a relationship between the security portfolio and the government security interest rate.[16] To the extent, moreover, that the policy of stabilizing the rate is undertaken with the objective of maximizing present and future demand for government debt, the inclusion of the government's borrowing requirement or debt outstanding in the private sector is rendered unnecessary. Our empirical results are broadly in line with this view. The variable to be considered is in some sense the discrepancy between the authorities' preferred rate and the 'ex-ante' rate of interest, and not the ex-post rate.

III.6. We specify this discrepancy to be related to two exogenous variables: (i) the Forward discount on sterling and (ii) the level of the U.S. short rate. The former variable is the outcome of speculation influenced by the demand for the currency, expectations of the domestic economy, and prospects for the external balance, etc. These arguments reflect and parallel closely the views of gilt-edge holders. In an open economy with a well-established international capital market, an overseas rate would be relevant in the portfolio decisions of institutions and persons holding substantial gilt-edged securities, and also in their formulations of the 'ex-ante' rate. These two variables (FDS and RUS) form a major part of our explanation of Bank Rate, and their inclusion could be viewed as generating bond holders' expectations of Bank Rate and hence the bond rate.

III.7. The other instruments under consideration, in particular Special Deposits and advances ceilings, are all postulated to affect the discrepancy. An imposition of advances ceilings increases the excess demand for advances at any administered rate of interest below the equilibrium rate. This increase may be eliminated either

---

[16] Unless, of course, the authorities behave systematically to variations in interest rates, in which case expectations are stable in their view, and the ex-post rate of change of the interest rate is a stable proportion of the ex-ante rate of change.

directly via unsatisfied borrowers selling gilt-edged securities, or indirectly via non-bank financial institutions meeting the demand via bidding for increased funds by offering higher terms.[17]

III.8. It has been generally accepted that special deposit calls have been met by the banks via a reduction of gilt-edged securities in their portfolio,[18] and further, that the Bank through its gilt-edged policy has obliged the banks' special deposit requirements via equivalent purchases of their government securities. This view is implicit in Norton's findings on the demand for government securities by the banks. Here, a negative coefficient of around one on special deposit calls is assumed to be effected via Bank purchases, and certain implications of this for policy are considered.[19] The behaviour of the banks in reducing their security holdings to meet special deposit calls has been established elsewhere.[20] However, our security-portfolio equation attempts to explain the Bank's holdings of securities, and here it is possible for the banks to reduce their security portfolio without the Bank increasing its own portfolio. In our model the Bank reacts to discrepancies between the desired bond rate change and the ex-ante bond rate change. If no such discrepancy exists, the Bank need not purchase securities that are off-loaded by the banks. A substantial off-loading will undoubtedly have an impact on the gilt-edged market and the Bank

---

[17] See Norton [17] for some empirical evidence of this proposition.

[18] See *Bank of England Quarterly Bulletin*, Dec. 1960.

[19] Norton arrives at the conclusion that the authorities' actions in the market may be destabilizing via the following steps: (i) banks reduce their securities holdings by the equivalent Special Deposit call, (ii) implicitly it is assumed that such reductions are met by Bank purchases, and (iii) the authorities supply function for government securities is specified with the interest rate on securities as the *dependent* variable, i.e. the policy instrument, and the security portfolio as an argument in the function, with a positive coefficient. Then, a rise in the security portfolio via (i) and (ii) causes an upward movement in interest rates via (iii). Anticipating this train of events, the public move out of bonds to avoid capital losses. This conclusion may be questionable for the following reasons: (a) assumption (ii) is an untested proposition and is not derived from any equation to explain the authorities' security portfolio; (b) the interest rate should be relevantly viewed as the authorities' intermediate target and the security portfolio as the instrument used to achieve the target variable. Then, the equation is specified the wrong way round and the results cannot be interpreted in the manner they are by Norton.

[20] See, for instance, 'The Portfolio Behaviour of Commercial Banks' by Parkin, Gray, and Barrett in *The Econometric Study of the United Kingdom*, ed. Hilton and Heathfield (London: Macmillan, 1970).

will therefore purchase securities in the first instance. However, within a quarter, the period of observation in this study, the Bank could neutralize these purchases or indeed reduce its portfolio to augment its policy stance. Thus the Governor of the Bank notes that 'it is open to the authorities—and the banks understand this— to ensure that the whole adjustment by the banks is not completed by such sale of gilts. *The initial call for Special Deposits can be supplemented by open-market operations, by action on interest rates, and in due course by further calls for Special deposits.*' ([9], our italics.) [21] There are three propositions to be tested: (i) that Special Deposit calls are offset, (ii) that the initial offset is neutralized via open-market sales, and (iii) that the authorities have also carried out net open-market operations.

III.9. Any slippage in the authorities advances ceilings cannot be readily countered by an immediate and commensurate reduction in the ceilings themselves. The Bank's security portfolio has the ideal characteristic of anonymity and immediate implementation to counter such slippages. Similarly, if the authorities regard the spread between the U.S. short rate and the U.K. short rate as a target variable to influence inflows of capital for balance-of-payments purposes, they may prefer to influence the spread via interest-rate charges through open-market operations in preference to altering Bank Rate in the first instance. We therefore consider Z_t, the discrepancy between actual advances and requests, and $(US/UK)_{t-1}$ as variables explaining the authorities' security portfolio.

The equation to be estimated is:

$$S_1 = \alpha_0 + \alpha_1 S_{2(t)} - \alpha_2 \Delta A^*_{(t)} + \alpha_3 RUS_{(t)}$$
$$+ \alpha_4 FDS_{(t)} + \alpha_5 ITC_{(t)} + \alpha_6 Z_{(t)} - \left(\frac{US}{UK}\right)_{t-1} + e_1$$

where S_2, ΔA^*, RUS, and FDS relate to the discrepancy between ex-post and ex-ante rates on securities,
ITC relates to the economic stabilization surrogate,
Z relates to the slippage in advance requests,
US/UK relates to the target ratio between U.S. and U.K. interest rates for balance-of-payments considerations.

---

[21] The quotation underlines the relevance of a simultaneous framework for explaining the setting of instruments by the monetary authorities.

Special deposits and advances ceilings

III.10. Special Deposits requirements and Advances Ceilings are not continuously set quarter by quarter—they are imposed for a number of periods ahead. Therefore, the values of all the arguments in these functions to some extent have to be anticipated by the authorities. This is not an unrealistic assumption, as the authorities generally undertake policy actions with a view of the likely situation in the immediate future. We have adopted the actual values of the explanatory variables instead of the authorities' forecast values of them, as this would involve imposing a naïve forecasting framework. The authorities have a considerable amount of additional information and judgement, which, we assume, produces a better forecast than would a naïve model.

III.11. Our own specification of the Bank's security-portfolio equation suggests that a considerable amount of the variation in that variable is explained by defensive operations. We may therefore expect the authorities to counter their involuntary actions on the reserve base, and hence on the money supply and availability of funds, via their quantitative instruments, Special Deposits and Advances ceilings. Both these instruments are primarily designed to affect the asset structures of the banks. However, in the case of Special Deposits, the base is immediately affected, though the net effect depends upon whether these calls are offset or otherwise by changes in the authorities' security portfolio. In both the Special Deposits and Advances Ceilings equation we introduce the authorities' security portfolio as arguments.[22] *A priori*, we would expect a positive sign for the coefficient in the S_2 equation, and a negative sign in the A^* equation. An additional element of simultaneity is introduced in the equations explaining S_2 and A^*—both these instruments are imposed in order to 'control' the level of advances in the economy, and we would therefore expect the authorities to set each instrument with reference to the value assumed by the other variable.

[22] Regression analysis will fail to distinguish between association and causality amongst the instruments, and so, if monetary policy generally has been expansive, one would derive highly significant coefficients. The obvious choice is to specify the *equations* in first-difference form. However, we refrain from doing so, because, when variables are subject to measurement error or revisions, this procedure magnifies the errors of observations, and both S_1 and A^* are subject to revision or measurement error.

III.12. As the Special Deposits variable reflects both the ratio imposed by the authorities and the level of deposits, we need to specify the authorities' function for deposits. This we specify somewhat simply as being a function of Bank Rate, as rates offered are administratively tied to it, and the ratio of the U.S. rate to the U.K. rate, to reflect overseas inflows in response to interest-rate differentials.[23] The operations of the Exchange Equalization Account are generally assumed to offset any inflows via reciprocal government borrowing in order to finance the currency conversion, thus neutralizing the effect on the money supply. Here we assume that a substantial proportion of private direct borrowing and overseas deposits were lent in sterling. Bain [1] notes that a 'second major impediment to monetary policy has been the growth of international short-term capital movements'. We expect that the authorities attempted over the period to neutralize the effects of overseas inflows on domestic liquidity by withdrawals through Special deposit calls on clearing banks. Such a situation would be plausible if, as we have suggested earlier, in the S_1 equation, the authorities treat US/UK as a target of policy for balance-of-payments considerations. Then, they would choose to offset the effects of this policy on the domestic availability of funds via special deposit 'leakage' on the base.

III.13. In a banking system subject to administered rates of interest, at any rate below the equilibrium rate equating the demand for and the supply of advances, there exists an excess demand for advances. The imposition of any advances ceilings in shifting the supply curve to the left increases the excess demand at a given rate of interest. Similarly, a rise in the authorities' security portfolio represents an increase in liquidity and a shift leftwards of the demand for bank advances. The announced ceilings on advances need not necessarily reflect the actual level of ceilings desired by the authorities, (A^{**}). It could incorporate an element to take account of the likely level of 'slippage' envisaged by the authorities, via the following relationship: $A^* = A^{**} - \alpha$ (excess demand for advances). If we suppose further that the excess demand is inversely related to Bank Rate and the Bank's security portfolio, we would expect the level of advances ceilings to be increased, the higher the Bank Rate and the security portfolio.

[23] See Hodjera, 'Short-term Capital Movements of the United Kingdom, 1963–1967', *J.P.E.*, Mar. 1971.

The equations to be estimated are:

$$S_2 = \alpha_{10} + \alpha_{11}(S_1)_t - \alpha_{12}(A^*)_t + \alpha_{13}(RB)_t$$
$$- \alpha_{14}\left(\frac{US}{UK}\right)_t + \alpha_{15}(ITC)_t + \alpha_{16}(S_2)_{t-1} + e_2$$

and

$$A^* = \alpha_{20} + \alpha_{21}(S_1)_t - \alpha_{22}(\Delta S_1)_t$$
$$- \alpha_{23}(S_2)_t + \alpha_{24}(ITC)_t + \alpha_{25}(RB)_t + e_3.$$

Bank rate

III.14. Traditionally, Bank rate variations have been interpreted to follow from (i) the authorities' economic stabilization objectives, (ii) external balance considerations, and (iii) debt management operations and the supplementation of quantitative restriction. These factors would suggest that, in addition to our economics stabilization surrogate, we could explain Bank rate changes mainly in terms of the other three instruments. However, preliminary attempts along these lines did not yield satisfactory results.

The function we have adopted to explain the Bank rate instrument is:

$$RB = \alpha_{30} - \alpha_{31}(ITC) + \alpha_{32}(FDS)_t + \alpha_{33}(RUS)_t$$
$$+ \alpha_{34}(LCRB) + \alpha_{35}(S_2D) + \alpha_{36}(RB)_{t-1} + e_4$$

where, in addition to the previously defined variables, $LCRB$ is an index of the cumulated days since the last change in Bank Rate, and S_2D is a dummy variable of changes in the special deposits ratio requirements.

The reason for the inclusion of the forward discount on sterling, and the U.S. short rate is pretty straightforward: these variables reflect the authorities' responses to balance-of-payments considerations. Further, we postulate that the authorities augment changes in special deposit ratio requirements by Bank rate changes.[24] The reason for including the index measuring the time elapsed since the last change in Bank Rate is as follows: the public's anticipation of a change in Bank Rate results in their 'discounting' such changes in their operations. Consequently, in order to achieve the desired impact, the Bank needs to change the rate by a larger amount.

---

[24] For an indication of this behaviour see the section on Special Deposits in the Governor's 1970 Jane Hodge Memorial Lecture [11].

As in the other equations, we represent the authorities' economic stabilization objectives by our surrogate fiscal measure. *A priori*, however, we would not expect this variable to be significant, as the authorities over the period of the study have not attached much importance to interest-rate effects on expenditures.

Estimation procedures

III.15. Our model of the authorities' behaviour incorporates an element of simultaneity. In principle, therefore, the method of ordinary least squares is inappropriate and the model needs to be estimated by instrumental variables and simultaneous estimation techniques. There is, of course, no clear-cut rule about the appropriateness of any particular estimator, as a formal model is open to a variety of interpretations, depending upon the stochastic properties assumed. The model is estimated by (i) ordinary least squares (OLS); (ii) two-stage least squares (TSLS); (iii) autoregressive two-stage least squares (ARTSLS), and (iv) full information maximum likelihood (FIML). A justification for the use of such a wide range of estimators (besides the availability of the programmes) is that such a procedure could, in yielding information about the stochastic nature of the model, indicate the appropriateness of the deterministic structure of the model. Parameter estimates are subject to substantial changes in size and sign, and such information is useful in assessing the conclusions derived from the empirical estimates.[25]

III.16. *Empirical results*

As indicated earlier, we argued that relating 'instruments' of monetary policy solely to the usual stabilization objectives, as does Fisher [7], does not provide a satisfactory framework for analysing the authorities' behaviour. This is confirmed by the results presented below.[26] In all cases the equations perform badly on the sign and

[25] Briefly, the properties of the estimators used are as follows: OLS in the presence of simultaneity and autocorrelation yields biased and inconsistent estimates. In these circumstances, TSLS and ARTSLS will give consistent estimates, where in the latter case the matrix of autocorrelation coefficients is assumed to be diagonal. FIML and autoregressive FIML have the properties of both consistency and efficacy although, as is well known, these estimators are particularly sensitive to specification errors. We are unable to report on autoregressive FIML results as these facilities were not available.

[26] The relevant results are in Table IV.10, eqns. 1, 2, and 3; Table IV.11, eqn. 1; Table IV.12, eqns. 1 and 2; and Table IV.13, eqn. 1.

significance criteria. These results could arise for one of two reasons: (a) the variables considered as instruments have not been utilized as such by the authorities, or (b) that relating the instruments directly to the ultimate objectives does not provide specification adequate for testing the authorities' preference function and model of the economy.

In an attempt to deal with the latter point, we have ourselves proposed a surrogate variable, ITC, to incorporate both the preference function and the model of the authorities. The results for this variable are interesting. *A priori*, as it is commonly accepted that bank advances have been the only major channel of monetary policy for stabilization purposes, one would expect only to find a significant relationship between ITC and advances ceilings—in the other equations, the coefficient would not be significantly differed from zero. However, whilst these conditions are satisfied for the advances ceilings and Bank rate equation, the results indicate that the authorities have offset fiscal policy in the security portfolio and Special Deposits equations. The OLS, TSLS, and FIML estimates yield negative coefficients for the security portfolio equation, and positive coefficients for the Special deposits equation. One explanation for these results is as follows—the monetary authorities generally believed that the Treasury typically reacted too late and by too much with fiscal actions, and in order, partially at least, to maintain the exchange rate, they undertook anonymous open-market operations and Special Deposit withdrawals, so as to reduce the base and liquidity. At the very least, the results confirm that the authorities only used their advances ceilings constraints for counter-cyclical stabilization purposes.

The simultaneous introduction of other policy instruments in our functions lead to satisfactory results. The TSLS and FIML estimates differ considerably from the OLS results, to suggest that simultaneity exists in the system. It is interesting to note that in the Bank security portfolio equation, the OLS results for the Special Deposits variable yields either a coefficient of one (the offsetting result), or insignificant results (neutralizing action), but that the simultaneous estimates are highly significant and negative, to suggest that the authorities in fact reinforced Special Deposit calls by undertaking net open-market operations. This result is at variance with that of earlier studies, which strongly suggested that the authorities offset Special Deposit calls by absorbing equivalent amounts of government securities from the banks. Our results would indicate that the non-bank private sector were net purchasers of government securities.

Overseas interest rates, *RUS*, the forward discount on sterling, *FDS*, and the rates of overseas to domestic rates, *RUS/RS*, clearly have a role in explaining the behaviour of the monetary authorities. This is not surprising, as one would expect such a result in an open economy operating under a fixed exchange rate. Proximately in the Mundell assignment framework, the monetary authorities concern themselves with maintaining external equilibria, whilst fiscal policy (with bank advances additionally) is used for internal equilibria. The Bank rate equation, which by any standards performs reasonably well, is dominated by external considerations, and, as is to be expected, in a situation where interest rates are not credited with having significant influence on expenditures, the stabilization surrogate is insignificant.

In order to give some consideration to serial correlation of the errors, the model was estimated by ARTSLS. This procedure assumes that the errors are generated by a first-order moving average scheme, and in that sense is a little restrictive. We noted earlier that advances ceilings and the Special Deposit ratio are not set continuously, but are undertaken for some time ahead. Consequently, the arguments in these two functions are strictly forecast values for the quarters in question. Our own equations are misspecified, to the extent that they use actual values of the arguments, and so one would expect some systematic component in the error terms. As it so turns out, of the four equations estimated, the Special Deposits and Advances Ceilings are the only equations which exhibit first-order autocorrelation. The results, however, hold for the ARTSLS case, with the exception of ITC in the Special Deposit equation, and one may view the autoregressive coefficient as providing additional information not included in the deterministic part of our model.

The model, as specified, is over-identified. However, the likelihood test for the over-identifying restrictions indicate that they are satisfied in the FIML case.

Conclusions

We have presented and estimated a model of the U.K. monetary authorities over the period 1959 to 1969, and the results are encouraging and suggestive. First, we may conclude that specific attention must be paid to broader objectives pursued by the authorities, other than those of economic stabilization. Then, it is important to recognize that variables conventionally assumed as 'instruments' of monetary policy have not in fact been treated as such by the authorities, and aggregates such as the money supply in the U.K. over this period may more appropriately be considered to be endogenously determined—a result, of course, that is not surprising for an open economy with a fixed exchange rate. Secondly, consideration has to be given to the interaction of behaviour on the part of the authorities, both in the specification and estimation of the model. Thirdly, the results reinforce the original plea by Wood [21], who pointed to the inadequacies of assuming the authorities' behaviour to be exogenous in large-scale economy-wide models. In particular, preliminary analysis of the type reported in this paper is required before variables can be acceptably treated as instruments of policy in such models.

In the way that the model is specified, it is not entirely satisfactory, as large and important areas of behaviour are subsumed behind the quasi-reduced-form equations representing the authorities' behaviour. However, whilst a considerable amount of empirical research is being undertaken into the demand for assets, relatively little attention has been paid to the supply side. This study represents a small initial step in that direction.

TABLE IV.10
Bank of England Security Portfolio
(t-ratios in brackets)

	Constant	LDV $S1_{(t-1)}$	Real variables (Y_m) $BP_{(t)}$	$P_{(t)}$	$U_{(t)}$	Exogenous financial variables (F_j) $FDS_{(t)}$	$RUS_{(t)}$	$Z_{(t)}$	$\left(\frac{RUS}{RS}\right)_{(t-1)}$	Fiscal surrogate $ITC_{(t)}$	Endogenous financial variables (Z_i) $S2_{(t)}$	$\Delta A^*_{(t)}$	R^2	DW	SE
OLS (1)	−245·24 (1·49)	0·66 (5·61)	−0·48 (2·01)	1185·92 (2·86)	−54·45 (1·33)								0·959	2·11 (DW68 = −0·55)[a]	91·41
(2)	−817·06 (4·41)		−0·60 (1·89)	3407·17 (20·42)	−70·44 (1·28)								0·924	0·68	122·66
(3)	−428·57 (2·92)		−0·65 (3·24)	2933·19 (22·03)	−73·27 (2·03)						1·28 (6·77)	0·18 (0·70)	0·971	1·36	77·74
(4)	2299·07 (10·40)					−38·72 (2·11)	215·18 (6·14)	−2·56 (3·92)		−1·53 (1·39)	1·03 (2·08)		0·907	0·80	139·77
(5)	2896·20 (11·42)					−12·74 (0·73)	269·95 (7·95)	−2·99 (5·16)	−780·08 (3·59)	−2·43 (2·47)	−0·12 (0·22)		0·932	1·41	121·17
(6)	2983·30 (11·60)					−11·21 (0·65)	259·48 (7·57)	−3·05 (5·33)	−742·85 (3·44)	−2·57 (2·64)	−0·36 (0·66)	−0·54 (1·43)	0·935	1·56	119·48
Simultaneous estimators TSLS	3491·93 (16·19)					−4·06 (0·31)	214·41 (7·91)	−3·52 (7·94)	−672·99 (3·99)	−3·64 (4·70)	−1·74 (3·57)	−2·83 (5·37)	0·964	1·83	89·56
Beta coefficients						0·014	0·70	0·45	0·30	0·60	0·37	0·40			
ARTSLS	no results quoted as no significant first order auto-correlation observed														
FIML	3931·97					−6·03 (0·16)	114·61 (1·71)	−3·42 (2·75)	−455·58 (0·96)	−4·40 (1·88)	−3·05 (1·82)	−5·58 (2·68)			

[a] $DW68 = (1 - \tfrac{1}{2}d)\sqrt{\dfrac{n}{1 - n.v(b_1)}}$, where d = Durbin-Watson statistic, n = number of observations, $v(b_1)$ = estimated variance of coefficient of lagged dependent variable.

TABLE IV.11

Special Deposits

(*t*-ratios in brackets)

	Constant	LDV $S2_{(t-1)}$	Real variables $Y_{(m)}$			Exogenous financial variables (F_t) $\frac{(RUS)}{(RS)_{(t)}}$	Fiscal surrogate $ITC_{(t)}$	Endogenous financial variables (Z_t)			R^2	DW	SE
			$BP_{(t)}$	$P_{(t)}$	$U_{(t)}$			$S1_{(t)}$	$A*_{(t)}$	$RB_{(t)}$			
OLS (1)	−11·19 (0·22)	0·95 (15·38)	−0·07 (0·96)	64·95 (1·40)	−35·50 (2·64)						0·908	1·23 (DW68 = 2·72)	29·62
(2)	75·13 (1·30)	0·62 (8·90)	0·08 (1·15)	−565·17 (4·13)	8·70 (0·72)			0·18 (4·27)	−0·02 (1·26)	25·48 (3·82)	0·961	2·07 (DW68 = −0·25)	20·09
(3)	−261·90 (4·12)	0·59 (7·91)				−76·62 (2·62)	0·30 (2·44)	0·19 (4·79)	−0·07 (5·09)	10·83 (1·66)	0·964	2·13 (DW68 = −0·48)	18·94
Simultaneous estimators TSLS	−491·65 (6·34)	0·34 (3·79)				−113·22 (4·00)	0·49 (4·19)	0·40 (6·36)	−0·13 (6·79)	−5·99 (0·77)	0·974	2·07 (DW68 = −0·28)	16·27
Beta coefficients		0·34				0·20	0·37	1·8	1·01	0·08		alpha 0·27 (2·6)	
ARTSLS	−288·3 (3·13)	0·43 (5·5)				−99·4 (1·9)	0·22 (1·1)	0·23 (4·9)	−0·07 (3·9)	6·9 (0·75)			
FIML	−530·16	0·43 (2·53)				−66·48 (2·53)	0·62 (1·83)	0·38 (2·04)	−0·13 (2·13)	0·96 (0·09)			

TABLE IV.12
Advances Ceilings
(t-ratios in brackets)

	Constant	LDV $A^*(t-1)$	Real variables (Y_m)			Fiscal surrogate	Endogenous financial variables (Z_t)				R^2	DW	SE
			$BP(t)$	$P(t)$	$U(t)$		$S1(t)$	$\Delta S1(t)$	$S2(t)$	$RB(t)$			
OLS (1)	418·95 (3·27)	1·00 (29·19)	0·02 (0·09)	−372·48 (1·68)	39·91 (1·44)						0·994	1·13 (DW68 = 2·89)	59·61
(2)	−2243·69 (5·15)		−2·52 (3·37)	5636·01 (14·37)	−168·24 (1·30)						0·857	0·15	228·36
(3)	−4075·70 (11·42)					5·30 (7·22)	2·72 (20·53)	−1·24 (4·92)	−3·66 (9·61)	46·28 (1·18)	0·964	1·08	147·45
Simultaneous estimators TSLS	−4157·22 (15·92)					5·03 (9·31)	2·85 (28·08)	−0·45 (1·91)	−3·64 (12·69)	−11·70 (0·36)	0·981	0·71	107·73
Beta co-efficients ARTSLS	−2993·2 (7·50)					0·48 / 3·61 (5·06)	1·6 / 2·21 (12·68)	0·05 / −1·01 (5·90)	0·45 / −3·74 (9·84)	0·02 / 47·66 (1·49)		alpha = 0·21 (2·61)	
FIML	−4181·87					4·82 (3·96)	3·01 (12·91)	0·70 (0·96)	−3·04 (4·27)	−111·43 (1·39)			

TABLE IV.13

Bank Rate

(*t*-ratios in brackets)

	Con-stant	LDV $RB(t-1)$	Real variables (Y_m)			Exogenous financial variables (Z_i)				Fiscal surrogate ITC(t)	R^2	DW	SE
			$BP(t)$	$P(t)$	$U(t)$	$FDS(t)$	$RUS(t)$	$LCRB(t)$	$S2D$				
OLS (1)	−1·76 (2·01)	0·58 (4·92)	−0·002 (1·78)	4·20 (3·26)	−0·46 (1·91)						0·860	1·63 (DW68 = 1·86)	0·50
(2)	1·36 (1·36)	0·32 (3·47)	−0·002 (2·31)	0·006 (0·01)	0·09 (0·52)	−0·16 (3·50)	0·27 (2·76)	0·01 (4·26)	0·47 (3·86)		0·955	2·06 (DW68 = 0·24)	0·30
(3)	1·35	0·35				−0·21	0·28	0·01	0·49	0·001	0·948	1·99 (DW68 = 0·04)	0·31
(4)	1·59 (5·93)	0·33 (3·77)				−0·20 (4·74)	0·25 (4·83)	0·01 (3·88)	0·50 (4·32)		0·947	1·94 (DW68 = 0·24)	0·31
Beta coefficients		0·33				0·23	0·27	0·28	0·16				
Simultaneous estimators FIML	1·61	0·33 (4·16)				−0·20 (5·31)	0·25 (5·16)	0·01 (4·31)	0·50 (4·73)				

TABLE IV.14
TSLS and FIML Results
(t-ratios in brackets)

	S1 TSLS	S1 FIML	S2 TSLS	S2 FIML	A* TSLS	A* FIML	RB TSLS	RB FIML
Endogenous variables (Z_i)								
$S1_{(t)}$					2·85 (28·08)	3·01 (12·91)		
$S2_{(t)}$	−1·74 (3·57)	−3·05 (1·82)			−3·64 (12·69)	−3·04 (4·27)		
A^*_t			−0·13 (6·79)	−0·13 (2·13)				
$RB_{(t)}$			−5·99 (0·77)	0·96 (0·09)	−11·70 (0·36)	−11·43 (1·39)		
$\Delta S1_{(t)}$					−0·45 (1·91)	0·70 (0·96)		
ΔA^*_t	−2·83 (5·37)	−5·58 (2·68)						
LDV $S2_{(t-1)}$			0·34 (3·79)	0·43 (2·53)				
$RB_{(t-1)}$							0·33 (3·77)	0·33 (4·16)
$ITC_{(t)}$	−3·64 (4·70)	−4·40 (1·88)	0·49 (4·19)	0·62 (1·83)	5·03 (9·31)	4·82 (3·96)		
Exogenous financial variables (F_j)								
$FDS_{(t)}$	−4·06 (0·31)	−6·03 (0·16)					−0·20 (4·74)	−0·20 (5·31)

$RUS_{(t)}$	214·41 (7·91)	114·61 (1·71)					0·25 (4·83)	0·25 (5·16)
$Z_{(t)}$	−3·52 (7·94)	−3·42 (2·75)						
$RUS/RS_{(t)}$			−113·22 (4·00)	−66·48 (2·53)				
$RUS/RS_{(t-1)}$	−672·99 (3·99)	−455·58 (0·96)						
$LCRB_{(t)}$							0·01 (3·88)	0·01 (4·31)
$S2D$							0·50 (4·32)	0·50 (4·73)
Constant	3491·93 (16·19)	3931·97	−491·65 (6·34)	−530·16	−4157·22 (15·92)	−4181·87	1·59 (5·93)	1·61
R^2	0·964		0·974		0·981		0·947	
DW	1·83		2·07 (DW68 = −0·28)		0·71		1·94 (DW68 = 0·24)	
SE	89·56		16·27		107·73		0·31	
Percentage of mean value	2·89		12·80		2·58		5·26	

DATA   DEFINITIONS AND SOURCES

S1   Bank of England Security Portfolio, £ million not seasonally adjusted. Government Securities held in the Issue and Banking Departments; average of third Wednesday in the month.
          Source: *Bank of England Quarterly Bulletin.*

S2   Bank of England's calls for Special Deposits from London Clearing Banks and Scottish Banks, £ million not seasonally adjusted; average of third Wednesday in the month.
          Source: *Bank of England Quarterly Bulletin.*

A*   Advances ceilings, £ million, seasonally adjusted L.C.B. advances, other than to Nationalized Industries, plus the estimated maximum permitted change during the quarter.
          Sources: *Bank of England Quarterly Bulletin* (for advances); R. F. G.
                    Alford, 'Indicators of direct controls on the U.K. capital
                    market, 1951–1967' (for estimated maximum permitted
                    change).

RB   Weighted average of Bank Rate during the quarter.

BP   U.K. Balance of Payments (current account including invisibles) £ million seasonally adjusted.
          Source: *N.I.E.R.*

P   G.D.P. price deflator (1958 = 1·0), seasonally adjusted from final expenditure on goods and services.

U   Unemployment (per cent) total manufacturing industry, U.K. Seasonally adjusted.
          Source: *Ministry of Labour Gazette.*

ITC   Cumulative effect of the estimated first-round impact of discretionary tax changes on G.D.P. at factor cost. £ million at current prices.
          Based on Godley and Hopkin, *N.I.E.R.*, May 1965.

FDS   Forward Discount on sterling. Three months' forward margins in London; U.S. dollars (per cent p.a.). Average of end-month figures.
          Sources: *The Economist* and *Financial Statistics.*

RUS   Unweighted tender rate on new three-month bills issued within the quarter New York (per cent p.a.).
          Sources: International Financial Statistics and *N.I.E.R.*

Z   Index of discrepancy between observed advances and the theoretical ceiling on advances (A* above).

RS   Weighted averages of discount rates at the weekly allotment of 91-day U.K. Treasury Bills (per cent p.a.).
          Source: *Financial Statistics.*

LCRB   Number of days since the last change in Bank Rate multiplied by the deviations of Bank Rate from its mean value over the sample period. Index based on 620 = 100.

S₂D   Dummy variable representing the timing of calls for and releases of Special Deposits (S_2). It takes the value +1·0 for calls of 1% of gross deposits and the value −1·0 for releases of 1% during the quarter when they are announced by the authorities. Otherwise, the value is zero.

Sample period: 1959(4)–1970(1), 42 quarterly observations.

REFERENCES

[1] BAIN, A. D., 'Monetary Policy', paper presented to the British Association for the Advancement of Science, Leeds, 1967.

[2] BRAINARD, W. C., 'Uncertainty and the Theory of Policy', in Brunner, K. (ed.), *Targets and Indicators of Monetary Policy*, 1969.

[3] CHRIST, C. F., 'Econometric Models of the Financial Sector', *Journal of Money, Credit and Banking*, May 1971.

[4] CHRISTIAN, J. W., 'A Further Analysis of the Objectives of American Monetary Policy', *Journal of Finance*, June 1968.

[5] CROUCH, R. L., 'A Model of the U.K.'s Monetary Sector', *Econometrica*, 1967.

[6] DEWALD, W. G., and JOHNSON, H. G., 'An Objective Analysis of the Objectives of American Monetary Policy, 1952–1961', in Carson, D. (ed.), *Banking and Monetary Studies*, 1963.

[7] FISHER, D., 'The Instruments of Monetary Policy and the Generalised Trade-Off Function for Britain, 1955–1968', *Manchester School*, Sept. 1970.

[8] GOODHART, C. A. E., 'The gilt-edged market', in Johnson, H. G., et al. (eds.), *Readings in British Monetary Economics*, 1972.

[9] GOVERNOR OF THE BANK OF ENGLAND, 'Monetary Management in the U.K.', the 1970 Jane Hodge Memorial Lecture, *Bank of England Quarterly Bulletin*, Mar. 1971.

[10] HARVILESKY, T., 'A Test of Monetary Policy Action', *J.P.E.*, June 1967.

[11] HENDRY, D. F., 'Stochastic Specification in an Aggregate Demand Model of the U.K.', presented to the Econometric Congress, Barcelona, June 1971.

[12] HOLMES, A. R., 'Operational Constraints on the Stabilization of Money Supply Growth', in *Controlling Money Aggregates*, Federal Reserve Bank of Boston, 1969.

[13] HOPKIN, W. A. B., and GODLEY, W. A. H., 'An analysis of tax changes', *National Institute Economic Review*, May 1965.

[14] KAUFMAN, G. G., and LAURENT, R. D., 'Three Experiments with Simulating a Modified F.R.B.–M.I.T. model', *F.R.B.* of Chicago, *Business Conditions*, 1969.

[15] KERAN, M. W., Reply to Comments on the 'St. Louis Position', *F.R.B. of St. Louis Review*, Aug. 1969.

[16] —— and BABB, C. T., 'An Explanation of Federal Reserve Actions, 1933–1968', *F.R.B. of St. Louis Review*, July 1969.

[17] NORTON, W. E., 'Debt management and monetary policy in the U.K.', *Economic Journal*, Sept. 1969.

[18] SHEPHERD, J. R., and SURREY, M. J. C., 'The short-term effects of tax changes', *N.I.E.R.*, Nov. 1968.

[19] THEIL, H., *Economic Forecasts and Policy*, North Holland, Amsterdam, 1970.

[20] WALTERS, A. A., 'Monetary Multipliers in the U.K., 1180–1962', *Oxford Economic Papers*, Nov. 1966.

[21] WOOD, J. H., 'A Model of Federal Reserve Behaviour', in Horwich, G. (ed.), *Monetary Process and Policy: A Symposium*, 1967.

[22] WORSWICK, G. D. N., Introduction to Surrey, M. J. C., 'The Analysis and Forecasting of the British Economy', *N.I.E.S.R. Occasional Papers*, xxv, 1971.

AN ECONOMETRIC MODEL OF THE U.K. FINANCIAL SECTOR: SOME PRELIMINARY FINDINGS*

G. CLAYTON, J. C. DODDS,
J. L. FORD, and D. GHOSH
(*University of Sheffield*)

I. Introduction

RECENTLY there has been increased interest in the economic significance of financial intermediaries at the theoretical and policy levels. The major impetus for this interest at the theoretical level has been the work of Gurley and Shaw [10], who have attempted to broaden the concept of money by suggesting that claims against all types of financial intermediaries possess the character of money in varying degree. In effect, they have questioned the orthodox theoretical practice of confining the concept of money to non-interest-bearing claims against government and commercial banks.[1] In

* We gratefully acknowledge the financial support we have received for this project from the Social Science Research Council and from the Esmee Fairbairn Charitable Trust (which is currently financing the research work of J. L. Ford). We would like to express our thanks to our colleague Professor R. J. Nicholson, who kindly read the first draft of this paper and who so willingly put his expertise in econometrics at our disposal. In similar vein we thank J. Stewart, University of Manchester, who, additionally, made available to us several important programmes. Thanks are also due to Charles Carter and Lawrence R. Klein, who commented on their over-all impression of the value of what we were trying to do, and on how we might go about developing the model. However, we must add the usual rider that we alone are responsible for any omissions from, and commissions in, this paper.

[1] The recent work of Sir John Hicks [11]—even though it has met with some strong strictures—lends weighty support to the view that the *sine qua non* of money is not that it is non-interest-bearing. It is rather that—ignoring changes in the purchasing power of money—it has a *certain* 'return'. We know full well that, for investors, *ceteris paribus*, the liabilities of non-bank financial intermediaries offer that kind of 'return': 'There is thus no reason, so long as we are solely concerned with the Speculative Motive, why savings deposits and such like, which have a certain value at the 'next decision-point', should not reckon

short, they argue that a comprehensive 'financial theory' is necessary to account for all the significant factors which may contribute to liquidity in an economy.

Publication of the Radcliffe Report [5] provided the major stimulus for increased interest in financial intermediaries at the policy level. The Report advanced the view that the existence of non-bank financial intermediaries is likely to have an impact on the effectiveness of monetary policy. They cited two main factors to support this contention. First, they called attention to the liquidity of the liabilities of a wide variety of non-bank financial intermediaries. This led them to question the adequacy of relying on policy instruments which operate solely on the supply of money and to emphasize the importance of influencing the general liquidity of the economy, since they regarded the latter as affecting 'decisions to spend'. From the point of view of policy, then, attempts to reduce the level of planned expenditures by reducing the supply of money may be largely frustrated because the total stocks of liquid assets may be only slightly affected. (See [4].)

The second strand to their argument is linked to their view that there is no 'reason for supposing, or any experience in monetary history indicating, that there is any limit to the velocity of circulation' ([5], para. 391). Non-bank financial intermediaries can, in principle, undermine monetary policy by raising the income velocity of circulation when the authorities are seeking to restrain the expansion of the level of money income by stabilizing the stock of bank deposits and currency. The non-bank financial intermediaries are in a position to mobilize idle balances and return them into active circulation by making their liabilities relatively more attractive to hold, by increasing their prospective rate of return. 'The extent to which the activities of the intermediaries are destabilizing will depend on the elasticity of substitution between idle money and time deposits held as part of the permanent portfolios of spending units and their own debt, and the extent to which they are prepared to

---

as money, even if they bear interest' ([11], p. 27). Even though the question of what does, or does not, constitute 'money' is implicitly germane to our present studies, we must leave the matter here. However, it is well worth noting that ultimately what *is* to be regarded as 'money' might have to be decided on empirical evidence, as D. Laidler [12] has argued. Development of our present model will, by implication, allow us to offer some new evidence on this important issue.

allow the prospective rate of return on their own debt to continue to rise' ([2], p. 213).

Theoretical work undertaken since the publication of the Radcliffe Report has indeed emphasized this central theme of substitution among different assets in the portfolios of the public or of financial institutions in general. For example, J. Tobin and W. C. Brainard [18] have extensively developed simplified models to show how the existence of some non-bank financial intermediaries has implications for monetary policy; for example, under the assumption of substitutability 'a billion dollar change in the supply of currency and bank reserves would have more effect on the economy if asset substitutions were prevented' ([18], p. 111).

The Tobin–Brainard models are *general equilibrium* models. To provide, or even to attempt to provide, worthwhile answers to questions, for example, of whether or not, and how, non-bank financial intermediaries impair monetary policy, and of how monetary policy in the round, as it were, affects the financial system, it seems to us that it is of paramount importance to construct models of that nature. Accordingly, we have developed such a model for the United Kingdom, for the period second quarter 1964 to first quarter 1970, basing it on the balance-sheet framework utilized by Tobin and Brainard.

The purpose of this paper is to present a pilot version of the model and to use it to evaluate the effect of certain instruments of monetary policy on the financial system, with particular, but not sole, emphasis on the implications for such policy of the existence of non-bank financial intermediaries. We attempt this in the full knowledge of all the risks attendant upon such a venture,[2] approaching our task in the spirit of the Chinese proverb which states that 'a journey of even one thousand miles must begin with the first step'.

We proceed as follows. In Section II we develop the model, noting the special features of some of its sectors; Section III discusses the problems of estimating the model and the limitations of our approach, especially in this initial study. This discussion is followed in

---

[2] For example, R. J. Ball has remarked that: 'While a full general equilibrium model is in principle desirable, the value of its development depends on the extent to which positive conclusions can be derived from it. From an *a priori* point of view, the difficulty is that in the absence of quantitative knowledge that is at present inadequate it is hardly possible to place sufficient restrictions, *a priori*, on the absolute and relative magnitudes of effects of changes in asset prices on margins of substitution, to derive many clear-cut conclusions' ([2], footnote 2, p. 213).

Section IV by a presentation and analysis of the preliminary results derived from the model together with the tentative policy implications that these results suggest. Finally, in Section V we make some brief observations as to how the present model *per se* can be improved, and as to how it can be extended.

II. The model

The present version of our model is epitomized in Table IV.15. So we have, in effect, a nine-sector model which contains sixteen categories of assets/liabilities. We would obviously not dispute the contention that ultimately disaggregation of this model both by sectors (in effect sectors 1, 4, 6, and 9) and by assets/liabilities (in particular, items 3–6, 8, 9–10, 12, and 16) is desirable if we are to explain fully the behaviour of the U.K. financial system, *per se*—let alone the repercussions of its behaviour on the real parts of the economy. However, given that this is an initial exercise it has been convenient, and given the availability of data it has been necessary, to constrain the model to its present dimensions and, in the process, to carry out a considerable degree of amalgamation of institutions. The data position is such, in fact, at the moment that we have to employ *first differences* of all variables in the model since there is a shortage of stock data for numerous assets/liabilities in the model.

It is necessary to formulate behaviouristic functions for each sector in the model, and to do so we begin with an individual institution in a given sector and consider its balance sheet. We presuppose that some kind of portfolio and debt adjustment theory is applicable to account for the form the given institution's balance sheet assumes. In effect, it has been assumed implicitly that the objective of an institution is to maximize its 'expected net revenue' or 'expected utility of net revenue'.[3] Each institution then starts any period with

[3] In a sense we are following the path laid down by many others, especially, initially, by Tobin [19] and Markowitz [13]. Explicit specification of portfolio-selection and debt-management problems on these lines, and investigation of their econometric properties can be found, for example, in the recent papers by J. M. Parkin (e.g. see [14]). There Parkin employs the Freund utility function (see [7]), which is the only one of manageable proportions available in the literature. Despite the fact that that utility function does not possess the and 'absolute risk-aversion' property suggested by J. W. Pratt [15] and K. J. Arrow [1], it might be the kind of utility function that could usefully be adopted in a more explicit treatment of portfolio behaviour in our model.

Model of Financial Intermediation in the U.K.

Assets/Liabilities	1 Public Sector	2 Discount Houses	3 Deposit Banks	4 Other Banks	5 Building Societies	6 Other Financial Institutions	7 Industrial and Commercial	8 Personal Sector	9 Overseas Sector	Rates
Currency 1	$-\bar{a}_{11}$							a_{18}		$\bar{r}_1\,(-\dot{P}_e)$
Treasury Bills 2	$-\bar{a}_{21}$	a_{22}	a_{23}	a_{24}	a_{25}	a_{26}	a_{27}		a_{29}	r_2
British Government Securities 3	$-\bar{a}_{31}$	a_{32}	a_{33}	a_{34}	a_{35}	a_{36}		a_{38}	a_{39}	r_3
National Savings 4	$-\bar{a}_{41}$					a_{46}		a_{48}		$\bar{r}_4$
Call Loans 5		$-a_{52}$	a_{53}	a_{54}			a_{57}	a_{58}	a_{59}	r_5
Local Authority Debt 6	$-\bar{a}_{61}$	a_{62}	a_{63}	a_{64}	a_{65}	a_{66}	a_{67}	a_{68}	a_{69}	r_6
Deposits with Deposit Banks 7	a_{71}		$-\bar{a}_{73}$		a_{75}	a_{76}	a_{77}	a_{78}	a_{79}	$\bar{r}_7$
Deposits with Other Banks 8	a_{81}			$-\bar{a}_{84}$		a_{86}	a_{87}	a_{88}	a_{89}	$\bar{r}_8$
Shares and Deposits 9					$-\bar{a}_{95}$			a_{98}		r_9
Deposits with Other Financial Institutions 10						$-\bar{a}_{10\cdot6}$	$a_{10\cdot7}$	$a_{10\cdot8}$	$a_{10\cdot9}$	r_{10}
Advances by Deposit Banks 11	$-\bar{a}_{11\cdot1}$		$a_{11\cdot3}$			$-\bar{a}_{11\cdot6}$	$-\bar{a}_{11\cdot7}$	$-\bar{a}_{11\cdot8}$	$-\bar{a}_{11\cdot9}$	$\bar{r}_{11}$
Advances by Other Banks 12	$-a_{12\cdot1}$			$a_{12\cdot4}$		$-a_{12\cdot6}$	$-a_{12\cdot7}$	$-a_{12\cdot8}$	$-a_{12\cdot9}$	$\bar{r}_{12}$
Discounts and Advances 13	$a_{13\cdot1}$	$-a_{13\cdot2}$								r_{13}
Commercial Bills 14	$a_{14\cdot1}$	$a_{14\cdot2}$	$a_{14\cdot3}$	$a_{14\cdot4}$		$a_{14\cdot6}$	$-a_{14\cdot7}$		$a_{14\cdot9}$	r_{14}
Mortgages 15					$a_{15\cdot5}$			$-a_{15\cdot8}$		r_{15}
Equity 16	$a_{16\cdot1}$	$a_{16\cdot2}$	$a_{16\cdot3}$	$a_{16\cdot4}$		$a_{16\cdot6}$	$-a_{16\cdot7}$	$a_{16\cdot8}$	$a_{16\cdot9}$	r_{16}
Changes in Net Worth (residual) 17		$\bar{A}_2$	$\bar{A}_3$	$\bar{A}_4$	$\bar{A}_5$	$\bar{A}_6$	$\bar{A}_7$	$\bar{A}_8$	$\bar{A}_9$	

$\bar{r}_1$ $(-\dot{P}_e)$ negative rate of inflation.
r_2 the rate on Treasury Bills.
r_3 the rate on British Government Bonds.
$\bar{r}_4$ the rate on National Savings.
r_5 the rate on Call Loans.
r_6 the rate on Local Authority Debt.
$\bar{r}_7$ the rate on Deposits with Deposit Banks.
$\bar{r}_8$ the rate for Deposits with Other Banks.

r_9 the rate on Building Society Shares.
r_{10} the rate for Deposits with Other Financial Institutions.
$\bar{r}_{11}$ the rate on Advances by Deposit Banks.
$\bar{r}_{12}$ the rate on Advances by Other Banks.
r_{13} Bank Rate.
r_{14} the rate on Commercial Bills.
r_{15} the Building Societies Mortgage rate.
r_{16} the rate on Equity.

a stipulated, i.e. given, endowment of net worth; it is then assumed to hold some expectations about the rates of return (expected interest rates plus expected changes in capital values) on the assets and liabilities that are relevant to its activities. Also, it is assumed to hold some expectation about the 'exogenous' items in its balance sheet. The institution then allocates its net worth between the given assets and takes up a debt position that, in the given circumstances, enables it to maximize its objective function.

The exogenous items in an institution's balance sheet are of two kinds. The first kind are those which are determined for the sector by 'the opposite side' of the market; and these are explicitly in the model. The second kind are those which are normally classified as 'other assets' or 'other liabilities', and these are only included in the model implicitly, in net worth.

Once the demand/supply functions for the institutions in a sector have been so derived they are aggregated—certain simplifying assumptions having been implicitly made—to obtain the sector demand/supply functions. Pooling those functions for all sectors enables us to write the market-clearing conditions for every category of asset/liability.

One important attribute of the selection of its optimum portfolio and debt position by a particular sector is that, because of the balance sheet constraint, any one of the (endogenous) assets and liabilities of the sector becomes a residual item. It is in order, therefore, to omit consideration of the behaviouristic equation for any asset/liability so classified. For convenience, Local Authority debt has been chosen to assume the role of a residual for all sectors since it is the only item that appears in the balance sheet of all sectors of the model.

It is fully appreciated that the allocation of the financial resources of some of the sectors of our model could well be influenced, even if not completely determined, by considerations and 'motives' other than those we have postulated. This is likely to be the case for Sector 1; it might well be true for Sectors 7, 8, and 9. However, it is necessary to include all these sectors in the model in order to close it. To do so the same hypothesis has to be advanced to explain their behaviour as has been advanced for the other sectors in the model. Consistent aggregation, of course, also requires that, to obtain the demand/supply equation for each type of asset/liability, all relevant sectors hold the same expectations about particular rates of return, and so on.

In the light of the above factors, the demand/supply functions for each sector can now be catalogued (where: a minus sign indicates a liability; a bar over a variable indicates that it is exogenous).

(1) *Public Sector*

The five demand/supply variables are: a_{71}; a_{81}; $-a_{12\cdot1}$; $a_{14\cdot1}$; and $a_{16\cdot1}$. It is hypothesized that they are functions of:

$$(\bar{r}_7, r_8, \bar{r}_{12}, r_{14}, r_{16}, -\bar{a}_{11}, -\bar{a}_{21}, -\bar{a}_{31}, -\bar{a}_{41}, -a_{61}, -\bar{a}_{11\cdot1}).$$

There is no separate equation for $a_{13\cdot1}$. This is because, in terms of our model, whatever quantity of Discounts and Advances is 'supplied' by the Discount Houses that quantity is 'demanded' by the Public Sector. We are unable to use any balance equation for this sector, since all the financial items in the balance sheet of each agent in this sector are not included in our model.

(2) *Discount Houses*

There are seven demand/supply variables for this sector, namely: a_{22}; a_{32}; $-a_{52}$; $-a_{13\cdot2}$; $a_{14\cdot2}$; $a_{16\cdot2}$; and $-a_{62}$. The first six are posited to be functions of:

$$(r_2, r_3, r_5, r_6, \bar{r}_{13}, r_{14}, r_{16}, \bar{A}_2);$$

and a_{62} is found, as follows, from the balance-sheet identity:

$$-(a_{62}) = a_{22} + a_{32} - a_{52} - a_{13\cdot2} + a_{14\cdot2} + a_{16\cdot2} - \bar{A}_2.$$

(3) *Deposit Banks*

Here the demand/supply variables: a_{13}; a_{23}; a_{33}; a_{53}; $a_{11\cdot3}$; $a_{14\cdot3}$; and $a_{16\cdot3}$, are assumed to be functions of:

$$(\bar{r}_1, r_2, r_3, r_5, r_6, \bar{r}_{11}, r_{14}, r_{16}, -\bar{a}_{73}, A_3).$$

While a_{63} is derived from the balance-sheet identity, which includes the exogenous variable $\bar{a}_{73}$:

$$-(a_{63}) = a_{13} + a_{23} + a_{33} + a_{53} + a_{11\cdot3} + a_{14\cdot3} + a_{16\cdot3} - \bar{a}_{73} - \bar{A}_3.$$

In this sector there may be objections to the use of $a_{11\cdot3}$ as an endogenous variable. We assume, when the volume of Bank Advances is controlled (the rate of interest on Bank Advances differs always from the Bank Rate by a constant), the demand for the asset on behalf of the Bank is indicated from the demand curve only and it is always

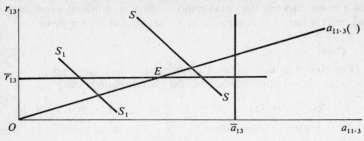

FIG. IV.4

less than, or equal to, $\bar{a}_{11.3}$, the ceiling imposed by the Authorities (see Fig. IV.4). Bank Advances are distributed among different sectors according to some criteria and those sectors form expectations about their allocation of Bank Advances. When the volume of the latter is not controlled, it is also assumed, as is also illustrated in Fig. IV.4, that the supply curve intersects the demand curve, $a_{11.3}(\ )$, at E or at a point to the right of E, but never to the left of E (for example, as it does with S_1–S_1).

(4) *Other Banks*

For this sector: a_{14}; a_{24}; a_{34}; a_{54}; $a_{12.4}$; $a_{14.4}$; and $a_{16.4}$ are held to be functions of:

$$(\bar{r}_1, r_2, r_3, r_5, r_6, \bar{r}_{12}, r_{14}, r_{16}, -\bar{a}_{8.4}, \bar{A}_4).$$

a_{64} is found once more from the balance-sheet identity.

(5) *Building Societies*

The variables: a_{15}; a_{25}; a_{35}; a_{75}; $-a_{95}$; and $a_{15.5}$ are taken to be functions of:

$$(\bar{r}_1, r_2, r_3, r_6, \bar{r}_7, r_9, r_{15}, \bar{A}_5)$$

Again, a_{65} is derived via the balance-sheet identity.

a_{95} *is* assumed to be a choice variable on behalf of the building societies. Obviously, they cannot refuse any deposit with them; but, given the relevant rate vector, they have a desired amount of shares and deposits and the equilibrium value may differ from the actual value by some margin. When this margin is high, i.e. when excess demand for shares and deposits is considerable, the interest rate adjusts itself to clear the market (see [8]).

(6) *Other Financial Institutions*

The demand/supply variables: a_{26}; a_{36}; a_{46}; a_{76}; a_{86}; $-a_{12 \cdot 6}$; $a_{14 \cdot 6}$; and $a_{16 \cdot 6}$ are assumed to be functions of:

$$(r_2, r_3, \bar{r}_4, r_6, \bar{r}_7, r_8, \bar{r}_{12}, r_{14}, r_{16}, -\bar{a}_{10 \cdot 6}, -\bar{a}_{11 \cdot 6}, \bar{A}_6).$$

a_{66} is obtained as a residual from the balance equation.

(7) *Industrial and Commercial*

The variables: a_{17}; a_{27}; a_{57}; a_{77}; a_{87}; $a_{10 \cdot 7}$; $-a_{12 \cdot 7}$; and $-a_{14 \cdot 7}$ are to be determined for this sector. They are assumed to be functions of:

$$(\bar{r}_1, r_2, r_5, r_6, \bar{r}_7, r_8, r_{10}, \bar{r}_{12}, r_{14}, -\bar{a}_{11 \cdot 7}, -\bar{a}_{16 \cdot 7}, \bar{A}_7).$$

a_{67} is found from the balance-sheet equation.

(8) *Personal Sector*

For this sector these variables have to be explained: a_{18}; a_{38}; a_{48}; a_{58}; a_{78}; a_{88}; a_{98}; $a_{10 \cdot 8}$; $-a_{12 \cdot 8}$; $-a_{15 \cdot 8}$; and $a_{16 \cdot 8}$. It is supposed that these are functions of:

$$(\bar{r}_1, r_3, \bar{r}_4, r_5, r_6, \bar{r}_7, r_8, r_9, r_{10}, \bar{r}_{12}, r_{15}, r_{16}, -\bar{a}_{11 \cdot 8}, \bar{A}_8).$$

$a_{6 \cdot 8}$ is obtained from the balance-sheet equation.

(9) *Overseas Sector*

The demand/supply magnitudes: a_{29}; a_{39}; a_{59}; a_{79}; a_{89}; $a_{10 \cdot 9}$; $-a_{12 \cdot 9}$; $a_{14 \cdot 9}$; and $a_{16 \cdot 9}$ are taken to be functions of:

$$(r_2, r_3, r_5, r_6, \bar{r}_7, r_8, r_{10}, \bar{r}_{12}, r_{14}, r_{16}, -\bar{a}_{11 \cdot 9}, \bar{A}_9).$$

a_{69} is solved for in the usual way.

The inclusion of this sector ideally calls for a detailed study of the variables that determine the flow of short-term capital into and out of the economy. At this stage such a study has not been undertaken: therefore, in some respects the demand/supply functions for the Overseas Sector are only partially specified. The functions are not so much *ad hoc* as incomplete. To close the model—as noted previously—some functions must be postulated for this sector.

Market-clearing Equations

Demand	Supply
$a_{13}(\ ) + a_{14}(\ ) + a_{15}(\ ) + a_{17}(\ ) + a_{18}(\ )$	$= \bar{a}_{11}$
$a_{22}(\ ) + a_{23}(\ ) + a_{24}(\ ) + a_{25}(\ ) + a_{26}(\ ) + a_{27}(\ ) + a_{29}(\ )$	$= \bar{a}_{21}$
$a_{32}(\ ) + a_{33}(\ ) + a_{34}(\ ) + a_{35}(\ ) + a_{36}(\ ) + a_{38}(\ ) + a_{39}(\ )$	$= \bar{a}_{31}$

Demand   *Supply*

$$a_{53}(\ ) + a_{54}(\ ) + a_{57}(\ ) + a_{58}(\ ) + a_{59}(\ ) \qquad\qquad\qquad = a_{52}(\ )$$

$$a_{62}(\ ) + a_{63}(\ ) + a_{64}(\ ) + a_{65}(\ ) + a_{66}(\ ) + a_{67}(\ ) + a_{68}(\ ) + a_{69}(\ ) \quad = \bar{a}_{61}$$

$$a_{98}(\ ) \qquad\qquad\qquad\qquad\qquad\qquad\qquad\qquad\qquad\qquad\qquad = a_{95}$$

$$a_{12\cdot4}(\ ) \qquad\qquad = a_{12\cdot1}(\ ) + a_{12\cdot6}(\ ) + a_{12\cdot7}(\ ) + a_{12\cdot8}(\ ) + a_{12\cdot9}(\ )$$

$$a_{14\cdot1}(\ ) + a_{14\cdot2}(\ ) + a_{14\cdot3}(\ ) + a_{14\cdot4}(\ ) + a_{14\cdot6}(\ ) + a_{14\cdot9}(\ ) \qquad = a_{14\cdot7}(\ )$$

$$a_{15\cdot5}(\ ) \qquad\qquad\qquad\qquad\qquad\qquad\qquad\qquad\qquad\qquad = a_{15\cdot8}(\ )$$

$$a_{16\cdot1}(\ ) + a_{16\cdot2}(\ ) + a_{16\cdot3}(\ ) + a_{16\cdot4}(\ ) + a_{16\cdot6}(\ ) + a_{16\cdot8}(\ ) + a_{16\cdot9}(\ )\ \bar{a}_{16\cdot7}$$

Looking at the model in its entirely, we find that we have an equal number of *independent* 'equations' and variables (85). On the supposition that the behaviouristic functions are linear, it follows that should there be a solution to the system, it will be unique. We do, in fact make such a supposition.

III. Estimation

It can be readily seen from the description of our model that each equation has a number of (expected) returns as explanatory variables. These returns here are proxied by actual rates of interest. Some of the latter are exogenous to the model, namely Bank Rate (r_{13}) and the rates linked to it $(\bar{r}_7, \bar{r}_{11},$ and $\bar{r}_{12})$. However, since the vector of interest rates in the model contains a set of endogenous rates, these latter are jointly determined together with the various assets and liabilities. Therefore, an estimator for a simultaneous-equation system is called for. One obvious method to employ is that of Two-Stage Least Squares (2SLS) and this is what we have used.[4]

In fact, *prima facie* one would expect, since the model detailed in Section II, has so many exogenous variables, that each of the 67 behaviouristic, i.e. here 'stochastic', equations is well identified. Application of the standard conditions for identifiability confirms this view.[5]

---

[4] The word 'obvious' is important here. We fully appreciate that other, possibly better, estimators for simultaneous systems exist. However, because: of the kind of data we have at our disposal; the present version of the model is a pilot study; of the fact that we have no suitable software on hand at present, we have chosen to use 2SLS.

[5] In the present circumstances we may invoke the order conditions for identifiability. It will be recalled that, adopting the conventional notation, this is: $K^{**} \geq M^* - 1$, where K^{**} is the number of exogenous variables excluded from, and M^* is the number of endogenous variables included in, the given equation. We have made no attempt to test for identification *a posteriori* by seeing if the rank conditions still holds; for, logically, identification must *precede* estimation.

So our estimator can be described as follows, given that we have: 28 observations;[6] 24 exogenous variables (25 including the sum vector for the constants); and 67 dependent variables:
Structural equations:

$$\underset{Y}{28 \times 67} \quad \underset{\Gamma}{67 \times 67} \quad + \quad \underset{X}{28 \times 25} \quad \underset{B}{25 \times 67} \quad + \quad \underset{E}{28 \times 67} \quad = \quad \underset{0}{28 \times 67}$$

$$\text{or} \quad Y = -XB\Gamma^{-1} - E\Gamma^{-1}$$
$$= X\Pi + V$$

For *stage one*: $\hat{\Pi}_1 = (X'X)^{-1}X'Y$ and, $\hat{Y} = X\hat{\Pi}_1$.

Stage two: We use $\hat{Y}$ wherever a jointly determined variable appears as an argument in a structural equation.

Having estimated the structural equations by 2SLS we can calculate the 'derived reduced-form coefficient matrix' (see Goldberger [9], pp. 364–71) $\hat{\Pi}_2$, and utilize it to investigate the multiplier effects in our model. In effect:

$$25 \times 85 \quad 25 \times 85 \quad 85 \times 85$$
$$\hat{\Pi}_2 = -\hat{B}_1\hat{\Gamma}_1^{-1}.$$

Here estimates of B and Γ^{-1} from the 2SLS have been supplemented with the coefficients on the exogenous and endogenous variables, respectively, that figure in the 18 identities in our model (i.e. the 10 market-clearing equations and the 8 balance-sheet equations). The derived reduced form $\hat{\Pi}_2$ will not coincide with $\hat{\Pi}_1$ in our model since all equations are over-identified; and it will be asymptotically more efficient than $\hat{\Pi}_1$.[7]

In the above we have incorporated a constant in all the stochastic

---

[6] Detailed information on the definition of variables in the model and on the data sources employed can be made available to interested readers in mimeographed form (about five foolscap pages). Requests should be made to: Miss Linda Henderson, Secretary, Research Section, Division of Economic Studies, 21 Northumberland Road, Sheffield, S10 2TX.

[7] Goldberger, for example, argues as follows: 'It should be noted that in general—i.e., unless all structural equations are just—identified— ... $\hat{\Pi}_2$ does not coincide with ... $\hat{\Pi}_1$ ... The direct reduced form $\hat{\Pi}_1$ is obtained by regressing each current endogenous variable on all predetermined variables, without using any restrictions. In contrast, ... $\hat{\Pi}_2$ will clearly incorporate these restrictions which were used in estimating the structural equations ... [it] incorporates more *a priori* information and hence will be more efficient, at least asymptotically' ([9], p. 365).

equations. However, given that the data we are using are first differences of the relevant stock figures one could argue that constants should be omitted from all estimated equations, if those equations are to be derived faithfully from the stock, or 'level', equations.[8] In the 2SLS estimates we have not omitted the constant terms, or restricted them to be zero: but we expect the (asymptotic) standard errors of those terms to be such as to indicate that they are effectively (that is, statistically speaking) zero.

It can be seen from the functions presented in Section II that many of the equations to be estimated contain several interest rates, and it is therefore likely that the equations will exhibit a fair degree of multi-collinearity (even in first difference form). One way of obviating this problem in a system such as the one here would be to impose certain restrictions on the estimates of the vector of coefficients at the second stage. This would also lessen the difficulties caused by the fact that we have relatively few degrees of freedom for some of the equations in the model, since we only have 28 observations.

To be precise we could impose upon the demand/supply equations of a given sector certain restrictions on 'the interest-rate effects', that follow from economic theory. These restrictions are those of symmetry, and of row sums of zero (or by implication of column sums of zero), on the interest-rates coefficient matrix. Formally, for a given sector k, these restrictions can be stated as:

$$\frac{\partial a_{ik}}{\partial r_j} = \frac{\partial a_{jk}}{\partial r_i}, \quad \text{for all } i \text{ and } j;$$

and,

$$\sum_{j=1}^{n} \frac{\partial a_{ik}}{\partial r_j} r_j = 0, \quad \text{for all } i.$$

We are confronted by some difficulties, however, when we try to impose such restrictions. It can be seen from Section II that only for Sectors 2, 3, 4, and 5, do we have only one of the four interrelated exogenous interest rates, $\bar{r}_7$, $\bar{r}_{11}$, $\bar{r}_{12}$, and $\bar{r}_{13}$, in the given equations. The other sectors' equations contain $\bar{r}_7$ and $\bar{r}_{12}$. Since $\bar{r}_{12}$ differs from $\bar{r}_7$, via the Bank Rate, by a constant (the same constant at any point of time), it is obviously necessary to exclude either of them from the to-be-estimated equations to avoid 'singularity'.

For any sector which contains $\bar{r}_7$ and $\bar{r}_{12}$ in its behaviouristic

[8] This naturally assumes that there is no time-trend in the 'level' equations.

equations the complete set of symmetry restrictions and the Cournot aggregation condition can be imposed *if*, and only if, the particular equations contain a constant. For it is the latter that takes-up the coefficient on the omitted rate of interest, $\bar{r}_7$ or $\bar{r}_{12}$. So that the required conditions can be imposed as if the omitted interest rate were present.

In our equations no more than two of the interdependent exogenous interest rates appear at any one time; so, in principle, we could apply the relevant 'demand theory restrictions'. *But*, since our equations have had to be cast in first difference form for estimating purposes, we have, as we have noted previously, to assume that the constant terms are zero. Wherever we can impose the restrictions in full we should add the further restrictions that the constant terms in the estimated equations are zero. For, furthermore, if one thinks of the kind of utility function which might be imputed to be behind the application of portfolio- and debt-management theory to any sector in the model, from which one could derive the restrictions now being considered, that utility function will probably be such that it produces 'level' equations which themselves contain *no* constant terms.

Given these points, it follows therefore that at the second stage only the stochastic equations for Sectors 2, 3, 4, and 5 can be, and have been, estimated using the 'demand theory restrictions'. To impose those restrictions the equations for a sector have to be stacked.[9] To calculate the vector of coefficients it is necessary to have an estimate of Φ, the contemporaneous variance–covariance matrix of the errors from the equations (where $\Phi = \Omega \otimes I$ in conventional notation). We have followed the suggestion of A. Zellner [21] and have let Ω be proxied by the residual variance–covariance matrix from the unrestricted (i.e. proper 2SLS) estimates of the equations for a given sector.[10]

---

[9] The restricted least squares estimates for a given sector have to be obtained by solving for all of its demand/supply magnitudes simultaneously. That is, now for any sector the residual equation for the 2SLS estimates, that for Local Authority Debt, has also to be estimated. Only in this way is it possible to impose conditions of symmetry *and* the aggregation conditions.

[10] The method we have used to re-estimate the equations for Sectors 2, 3, 4, and 5 is, in fact, similar to three stage least squares (3SLS). However, it differs from 3SLS in the calculation of Ω on two counts: (i) at the first stage of RLS some $\hat{Y}$'s rather than the true values of Y have been used in the calculation of the residuals; (ii) exclusion restrictions are not utilized in the calculation of the residuals. The second point represents a minor difference, while the first point represents a substantial difference, between our estimator and 3SLS.

Limitations

Leaving on one side the quality of the kind of data we have employed in this pilot model, the latter has several limitations, some of which may be noted in the following:

(i) The model is couched in a comparative statics framework. It has been assumed that all observed values of the variables in the model are equilibrium values; so that the whole system adjusts itself to a change in any exogenous or policy variable within a unit of time, namely, one quarter of a year in this version of the model. There is then no 'stock-adjustment', dynamic, mechanism present in any part of the system.

(ii) Expected returns, as mentioned earlier in the paper, are assumed to be adequately proxied by actual interest rates. For no part of the system do we postulate any 'adaptive expectations' hypotheses.

(iii) Because so far the data we have collated is only in first-difference form it it not possible to impose all the restrictions on the estimates of the structural coefficients that could be possibly justified in the light of our approach to the description of the portfolio and debt behaviour of the financial sectors in the model. Although how serious an actual, as opposed to a potential, limitation this is likely to be can be gauged, to some extent, by consideration of the RLS results for Sectors 2, 3, 4, and 5.

(iv) Even if it were possible to impose all relevant restrictions throughout the system this would not be sufficient to guarantee that it was stable. For, in addition to those linear restrictions, we would have to include information to the effect that all the market demand/supply variables should be substitutes for each other (except in very special circumstances: see Brainard [3]). This clearly involves us in solving a quadratic programming problem (see Goldberger [9] and H. Theil [17]): even when we cast the model in stock terms and impose all linear restrictions, we have no software available at this time to allow us to impose the extra inequality constraints.

(v) The multiplier derived from this model, as already implied above, will be of a special kind. In effect, because of the nature of our model it will be a simple comparative statics multiplier: it cannot contain any dynamic, or 'time-delay', effects.

(vi) As noted in Section II, some of the sectors in the model, particularly the Overseas Sector, need to be amplified. A more rigorous and explicit treatment of that sector would undoubtedly reveal that additional independent variables would need to be incorporated in the demand/supply equations of that sector.

(vii) However, to close the model after such a step would probably require at least including *the real sector* of the U.K. economy in the model. Indeed, if it can be achieved, the ideal state of affairs would be to add income (separated out also into consumption and investment) to this model or any development of it. Some theoretical work on how this might be accomplished has, in fact, already been done by Tobin and Brainard [20].

IV. Empirical findings

The basic, that is without-restrictions, 2SLS results obtained from estimating the 67 stochastic equations in the model are catalogued in Tables 1–9 (see Appendix), for Sectors 1–9, respectively. In the presentation of the results the figures in parentheses under a given coefficient are its 'asymptotic t-value'; an asterisk above a coefficient indicates that, in terms of the latter, the coefficient is significant at the 5 per cent level or better; R^2 is the coefficient of multiple determination; $\bar{R}^2$ is that coefficient adjusted for degrees of freedom; and F is an analysis-of-variance test-statistic, to indicate whether or not R^2 is significantly different from zero—strictly speaking, the F-statistic is not applicable given the present estimator, but it can be used as a rough guide to the statistical significance of the goodness of fit.

In commenting on the 2SLS results we proceed by considering the sectors *seriatim*. Interest rate $\bar{r}_{12}$ has been omitted from all equations in the Public Sector. Now that the interest rates are couched in first-difference form, of course, $\Delta \bar{r}_{12} = \Delta \bar{r}_7$. In terms of (significant) goodness of fit only two equations in this sector are of value; namely those seeking to explain the Public Sector's demand for Commercial Bills and its demand for Deposits with Other Banks. There are also five significant coefficients in the demand equation for Commercial Bills. The own rate of interest is positive in that equation, as it is in the demand equation for Deposits with Other Banks, and both own-rate coefficients are statistically speaking significantly different from zero. Effectively, the constant terms in those equations, and in the remaining three equations for the Public Sector, *are* zero. But the three other demand equations, namely for Deposits with Deposit Banks, Discounts and Advances, and Equity, appear to be not very well specified; the signs and significance of the coefficients in these equations leave much to be desired.

For Discount Houses the demand for Treasury Bills is explained extremely well by the equation we have specified; having a highly significant goodness of fit of some 90 per cent. However, only two coefficients are significant at the 5 per cent level or better, namely, those on net worth and on the own rate of interest. Changes in the latter also invoke a positive response in the demand for Treasury Bills. Also we might note that numerically the coefficient on the own rate of interest comes close to the partial equilibrium estimate of it (see J. M. Parkin [14]). The demand equations for Commercial Bills and British Government Securities are also reasonably well determined. The equation for Commercial Bills has five coefficients which are significantly different from zero—though the own rate coefficient is negative. For the British Government Securities equation the only significant coefficient is that on the Treasury Bill rate, which has a negative sign. The equation for Call Loans has a fair over-all performance. Those for Deposits and Advances and for Equity have not been well specified—although both have two significant coefficients. However, the own-rate coefficient for Deposits and Advances is (significantly) negative; while that for Equity is not significant at all.

As far as the Deposit Banks are concerned, the equations for Call Loans, Commercial Bills, and Equity do not produce very satisfactory results. The other equations are tolerably well determined—although there is only one good over-all result, that for British Government Securities. Even there, only two coefficients are statistically different from zero; and the own-rate coefficient is negative, although effectively zero.

Matters improve somewhat when we examine the results for Other Banks. For this sector there are two equations with high, and significant, R^2's. It would be hard to improve on the over-all performance ($\bar{R}^2 = 0.98$) of the equation for Advances by Other Banks! But in that equation the own-rate coefficient is negative and statistically speaking zero. For the British Government Securities equation also the own-rate coefficient is not statistically significantly different from zero. Similarly in both these equations the constant term is significantly different from zero, as is the constant in the equation for Equity. But that equation and those for Currency, Treasury Bills, Call Loans, and Commercial Bills are not well determined.

With the possible exception of the equations for Deposits with

Deposit Banks, the equations for Building Societies have performed rather badly. In three of the six equations the constant terms are significantly different from zero. Only one equation, that for Treasury Bills, has a significant, and positive, own-rate coefficient.

For the Other Financial Institutions Sector there are only two equations which produce reasonable, and significant, over-all results. These are the equations for Deposits with Other Banks and British Government Securities. In the former equation the own-rate coefficient is positive and significant; but in the latter equation it is negative and insignificant. The equations for Equity, National Savings, and Deposits with Deposit Banks have fairly good R^2's but not so good $\bar{R}^2$'s. But only in the National Savings equation is the own-rate coefficient significant and positive. In the Equity and Deposits with Deposit Banks equations the signs of the own-rate coefficients are perverse; and those coefficients are really zero. Likewise, in all equations the constant terms are effectively zero.

In terms of R^2, apart from the equation for currency, the set of results obtained for the Industrial and Commercial Sector is quite good. However, in line with the pattern that has been established up to now, in terms of statistically significant over-all relationships and of $\bar{R}^2$ only two equations are well determined for this sector. These are the equations for Deposits with Deposit Banks and the equation for Deposits with Other Financial Institutions. But in both of those equations the own-rate response is perverse and insignificantly different from zero. In no equation, in fact, in this sector is the own rate response other than zero, statistically speaking. Furthermore, two out of the eight equations have constant terms that are significantly other than zero.

The Personal Sector also has few well-specified equations. Two equations have high and significantly different from zero, R^2's and high $\bar{R}^2$'s; namely the equation for British Government Securities and the equation for Deposits with Deposit Banks. In the former equation the own-rate response is perverse, and statistically very much different from zero. While in the latter equation the own-rate coefficient, similarly highly significant, is positive. However, in only one other equation, that for Deposits with Financial Institutions, is the own-rate response significantly different from zero, where it is, in effect, positive. In seven out of the eleven equations in this sector the coefficient on the own-rate is perverse. But only two of the equations contain constants which are statistically different from zero.

We come now to the final sector in the model, the Overseas Sector. Here a broad view of the results confirms the doubts raised earlier about the specification of the equations for this sector. There are at best only two well-specified equations. The Treasury Bill equation is a good one and exhibits a highly significant relationship; however, the coefficient on the own-rate is negative and effectively zero. Only for the Equity equation is the own-rate response positive and significant. But the results for this sector possess one favourable attribute in that in only two out of eight equations is the constant term significantly different from zero.

Sectors 2, 3, 4, and 5, as indicated in Section II of this paper, were re-estimated at the second stage using RLS. The object of such an exercise being, it will be recalled, to obtain better determined estimates of the parameters for each sector; thereafter, if appropriate, such estimates can be used as replacements for the appropriate 2SLS estimates in deriving the multiplier.

The RLS results all appear to be very inferior to the 2SLS estimates. However, we need some kind of test that will enable us to judge which are the better results; indeed, in our situation, we need to be able to decide which is the better *set* of estimates. Although an *F*-test is applicable to RIS estimates *per se*, it is not strictly speaking correct to use such a test with our present estimating technique, since it is based on 2SLS. But some test statistic is necessary, even if it can at best only provide an approximate indicator as to which is the better set of estimates. The test statistics we have employed, which we may call an '*F*-test', is that devised by J. Stewart [16], which is an *F*-test that is appropriate for RLS estimates. It is on the basis of that test statistic that we have decided to reject for present purposes the RLS results in favour of the 2SLS results.[11] Clearly, at whatever appropriate level of significance we choose, the aim is to discover that F is statistically speaking not different from zero. In the present situation it is certainly very different from zero; but it is worth noting that the '*F*' values are only of the order of 10–20, which compare extremely favourably with *F*-tests on restrictions of the

---

[11] *For current requirements* it can be shown that the '*F*-test' can be epitomized by this formula (see [16]):

$$F = \frac{S_* - m(n - k)}{g}.$$

Here: S_* is the weighted gross sum of squares of the residuals in the 'restricted model'; m is the number of equations in the model; $(n - k)$ is the degrees of freedom in each equation; and g is the number of restrictions in the model.

present kind that we have imposed, for example, in other work on portfolio behaviour. Since the restrictions are not satisfied, and since some of the over-all results are worthless, from the application of RLS, we have not deemed it opportune to include coefficients from the RLS estimates in the calculation of the multiplier. Also, we have refrained from quoting the results here.

We have then performed the calculation of the multiplier by using the coefficients from the 2SLS estimates. Despite the fact that *prima facie* the over-all impression might be formed that those estimates are a 'mixed bag', on reflection they will no doubt be judged to be not too bad, and therefore of some value in giving us possible (first-step) insight into the working of monetary policy. For it must be remembered that they are *first difference* results.

Two multipliers have, in fact, been calculated. One is based on all the coefficients from the 2SLS results, whether they are significantly different from zero or not; while the other ignores those coefficients that are insignificant at the 15 per cent level. We refer in what follows to some of the results derived from both multipliers. However, objections can be raised on theoretical grounds against the second type of multiplier. The coefficients that are actually used in the calculation of the multiplier will be affected by the values of the omitted coefficients. For, as Tobin and Brainard [20] have correctly argued, even if, say, one interest rate appears not to be significant in influencing a demand/supply variable for a particular sector, it must be included in that equation because any effects it might have on the demand/supply variable would otherwise be being attributed to the other interest rates in the equation.

Because of their dimension the two multipliers' matrices have not been quoted in full. Also, importantly, to so quote such a matrix only has relevance if we are trying to predict the multiplier effects on the various parts of the Financial Sector, of a unit change in, say, a policy variable on the assumption that no other exogenous variable changes. For the effects of a change in a given exogenous on the system can only be 'predicted' if some expectation is made about changes in the remaining exogenous variables. It is necessary then, as it were, to process the multiplier matrix before it becomes operational.

To limit the computation involved, multiplier effects were calculated from the two multiplier matrices for the four policy variables only (Bank Rate, Currency, Treasury Bills, and Government Bonds). Here, furthermore, for reasons of space, we report on a change in only one of those variables, namely, Bank Rate, which we assume rises by one per cent. The Bank Rate is to be envisaged as a very important policy variable in that an upward adjustment of it is intended, usually without question, to signal the beginning of a period of monetary restraint.

In examining the policy effects in the model, we have not experimented with alternative methods of 'estimating' the expected values of the remaining exogenous variables. Rather we have decided to adopt one method only, and that method is the same for all exogenous variables, no matter which sector forms the relevant expected value. To be precise, the expected values are taken to be the mean value of the variable over our sample period. Clearly, objections can be levelled at such a choice—but a choice has to be made. Out of the approaches we considered (e.g. 'take last sample value'; 'take the first out-of-the-sample-period-observation') the present one seemed the most reasonable. After all, in many ways, use of it can be rationalized on the same kind of grounds that are implicitly invoked when elasticities are calculated 'at the point of sample means'.

In Table IV.16 we have catalogued the signs of the changes in the 85 endogenous variables based upon 'multiplier one', as Bank Rate is increased by one per cent. Something like 50 per cent of the multiplier effects are numerically outside the bounds that we believe *a priori* to be reasonable: so we have refrained from quantifying the multiplier effects in Table IV.16.

In commenting on Table IV.16 let us begin with the interest-rate changes. These rates rise: Treasury Bill rate; rate on Deposits paid by Other Banks; rate paid on Deposits by Other Financial Institutions; rate charged for Mortgages; and the return on Equity. The rates that decline are: that on British Government Securities; the Call Loan rate; that on Local Authority Debt; that on Building Society Shares and Deposits; and that on Commercial Bills. Thus not all the interest-rate changes are in the direction that we would usually expect them to be (e.g. the change in Call Loan Rate).

Relative interest-rate movements have, of course, to be based on the quantitative multiplier effects of a change in Bank Rate. For what they are worth, then, the interest-rate movements are as follows. For those that have risen the (descending) order of increase is (rate on): Equity; Mortgages; Deposits with Other Banks; Treasury Bills; Deposits with Other Financial Institutions. Similarly for those rates that have fallen the (descending) order of decrease is: Commercial Bills; Local Authority Debt; Call Loans; British Government Securities; and Shares and Deposits.

Table IV.16

Movements in the Endogenous Variables as Bank Rate rises by one per cent

a_{71}	+	a_{75}	+	$a_{15.8}$	+
a_{81}	−	$-a_{95}$	−	$a_{16.8}$	−
$a_{12.1}$	+	$a_{15.5}$	+	a_{29}	+
$a_{14.1}$	−	a_{26}	+	a_{39}	+
$a_{16.1}$	+	a_{36}	−	a_{59}	−
a_{22}	−	a_{46}	−	a_{79}	+
a_{32}	+	a_{76}	−	a_{89}	+
$-a_{52}$	−	a_{86}	+	$a_{10.9}$	+
$-a_{13.2}$	−	$-a_{12.6}$	−	$a_{12.9}$	0
$a_{14.2}$	+	$a_{14.6}$	−	$a_{14.9}$	0
$a_{16.2}$	0	$a_{16.6}$	+	$a_{16.9}$	−
a_{13}	0	a_{17}	−	r_2	+
a_{23}	+	a_{27}	+	r_3	−
a_{33}	+	a_{57}	+	r_5	−
a_{53}	+	a_{77}	+	r_6	−
$a_{11.3}$	+	a_{87}	+	r_8	+
$a_{14.3}$	+	$a_{10.7}$	+	r_9	−
$a_{16.3}$	+	$a_{12.7}$	+	r_{10}	+
a_{14}	+	$a_{14.7}$	+	r_{14}	−
a_{24}	−	a_{18}	−	r_{15}	+
a_{34}	+	a_{38}	−	r_{16}	+
a_{54}	−	a_{48}	+	a_{62}	+
$a_{12.4}$	+	a_{58}	−	a_{63}	−
$a_{14.4}$	−	a_{78}	−	a_{64}	−
$a_{16.4}$	+	a_{88}	+	a_{65}	−
a_{15}	+	a_{98}	+	a_{66}	−
a_{25}	−	$a_{10.8}$	+	a_{67}	0
a_{35}	+	$a_{12.8}$	−	a_{68}	−
				a_{69}	0

As can be appreciated from Table IV.16 these interest-rate changes have provoked a considerable degree of portfolio adjustment. A great deal of the adjustments that have occurred can be accounted for in terms of the interest-rate changes mentioned above. But this is not always the case.

We might take a brief look at one of the sectors—the Personal Sector. The items which have declined it its balance sheet are: Currency; Advances by Other Banks; Equity; Call Loans; British Government Securities; and Deposits with Deposit Banks. Matching these items *one by one* with changes in their rates of return we find that on this *ceteris paribus* assumption only two items, those for Equity and Deposits with Deposit Banks, move in a perverse fashion (recall that the return on Currency is the negative rate of inflation

$\bar{r}_1$: the 'expected value' of inflation is positive for calculation of the multiplier effects). Even if we were to invoke changes in relative interest rates, or in interest differentials, as we should more correctly do, we would still find it difficult to explain these negative changes in the Personal Sector's holdings of Equity and Bank Deposits.

The items which have increased in the balance sheet of the Personal Sector are: Deposits with Other Banks; Shares and Deposits with Building Societies; Mortgages; Deposits with Other Financial Institutions; and National Savings. The seemingly 'perverse' items here are: the increased holdings of Shares and Deposits in Building Societies and the increased demand for Mortgages.

Turning now to the effects of a unit increase in Bank Rate via 'multiplier two', the results are reported in Table IV.17. There, for all variables except interest rates, we have quoted the quantitative

TABLE IV.17

Changes in the Endogenous Variables as Bank Rate rises by one per cent

a_{71}	142·2	a_{75}	−61·7	$a_{15 \cdot 8}$	111·2
a_{81}	9·79	$-a_{95}$	237	$a_{16 \cdot 8}$	−229·2
$a_{12 \cdot 1}$	13·6	$a_{15 \cdot 5}$	−198·5	a_{29}	39·9
$a_{14 \cdot 1}$	−254	a_{26}	0	a_{39}	−8·64
$a_{16 \cdot 1}$	0	a_{36}	8·48	a_{59}	−3·35
a_{22}	190	a_{46}	−83·6	a_{79}	−116·4
a_{32}	37·8	a_{76}	−74·9	a_{89}	0
$-a_{52}$	−90·5	a_{86}	464·7	$a_{10 \cdot 9}$	70·2
$-a_{13 \cdot 2}$	−202·3	$-a_{12 \cdot 6}$	68·8	$a_{12 \cdot 9}$	−73
$a_{14 \cdot 2}$	28·1	$a_{14 \cdot 6}$	−48	$a_{14 \cdot 9}$	−0·57
$a_{16 \cdot 2}$	−79·5	$a_{16 \cdot 6}$	−190	$a_{16 \cdot 9}$	−20·3
a_{13}	−16·52	a_{17}	−25	r_2	+
a_{23}	13·35	a_{27}	−411·6	r_3	−
a_{33}	−45·6	a_{57}	45·1	r_5	+
a_{53}	0	a_{77}	37·2	r_6	−
$a_{11 \cdot 3}$	−99·4	a_{87}	−38·5	r_8	−
$a_{14 \cdot 3}$	0	$a_{10 \cdot 7}$	293·8	r_9	+
$a_{16 \cdot 3}$	−18·02	$a_{12 \cdot 7}$	282·7	r_{10}	+
a_{14}	−0·88	$a_{14 \cdot 7}$	284·6	r_{14}	+
a_{24}	1·1	a_{18}	27·58	r_{15}	+
a_{34}	−137·5	a_{38}	−52·8	r_{16}	+
a_{54}	0	a_{48}	−12·23	a_{62}	13
$a_{12 \cdot 4}$	−418	a_{58}	37·9	a_{63}	−142
$a_{14 \cdot 4}$	−30·6	a_{78}	99·8	a_{64}	−593
$a_{16 \cdot 4}$	−96·3	a_{88}	0	a_{65}	2·5
a_{15}	−14·5	a_{98}	−190	a_{66}	−540
a_{25}	−20·6	$a_{10 \cdot 8}$	0	a_{67}	−138
a_{35}	−17·9	$a_{12 \cdot 8}$	7	a_{68}	411·4
				a_{69}	795

multiplier effects. For some interest rates (r_9, r_{10}, and r_{15}) the latter are eminently sensible, for some others, however, they are not. The reason for this—apart from the possible implications of having removed so many coefficients from the Γ and B matrices—could well be the kind of model we have. For one of its characteristics, as noted earlier in the paper, is that it 'forces' the system to adjust to an exogenous shock within one period. To make such an adjustment possible it is self-evident that interest rates have to change, but it is also likely that they have to change by far wider margins than seems sensible to enable the system to attain its next equilibrium point in such a short space of time. Recall as well, that, taking the model as it stands, the multiplier effects it generates depend upon the values we have assumed for the 23 exogenous variables besides the Bank Rate.

Ceteris paribus, 'multiplier two' produces effects for the majority of the endogenous assets/liabilities in the model which are very realistic in a quantitative sense. In fact, only for variables such as: a_{86}; a_{27}; $a_{10.7}$; $a_{14.7}$; and a_{79} (apart from possibly the assets with zero multiplier effects) are the results numerically speaking near to being outside realistic limits.

A comparison of Tables IV.16 and IV.17 reveals that about 50 per cent of the signs of the multiplier effects are the same. There are important differences when we examine the signs for the interest rates. Now, however, the rate on Call Loans has the correct *a priori* sign; so too does that on Building Society Shares and Deposits. But the rate on Deposits with Other Banks is reduced rather than increased. Once again, however, not all the asset-switching in the system can be explained by the interest-rate changes.

We may again look at the balance sheet of the Personal Sector. Here, comparing changes in own-returns with asset/liability changes we can see that in only five instances are the asset/liability changes in the right direction. This is also true if we accept the quantitative interest rate multiplier effects and examine asset/liability changes in the light of adjustments in interest-rate differentials. The correct changes concern: British Government Securities; Call Loans; Deposits with Deposit Banks; Advances by Other Banks; and Mortgages.

'Multiplier one' allows us to account for changes in the portfolio adjustment of the Personal Sector better than does 'multiplier two'. But the latter produces more sensible interest changes and quantitative asset/liability changes than does the former. On the whole it seems to enable us to explain the balance-sheet adjustment of all sectors collectively somewhat better than does 'multiplier one'.

Once the present model has been developed and it produces more meaningful multiplier effects for interest-rate changes, it will become possible to use it to provide a quantitative assessment of certain categories of monetary policy. It will then be possible to give some more definite indication on an issue upon which we focused attention in Section I of this paper. We refer to the question as to whether or not non-bank financial intermediaries can negate, or neutralize, monetary policy. However, we can present the evidence on this matter for an increase in Bank Rate of 1 per cent, under the assumptions we have made, in terms of 'multiplier one' and 'multiplier two'.

To consider the question we might look at it in this kind of way. As Bank Rate is raised, the supposition is that the authorities are seeking, via changes in certain key rates (the other exogenous interest rates tied to Bank Rate), to influence interest rates generally and to reduce the liquidity of the economy by reducing the supply of money, or at least by constraining its rate of growth. But what happens to the supply of money and to the stock of liquid assets in the economy, in terms of 'multiplier one'? The answer is: money supply (Currency + Deposits at Deposit Banks) rises; while the liabilities of non-bank financial intermediaries falls. But the net effect of these changes happens to be positive.

However, it must be stated that if we exclude the Public Sector's holdings of Deposits with Deposit Banks and its Deposits with Other Banks, it is revealed that the money supply falls while the non-bank financial intermediaries' liabilities rise. The net effect is still positive. We are not arguing that we should so discard the activities of the Public Sector: the basis on which we might do so might be questionable although possibly justifiable. But, in any event, our concern over the efficacy of monetary policy lies in evaluating its effect on the *Private Sector* of the economy and not on the *Public Sector*. In the light of the joint activities of the Industrial and Commercial and the Personal Sector then the multiplier effects of 'multiplier one' come close to establishing a *prima facie* case that the non-bank financial intermediaries can negate monetary policy.

This conclusion is very much underlined when the results obtained via 'multiplier two' are analysed. This can be seen from Table IV.17. *In toto*, money supply *decreases* by about 4 units. The liabilities of non-bank financial intermediaries *increase* by approximately 610 units, even allowing for the perverse item, Building Society Shares and Deposits, *and* for the holdings of liquid assets by the Public Sector. Once the latter's activities are excluded the over-all result is even more in favour of the non-bank financial intermediaries.

To summarize, it is quite apparent that this kind of model has much to offer in enabling us to discover the various effects of monetary policy. But we would not place too much emphasis on the *quantitative* multiplier effects we have derived from it; and it should be stated that the present multiplier effects represent the outcome really of 'an exercise'. For any predictions about monetary policy depend, *inter alia*, upon the assumptions made about that policy and about the remaining exogenous variables in the model. In that regard, rather than investigating the effects of changes in any one of the four policy variables, it might, for example, be more instructive for real-world policy decisions to analyse the consequences of a 'package deal' monetary policy. For instance, we might assume that, in order to restrain economic activity, the authorities will: increase Bank Rate; reduce the supply of Treasury Bills; reduce the stock of Currency; and increase the supply of Government Securities.

V. Further work on the model

There is no need to say very much about 'further work on the model', for we have, by implication, made some remarks with regard to developments of this model, in listing the 'limitations' of our present approach in Section III. Our long-term aim is to rescind all of those limitations, or as many as we can. As a first objective, though, we would like to be able to re-estimate the present model using stock data, and to do so on the basis of more observations. For one obvious drawback to estimating the present model is that we have so few observations. If we cannot increase the latter, it may be necessary, in order to economize on degrees of freedom, to amalgamate some sectors, for example, the Banking Sector.

However, we hope that this will not be the case, for as we attempt to make the treatment of portfolio- and debt-management more explicit for each sector and to dynamize the model, we would be seeking to disaggregate the model rather than to carrying out further aggregation. In this regard we would like to be able to disaggregate the Other Financial Institutions Sector in view of our interest in the effects of non-bank financial intermediaries on the working of monetary policy.

With reference to such policy, something we did not mention in Section III, although some reference has been made to it in Section IV, is that two 'quantitative' policy instruments have been omitted from this initial model. The one is Special Deposits and the other is the Funding of Government Debt. The former will almost certainly become assimilated into the model when we treat portfolio behaviour more explicitly; and the latter we hope can be accommodated in the model at the present stage, or when stock data are collated, by separating British Government Securities into 'short-term' and 'long-term'. Once this has been achieved, even the present kind of model will allow us to examine the effect of changes in the maturity of the Debt on 'the term structure of interest rates';[12] and to do so for the first time in a general equilibrium framework.

POSTSCRIPT
G. CLAYTON, J. C. DODDS, AND J. L. FORD

It is now over two years since this model was specified. In the period since the Conference we have been working along the kind of lines indicated in Section V of this paper, in an endeavour to remove some of the limitations inherent in the pilot model. Details of this work can be obtained on request from the above-named.

---

[12] This is also an area in which we have been working see, for example, the recent paper [6]. In a monograph which is currently being written, and which is to be published early in 1974, [22], a chapter is being devoted to the 'market segmentation' theory of the term structure. It is hoped that we shall be able to report there on some initial 'general equilibrium findings' on that theory.

Appendix

TABLE 1

Public (Sector 1)

	Constant	$\Delta \bar{r}_7$	Δf_8	Δf_{14}	Δf_{18}	$\bar{a}_{1\cdot1}$	$\bar{a}_{2\cdot1}$	$\bar{a}_{3\cdot1}$	$\bar{a}_{6\cdot1}$	$\bar{a}_{11\cdot1}$	R^2	$\bar{R}^2$	F
$a_{7\cdot1}$	−1·74 (0·13)	−128·1 (1·94)	−11·1 (1·2)	140·5 (2·05)	−13·9 (0·6)	−0·014 (0·2)	0·02 (1·1)	0·001 (0·08)	0·002 (0·02)	−0·1 (0·4)	0·36	0·05	1·15
$a_{8\cdot1}$	0·75 (0·3)	18·9 (1·4)	6·9 (3·6)	−25·6 (1·8)	5·73 (1·2)	−0·02 (1·4)	−0·00002 (0·05)	−0·006 (1·5)	−0·005 (0·3)	−0·02 (0·51)	0·62	0·43	3·3
$-a_{12\cdot1}$	0·6 (0·4)	1·05 (0·15)	2·69 (2·7)	−2·02 (0·3)	−0·35 (0·14)	0·008 (1·15)	0·0009 (0·5)	−0·005 (2·2)	0·013 (1·3)	−0·03 (1·3)	0·48	0·22	1·9
$a_{14\cdot1}$	−0·75 (0·4)	−19·5 (2·3)	−0·89 (0·7)	23·7 (2·7)	−5·46 (1·78)	0·02 (2·5)	0·005 (2·03)	0·007 (2·85)	−0·001 (0·09)	−0·008 (0·3)	0·7	0·56	4·78
$a_{16\cdot1}$	4·66 (1·0)	1·96 (0·09)	2·81 (0·9)	−5·4 (0·24)	−6·74 (0·85)	0·007 (0·3)	0·004 (0·6)	0·009 (1·5)	−0·01 (0·3)	0·05 (0·7)	0·36	0·04	1·13

Table 2
Discount Houses (Sector 2)

	Constant	$\bar{A}_2$	$\Delta \dot{r}_2$	$\Delta \dot{r}_3$	$\Delta \dot{r}_5$	$\Delta \dot{r}_{13}$	$\Delta \dot{r}_{14}$	$\Delta \dot{r}_{16}$	$\Delta \dot{r}_6$	R^2	$\bar{R}^2$	F
$a_{2\cdot2}$	−30·1 (1·96)	0·86 (12·0)	296·3 (2·5)	55·7 (0·8)	59·6 (0·8)	−484·0 (1·98)	137·2 (0·8)	−33·8 (0·8)	−10·52 (0·8)	0·9	0·87	26·7
$a_{3\cdot2}$	13·3 (0·8)	−0·014 (0·2)	−295·5 (2·5)	−132·5 (1·87)	−7·58 (0·01)	419·4 (1·7)	−121·3 (0·7)	69·5 (1·7)	90·0 (2·1)	0·64	0·5	5·1
$a_{6\cdot2}$	1·26 (0·5)	−0·012 (0·9)	−0·14 (0·007)	−23·7 (1·96)	36·3 (2·7)	−81·7 (1·96)	48·2 (1·7)	−7·4 (1·1)	15·7 (1·4)	0·54	0·37	3·3
$a_{13\cdot2}$	−8·9 (1·7)	0·05 (1·86)	51·9 (1·3)	−15·2 (0·6)	19·4 (0·7)	−265·5 (3·1)	216·3 (3·8)	−5·4 (0·4)	18·7 (1·1)	0·47	0·29	2·58
$a_{14\cdot2}$	8·5 (1·8)	0·07 (3·2)	−64·1 (1·7)	88·1 (4·0)	−67·2 (2·75)	233·3 (3·1)	−115·9 (2·3)	−18·1 (1·4)	−1·25 (0·03)	0·72	0·62	7·2
$a_{16\cdot2}$	0·61 (0·5)	−0·001 (0·2)	−18·2 (2·1)	−11·5 (2·1)	−3·13 (0·5)	36·0 (1·95)	−19·0 (1·5)	0·09 (0·03)	5·27 (0·8)	0·26	−0·005	0·98

TABLE 3
Deposit Banks (Sector 3)

	Constant	$\bar{A}_3$	$\bar{a}_{7.3}$	$\Delta\bar{r}_1$	Δt_2	Δt_3	Δt_5	Δt_6	$\Delta\bar{r}_{11}$	Δt_{14}	Δt_{16}	R^2	$\bar{R}^2$	F
$a_{1.3}$	−34·6 (1·9)	0·13 (1·3)	−0·36 (3·7)	35·2 (1·1)	3·7 (0·03)	−22·7 (0·3)	4·2 (0·05)	28·9 (0·6)	−25·6 (0·01)	13·7 (0·01)	−6·36 (0·2)	0·59	0·35	2·4
$a_{2.3}$	−62·6 (1·7)	0·21 (1·0)	−0·38 (1·9)	−117·7 (1·9)	34·6 (0·1)	143·5 (1·0)	−45·0 (0·25)	−106·0 (0·25)	166·0 (0·3)	−141·3 (0·45)	1·0 (0·01)	0·62	0·4	2·8
$a_{3.3}$	−14·8 (1·0)	0·18 (2·2)	−0·27 (3·5)	−39·6 (1·6)	−153·2 (1·4)	−68·8 (1·2)	14·9 (0·2)	47·6 (1·3)	142·0 (0·7)	−90·6 (0·7)	−23·7 (0·8)	0·7	0·52	3·9
$a_{5.3}$	5·74 (0·7)	0·005 (0·1)	−0·035 (0·8)	−12·3 (0·8)	−40·7 (0·6)	−17·0 (0·5)	−31·7 (0·8)	−3·02 (0·1)	132·0 (1·1)	−57·1 (0·8)	20·8 (1·1)	0·41	0·06	1·2
$a_{11.3}$	72·7 (1·9)	0·44 (2·1)	−0·008 (0·04)	127·4 (2·02)	76·8 (0·3)	102·0 (0·7)	8·8 (0·05)	−21·3 (0·2)	−92·1 (0·2)	52·3 (0·2)	27·4 (0·35)	0·66	0·46	3·3
$a_{14.3}$	17·5 (1·9)	0·07 (1·3)	−0·02 (0·5)	−2·1 (0·14)	−21·5 (0·3)	−36·9 (1·0)	−8·0 (0·2)	26·3 (1·1)	−25·6 (0·2)	43·5 (0·5)	−1·5 (0·08)	0·32	−0·07	0·82
$a_{16.3}$	3·75 (1·7)	0·019 (1·5)	−0·02 (1·4)	3·48 (0·9)	−6·25 (0·4)	5·14 (0·6)	−12·1 (1·1)	1·5 (0·3)	53·0 (1·6)	−41·4 (2·13)	5·8 (1·2)	0·41	0·06	1·2

TABLE 4
Other Banks (Sector 4)

	Constant	$\bar{a}_{8\cdot4}$	$\bar{A}_4$	$\Delta\bar{r}_1$	$\Delta\hat{r}_2$	$\Delta\hat{r}_3$	$\Delta\hat{r}_5$	$\Delta\hat{r}_6$	$\Delta\bar{r}_{12}$	$\Delta\hat{r}_{14}$	$\Delta\hat{r}_{16}$	R^2	$\bar{R}^2$	F
$a_{1\cdot4}$	0·3 (1·7)	0·0002 (1·0)	0·001 (1·3)	−0·05 (0·3)	−0·4 (0·3)	0·4 (0·6)	0·05 (0·1)	−0·29 (0·9)	3·2 (1·6)	−2·8 (1·9)	0·06 (0·2)	0·35	−0·03	0·91
$a_{2\cdot4}$	−1·03 (0·2)	0·001 (0·2)	0·05 (2·2)	−1·29 (0·3)	36·5 (1·2)	−12·7 (0·6)	24·3 (1·4)	−2·8 (0·3)	−53·6 (0·9)	6·7 (0·2)	−11·2 (1·2)	0·47	0·15	1·5
$a_{3\cdot4}$	19·3 (2·21)	0·03 (2·13)	−0·06 (1·5)	−0·6 (0·06)	−197·9 (3·8)	7·6 (0·2)	6·26 (0·2)	35·0 (2·2)	264·1 (2·6)	−138·8 (1·9)	41·7 (2·7)	0·76	0·6	5·25
$a_{5\cdot4}$	−4·65 (1·5)	−0·01 (3·1)	−0·04 (2·8)	−4·76 (1·5)	9·46 (0·5)	−8·1 (0·7)	0·11 (0·01)	−8·91 (1·63)	−4·78 (0·14)	3·97 (0·16)	−10·1 (1·86)	0·63	0·41	2·84
$a_{12\cdot4}$	−107·1 (4·1)	−1·03 (28·0)	0·44 (3·7)	−27·1 (1·0)	256·3 (1·6)	−9·9 (0·1)	−124·1 (1·4)	−50·5 (1·1)	−521·4 (1·7)	498·7 (2·3)	−58·7 (1·3)	0·99	0·98	153·3
$a_{14\cdot4}$	−3·77 (1·71)	−0·004 (1·2)	−0·02 (1·85)	−2·98 (1·3)	−5·2 (0·4)	−2·68 (0·3)	0·57 (0·08)	−0·2 (0·05)	−28·2 (1·1)	29·1 (1·6)	−4·2 (1·1)	0·43	0·01	1·3
$a_{16\cdot14}$	15·3 (2·2)	0·0001 (0·01)	0·07 (2·4)	−0·05 (0·07)	4·9 (0·1)	−7·5 (0·3)	46·0 (2·03)	79·0 (0·6)	−26·0 (0·3)	−29·7 (0·5)	13·9 (1·1)	0·45	0·13	1·4

TABLE 5
Building Societies (Sector 5)

	Constant	$\bar{A}_5$	$\Delta \bar{r}_1$	$\Delta \dot{r}_2$	$\Delta \dot{r}_3$	$\Delta \dot{r}_6$	$\Delta \dot{r}_7$	$\Delta \dot{r}_9$	$\Delta \dot{r}_{15}$	R^2	$\bar{R}^2$	F
$a_{1.5}$	1·3 (0·9)	0·09 (2·4)	−1·75 (0·6)	−12·6 (1·2)	6·1 (1·1)	−3·64 (1·0)	14·3 (1·8)	1·0 (0·07)	−6·4 (0·8)	0·47	0·24	2·09
$a_{2.5}$	−0·67 (1·1)	−0·0071 (0·5)	0·62 (0·5)	10·4 (2·4)	−4·46 (2·02)	−2·1 (1·4)	−7·2 (2·2)	14·5 (2·4)	−4·3 (1·3)	0·51	0·3	2·4
$a_{3.5}$	18·9 (2·6)	−0·41 (2·3)	−6·15 (0·5)	−6·99 (0·1)	−34·1 (1·3)	−21·3 (1·2)	29·7 (0·8)	41·7 (0·6)	56·3 (1·5)	0·42	0·17	1·7
$a_{7.5}$	1·3 (0·3)	0·4 (3·1)	−3·82 (0·4)	−33·5 (1·0)	23·3 (1·3)	−9·2 (0·7)	40·7 (1·5)	24·3 (0·5)	−43·8 (1·6)	0·57	0·39	3·2
$-a_{9.5}$	−237·0 (9·7)	0·38 (0·6)	51·4 (1·1)	188·8 (1·0)	−57·8 (0·6)	44·8 (0·7)	−182·3 (1·4)	142·6 (0·6)	−24·8 (0·2)	0·15	−0·21	0·4
$a_{15.5}$	198·5 (12·3)	0·11 (0·3)	−24·2 (0·8)	−95·5 (0·8)	17·6 (0·3)	12·4 (0·3)	62·8 (0·7)	−131·0 (0·8)	28·32 (0·3)	0·06	−0·3	0·16

TABLE 6
Other Financial Institutions (Sector 6)

	Constant	Δf_2	Δf_3	$\Delta \bar{r}_4$	Δf_6	$\Delta \bar{r}_7$	Δf_8	Δf_{14}	Δf_{16}	$\bar{a}_{10\cdot6}$	$\bar{a}_{11\cdot6}$	$\bar{A}_6$	R^2	$\bar{R}^2$	F
$a_{2\cdot6}$	-6·11 (0·6)	7·41 (0·5)	7·28 (0·9)	14·4 (1·46)	0·22 (0·04)	-25·7 (0·96)	-21·1 (0·78)	6·82 (0·37)	2·83 (0·52)	-0·21 (0·53)	0·13 (1·4)	0·26 (0·62)	0·54	0·22	1·7
$a_{3\cdot6}$	5·5 (0·73)	-186·8 (1·85)	-65·7 (1·07)	-27·7 (0·39)	94·1 (2·53)	184·2 (0·95)	-28·7 (1·46)	-71·8 (0·55)	-8·76 (0·25)	-0·15 (0·54)	-0·25 (0·38)	0·27 (0·89)	0·69	0·48	3·3
$a_{4\cdot6}$	-23·3 (1·9)	0·99 (0·06)	-11·5 (1·2)	40·3 (3·6)	-15·5 (2·6)	-42·7 (1·4)	8·11 (2·6)	21·7 (1·0)	-5·07 (0·82)	0·08 (1·8)	0·23 (2·1)	-0·11 (2·2)	0·61	0·34	2·3
$a_{7\cdot6}$	2·91 (0·17)	-35·6 (1·6)	22·2 (1·6)	3·12 (0·2)	-12·2 (1·5)	-49·7 (1·1)	-5·9 (1·3)	-8·5 (0·3)	-6·2 (0·7)	-0·01 (0·2)	-0·03 (0·2)	0·04 (0·5)	0·60	0·32	2·2
$a_{8\cdot6}$	-7·1 (0·16)	-11·6 (0·2)	59·3 (1·7)	23·6 (0·6)	-16·2 (0·8)	186·1 (1·7)	23·1 (2·1)	-215·7 (2·9)	17·8 (0·8)	-0·02 (0·1)	0·37 (1·0)	-0·12 (0·7)	0·71	0·52	3·6
$a_{12\cdot6}$	-46·1 (1·6)	23·5 (0·6)	-72·4 (3·2)	36·0 (1·4)	-5·3 (0·4)	-150·7 (2·1)	9·1 (1·2)	116·5 (2·4)	24·5 (1·7)	-0·22 (2·1)	-0·11 (0·5)	0·27 (2·4)	0·57	0·28	1·9
$a_{14\cdot6}$	1·76 (0·1)	-1·42 (0·07)	-17·9 (1·4)	19·1 (1·3)	-4·4 (0·6)	-12·4 (0·3)	2·5 (0·6)	-5·7 (0·2)	-2·6 (0·3)	0·01 (0·2)	0·1 (0·7)	-0·3 (0·4)	0·47	0·14	1·3
$a_{16\cdot6}$	47·4 (0·8)	71·4 (0·9)	-66·1 (1·4)	-65·7 (1·2)	-38·1 (1·3)	-76·2 (0·51)	-5·0 (0·33)	131·6 (1·3)	-39·9 (1·3)	-0·5 (2·1)	-1·3 (2·4)	0·46 (1·9)	0·65	0·41	2·7

TABLE 7

Industrial and Commercial (Sector 7)

	Constant	$\bar{a}_{11\cdot7}$	$\bar{a}_{16\cdot7}$	$\bar{A}_7$	$\Delta\bar{r}_1$	$\Delta\ell_2$	$\Delta\ell_5$	$\Delta\ell_6$	$\Delta\ell_8$	$\Delta\ell_{10}$	$\Delta\ell_{14}$	$\Delta\bar{r}_7$	R^2	$\bar{R}^2$	F
$a_{1\cdot7}$	25·0 (1·7)	−0·01 (0·07)	0·21 (0·9)	−0·02 (0·2)	−16·2 (0·7)	−12·2 (0·16)	20·8 (0·3)	−17·2 (0·6)	−1·24 (0·08)	−127·5 (1·1)	45·8 (0·4)	21·6 (0·14)	0·27	−0·2	0·5
$a_{2\cdot7}$	−7·0 (1·6)	0·11 (2·3)	0·10 (1·4)	−0·04 (1·6)	−2·12 (0·3)	−16·7 (0·7)	42·8 (1·9)	−11·3 (1·3)	5·9 (1·2)	59·8 (1·6)	14·9 (0·5)	−37·5 (0·8)	0·58	0·29	2·0
$a_{5\cdot7}$	−2·25 (0·5)	0·007 (0·4)	0·03 (1·4)	−0·005 (0·6)	4·4 (1·8)	23·8 (2·9)	7·0 (0·9)	0·66 (0·2)	−2·6 (1·5)	9·31 (0·8)	5·61 (0·5)	−30·0 (1·9)	0·55	0·23	1·75
$a_{7\cdot7}$	−0·05 (0·02)	−0·51 (1·7)	−0·5 (1·2)	0·51 (3·4)	−33·7 (0·8)	89·6 (0·6)	128·2 (0·9)	−30·4 (0·6)	−58·3 (1·9)	69·1 (0·3)	13·4 (0·7)	−304·0 (1·0)	0·76	0·59	4·5
$a_{8\cdot7}$	38·5 (2·4)	−0·06 (0·4)	0·066 (0·3)	0·12 (1·3)	22·7 (0·9)	−59·4 (0·7)	−35·5 (0·4)	9·8 (0·3)	12·1 (0·7)	−16·5 (0·1)	49·2 (0·4)	53·8 (0·3)	0·48	0·13	1·4
$a_{10\cdot7}$	7·2 (1·6)	0·01 (0·2)	0·1 (1·6)	0·04 (1·6)	1·69 (2·4)	11·3 (0·5)	26·6 (1·2)	−16·96 (1·9)	20·52 (4·1)	−24·0 (0·7)	14·0 (0·4)	−34·7 (0·7)	0·74	0·56	4·1
$a_{12\cdot7}$	−41·5 (2·2)	−29·2 (1·4)	−0·64 (2·2)	0·17 (1·6)	9·06 (0·3)	60·1 (0·6)	−205·2 (2·1)	52·5 (1·4)	−70·5 (0·03)	−153·0 (1·0)	−160·0 (1·2)	246·1 (1·2)	0·47	0·11	1·29
$a_{14\cdot7}$	−17·5 (1·4)	−0·03 (0·2)	−0·08 (0·4)	0·024 (0·3)	−15·1 (0·7)	−121·5 (1·8)	34·0 (0·5)	−19·7 (0·8)	23·8 (1·7)	147·1 (1·4)	−106·1 (1·2)	161·2 (1·2)	0·50	0·16	1·47

TABLE
Personal

	Constant	$\bar{a}_{11\cdot8}$	$\bar{A}_8$	$\Delta\bar{r}_1$	$\Delta\dot{r}_3$	$\Delta\dot{r}_5$	$\Delta\dot{r}_6$	$\Delta\dot{r}_8$
$a_{1\cdot8}$	−6·7 (0·5)	−0·024 (0·35)	0·072 (2·3)	−4·4 (0·54)	22·6 (1·4)	−70·6 (2·9)	−0·71 (0·08)	−5·0 (0·6)
$a_{3\cdot8}$	−56·0 (0·9)	−0·25 (0·8)	0·2 (1·4)	46·3 (1·2)	−337·7 (4·7)	141·8 (1·23)	96·5 (2·1)	33·1 (0·9)
$a_{4\cdot8}$	17·0 (0·4)	−0·26 (1·0)	0·044 (0·39)	−8·7 (0·3)	16·2 (0·29)	−71·2 (0·8)	67·3 (1·85)	−20·3 (0·7)
$a_{5\cdot8}$	15·0 (0·9)	0·018 (0·19)	−0·075 (1·7)	8·3 (0·7)	66·9 (3·1)	−5·36 (0·16)	18·65 (1·34)	−15·0 (1·34)
$a_{7\cdot8}$	20·0 (0·5)	−0·77 (3·3)	0·32 (3·0)	−80·2 (2·9)	65·8 (1·23)	−167·5 (2·0)	−95·6 (2·8)	3·1 (0·1)
$a_{8\cdot8}$	−5·2 (0·3)	0·006 (0·08)	0·03 (0·76)	5·0 (0·5)	40·5 (2·03)	−36·5 (1·2)	−3·5 (0·27)	−3·4 (0·3)
$a_{9\cdot8}$	30·3 (0·4)	−0·32 (0·8)	0·47 (2·7)	−91·3 (2·0)	−21·8 (0·2)	75·0 (0·5)	−68·4 (1·2)	12·5 (0·28)
$a_{10\cdot8}$	193·0 (4·7)	−0·26 (1·2)	0·36 (3·65)	−20·7 (0·8)	33·1 (0·66)	−47·2 (0·6)	5·5 (0·17)	15·2 (0·6)
$-a_{12\cdot8}$	4·9 (0·9)	0·05 (1·8)	−0·03 (2·2)	4·8 (1·3)	8·2 (1·17)	1·9 (0·2)	−1·56 (0·35)	−8·14 (2·2)
$-a_{15\cdot8}$	−68·0 (1·4)	0·38 (1·4)	−0·27 (2·3)	48·6 (1·57)	−7·9 (0·1)	51·6 (0·55)	−1·45 (0·04)	−7·23 (0·2)
$a_{16\cdot8}$	−164·0 (4·6)	0·25 (1·3)	−0·05 (0·6)	19·5 (0·9)	−48·0 (1·1)	161·5 (2·4)	−25·4 (0·9)	27·3 (1·92)

8

(Sector 8)

$\Delta \hat{r}_9$	$\Delta \hat{r}_{10}$	$\Delta \hat{r}_{15}$	$\Delta \hat{r}_{16}$	$\Delta \bar{r}_4$	$\Delta \bar{r}_7$	R^2	$\bar{R}^2$	F
−23·5 (0·4)	−53·3 (1·2)	2·24 (0·08)	−3·37 (0·3)	−1·59 (0·08)	65·2 (3·0)	0·68	0·38	2·3
124·7 (0·5)	−295·7 (1·45)	−8·23 (0·6)	62·9 (1·2)	−9·16 (0·1)	−230·4 (2·3)	0·79	0·59	4·0
−110·9 (0·55)	−17·5 (0·1)	13·2 (0·13)	24·3 (0·6)	−47·5 (0·6)	−4·1 (0·05)	0·37	−0·2	0·64
20·0 (0·3)	58·1 (0·95)	20·4 (0·5)	10·8 (0·7)	−30·7 (1·1)	−20·9 (0·7)	0·63	0·3	1·9
−172·3 (0·9)	−252·5 (1·67)	−150·5 (1·5)	−7·3 (0·2)	124·1 (1·8)	249·9 (3·4)	0·85	0·7	5·9
60·5 (0·86)	68·7 (1·2)	−63·9 (1·7)	−27·0 (1·9)	28·5 (1·1)	49·4 (1·8)	0·58	0·19	1·47
−478·5 (1·5)	278·0 (1·12)	166·1 (1·03)	51·16 (0·8)	19·3 (0·17)	−58·4 (0·5)	0·52	0·08	1·18
−160·1 (0·9)	400·0 (2·8)	55·4 (0·6)	18·3 (0·5)	73·0 (1·1)	3·75 (0·05)	0·65	0·3	2·0
55·9 (2·24)	−1·52 (0·08)	3·94 (0·3)	−2·23 (0·4)	5·39 (0·6)	5·44 (0·6)	0·49	0·008	1·0
276·3 (1·3)	−293·1 (1·7)	−32·6 (0·3)	−16·5 (0·4)	−75·3 (0·9)	−27·5 (0·3)	0·43	−0·09	0·8
14·4 (0·1)	−60·0 (0·5)	−3·9 (0·05)	−47·0 (1·5)	61·5 (1·1)	−109·8 (1·8)	0·57	0·17	1·4

TABLE
Overseas

	Constant	$\bar{a}_{11\cdot9}$	$\bar{A}_9$	Δf_2	Δf_3	Δf_5	Δf_6
$a_{2\cdot9}$	$-62\cdot7$ $(1\cdot3)$	$0\cdot53$ $(0\cdot2)$	$0\overset{\bullet}{\cdot}97$ $(4\cdot9)$	$-53\cdot0$ $(1\cdot0)$	$29\cdot5$ $(0\cdot2)$	$-92\cdot2$ $(0\cdot4)$	$-110\cdot2$ $(1\cdot27)$
$a_{3\cdot9}$	$21\cdot0$ $(1\cdot4)$	$-0\cdot5$ $(0\cdot6)$	$0\cdot07$ $(1\cdot1)$	$4\cdot14$ $(0\cdot2)$	$-30\cdot2$ $(0\cdot6)$	$-58\cdot0$ $(0\cdot8)$	$47\cdot5$ $(1\cdot7)$
$a_{5\cdot9}$	$-0\cdot06$ $(0\cdot02)$	$0\cdot007$ $(0\cdot04)$	$-0\cdot02$ $(1\cdot7)$	$3\cdot5$ $(1\cdot0)$	$-16\cdot7$ $(1\cdot7)$	$3\cdot9$ $(0\cdot3)$	$0\cdot47$ $(0\cdot1)$
$a_{7\cdot9}$	$3\cdot95$ $(0\cdot4)$	$0\cdot45$ $(0\cdot8)$	$-0\cdot07$ $(1\cdot6)$	$-0\cdot18$ $(1\cdot6)$	$39\cdot0$ $(1\cdot2)$	$-56\cdot8$ $(1\cdot3)$	$-28\cdot7$ $(1\cdot6)$
$a_{8\cdot9}$	$340\overset{\bullet}{\cdot}2$ $(2\cdot5)$	$-9\cdot97$ $(1\cdot3)$	$-1\cdot1$ $(1\cdot9)$	$171\cdot4$ $(1\cdot1)$	$97\cdot4$ $(0\cdot2)$	$143\overset{\bullet}{\cdot}0$ $(2\cdot3)$	$165\cdot3$ $(0\cdot7)$
$a_{10\cdot9}$	$-2\cdot23$ $(0\cdot2)$	$0\cdot45$ $(0\cdot7)$	$-0\cdot03$ $(0\cdot7)$	$-5\cdot9$ $(0\cdot5)$	$-34\cdot7$ $(1\cdot0)$	$75\cdot0$ $(1\cdot6)$	$-24\cdot2$ $(1\cdot3)$
$-a_{12\cdot9}$	$-293\overset{\bullet}{\cdot}0$ $(2\cdot2)$	$9\cdot03$ $(1\cdot2)$	$1\cdot13$ $(1\cdot9)$	$-111\cdot9$ $(0\cdot7)$	$22\cdot9$ $(0\cdot05)$	$-1363\overset{\bullet}{\cdot}1$ $(2\cdot2)$	$-80\cdot2$ $(0\cdot3)$
$a_{14\cdot9}$	$-10\cdot8$ $(1\cdot3)$	$0\cdot31$ $(0\cdot6)$	$-0\cdot009$ $(0\cdot3)$	$-6\cdot35$ $(0\cdot7)$	$24\cdot4$ $(0\cdot9)$	$-1\cdot2$ $(0\cdot03)$	$13\cdot7$ $(0\cdot9)$
$a_{16\cdot9}$	$6\cdot64$ $(0\cdot7)$	$-1\overset{\bullet}{\cdot}46$ $(2\cdot6)$	$0\cdot04$ $(0\cdot9)$	$12\cdot6$ $(1\cdot2)$	$-114\overset{\bullet}{\cdot}7$ $(3\cdot7)$	$25\cdot3$ $(0\cdot6)$	$4\cdot7$ $(0\cdot3)$

9

(*Sector 9*)

$\Delta \dot{r}_8$	$\Delta \dot{r}_{10}$	$\Delta \dot{r}_{14}$	$\Delta \dot{r}_{16}$	$\Delta \bar{r}_7$	R^2	$\bar{R}^2$	F
161·0 (2·9)	44·4 (0·09)	330·2 (1·0)	−255·0 (2·7)	−87·4 (0·2)	0·82	0·69	6·4
−7·8 (0·4)	−154·1 (1·0)	−34·2 (0·3)	33·9 (1·1)	42·2 (0·35)	0·29	−0·2	0·6
3·86 (1·1)	−4·14 (0·1)	7·18 (0·3)	−12·8 (2·2)	−5·3 (0·2)	0·47	0·11	1·3
−15·5 (1·36)	100·4 (1·0)	−43·0 (0·6)	−12·6 (0·6)	123·1 (1·6)	0·5	0·15	1·4
180·3 (1·1)	557·0 (0·4)	−1500·0 (1·6)	280·4 (1·1)	−128·5 (0·12)	0·61	0·34	2·27
−9·9 (0·8)	119·0 (1·1)	160·0 (2·2)	14·9 (0·7)	−200·6 (2·4)	0·51	0·18	1·54
−323·2 (2·05)	−483·0 (0·35)	996·4 (1·1)	−122·5 (0·5)	446·2 (0·4)	0·62	0·35	2·35
−6·1 (0·6)	−34·3 (0·4)	91·7 (1·6)	−1·6 (0·1)	−95·7 (1·5)	0·41	0·006	1·0
16·9 (1·5)	−196·6 (1·98)	−10·3 (0·15)	75·8 (4·0)	−38·1 (0·5)	0·69	0·47	3·2

REFERENCES

[1] ARROW, K. J., *Aspects of the Theory of Risk-Bearing*, Yrjo Jahnsson Lectures (Helsinki, 1965).

[2] BALL, R. J., *Inflation and the Theory of Money* (London: Allen & Unwin, 1964).

[3] BRAINARD, W. C., ch. 4 in D. Hester and J. Tobin (eds.), *Financial Markets and Economic Activity* (New York: Wiley, 1967).

[4] CLAYTON, G. 'British Financial Intermediaries in Theory and Practice', *Economic Journal*, Dec. 1962.

[5] COMMITTEE ON THE WORKING OF THE MONETARY SYSTEM (Radcliffe Committee), Cmnd. 827 (London: H.M.S.O., 1959).

[6] FORD, J. L., and DODDS, J. C., 'Expectations, Uncertainty and the Term Structure of Interest Rates', in C. F. Carter and J. L. Ford (eds.), *Uncertainty and Expectations in Economics: Essays in Honour of G. L. S. Shackle* (Oxford: Blackwell, 1972).

[7] FREUND, R. 'The Introduction of Risk into a Programming Model', *Econometrica*, July 1956.

[8] GHOSH, D., and PARKIN, J. M. 'A Theoretical and Empirical Analysis of the Portfolio, Debt and Interest Rate Behaviour of Building Societies', in the *Manchester School*, Sept. 1972.

[9] GOLDBERGER, A. S., *Econometric Theory* (New York: Wiley, 1964).

[10] GURLEY, J. G., and SHAW, E. S., 'Financial Aspects of Economic Development', *American Economic Review*, vol. lxv, No. 4 (1955); *Money in a Theory of Finance* (Washington, D.C.: The Brookings Institution, 1960).

[11] HICKS, Sir John, *Critical Essays in Monetary Theory* (Oxford: The Clarendon Press, 1967).

[12] LAIDLER, D. E. W., 'The Definition of Money', *Journal of Money, Credit and Banking*, 1970.

[13] MARKOWITZ, H., *Portfolio Selection* (New York: Wiley, 1959).

[14] PARKIN, J. M., 'Discount House Portfolio and Debt Selection Behaviour', *Rev. Econ. Studs.*, Oct. 1970.

[15] PRATT, J. W., 'Risk Aversion in the Small and in the Large', *Econometrica*, 32, 1964.

[16] STEWART, J., 'Testing Restrictions of the GLS Model as applied to Multivariate Restricted Least Squares', unpublished note, Nov. 1970.

[17] THEIL, H., *Principles of Econometrics* (London: North-Holland, 1971).

[18] TOBIN, J., and BRAINARD, W. C., ch. 3 in D. Hester and J. Tobin (eds.), *Financial Markets and Economic Activity* (New York: Wiley, 1967).

[19] TOBIN, J., 'Liquidity Preference as Behaviour Towards Risk', *Rev. Econ. Studs.*, Feb. 1958; 'The Theory of Portfolio Selection',

ch. 1 in F. H. Hahn and F. P. R. Brechling (eds.), *The Theory of Interest Rates* (London: Macmillan, 1965).

[20] ——, and BRAINARD, W. C., 'Pitfalls in Financial Model Building', *American Economic Review*, May 1968.

[21] ZELLNER, A., 'An Efficient Method of Estimating Seemingly Unrelated Regressions and Tests for Aggregation Bias', *Journal of the American Statistical Association*, June 1962.

[22] DODDS, J. C., and FORD, J. L. *'Expectations, Uncertainty and the Term Structure of Interest Rates*, Forthcoming (London: Martin Robertson, 1974).

THE TERM STRUCTURE OF INTEREST RATES— A CROSS-SECTION TEST OF A MEAN-VARIANCE MODEL*

W. R. WHITE *and* J. P. BURMAN

(*Economic Section, Bank of England*)

I. Introduction

THERE are three factors which are commonly mentioned when attempts are made to identify the determinants of the term structure of interest rates: investors' expectations about future interest-rate levels, liquidity preference, and market segmentation (or preferred habitats). The second of these factors can be thought of as a variant of the third. In this paper a test is presented of a model which incorporates both expectations and liquidity preference. Evidence indicating the importance of market segmentation is only derived, by inference, from observed deficiencies in the predictive ability of the model specified. Data in the test are taken from the market in British Government Securities (B.G.S.).

A. *Previous work on the term structure*

Although great efforts have been made, particularly in recent years, to identify the influence of expectations and liquidity preference on the term structure, no final consensus has yet been reached. This reflects the fact that most empirical work to date has been subjected to criticisms of one sort or another, either on grounds of underlying theory or empirical procedures.

The largest part of the empirical work done in both the U.K. and U.S. has consisted of tests of those two variants of the 'traditional theory' of the term structure; the pure expectations hypothesis and

* Our thanks are due to Mrs. Jenny Sims, who wrote the computer programs, and to Michael Hamburger, A. D. Crockett, C. A. E. Goodhart, and L. D. D. Price, who commented either on this or earlier drafts. The views presented in this paper are the authors' own, and can in no way be assumed necessarily to represent the views of the Bank.

the liquidity preference hypothesis (as described by Hicks). The main assumptions and conclusions of these hypotheses need only brief review here.[1] The pure expectations version assumes that investors (who have no security preferences and pay no transactions costs) attempt to maximize investment returns over their *holding period*—defined as the span of time they intend to be invested in bonds. In consequence of their resulting investment behaviour,

(a) Forward short rates implicit in ruling long bond rates are unbiased estimates of the short rates expected by the market to prevail in future periods.

(b) The expected holding-period yield is the same on all securities regardless of length of holding period.

Hick's liquidity preference theory says there is a 'constitutional weakness' in the long end of the bond market. Thus 'biased upwards' must be substituted for 'unbiased' in (a) above, and 'adjusted for liquidity premia' must be substituted into (b) after 'expected holding-period yields'.

A number of authors have contended that the behavioural assumptions of the traditional theory are not supported by available evidence on how investors in the U.K. and U.S. bond markets actually appear to manage their portfolios.[2] Two points have been stressed. First, investors appear to diversify their bond portfolios. There is little evidence of the 'plunging into single securities' implied by the traditional theory. Second, to the extent investors incorporate expectations of future price or interest-rate movements into their investment decisions, these appear to be expectations about security prices at the end of a single, short-term *decision period*—defined as a span of time over which alternative courses of action are compared. Nor does there seem any clear indication that they generate these price expectations so as to ensure consistency with any expectations they (might) have about forward rates in the further future. Grossman [13] and Wood [35] have pointed out that there are no theoretical grounds for expecting such consistency.[3] Finally, the liquidity preference version of the traditional theory has been specifically accused of lacking a rigorous micro-economic foundation in investor response to uncertainty.

[1] See Conard [6], pp. 290–3.
[2] See Malkiel [20] and White [33] for U.S. and U.K. evidence respectively, and Malkiel [20] for a discussion of criticisms of the traditional theory.
[3] See Grossman [13], p. 495. The point also seems consistent with the central theme of Keynes's comments about long-term expectations in the bond market. See [17], ch. 12.

There has too been criticism of the empirical methodology associated with many tests of the traditional theory. The use of the forward-rate concept has proved particularly troublesome. Those (like Meiselman [21]) who have desired to test directly conclusion (a), above, have first had to face the difficult (perhaps impossible) task of obtaining accurate measurements of forward rates from ruling market rates on long bonds.[4] Secondly, there has been the necessity to generate proxy measures for investors' (unobserved) expectations about the various future short rates. Neither of these problems has yet been satisfactorily resolved.

Perhaps in part because of the above criticisms, most very recent empirical work on the term structure has followed in a new tradition pioneered by Malkiel [20] and Modigliani and Sutch [22]. While mathematically consistent with the 'traditional' theory (if the security preference question is ignored), a successful outcome to their respective tests is also consistent with a somewhat different hypothesis; namely, investors choose between securities on the basis of relative returns over a single short-term decision period. Prices of securities adjust to ensure equality of decision-period returns on all securities. While this hypothesis seems an advance on previous work, important difficulties relating to empirical procedures nevertheless remain. These reduce the usefulness of the Malkiel, Modigliani–Sutch work for analysing events in the market for British Government Securities. These difficulties seem better considered using the Modigliani–Sutch model. It has attained a central position in the literature. For convenience, the security preference question is ignored throughout.

Modigliani–Sutch have presented their work as a test of conclusion (b) of the traditional theory (see p. 363). Two securities are considered; a 3-month bill and an n period bond. The holding period is arbitrarily set at 3 months (also interpretable as the length of 1 decision period, as defined above). Over this period the returns on the two securities should be identical. Assuming that the redemption yields on the two securities adequately proxy interest incomes (i.e. both securities stand near par), and that the 3-month bill is redeemed at par, the testable hypothesis reduces to

$$r = R(n) + K(n), \qquad (1)$$

---

[4] Malkiel [20], pp. 44–9, describes the problem in detail. Various others have discussed the specific complications to forward rate calculations caused by coupon payments.

where r and $R(n)$ are the redemption yields on the shorter and longer security respectively. $K(n)$ is the expected capital gain on the latter over the 3-month period. Since $K(n)$ has an exact mathematical relationship with the change expected in $R(n)$ by the end of the period $\{\Delta R(n)^e\}$, this reduces further to

$$R(n) = r - V\,\Delta R(n)^e \qquad (2)$$

where V is determined by the mathematical relationship just referred to.[5] Modigliani and Sutch construct a proxy for $\Delta R(n)^e$ and test whether, *over time*, the postulated equality of the 3-month holding-period yields holds in fact.

The following characteristics of this model reduce its usefulness, particularly for examining the U.K. term structure:

(a) The regression used by Modigliani–Sutch

$$R(n) - r = -V\{\Delta R(n)^e\} + \alpha + \text{error term}$$

assumes the constancy of V (estimated as a parameter) over the data period. This value should rather be calculated directly, upon which the constancy assumption is seen to be seriously violated if U.K. data are used. For $3\frac{1}{2}\%$ War Loan, the end-January values in 1955, 1962, and 1970 were respectively $0\cdot275$, $0\cdot175$, and $0\cdot102$ (assuming $R(n)^e$ is small).

(b) The test depends centrally on the proxy for expected interest-rate movements being correct. Modigliani–Sutch, Malkiel (and Rowan and O'Brien [26] in a similar test using U.K.

---

[5] The gross redemption yield (y) on a bond with given coupon (c), period to maturity (n) and price (P) is defined by the formula

$$P = \frac{c}{(1 + y)} + \cdots + \frac{c + 1}{(1 + y)^n}$$

where 1 is the repayment (nominal) value of the security. For any given security, at any time, a given change in y implies a certain absolute and percentage change in price. A term commonly used in the market for B.G.S., to measure the latter, is *Volatility*; defined as $1/P.\mathrm{d}P/\mathrm{d}y$. It can be easily demonstrated that

$$\frac{\mathrm{d}V}{\mathrm{d}n} > 0; \qquad \frac{\mathrm{d}^2V_2}{\mathrm{d}n} < 0; \qquad \frac{\mathrm{d}V}{\mathrm{d}c} < 0.$$

This implies, given the assumption that the yields on all securities move by the same amount, that longer stocks and stocks with smaller coupons should *(ceteris paribus)* demonstrate larger price movements than shorter and higher coupon securities respectively. The calculated Volatility of a stock is not constant, but varies with P, c, y, and n. Finally, the measure V in the text is an interval measure of Volatility (given a change in yield from $R(n)$ to $R(n^e)$).

data) all suggest using long distributed lags of past interest rates. This particular approach involves many special problems, given both the difficulty of obtaining correct statistical estimates for distributed lag functions (see Griliches [12]) and the difficulty of giving correct economic interpretation to these lag structures once obtained (see Hamburger [14] on the conclusions reached by Rowan and O'Brien, and Fand's comments [10] regarding Modigliani and Sutch). There must too be some doubt about a U.K. proxy for expected interest-rate changes which ignores such factors (among others) as interest rates abroad, anticipated monetary policy, and the balance-of-payments situation. Finally, use of this proxy demands that investors form their expectations in the same way over relatively long periods of time and under diverse circumstances. These possibilities seem unlikely, and conflict with what little evidence is available on how U.K. investors predict future interest rates.[6]

Finally, it can be noted that White [34] has conducted extensive tests of their model, using U.K. data, and these gave quite unsatisfactory results. Hamburger [14] has also reported results which specifically deny the usefulness of distributed lag models in explaining the U.K. term structure.

B. *A suggested new approach*

The points above imply that there is room for further work in this area. Accordingly, this paper suggests an approach to the term-structure problem which is novel in three central respects: the hypothesis to be tested, the means used to generate expectations about future interest rates, and the procedure used to test the hypothesis.

The hypothesis to be tested is set out in Section II.A below. Relative prices on B.G.S. are assumed to be determined by the Lintner [19]–Sharpe [27] model of capital-asset pricing. In this model both risk-aversion and investors' expectations about security prices (redemption yields) at the end of a single decision period play a central role. The Lintner–Sharpe model is a variant of the Mean-Variance model, where the latter is broadly defined to include all models in which investors demonstrate aversion to uncertainty about capital values expected at the end of the single decision period ('Tobin–Markowitz' risk). The Lintner–Sharpe model has certain

---

[6] See White [34], chs. 8–10, also Hamburger [14].

similarities to the term-structure models developed by Malkiel, Modigliani and Sutch, and Rowan and O'Brien. It is also similar in an important respect to 'liquidity preference' models. As will be seen below, the Lintner–Sharpe model implies that longer-term securities are 'riskier' than shorter-term securities, and should (*ceteris paribus*) have a higher gross redemption yield.

The second important assumption underlying the model tested is also set out in Section II.A; namely, that investors predict end-period security prices by predicting the level and shape of the expected yield curve. Equally important, they expect that this curve will have some simple shape. Finally in Section II.A, some consideration is given to investors' subjective assessment of the 'risk' associated with individual B.G.S. Section II concludes with a discussion of the shape of the family of yield curves implied by all the assumptions mentioned above.

In Section III the suggested new approach to testing the hypothesis is described. The hypothesis, if correct, should apply at any time to the determination of all the rates observed in the market for British Government Securities. Thus different cross-section data, commonly for 20–30 B.G.S. in each case, are utilized in a test which is repeated for end-quarter dates over the period 1962(1)–1970(3). The first advantage of the cross-section approach is that it directs attention to the whole shape of the yield curve, including the relative prices of high and low coupon issues. Compared to most recent time-series tests, which look solely at the relative yield levels of a long and a short stock, this is desirable. It provides a great increase in information and more degrees of freedom for testing. It moreover allows (or perhaps demands) explicit consideration of some of the problems implied by tax conditions. These problems have been almost wholly ignored in previous term-structure work. Finally, the giving of attention to the whole curve provides a theoretical basis for the construction of 'hypothetical' yield curves, which have numerous practical applications. The monetary authorities, for example, might usefully consult them: when pricing new B.G.S. issues, when determining in what part of the maturity-coupon spectra most cheaply to place new issues, or when deciding on what terms to lend to public sector and other borrowers. Brokers and investment analysts might find them useful as a reference point for determining the relative 'cheapness' or 'dearness' of various securities.

The second advantage of the cross-section approach relates to the problem described by Malkiel: 'The lack of independent evidence concerning expectations of future interest rates has been the chief obstacle to effective empirical testing of "theories incorporating an" expectations hypothesis.'[7] The test described in Section III does not demand such independent evidence about expectations, though (as noted above) it does need the strong assumption that prices expected at the end of the decision period are consistent with a yield curve having some relatively simple shape. Given this, the cross-section test below generates measures of the expected B.G.S. rates at the end of the decision period, as well as a measure of the length of this period. The usefulness of such series, both for other portfolio studies and for further investigations (why do investors' expectations change ?), would seem obvious.

In Section IV of the paper, test results are presented and interpreted. In Section V conclusions are drawn and suggestions made for further research. All mathematical expositions of the arguments are gathered together in appendices.

II. Specification of the basic model—a mean-variance framework for the market in B.G.S.

A. *The initial assumptions*

THE LINTNER–SHARPE HYPOTHESIS. Explaining the determination of the term structure of rates in the market for B.G.S. is equivalent to explaining the determination of the relative prices of individual securities. To deal with such problems, Lintner [19] and Sharpe [27] among others, have developed a theoretical model which explicitly recognizes the existence of capital uncertainty in financial markets. This model, as originally presented, was based on the following assumptions about investment behaviour.

(a) All investors are single-period expected utility of terminal wealth maximizers, who choose among alternative portfolios solely on the basis of expected mean and variance of portfolio return. All investors have the same decision horizon.

(b) All investors make identical predictions about expected means, variances, and co-variances of decision-period returns among assets.

(c) All investors can borrow or lend as much as they wish at an exogenously given riskless rate of interest. There are no restrictions on short selling.

7 Malkiel [20], p. 30.

(d) The market in securities is perfect (neither transaction costs, information shortages, taxes, or security preferences influence investment behaviour).

(e) The quantities of all assets are given.

On this basis the Lintner–Sharpe model produces equilibrium equations which have to be met if the markets in all securities are to be cleared. These equations (derived formally as equation (10) in Appendix A) are:

$$\frac{r_i + (P_i^E - P_i)}{P_i} - c \left[\sum_{j=1}^{n} \frac{X_j \sigma_{ij}}{P_i P_j} \right] = \lambda \quad \text{(for all } i = 1 \ldots n) \quad (3)$$

or

$$x_i - cZ_i = \lambda \quad \text{(for all } i = 1 \ldots n), \quad (4)$$

where i refers to the ith security, c is a parameter, and

r = interest (or coupon) return over the decision period,

P^E = expected price at the end of the decision period (a weighted average of the views of all investors),

P = actual price,

X_j = the market's aggregate holdings of the jth security at market values,

σ_{ij} = co-variance of the returns expected on the ith and jth securities (a weighted average of the views of all investors),

λ = certainty equivalent yield (risk-free rate of interest),

x = decision-period yield,

Z = risk premium.

Security prices (and thus redemption yields) are assumed to adjust to satisfy these conditions.

The applicability of equation system (3) to the market for B.G.S. constitutes the central hypothesis tested in this paper. Restricting the analysis to B.G.S. alone, to the exclusion of other securities, presumes that decisions about the optimal structure of B.G.S. portfolios are made independently of decisions about other kinds of investments.[8]

[8] The theoretical circumstances in which this stepwise investment procedure is optimal, for an investor who is an expected utility of terminal wealth maximizer, are given in Cass and Stiglitz [5]. In the event, interviews with institutional portfolio managers and stockbrokers indicate that such procedures are commonly followed. The underlying reason seems to be administrative convenience and the necessity for specialization in highly technical areas.

Although the ultimate test of a theory's usefulness is how well it conforms to the data (to be tested below), and not the apparent realism of the underlying assumptions, some comments on this latter question seem called for. Assumption (a) is central to the model. It implies that all investors act as the normative Tobin–Markowitz model says they should. Since for all *practical* purposes this constitutes the 'modern theory of portfolio selection',[9] it seems a reasonable starting place. Tobin [32] has demonstrated that this mean-variance model is applicable when investors' utility functions are quadratic (over the relevant range) or when the probability distributions of portfolio returns are Normal. Fama[10] has noted that, for analytical purposes, this Normality assumption is an acceptable approximation to reality (at least in the U.S. equity and bond markets). As for the assumption that investors make security choices on the basis of expected utility at the end of a single decision period, regardless of the length of the holding period over which they wish to maximize expected utility from holding B.G.S., there is micro-evidence that this may adequately describe the behaviour of many of the large institutions that dominate the B.G.S. market.[11] Certainly, as is well known,[12] in the assumed absence of transactions costs such behaviour is also rational for those ultimately concerned only with their wealth position at the end of the holding period.[13]

Lintner [19] has shown that assumption (b), which does seem *a priori* unacceptable, is in no way crucial to the establishment of equilibrium price conditions. Given disagreement, the elements P_i^E and σ_{ij}, in (3) above, become complex weighted averages of the views of all investors. Likewise, assumption (c) has been shown by Black [1] to be stronger than necessary.

As for assumptions (d) and (e), available evidence about market conditions does not support them. In particular, taxes and transactions costs do not seem unimportant. Nor do the monetary authorities appear to set the supply of securities exogenously (rather there is evidence that the authorities have tended to stabilize price movements in the market for B.G.S., which implies the necessity for explicit introduction of supply functions for individual securities

---

[9] Jensen [16], pp. 1–2, and Sharpe [28], pp. 3–4.
[10] See Fama [8], p. 30, footnote 6.
[11] White [33].   [12] Tobin [32], Wood [35].
[13] Fama [9] has also established quite general conditions under which single-period utility maximization will be optimal for a consumer/investor ultimately concerned in maximizing his expected utility of lifetime consumption.

into the model). Finally, many practising investors would argue strongly for the existence of security preferences on institutional and other grounds. None of these factors, with the exception of the tax problem, has in fact been incorporated into the model to be tested. As has been common in nearly all term-structure studies (most of which also make assumptions (d) and (e)), the failure of the Basic Model to satisfy the data is taken as indication that these neglected factors are important in the determination of security prices.

One final point remains to be made about the *a priori* acceptability of the Lintner–Sharpe model, as summarized in (3). Its general conclusion that the expected returns on all securities, adjusted for risk (*somehow* defined), must be equal over a single decision period is also the hypothesis tested by Malkiel [20], Modigliani and Sutch [22], Rowan and O'Brien [26], and Bierwag and Grove [2]. A test of the Lintner–Sharpe model can then be interpreted, if preferred, as a test of these other hypotheses but with 'risk' specifically defined to reflect investors' aversion to capital uncertainty.

THE DETERMINANTS OF EXPECTED FUTURE BOND PRICES AND MEASURES OF RISK. The hypothesis described by equation (3) is not empirically testable without prior knowledge of the end-decision-period expected price (P_i^E) and the risk premium (Z_i) associated with each security. These are unobservable.

Previous studies have generated P_i^E in one of two ways. Economists have favoured the use of distributed lag functions of past price and interest-rate movements. The problems attendant to this approach have been discussed in Section I. Business and financial analysts [14] have tended to assume that ex-ante expectations bear some relationship to ex-post realizations. In this paper a third, no less plausible, assumption is made. The market expects the various P_i^E to be consistent with a yield curve having some simple shape. This simplicity accords with market practice, where expectations are rarely summarized using any more than one word; bearish, bullish, uncertain, etc.

The first possibility given extensive consideration (though the assumption is later relaxed) is that investors expect the yield curve, at the end of the decision period, to be flat. This suggestion has its origins in the term-structure work of Malkiel.[15] More important,

---

[14] Jensen [16] cites a number of examples.
[15] Malkiel suggests ([20], pp. 59–67), that investors, when calculating expected decision-period returns from alternative security holdings, utilize

it is implied by the widely used Cagan–Friedman model for generating expectations from past interest-rate levels.[16] Their implicit assumption is simply made explicit in our test. From the theoretical point of view, moreover, the assumption appears reasonable. It can be thought of as a synthesis of the 'traditional' approach and the single-period approach to term structure analysis. That is, it is consistent with the hypothesis that individual investors try to predict forward rates 'to Kingdom come' but, beyond the end of the decision period, feel incapable of doing so with any certainty. The best prediction these individual investors can make is 'no further change', which implies equal forward rates for all periods longer than the decision period, and a level expected yield curve at the end of the decision period. Finally, even if some investors do feel capable of predicting beyond the end of the decision period, an expected level yield curve may still be assumed if the views of 'bears' and 'bulls', about the further future, are presumed to cancel each other out.

For empirical justification of this initial assumption, recourse can be had to the observations of market participants. At least two investment analysts[17] have done studies (for differing practical reasons) which begin with the assumption that expected decision-period returns on various B.G.S. must be equal. They conclude with a test of whether the expected yield curve (at the end of the decision

---

the concept of expected-level yield curves. One forms an upper limit for expected rates, and one forms a lower limit.

[16] The Cagan–Friedman model is

$$R^*_{n, t-1, t} = c \sum (1 - c)^x R_{n, t-1-x}$$

where $R^*_{n, t-1, t}$ is the spot rate expected to rule in period t on an n period security, as of period $t - 1$. Telser [30], p. 552, points out that this model implies

$$R^*_{n, t-1, t} = R^*_{n, t-1, t+1} = \cdots = R^*_{n, t-1, t+n}.$$

Then, given that the predicted rate for t, as of $t - 1$, on a one-period bond $(R^*_{1, t-1, t})$ = the one-period forward rate $(r_{1, t-1, t})$, if the traditional theory of the term structure is correct, we have

$$r_{1, t-1, t} = r_{1, t-1, t+1} = r_{1, t-1, t+1} = \cdots = r_{1, t-1, t+n}.$$

That is, all forward rates are equal. The yield curve predicted for time t is level. Roll [25], p. 37, has also pointed this out: 'Only a flat yield curve has the same expected shape next period. Yield curves with any other shape will tend to change shape from period to period.'

[17] The analysts referred to are J. M. Brew and B. H. Fison. Each is a partner, occupied with B.G.S. dealings, with a large City stockbroking firm specializing in B.G.S. Brew is author of numerous papers on investment policy.

period), implicit in the ruling term structure, is level. J. M. Brew has stated, concerning expected level yield curves, 'In my practical experience gilt-edged investors are very often thinking in precisely this way,'[18] and has commented on the results of his calculations that 'It is remarkable how often in the British Market, and particularly at the long end, a sloping yield curve exists which is equivalent to a level yield curve at some different rate of interest.'[19] B. H. Fison has reported similar results.[20] Finally, it can be shown that the methods of plotting hypothetical yield curves, already used by some of the largest stockbroking firms specializing in B.G.S., have implicit in them a strong version of the expected level yield curve hypothesis.[21]

Turning to investors' subjective assessment of the risk premium attached to each B.G.S., at each of the dates considered, such measures were initially provided using the formula described in (3) above. The price co-variance estimates were derived from a sample comprising the eight preceding quarters. These initial calculations were, however, adjusted before use to reflect two facts. A security maturing at the end of the decision period should have no capital uncertainty attached to it. Risk premia calculated from past data will systematically over-estimate the 'riskiness' of bonds which are constantly shortening in life.[22] Use of risk premia calculated in this way is intended to constitute a test of the Lintner–Sharpe hypothesis.

There is one troublesome point about the risk measure, Z_i. Observation of portfolio managers indicates that they do not commonly calculate such measures in practice. The measure of a security's 'riskiness' that is most widely used is Volatility. This is defined mathematically as the percentage change in a security's

---

[18] Brew [3], p. 9.   [19] Brew [4], p. 7.   [20] Private correspondence.

[21] A number of stockbroking firms fit yield curves by purely empirical methods. Certain of these (for example, Phillips and Drew, Grieveson-Grant, Hoare and Co.) regress gross redemption yields against the inverse of Volatility and higher order terms of Volatility (see footnote 5). Abstracting from risk, this is exactly the equilibrium interest-rate condition that would be implied by the theory in the text, if all investors expected an instantaneous move to a flat yield curve at some new interest-rate level. The proof of this follows directly from the mathematical exposition on page 386 below. Set $c = 0$ in equation (11) and replace the denominator by the Taylor series expansion of $P = f(y)$ around Y.

[22] This is because, in practice, the percentage price fluctuations of securities tend strongly to vary directly in size with their period to maturity. A scaling factor, reflecting this observed phenomenon, was used to adjust Z_i.

price given a small change in the security's gross redemption yield. This measure of risk (defined as Z_i^*) rises at a decreasing rate with period to maturity (see footnote 5). To investigate the importance of this, the test below was rerun for all data periods using Z_i^* in place of Z_i.[23] Use of Z_i^* in the test still implies that investors are primarily concerned with capital uncertainty and single period portfolio returns. Yet, since it also implies that investors ignore price co-variance elements in their assessment of risk, it does in theory undercut the foundations of the Lintner–Sharpe hypothesis.

B. *The implied shape of the yield curve*

The main features of the hypothesis to be tested—namely, the equality of certainty equivalent yields on all securities over the decision period, and the expectation of a level gross redemption yield curve at the end of the decision period—imply yield curves of a particular family of shapes. This is discussed formally in Appendix B. For the purpose of describing these curves it is best to simplify initially; thus the assumption is made for the moment that all stocks stand at par (so that the coupon on any stock equals its gross redemption yield) and all risk premia are zero.

The yield curve implied by this is monotonically increasing or decreasing, depending on whether expected capital gains are negative or positive. The curve rises (or falls) at a decreasing rate, thus tending to flatness at the long end. Introducing the risk premia does (in theory at least) allow for humped yield curves. Both Z_i and Z_i^* were found to be positively related with the period to maturity of the ith security. Superimposing such a curve of rising risk premia on a yield curve sloping downwards in expectation of a fall in rates could result in a curve which sloped up at the short end and down at the long. A humped curve opening in the other direction would not be consistent with the theory.

The effect of coupon differences on gross redemption yields can be described by analogy. Low coupon issues are 'effectively longer' than high coupon securities of the same maturity. Thus when rates are expected to rise, they should have a higher gross redemption yield than securities with higher coupons, just as yield curves slope

[23] As is noted in footnote 5, the measured Volatility of a security varies with its gross redemption yield. The Volatility measures (Z_i^*) used in the test were calculated assuming the securities' *expected* yield at the end of the decision period. The Z_{ij}^* thus indicate the effect on a security's price (and therefore on its decision period return) of a small error in predicting its expected interest rate.

upwards in that situation. The opposite relationship should occur when rates are expected to fall. This effect is entirely due to expectations. Beyond this, low coupon securities should normally tend to have higher gross redemption yields on the grounds that, being 'effectively longer', they tend to be 'riskier'. Finally, it should be stressed that neither of these effects should be expected to dominate those coupon effects which emerge because of differences between income- and capital-gains tax rates. This is referred to in Section III.B below.

III. A cross-section test of the basic model

A. *The general nature of the test*

The hypothesis to be tested is that, at any time, the 'certainty-equivalent yield' (the expected decision-period yield adjusted for risk) on all securities is the same. That is

$$\frac{r_i + P_i^E - P_i}{P_i} - cZ_i = \lambda \quad \text{(for all } i\text{)} \tag{5}$$

where all definitions are as on page 369 above. This hypothesis reduces to

$$\frac{r_i + f(Y, t_0) - P_i}{P_i} - cZ_i = \lambda \quad \text{(for all } i\text{)} \tag{6}$$

upon introduction of the basic assumption that P_i^E is a function of the ith security's expected gross redemption yield (Y on *all* stocks) at the end of the decision period (t_0 for all investors). Given values for the parameters Y, t_0, c, and λ, plus observed values for r_i and Z_i (or Z_i^*), the value of P_i required to satisfy (6) can be immediately calculated ($\hat{P}_i$).[24] From $\hat{P}_i$ a required value for the gross redemption yield of the ith security ($\hat{y}_i$) follows identically (see footnote 5).

The evident problem is that the four parameters noted above are unknown. This was resolved by assuming that the differences (error terms) between the required ($\hat{y}_i$) and the observed gross redemption yields (y_i) are independent random variables drawn from the same Normal distribution.[25] Then a Likelihood function of observing

---

[24] The actual formulae used to calculate expected holding period yields were kindly provided by Mullens and Co. These formulae took explicit account of the discrete payment of coupons.

[25] An alternative procedure would assume $\hat{P}_i - P_i = \varepsilon_i$, for all i, where $\varepsilon_i \sim N(0, \sigma^2)$. The relationship between prices and interest rates, described in footnote 5, implies that whatever Normality assumption is correct, the error

these error terms can be constructed, whose value is maximized by minimizing the error sum of squares, $\sum_{i=1}^{a} (\hat{y}_i - y_i)^2$ with respect to the four parameters noted above. Thus the parameter estimates, as well as the $\hat{y}_i$, emerge as output from the test. This cross-section test was repeated (after adjustment for certain complications noted below) for a number of dates. The Powell iterative routine [24] for minimizing the sums of squares of non-linear functions was used.

B. *Some pre-test complications*

TAXES. At least three ways in which tax considerations can influence the demand for securities can be distinguished. In practice these appear to have a substantial effect on bond yields. The test above was adapted to accommodate these complications.

The first point, which would seem self-evident, is that tax-paying investors are concerned with net rather than gross decision-period yields. Accepting this, defining α and B as the tax rates on income and capital gains paid by the 'typical investor',[26] and further defining $\rho = (1 - B)/(1 - \alpha)$, it can be shown that the new equilibrium condition which the price of any security must meet is[27]

$$\frac{(1/\rho)r_i + (P_i^E - P_i)}{P_i} - c(1 - B)Z_i = \frac{\lambda}{\rho} \tag{7}$$

or

$$x_i^* - c^* Z_i = \lambda^*. \tag{8}$$

This new version of the hypothesis has only one new parameter ρ to be actually estimated. The important point is that the test can be conducted without any prior knowledge of the widely differing tax rates paid by investors active in the market. Nor do changes in tax rates over time affect the test. These simply result in a changing estimated value for ρ.

If the effective rate of tax on capital gains is less than that on

---

terms generated by the non-valid procedure should, when the securities are arranged in order of term to maturity, be heteroscedastic. There was no evidence of this in the test conducted.

[26] The fiction of a typical investor is useful, and in no way affects the test. As with the proof that P_i^E is a weighted average of the views of all investors, it can be demonstrated that the actual tax rates paid by the typical investor are a weighted average of the rates paid by all investors.

[27] To prove this, re-estimate the equilibrium price conditions, as in Appendix A, but define the decision-period return as being net of taxes. Note that this implies full tax offsets for capital losses.

income, as it has been for some years in the U.K., considering (7) as the new equilibrium condition has an important implication. If security prices are expected to rise, then the gross redemption yield on low coupon securities should be lower than that of high coupon securities (of equal maturity). The opposite relationship should be established when prices are expected to fall.[28] Finally, it should be stressed that the passage of time causes the price of most B.G.S. to rise towards their redemption value (par). A bias towards observing the former phenomenon might then be expected. The longer investors' decision period, the greater the influence this last factor will have.

Casual observation reveals that low coupon securities do always have lower gross redemption yields than their high coupon equivalents, though the gap frequently varies in size. While this can be partially explained using the argument from (7) above, the phenomenon is so consistent as to imply one of two conclusions. Either some investors have a 'preference' for low coupon securities (which preference might be explained on various grounds), or investors consistently invest in the belief that this relationship will be observed at the end of the decision period. In the test below, these possibilities were admitted (a second influence of taxes on bond yields) by postulating that investors expect a level *net* redemption yield curve at the end of the decision period. Grossing up these net yields, using the capital-gains tax rate and the ρ element (to establish the 'effective' income tax rate for the grossing-up calculation[29]), yields a pattern of expected grossed-up redemption yields with the following

[28] Consider equation (7). Suppose that all markets are in equilibrium with α and B positive and that an increase in ρ is effected by abolishing capital gains tax ($B = 0$). Suppose too that $P_i^E - P_i > 0$. Consider a hypothetical stock paying no coupons. For this stock a decline in B lowers the *absolute* value of λ/ρ. The equilibrium condition can continue to be met only by a rise in P_i. A similar decline in λ/ρ would occur for a stock bearing a coupon, but the necessity for a large increase in P_i would be diminished by the decline in $(1/\rho)r_i$. Thus the required price rise would be less than in the case of the couponless stock, and the decrease in the gross redemption yield would be accordingly smaller. A positive gap between the rate on the high coupon and low coupon security would be observed. In the case where $P_i^E - P_i < 0$, the decline in $(1/\rho)(r_i)$ would increase the absolute value of the left side of (7). A larger price increase would be required to restore equilibrium in the case of the stock bearing coupons than would be necessary for the couponless stock.

[29] Using ρ in this calculation implies that, when different capital-gains tax rates apply, people expect low coupon securities to stand at correspondingly different gross redemption yields relative to high coupon securities.

desirable properties. Longer stocks are expected to have slightly higher yields than shorter stocks (assuming identical coupons).[30] This might be considered an improvement on the hypothesis of an expected perfectly level curve. High coupon securities are expected to have higher grossed-up redemption yields than low coupon securities of identical time to maturity.

The third tax complication is caused by Neutral Zone stocks; these stocks existed between April 1965 and April 1969.[31] All such stocks were omitted from the test when their prices were within the Neutral Zone or within four points of it.[32]

A PRE-HORIZON MODEL. Define the end of the decision period as *the horizon*. The Basic Model described above cannot be used to establish equilibrium prices on securities maturing before this date. Assuming the correctness of the model, this establishes a point where there must be segmentation (that is, discontinuity) in the market for B.G.S. The following points relate solely to the portfolio made up of these pre-horizon B.G.S.

Equilibrium prices and gross redemption yields for such pre-horizon securities were generated from the traditional pure expectations theory. The procedure is described in detail in Appendix C. These equilibrium prices were calculated to ensure an equality of expected holding-period returns on alternative sequences of pre-horizon investments, for whatever length of holding period (necessarily less than or equal to the horizon). The expected forward rates, needed to establish equilibrium prices, were generated in the course of the test. This is also described in Appendix C. The central assumption used in this regard was that the structure of forward rates had a shape simple enough to be estimated by a cubic function of time to maturity. Given certain constraints on these forward rates (discussed below) only one new parameter, A_3, actually had to be estimated in the course of the test. Dealing with the pre-horizon securities in this manner seemed to offer two advantages. First, it

[30] J. M. Brew provided the proof of this.

[31] Statutory provisions to tax all long-term capital gains were announced on 6 April 1965. Certain B.G.S. were made subject to special provisions, and were described as 'Neutral Zone securities'. Such securities, issued before 1 Apr. 1965, were not subject to the gains tax when a price rise occurred in the region between the lowest issue price and the redemption price.

[32] Stockbrokers consulted on this point were of the view that (especially on rising markets) the attraction of a possible tax-free gain began to have an effect on demand when stocks were three to four points below the entrance to the Neutral Zone.

allows for investors to predict non-equal forward rates over the relatively near future. Second, it presumes that investors manage their portfolio of pre-horizon securities in a way which is, at least mathematically, equivalent (ignoring risk) to the way they handle their main portfolio, made up of securities maturing after the horizon.

The problem with proposing a pre-horizon model to supplement the Basic Model is that it opens the way to inconsistencies. At least two issues need discussion. The first of these relates to investors' expectations about future interest rates. The pre-horizon model generates forward rates stretching up to, and including, the horizon. The Basic Model, with its assumption of an expected yield curve at the horizon, implicitly forecasts forward rates from the horizon date onwards. There are then two predicted forward rates for the horizon and, assuming that the same investors manage both the pre- and post-horizon portfolios, these predictions must be identical. The test producure in fact ensured this equality. A smooth (differentiable) transition between the series of forward rates generated by the two models was also imposed.

The second and more important issue involves the real meaning of the horizon parameter in the context of a joint test of the Basic Model and the pre-horizon model. The horizon has three functions. It gives the length of the decision period used in the Basic Model (t_D). It marks a point of segmentation between shorter stocks and longer stocks (t_S). And it further marks the point at which the expected future short rates must become equal (t_H). Are these three meanings consistent? Investigation reveals they need not be. On the one hand, if segmentation exists in the bond market only because investors have a decision period longer than the time to maturity of the shortest B.G.S. (thus precluding choice between these short securities using the same criteria as determines the choice between longer securities) then the segmentation point must equal the length of the decision period $(t_S = t_D)$. Conversely, if segmentation exists for institutional or other reasons (e.g. banks dominate the short market and Insurance Companies, the long) then a divergence between the value of t_S and t_D could occur. The way in which evidence of this might be expected to appear in the empirical tests would be through estimated values of the horizon which seemed implausibly large for a decision period. In effect, the horizon parameter would rise to allow different models (the pre-horizon and Basic Models respectively) to apply to different, and discontinuous, sections of the market for B.G.S.

Another problem is that the length of the decision period (t_D) can differ from that point in the future at which investors feel all subsequent forward rates must be equal (t_H). If t_H is less than t_D there would not seem to be an estimation problem. Expected equal forward rates, before the end of the decision period, can in fact be accommodated in the pre-horizon model (there being nothing to prevent the estimated cubic being approximately flat in the region preceding the horizon). Conversely, if investors do not expect a level yield curve to prevail, until some date further in the future than the end of their decision period $(t_H > t_D)$, they expect a non-level yield curve at the end of the decision period. It seems likely that, in the test below (which assumes $t_H = t_D$), this will also show up empirically in a relatively long horizon measurement. Given that two possible causes of large estimates for this horizon parameter have been distinguished above, further tests would have to be done to distinguish the operative factor.

C. *Estimation procedures and data utilized*

After adjusting the Basic Model for tax considerations, and incorporating the pre-horizon model into the analysis, a test of the resulting model should have been carried out so as to estimate six parameters (four from the Basic Model, one for taxes, and one for the pre-horizon model) using the general procedures described in Section III.A above. Technical considerations led to two parameters being pre-set; namely, c (the marginal rate of substitution between risk and return in investors' common utility function) and ρ (the tax parameter). These seemed, *a priori*, the most likely to be constant over successive data periods.[33] ρ was variously assigned three different values, depending on the level of long-term capital-gains tax at the time, so as to minimize the error sum of squares in the test. The value of c was alternatively set at $0 \cdot 00$ and $0 \cdot 01$ in order to make explicit the contribution of the risk premium. The latter value

---

[33] This is a judgement about relative rather than absolute stability. Empirical investigation has in fact indicated that ρ does vary over time. The theoretical work of Lintner–Sharpe *et al.* indicates that c too should vary. While this latter point might be thought particularly worrisome, it seems doubtful in practice whether the imposition of constancy on c detracts from the test. As is reported below, parameters c and Y are affected by a problem akin to multi-collinearity. The Likelihood function estimated appears to have its maximum along a ridge in the c, Y plane. Presetting c does not then greatly (if at all) reduce the goodness of fit of the model.

implies (given the values fed in for the risk premia) that risk-aversion leads, in equilibrium, to expected decision-period returns on the longest stocks being approximately 1 per cent per annum above the expected decision-period returns on the shortest stocks. With these two parameters pre-set, the Powell [24] routine was used to search for the remaining parameters as described above. Extensive testing was done to ensure that, so far as possible, no purely local maxima in the Likelihood function were recorded in the results below.

Various end-quarter dates between 1963(1) and 1970(4) were chosen for testing in two groups. In general, the first group (*Group 1*) comprised most end-quarter dates where the yield curve had some significant slope. This preoccupation with sloping curves reflected a belief that they contain more information about investment behaviour. It can be shown (if risk-aversion is ignored) that the 'horizon' parameter is completely indeterminate if the yield curve is flat.[34] All other dates investigated were reported as *Group 2* results. The only end-quarter dates ultimately rejected from consideration were those where the term structure was suspected to be influenced by factors militating against an equilibrium solution. These comprised 1 January, 1 April, and 1 June 1965, and 1 April 1969, at which times there was speculation in the market about changes in capital-gains tax provisions.

For each chosen date a sample of B.G.S. was decided upon for the cross-section test. In practice all securities were used save those with sinking fund provisions, those which had been in the market for less than two years,[35] those with less than one year to maturity,[36] and all irredeemables except War Loan. Information about prices and dividend yields were taken from Mullens's daily stock sheet. On average 30 stocks were used for each of the 32 cross-section tests, giving over 960 observations in all.

[34] In Appendix B it is shown that the yield curve is flat if $Y = x$ (ignoring risk). Setting $Y = x$ in line (6) of Appendix B reveals that all the elements in t_0 (the horizon) cancel out.

[35] This was necessary since the method used to calculate the risk premia (Z_i) required price data from eight previous quarters. The rule had too the effect of excluding tap stocks. Occasionally, when prices are falling, the Authorities do not lower the tap price. In this situation the tap is 'non-operative'.

[36] Such very short securities are subject to short-term capital-gains tax upon their sale or maturity. Since, in the analysis, no specific provision is made for this particular tax, it was thought advisable to leave out such stocks.

IV. Test results

The parameter estimates and measures of goodness of fit for the Group 1 and Group 2 dates combined are given in Table IV.18. Group 1 results are denoted by an asterisk. It will be recalled that 3 variants of the empirical model were tested; c was set alternatively at 0·00 (*Variant 1*) and 0·01 (*Variant 2*). In the latter case, the risk premia used were alternatively Z_i (*Variant 2a*) and Z_i^* (*Variant 2b*). Only the best-fitting results, provided by Variant 2b, are reported in Table IV.18, though a consideration of the relative performance of all 3 variants of the model figures centrally in the discussion.

Three issues are considered below. This constitutes an attempt to identify the separate influence of those 3 factors most commonly mentioned when attempts are made to identify the determinants of the term structure of interest rates. In A consideration is given to how well the estimated model—which assumes the importance of both expectations and liquidity preference—fits the data. In B an attempt is made to establish the separate influence of liquidity preference. In C the question of market segmentation is looked at more directly.

A. *Goodness of fit*

From Table IV.18 it can be calculated that over all data periods, the standard error of the estimated gross redemption yields is less than 20 basis points (0·2 per cent in terms of gross redemption yields). When the four most recent dates are excluded, moreover, this falls to 16·9 basis points. These figures seem to compare favourably with results reported by other researchers.[37]

As for the $\bar{R}^2$ statistics, these are at first glance somewhat discouraging. Though high in the periods 1962–4 and 1970, they are very low in the intervening period. Yet these individual figures give a somewhat misleading picture of the model's explanatory powers. In general, low $\bar{R}^2$ are associated with yield curves having very little slope. Conversely, higher $\bar{R}^2$ generally occur when the yield curve does have some slope, and there is in consequence rather more

[37] While there are evident difficulties in comparing the results of cross-section and time-series tests of an hypothesis, such a comparison may provide some perspective. Modigliani and Sutch [22] and de Leeuw [18] reported standard errors of estimate of 9·3 and 34 basis points respectively. They used quarterly U.S. corporate bond data. The former referred to their figure as 'remarkably low'. Rowan and O'Brien [26], using quarterly data from the market in B.G.S., reported a standard error of estimate of 19 basis points (approximately) for most of their equations.

TABLE IV.18

Results

Model Variant 2b

Dates	Y	t_0	(CEY)	A_3	S.D.	$\bar{R}^2$ [a]
2.1.62	6·3334	4·8519	6·1792	0·00015	0·000946	0·85540
2.4.62	6·3592	4·0224	5·7851	0·00015	0·001461	0·88194
2.7.62*	6·5062	2·8115	5·1097	−0·00378	0·001087	0·95676
1.10.62*	5·2067	4·9755	4·5461	−0·00015	0·001440	0·90541
2.1.63*	5·4370	3·8096	4·6170	−0·00066	0·001015	0·95065
1.4.63*	5·6986	4·7931	5·1617	0·00014	0·001077	0·94117
1.7.63*	5·2602	3·4024	4·6088	−0·00053	0·000810	0·91461
1.10.63*	5·1606	5·0000	4·6245	−0·00005	0·001338	0·84983
2.1.64	5·5590	5·0000	5·0334	0·00010	0·001391	0·84860
1.4.64	5·6156	4·9914	5·3835	0·00021	0·001359	0·76474
1.7.64	5·9281	3·9076	5·4156	−0·00010	0·001370	0·82766
1.10.64	5·8256	4·9461	5·7355	0·00032	0·001169	0·69301
4.1.65						
1.4.65						
1.7.65						
1.10.65	6·2095	1·0002	7·3097	0·34255	0·001738	0·37463
3.1.66	6·5428	1·0000	6·5462	0·07206	0·001882	−0·03177
1.4.66	6·6902	1·5833	6·9357	0·02620	0·001528	−0·06057
1.7.66	6·8994	2·3924	6·9362	0·00443	0·001754	−0·04610
3.10.66	6·9340	5·0000	7·0318	0·00011	0·002032	0·17262
3.1.67	6·5840	1·0576	7·3857	0·15690	0·002315	0·25710
3.4.67	6·3586	1·0000	6·5260	0·10128	0·002296	0·00256
3.7.67*	6·8189	2·7868	6·2704	−0·00048	0·001348	0·80131
2.10.67*	6·9447	1·8717	6·5238	0·00061	0·001292	0·35023
2.1.68*	6·9910	1·8606	7·7918	0·01528	0·001309	0·63425
1.4.68*	7·1859	1·4447	7·5551	0·02139	0·001216	0·11480
1.7.68*	7·8739	1·0793	7·8419	0·01960	0·001568	−0·30614
1.10.68	7·2714	4·4365	7·4566	0·00055	0·003113	0·03736
2.1.69*	8·1019	1·2021	7·7431	0·00067	0·001668	0·23855
1.4.69						
1.7.69	9·4734	2·1174	10·7951	0·03061	0·003087	−0·05496
1.10.69	9·144	3·3955	10·5471	0·00651	0·003493	0·09975
31.12.69*	9·4667	1·0000	10·1091	0·28709	0·004327	−0·12472
1.4.70*	8·9217	3·3940	8·6502	0·00094	0·003817	0·61905
1.7.70*	9·8139	4·9999	8·7172	0·00013	0·004461	0·79623
1.10.70*	9·6348	4·9968	8·2307	0·00052	0·003077	0·89719

Y = height of expected level yield curve at t_0.

t_0 = time to horizon (constrained at 5 years).

(CEY) = certainty − equivalent yield.

A_3 = parameter generating profile of expected future short rates in pre-Horizon Model.

S.D. = standard deviation of error (basis points/100).

[a] The absence of a constant term in this non-linear model implies that the $\bar{R}^2$-statistic need not be greater than zero.

* Group 1 results.

TABLE IV.19
$\bar{R}^2$ *and Yield Curve Slope*
(Group 1 data)

Date	$\bar{R}^2$	$\{Y/(CEY)\} - 1$	Date	$\bar{R}^2$	$\{Y/(CEY)\} - 1$
2.7.62	0·96	0·29	2.1.68	0·63	−0·08
1.10.62	0·91	0·22	1.4.68	0·11	−0·03
2.1.63	0·95	0·21	1.7.68	−0·31	0·00
1.4.63	0·94	0·16	2.1.69	0·24	0·03
1.7.63	0·91	0·12	31.12.69	−0·12	−0·06
3.7.67	0·84	0·16	1.7.70	0·80	0·16
2.10.67	0·35	0·08	1.10.70	0·90	0·20

variance between B.G.S. yields to be explained. This association is made evident in Table IV.19, where the deviation of the ratio $Y/(CEY)$ from 1 is used as a measure of yield curve slope (see Appendix B). As the absolute value of this latter measure increases, so too does the $\bar{R}^2$ statistic. A statistic which avoids this possibility of confusion, by giving a single measure of the over-all goodness of fit provided by the model, is defined here as the *composite* $\bar{R}^2$, denoted by $\bar{R}^2_C$. This is the ratio of the explained sum of squares, from a number of dates, over the total sums of squares to be explained (all corrected for degrees of freedom). This calculation gives more satisfying and less ambiguous results.

	All Group 1 Dates	All Group 2 Dates	All Dates
$\bar{R}^2_C =$	0·782	0·447	0·699

The results summarized above, plus the observation that the parameter estimates seem, *a priori*, sensible (with the exception of t_0, which will be discussed below), are consistent with the following provisional conclusion. There is a certain minimum level of dispersion, between the yield levels on B.G.S., which even the best variant of the empirical model cannot explain. Such dispersion is evident both when the yield curve has some slope and when it is flat. It seems probable that such factors as imperfectly accounted for tax provisions, the impact of 'neutral zone' and 'tap stocks', the influence of transaction costs, security preferences, market segmentation (especially between shorter and longer stocks), and expectations of non-level yield curves at the end of the decision period, all contribute to this. Comments on the last three possibilities in this list are extended below. What also seems implied by the results, however, is that in most cases where the dispersion of yields rises above this minimum level—owing specifically to a change in the slope or general shape of the yield curve—the model tested seems largely capable of explaining this increase. Though there were occasions when this was apparently not true (particularly in 1969), the evidence thus far reviewed seems consistent overall with the conclusion that expectations and aversion to capital uncertainty play an important role in the determination of relative B.G.S. yields and the term structure of rates.[38]

B. *Tobin–Markowitz risk-aversion*

The specific contribution of risk-aversion, defined in the Tobin–Markowitz tradition, to the model's explanatory power was investigated through a comparison of the Variant 1 ($c = 0.00$) and Variant 2b ($c = 0.01$) results. Since, as noted above, the measure of risk used for Variant 2b (Z_i^*) tends empirically to increase with the maturity of the stock being considered (as indeed does Z_i) any indication that these risk premia influence the term structure also implies that investors demonstrate liquidity preference (i.e. a preference for shorter as opposed to longer B.G.S.). Variant 2b did give a better fit overall ($\bar{R}^2$ higher in 24 of the 33 cross-section tests), yet the difference was at best marginal. The standard error of the estimates (averaged over all data periods) in fact fell by only 1 basis point upon inclusion of the risk premium. This would lead to the conclusion that Tobin–Markowitz risk-aversion makes no significant contribution were it not for a problem, akin to multi-collinearity, which affects the parameter c and the parameter Y (measuring the height of the expected level yield curve). In every case when c

[38] It is beyond the scope of this paper to turn to any rigorous time-series analysis. Yet the following simple argument supports the conclusion in the text. If the hypothesis tested is true, the slope of the yield curve (measured by $Y/(CEY)$ as described in Appendix B) changes as expectations change. Now there are at least 2 independent measures which also indicate investors' expectations at particular times; net sales of stock by the Authorities, and past interest-rate changes. Assuming the correctness of the hypothesis, a negative correlation should exist between increasing $Y/(CEY)$ (growing bearishness) and net sales of B.G.S. (bullishness). Over the data period 1962(1)–1970(4) the zero order correlation coefficient was in fact -0.45. Assuming investors extrapolate past interest-rate changes in forming expectations, a positive correlation should exist between $Y/(CEY)$ and the change in long bond rates (a rise in both indicates bearishness). The correlation coefficient was 0.174. These simple results tend rather to confirm the hypothesis than deny it.

was raised from 0·00 to 0·01, the value for Y fell, while the goodness of fit normally changed only slightly. The underlying reason for this can be explained using a simple version of the Basic Model presented above.

Suppose that all gross redemption yields (y_i) are at their equilibrium levels, such that if all yields rose instantaneously to a given constant yield level (Y) the certainty equivalent return (λ) on all stocks would be equal. Then for the ith stock (after dropping the i subscript)

$$\frac{P^{\mathrm{E}} - P}{P} = \lambda + cZ^* \tag{9}$$

$$(y - Y) \frac{P^{\mathrm{E}} - P}{y - Y} \frac{1}{P} = \lambda + cZ^* \tag{10}$$

$$y = \frac{\lambda + cZ^*}{\dfrac{(P^{\mathrm{E}} - P)}{y - Y} \dfrac{1}{P}} + Y \tag{11}$$

where all definitions are as on page 369 above. If the element $(P^{\mathrm{E}} - P)/(y - Y)$ is now approximated by the derivative of P with respect to y (calculated at Y), and if Z^* is recalled as being identical to the Volatility measurement of the ith security (again calculated at Y), cancelling leaves

$$y = \frac{\lambda}{\dfrac{(P^{\mathrm{E}} - P)}{y - Y} \dfrac{1}{P}} + c + Y.$$

The same equilibrium interest can result from any combination of c and Y (moreover much the same result holds if Z is used rather than Z^*, since in practice these series are very similar). The implication of this is that the separate influences of expectations and risk-aversion can be identified only by the second and higher order effects of using a more accurate (Taylor series expansion) proxy for $(P^{\mathrm{E}} - P)/(y - Y)$. It also implies that, even with a perfectly accurate calculation of expected capital gain (as is true in the test, assuming a correct choice of Y), the scope for improving the model's performance by introducing the risk element is slight. In this context, the consistent tendency of Variant 2b (implying risk-aversion) to out-perform Variant 1 (no risk-aversion) might be thought meaningful.

Another important issue is raised by the superior performance of Variant 2b (using Z_i^*) to Variant 2a (using Z_i). Since the latter risk premia are implied by the Lintner–Sharpe theory, while the former is only an *ad hoc* measure of risk (though still associating risk with capital uncertainty), this finding implies that the Lintner–Sharpe model is incorrect. Investors apparently do not choose B.G.S. portfolios which are 'efficient' in the Tobin–Markowitz sense, since they fail to consider the impact which price covariance can make on the risk associated with the purchase of individual securities. Though this does correspond to the empirical findings of Douglas and Lintner,[39] using U.S. equity-market data, anything more than a provisional conclusion on the general applicability of the Lintner–Sharpe hypothesis to speculative markets, would seem unwarranted. Again the problem is one akin to multi-collinearity. The ranking of B.G.S., according to the size of their associated Z_i^*, gives virtually the same ranking as when Z_i is used. The implication is that the 'inefficiency' implied by the use of Z_i^* may be very small in the case of B.G.S. This would not necessarily be the case in other speculative markets, and the incentive to act 'efficiently' might be correspondingly greater.

C. *Market segmentation and security preferences*

It seems useful to distinguish between two concepts, segmentation proper and security preferences. The former is an extreme version of the latter and implies that securities with certain different characteristics are traded in effectively different (discontinuous) markets. Security preferences imply a willingness on the part of some investors to pay higher prices for securities with certain characteristics than for securities (otherwise identical) not possessing those characteristics.

A number of points in the test results reflect on the question of segmentation between shorter and longer B.G.S. The first of these has to do with the very high parameter estimates recorded for t_0 (the horizon) in Table IV.18. Its average value was 3·1 years, and on 11 of 32 occasions it rose above 4·5 years.[40] Recalling the

---

[39] See Douglas [7].

[40] The variability of t_0 also needs explanation. The less steep the slope of the yield curve, the more indeterminate is t_0 (see footnote 34). In such circumstances the parameter t_0 remains at or near its starting-point for the iterations (1 year). When the yield curve slope increases, this parameter becomes more determinate, and rises for reasons discussed in the text (segmentation).

discussion in Section III.B above, where it was pointed out that t_0 could have three possibly inconsistent interpretations, these results lead to one of three conclusions: (i) the decision period is very long, or (ii) the market expects a non-level yield curve at the end of the decision period, or (iii) segmentation exists for institutional or other reasons not related to the underlying theory. Acceptance of conclusion (iii) follows from rejection of the other two possibilities.

Interpretation (i) was thought inconsistent with the results of tests of the model using only securities having more than 6 years to maturity (thus generally avoiding the segmentation problem). The average length of the horizon parameter fell to 2·6 years. There were only 3 dates out of 32 when the value rose above 4·5 years. Less formally, decision periods in the region of 5 years simply seem unrealistic. Indeed, in a questionnaire survey of over forty Pension Fund and Insurance Company investment managers (whose behaviour should most closely approximate to that assumed by the Basic Model) all but two stated that their decision period was normally less than 2 years.

Interpretation (ii) was also rejected from bearing primary responsibility for the high parameter estimates, although only after the model had been retested for four dates seriously troubled by this problem. In these further tests the assumption of an expected level yield curve, was replaced by the assumption that investors expected the yield curve to have the shape it 'normally' had over the period 1962–70. Past data (averaged) were used to generate a 'normal' yield curve, and the parameter describing its shape was estimated and introduced as a known constant value into the model to be tested. The comparative results are listed in Table IV.20. All definitions are as in Table IV.18 above. While it is clear that this alternative formulation appears substantially to improve the fit in 3 of the 4 cases, the evidence taken above to imply segmentation continues to emerge. In 3 of the 4 cases the length of the horizon parameter (t_0) rose to the maximum length permitted by the program (5 years). These considerations lead to the conclusion that interpretation (iii) above is the most acceptable.

A second result indicating segmentation emerged after the model had been retested using only securities having more than 6 years to maturity. As Table IV.21 indicates, there were substantial differences between the resulting parameter estimates and those observed in Table IV.18. If the market in B.G.S. were fully continuous, this would not be expected to occur. Moreover, similarly

TABLE IV.20

Alternative Test Results

	$\bar{R}^2$	S.D.	t_0	(CEY)	D–W statistic[c]
1.10.62 [a]	0·934	0·0013	5·000	4·519	0·699
[b]	0·948	0·0011	3·211	3·910	0·846
1.10.63 [a]	0·855	0·0014	5·000	4·635	0·499
[b]	0·927	0·0011	5·000	4·358	1·131
1.4.70 [a]	0·506	0·0034	2·909	8·734	0·410
[b]	0·766	0·0028	5·00	8·294	0·593
1.10.70 [a]	0·918	0·0028	5·000	8·320	0·823
[b]	0·907	0·0034	5·000	8·431	0·639

[a] Assumes level expected yield curves. Values differ from Table IV.18 results owing to minor alterations in the data input.
[b] Assumes sloping ('normal') expected yield curves.
[c] Securities listed in order of time to maturity.

TABLE IV.21

Alternative Test Results

(Averages over Group 1 data periods)

	P.S.1	P.S.2	Mean abs. diff.
Y	7·189	7·296	0·293
t_0	3·129	2·593	1·670
(CEY)	6·756	6·017	1·125

P.S.1: portfolio including all B.G.S.
P.S.2: portfolio like P.S.1 but excluding all
stocks of less than 6 years to maturity.

large differences in the parameter estimates were also observed when the model was retested (for 4 dates) using the alternative assumption of a 'normal' expected yield curve.

As for security preferences, as defined above, these are first indicated by the evidence implying long/short segmentation in the market for B.G.S. They seem further indicated by systematic deviations of actual from calculated values of gross redemption yields. The possibility of this latter phenomenon being a consequence of the market expecting a non-level yield curve at the end of the decision period is considered later. Evidently not all of the 960 data residuals can be discussed separately, but a few general observations seem possible.

In spite of the model being generally supported by the data, on some occasions it does leave quite high residual variances. This has been particularly true in recent years. Moreover, as Table IV.22 indicates, when the residuals are listed in the order of their period to maturity, they are sometimes highly serially correlated. This problem particularly arises in 1962, 1963, and 1970, years when in fact the goodness of fit $(\bar{R}^2)$ was highest. In Charts IV.1 and IV.2 are presented two examples of the most common residual pattern. The outstanding characteristic is the way the model generates too high gross redemption yields for shorter securities and too low gross redemption yields for longer securities. This implies a 'preference for liquidity' which cannot be explained on grounds of 'Tobin–Markowitz' risk-aversion alone, at least as proxied above (i.e. with Z_i and Z_i^*). There is also a tendency in recent years, as seen for example in Chart IV.2, for the very longest stocks to stand at a lower gross redemption yield than that implied by the model. This could be a consequence of the apparent preferences of Insurance Companies and Pension Funds. They desire longer as opposed to shorter B.G.S. to 'match' against their long-term liabilities.

TABLE IV.22

Durbin–Watson Statistics

Group 1 Residuals taken in order of increasing time to maturity of the security

Date	D–W	Date	D–W
2.7.62	0·667	2.1.68	1·933
1.10.62	0·479	1.4.68	1·568
2.1.63	1·073	1.7.68	2·042
1.4.63	1·525	2.1.67	2.206
1.7.63	0·902	31.12.69	0·899
1.10.63	0·418	1.4.70	1·235
3.7.67	2·292	1.7.70	0·875
2.10.67	2·281	1.10.70	0·417

A second piece of evidence implying security preferences is provided by the instances (again seen particularly in the more recent data periods considered) when supply constraints have been correlated with particularly large negative residuals at the short end. Two typical examples of this are reported in Table IV.23. It is apparent that all securities listed in Table IV.23, except 3% Savings 1965/75, constituted relatively small issues. For comparison,

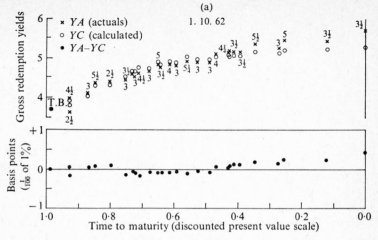

CHART IV.1

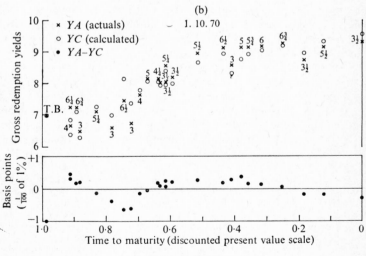

CHART IV.2

TABLE IV.23

	Residual		Amount issued
	(1.7.70)	(1.10.70)	(£m.)
3% Gas 1968/73	−0·349		136
5¼% Conversion 1974	−0·393	−0·262	299
3% Savings 1965/75	−0·570	−0·471	1,073
6½% Treasury 1976	−1·062	−0·749	300
4% Transport 1972/77	−0·332	−0·218	242

the average size of issue for all securities in the market for B.G.S. (as of July 1970) was almost £500 million. As for 3% Savings 1965/75, the 'amount issued' figure gives a misleading impression of the 'effective' supply of this security to the market place. 3% Savings was issued during the Second World War, much like a National Savings security today. An unusually large proportion of it remains in the hands of small private investors, who tend to hold such securities until near maturity.[41] The pattern of these residuals also seems consistent with informal observations commonly put forward by market operators; namely, that the Clearing Banks attempted to have some part of their holdings of short B.G.S. maturing in each near-future year, and that they were willing (if necessary) to pay a higher price for needed securities. Market operators extend this observation by stating that the Banks preferred high coupon issues. This seems substantiated by the very large negative residual attached (in Table IV.23) to 6½% Treasury 1976, which stock was flanked by two low coupon issues.

Turning finally to the suggestion that all these observations, taken above to imply the existence of security preferences, are rather a consequence of the assumption of an expected level yield curve, the four data periods noted in Table IV.20 were chosen for further investigation. The model was retested using the alternative assumption of a 'normal' expected yield curve. The Durbin–Watson statistics, which were originally very low, were only slightly altered by

[41] As of 1 July 1970, some 31·5% of the nominal amounts of 3% Savings 1965/75 outstanding were in the hands of private holders. This contrasted with a level of 15·3% for all B.G.S. in aggregate. Moreover, turnover in 3% Savings was also below that in other short stocks (0–5 years to maturity). The ratio of inter-sector transactions (using the Bank of England security register's sectoral classifications) to total amounts outstanding was 3·3% for 3% Savings (average figure for the July, Aug., Sept. 1970 register data), while the comparable ratio for all other stocks was 7·3%.

this new specification. The same was true of the pattern of the residuals. These results do not then lead to a rejection of the conclusion above. The evidence seems consistent with a market preference for certain securities.

V. Conclusions and suggestions for further research

The primary purpose of this paper was to investigate the determinants of the term structure of interest rates in the market for B.G.S. A new cross-section approach to the data was used, premissed on the belief that investors expect end-decision-period yield curves to have some simple shape. The theoretical model tested was based on the mean-variance framework suggested by Tobin and Markowitz and developed by Lintner and Sharpe. Yet it had certain characteristics in common with the models tested by Malkiel, Modigliani and Sutch, and Rowan and O'Brien.

The main conclusions implied by the test results reported in Section IV can be quickly summarized. Both expectations about security price changes and aversion to capital uncertainty appear to play a role in the determination of the term structure. The evidence for the latter factor being important is, however, rather slight. Nor do the risk premia associated with individual B.G.S. conform exactly to those suggested by the Lintner–Sharpe hypothesis. The evidence is also consistent with there being some discontinuity between the markets for shorter and longer securities, and with some investors demonstrating security preferences. The predominant characteristic in this last regard seems to be a 'preference for liquidity'. Finally, differences in the gross redemption yields of securities of near-equal period to maturity seem largely determined by tax considerations.

Suggestions for any further research in the same vein as this paper must begin with such improvements of the above model as the explicit recognition of segmentation and the introduction of non-level expected yield curves. This done, a separate investigation might first be initiated on why investors' expectations (as indicated by the term structure) change over time. In this regard, the role played by the Authorities, in particular the leads given by their pricing of tap stocks, could perhaps be isolated; as might be the role played by past interest-rate levels and movements. Such information would have relevance to such policy questions as the 'stability' of the market for B.G.S., with all its implications for monetary policy.

Finally, some more extensive consideration of security preferences might also prove of immediate practical and theoretical value. A first step might be a formal analysis of the relationship between test residuals and size of issue.

Appendices

A. *Equilibrium conditions in the market for B.G.S.*

Given assumptions (a)–(e) in Section II.A of the text, equilibrium condition (3) can be derived as follows. A more rigorous presentation can be found in Mossin [23], who also discusses the various implications of investors behaving as described here.

Consider first an individual investor who wishes to allocate his total wealth (W_0), over n different B.G.S., so as to maximize his expected utility at the end of a single decision period. The market value of his purchase of the ith security is defined as X_i, where $i = 1 \ldots n$. Suppose the investor has a utility function of the form.[1]

$$U = a_0 - a_1 e^{-bW} \qquad (A.1)$$

where U and W are utility and terminal wealth respectively. Then

$$E(U) = E(a_0 - a_1 e^{-bW}) \qquad (A.2)$$

$$= a_0 - a_1 e^{-bU_w + b^2\sigma_w^2} \qquad (A.3)$$

assuming W is Normally distributed[2] with mean U_w and variance σ_w^2. Maximizing $E(U)$ is accomplished by maximizing

$$E(U)^* = U_w - b\sigma_w^2. \qquad (A.4)$$

Expressions for U_w and σ_w^2 can be easily calculated as below, upon noting that P_i is the market price of the ith security, and that r_i

[1] There is little empirical evidence available about the exact form of investors' utility function. The main criteria for choosing a function as a basis for analysis are that it has *a priori* sensible implications for investment behaviour, and that it produces operational results. For the former, the above function implies $dU/dw > 0$ and $d^2u/d^2w^2 < 0$. Thus the investor is taken to be a risk averter. The function also implies constant absolute risk-aversion in the Pratt–Arrow sense. While theoretically somewhat unsatisfactory, this assumption does have practical advantages. The fact that b (in (A.1) above) can be taken as constant, rather than as a function of P_i, greatly simplifies calculation of equilibrium conditions, particularly if it is also desired to admit heterogeneous expectations into the model. See Jensen [15], pp. 49–50.

[2] This assumption can be justified either through use of the Central Limit Theorem, or by making the prior assumption that B.G.S. returns have independent Normal distributions.

and $E(g_i)$ are respectively the coupon return (non-stochastic) and expected capital gain/loss (stochastic) anticipated over the decision period on the ith security.

$$U_w = \mathbf{m'x} \tag{A.5}$$

$$\sigma_w^2 = \mathbf{x'}V\mathbf{x}, \tag{A.6}$$

where:

$$\mathbf{m'} = \left(1 + \frac{r + E(g_1)}{P_1}, 1 + \frac{r_2 + E(g_2)}{P_2}, \ldots, 1 + \frac{r_n + E(g_n)}{P_n}\right)$$

$$\mathbf{x'} = (X_1, X_2, \ldots, X_n)$$

and V is defined as an $n \times n$ matrix comprising the variance–covariance matrix of the capital gains/losses on each of the n securities, with each element weighted by the appropriate prices.

Substituting (A.5) and (A.6) into (A.4), and maximizing subject to the over-all portfolio constraint $(\mathbf{i'x} = W_0)$, yields

$$\mathbf{m} - 2bV\mathbf{x} + \bar{\lambda}\mathbf{i} = 0 \tag{A.7}$$

$$\mathbf{i'x} - W_0 = 0, \tag{A.8}$$

where $\bar{\lambda}$ is a Lagrangean multiplier. This is a true maximum if V is assumed positive definite. From (A.7) and (A.8) the individual's demand functions, for the individual B.G.S., follow immediately.

$$\mathbf{x} = (2b)^{-1}\left(V^{-1} - \frac{V^{-1} - \mathbf{ii'}V^{-1}}{\mathbf{i'}V^{-1}\mathbf{i}}\right)\mathbf{m} + \left(\frac{V^{-1}\mathbf{i}}{\mathbf{i'}V^{-1}\mathbf{i}}\right)W_0. \tag{A.9}$$

Assuming that all investors are identical in every respect is a useful (though not strictly necessary) simplification, which allows (A.9) to be interpreted as the market's aggregate demand equations for individual B.G.S. With these aggregate demand functions specified, the further assumptions that the supplies of securities can be taken as given, and that the market always clears to absorb these, allow attention to be directed back to equation system (A.7). These equations can now be interpreted as the market clearing conditions for the individual B.G.S. Recalling that the expected capital gain/loss component in $\mathbf{m}$ is defined as the difference between the present price of the security (P_i) and its expected price at the end of the decision period (P_i^{E}), (A.7) is seen to be a system of n

equations in the $n + 1$ unknowns comprising the various P_i and $\bar{\lambda}$ (assuming that all the other elements in (A.7) are known). Since this system is underdetermined, it can be solved only for relative prices (and relative gross redemption yields) and not absolute prices. The equilibrium conditions reported in the text can be derived by assuming that $\bar{\lambda}$ can be taken as known. Then

$$\frac{r_i + (P_i^E - P_i)}{P_i} - 2b \left[\sum_{j=1}^{n} \frac{X_j \sigma_{ij}}{P_i P_j} \right] = \lambda \qquad \text{(A.10)}$$

for all i ($i = 1 \ldots n$) where λ ($\lambda = \bar{\lambda} - 1$) is here defined as the Certainty–Equivalent Yield on the ith security. To assume λ is known is consistent with assuming the price of a risk-free asset is given exogenously.

B. *The implied shape of the yield curve*

Consider the following definitions

$i = i$th security,	P^E = price expected at t_0,
P = market price,	Y = gross redemption yield expected on *all* stocks at t_0,
t_i = maturity date of ith stock,	
t_0 = end of decision period,	y = gross redemption yield,
r = coupon,	x = expected decision-period return.

Begin by assuming that all securities stand at par, that risk premia and tax complications can be ignored, and that interest accumulates continuously. Then at any chosen time, for any security,

$$P_i^E = \int_{t_0}^{t_i} e^{-Y(t - t_0)} r_i \, dt + e^{-Y(t_i - t_0)}; \qquad \text{(B.1)}$$

where the price of security i at maturity (t_i) is assumed to be 1. Given this, the expected decision-period return on the security is calculated:

$$P_i = \int_0^{t_0} e^{-x_i t} r_i \, dt + e^{-x_i t_0} . P_i^E \qquad \text{(B.2)}$$

$$P_i = \frac{r_i}{x_i} (1 - e^{-x_i t_0}) + e^{-x_i t_0} . P_i^E. \qquad \text{(B.3)}$$

Integrating (B.1) and substituting into (B.3), then incorporating both the hypothesis that the decision period return on all securities is equal (i.e. all $x_i = x$)[1] and the assumption that all securities stand at par, yields

$$1 = \frac{y_i}{x}(1 - e^{-xt_0}) + e^{-xt_0}\left\{\frac{y_i}{Y}(1 - e^{-Yt'}) + e^{-Yt'}\right\},$$
(B.4)

where $t_i - t_0 = t'$. Dropping the i subscript, considering y as a continuous function in t, and rearranging gives:

$$y\left\{\frac{1}{x}(1 - e^{-xt_0}) + \frac{e^{-xt_0}}{Y}(1 - e^{-Yt'})\right\} = 1 - e^{-xt_0 - Yt'}$$
(B.5)

or

$$y = \frac{Y(1 - Ae^{-Yt'})}{B - Ae^{-Yt'}}$$
(B.6)

where $A = e^{-xt_0}$, $B = Y/x(1 - e^{-xt_0}) + e^{-xt_0}$. And from (B.6)

$$\frac{dy}{dt} = \frac{AY^2 e^{-Yt'}(B - 1)}{(B - A e^{-Yt'})^2}.$$
(B.7)

This derivative will be positive for all values of t (i.e. the yield curve will slope upwards throughout its length) if $B > 1$. This requires in turn, $Y > x$. Conversely, the curve will slope downwards for all values of t if $Y < x$, and will be flat if $Y = x$. Finally, it can be easily shown that $d^2y/dt^2 < 0$ for all t. The yield curve (recalling the assumption that all $Z_i = 0$) is therefore monotonic.

A humped yield curve is possible when risk premia are introduced. The equilibrium condition is in this case

$$x_i - cZ_i = \lambda$$
(B.8)

for all i. Assuming x and Z to be continuous functions in t, we have

$$x(t) = \lambda + cZ(t).$$
(B.9)

Substituting for $x(t)$ in (B.5), and proceeding analogously to lines (B.5)–(B.7) above, the implied yield curve is seen to have the following properties. At any point t

$$\frac{dy}{dt} > 0 \quad \text{if } Y > \lambda + cZ(t),$$
(B.10)

---

[1] Since the equilibrium condition is $x_i - cZ_i = \lambda$ for all i, and we assume here that all the Z_i are zero, then the equality of the x_i is necessary.

$$\frac{dy}{dt} < 0 \quad \text{if } Y < \lambda + cZ(t). \tag{B.11}$$

Evidently if $Z(t)$ were relatively small for low values of t, and large for larger values of t (as is indicated by the empirical evidence), then the derivative, dy/dt, could change sign in cases where $Y < x$.

C. *A pre-horizon model based on the pure expectations hypothesis*

The underlying behavioural assumptions and the two principal conclusions of the traditional pure expectations hypothesis have been summarized in the text. Equilibrium prices (and gross redemption yields) for pre-horizon securities were generated on the assumption that both these principal conclusions (see (a) and (b) on p. 363, above) were always met. For simplicity, the exposition of procedures below abstracts from coupon payments, tax considerations, and as well assumes continuous accumulation of interest. Such simplifications were not assumed in the actual test.

Suppose an investor has a capital sum ($=1$) to invest over period $(t + \delta t)$; and there are two investment possibilities open to him. He can (Policy 1) invest in a security (assumed) standing at par, paying interest continuously at a rate $y(t)$ and maturing at t, with subsequent investment in a short-term security for time δt, paying interest at the rate then *expected* to prevail $\{Y(t)\}$. Or he can invest immediately (Policy 2) in a stock maturing at time $(t + \delta t)$ and paying interest at the rate $(y + \delta y)$. Traditional theory says the return over the period $(t + \delta t)$ should be equal from both investment policies. Thus, if the returns from the Policy 1 investments were discounted back to their present value, by the Policy 2 rate of return, the original value ($=1$) would emerge. This demands

$$\int_0^t y(t)\, e^{-(y+\delta y)\theta}\, d\theta + Y(t)\, e^{-(y+\delta y)t}\, \delta t + e^{-(y+\delta y)(t+\delta t)} = 1 \tag{C.1}$$

$$\frac{y}{y+\delta y}\{1 - e^{-(y+\delta y)t}\} + Y(t)\, e^{-yt}\, \delta t = 1 - e^{-yt}(1 - t\,\delta y - y\,\delta t)$$
$$\text{(to the first order)} \tag{C.2}$$

$$y\{1 - e^{-yt}(1 - t\,\delta y)\} + Y(t)y\, e^{-yt}\, \delta t$$

$$= y\{1 - e^{-yt}\} + y\, e^{-yt}(t\,\delta y + y\,\delta t) + \delta y(1 - e^{-yt}) \tag{C.3}$$

and cancelling, dividing through by δt, and letting $\delta t \to 0$

$$yt \, e^{-yt} \frac{dy}{dt} + Y(t)y \, e^{-yt}$$

$$= yt \, e^{-yt} \frac{dy}{dt} + y^2 \, e^{-yt} + \frac{dy}{dt} (1 - e^{-yt}) \quad \text{(C.4)}$$

$$\frac{dy}{dt} = \frac{y(t)\{Y(t) - y(t)\}}{1 - e^{-yt}} \, e^{-yt}. \quad \text{(C.5)}$$

This expression, given $Y(t)$, can be integrated over the region 0 to t_0 (the horizon) to yield $y(t)$—the required gross redemption yield $\{\hat{y}(t)\}$ on all securities maturing prior to the horizon. The calculated value for $y(t_0)$ is taken as being equal to λ (the certainty-equivalent yield) in the test of the whole model.

For the integration above, values of $Y(t)$, expected future short-term rates, are required. These were generated using the following assumptions. Let the profile of forward (expected) short rates have some simple shape; namely,

$$Y(t) = A_0 + A_1 t + A_2 t^2 + A_3 t^3. \quad \text{(C.6)}$$

Then assume

1. A_0 = present Treasury Bill rate. The expected rate at $t = 0$ must equal the present rate.
2. $Y(t_0) = Y$. The yield expected to prevail on short-term securities purchased at t_0 must equal the expected yields on all other stocks. This is consistent with an expected level yield curve at the horizon.
3. $(dY/dt)_{t_0} = 0$. This gives a smooth transition to constant expected yields beyond the horizon.

This leaves only one parameter (defined in the test as A_3) to be actually estimated in (C.6) above. It was calculated from the data, after appropriate substitution of (C.6) into the main body of the test, by the iterative procedure used to find values for all the other parameters in the model. Again, actual yields were assumed to equal equilibrium yields plus a Normally distributed error term.

Finally, it can be seen from (C.5) above that the measure of dy/dt generated for $t = t_0$ by the pure expectations hypothesis, is identical to that value of dy/dt at t_0 generated by the Basic Model (abstracting from risk). This is clear if line (C.5) is compared with line (B.7) in Appendix B and it is recalled that $y(t_0) = x$ and $Y(t_0) = Y$. This constitutes an illustration that the two approaches to explaining the yield curve are mathematically equivalent.

REFERENCES

[1] BLACK, F., 'Capital Market Equilibrium with Restricted Borrowing' (1970: forthcoming in the *Journal of Business*).

[2] BIERWAG, G. O., and GROVE, M. A., 'A Model of the Term Structure of Interest Rates', *Rev. Econ. Stats.*, 1967, pp. 50–62.

[3] BREW, J. M., 'Gilt-Edged Yield Curves', *Investment Analyst*, 1966, pp. 3–22.

[4] —— 'The Term Structure of Interest Rates and the Expectations Hypothesis' (mimeo).

[5] CASS, D., and STIGLITZ, J. E., 'The Structure of Investor Preference and Asset Returns, and Separability in Portfolio Allocation: A Contribution to the Pure Theory of Mutual Funds', *Journal of Economic Theory*, 1970, pp. 122–60.

[6] CONARD, J. W., *An Introduction to the Theory of Interest* (Berkeley, Calif., 1959).

[7] DOUGLAS, G. W., *Risk in the Equity Markets: an Empirical Appraisal of Market Efficiency* (Yale Economic Essays, 1969), pp. 3–45.

[8] FAMA, E. F., 'Risk Return and Equilibrium: Some Clarifying Comments', *Journal of Finance*, 1967, pp. 29–40.

[9] —— 'Multiperiod Consumption—Investment Decisions', *American Economic Review*, 1970, pp. 163–74.

[10] FAND, D., 'Comment', *J.P.E.*, 1967, pp. 565–8.

[11] GRANGER, C. W. J., 'Empirical Studies of Capital Markets' (1971: forthcoming in *Proceedings of the Venice Seminar on Mathematical Methods in Investment and Finance*).

[12] GRILICHES, Z., 'Distributed Lags: a Survey', *Econometrica*, 1967, pp. 16–59.

[13] GROSSMAN, H., 'Expectations, Transaction Costs and Asset Demands', *Journal of Finance*, 1971, pp. 491–506.

[14] HAMBURGER, M. J., 'Expectations, Long-Term Interest Rates and Monetary Policy in the United Kingdom', *Bank of England Quarterly Bulletin*, Sept. 1971, pp. 354–71.

[15] JENSEN, M. C., 'Risk, The Pricing of Capital Assets and the Evaluation of Investment Portfolios', *Journal of Business*, 1969, pp. 167–247.

[16] —— 'The Foundations and Current State of Capital Market Theory' (1971: forthcoming in *Studies in the Theory of Capital Markets* (Praeger)).

[17] KEYNES, J. M., *General Theory of Employment, Interest and Money* (London, 1961).

[18] DE LEEUW, F., 'A Model of Financial Behaviour', in J. S. Duesenberry, G. Fromm, L. R. Klein, and E. Kuh (eds.), *The Brookings Quarterly Econometric Model of the United States* (Amsterdam, 1965), pp. 465–530.

[19] LINTNER, J., 'Security Prices, Risk and Maximal Gains from Diversification', *Journal of Finance*, 1965, pp. 587–615.

[20] MALKIEL, B. G., *The Term Structure of Interest Rates* (Princeton, N.J., 1966).

[21] MEISELMAN, D., *The Term Structure of Interest Rates* (Englewood Cliffs, N.J., 1962).

[22] MODIGLIANI, F., and SUTCH, R., 'Debt Management and the Term Structure of Interest Rates', *J.P.E.*, Aug. Supp., 1967, pp. 569–95.

[23] MOSSIN, J., 'Equilibrium in a Capital Asset Market', *Econometrica*, 1966, pp. 768–83.

[24] POWELL, M. J. D., 'A Method for Minimising a Sum of Squares of Non-Linear Functions without Calculating Derivatives', *Computer Journal*, 1965.

[25] ROLL, R., *The Behaviour of Interest Rates* (London, 1970).

[26] ROWAN, D. C., and O'BRIEN, R. J., 'Expectations, the Interest Rate Structure and Debt Policy', in K. Hilton and D. Heathfield (eds.), *The Econometric Study of the United Kingdom* (Edinburgh, 1970).

[27] SHARPE, W. F., 'Capital Asset Prices. A Theory of Market Equilibrium under Conditions of Risk', *Journal of Finance*, 1964, pp. 425–42.

[28] —— *Portfolio Theory and Capital Markets* (London, 1970).

[29] SOCIETY OF INVESTMENT ANALYSTS, *Report on Gilt-Edged Yields* (private circulation, 1960).

[30] TELSER, L. G., 'A Criticism of Some Recent Empirical Research on the Explanation of the Term Structure of Interest Rates', *J.P.E.*, 1967, pp. 546–61.

[31] TOBIN, J., 'Liquidity Preference as Behaviour towards Risk', in Cowles Foundation Monograph 19 (New York, 1967).

[32] —— 'The Theory of Portfolio Selection', in F. H. Hahn and F. P. R. Brechling (eds.), *The Theory of Interest Rates* (London, 1965), pp. 3–51.

[33] WHITE, W. R., 'Expectations, Investment and the U.K. Gilt-Edged Market—Some Evidence from Market Participants', *Manchester School*, 1971, pp. 293–317.

[34] —— 'The Authorities and the United Kingdom Gilt-Edged Market 1952–66', unpublished Ph.D. Thesis, University of Manchester, 1969.

[35] WOOD, J. H., 'Expectations and the Demand for Bonds', *American Economic Review*, 1969, pp. 183–92.

A MODEL OF
COMMERCIAL BANK LOAN
AND INVESTMENT BEHAVIOUR

J. H. WOOD*
(*University of Birmingham*)

I. Introduction

The primary objective of this study is the development of a theoretical framework that will be useful in the explanation of certain observed phenomena relating to commercial banks in the United States. These phenomena are summarized in Table IV.24, in which aggregate commercial bank loans and security holdings are listed along with rates of return on bank loans and securities at post-World War II cyclical peaks and troughs. Except for 1966–7, peak and trough months are those of the National Bureau of Economic Research. Although the N.B.E.R. has not awarded official recognition to the mini-recession of 1966–7, I have added what appear to be reasonable peak and trough months corresponding to that slowdown in economic activity.

Perhaps the most striking feature of these data are the strong upward trends in interest rates and bank loans. However, it is the cyclical variation in these figures that I wish to examine. Note that both the loan rate, r, and the yield on securities, y, rise during expansions and fall during recessions. But the cyclical variability of y exceeds that of r so that the difference $r-y$ tends to decrease in expansionary periods and increase during recessions. These movements in the rate differential during, for example, expansions would

* I wish to express my appreciation to former colleagues in the Finance Department of the University of Pennsylvania for many helpful discussions and to the Federal Reserve Bank of Philadelphia for generous financial assistance and for the use of its computational and typing facilities. A National Science Foundation Grant was also helpful. Programming assistance was ably supplied by Judy Helmuth, Bunny Jablon, Cyndy Tyler, and David de Carlo. My greatest debts are to Michael D. McCarthy and Maurice Dupre for help in the mathematical portions of the study.

TABLE IV.24

Interest Rates and Bank Portfolios in Post-war Business Cycles

	Month	L	G	$\frac{L}{L+G}$	r	y	r − y
(P)	11.48	41.3	71.7	0.365	2.63	1.89	0.74
(T)	10.49	41.3	77.0	0.349	2.63	1.61	1.02
(P)	7.53	65.3	75.8	0.463	3.73	2.91	0.82
(T)	8.54	66.6	81.7	0.449	3.58	1.72	1.86
(P)	7.57	91.1	73.7	0.553	4.54	4.17	0.37
(T)	4.58	92.1	80.3	0.534	4.38	2.48	1.90
(P)	5.60	111.0	75.8	0.594	5.35	4.56	0.79
(T)	2.61	114.7	82.2	0.583	4.98	3.63	1.35
(P[a])	10.66	206.5	102.3	0.669	6.30	5.88	0.42
(T[a])	3.67	211.4	108.2	0.661	6.02	4.88	1.14
(P)	11.69	270.1	124.5	0.685	8.78	8.39	0.39
(T)	11.70	282.1	138.4	0.671	7.91	6.49	1.42

L = Loans of all commercial banks in billions of dollars.
G = Security holdings of all commercial banks in billions of dollars.
r = Rate of interest on short-term business loans, per cent per annum.
y = Weighted average of yields to maturity on securities, per cent per annum.
The weights used are the average proportions of U.S. Government securities of different maturities and of state and local Aaa bonds held by banks during the post-war period.
   If variable weights had been used (the weights varying with the proportions of bank security holdings) the values of y, beginning in Nov. 1948, would have been 1·76, 1·48, 2·79, 1·69, 4·11, 2·41, 4·57, 3·56, 6·44, 5·31, 9·68, 7·09. The qualitative nature of the cyclical variation of $r-y$ discussed in the text is not changed by the use of variable weights.

[a] All months except Oct. 1966 and Mar. 1967 are turning-points of American business cycles as selected by the National Bureau of Economic Research. The 1966–7 'mini-recession' has been added.
Sources and descriptions of the data are contained in the Appendix.

appear to cause securities to become more attractive relative to loans as bank investments. Yet bank holdings of securities relative to loans decrease during expansions. Conversely, during recessions, bank holdings of loans relative to securities decrease at the same time that rates of return on loans are rising relative to yields on securities.

   These phenomena cannot be called paradoxical because there exist several more-or-less plausible explanations of the data. One of these explanations is based on the assumption that 'banks play a fairly passive role in the lending process', i.e. that 'the initiative in the bank-loan market lies with the borrower, not with the banks'[1] (Galbraith, 1963, p. 20). Another explanation takes into account the fact that the observed rates r and y are not likely to be equal to expected rates of return on loans and securities, which we may denote as $\bar{r}$ and $\bar{y}$. If the riskiness of loans as evaluated by bankers is inversely related to the level of economic activity, then observed variations in contract loan rates understate the variability of expected rates of return on loans. Furthermore, if bankers expect recent changes in security yields to continue in the same direction in the future, then the variability of $\bar{y}$ is less than that of y. Consequently, it is possible that the rate differential $\bar{r}-\bar{y}$ moves in the same direction as economic activity and as bank loans as a proportion of total earning assets. On the other hand, if bankers formulate interest-rate expectations in such a way that movements away from a 'normal' rate are expected to be reversed, then observed cyclical variations in y understate those in $\bar{y}$.

An alternative explanation of the data in Table IV.24 may be described as follows. If, at times of increases in economic activity and upward pressures on interest rates, bank asset preferences tend to change in such a way that their loan demand shifts upward at the expense of their demand for securities, we may observe loan rates rising less than security yields simultaneously with increases in bank loans relative to bank security holdings. Such a rationalization of the data, if it is to be complete, must include an explanation of why bank asset demands shift in such a cyclical manner. The theory of commercial bank behaviour developed below may be viewed as an attempt at such an explanation. A theory is presented that takes as its point of departure the bank–customer relationship introduced to the literature on banking theory and practice by Donald R. Hodgman (1961, 1963). The objective is to determine whether the empirical regularities shown in Table IV.24 can be explained within the framework of a dynamic model of commercial bank asset choice that is built upon the customer relationship.

A model of individual bank behaviour is developed in Parts II–IV. This model is based upon two related observations regarding differences between the markets for loans and securities as viewed

---

[1] Galbraith is here summarizing a view put forth in detail by Schumpeter (1939), pp. 641–3. A special case of this passive or accommodating approach to bank lending is the 'real bills doctrine'. For a comparison of the empirical implications of 'accommodation' and 'profit-maximizing' theories of bank behaviour, see Andersen and Burger (1969).

by a bank: (i) The bank is a perfect competitor in the securities market but an imperfect competitor in the market for bank loans; (ii) Owing to the nature of the bank–customer relationship, the loan demand confronting a bank currently is dependent not only upon current loan rates but also upon the quantities of loans extended by the bank in earlier periods. This is not true of the securities market—current yields on securities are independent of the individual bank's past investment in securities. As a consequence, in choosing its loan/security portfolio, the profit-maximizing bank takes into account not only current loan demand but also the influence of current loans extended on future loan demand. A further dynamic consideration concerns deposits. If the bank pursues a liberal loan policy currently, the result is an increase in the future supply of deposits as well as in the future demand for loans. The principal implication of these dynamic loan and deposit aspects of the customer relationship is that banks raise loan rates less and increase the quantity of loans more during periods of economic expansion than would be the case in the absence of the customer relationship.[2]

In Parts II–IV, quantitative significance is attached to the dynamic characteristics of the customer relationship in order to derive the conditions under which the customer relationship is by itself sufficient to explain the data in Table IV.24. Part V is concerned with aggregation and estimation. The demands by the non-bank public for loans and deposits of individual banks are summed and the parameters of the resulting aggregate demands are estimated. The implications of these estimates for our theory of bank behaviour are discussed in Part VI.

[2] No mention has been made of 'credit rationing' or the 'availability doctrine' as possible explanations of cyclical variations in commercial bank portfolios. To the extent that the literature discussing these concepts has had anything to say about bank choices between loans and securities in the aggregate, it has been in connection with attempts to explain phenomena that are the reverse of those illustrated in Table IV.24; i.e. explanations of why banks might wish to move out of loans into securities during periods of rising interest rates. For a review of this literature, see Kane and Malkiel (1965). Neither is the 'lock-in effect' discussed because it too is an explanation of phenomena that have not in fact been observed in the period since World War II; viz. why banks are reluctant to sell securities during periods of rising interest rates. If credit rationing or the lock-in effect have been factors affecting bank choices between loans and securities, it is apparent from the data that they have been dominated by other forces. For discussions of the lock-in effect, see Chase (1962) and Kane and Malkiel (1965).

II. Dynamic loan demand: the loan–customer relationship

II.1. Introduction and assumptions

This Part begins the development of a micro-economic model of commercial bank portfolio selection in a regime in which the individual bank's behaviour today influences its ability to earn profits tomorrow. Specifically, the current accommodation of prospective borrowers induces some of those customers to maintain recurrent or continuing loan and/or deposit relations with the bank. Hodgman and others have emphasized the intertemporal relationship between current loans and future deposits. We shall consider that aspect of the bank's operations (i.e. the dynamic deposit relation) in Part III. The discussion will initially be devoted exclusively to the intertemporal loan relationship.

The model presented below is exceedingly simple within any single period. All of the complications are of an intertemporal nature. The following simplifying assumptions are made: (a) The sole objective of the bank is profit maximization. (b) We abstract from all problems associated with risk and uncertainty. (c) Only two earning assets are available to the bank—homogeneous one-period securities and homogeneous one-period loans. No distinction is drawn between bond, bill, certificate, and note obligations of the U.S. and state and local governments or between the various types of loans to different classes of borrowers. (d) The only variable dimension of loans and securities is the rate of return net of costs and taxes, where the costs of making loans and investing in securities are assumed to be proportional to the dollar values of loans extended and securities purchased. (e) The individual bank is a price-taker in the securities market but an imperfect competitor in the market for loans. (f) The bank holds no excess reserves. Nor does it borrow from the Federal Reserve or from other banks. These assumptions will be relaxed in Part IV. (g) The bank is small relative to its marketing area, so that it expects to lose all of the deposits that it creates in connection with loans. Security purchases and loans deplete the bank's reserves in the same fashion. (h) We abstract until Part IV from the effects on our bank of rates charged and loans extended by other banks. (i) All items on the liability side of the bank's balance sheet are fixed. Deposits are homogeneous. Costs of servicing deposits plus interest on deposits equals service charges, so that net revenue from deposits is zero. There is no retention of profits, so that the bank's capital is fixed. Deposit variation is introduced in Part III. (j) Consistent with the assumption of one-period assets and the additional assumption of rapid receipt, processing and application of new information, we assume that the allocation of the bank's portfolio between loans and securities is optimal in each period. There is no stock-adjustment process.

II.2. The one-period model

Under the assumptions set out above, profit maximization means the maximization of total net revenue from securities and loans. Consider for a moment the one-period case, which results either from the assumption that the bank cares nothing about the future or that its current behaviour has no effect on the constraints that it will face in the future. Under these conditions, the bank maximizes profit when it sets its loan rate such that loans are extended to the point at which marginal returns from loans and securities are equal. This occurs at r_1^0 and l_1^0 in Fig. IV.5a, where l_1 denotes loans as a proportion of total earning assets. The optimal proportion of securities in the portfolio under these conditions is $g_1^0 = 1 - l_1^0$. It is conceivable that the loan marginal revenue curve $L_1 M_1$ might either (i) intersect y at a point $l > 1$, in which case the optimal portfolio would be $l^0 = 1$, or (ii) intercept the vertical axis at a point below y, in which case the optimal portfolio would be $g^0 = 1$. We will assume throughout this study that neither of these corner solutions occurs. The bank's portfolio is always diversified between loans and securities.

II.3. The multi-period model

It is well known that 'the majority of business loans, although nominally of short maturities, have been converted into longer-term credit in effect through the practice of continuous renewals' (Federal Reserve Bank of Cleveland, 1956, pp. 99–100). This observation, along with the results of Hodgman's survey, discussed in Part III below and the frequent discussions of the importance of the customer relationship by bankers, suggests that the current extension of credit to prospective borrowers may exert an impact on the future demand for funds from the bank; the more loans that a bank extends in the current period, the greater will be the demand for credit facing the bank in the future. This effect is more pronounced the greater are search costs and other costs to borrowers of transferring business from one bank to another. We have thus introduced the second distinction, from the bank's viewpoint, between loan and security investments—the loan–customer relation. Not only is there an inverse relation between loan volume and the loan rate in the current period, the current quantity of loans extended influences the strength of future loan demand. Neither of these characteristics applies to the bank's operations in securities. The profitability of future transactions in securities is not affected by the failure of the bank to buy another bond today. However, by a decision not to accommodate a prospective private borrower, the bank not only forgoes the revenue from that loan, the disappointed borrower may take his business elsewhere in future periods.

The loan–customer relation works both ways. Firms maintain a continuing relationship with the bank, at times even borrowing more than an optimal amount from the short-run standpoint of the firm, with a view toward accommodation in the future, particularly in times of credit stringency. Banks are also interested in a continuing relationship and will at times extend loans beyond that amount consistent with the maximization of current profit. This latter point, the bank's side of the loan–customer relation, is the subject of this study.

Assume that the bank desires to maximize the sum of discounted profits, where β is the discount factor $(0 \leq \beta \leq 1)$ and all variables are expressed as proportions of the sum of earning assets.[3] The profit equation is

$$\pi = \sum_{t=1}^{T} \beta^{t-1}(r_t l_t + y_t g_t), \tag{1}$$

where the bank's horizon is T periods and

$l_t, g_t =$ loans and securities, respectively, in the bank's portfolio in the tth period as proportions of total loans and securities $(t = 1, 2, \ldots, T)$.

$r_t, y_t =$ rates of return in the tth period on loans and securities, respectively.

Given that the bank's deposits, reserve ratio, and capital (and therefore earning assets) are fixed—assumptions (f)–(i)—the balance-sheet restraint is unchanged over time:

$$l_t + g_t = 1 \quad (t = 1, 2, \ldots, T). \tag{2}$$

[3] β will depend upon rates of return on investments alternative to those on bank capital and may be regarded as an independent variable from the standpoint of the bank. A fixed β will be assumed throughout the study even when other dependent and independent variables are permitted to vary over time in order to preserve the quadratic form of the objective function and therefore the simplicity of the results.

The argument at the beginning of this section suggests that the loan demand confronting the bank in the tth period may be written as follows:

$$l_t = l(r_t, y_t, z_t, l_{t-1}, l_{t-2}, \ldots, l_{t-n}) \quad (t = 1, 2, \ldots, T') \quad (3)$$

where it is assumed that current loans influence future loan demands over n periods. An index of economic activity, z_t, is assumed to be an indicator of the strength of loan demand. Current and future economic activity are assumed to be unaffected by the policies of the individual bank; i.e. z_t is exogenous to the bank. Loan demand in the tth period is negatively related to the loan rate, r_t, and positively related to the security rate, y_t, in that period. The higher is y_t, the less likely it is that those requiring funds will sell securities in order to raise the needed money and the more likely it is that they will ask for loans. As pointed out in assumption (e), y_t is also exogenous to the bank.

First consider the two-period case ($T = n = 2$). The bank will select r_t, l_t, and g_t for $t = 1, 2$ in such a way as to maximize the objective function (1) subject to the balance-sheet and market restraints (2) and (3). This maximization procedure yields the following marginal conditions:

$$\left(r_1 + \frac{l_1}{\partial l_1 / \partial r_1}\right) - \frac{\beta l_2}{\partial l_2 / \partial r_2} \frac{\partial l_2}{\partial l_1} = y_1, \quad (4)$$

$$r_2 + \frac{l_2}{\partial l_2 / \partial r_2} = y_2. \quad (5)$$

The left-hand side of (5) is marginal revenue from loans in the second period. Since y_2 is marginal revenue from second-period security purchases, equation (5) indicates that the bank plans to extend loans in the second period (select r_2) such that marginal returns from loans and securities will be equalized. Since, in the present example, the bank's horizon ends with the second period, there are no additional factors influencing the bank's decision.

But we see from equation (4) that, where $\partial l_2 / \partial r_2 < 0$ and $\partial l_2 / \partial l_1 > 0$ so that the term outside the parentheses on the left-hand side of (4) is positive, the bank maximizes profit by arranging its first-period portfolio such that first-period marginal revenue from loans (the term in parentheses in (4)) is less than that from bonds (y_1). That is, the bank extends more loans in the first-period than would be the case if it considered only first-period profit. It does this because, by thus expanding loans, it induces an increase in loan demand and therefore profit in the second period. The greater is the strength of the loan-customer relationship, $\partial l_2 / \partial l_1$, the greater is the present value of a dollar's worth of second-period profits, β, and the more inelastic is second-period loan demand for given r_2,[4] the more incentive does the bank have to extend loans beyond the single-period optimum.

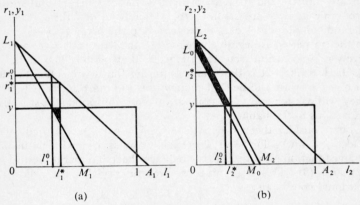

(a)   (b)

FIG. IV.5. Bank Portfolios in the Two-Period Case

The parameters underlying these Figures are, where $z_1 = z_2$ is included in the constant term of the loan demand function and we abstract from the influence of y_t on loan demand:

$$l_t = 1 - 10r_t + 0.2l_{t-1}; \qquad y_1 = y_2 = y = 0.05; \qquad l_0 = 0.5; \qquad \beta = 1.$$

The solutions are approximately (r_2^0 is not shown):

$$l_1^0 = 0.300; \qquad l_2^0 = 0.280; \qquad r_1^0 = 0.0800; \qquad r_2^0 = 0.0780$$
$$l_1^* = 0.328; \qquad l_2^* = 0.282; \qquad r_1^* = 0.0772; \qquad r_2^* = 0.0783$$

These results are illustrated in Fig. IV.5. L_1A_1 is the loan demand confronting the bank in the first period and L_1M_1 is the corresponding marginal revenue curve. The marginal revenue (=average revenue) from security purchases is perfectly elastic at y ($=y_1 = y_2$), where for simplicity it is assumed that the bank expects the bond

[4] The increased loan demand in period two induces an increase in r_2. The less elastic (in absolute value) is second-period loan demand, $(\partial l_2 / \partial r_2)(r_2 / l_2)$; the greater will be the addition to second-period revenue resulting from the increase in r_2. The effect of l_1 on second-period revenue is due partly to the shift in l_2 due to $\partial l_2 / \partial l_1$ and partly to the movement along the new demand curve due to the rise in r_2.

rate in the second period to be equal to the rate currently prevailing. It is also assumed that the bank expects $z_1 = z_2$.

If the bank were interested only in first-period profit ($\beta = 0$) or if future loan demand were independent of current loans extended ($\partial l_2 / \partial l_1 = 0$) the bank would set a loan rate r_1^0 and extend a quantity of loans l_1^0 (as a proportion of its earning assets) at which the marginal revenue from loans equals that from securities. But, as seen from equation (4), when dynamic considerations are introduced the bank increases loans beyond l_1^0. In Fig. IV.5, maximization of the sum of discounted profits implies a first-period loan rate $r_1^* < r_1^0$ and first-period loans of $l_1^* > l_1^0$. This increase in loans in the amount $l_1^* - l_1^0$ reduces first-period profit below the maximum attainable by the amount indicated by the shaded area in Fig. IV.5a. The number 1 on the horizontal axis indicates the maximum possible value of l_t as a proportion of the bank's investment fund. Thus, $1 - l_1^* = g_1^*$ is the optimal first-period investment in securities.

The loan demand facing the bank in the second period is $L_2 A_2$ and the corresponding marginal revenue curve is $L_2 M_2$. If the bank had maximized first-period profit by setting $r_1 = r_1^0$ and $l_1 = l_1^0$, second-period marginal revenue would have been $L_0 M_0$ ($L_0 A_0$ is not shown). The increment in second-period profit resulting from the bank's policy of setting l_1 at l_1^* rather than l_1^0 is indicated by the shaded area in Fig. IV.5b. The increment in revenue from second-period loans is the shaded area plus the rectangle with height $0y$ and base $l_2^0 l_2^*$. Since the introduction of the dynamic element into loan demand has reduced optimal g_2 from $1 - l_2^0$ to $1 - l_2^*$, the decrease in second-period revenue from securities is measured by this same rectangle.[5]

Equation (4) indicates that the extent to which the bank is able to increase total profit by reducing first-order profit depends upon, among other factors, the discount factor β and the strength of the dynamic relation, $\partial l_2 / \partial l_1$. If these factors are sufficiently strong, it will pay the bank to put all of its funds into loans; we will have a corner solution at $l_1^* = 1$. On the other hand, if $\partial l_2 / \partial l_1$ were negative and large in absolute value, we would obtain a corner solution at $l_1^* = 0$. Thus, if the first-order conditions (4) and (5) are to be consistent with a maximum, β and $\partial l_2 / \partial l_1$ must not be overly large in absolute value. It will be seen in the linear two-period case that

---

[5] The second-period revenue pertinent to the bank's decision is that shown in Fig. IV.5b times the discount factor β.

an interior maximum requires $\beta(\partial l_2/\partial l_1)^2 < 4$. This is a necessary but not a sufficient condition for an interior maximum; the bank might also have an undiversified portfolio for either very strong or very weak demand functions even if $\partial l_2/\partial l_1$ and β satisfy the above restriction. As indicated in section II.2, we will consider in this study only those demand functions that yield interior solutions; i.e. we will assume the inequality restraints $0 < l_t, g_t < 1$ always to be satisfied.

It will be remembered from the discussion in Part I that the motivation of this study was the desire to explain movements over the business cycle of loans as a proportion of bank earning assets, l_t, in relation to the differential between loan and security rates, $r_t - y_t$. On the basis of the groundwork developed above, we are now able to bring the model to bear on this problem. Linear loan demands will be used for reasons of simplicity. The loan demand function (3) is written in linear form as follows:

$$l_t = a - br_t + cz_t + uy_t + \gamma \sum_{i=1}^{n} d^i l_{t-i} \quad (t = 1, 2, \ldots, T) \quad (6)$$

where $b, c, u, \gamma, d \geq 0$. It would be difficult to reconcile this function with any kind of reasonable behaviour for d greater than unity. And we shall see below that the second-order conditions for a maximum for $T > 2$ require in most circumstances that $d < 1$. A dynamic loan relation in the form of a distributed lag with geometrically declining weights $(0 \leq d < 1)$ has been used partly because the calculation and interpretation of results is simplest for this type of lag distribution. Such a lag form has also been used because it seems reasonable to suppose that the loan–customer relation is strongest for those customers that have most recently transacted business with the bank.

In order to be able to ascertain the bank's responses (i.e. responses of l_1 and r_1) to variations in current economic activity, z_1, we must determine the process by which the bank formulates its expectations of future events. Specifically, we must state the manner in which the bank revises its expectations of future levels of economic activity and returns on securities in response to observed changes in current economic activity. Let us assume that the bank expects the one-period rate of return on securities and the level of economic activity to be linearly related over time such that

$$\frac{\partial y_t}{\partial z_t} = f \quad (t = 1, 2, \ldots). \quad (7)$$

Our model allows us to examine variations in l_t, r_t, and g_t in response to variations in z_t and y_t separately. But the model equally permits the analysis of bank responses to joint movements in y_t and z_t—once account is taken of the fact that movements in y_t and z_t tend to be closely related over time.

Let us further assume, following a procedure used by Metzler (1941) and Enthoven (1956), that the bank revises its expectations of future economic activity in response to observed changes as follows:

$$z_{t+1} = z_t + w(z_t - z_{t-1}) \quad (t = 1, 2, \ldots). \tag{8}$$

Letting the current period be $t = 1$ and deriving expected z_t from (8) by extrapolation gives

$$z_t = \left(\frac{1 - w^t}{1 - w}\right) z_1 - \left(\frac{w - w^t}{1 - w}\right) z_0 \tag{9}$$

Hence, $\qquad\qquad\qquad\qquad (0 \le w < 1; t = 1, 2, \ldots).$

$$\frac{\partial z_t}{\partial z_1} = \frac{1 - w^t}{1 - w} \tag{10}$$

It must be emphasized that (7) and (10) are merely empirical regularities that the bank's decision-makers expect to occur over time and imply nothing about causation.

Under the conditions set forth in (6), (7), and (10), the response of the profit-maximizing bank to an increase in current economic activity, z_1, and hence loan demand, will be as follows: First, in the absence of dynamic elements (γd and/or β equal to zero), there will be increases in current loan and security rates, r_1 and y_1, and in bank loans as a proportion of total earning assets, l_1. For purposes of this discussion, let the initial values of these variables be r_1', y_1', and l_1' and let the levels of these variables after the increase in z_1 but before the introduction of dynamic considerations be $r_1'' > r_1'$, $y_1'' > y_1'$, $l_1'' > l_1'$. When future profits and the dynamic aspects of loan demand are considered, the bank has additional reason to increase l_1. What has happened is that, at every loan rate, there is an increased demand for the bank's funds. The bank is faced with a rise in the number of prospective customers. The greater are γ, d, and β, the more incentive will the bank have to accommodate not only the increased number of borrowers at the loan rate, r_1'', but also those who would like to borrow at rates lower than r_1''. Consequently, the bank will set its loan rate at $r_1''' < r_1''$ in the expectation of extending a quantity of loans equal to $l_1''' > l_1''$. The greater are γ, d, and β, the smaller will be r_1'''. It may even happen that the increase in r_1 from its initial position, $r_1''' - r_1'$, will be less than the increase in the rate on securities, $y_1'' - y_1'$. If this is the case, we will see a shift by the bank out of securities into loans at the same time that the rate of return on loans declines relatively to that on securities.

The effects of variations in economic activity on relative rates and the bank's portfolio described above may occur even in the presence of 'static' expectations $(w = 0)$; i.e. where induced expectations are zero and the existing z is expected to persist. But if the bank's expectations are 'extrapolative' $(w > 0)$, the bank has further reason to hold r_1 at a relatively low level in order to increase l_1.

Now let us examine more closely the bank's response to economic activity in the linear two-period case. The purpose is to determine those values of γ, d, β, and w that are consistent with alternative patterns of commercial bank loan-rate and portfolio behaviour. The following calculations are performed: First maximize (1) subject to (2) and (6) with respect to l_t, r_t, g_t $(t = 1, 2)$; then solve for the optimal values of the bank's decision variables—l_t^*, r_t^*, g_t^*; substitute (7) and (10) into this solution and differentiate with respect to z_1. As in any intertemporal model, while current decisions and future plans (portfolios) are simultaneously determined in such a way as to maximize the objective function, only current decision variables (l_1^*, r_1^*, g_1^*) are sure of being implemented. Future portfolios and loan rates may or may not assume the values chosen in the first (current) period, depending upon whether or not the bank's expectations are fulfilled. The decision process is repeated each period, based upon new information and revised expectations. The portfolio that is implemented in any period is always that which corresponds to period $t = 1$.

The results are as follows, where the derivative of g_1^* is not shown because it is simply $\partial g_1^*/\partial z_1 = -\partial l_1^*/\partial z_1$:

$$\frac{\partial l_1^*}{\partial z_1} = \frac{(c + uf - bf)}{2} \frac{\{4 + 2\gamma d\beta(1 + w)\}}{\{4 - (\gamma d)^2\beta\}} \tag{11}$$

$$\frac{\partial r_1^*}{\partial z_1} = \frac{(c + uf)\{2 - (\gamma d)^2\beta - \gamma d\beta(1 + w)\} + bf\{2 + \gamma d\beta(1 + w)\}}{b\{4 - (\gamma d)^2\beta\}}. \tag{12}$$

But we are interested not so much in variations in r_1^* as in variations in r_1^* relative to y_1. From (7) and (12) we have

$$\frac{\partial r_1^*}{\partial z_1} - \frac{\partial y_1}{\partial z_1} = \frac{\partial r_1^*}{\partial z_1} - f$$

$$= \frac{(c + uf - bf)}{2b} \frac{\{4 - 2(\gamma d)^2\beta - 2\gamma d\beta(1 + w)\}}{\{4 - (\gamma d)^2\beta\}}. \quad (13)$$

The second-order conditions for a profit maximum are
$$b, \{4 - (\gamma d)^2\beta\} > 0. \quad (14)$$
The condition $\{4 - (\gamma d)^2\beta\} > 0$ was discussed above. The condition $b > 0$ requires that the loan demand function be downward sloping.

The term $c + uf - bf$ is positive if the shift in the marginal revenue curve for loans in period t as the result of a movement in z_t exceeds the shift in marginal revenue from securities in period t.[6] It will be assumed for purposes of discussion that $c + uf - bf$ is in fact positive; empirical support for this assumption will be given in Part V.

The second of each of the terms on the right-hand sides of (11) and (13) indicate the strength of the customer relationship. Both are equal to unity when γd or β is zero: we have the one-period result in such a case and $\partial l_1^*/\partial z_1$ and $\partial(r_1^* - y_1)/\partial z_1$ are of the same sign. The model is not capable of explaining the data in Table IV.24 in the one-period case. When we introduce γ, d, and β, parameters measuring the strength of the customer relationship and the present value of second-period profit, the responses of l_1^* and $r_1^* - y_1$ to variations in z_1 are respectively increased and reduced. These responses are more pronounced the greater are γ, d, β, and w. Assuming the sufficient conditions for a maximum to be satisfied and $(c + uf - bf) > 0$, then $\partial l_1^*/\partial z_1 > 0$ for all γ, d, β, $w \geq 0$ and

$$\frac{\partial r_1^*}{\partial z_1} - \frac{\partial y_1}{\partial z_1} \gtreqless 0 \quad \text{as} \quad \{2 - (\gamma d)^2\beta - \gamma d\beta(1 + w)\} \gtreqless 0. \quad (15)$$

In the simple case in which $\beta = 1$ and $w = 0$, (15) exceeds, equals, or is less than zero as γd is less than, equal to, or greater than unity. That is, for $(\beta, w) = (1, 0)$, our two-period model of intertemporal loan demand and profit maximization is able to explain the data in Table IV.24 for $1 < \gamma d < 2$. If, taking another example, $(\beta, w) = (0.9, 0.5)$, the two-period model is consistent

[6] For given l_t and g_t, the effects of a change in z_t on the marginal revenues from loans and securities are $(c + uf)/b$ and f, respectively.

with the data for (approximately) $0·92 < \gamma d < 2·11$. Other combinations of d, β, and w (assuming $\gamma = 1$) such that $\partial(r_1^* - y_1)/\partial z_1 \leq 0$ may be seen in Table IV.25.

Let us compare the above results with those of the three-period case when $\gamma = 1$. When $T = n = 3$, for (γ, β, w) first equal to $(1, 1, 0)$ and then $(1, 0·9, 0·5)$, $\partial(r_1^* - y_1)/\partial z_1 < 0$ and the second-order conditions are satisfied first for (approximately) $0·60 < d < 1$ and then for $0·55 < d < 1·05$. Further comparisons may be seen in Table IV.25.

If we let the bank's horizon approach an infinite length and assume that current loans influence future loan demands over an infinitely long duration ($n = T \to \infty$), the following results are obtained:[7]

$$\frac{\partial l_1^*}{\partial z_1} \to \frac{(c + uf - bf)}{2} \frac{2\{(1 + v)(1 - d\beta w) - d\beta V_1'\}}{\rho V_1 V_1'} \tag{16}$$

$$\frac{\partial r_1^*}{\partial z_1} - \frac{\partial y_1}{\partial z_1} \to \frac{(c + uf - bf)}{2b}$$

$$\times \frac{2(V_1''[(1 + v)\{1 - (1 + \gamma)d\beta w\} - (1 + \gamma)d\beta V_1'] - (1 + \gamma)\gamma d^2\beta V_1 V_1')}{\rho V_1 V_1'\{1 + v + 2x(1 + \gamma)d\beta^{1/2}\}} \tag{17}$$

as $T \to \infty$, where

$$V_1 = (1 + v + 2x\beta^{1/2}); \qquad V_1' = (1 + v + 2xw\beta^{1/2});$$
$$V_1'' = (1 + v + 2xd\beta^{1/2}); \qquad \rho = \{1 + (1 + \gamma)d^2\beta\};$$
$$x = -(2 + \gamma)d\beta^{1/2}/2\rho; \qquad v = (1 - 4x^2)^{1/2}.$$

The second-order conditions for a profit maximum require that, continuing to consider only non-negative values of γ, d, and β,

$$b, \{1 - (1 + \gamma)d\beta^{1/2}\} > 0. \tag{18}$$

No new assumptions are required for the infinite-horizon case to have finite limits. The finiteness of (16) and (17) follows from (i) the geometrically declining weights of the loan demand function, (ii) $0 \leq w < 1$, and (iii) the satisfaction of (18). This last condition implies that $(1 - 4x^2) > 0$, so that (16) and (17) contain no complex numbers.

For (γ, β, w) first equal to $(1, 1, 0)$ and then $(1, 0·9, 0·5)$, $\partial(r_1^* - y_1)/\partial z_1 < 0$ and the second-order conditions are satisfied

---

[7] The results of the models presented in Parts II–IV of this paper are derived for the general (T-period) and infinite-horizon ($T \to \infty$) cases in a forthcoming monograph.

as $T \to \infty$ first for (approximately) $0.43 < d < 0.50$ and then for $0.41 < d < 0.53$. In comparing the results of the two-, three-, and infinite-horizon cases, it is seen that, for given γ, β, and w, the values of d that (i) enable the model to explain the data and (ii) are consistent with the second-order conditions are inversely related to the length of the bank's horizon. This is because the more future periods for which (i) profits enter the objective function and (ii) current loans influence future loan demand the more reason will the bank have to accommodate increases in current loan demand. A liberal lending response currently, though it may not be conducive to short-term profit maximization, will induce repercussions favourable for bank profits in the near and distant future, these repercussions being stronger or weaker as γ, d, and w are large or small and being more or less important to the bank as β is large or small.

Further examples of the implications of our model of intertemporal loan demand are listed in Table IV.25. This Table illustrates the strength of the impact of the loan–customer relationship on the responsiveness of commercial bank portfolio and interest-rate policies to variations in economic activity. The importance of the customer relationship is best expressed in terms of the magnitudes of L_T and R_T $(T = 1, 2, \ldots)$ where, for example, L_T $(T = 2, \infty)$ represents the second of the two terms on the right-hand sides of (11) and (16) and R_T $(T = 2, \infty)$ represents the analogous terms in (13) and (17). Thus our results may be expressed as follows:

$$\frac{\partial l_1^*}{\partial z_1} = \frac{(c + uf - bf)}{2} L_T \tag{19}$$

$$(T = 1, 2, \ldots).$$

$$\frac{\partial r_y^*}{\partial z_1} - \frac{\partial y_1}{\partial z_1} = \frac{(c + uf - bf)}{2b} R_T \tag{20}$$

All of the dynamic or intertemporal properties of the model are incorporated in L_T and R_T, which are both equal to unity for γ, d, and/or β equal to zero and/or $T = 1$. L_T is a monotonically increasing function and R_T is a monotonically decreasing function of γ, d, β, and T provided that γ, d, $\beta > 0$, and $T > 1$. Table IV.25 shows values of R_T for $\gamma = 1$ and selected values of d, β, and w for $T = 2, 3, \infty$. L_T is not shown because $L_T + R_T = 2$ in all cases.

The results shown in Table IV.25 illustrate the fact that it is at least conceptually possible to test within the framework of the model developed in the preceding pages the hypothesis that the loan–customer relationship is sufficient to explain those aspects of

TABLE IV.25

Impact of the Loan–Customer Relationship on $\partial(r_1^* - y_1)/\partial z_1$ for various β, w, d ($\gamma = 1$)

d	$\beta = 0.5;\ w = 0$			$\beta = 0.5;\ w = 0.5$			$\beta = 0.5;\ w = 0.9$		
	R_2	R_3	R_∞	R_2	R_3	R_∞	R_2	R_3	R_∞
0	1·0000	1·0000	1·0000	1·0000	1·0000	1·0000	1·0000	1·0000	1·0000
0·1	0·9737	0·9717	0·9716	0·9612	0·9578	0·9575	0·9512	0·9459	0·9453
0·2	0·9447	0·9361	0·9346	0·9196	0·9050	0·9021	0·8995	0·8773	0·8720
0·3	0·9128	0·8916	0·8852	0·8748	0·8394	0·8276	0·8445	0·7914	0·7696
0·4	0·8776	0·8357	0·8156	0·8265	0·7578	0·7216	0·7857	0·6843	0·6175
0·5	0·8387	0·7647	0·7085	0·7742	0·6555	0·5560	0·7226	0·5499	0·3674
0·6	0·7958	0·6731	0·5093	0·7173	0·5250	0·2424	0·6544	0·3793	−0·1392
0·7	0·7483	0·5551	−0·3095	0·6551	0·3549	−1·1024	0·5806	0·1581	−2·6340
0·8	0·6957	0·3874	...	0·5870	0·1263	...	0·5000	−0·1374	...
0·9	0·6370	0·1534	...	0·5118	−0·1948	...	0·4117	−0·5499	...
1·0	0·5714	−0·2000	...	0·4286	−0·6750	...	0·3143	−1·1630	...

d	$\beta = 0.9;\ w = 0$			$\beta = 0.9;\ w = 0.5$			$\beta = 0.9;\ w = 0.9$		
	R_2	R_3	R_∞	R_2	R_3	R_∞	R_2	R_3	R_∞
0	1·0000	1·0000	1·0000	1·0000	1·0000	1·0000	1·0000	1·0000	1·0000
0·1	0·9526	0·9462	0·9452	0·9301	0·9189	0·9170	0·9121	0·8949	0·8914
0·2	0·9001	0·8720	0·8614	0·8547	0·8068	0·7869	0·8184	0·7457	0·7080
0·3	0·8415	0·7713	0·7195	0·7726	0·6550	0·5586	0·7175	0·5413	0·3531
0·4	0·7759	0·6333	0·4206	0·6826	0·4487	0·0557	0·6079	0·2629	−0·5453
0·5	0·7020	0·4389	−0·9071	0·5828	0·1617	−2·3427	0·4874	−0·1236	−6·2091
0·6	0·6181	0·1522	...	0·4712	−0·2563	...	0·3536	−0·6833	...
0·7	0·5221	−0·3039	...	0·3450	−0·9129	...	0·2034	−1·5572	...
0·8	0·4112	−1·1284	...	0·2009	−2·0869	...	0·0327	−3·1100	...
0·9	0·2819	−3·0366	...	0·0342	−4·7819	...	−0·1639	−6·6572	...
1·0	0·1290	−12·0345	...	−0·1613	−17·4267	...	−0·3935	−23·2487	...

d	$\beta = 0.98; w = 0$			$\beta = 0.98; w = 0.5$			$\beta = 0.98; w = 0.9$		
	R_2	R_3	R_∞	R_2	R_3	R_∞	R_2	R_3	R_∞
0	1·0000	1·0000	1·0000	1·0000	1·0000	1·0000	1·0000	1·0000	1·0000
0·1	0·9484	0·9408	0·9394	0·9239	0·9106	0·9081	0·9042	0·8839	0·8792
0·2	0·8911	0·8578	0·8436	0·8416	0·7847	0·7581	0·8021	0·7157	0·6647
0·3	0·8271	0·7434	0·6712	0·7520	0·6118	0·4770	0·6919	0·4819	0·2144
0·4	0·7552	0·5842	0·2585	0·6532	0·3729	−0·2329	0·5716	0·1582	−1·1358
0·5	0·6738	0·3553	−5·1384	0·5433	0·0337	−10·5568	0·4389	−0·3001	−34·6741
0·6	0·5808	0·0076	...	0·4196	−0·4750	...	0·2906	−0·9837	...
0·7	0·4738	−0·5725	...	0·2789	−1·3131	...	0·1230	−2·1027	...
0·8	0·3491	−1·7147	...	0·1167	−2·9465	...	−0·0693	−4·2708	...
0·9	0·2022	−4·9470	...	−0·0729	−7·5355	...	−0·2929	−10·3355	...
1·0	0·0265	−72·0057	...	−0·2980	−102·3836	...	−0·5576	−135·3874	...

d	$\beta = 1; w = 0$			$\beta = 1; w = 0.5$			$\beta = 1; w = 0.9$		
	R_2	R_3	R_∞	R_2	R_3	R_∞	R_2	R_3	R_∞
0	1·0000	1·0000	1·0000	1·0000	1·0000	1·0000	1·0000	1·0000	1·0000
0·1	0·9474	0·9394	0·9380	0·9223	0·9085	0·9058	0·9023	0·8810	0·8761
0·2	0·8889	0·8542	0·8389	0·8384	0·7791	0·7505	0·7980	0·7080	0·6532
0·3	0·8235	0·7363	0·6579	0·7468	0·6006	0·4544	0·6854	0·4665	0·1751
0·4	0·7500	0·5714	0·2087	0·6458	0·3532	−0·3226	0·5625	0·1310	−1·3289
0·5	0·6667	0·3333	...	0·5333	0·0	...	0·4267	−0·3467	...
0·6	0·5714	−0·0312	...	0·4066	−0·5338	...	0·2747	−1·0645	...
0·7	0·4615	−0·6471	...	0·2621	−1·4243	...	0·1026	−2·2544	...
0·8	0·3333	−1·8889	...	0·0952	−3·2020	...	−0·0952	−4·6162	...
0·9	0·1818	−5·6316	...	−0·1003	−8·5226	...	−0·3260	−11·6546	...
1·0	0·0	...	...	−0·3333	...	...	−0·6000	...	...

commercial bank behaviour depicted in Table IV.24, i.e. the joint occurrence of $\partial l_1^*/\partial z_1 > 0$ and $\partial(r_1^* - y_1)/\partial z_1 < 0$. Some empirical examinations of this hypothesis are presented in Part V. But we will first examine the implications of (i) another aspect of the customer relationship in Part III and (ii) interbank competition in Part IV.

III. Dynamic deposit supply: the deposit relationship

III.1. Introduction and assumptions

Few of the characteristics of the model presented in Part II are peculiar to commercial banks. That model has much wider applicability than merely to banks or even to financial institutions. It must be true of many imperfectly-competitive firms with multiperiod horizons that customer relationships exist such that future demands depend not only upon future prices and incomes but also upon current sales and, hence, current prices. However, while it may be common for demand for the future output of a firm to depend upon current output, it is probably less common for the future supply of inputs to the firm to be functionally related to current output. Yet, some writers have contended that such an intertemporal relationship between output demand and input supply is one of the most important distinguishing characteristics of commercial banks (Hodgman, 1961, 1963; Kane and Malkiel, 1965). In fact, the term 'customer relationship' as used by these authors as well as by bankers usually applies to the relationship over time of current loans to future deposits for a given bank customer. This loan–deposit connection is in the present study designated the 'deposit relationship' in order to distinguish it from the 'loan-customer relationship' discussed in Part II.

In his important book, Hodgman presents the results of a series of interviews with bankers. One of the questions asked by Hodgman was: 'What criteria do bankers apply in deciding whether or not to make a loan which has been requested?' (1963, p. 24). There are, of course, many criteria applied by bankers in the process of loan selection, but the 'criterion with highest priority is that of the deposit relationship'. The deposit relationship involves more than compensating balances, which 'has been interpreted simply as a device to secure a higher effective rate of interest on the specific loan'. The dominant consideration with respect to deposits in the evaluation of loan requests by banks is not 'the current ratio of deposit to loan'. Rather, banks want 'long-term deposit relationships'. The 'significance of the deposit criterion stems from the importance of deposits as the primary determinant of the individual bank's lending capacity' (pp. 24–5). In short, other characteristics of prospective borrowers being equal, the bank will select those loan applicants who are most likely to maintain long-term deposit relationships with the bank—deposit relationships extending beyond the maturities of loans and which cannot be guaranteed by compensating balance requirements.

As with the loan–customer relationship, the deposit relationship influences both bank and customer behaviour, though the former is emphasized in this study. Banks extend more loans, especially to commercial and industrial borrowers, than would otherwise be the case because of the possibility of developing long-term deposit relationships with these customers. In fact, in the absence of the deposit relationship and in terms of other important criteria for loan selection—net rate of return, risk, and liquidity—commercial and industrial loans would be far down the list of loans preferred by banks.[8] The other side of the deposit relationship is that firms keep more deposits with their banks than they would in the absence of the intertemporal relationship between deposits and the granting of loan requests by banks. By maintaining a sizeable deposit balance with its bank, a firm counts on being able to arrange in the future for loans at favourable rates and, more importantly, hopes to enjoy a preferred status during periods of tight money.

III.2. *The model*

Deposit variation will now be introduced within the framework of the model presented in Part II. As before, deposits are homogeneous and there is no net gain or loss accruing from service charges and interest costs on deposits. The bank is interested in deposits only as the source of loanable funds. We retain the profit equation (1) and the intertemporal loan demand function (3). However, the balance-sheet restraint (2) must now be replaced by one in which deposits are permitted to vary over time. Let the bank's balance sheet in period t be written as follows, where q_t denotes deposits of the individual bank in period t as a proportion of first-period earning assets, k is the required-reserve ratio on deposits, and κ is the bank's capital:

$$l_t + g_t = (1 - k)q_t + \kappa \quad (t = 1, 2, \ldots, T). \tag{21}$$

[8] Hodgman (1963, pp. 16–20, 24–5). See especially Table 1, p. 18.

We continue to abstract from excess reserves and bank borrowing from the Federal Reserve. We also retain the assumption that bank profits are paid to the owners as they accrue, so that κ is invariant over time. Since all dollar values are expressed as proportions of first-period earning assets, $l_1 + g_1 = 1$.

The supply of deposits to the bank depends upon its past loans, i.e. upon the degree to which it has satisfied and/or attracted prospective borrowers who have kept or would be willing to keep deposits with the bank because of the accommodation of their loan demands. Deposits in the individual bank will in addition be positively related to total deposits in the banking system, $q_t + q_t^0$, where q_t^0 denotes deposits in other banks as a proportion of the earning assets of our bank. In order to simplify the argument, we abstract from the direct effects of current deposits on future deposit supplies and loan demands; firms and households choose their depositories and lenders on the basis of convenience and service (assumed to be constant), loan rates, and the past accommodation of loan demands. The supply of deposits to the bank in the tth period may under the above assumptions be written as follows:

$$q_t = q(q_t + q_t^0, l_{t-1}, l_{t-2}, \ldots, l_{t-n}) \quad (t = 1, 2, \ldots, T). \quad (22)$$

Now assume that the Federal Reserve fixes total deposits in the banking system in response to economic activity with a one-period lag. This assumption implies that total deposits are independent of current income and interest rates even though the public's demand for deposits depends upon these variables. The Federal Reserve offsets the effects of current influences on the quantity of deposits in its efforts to fix deposits—a proximate objective—at that level which it considers conducive to the attainment of its ultimate objectives—always acting in response to events with a one-period lag. The aggregate supply of deposits may as a consequence be written as follows:[9]

$$q_t + q_t^0 = \sigma(z_{t-1}) \quad (t = 1, 2, \ldots). \quad (23)$$

Now let the bank maximize profits (1) subject to the market restraints (3) and (22), its balance-sheet restraint (21), and the

[9] This assumes a type of Federal Reserve behaviour similar to that in Wood (1967). It might be considered more reasonable to suppose that the Federal Reserve, instead of being concerned with levels, controls changes in deposits in response to lagged changes in economic activity. Such an assumption would not alter the results discussed below, the key requirement for our purposes being that current q is independent of current z.

Federal Reserve behavioural equation (23). The resulting marginal conditions may be written in the two-period case as follows:

$$\left(r_1 + \frac{l_1}{\partial l_1/\partial r_1}\right) - \frac{\beta l_2}{\partial l_2/\partial r_2}\frac{\partial l_2}{\partial l_1} + \beta(1 - k)y_2\frac{\partial q_2}{\partial l_1} = y_1. \quad (24)$$

$$r_2 + \frac{l_2}{\partial l_2/\partial r_2} = y_2. \quad (25)$$

Equation (25) is identical to (5). The decision in the second period is equivalent to the first-period decision discussed in Part II because the bank's horizon in the present example ends with the second period. Equation (24) differs from (4) by the addition of the last term on the left side of (24). This term is the present value of the added revenue from second-period security investments due to a marginal increase in first-period loans. The magnitude of this term is a measure of the effect of the intertemporal loan-deposit relationship on the bank's current behaviour. The greater is this term, the more incentive will the bank have to extend first-period loans beyond that point at which first-period profit would be maximized. The derivative $\partial q_2/\partial l_1$ is the increase in second-period deposits in response to an increase in first-period loans, $(1 - k)$ is the proportion of the deposit increase that is invested, y_2 is the rate of return on those investments and β is the factor by which second-period earnings are discounted.

The bank now has two reasons to extend loans beyond the single-period optimum—the loan–customer relationship and the deposit relationship, the magnitudes of which are measured by the second and third terms, respectively, on the left side of (24). The effects of these considerations on the bank's first-period decision are illustrated in Fig. IV.6a. The parameters underlying this Figure are identical to those upon which Fig. IV.5 is based except for the addition of a term in $\partial q_2/\partial l_1$. Note that the addition of the deposit relationship has induced an increase in first-period loans beyond the point at which the loan–customer relationship was the only dynamic element in the model; i.e. comparing Figs. IV.5a and IV.6a, we see that $l_1^{**} > l_1^* > l_1^0$ and $r_1^{**} < r_1^* < r_1^0$.

While our main concern is with the bank's first-period behaviour, the impact of that behaviour on the size and composition of its second-period portfolio is also of interest. This impact is illustrated in Fig. IV.6b. As in Fig. IV.5b, L_0M_0 denotes the second-period marginal revenue from loans that would have existed if the bank had maximized first-period profit by extending a quantity of first-period loans, l_1^0. The second-period marginal and average revenues that prevail as the result of the quantity of first-period loans l_1^{**} are $L_2'M_2'$ and $L_2'A_2'$ in Fig. IV.6b because $l_1^{**} > l_1^0$ as the result of the addition of the customer relationship. The net addition to second-period revenue resulting from the increased loan demand is

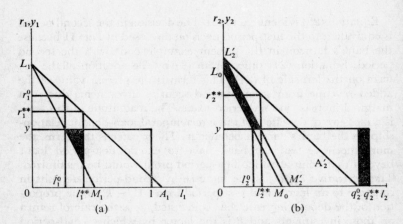

(a)   (b)

FIG. IV.6. Bank Portfolios in the Two-Period Case: the Deposit Relationship

The parameters underlying these Figures are, where we abstract from the influence of y_t on loan demand, $z_1 = z_2$ is included in the constant term of the loan demand function, $q_t + q_t^0$ is included in the constant term of the deposit supply equation, and $k = \kappa = 0$:

$$l_t = 1 - 10r_t + 0.2l_{t-1}; \qquad q_2 = 1 + 0.5l_1;$$
$$y_1 = y = \underline{y} = 0.05; \qquad l_0 = 0.5; \qquad \beta = 1.$$

The solutions are approximately (r_2^0 is not shown):

$$l_1^0 = 0.300; \quad l_2^0 = 0.280; \quad r_1^0 = 0.0800; \quad r_2^0 = 0.0780; \quad q_2^0 = 1.150$$
$$l_1^{**} = 0.455; \quad l_2^{**} = 0.295; \quad r_1^{**} = 0.0645; \quad r_2^{**} = 0.0795; \quad q_2^{**} = 1.2275$$

indicated by the shaded area between L_0M_0 and $L_2'M_2'$. There has also been an increase in deposits in the amount $q_2^{**} - q_2^0$ because $\partial q_2/\partial l_1 > 0$. The increase in second-period revenue due to this increase in deposits is equal to $(1 - k)$ times the increase in deposits times the rate of return on second-period securities, y_2.

Let us now examine the effects of variations in economic activity on first-period loans and interest rates. As in Part II, we linearize the model for reasons of simplicity. Thus we again utilize the linear loan demand and expectations equations—(6), (7), (10)—and rewrite (22) and (23) as follows:

$$q_t = a_1 + \alpha \sum_{i=1}^{n} h^i l_{t-i} + s(q_t + q_i^0) \qquad (26)$$
$$(t = 1, 2, \ldots, T)$$

$$q_t + q_i^0 = a_2 + \sigma z_{t-1} \qquad (27)$$

where h, $s \geq 0$ and no restrictions are placed on the signs of a_1, a_2, σ. As with γ and d in the intertemporal loan demand function (6), α and h together indicate both the strength of the impact of past actions on current conditions and the rapidity with which this impact declines in importance as the periods to which the weights apply recede into the past. It is reasonable to suppose that $0 < h < 1$, i.e. that the deposit relationship is strongest for those customers who have most recently obtained loans from the bank.

Again consider the two-period case, in which the bank maximizes the discounted sum of first- and second-period profits with respect to r_t, l_t, g_t, q_t ($t = 1, 2$)[10] subject to (6), (21), (26), and (27). Differentiating the solution with respect to z_1 and using (7) and (10), we obtain the following results:

$$\frac{\partial l_1^{**}}{\partial z_1}$$
$$= \frac{(c + uf - bf)\{4 + 2\gamma d\beta(1 + w)\} + 4bf(1 - k)\alpha h\beta(1 + w)}{2\{4 - (\gamma d)^2\beta\}}. \qquad (28)$$

$$\frac{\partial r_1^{**}}{\partial z_1} - \frac{\partial y_1}{\partial z_1}$$
$$= \frac{(c + uf - bf)\{4 - 2(\gamma d)^2\beta - 2\gamma d\beta(1 + w)\}}{2b\{4 - (\gamma d)^2\beta\}}. \qquad (29)$$

Two asterisks are used to indicate the optimal solutions corresponding to both the loan and deposit relationships as distinct from the solutions corresponding only to the loan relationship discussed in Part II. The second-order conditions for a maximum are the

[10] It is seen from (22) and (23) or (26) and (27) that q_1 is predetermined. Hence, we maximize with respect to q_t only for $t > 1$.

same as in Part II.[11] Comparing (28) and (29) with (11) and (13), we see that the deposit relationship gives the bank additional reason to increase loans by moderating the extent to which it increases its loan rate in response to an increase in current economic activity, z_1. The increase in l_1 in response to an increase in z_1 will be greater the greater is $\partial q_2/\partial l_1 = \alpha h$, the greater is the present value of a dollar's worth of second-period profits, β, the more is the second-period rate of return on bonds expected to increase in response to the current increase in economic activity, $f(1 + w)$, and the greater is the proportion of the increase in deposits that can be invested in securities, $(1 - k)$.

The ability of our model to explain the data in Table IV.24 is increased by the addition of the deposit relationship. Even if γ and d are small, sufficiently large values of α and h will induce movements in $r_1 - y_1$ that are inversely related to z_1. For example, in the special case in which $\gamma d = 0$, it is seen from (29) that

$$\frac{\partial r_1^{**}}{\partial z_1} - \frac{\partial y_1}{\partial z_1} \gtreqless 0 \quad \text{as} \quad (c + uf - bf) \gtreqless bf(1 - k)\alpha h\beta(1 + w). \quad (30)$$

Unlike the dynamic loan demand case ($\gamma d > 0$; $\alpha h = 0$), the selection of values of the dynamic parameters (α, h, β, w in this case) is not sufficient to determine the direction of the inequality (30). We must also obtain estimates of b, c, f, u, and k. These will be discussed in Parts V and VI.

Letting the bank's horizon become infinitely long and assuming that current loans influence future loan demands and deposit supplies over an infinitely long duration ($n = T \to \infty$), we obtain:

$$\frac{\partial l_1^{**}}{\partial z_1} \to \frac{(c + uf - bf)}{2} L_\infty$$

$$+ \frac{f(1 - k)\alpha h\beta[\{1 - d\beta(1 + w - h\beta w)\}V_1' + w(1 + v)(1 - h\beta)(1 - d\beta w)]}{\rho V_1 V_1'(1 - h\beta)(1 - h\beta w)} \quad (31)$$

[11] Unlike $\partial l_2/\partial l_1 = \gamma d$, $\partial q_2/\partial l_1 = \alpha h$ does not enter the second-order conditions. As seen in Figs. IV.5 and IV.6, equal increments in l_1 cause first-period profit π_1 to decline at an increasing rate. (This follows from the assumption of a linear loan demand.) And because of the upward influence of l_1 operating through γd on future optimal values of both l_t and r_t, increments in l_1 induce increases in future π_t at increasing rates. Hence the expression of the sufficient conditions for a finite profit maximum in terms of γd and β. However, increments in l_1 induce increases in future profits via the deposit relationship at a constant rate. Hence, if (14) is satisfied, a finite solution is obtained no matter what the value of αh provided only that β, $(1 - k)$, αh, and y_t ($t = 2, 3, \ldots$) are finite.

$$\frac{\partial r_1^{**}}{\partial z_1} - \frac{\partial y_1}{\partial z_1} \rightarrow \frac{(c + uf - bf)}{2b} R_\infty$$

$$- \frac{f(1 - k)\alpha h\beta[\{1 - d\beta(1 + w - h\beta w)\}V_1' + w(1 + v)(1 - h\beta)(1 - d\beta w)]}{\rho V_1 V_1'(1 - h\beta)(1 - h\beta w)} \quad (32)$$

as $T \rightarrow \infty$, where L_∞ and R_∞ were defined in connection with (19) and (20).

Given the satisfaction of the second-order conditions for a profit maximum and $0 \leq w < 1$, the only additional assumption needed to assure finite limits of (31) and (32) is $h\beta < 1$. Setting $d = 0$, we see that

$$\frac{\partial r_1^{**}}{\partial z_1} - \frac{\partial y_1}{\partial z_1} \gtreqless 0 \quad \text{as} \quad (c + uf - bf)$$

$$\gtreqless \frac{bf(1 - k)\alpha h\beta(1 + w - h\beta w)}{(1 - h\beta)(1 - h\beta w)}. \quad (33)$$

The relative strengths of the deposit relationship in the two-period and infinite–horizon cases may be seen from comparisons of (30) and (33). As expected, the ability of the deposit relationship to induce reductions in $r_1 - y_1$ simultaneously with increases in l_1 during economic expansions (and conversely during contractions) is strengthened by lengthening the bank's horizon.

IV. Interbank competition

IV.1. Introduction and assumptions

We have heretofore ignored the effects of actions of other banks on the behaviour of the individual bank. Such abstraction is permissible in situations in which (i) we wish to analyse the reactions of a single bank to events which affect that bank but which do not disturb its competitors or (ii) each bank is a monopolist in its own marketing area. However, we are interested in the reactions of banks to swings in economic activity, which affect most banks simultaneously. Furthermore, it is not likely, except perhaps in small towns in unit banking areas, that banks are free of competitive restraints. Consequently, a useful extension of the model developed in Parts II and III will be to admit competition. Perfect competition among banks in the loan market will not be considered. Given our assumption of certainty, the perfectly elastic loan demand facing banks that perfect competition implies would do away with portfolio diversification. Neither will we consider any of the many interesting forms of oligopolistic competition. While either perfect competition or oligopoly might be applicable to some types of loans and certain classes of banks, the simplest and most straightforward way in which competition can be introduced into the present model is in a form similar to Chamberlin's (1956) monopolistic competition. That is, each bank is sufficiently small relative to the total loan market that its actions have no discernible impact on any other bank or on the banking system. However, shifts in the behaviour of banks in the aggregate influence the market restraints (loan demand and deposit supply) confronting the individual bank. Each bank is in competition with other banks in the aggregate but not with any other single bank.

The implications of these assumptions for the decision process of the individual bank are as follows: (i) Given values of variables that are exogenous to banks $(z_t, y_t; t = 1, 2, \ldots, T)$, each bank can treat the behaviour of other banks as given and proceed to maximize profit in the manner described in Parts II and III. It need not be concerned with the effects of its actions on other banks or, hence, the reactions of other banks. (ii) However, when these exogenous variables are disturbed, the individual bank must, in formulating its own response, take into account the expected reactions of other banks to those disturbances. This is so because the behaviour of other banks in the aggregate affects the individual bank.

The above assumptions are given operational meaning in the following equations. Let the loan demand confronting the individual monopolistically competitive bank be written as follows, where r_t^0 is the average loan rate of other banks in the tth period and l_t^0 is the aggregate of loans extended by all other banks in the tth period:

$$l_t = a - br_t + b_0 r_t^0 + cz_t + uy_t + \gamma \sum_{i=1}^{n} d^i l_{t-1} - \gamma_0 \sum_{i=1}^{n} d^i l_{t-i}^0$$

$$(t = 1, 2, \ldots, T). \quad (34)$$

The newly-introduced coefficients, b_0 and γ_0, are assumed to be non-negative. Since it is further assumed that banks are identical in size and behaviour, no identifying indices pertaining to banks are used. Assume $b - b_0$, $\gamma - N\gamma_0 \geq 0$, where the size of the individual bank relative to other banks is $1/N$; i.e. $l_{t-1} = l_{t-1}^0/N$ $(i = 1, 2, \ldots, n; t = 1, 2, \ldots, T)$. This means that, if the inequality holds, equal reductions in loan rates by all banks induce increases in loans demanded from all banks currently (and, hence, from the banking system) and also increases in future loan demands via the loan–customer relationship. That is, reductions in loan rates attract borrowers to the banking system through increased borrowing by non-financial economic units and/or the attraction of business from other types of financial intermediaries. It is assumed for reasons of simplification that the geometrically declining weights d^i attached to loans of other banks, l^0_{t-1}, are the same as the weights for past loans of the individual bank. The implications of this assumption are that (i) the relative impacts of past loans by our bank and by other banks on the loan demand confronting our bank depends entirely on the size of γ relative to γ_0 and (ii) the rapidity with which the importance of past loans on current loan demand declines as the lag, i, increases is the same for l_{t-i} and l^0_{t-1}.

It is seen from (34) that banks compete both through loan rates and the customer relationship. A bank loses current borrowers by charging a high loan rate, r_t, relative to the average loan rate of other banks, r^0_t, and loses future customers by extending a small quantity of current loans, l_t, relative to the loans extended by other banks, l^0_t. Competition for deposits via the deposit relationship also exists. The supply of deposits to the individual bank depends upon the past loans of that bank and of other banks and upon total deposits in the banking system:

$$q_t = a_1 + \alpha \sum_{i=1}^{n} h^i l_{t-i} - \alpha_0 \sum_{i=1}^{n} h^i l^0_{t-i} + s(q_t + q^0_t)$$

$$(t = 1, 2, \ldots, T). \quad (35)$$

It is assumed that α_0, $\alpha - N\alpha_0 \geq 0$. Increases in loans by other banks attract not only prospective borrowers but also depositors away from the individual bank. But equal increases in loans by all banks will, if $\alpha - N\alpha_0 > 0$, induce increases in the public's future demands for bank deposits in the aggregate; prospective depositors will be attracted from other types of assets and institutions.[12]

Before incorporating (34) and (35) into the decision process of the individual bank, let us introduce the demand by the bank for

---

[12] Although, in the presence of the deposit relationship, an expansion of bank loans currently induces increased deposit demands in future periods by the public, aggregate bank deposits in any current or future period are assumed to be determined by the Federal Reserve.

free reserves. This aspect of the bank's portfolio decision is considered for the sake of completeness only and in such a way as not to complicate our analysis of the choice among earning assets. Let the bank's demand for free reserves be written as follows:

$$e_t = a_3 - \delta y_t \quad (t = 1, 2, \ldots, T) \tag{36}$$

where e_t denotes the bank's holdings of free reserves as a proportion of earning assets plus free reserves in the tth period and we assume that $a_3, \delta > 0$. The bank desires to be liquid, but there is a cost to liquidity in terms of forgone profit. Given that the bank extends loans up to the point at which the marginal revenue from loans equals the infinitely elastic marginal revenue from securities, the opportunity cost of holding excess reserves is the rate of return on securities. Hence, the demand for free reserves is negatively related to y_t, where the Federal Reserve's discount rate is assumed fixed. Equation (36) has been expressed in linear form in order to simplify the calculations and interpretation.

With the addition of free reserves, the bank's balance sheet becomes

$$l_t + g_t + e_t = (1 - k)q_t + \kappa \quad (t = 1, 2, \ldots, T). \tag{37}$$

Now introduce a new scale factor $F_1 = L_1 + G_1 + E_1$, where L_t, G_t, and E_t are dollar values in period t of the individual bank's loans, securities and free reserves, respectively. In Parts II and III, we denoted all dollar values as proportions of the first-period earning assets of the individual bank, $L_1 + G_1$. From this point on, all dollar values are expressed as proportions of the first-period earning assets plus free reserves of the individual bank, F_1. This includes both coefficients and variables relating to the behaviour of individual banks (e_t, a_3, and δ in addition to those introduced in Parts II and III) and those measuring the actions of other banks (b_0, l_{t-1}^0, and q_t^0). We know from (27) and (35) that q_1 is predetermined. Hence, from (37) and given fixed k and κ, F_1 is also predetermined. But, from (36), E_1 and, hence, $L_1 + G_1$ are subject to the bank's control. The responses of l_1 to variations in z_1 that will be derived below are proportional not to earning assets as in Parts II and III but to earning assets plus free reserves. This approach does not affect the qualitative nature of the data shown in Table IV.24.

IV.2. *The general model and the two-period solution*

Under the monopolistically competitive conditions described in the preceding section, the bank will maximize the sum of discounted profits (1) with respect to its decision variables r_t, l_t, g_t, q_t, e_t ($t = 1, 2, \ldots, T$) subject to the market loan and deposit restraints (34) and (35), its liquidity restraint (36), the balance-sheet restraint (37), the Federal Reserve's behavioural equation (27), and the exogenously (to the bank) determined values of z_t, r_t^0, and q_t^0 ($t = 1, 2, \ldots, T$). In formulating its intertemporal portfolio plan, the individual bank must now forecast not only future levels of economic activity and security yields, but also the future actions of other banks, r_t^0 and q_t^0, since these variables enter the loan demands and deposit supplies with which the bank will be confronted in the future.

This constrained optimization procedure yields profit-maximizing values for the decision variables—r_t^*, l_t^*, g_t^*, q_t^*, e_t^* ($t = 1, 2, \ldots, T$). Now, as in Parts II and III, let us examine the effects of variations in current economic activity z_1 on $r_1^* - y_1$ and l_1^*. Variations in economic activity cause the bank to revise its expectations regarding future economic activity and security yields. Our assumptions with regard to the pattern of these revisions are specified in equations (7) and (10). Further, the individual bank knows that cyclical expansions and contractions will influence not only its own behaviour but also the behaviour of other banks, with whom it is in competition. Thus, the alteration by the bank of its decision variables must be based on expectations regarding the current and future reactions of other banks to the observed change in economic activity. I will utilize the simplest possible assumption with regard to the individual bank's conception of the behaviour of other banks. I will suppose that our bank expects other banks to react to changes in z_1 in precisely the same way that it does. This means that, where r_t^0 is the average loan rate of other banks that our bank expects to prevail in the tth period,

$$\frac{\partial r_t^0}{\partial z_1} = \frac{\partial r_t}{\partial z_1} \quad (t = 1, 2, \ldots, T). \tag{38}$$

Suppose there are $N + 1$ banks in the system. Under the assumption of an identical response of all banks to z_1, since there are N 'other' banks, variations in l_t in response to z_1 are $1/N$ times variations in l_t^0, where l_t^0 is the aggregate of loans of other banks:

$$\frac{\partial l_t^0}{\partial z_1} = N \frac{\partial l_t}{\partial z_1} \quad (t = 1, 2, \ldots, T). \tag{39}$$

Let us examine the implications of these assumptions for the reaction of the individual bank to a change in z_1. First consider the two-period case by setting $T = 2$:

$$\frac{\partial l_1^*}{\partial z_1}$$

$$= \frac{b\{c + uf - (b - b_0)f\}\{2b - b_0 + (b - b_0)\gamma d\beta(1 + w)\} + bf(b - b_0)(2b - b_0)(1 - k)\alpha h\beta(1 + w)}{(2b - b_0)^2 - b(b - b_0)(\gamma - \gamma_0')\gamma d^2\beta} \quad (40)$$

$$\frac{\partial r_1^*}{\partial z_1} - \frac{\partial y_1}{\partial z_1}$$

$$= \frac{\{c + uf - (b - b_0)f\}[2b - b_0 - b\beta\gamma d\{(\gamma - \gamma_0')d + 1 + w\}] - bf(2b - b_0)(1 - k)\alpha h\beta(1 + w)}{(2b - b_0)^2 - b(b - b_0)(\gamma - \gamma_0')\gamma d^2\beta} \quad (41)$$

where $\gamma_0' = N\gamma_0$. Equations (40) and (41) reduce to (28) and (29), respectively, for $b_0 = \gamma_0 = 0$. Now let us compare the responses of the individual bank to variations in economic activity under competitive and non-competitive conditions. The points that I wish to make will be more easily followed if (40) and (41) are simplified by letting $\gamma = \beta = 1$ and $w = h = 0$. Further assume that $b_0/b = \gamma_0/\gamma = \eta$, where, from the discussion following (34), $0 \leq \eta \leq 1$. The proportion η may be considered a measure of the intensity of competition in the market for bank loans. Under these assumptions, (40) and (41) reduce to the following:

$$\frac{\partial l_1^*}{\partial z_1} = \frac{\{c + uf - (1 - \eta)bf\}\{2 - \eta + (1 - \eta)d\}}{(2 - \eta)^2 - (1 - \eta)^2 d^2} \quad (40.1)$$

$$\frac{\partial r_1^*}{\partial z_1} - \frac{\partial y_1}{\partial z_1}$$

$$= \frac{\{c + uf - (1 - \eta)bf\}\{2 - \eta - d - (1 - \eta)d^2\}}{b\{(2 - \eta)^2 - (1 - \eta)^2 d^2\}}. \quad (41.1)$$

For small values of d, both $\partial l_1^*/\partial z_1$ and $\partial(r_1^* - y_1)/\partial z_1$ are greater in the presence of competition ($\eta > 0$) than in the non-competitive case ($\eta = 0$). The reason for this is as follows: As z_1 increases, other banks find it profitable to increase both their loans, l_1^0, and their loan rates, r_1^0, due to the upward shift in loan demand. Therefore, the loan demand confronting our bank is higher than it otherwise would have been due to the effect of $b_0 r_1^0 = \eta b r_1^0$ in equation (34). This result is easily seen in the special case in which $d = 0$ and η is either unity or zero:

$$\frac{\partial l_1^*}{\partial z_1} = \begin{cases} (c + uf), & \eta = 1 \\ \dfrac{(c + uf - bf)}{2}, & \eta = 0 \end{cases} \quad (d = h = 0) \quad (40.2)$$

$$\frac{\partial r_1^*}{\partial z_1} - \frac{\partial y_1}{\partial z_1} = \begin{cases} \dfrac{(c + uf)}{b}, & \eta = 1 \\ \dfrac{(c + uf - bf)}{2b}, & \eta = 0 \end{cases} \quad (d = h = 0). \quad (41.2)$$

This result is reversed as the customer relationship becomes more important, i.e. as d increases. The larger is d the less will other banks increase their loan rates, r_1^0, in order to achieve greater increases in their loans, l_1^0. Consequently, the loan demand facing the individual bank shifts upward in response to an increased z_1 by smaller amounts under competition the larger is d. That is, the larger is d the less will be the amounts by which $\partial l_1^*/\partial z_1$ and $\partial(r_1^* - y_1)/\partial z_1$ under competition exceed these derivatives in the absence of competition. In fact, there is a value of $d = d'$ such that $\partial l_1^*/\partial z_1$ is the same under competitive and non-competitive conditions. When $d > d'$, $\partial l_1^*/\partial z_1$ for $\eta > 0$ is less than $\partial l_1^*/\partial z_1$ for $\eta = 0$. The precise value of d' depends upon the parameters of the model. In the present example ($\gamma = \beta = 1$, $w = h = 0$), $d' = (c + uf + bf)/(c + uf)$. In general, d' will depend upon γ, β, w, and h as well as c, u, f, and b.

In our simple example the value of d such that $\partial(r_1^* - y_1)/\partial z_1$ is the same under competitive and non-competitive conditions is unity. This result is independent of c, u, f, and b but is contingent upon $\gamma = \beta = 1$ and $w = h = 0$. It may be remembered from (15) that in the two-period case under these assumptions, $\partial(r_1^* - y_1)/\partial z_1 \gtreqless 0$ as $d \lesseqgtr 1$. Thus, in this special case, the introduction of competition has no effect upon the value of d for which $\partial(r_1^* - y_1)/\partial z_1 = 0$.

In situations in which γ, β, and/or $(1 + w)$ are different from unity, the value of d that renders $\partial(r_1^* - y_1)/\partial z_1 = 0$ is dependent upon η. For example, if $\gamma = 1$, $w = 0.5$ and $\beta = 0.9$, $\partial(r_1^* - y_1)/\partial z_1 \gtreqless 0$ as $d \lesseqgtr 0.87$ and $d \lesseqgtr 0.74$ (approximately) for $\eta = 0.5$ and $\eta = 1$, respectively. These results may be compared with the non-competitive case discussed in section II.3 in which the critical value of d under these conditions was 0.92.

The comparison of the effects of the deposit relationship, αh, on the individual bank's response to variations in economic activity under competitive and non-competitive conditions is simpler than for γd. As seen in (34) when $d = 0$, the greater is η the greater will be the increase in the loan demand facing the individual bank (due to $b_0 r_t^0 = \eta b r_t^0$) when other banks raise their loan rates in response to an increase in z_1. As a consequence, $\partial l_1^* / \partial z_1$ is positively related to η. For the same reason, the greater is η the greater is $\partial r_1^* / \partial z_1$ and the higher is the value of αh required to cause $\partial (r_1^* - y_1)/\partial z_1 = 0$.

IV.3. An infinitely long horizon

Under competitive conditions, letting the bank's horizon approach an infinite length and retaining the assumptions specified in sections IV.1 and IV.2, the response of the individual bank to variations in z_1 may be written as follows:

$$\frac{\partial l_1^*}{\partial z_1}$$

$$\rightarrow \frac{2b}{(2b - b_0)\rho VV'}\bigg(\{c + uf - (b - b_0)f\}\{(1 + v)(1 - d\beta w) - d\beta V'\}$$

$$+ \frac{(b - b_0)(1 - k)f\alpha\beta h}{\times [\{1 - d\beta(1 + w - h\beta w)\}V' + w(1 + v)(1 - h\beta)(1 - d\beta w)]}{(1 - h\beta)(1 - h\beta w)} \bigg)$$

$$(42)$$

$$\frac{\partial r_1^*}{\partial z_1} - \frac{\partial y_1}{\partial z_1} \rightarrow \frac{2}{(2b - b_0)\rho VV'}$$

$$\times \left\{ \frac{[c + uf - (b - b_0)f](V''\{(1 + v)[1 - (1 + \gamma)d\beta w]}{\{1 + v + 2x_1(1 + \varepsilon)d\beta^{1/2}\}}{-(1 + \gamma)d\beta V'\} - (1 + \gamma)d^2\beta\varepsilon VV')}{\{1 + v + 2x_1(1 + \varepsilon)d\beta^{1/2}\}} \right.$$

$$\left. - \frac{b(1 - k)f\alpha\beta h[V'\{1 - d\beta(1 + w - h\beta w)\}}{+ w(1 + v)(1 - h\beta)(1 - d\beta w)]}{(1 - h\beta)(1 - h\beta w)} \right\}$$

$$(43)$$

as $T \rightarrow \infty$, where

$$V = (1 + v + 2x_1\beta^{1/2});$$
$$V' = (1 + v + 2x_1w\beta^{1/2});$$
$$V'' = (1 + v + 2x_1d\beta^{1/2});$$

$$\varepsilon = \gamma - \gamma_0';$$

$$\rho = \left[1 + \frac{\{b\varepsilon + \gamma(b - b_0)\}d^2\beta}{2b - b_0} \right];$$

$$x_1 = -\left[1 + \frac{\gamma(b - b_0)}{2b - b_0} \right] \frac{d\beta^{1/2}}{\rho}$$

$$x_2 = -\left(1 + \frac{b\varepsilon}{2b - b_0} \right) \frac{d\beta^{1/2}}{\rho}, \qquad v = (1 - 4x_1x_2)^{1/2}.$$

Letting $\alpha h = 0$, equations (40)–(43) may be written as follows where (40)–(41) and (42)–(43) correspond to $T = 2$ and $T \to \infty$, respectively:

$$\frac{\partial l_1^*}{\partial z_1} = \frac{b\{c + uf - (b - b_0)f\}}{(2b - b_0)} L_T^0 \qquad (44)$$

$$(T = 1, 2, \ldots).$$

$$\frac{\partial(r_1^* - y_1)}{\partial z_1} = \frac{\{c + uf - (b - b_0)f\}}{(2b - b_0)} R_T^0 \qquad (45)$$

L_T^0 and R_T^0 embody the dynamic properties of the loan–customer relationship under competitive conditions. Equations (44)–(45) reduce to (19)–(20) when $b_0 = \gamma_0 = 0$. Values of R_T^0 ($T = 2, \infty$) for $\gamma = 1$, $\eta = 0.5$ and selected β, w, and d are listed in Table IV.26. L_T^0 may be calculated from Table IV.26 using the knowledge that $L_T^0 = 1$ when $d = 0$ and $\partial L_T^0/\partial d = -(1 - \eta)(\partial R_T^0/\partial d)$.

TABLE IV.26

Impact of the Loan–Customer Relationship on $\partial(r_1^* - y_1)/\partial z_1$ under Competition for various β, w, d ($\gamma = 1$; $\eta = 0.5$)

	$\beta = 0.5$; $w = 0$		$\beta = 0.5$; $w = 0.5$		$\beta = 0.5$; $w = 0.9$	
d	R_2	R_∞	R_2	R_∞	R_2	R_∞
0	1·0000	1·0000	1·0000	1·0000	1·0000	1·0000
0·1	0·9655	0·9631	0·9489	0·9445	0·9355	0·9288
0·2	0·9287	0·9175	0·8953	0·8758	0·8686	0·8379
0·3	0·8894	0·8605	0·8392	0·7890	0·7990	0·7191
0·4	0·8475	0·7869	0·7803	0·6758	0·7265	0·5585
0·5	0·8028	0·6877	0·7183	0·5217	0·6507	0·3305
0·6	0·7551	0·5445	0·6531	0·2964	0·5714	−0·0192
0·7	0·7042	0·3088	0·5842	−0·0792	0·4883	−0·6357
0·8	0·6498	...	0·5115	...	0·4009	...
0·9	0·5916	...	0·4346	...	0·3089	...
1·0	0·5294	...	0·3529	...	0·2118	...

TABLE IV.26—*continued*

d	$\beta = 0.9; w = 0$		$\beta = 0.9; w = 0.5$		$\beta = 0.9; w = 0.9$	
	R_2	R_∞	R_2	R_∞	R_2	R_∞
0	1·0000	1·0000	1·0000	1·0000	1·0000	1·0000
0·1	0·9379	0·9294	0·9079	0·8930	0·8839	0·8603
0·2	0·8715	0·8299	0·8112	0·7381	0·7631	0·6443
0·3	0·8002	0·6806	0·7094	0·4984	0·6367	0·2816
0·4	0·7236	0·4314	0·6016	0·0841	0·5041	−0·4135
0·5	0·6410	−0·0808	0·4872	−0·8026	0·3641	−2·1277
0·6	0·5519	...	0·3651	...	0·2158	...
0·7	0·4553	...	0·2345	...	0·0578	...
0·8	0·3504	...	0·0940	...	−0·1111	...
0·9	0·2361	...	−0·0577	...	−0·2927	...
1·0	0·1111	...	−0·2222	...	−0·4889	...

d	$\beta = 0.98; w = 0$		$\beta = 0.98; w = 0.5$		$\beta = 0.98; w = 0.9$	
	R_2	R_∞	R_2	R_∞	R_2	R_∞
0	1·0000	1·0000	1·0000	1·0000	1·0000	1·0000
0·1	0·9324	0·9222	0·8997	0·8818	0·8736	0·8451
0·2	0·8600	0·8092	0·7944	0·7048	0·7419	0·5955
0·3	0·7823	0·6323	0·6833	0·4176	0·6041	0·1506
0·4	0·6986	0·3153	0·5656	−0·1181	0·4592	−0·7877
0·5	0·6082	−0·4415	0·4403	−1·4594	0·3060	−3·5975
0·6	0·5104	...	0·3064	...	0·1432	...
0·7	0·4042	...	0·1626	...	−0·0306	...
0·8	0·2884	...	0·0075	...	−0·2173	...
0·9	0·1617	...	−0·1608	...	−0·4187	...
1·0	0·0224	...	−0·3441	...	−0·6374	...

d	$\beta = 1; w = 0$		$\beta = 1; w = 0.5$		$\beta = 1; w = 0.9$	
	R_2	R_∞	R_2	R_∞	R_2	R_∞
0	1·0000	1·0000	1·0000	1·0000	1·0000	1·0000
0·1	0·9310	0·9204	0·8977	0·8789	0·8710	0·8412
0·2	0·8571	0·8038	0·7902	0·6962	0·7366	0·5826
0·3	0·7778	0·6193	0·6768	0·3958	0·5960	0·1145
0·4	0·6923	0·2824	0·5566	−0·1761	0·4480	−0·8986
0·5	0·6000	...	0·4286	...	0·2914	...
0·6	0·5000	...	0·2917	...	0·1250	...
0·7	0·3913	...	0·1445	...	−0·0529	...
0·8	0·2727	...	−0·0144	...	−0·2440	...
0·9	0·1429	...	−0·1868	...	−0·4505	...
1·0	0·0	...	−0·3750	...	−0·6750	...

V. Aggregation and estimation

V.1. Introduction

The model developed in Parts II–IV might be put to at least two uses. First, given their forecasts of interest rates and levels of economic activity and their estimates of the parameters of the loan–demand and deposit–supply equations, including those parameters pertaining to the customer relationship, bankers might find the model useful in the determination of optimal interest-rate and investment strategies. The model also bears on the conduct of monetary policy. The stronger is the customer relationship the more will bank loans and security yields increase and the less will be the rise in loan rates during periods of economic expansion as banks shift out of securities into loans. As a consequence, the Federal Reserve's estimate of the strength of the customer relationship should affect its decisions regarding actions to be taken for the purpose of influencing interest rates and bank credit.

The model is useful for either of these purposes or merely for an increased understanding of bank behaviour only if the parameters are quantified. This brings us to the problem of estimation. The values of the parameters that we would like to know are those used by bankers in the course of formulating their decisions, which are not necessarily the true values. For example, a banker's estimate of loan demand may differ from the true function. It is conceivable that bankers operate under the assumption that the customer relationship is strong (weak) when it is in fact weak (strong). But, again, what is relevant to the interest-rate and investment decisions of the bank is its estimate, however incorrect, of the strength of the customer relationship. These considerations suggest that the best estimates of the model's parameters would be based on data obtained from in-depth interviews with a number of bankers over a period of time sufficiently long to encompass several business cycles. However, such data are not available and would be costly to acquire. Consequently, I have decided to rely on standard regression techniques based on published data, which, if the parameters of their constraints as estimated by banks are correct and the assumptions underlying the regression model are satisfied, will produce unbiased and consistent estimators of the parameters in which we are interested. However, as with most models involving distributed lags, the presence of serial correlation in the error terms causes the least-squares estimates to be both biased and inconsistent.

Despite this very serious difficulty, because the empirical implications of the model derived in Parts II–IV are so clear-cut, I have proceeded with regression analysis in the hope of obtaining at least a rough impression of the strength of the customer relationship and its influence on bank behaviour.

V.2. Aggregation

The model developed in Parts II–IV is a model of the behaviour of an individual bank. Therefore, the estimation of the parameters of that model would at first thought appear to require the use of micro-bank data. However, in a highly integrated economy such as that existing in the United States, variations in economic activity, loan demand, Federal Reserve credit, and interest rates are diffused throughout the various sectors in extremely rapid fashion. This is particularly true of the banking system. Trend and cyclical movements in loan rates and the sizes and compositions of the assets and liabilities of commercial banks widely separated in geography, size, and regulatory restraints are regularly observed to proceed at similar rates and to have contemporaneous turning-points. These considerations suggest that the analysis of data obtained by summing over banks may not yield results substantially different from an analysis of disaggregated data.

The demand for loans in dollars from the jth bank in the tth period is

$$L_{jt} = A_j - B_j r_{jt} + B_{0j} r_{jt}^0 + C_j z_t + U_j y_t$$
$$+ \gamma_j \sum_{i=1}^{n} d_j^i L_{j,t-1} - \gamma_{0j} \sum_{i=1}^{n} d_j^i L_{j,t-i}^0 + \xi_{jt}$$
$$(j = 1, \ldots, N+1; t = 1, \ldots, T) \quad (46)$$

where ξ_{jt} is the error term. If we assume identical banks, including $r_{jt} = r_{jt}^0$ and $L_{j,t-i}^0 = N L_{j,t-i}$ $(j = 1, \ldots, N+1)$, summing (46) over j gives the following aggregate demand for bank loans:

$$L_t = A - (B - Bo)r_t + Cz_t + Uy_t + \varepsilon \sum_{i=1}^{n} d^i L_{t-i} + \xi_t \quad (47)$$

where $\varepsilon = \gamma - N\gamma_0$, $A = \sum A_j$, $B = \sum B_j, \ldots, \xi_t = \sum \xi_{jt}$.

Following a similar procedure, the aggregate demand for bank deposits may be written

$$Q_t = A_4 - B_1 r_t - U_1 y_t + C_1 z_t + \Psi \sum_{i=1}^{n} h^i L_{t-i} + \zeta_t \quad (48)$$

where $\Psi = \alpha - N\alpha_0$, $A_4 = \sum A_{4j}, \ldots, \zeta_t = \sum \zeta_{jt}$. The relevant loan rate is the average rate on all bank loans. It is expected that the demand for bank deposits is positively related to economic activity and negatively related to rates of return on competing assets so that $B_{1j}, U_{1j}, C_{1j} > 0$.[13]

V.3. Estimation

It is well known that distributed-lag equations such as (47) and (48) may be transformed as follows, where $0 \le d$, $h < 1$ and $n \to \infty$:

$$
\begin{aligned}
(L_t - dL_{t-1}) = {} & (1 - d)A - (B - B_0)(r_t - dr_{t-1}) \\
& + C(z_t - dz_{t-1}) + U(y_t - dy_{t-1}) \\
& + \varepsilon dL_{t-1} + (\xi_t - d\xi_{t-1})
\end{aligned} \tag{49}
$$

$$
\begin{aligned}
(Q_t - hQ_{t-1}) = {} & (1 - h)A_4 - B_1(r_t - hr_{t-1}) \\
& - U_1(y_t - hy_{t-1}) + C_1(z_t - hz_{t-1}) \\
& + \psi hL_{t-1} + (\zeta_t - h\zeta_{t-1}).
\end{aligned} \tag{50}
$$

We must face up to several problems before proceeding with the estimation of the parameters entering (49) and (50). First, note that d and h are over-identified in the coefficients of the variables. As a way out of this difficulty, Nerlove (1960) has suggested the following procedure: With respect to (49), for example, assume different values of d, compute the least-squares regression of the weighted difference of L on dL_{t-1} and the weighted differences of r, z, and y for each d and determine the coefficient of multiple correlation, R^2, as a function of d. The value of d corresponding to the maximum R^2 is the maximum-likelihood estimate, and the values of the other coefficients, given this value of d, are their maximum-likelihood estimates. This method produces unique estimates of d, A, $B - B_0$, C, U, and ε subject to the requirement that the error terms of (49) be normally and independently distributed. The application of the same procedure to (50) produces unique maximum-likelihood estimates of h, A_4, B_1, U, C, and ψ if the error terms in (50) are normally and independently distributed. Since the model requires $0 \le d$, $h < 1$, regressions were computed for $d, h = 0, 1, 0\cdot2, \ldots, 0\cdot9$ and for purposes of comparison, $d, h = 1$.

---

[13] Although it was assumed in Parts III and IV that, owing to the nature of the Federal Reserve's behaviour, aggregate bank deposits in the current period are predetermined, the public's demand for deposits is nevertheless dependent upon current endogenous variables.

Our theory implies nothing about the period of observation except, loosely, that it should be sufficiently long to permit banks to adjust to new information, yet short enough to enable us to capture the dynamic properties of the customer relationship. Dictated largely by data availability, the use of quarterly data is not obviously inconsistent with these criteria.

We must now decide upon empirical counterparts to the interest rates, r_t and y_t, used in the theoretical model. The use of quarterly data and the assumption that banks maximize expected profits imply a convenient empirical specification of y_t. If we are to be consistent with the assumptions of the model and the chosen period of observation, we must require banks to select their security portfolios such that quarterly expected returns on the securities held are equal. But the quarterly return on one of the securities held by banks is known with certainty—that on three-month Treasury bills. Therefore, given the requirements stated above, the expected quarterly return on security portfolios is equal to the three-month Treasury bill rate, henceforth denoted by $\bar{y}_t$.

Loan rates used in the empirical analysis are based on the Federal Reserve's 'Quarterly Survey of Interest Rates on Business Loans' of commercial banks in thirty-five cities. However, contract rates, even if accurately reported, are not those relevant to our model, which requires expected returns. In the absence of time-series on loan defaults, the contract loan rate was adjusted for default risk using the differential between Moody's Baa and Aaa corporate bond rates.[14] The procedure by which the adjusted loan rate (expected rate of return on loans), $\bar{r}$, was derived is described in the Appendix. The use of $\bar{r} - \bar{y}$ produces only one qualitative change from the data shown in Table IV.24. On the dates shown in that Table, $\bar{r} - \bar{y}$ assumes the following values: 0·80, 0·81, 1·11, 2·04, 0·64, 2·18, 1·24, 1·76, 0·28, 1·04, 0·64, 1·31.

Quarterly averages of $\bar{r}$, $\bar{y}$, and $\bar{r} - \bar{y}$ for the period 1948(2)–1970(4) are depicted in Fig. IV.7 along with the risk adjustment on bank loans, r_r, which is roughly equal to the difference between the Baa and Aaa corporate bond rates. Also shown are averages of

---

[14] As one would expect if Aaa bonds are relatively free of default-risk and if the market's estimate of the riskiness of Baa borrowers is inversely related to economic activity, the difference between the Baa and Aaa rates tends to be higher at N.B.E.R. troughs than at peaks. On the dates listed in Table IV.24, this difference, which moves oppositely to the N.B.E.R.'s definition of economic activity eight of eleven times, takes the following values: 0·69, 0·75, 0·58, 0·62, 0·74, 1·07, 0·82, 0·80, 0·69, 0·72, 0·90, 1·33.

$l = L/F$[15] and alternative definitions of our index of economic activity, z: gross national product in constant (1958) dollars, GNP, and quarterly averages of the Federal Reserve Board's index of industrial production (1957–9 = 100), IP, both seasonally adjusted. Interpreting Fig. IV.7 within the framework of the model developed in Parts II–IV, these data (like those in Table IV.24) suggest a strong customer relationship. That is, the data appear to be consistent with values of γ, d, α, h, β, and w sufficiently large to cause $\partial(\bar{r}_1 - \bar{y}_1)/\partial z_1 < 0$ where $\bar{r}$ and $\bar{y}$ in the empirical analysis correspond to r and y in Parts II–IV.

TABLE IV.27

Loan Demand: Seasonally Adjusted, Unscaled, GNP

		Dependent variable $= L_t - dL_{t-1}$				
d	Constant	$\bar{r}_t - d\bar{r}_{t-1}$	$z_t - dz_{t-1}$	$\bar{y}_t - d\bar{y}_{t-1}$	dL_{t-1}	$\bar{R}^2/D$
0	−83·87	−2·24	0·399	2·05		0·99420
	(−29·99)	(−1·86)	(36·89)	(2·28)		
0·1	−14·31	−2·15	0·086	0·65	7·51	0·99946
	(−6·44)	(−5·89)	(7·70)	(2·40)	(29·49)	5·49
0·2	−13·90	−2·28	0·093	0·71	3·27	0·99931
	(−6·41)	(−5·64)	(7·71)	(2·40)	(26·56)	5·34
0·3	−13·33	−2·38	0·102	0·75	1·87	0·99908
	(−6·34)	(−5·26)	(7·66)	(2·34)	(23·66)	5·17
0·4	−12·55	−2·44	0·111	0·77	1·17	0·99873
	(−6·20)	(−4·73)	(7·54)	(2·20)	(20·77)	4·97
0·5	−11·53	−2·38	0·121	0·74	0·76	0·99810
	(−5·99)	(−4·02)	(7·33)	(1·94)	(17·95)	4·82
0·6	−10·18	−2·13	0·131	0·65	0·49	0·99691
	(−5·73)	(−3·10)	(7·02)	(1·56)	(15·27)	4·69
0·5	−8·36	−1·59	0·140	0·48	0·30	0·99426
	(−5·39)	(−2·00)	(6·63)	(1·06)	(12·91)	4·60
0·8	−5·89	−0·74	0·145	0·26	0·17	0·98679
	(−4·87)	(−0·84)	(6·11)	(0·53)	(11·14)	4·54
0·9	−2·78	0·20	0·140	0·08	0·08	0·95097
	(−3·69)	(0·22)	(5·39)	(0·15)	(10·07)	4·53
1·0		0·99	0·126	0·00	0·01	0·69807
		(1·09)	(4·77)	(0·00)	(6·84)	4·63

t-ratios are in parentheses; $\bar{R}^2$ is the coefficient of determination adjusted for degrees of freedom; D is the Durbin statistic.

[15] L is total loans and F is total earning assets plus free reserves of all commercial banks. Since the total assets of member banks comprise approximately five-sixths of total commercial bank assets, member bank free reserves have been raised by a factor of one-fifth to get a comparable figure for all commercial banks.

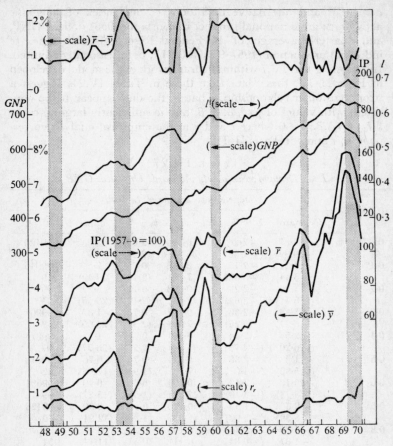

FIG. IV.7. $\bar{r}-\bar{y}$, l, GNP, IP, $\bar{r}$, $\bar{y}$, r_r

Table IV.27 lists the results of regressions based on equation (49) for $d = 0, 0\cdot1, 0\cdot2, \ldots, 1\cdot0$ when $\bar{r}$, $\bar{y}$, and GNP are substituted for r, y, and z, respectively. The data entering these regressions possess the following characteristics (sources and more detailed definitions are contained in the Appendix):

Quarterly data were used for the *period 1948(2)–1970(4)*; the beginning of the sample period being dictated by the date on which an end-of-month series on total commercial bank loans first became available

(January 1948); prior to that time, these data usually were available for only two dates each year. Given the one-period lags appearing in the regressions, this gives us *ninety observations*.

Except for interest rates, which show little or no seasonal variation, the data are *seasonally adjusted*.

L is an estimate of quarterly averages of total commercial bank loans based on straight-line interpolation of end-of-month figures—in billions of dollars deflated by the GNP price deflator (1958 = 100).

GNP is in billions of constant (1958) dollars at annual rates.

$\bar{y}$ is a quarterly average of daily figures of the three-month Treasury bill rate measured in percentages at annual rates. $\bar{r}$ is an estimate of the quarterly average of business loan rates, adjusted for default risk, derived by straight-line interpolation of data for the first fifteen days of one month in each quarter.

Looking ahead to Table IV.28, Q is a quarterly average of monthly data on total bank deposits, both time and demand (net of inter-bank deposits).

Referring to Table IV.27, we see that the maximum $\bar{R}^2$ corresponds to $d = 0.1$, with $\bar{R}^2$ falling monotonically as d increases from 0.1 to 1.0. When $d = 0.1$, all of the estimated coefficients are significant and have the expected signs; i.e. $(B \overset{\wedge}{-} B_0), \hat{C} \, \hat{U}, \hat{\epsilon} > 0.$[16,17] However, the form in which the error term enters (49) suggests that we should expect the errors to be autocorrelated, and this in fact turns out to be the case. The Durbin–Watson test for autocorrelation is not applicable to (49), which contains the lagged dependent variable as an explanatory variable. But Durbin (1970) has provided a large-sample test that may be used under these conditions. The procedure involves the test of the quantity $D = (1 - \tfrac{1}{2}D_w)\{n/(1 - n\hat{V})\}^{1/2}$ as a standard normal deviate, where

[16] Regressions were also computed (i) using IP instead of GNP, (ii) with a time trend, (iii) on seasonally unadjusted data and seasonal dummies, and (iv) with all variables divided by F (this meant the suppression of the constant and the substitution of F_t^{-1}). Regressions were computed for all sixteen combinations of these four approaches. In every case, the maximum $\bar{R}^2$ corresponded with $d = 0.1$ and there were no important differences between the estimates shown in Table IV.27 and those in the other fifteen sets of regressions.

[17] The negative constant poses no problem. If we think of L_t as a function of r_t given the values assumed by the other variables affecting loan demand, the estimates in all eleven regressions in Table IV.27 imply a positive intercept of this function for all values of $\bar{r}$, $\bar{y}$, and z (=GNP) in our sample. A negative constant implies, for example, that if $z_t = \bar{r}_t = L_{t-1} = L_{t-2} = \cdots = 0$, loan demand would be so weak that people would have to be paid to borrow.

D_w is the Durbin–Watson statistic, n is the number of observations, and $\hat{V}$ is the estimate of the variance of the estimated regression coefficient of the lagged dependent variable.[18] Values of D are shown in the last column of Table IV.27 (except for $d = 0$, when D is not applicable). These very large values of D compel us to reject the hypothesis of no serial correlation. The presence of positive serial correlation in the error term of (49) causes inefficient estimates of the coefficients, biased estimates of the standard errors resulting in upward bias of the t-statistics, upward bias in the estimate of ε and, further, the use of Nerlove's iterative maximum-likelihood procedure is invalidated.

TABLE IV.28

Deposit Demand: Seasonally Adjusted, Unscaled, GNP

| h | Constant | Dependent variable = $Q_t - hQ_{t-1}$ | | | | $\bar{R}^2/D_w$ |
		$\bar{r}_t - hr_{t-1}$	$z_t - hz_{t-1}$	$\bar{y}_t - h\bar{y}_{t-1}$	hL_{t-1}	
0	16·69	−14·45	0·455	4·79		0·96948
	(2·90)	(−5·81)	(20·42)	(2·58)		0·3985
0·1	86·95	−14·21	0·085	3·02	8·86	0·97738
	(6·75)	(−6·72)	(1·32)	(1·91)	(6·00)	0·5951
0·2	75·67	−14·18	0·094	2·93	3·87	0·97571
	(6·55)	(−6·58)	(1·45)	(1·87)	(5·88)	0·7558
0·3	64·48	−14·08	0·104	2·79	2·20	0·97308
	(6·27)	(−6·35)	(1·60)	(1·78)	(5·71)	0·9653
0·4	53·41	−13·83	0·116	2·58	1·38	0·96877
	(5·89)	(−5·99)	(1·76)	(1·65)	(5·45)	1·2288
0·5	42·54	−13·35	0·131	2·27	0·88	0·96130
	(5·38)	(−5·47)	(1·93)	(1·44)	(5·08)	1·5425
0·6	32·02	−12·51	0·148	1·83	0·56	0·94726
	(4·74)	(−4·78)	(2·09)	(1·15)	(4·58)	1·8873
0·7	22·23	−11·23	0·167	1·27	0·33	0·91760
	(4·03)	(−3·97)	(2·22)	(0·78)	(4·01)	2·2273
0·8	13·71	−9·61	0·181	0·69	0·18	0·84306
	(3·32)	(−3·19)	(2·23)	(0·42)	(3·52)	2·5153
0·9	6·57	−8·19	0·178	0·33	0·09	0·60830
	(2·60)	(−2·63)	(2·04)	(0·20)	(3·28)	2·6993
1·0		−7·50	0·145	0·41	0·01	0·16723
		(−2·44)	(1·63)	(0·25)	(2·34)	2·7399

t-ratios are in parentheses; $\bar{R}^2$ is the coefficient of determination adjusted for degrees of freedom; D_w is the Durbin–Watson statistic.

[18] Since the estimated coefficient of L_{t-1} in (49) is $\varepsilon\hat{d}$, the values of $\hat{V}$ calculated for Table IV.27 are $d^2\hat{V}(\hat{\varepsilon})$; $d = 0·1, 0·2, \ldots, 1·0$.

Table IV.28 lists regressions computed for equation (50) for $h = 0, 0\cdot1, 0\cdot2, \ldots, 1\cdot0$ with the same regressors as those used in Table IV.27. The maximum $\bar{R}^2$ corresponds to $h = 0\cdot1$, with $\bar{R}^2$ falling monotonically as h increases from $0\cdot1$ to $1\cdot0$.[19] When $h = 0\cdot1$, $\hat{B}_1$ and $\hat{\Psi}$ are significant with the expected signs, $\hat{C}_1$ has the expected sign but is not significant, and $\hat{U}_1$ neither has the expected sign nor is significant. The Durbin–Watson ratio is used to test for serial correlation of the error term since the lagged dependent variable does not enter (50). The low value of D_w corresponding to $h = 0\cdot1$ means that, as for the loan–demand equation, Nerlove's iterative maximum-likelihood procedure is not applicable.

Although our ordinary-least-squares results are in some respects encouraging, the problems raised by serially correlated errors require the results shown in Tables IV.27 and IV.28 to be regarded only as a progress report. The next step in the estimation of the parameters of the customer relationship will be the application of some of the recent advances in the estimation of distributed-lag models in the presence of serial correlation.[20]

VI. Theoretical implications of the estimates

The question remains: Is the customer relationship sufficiently strong to account for the opposite movements in $r - y$ and l shown in Table IV.24? I will attempt to throw a little light on this question by means of an examination of the conditions under which the estimates reported in Part V are consistent with the results $\partial(r_1^* - y_1)/\partial z_1 < 0$, $\partial l_1/\partial z_1 > 0$ as discussed in Part IV (the

[19] As for (49), sixteen sets of regressions were computed for (50). In twelve cases, the maximum $\bar{R}^2$ corresponded with $h = 0\cdot1$. When the data were expressed as proportions of F and a time trend was added, the maximum $\bar{R}^2$ corresponded with $h = 0$.

[20] One of the problems that arises in the interpretation of distributed-lag models is that models with quite different theoretical justifications are often empirically indistinguishable, especially in the presence of serial correlation. This is the case for models embodying (i) adaptive expectations or (ii) partial adjustment or (iii) for contemporaneous models with serially correlated residuals. This problem has been discussed by Griliches (1967) and others. It is encouraging to note that the model developed in this paper is at least conceptually distinguishable from models (i)–(iii). As these models have typically been formulated, although in some circumstances empirically indistinguishable from one another, they imply empirical forms that are different from either (49) or (50).

usefulness of this exercise being inversely related to the degree of bias in the estimates). As in Part IV, let $b_0/b = N\gamma_0/\gamma = \eta$ be a measure of the intensity of competition in the market for bank loans, and let the same parameter apply to deposit demands so that $N\alpha_0/\alpha = \eta$. In the unscaled regressions (49) and (50), the upper-case coefficients C, $B - B_0$, and U correspond to their lower-case counterparts in Part IV.[21] Using these upper-case parameters, we see from (40)–(43) that bank responses to variations in economic activity (GNP) depend upon C, $B - B_0 = B(1 - \eta)$, U, d, h, $(\gamma - N\gamma_0) = \gamma(1 - \eta) = \varepsilon$, $(\alpha - N\alpha_0) = \alpha(1 - \eta) = \psi$, k, f, β, w. From Tables IV.27 and IV.28, estimates of the first seven of these parameters are approximately 0·086, 2·15, 0·65, 0·1, 0·1, 7·5, 8·8.[22] The average reserve requirement ratio on all bank deposits during the period 1948–70 was approximately equal to 0·11, which was used as an estimate of k. An estimate of f was obtained from a regression of the Treasury bill rate on GNP, the data and sample period being the same as those in the regressions in Tables IV.27 and IV.28. This provided an estimate of $\partial\bar{y}/\partial z = \hat{f} = 0.012$.[23]

---

[21] By 'unscaled' I mean not divided through by bank earning assets plus free reserves, F_t. The use of estimated coefficients based on unscaled regressions does not affect the nature of the results in Parts II–IV. Given these estimates, equations in $\partial(r_1 - y_1)/\partial z_1$ are unchanged except for the substitution of C, B, B_0, and U for c, b, b_0, and u; the equations in $\partial l_1/\partial z_1$ become, using the upper-case parameters, $\partial L_1/\partial z_1 = F_1 \, (\partial l_1/\partial z_1)$. The scaled regressions also give estimates of upper-case rather than lower-case coefficients since the variables rather than the coefficients are expressed as proportions of F_t in these regressions.

[22] Estimates of these parameters based on regressions identical to (49) and (50) except that all variables were expressed as proportions of F_t were 0·075, 1·43, 1·56, 0·1, 0·1, 7·2, 8·3.

[23] That is, during the period 1948–70, the Treasury bill rate has tended to change by slightly more than one basis point for each billion dollar change in GNP. The $\bar{R}^2$ for the regression was 0·87 and the t-statistic for $\hat{f}$ was 23·8.

We have assumed throughout (see the discussion in connection with Fig. IV.6) that $\{c + uf - (b - b_0)f\} = \{C + Uf - (B - B_0)f\}/F > 0$. This assumption is supported by our estimates, which give a value of $\{C + Uf - (B - B_0)f\} = 0.068$. The dimensions and scaling of the variables and coefficients raise no problem with respect to the sign of this term provided only that r and y are scaled in the same way and that y and z have the same scales both in the regressions in Table IV.27 and in the regression upon which the estimate of f is based. The parameters C, $(B - B_0)f$, and Uf have identical dimensions and scales; viz. $\partial L/\partial z$, $(\partial L/\partial r)(\partial y/\partial z)$, and $(\partial L/\partial y)(\partial y/\partial z)$, respectively. For example, the measurement of L and/or z in thousands rather than billions of dollars or r and y in basis points rather than percentages would alter the terms C, $(B - B_0)f$, and Uf in identical proportions.

The implications of these estimates for bank behaviour are conditional upon values assumed with respect to η, β, and w, for which our empirical analysis has not provided independent evidence. The nature of the expectations equation (10) requires $0 \leq w < 1$. The discount factor may assume any value in the range $0 \leq \beta \leq 1$. Given the maximum possible $\beta = 1$ and the estimates of d and ε, the range of admissible η is dictated by the second-order conditions which, when $T \to \infty$, include the statement $(1 + \gamma)d\beta^{1/2} < 1$ or $\{1 + 7 \cdot 5/(1 - \eta)\}(0 \cdot 1)(1) < 1$ or $\eta < \frac{1}{6}$ (i.e. $\gamma < 9$).[24]

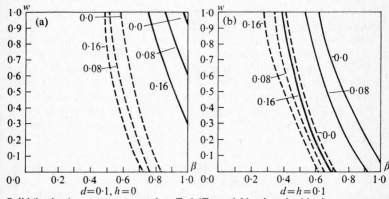

Solid (broken) curves correspond to $T = 2$ ($T \to \infty$) Numbers beside the curves indicate values of η. When $\eta = 0$, $0 \cdot 08$, $0 \cdot 16$, $(\gamma, \alpha) \approx (7 \cdot 5, 8 \cdot 8), (8 \cdot 2, 9 \cdot 6), (8 \cdot 9, 10 \cdot 5)$

FIG. IV.8. Values of β and w Consistent with $(r_1 - y_1)/z_1 = 0$. Given the Estimates in Tables IV.27–IV.28

The curves in Fig. IV.8 are loci of combinations of β and w for the estimates listed above and selected $\eta = 0$, $0 \cdot 08$, $0 \cdot 16$ (i.e. $\gamma = \varepsilon/(1 - \eta) = 7 \cdot 50$, $8 \cdot 15$, $8 \cdot 93$; $\alpha = \psi/(1 - \eta) = 8 \cdot 80$, $9 \cdot 57$, $10 \cdot 47$) such that $\partial(r_1 - y_1)/\partial z_1 = 0$ for $T = 2$, ∞.[25] Figure IV.8a

Since the calculations upon which Fig. IV.8 is based use these terms in the form $\{C + Uf - (B - B_0)f\}/Bf$, those calculations are independent of the units in which the variables entering the regressions are expressed.

[24] See (18) in Part II. Values of $\beta < 1$ permit the consideration of values of $\eta > \frac{1}{6}$ (i.e. $\gamma > 9$). However, in order to be able to treat the full ranges of β and w in Fig. IV.8, only values of $\eta < \frac{1}{6}$ are used.

For $\beta = 1$ and $T = 2$, values of $\eta < \frac{5}{8}$ ($\gamma < 20$) are admitted by the second-order condition when $d = 0 \cdot 1$, $\varepsilon = 7 \cdot 5$. But only values of η consistent with all β and T and our estimates of d and ε are considered in Fig. IV.8.

[25] $\partial l_1/\partial z_1 > 0$ for all values of the parameters considered.

shows these loci for $d = 0.1$, $h = 0$, i.e. in the absence of the deposit relationship. Figure IV.8b shows these loci for $d = h = 0.1$. The solid curves correspond to $T = 2$ and the dashed curves to $T \to \infty$. All of these curves approach the vertical axis asymptotically as $\beta \to 0$. Combinations of β and w lying above the curves imply $\partial(r_1 - y_1)/\partial z_1 < 0$. Curves for $d = 0$, $h = 0.1$ are not shown because, except in the case $\eta = 0.16$ and $T \to \infty$, no combinations of w, $\beta \le 1$ are consistent with $\partial(r_1 - y_1)/\partial z_1 = 0$. For this exception, values of $w > 0.979$, $\beta > 0.990$ are required. Thus, our estimates suggest that the loan–customer relationship discussed in Part II exerts a greater impact on bank behaviour than the deposit relationship introduced in Part III.

Considering the case where $T \to \infty$, Fig. IV.8b shows that, given the estimates in Tables IV.27 and IV.28, all values of $0 \le w < 1$ and $0 \le \eta \le 0.16$ imply $\partial(r_1 - y_1)/\partial z_1 \le 0$ for all values of $\beta \ge 0.725$. It is seen in Fig. IV.8a that, under these same conditions except that the deposit relationship is excluded $(h = 0)$, $\partial(r_1 - y_1)/\partial z_1 \le 0$ for $\beta \ge 0.835$. It is unlikely that the true value of β is lower than 0.95.[26] Therefore, the estimates reported in Part V, when applied to the model developed in Parts II–IV, support the hypothesis that the customer relationship is sufficient to explain those aspects of bank behaviour discussed in Part I. However, given the shortcomings of these estimates (especially the upward bias in $\hat{\epsilon}$) due to serially correlated residuals, a more conclusive evaluation of the strength of the customer relationship must await further empirical work.

Data appendix

A.1. Data used in Table IV.24

Loans (L) *and security holdings* (G) of banks, seasonally adjusted in billions of dollars, are derived from those reported in the Federal Reserve Board's series, 'Loans and Investments', available in the *Federal Reserve Bulletin* (*FRB*). Especially see *FRB*, Aug. 1968, pp.

[26] Member bank after-tax income as a percentage of total capital accounts has averaged 8.7 per cent on an annual basis since 1948, varying between a low of 7.2 per cent in 1948 and a high of 10.4 per cent in 1970. (For example, see the *Federal Reserve Bulletin*, June 1971, pp. 445–51.) Using the generous figure of 12 per cent per annum as the appropriate rate of discount on bank profits and converting this to a quarterly basis to be consistent with the estimates upon which Fig. IV.8 is based, we arrive at a value of β equal to (approximately) 0.97.

A-94–A-97. The reported data are end-of-month figures; the data in Table IV.24 are estimated monthly averages, being simply unweighted averages of end-of-month figures. These data were revised beginning June 1969, the revision and the differences between the new and old series being discussed in *FRB*, Aug. 1969, pp. 642–6. The old and new series were both reported for June 1969 and, on the assumption that the ratios of the old and new series of L and $L + G$ have remained unchanged since that time, I have made the new series comparable with the old. The ratios of the old to the new series are 0·988 for $L + G$ and 0·982 for L.

The rate on short-term business loans of banks (r) is a monthly average derived from a straight-line interpolation of the Federal Reserve's 'Quarterly Survey of Interest Rates on Business Loans', available in *FRB*. Especially see *FRB*, May 1967, pp. 721–7. Until February 1967, this series was based on a survey of 19 centres for the first 15 days of March, June, September, and December; since that time, it has been based on a survey of 35 centres for the first 15 days of February, May, August, and November. It was reported (see *FRB*, May 1967) that, in February 1967, the new series was five basis points higher than the old. I have subtracted five basis points from the 1967–71 data to make the new and old series consistent. This and other interest-rate series contain little or no seasonal variation and have not been seasonally adjusted.

The average yield on securities (y) is a weighted average of the following yield series (with weights in parentheses): (i) market yield on 3-month Treasury bills (0·1115); (ii) average yield on selected 9–12 month U.S. note and bond issues (0·1115); (iii) average yield on selected 3–5 year U.S. note and bond issues (0·484); (iv) average yield on selected U.S. long-term issues (0·061); (v) an estimate of the monthly average of yields on 5–10 year prime municipal bonds (0·232). These weights are based on the observation that the average proportions of U.S. 0–1, 1–10, and over-ten year securities and state and local government securities in the security portfolios of commercial banks during 1948–70 were 0·223, 0·484, 0·061, and 0·232, respectively. An unweighted average of (i) and (ii) was used as an estimate of the average yield on U.S. 0–1 year securities, the average yield on U.S. 1–10 securities is estimated by (iii). Series (i)–(iv) are monthly averages of daily figures as they appear in *FRB*. Data reported by Robinson (1960, p. 88), Rothwell (1966), and Rabinowitz (1969, pp. 236–7) suggest that the average maturity of state and local government securities held by commercial banks during the period 1956–65 was between six and nine years. An estimate of the yield on this type of security was derived by averaging yields on 5- and 10-year prime municipal bonds as reported in Salomon Brothers and Hutzler (1969, 1971). Estimates of monthly averages were obtained by averaging first-of-month data. The Salomon Brothers' data begin with 1950; data for 1948–9 were extrapolated from the relationship existing during 1950–70 between these data and Moody's Aaa state and local yield series. Municipal yields were doubled in order to make their yields comparable with those on U.S. securities on an after-tax basis.

A.2. Derivation of $\bar{r}$

Let R_A and R_B denote Moody's series on long-term taxable, nonconvertible seasoned corporate bonds rated Aaa and Baa, respectively. (For detailed descriptions of these series see Board of Governors of the Federal Reserve System, *Supplement to Banking and Monetary Statistics*, Section 12, 1966, p. 15.) On the assumption that the risk of default on a Baa bond increases with the maturity of the payment, suppose the expected payment in the ith period on a Baa bond to be $(1 + r_r)^{-i}$ of the contracted payment. The price of an Aaa bond is, where c = coupon, V = principal and m = term to maturity,

$$P_A = \sum_{i=1}^{m} c(1 + R_A)^{-i} + V(1 + R_A)^{-m}, \qquad (A.1)$$

and the price of a risky but otherwise identical security is

$$P_B = \sum_{i=1}^{m} c\{(1 + r_r)(1 + R_A)\}^{-i} + V\{(1 + r_r)(1 + R_A)\}^{-m}$$

$$= \sum_{i=1}^{m} c(1 + R_B)^{-i} + V(1 + R_B)^{-m}. \quad (A.2)$$

We do not observe r_r directly, but (A.1) and (A.2) give us observations on R_A and R_B. Thus,

$$(1 + R_B) = (1 + r_r)(1 + R_A) \quad \text{or} \quad r_r = \frac{R_B - R_A}{1 + R_A}. \quad (A.3)$$

For one-period investments, such as we have assumed bank loans to be, a measure of the expected rate of return is

$$\bar{r} = \frac{L(1 + r)(1 + r_r)^{-1} - L}{L} = \frac{r - r_r}{1 + r_r}. \qquad (A.4)$$

The definition of $\bar{r}$ shown in (A.4) assumes R_A, R_B, and r to be one-period (quarterly) rates of return. If we follow convention by using annual rates, the expected rate of return on one-period loans, where all rates are expressed in annual terms, is

$$\bar{r} = \frac{4(r - r_r)}{4 + r_r}, \quad \text{where} \quad r_r = \frac{4(R_B - R_A)}{4 + R_A}. \tag{A.5}$$

This approach has assumed the preponderance of bank loans to be risky. To the extent that this is not so, our risk adjustment is overstated, the extent of the bias depending upon the size of r_r and the parameters of the demand functions for risky and riskless loans.

A.3. Data used in Figure IV.7 and the regressions (Tables IV.27–IV.28)

r, r_r, $\bar{r}$, $\bar{y}$: r is a quarterly average of the monthly figures calculated as described in section A.1. r_r and $\bar{r}$ are quarterly averages as defined in section A.2 when r, R_A, and R_B are quarterly averages. $\bar{y}$ is a quarterly average of daily market yields on 3-month Treasury bills (see section A.1).

L, l: L is a quarterly average of the monthly averages estimated as described in section A.1. $l = L/(L + G + E)$ is based on quarterly averages of L, G, and E, where E is member bank excess reserves raised by a factor of one-fifth since member bank assets are approximately five-sixths of assets of all commercial banks. L has been deflated by the *GNP price deflator*, 1958 = 100. Source: *The National Income and Products Accounts of the U.S.*, *1929–65* and the *Survey of Current Business*.

IP is a quarterly average of the Federal Reserve Board's monthly Index of Industrial Production (1957–9 = 100), seasonally adjusted. Source: *Business Statistics, Supplement to Survey of Current Business*, U.S. Department of Commerce, *FRB*.

GNP is gross national product in billions of constant (1958) dollars, seasonally adjusted quarterly totals at annual rates. Sources: *Business Statistics; Survey of Current Business*.

Q is a quarterly average of the sum of the monthly series on the public's demand and time deposits (seasonally adjusted) plus government deposits (seasonally unadjusted) in billions of dollars deflated by the GNP price deflator, 1958 = 100. For detailed descriptions and lists of data, see *FRB*, Oct. 1966, Dec. 1970.

REFERENCES

ANDERSEN, L. A., and BURGER, A. E. (1969). 'Asset Management and Commercial Bank Portfolio Behavior: Theory and Practice', *Journal of Finance*, May, pp. 207–22.

CHAMBERLIN, E. H. (1956). *The Theory of Monopolistic Competition*, 7th edn. (Cambridge, Mass.: Harvard University Press).

CHASE, S. B. (1962). 'Bank Reactions to Securities Losses', in D. R. Cawthorne *et al.* (eds.), *Essays on Commercial Banking* (Federal Reserve Bank of Kansas City), pp. 87–98.

DURBIN, J. (1970). 'Testing for Serial Correlation in Least-Squares Regression When Some of the Regressors are Lagged Dependent Variables', *Econometrica*, May, pp. 410–21.

ENTHOVEN, A. C. (1956). 'Monetary Disequilibrium and the Dynamics of Inflation', *Economic Journal*, June, pp. 256–70.

FEDERAL RESERVE BANK OF CLEVELAND (1956). 'Continuous Borrowing Through "Short-Term" Bank Loans', *Business Review*, Sept., pp. 99–101; reprinted in L. S. Ritter (ed.), *Money and Economic Activity*, 3rd edn. (Boston, Mass.: Houghton Mifflin, 1967).

GALBRAITH, J. A. (1963). *The Economics of Banking Operations: A Canadian Study* (Montreal: McGill University Press).

GRILICHES, Z. (1967). 'Distributed Lags: A Survey', *Econometrica*, Jan., pp. 16–49.

HODGMAN, D. R. (1961). 'The Deposit Relationship and Commercial Bank Investment Behavior', *Rev. Econ. Stats.*, Aug., pp. 257–68.

—— (1963). *Commercial Bank Loan and Investment Policy* (Champaign, Ill.: University of Illinois Press).

KANE, E. J., and MALKIEL, B. G. (1965). 'Bank Portfolio Allocation, Deposit Variability and the Availability Doctrine', *Q.J.E.*, Feb., pp. 113–37.

METZLER, L. A. (1941). 'The Nature and Stability of Inventory Cycles', *Rev. Econ. Stats.*, Aug., pp. 113–29.

NERLOVE, M. (1960). 'The Market Demand for Durable Goods: A Comment', *Econometrica*, Jan., pp. 132–42.

RABINOWITZ, A. (1969). *Municipal Bond Finance and Administration* (New York: Wiley).

ROBINSON, R. (1960). *Postwar Market for State and Local Government Securities* (New York: National Bureau of Economic Research).

ROTHWELL, J. C. (1966). 'The Move to Municipals', Federal Reserve Bank of Philadelphia, *Business Review*, Sept., pp. 3–7.

SALOMON BROTHERS AND HUTZLER (1969). *An Analytical Record of Yields and Yield Spreads, 1950–1968* (New York).

—— (1971). 1969–70 'Supplement' to op. cit., above.

SCHUMPETER, J. A. (1939). *Business Cycles: A Theoretical, Historical, and Statistical Analysis of the Capitalist Process* (New York: McGraw-Hill).

Wood, J. H. (1967). 'A Model of Federal Reserve Behavior', in G. Horwich (ed.), *Monetary Process and Policy* (Homewood, Ill.: Irwin).

MONETARY POLICY AND NEO-CLASSICAL INVESTMENT ANALYSIS*

FRANK BRECHLING

(*Northwestern University and University of Essex*)

I. Introduction

IN recent years there has been a considerable revival of interest in classical production and factor demand theory. The distinguishing feature of this theory is its dependence on an *explicit* optimization procedure by individual firms. Such explicit theorizing has great advantages because it enables us to develop, test, and compare all the implications of various alternative sets of assumptions. Prior to the development of the neo-classical model of investment behaviour, a substantial amount of empirical work was published which related investment expenditures to output, profits, liquidity, capacity utilization, the rate of interest, etc. in a more or less *ad hoc* fashion. The researchers rarely stated their models explicitly and frequently related jointly dependent variables to one another. By contrast, the neo-classical approach provides a framework for a much more precise and rigorous specification.

Since gross investment is a large and relatively volatile part of total effective demand, and since government policies are often aimed at controlling investment expenditure, our models of invest-

* This is a substantially revised version of a paper read to the Conference of the Money Study Group, held in Bournemouth on 21–5 Feb. 1972. I am much indebted to Michael Parkin, the official discussant of the paper, for his suggestions and comments. I have attempted to meet most of his critical points. Hence, some of his own comments may no longer seem relevant. The work underlying this paper is part of a larger research project which Dale Mortensen and I have been conducting and which is supported by an N.S.F. grant (No. GS 2190). I also wish to acknowledge gratefully a Ford Foundation Faculty Fellowship which enabled me to be on leave in 1970–1 in order to pursue this project. My intellectual indebtedness to Dale Mortensen is too large to be acknowledged in detail. The paper was written while I was on leave from Northwestern University at the University of Essex.

ment behaviour ought to yield predictions about the response of investment to changes in various instruments of economic policy. For the purposes of the present conference, monetary policy instruments are of most interest. Hence, an attempt is made in this paper to review and evaluate some recent neo-classical models of investment with a view to discovering how monetary factors might influence the level of investment expenditure.

Although a large number of authors have recently been working on neo-classical models of investment behaviour, only a few typical approaches can be discussed here. The starting-point is the neo-classical model used extensively by Jorgenson [6], in which all firms (i) are price takers in all output and input markets and (ii) choose their optimum levels of output, employment, and capital according to a multi-period profit-maximization principle. Although Jorgenson uses a multi-period optimization procedure, the latter does not yield an *optimal* lag structure according to which firms adjust their capital stocks. Consequently, monetary policy can affect investment *only through the effects of changes in the rate of interest on the optimal capital stock*.[1] This type of model and some of the relevant empirical tests will be discussed in Section II.

In Section III a slightly different type of neo-classical model will be discussed. In addition to Jorgenson's assumptions, it is now postulated that firms face non-linear costs of adjusting their stocks of capital. The assumption of non-linear adjustment costs leads to predictions about the optimal lag structure according to which the stock of capital is adjusted. Although monetary policy can again operate only through the rate of interest, changes in the latter now have a *twofold* effect on investment: first, they change the long-run (i.e. steady-state) level of the capital stock and, second, they affect the speed of adjustment of the stock of capital. In Section III, the latter effect will be discussed in some detail and some relevant empirical tests will be presented.

When a Cobb–Douglas production function is assumed and the reduced forms of the above two types of models are fitted to quarterly data for U.S. manufacturing industries (total, durables, and non-durables will be reported) the results are not very satisfactory. The structural parameters frequently have wrong signs, implausible magnitudes, and very large standard errors. It is possible that a

---

[1] Similarly, non-monetary economic policy measures can influence investment *only* through the optimal capital stock and *not* through changes in the speed of adjustment.

different type of production function will yield more satisfactory results. But in Section IV an alternative hypothesis will be explored: if the observed level of gross investment is supply-determined in some or all phases of the business cycle, then the neo-classical demand-for-investment theory by itself cannot be expected to explain movements in actual gross investment at all well. In Section IV some arithmetical examples of partially supply-constrained models will be constructed and neo-classical investment models will be fitted to them. The observed biases in the resulting estimates often have the same signs as the ones one must suspect in the actual estimates of the structural parameters.

The general conclusion which will be drawn from the empirical evidence is that the neo-classical demand-for-investment approach cannot as yet be regarded as a satisfactory basis for the formulation of monetary (or, for that matter, other types of economic) policy. This conclusion is in contrast to that reached by Jorgenson and his associates (see, for instance, Jorgenson, Hunter, and Nadiri [7]). The differences in the conclusions arise from the following differences in the econometric approaches: Jorgenson and his associates fit *one* structural equation of their theoretical model to the data and compare the goodness of fit (measured by the residual standard error, the autocorrelation in the residuals, predictive power, etc.) with those of alternative theories of investment. By contrast, the approach presented in the present paper is based on fitting one or more *reduced-form* equations of the theoretical model and of studying the signs, magnitudes, and statistical significance of the underlying parameters of the production function. It would appear that the neo-classical demand-for-investment approach performs comparatively well according to Jorgenson's (relatively weak) criteria, but that it is far from satisfactory according to the (relatively strong) criteria used in the present paper. In Sections II and III, it will be shown that 'wrong' signs, implausible magnitudes of parameters, and low statistical significance abound. Consequently, the general message of this paper is one of caution: there is need for a great deal of further theoretical and empirical analysis before a satisfactory model of investment behaviour, on which economic policy can be based, will be available.

II. The neo-classical model without adjustment costs

In this section of the paper two types of neo-classical models without adjustment costs will be developed and tested empirically. The first type is the profit-maximization model used extensively by Jorgenson and presented most concisely in [6] and the second type is a cost-minimization model. The reduced-form equations of both types of models will be derived and fitted to the data.

1. The profit-maximization model

The following standard neo-classical assumptions are made:

(i) Individual firms are assumed to be perfectly competitive long-run profit maximizers. All output and input prices are exogenous to the firms and they simply adjust their inputs of factors and their homogeneous output, so as to maximize the net worth of the firm.

(ii) The capital market is perfect in the following sense: at a given market rate of interest all firms can borrow as much as they wish, but before the end of the planning horizon all debts have to be repaid. Hence, the discounted sum of cash inflows from borrowing must equal that of cash outflows due to debt repayment.

(iii) There exists a meaningful technological relationship, called the production function, which relates the inputs of labour and capital to the homogeneous output of the firm.

(iv) Real capital is treated like 'putty'. It depreciates (or decays) at a certain proportionate rate, but both new and existing capital goods are traded freely in the same market (indeed, they are quite indistinguishable).

The firm's cash flow in each period (R_t) is defined as sales revenue minus wage payments and minus gross investment:

$$R_t = P_t f(K_t, N_t) - w_t N - q_t(\dot{K}_t + \delta K_t) \tag{1}$$

where P_t, w_t, q_t stand for the price of output, labour, and investment goods, respectively, K_t and N_t are the inputs of capital and labour, δ is the rate of depreciation, so that gross investment is equal to $\dot{K}_t + \delta K_t$.[2] The levels of K_t and N_t should be chosen so as to maximize the discounted sum of R_t:

$$V = \int_0^\infty R_t \, e^{-rt} \, dt \tag{2}$$

where r is the real rate of interest (that is the money rate minus the

---

[2] R_t does not contain borrowing and debt repayment, because their discounted sums have already been assumed to be equal.

expected rate of price inflation). Since R_t contains $\dot{K}$, the Euler Equation gives the appropriate first-order necessary conditions for a maximum. As will be remembered, the Euler Equation states that for $\bar{X} = \int g(x, \dot{x}, t)\, \mathrm{d}t$ to be maximum (or minimum), it is necessary that $\partial g/\partial x - \mathrm{d}(\partial g/\partial \dot{x})/\mathrm{d}t = 0$ for all t.[3] Applying this formula, we obtain:

$$P_t f_K(K_t^*, N_t^*) - q_t\delta - r_t q_t + \dot{q}_t = 0 \tag{3}$$

and

$$P_t f_N(K_t^*, N_t^*) - w_t = 0 \tag{4}$$

where f_K and f_N stand for the marginal products of capital and labour, respectively. These conditions are, of course, well known, especially when they are rearranged somewhat:

$$f_K(K_t^*, N_t^*) = \frac{q_t}{P_t}\left(r_t + \delta - \frac{\dot{q}_t}{q_t}\right) = c_t \tag{5}$$

$$f_N(K_t^*, N_t^*) = \frac{w_t}{P_t} = \bar{w}_t. \tag{6}$$

The great advantage of the above approach is that the rental of capital (c_t) has been derived from an explicit multi-period optimization procedure. It is the product of the real price of equipment and the sum of depreciation, interest, and the proportionate (capital goods) price decline. As is shown in Jorgenson and Stephenson [8], the introduction of profit taxes, together with allowances, changes the definition of c_t to

$$c_t = \frac{q_t}{P_t(1-u)}\left\{(1 - \bar{w}u)r + (1 - vu)\delta - (1 - xu)\frac{\dot{q}_t}{q_t}\right\}$$

where u is the average rate of profits tax, and $\bar{w}$, v, and x are the proportions of true interest charges, depreciation charges, and capital gains which are allowable for tax purposes. Clearly, if $\bar{w} = v = x = 1$, so that there is no distinction between true and allowable charges, changes in profits taxes have no influence on c_t.

If the production function $f(K_t, N_t)$ is sufficiently simple, equations (5) and (6) can be solved for K_t^* and N_t^*. The Cobb–Douglas production function is a particularly convenient one. Since it has

---

[3] In our application, $g = R_t\, \mathrm{e}^{-rt}$. Hence $\partial g/\partial \dot{K} = -q_t\, \mathrm{e}^{-rt}$, which is then differentiated with respect to t. The Euler Equation (and other conditions) can easily be derived from a discrete version of equation (2). See Brechling [1].

been widely used in Jorgenson's (*et al.*) empirical work, let us solve equations (5) and (6) for the following production function:

$$Q_t = A \, e^{\rho t} K_t^\alpha N_t^\beta \tag{7}$$

where ρ measures some exogenous technological progress and α and β are the elasticities of output with respect to capital and labour. As is well known, the optimum levels of capital, employment, and output turn out to be:

$$K_t^* = A^\gamma \alpha^{\gamma\alpha+1} \beta^{\gamma\beta} \, e^{\gamma\rho t} c_t^{-\gamma\alpha-1} \bar{w}_t^{-\gamma\beta} \tag{8a}$$

$$N_t^* = A^\gamma \alpha^{\gamma\alpha} \beta^{\gamma\beta+1} \, e^{\gamma\rho t} c_t^{-\gamma\alpha} \bar{w}_t^{-\gamma\beta-1} \tag{8b}$$

$$Q_t^* = A^\gamma \alpha^{\gamma\alpha} \beta^{\gamma\beta} \, e^{\gamma\rho t} c_t^{-\gamma\alpha} \bar{w}_t^{-\gamma\beta} \tag{8c}$$

where $\gamma = 1/(1 - \alpha - \beta)$. Equations (8a)–(8c) are the appropriate reduced-form equations for the postulated model: K_t^*, N_t^*, and Q_t^* are determined *jointly* by t, c_t, and $\bar{w}_t$. It can also be verified easily that equations (8a)–(8c) imply the following three *structural* equations:

$$K_t^* = \frac{\alpha}{\beta} \frac{\bar{w}_t}{c_t} N_t^* \tag{9a}$$

$$K_t^* = \alpha \frac{Q_t^*}{c_t} \tag{9b}$$

$$N_t^* = \beta \frac{Q_t^*}{\bar{w}_t}. \tag{9c}$$

Equations (8) and (9) show clearly that, in this type of neo-classical model, monetary policy can affect the rate of investment only through the influence of the rate of interest (r) on the optimum stock of capital (K^*). The latter influence can be obtained by differentiating (8a) with respect to r. Without the subscript t, and, expressed as an elasticity, this turns out to be:[4]

$$\frac{\partial K^*}{\partial r} \frac{r}{K^*} = -\left(\frac{1-\beta}{1-\alpha-\beta}\right)\left(\frac{r}{r+\delta-\dot{q}/q}\right). \tag{10}$$

---

[4] A slightly different formulation is obtained when profits taxes are considered explicitly:

$$-\left(\frac{1-\beta}{1-\alpha-\beta}\right)\frac{(1-\bar{w}u)r}{(1-\bar{w}u)r + (1-vu)\delta - (1-xu)\dot{q}/q}.$$

Although this type of theory does not deal explicitly with the relationship between current net investment and the optimum stock of capital, it is plausible to assume that $\partial I/\partial K^*$ is positive. For economically relevant cases, equation (10) should have a negative value, and, hence, $\partial I/\partial r$ should also be negative.

In his theoretical statement of the above neo-classical model, Jorgenson [6] derived reduced forms which are analogous to equations (8a)–(8c) (but they are not explicitly solved for the Cobb–Douglas production function). By contrast, in his empirical analyses of investment behaviour (for instance, [8]), he invariably uses the *structural equation* (9b) rather than the *reduced-form equation* (8a). The use of the structural equation (9b) has the following two disadvantages: first, as is well known, the inclusion of an endogenous variable as an independent variable may lead to simultaneous equation bias. Second, the structural equation (9b) provides an estimate of *only α* and *knowledge of α is insufficient to measure the full effects of changes in an exogenous variable*. This point is shown clearly by equation (10): since β appears on the right-hand side, its value must be known before the impact of r on K^* can be measured. The same point applies to a change in any economic policy variable. In other words, in order to be able to measure the full effects of changes in the exogenous variables, information on *both α and β* is required while the structural equation (9b) yields only a (biased) estimate of α. Hence, there seem to be strong theoretical reasons for preferring *reduced-form* over *structural-equation* estimation.

Inspection of the reduced-form equations (8a), (8b), and (8c) shows that each one could be used to estimate both α and β. Moreover, compared with the structural equation (9b), only one additional variable is required for purposes of estimation: namely, the wage rate, which is comparatively easily available. Thus there seem to be no compelling practical reasons for preferring structural over reduced-form equation estimation. Hence, in this paper, only reduced-form equation estimates will be presented.

When the above neo-classical theory of the *individual firm* is applied empirically to time-series of *industries*, some further serious theoretical difficulties arise: first, the model does not predict anything about the *number* of firms that will be in existence at any moment of time. If free entry in response to positive profits is assumed, then equations (8a), (8b), and (8c) imply either that there are an infinitely large number of very small firms (if $\alpha + \beta < 1$) or that there is only one firm (if $\alpha + \beta > 1$).[5] In the latter case, the single firm can hardly be assumed to act like a perfectly competitive profit-maximizer. Since neither result is supported by empirical evidence, free entry in response to positive profits should not be assumed, and some notion of minimum normal profits above which new entrants are attracted may have to be introduced. A full analysis of this problem would be beyond the scope of this paper. Hence, the existence of an industry equilibrium with n firms will simply be assumed.[6] The second problem which arises in connection with the analysis of industry time-series is a standard aggregation problem. Equations (8a), (8b), and (8c) all refer to individual firms and they have the general form of $Y_j = X_1^{\eta_{1j}} X_2^{\eta_{2j}}$ where j refers to the jth firm and the exogenous variables X_1 and X_2 (the prices) are the same for all firms. A sufficient condition for aggregation is that all firms have identical η_{1j} and η_{2j}. In that case, all firms would have identical levels of Y and the aggregate relationship is simply $nY = nX_1^{\eta_1} X_2^{\eta_2}$ or, in logarithmic form: $\ln (nY) = \ln n + \eta_1 \ln X_1 + \eta_2 \ln X_2$. Our data refer to (nY) and, hence, the right-hand side of the aggregate relationship ought to include n, the total number of identical firms in the industry.[7] In the empirical analysis to be presented below, n will be assumed to be either constant or a smooth function of time, so that it appears either in the intercept or in ρ'.

Although equations (8a), (8b), and (8c) could all be estimated, either separately or as a system, the present section contains only the estimates of the parameters of (8a).[8] The latter was transformed into logarithms and then an arbitrary rational distributed lag of the type discussed by Jorgenson [5] was imposed. The resulting estimating equation has the following form:

---

[5] It can easily be shown from equations (8a), (8b), and (8c) that profits are equal to $P_t(Q_t^* - \bar{w}_t N_t^* - c_t K_t^*) = P_t A^\gamma \alpha^{\gamma\alpha} \beta^{\gamma\beta} e^{\gamma\rho t} c_t^{-\gamma\alpha} \bar{w}_t^{-\gamma\beta} (1 - \alpha - \beta)$. They can vanish only if P_t declines to zero and/or c_t and $\bar{w}_t$ rise to infinity as more firms enter the industry.

[6] Jorgenson and Stephenson [8], who also analyse industry time-series, do not deal with the problem of industry equilibrium.

[7] One advantage of Jorgenson's method of structural-equation estimation is that the number of firms need not be included. If α and c are the same for all firms, it is clearly legitimate to aggregate equation (9b) across firms: $\sum_j K_j^* = d \sum_j Q_j^* / c$ and n need not be known.

[8] In Section III the results of fitting a two-equation model with interequation constraints will be reported.

$$\ln K_t = k + \rho't - \frac{1 - \beta}{1 - \alpha - \beta} \sum_{i=0}^{4} a_i \ln c_{t-i}$$

$$- \frac{\beta}{1 - \alpha - \beta} \sum_{i=0}^{4} b_i \ln \bar{w}_{t-i} \tag{11}$$

$$+ \sum_{i=1}^{3} d_i \ln K_{t-i} + \text{seasonal dummies} + u_t.$$

Moreover, the following two constraints were imposed in the estimation:

$$\sum_{i=0}^{4} a_i = 1 - \sum_{i=1}^{3} d_i \quad \text{and} \quad \sum_{i=0}^{4} b_i = 1 - \sum_{i=1}^{3} d_i.$$

They ensure that, in the steady state when c_t, w_t, and K_t are all constant, the distributed lag coefficients cancel out. Equation (10) was fitted to data for (i) all U.S. manufacturing industries, (ii) durable goods industries, and (iii) non-durable goods industries. Quarterly data, covering the period 1949–69 (83 observations) were used.[9] Seasonal shift dummies were used, but their coefficients are not reported.[10]

Table IV.29 contains the estimates of the parameters of equation (11). The R^2's are extremely high, but this is largely due to the strong influence of the lagged dependent variables (the d-coefficients) and of the seasonal dummies. For the present purposes the production function coefficients α and β, as well as their sum (the scale parameter s, presented in the last line of Table IV.29) are of special interest. The t-ratios of the α-coefficients are 0·066, 1·73, and 0·252. Thus only the α-coefficient for durable industries can be taken seriously. Its magnitude of 0·607 is, however, implausibly large. The t-ratios of the β-coefficients are somewhat larger, namely 0·066, 4·73, and 6·20; moreover, the magnitudes of the last two coefficients (0·86 and 0·79) are quite plausible.

As is well known, the neo-classical theory of the firm discussed here requires (in order that the second-order conditions for a maximum be satisfied) that the scale parameter $(s = \alpha + \beta)$ be less than

[9] The data were very similar to those used by Jorgenson and Stephenson (see [8], Appendix). The rental c_t contains Moody's Baa bond rate. Moreover, a new series of 'net interest' is now being published in the *National Income and Product Accounts* [12] (Table 1 for 1947–66 and Table 1.22 for 1967–70). w_t is the *straight-time* hourly rate of earnings and P_t is the wholesale price index. $\dot{q}$ was assumed to be constant. All data are available on request.

[10] Most of the seasonal shift dummies have very high t-ratios.

TABLE IV.29

Parameter Estimates of Equation (10)

	All manufacturing industries	Durable goods industries	Non-durable goods industries
ρ'	0·0000901 (0·0001905)	0·0000399 (0·0001687)	0·0002312 (0·0001433)
α	6·0768 (97·1226)	0·60766 (0·35614)	0·10290 (0·40869)
β	0·48048 (7·25195)	0·79527 (0·12817)	0·86157 (0·18215)
a_0	0·0978 (0·4881)	0·02906 (0·03315)	−0·00110 (0·01111)
a_1	−0·0898 (0·5165)	−0·01430 (0·04080)	0·00246 (0·02202)
a_2	0·1493 (0·8104)	0·02739 (0·04302)	−0·00301 (0·02678)
a_3	−0·1074 (0·5940)	−0·00530 (0·04060)	0·00246 (0·02221)
b_0	0·1014 (2·9591)	−0·02549 (0·04823)	0·00059 (0·00496)
b_1	−1·5086 (46·5399)	−0·03236 (0·06208)	0·00307 (0·02470)
b_2	1·5083 (46·5130)	0·03066 (0·05964)	−0·00404 (0·03251)
b_3	−0·3153 (9·7182)	−0·01792 (0·05738)	0·00184 (0·01470)
d_1	2·1397 (0·1229)	1·99267 (0·12725)	2·02422 (0·13155)
d_2	−1·3774 (0·2425)	−1·10225 (0·25040)	−1·23827 (0·25074)
d_3	0·2261 (0·1271)	0·08492 (0·13027)	0·21306 (0·13129)
R^2	0·99979	0·99974	0·99977
D–W	2·0894	2·1401	1·9696
s	6·5573 (90·2160)	1·40293 (0·26739)	0·96448 (0·28796)

Asymptotic standard errors are given in parentheses.

unity. For total manufacturing, the scale parameter is very badly determined and must, therefore, be ignored. For durable goods industries the parameter of 1·4 is rather high, but its two-standard-error range is about 0·7 to 1·9 which covers some theoretically admissible values. The scale parameter for non-durable industries of 0·96 with a two-standard-error range of about 0·4 to 1·5 is the most satisfactory result.

The parameter estimates reported above seem to be quite sensitive to minor changes in the specification of the model or in the data. Thus, in order to be able to assess the importance of the profits tax adjustments, equation (11) was fitted *without* the tax adjustments. The resulting values of α, β, s, and R^2 are presented in Table IV.30.

TABLE IV.30

Selected Parameters for Equation (11) without Tax Adjustments

	α	β	s	R^2
All manufacturing indus- tries	0·7392 (0·1893)	0·2319 (0·1766)	0·9711 (0·0639)	0·99982
Durable goods industries	0·3212 (1·8982)	−0·2359 (2·9112)	0·0853 (3·0844)	0·99974
Non-durable goods indus- tries	1·1325 (0·4935)	−0·1650 (0·4542)	0·9675 (0·1395)	0·99982

Thus the coefficients for all manufacturing industries are somewhat better determined when the tax variables are omitted; moreover, the scale parameter is now fairly plausible. On the other hand, the coefficients for both durable and non-durable goods industries are either very badly determined or have implausible magnitudes (with the exception of s for non-durables). But the most striking aspects of Tables IV.29 and IV.30 are the large differences in the parameters which are attributable to the tax adjustments in the rental of capital (c_t).

2. *The cost-minimization model*

While the above profit-maximization model has been used very extensively, there have been a number of other investigators (e.g. Coen and Hickman [3]) who have preferred a cost-minimization model. Accordingly, they have assumed that the typical firm takes its level of output (Q_t) as exogenous or predetermined and aims at minimizing the cost of producing it. The cost minimization relaxes some of the restrictive assumptions which underlie the profit-maximization one. The specific advantages of the cost-minimization approach are as follows:

(i) Since output is assumed to be exogenous (or predetermined) it is no longer necessary to suppose that individual firms are perfectly competitive price takers in the product market. No specific assumptions about the working of the output market need be made.

(ii) Since output is now given to the firm, the second-order conditions for a cost minimum do not require that firms operate in conditions of decreasing returns to scale $(\alpha + \beta < 1)$.

(iii) The cost-minimization approach focuses attention on the *pure* factor substitution effect of a change in relative factor prices. *Given the level of output*, what happens to the amount of capital (and labour) used when there is a change in relative factor prices? By contrast, the profit-maximization model allows for *both* a substitution and scale effect in response to a change of one of the (real) input prices. Hence, even if the assumption of exogenous (or predetermined) output is inappropriate and leads to simultaneous equation bias, the cost-minimization approach may generate some valuable information on the degree of factor substitutability, that is, on the slope of the isoquants.

Individual firms are still assumed to be price takers in the factor markets and, hence, their multi-period objective can be stated as:

$$\text{Min } \bar{C} = \int_0^\infty C_t \, e^{-rt} \, dt$$

$$\text{s.t.} \quad \text{(a)} \quad C_t = w_t N_t + q_t(\dot{K}_t + \delta K_t) \tag{12}$$

$$\text{(b)} \quad Q_t = f(N_t, K_t)$$

where w_t, q_t, δ, and Q_t are assumed to be either parameters or exogenous variables. As is well known, the necessary first-order condition for (12) to be a minimum is that the ratio of marginal products be equal to the ratio of factor prices: [11]

$$\frac{f_K(K_t^*, N_t^*)}{f_N(K_t^*, N_t^*)} = \frac{q_t}{w_t}\left(r_t + \delta - \frac{\dot{q}_t}{q}\right) = \frac{c_t}{w_t}. \tag{13}$$

[11] When adjustments for profits taxes are made, the price ratio in (13) becomes

$$\frac{q_t}{w_t(1-u)}\left\{(1 - \tilde{w}u)r + (1 - vu)\delta - (1 - xu)\frac{\dot{q}_t}{q_t}\right\}.$$

When the production function is assumed to be Cobb–Douglas, then the reduced form for K^* is:

$$K_t^* = \left\{ \left(\frac{\beta}{\alpha} \right)^\beta A^{-1} \, e^{-\rho t} \left(\frac{c_t}{w_t} \right)^{-\beta} Q \right\}^{1/(\alpha + \beta)}. \tag{14}$$

The elasticity of K^* with respect to the rate of interest r is:

$$\frac{\partial K^*}{\partial r} \frac{r}{K} = - \frac{\beta}{\alpha + \beta} \frac{r}{(r + \delta - \dot{q}/q)}. \tag{15}$$

Since the cost-minimization model allows only for factor substitution and *not* for a scale effect this elasticity is smaller (in absolute value) than the corresponding one in equation (10): for cost minimization $\beta/(\alpha + \beta) < 1$ while for profit maximization $(1 - \beta)/(1 - \alpha - \beta) > 1$ (for positive coefficients).

As in the case of profit maximization, equation (14) can be aggregated if there are n identical firms. It is again assumed that n is either constant or varies smoothly over time. Equation (14) was transformed into logarithms and an arbitrary rational distributed lag was imposed, so that the actual estimating equation was:

$$\ln K_t = k_0 + \rho' t + \frac{\beta}{\beta + \alpha} \sum_{i=0}^{4} a_i \ln \frac{w_{t-i}}{c_{t-i}} + \frac{1}{\beta + \alpha} \sum_{i=0}^{4} b_i \ln Q_{t-i}$$

$$+ \sum_{i=1}^{3} d_i \ln K_{t-i} + \text{seasonal dummies} + u_t. \tag{16}$$

The constraints

$$\sum_{i=0}^{4} a_i = \sum_{i=0}^{4} b_i = 1 - \sum_{i=1}^{3} d_i$$

were again imposed and the K_t and Q_t refer to industry aggregates. Output was defined as shipments plus inventory changes. The sample period was 1954–69 (59 observations).

It should perhaps be pointed out that in equation (16) the scale parameter $s = \alpha + \beta$ is identified by output while β is identified by the relative factor prices. The sign and magnitude of β—although it is the exponent of N—is thus of particular interest, because it is a crucial measure of the degree of factor substitutability.

In Table IV.31, the estimates of the parameters of equation (16) are presented. The estimates of β are *negative* and fairly significant in the case of total manufacturing and of durable goods industries. In the non-durable goods industries, both α and β are very small

TABLE IV.31

Parameter Estimates of Equation (16)

	All manufacturing industries	Durable goods industries	Non-durable goods industries
ρ'	-0.0003216 (0.0000958)	0.00002978 (0.00010209)	-0.0005884 (0.0001962)
α	0.76992 (0.12960)	1.12461 (0.16346)	0.16474 (0.19634)
β	-0.13538 (0.07858)	-0.25124 (0.10926)	0.07377 (0.10407)
α_0	0.1327 (0.0925)	0.1460 (0.0808)	-0.0578 (0.1289)
a_1	-0.0528 (0.0992)	-0.0579 (0.0904)	0.0307 (0.0997)
a_2	0.0728 (0.1004)	0.0560 (0.0870)	-0.0207 (0.0857)
a_3	-0.0869 (0.0952)	-0.0256 (0.0772)	0.1032 (0.1916)
b_0	0.0301 (0.0086)	0.0405 (0.0112)	0.0064 (0.0060)
b_1	0.0027 (0.0101)	-0.0060 (0.0146)	0.0088 (0.0070)
b_2	0.0246 (0.0104)	0.0361 (0.0150)	0.0016 (0.0053)
b_3	-0.0092 (0.0101)	-0.0078 (0.0147)	-0.0028 (0.0056)
d_1	1.4333 (0.1532)	1.4053 (0.1558)	1.8279 (0.1616)
d_2	-0.3441 (0.2651)	-0.4081 (0.2593)	-0.9173 (0.3035)
d_3	-0.1480 (0.1295)	-0.0781 (0.1275)	0.0712 (0.1583)
R^2	0.99991	0.99984	0.99987
D–W	2.1217	2.040	2.0313
s	0.63454 (0.06882)	0.87337 (0.07756)	0.23851 (0.11511)

Asymptotic standard errors in parentheses.

and statistically very insignificant. The scale parameters $(s = \alpha + \beta)$, presented in the last row of the Table, are plausible in the first two industries but very small in non-durable goods industries. The 'wrong' negative signs of β are especially disturbing because they imply that the isoquants of the production function have a positive slope.

When the tax adjustments are omitted, the estimates of the parameters of equation (16) are still highly implausible. They are presented in Table IV.32. According to the estimates, the isoquants for all three industries have positive slopes.

TABLE IV.32

Selected Parameter Values for Equation (16) without Tax Adjustments

	α	β	s	R^2
All manufacturing industries	0·7229 (0·2176)	−0·1886 (0·2019)	0·5343 (0·0490)	0·99990
Durable goods industries	1·4260 (0·3591)	−0·6259 (0·3337)	0·8001 (0·0665)	0·99984
Non-durable goods industries	−0·1767 (0·3018)	0·3801 (0·2656)	0·2035 (0·0788)	0·99988

This concludes the discussion of the multi-period neo-classical model of investment demand without adjustment costs. The optimal stock of capital (K^*) has been derived for both profit-maximization and cost-minimization models on the assumption that the production function is Cobb–Douglas. *Ad hoc* lag structures have been imposed on the appropriate reduced-form equation for K^* and reduced-form equation estimates of the exponents α and β have been obtained. As the figures in Tables IV.29–IV.32 show, the results are far from satisfactory. The majority of the coefficients have highly implausible magnitudes and signs or large standard errors. Moreover, some seem to be very sensitive to minor differences in specification. The main conclusion to be drawn from this analysis is that these two types of neo-classical models do not perform well, and that it would be premature to use them as the basis for the formulation of economic policy. Jorgenson and his associates [7] have reached a less pessimistic conclusion. But their views have been based on the relatively weak criterion of the comparative performance of one structural equation of the model. In this paper a more severe criterion for judging the neo-classical model has been used: Does the estimation of one reduced form of the model yield plausible and statistically significant values of the parameters? Unfortunately, the preliminary answer must be no.

III. The neo-classical model with adjustment costs

The neo-classical model discussed in Section II does not provide an optimal lag structure according to which the individual firm should adjust its current capital stock to the long-run optimal stock. If, however, non-linear adjustment costs are postulated, then a lag structure can be derived from the optimizing behaviour of the firm. This type of model was analysed in a seminal article by Eisner and Strotz [4] and it has been refined by, among others, Lucas [9], Treadway [13], and Brechling and Mortensen [2]. In this section of the paper, some properties and estimates of this type of model will be reported: first, the role of the rate of interest will be analysed in a simple version of this model and, second, some parameter estimates of a multi-input version of this model will be presented.

1. The role of the rate of interest in adjustment cost models

Let us amend the revenue function of an individual firm by deducting a cost of changing the capital stock. Equation (1) then becomes:

$$R_t = P_t f(K_t, N_t) - w_t N - q_t({}_t \dot{K} + \delta K) - C(\dot{K}_t). \qquad (17)$$

It is intuitively plausible that non-linear $C(\dot{K}_t)$ functions will lead to slow adjustments: if large changes in K_t are much more expensive than small changes, then the firm will have a strong inducement to adjust slowly. Moreover, it is sensible to postulate that costs of adjustment are positive for *both* positive and negative $\dot{K}$.[12] Consequently it will be assumed that $C'(\dot{K}) \gtrless 0$ as $\dot{K} \gtrless 0$ and $C''(\dot{K}) > 0$. If the firm is assumed to maximize the present value of equation (17), namely $V = \int_0^\infty R_t \, e^{-rt} \, dt$, then the Euler Equation requires that:

$$P_t f_K(K_t^*, N_t^*) - r_t C'(\dot{K}_t^*) + C''(\dot{K}_t^*)\ddot{K}_t^*$$
$$= q_t(r_t + \delta - \dot{q}_t/q_t) = P_t c_t. \qquad (18)$$

[12] Equation (17) illustrates that the term $q_t \dot{K}_t$ acts like a linear adjustment cost which becomes negative for negative $\dot{K}_t$.

(In addition, the marginal product of labour must be equal to its real wage, as postulated by equation (4).) As is well known, for V to be a maximum it is also necessary that $C''(\dot{K}) \geq 0$ (the Legendre condition) which is satisfied by assumption and that $\lim_{t \to \infty} C'(\dot{K}) \, e^{-rt} = 0$ (the Transversality condition).

The following three points about equation (18) are of interest: (i) As already mentioned, linear adjustment costs—which imply $C''(\dot{K}) = 0$ and $C'(\dot{K}) = \text{constant}$—would lead to an equation similar to (5), except that c_t would contain another term. (ii) If $C'(0) = 0$, then, in the steady state when $\dot{K} = \ddot{K} = 0$, equations (5) and (18) become identical. Hence, equation (5) should be regarded as a long-run condition. (iii) It is clear that the rate of interest influences K_t^* not only through the rental c_t but also through the second term of the left-hand side. Hence, *both the steady state solution and the path towards the steady state are affected by changes in the rate of interest.*

For the present purpose, the dual role of the rate of interest is of special interest. Let us examine it further by making the following assumptions which allow us to convert equation (18) into a *linear* equation: first, let the production function be quadratic and separable, so that $f_K(K_t^*, N_t^*) = \beta + \gamma K_t^*$ ($\gamma < 0$). Second, let the cost-of-adjustment equation be approximately quadratic, so that $C'(\dot{K}_t^*) = b\dot{K}_t^*$ and $C''(\dot{K}_t^*) = b$. Third, let the rate of interest and the prices be constant over the planning period. On these assumptions equation (18) becomes:

$$\ddot{K}_t^* - r\dot{K}_t^* + p\gamma K_t^* + p(\beta - c) = 0 \qquad (19)$$

where the small-case p stands for P/b. The roots of this second-order equation are:

$$\lambda = \tfrac{1}{2}r \pm \tfrac{1}{2}(r^2 - 4p\gamma)^{1/2}. \qquad (20)$$

Since $\gamma < 0$ and both r and p are positive, it follows that (i) both roots must be real and (ii) there must be one positive (unstable) and one negative (stable) root. Thus if both λ's were allowed to remain in the general solution of equation (19), the unstable root would dominate. But this process would not satisfy the transversality condition and, hence, the unstable root must be excluded.[13]

---

[13] Let $\tilde{\lambda}$ be the unstable root: $\tilde{\lambda} = \tfrac{1}{2}r + \tfrac{1}{2}(r^2 - 4p\gamma)^{1/2}$ which is larger than r. The general solution of (19) becomes $K_t - K^{**} = B \, e^{\tilde{\lambda}t}$ when the stable root is dominated. Hence $\dot{K}_t = \tilde{\lambda}B \, e^{\tilde{\lambda}t}$. Thus, the transversality condition $\lim_{t \to \infty} \tilde{\lambda}bB \, e^{(\tilde{\lambda} - r)t} = 0$ cannot hold (because $\tilde{\lambda} > r$).

Let the general solution be $K_t - K^{**} = A e^{\lambda t} + B e^{\bar{\lambda} t}$ where λ and $\bar{\lambda}$ are the stable and unstable roots, respectively. K_0 is given to the firm. Hence, $K_0 - K^{**} = A + B$ and $K_1 - K^{**} = A e^{\lambda} + B e^{\bar{\lambda}}$ must hold and K_1^* is *chosen* such that B is equal to zero. Hence, $A = K_0 - K^{**}$, $K_1^* - K^{**} = (K_0 - K^{**}) e^{\lambda}$ and, in general:

$$K_1^* - K^{**} = (K_0 - K^{**}) e^{\lambda t} \tag{21}$$

and

$$\dot{K}_t^* = \lambda(K_0 - K^{**}) e^{\lambda t} = \lambda(K_t^* - K^{**}) \tag{22}$$

where

$$K^{**} = -\frac{\beta + c}{\gamma} \tag{23}$$

The twofold influence—through K^{**} and through λ—can now be analysed more precisely. Specifically, let us differentiate $\dot{K}^*$ with respect to r:

$$\frac{\partial \dot{K}^*}{\partial r} = -\lambda \frac{\partial K^{**}}{\partial r} + (K_t^* - K^{**}) \frac{\partial \lambda}{\partial r}$$

$$= -\lambda \frac{1}{\gamma} \frac{q}{P} + \tfrac{1}{2}(K_t^* - K^{**})\{1 - r(r^2 - 4b\gamma)^{-1/2}\}. \tag{24}$$

Since $\lambda < 0$ and $\gamma < 0$, equation (20) implies that (i) a rise in r will always reduce K^{**} and this partial effect on $\dot{K}_t^*$ will always be negative, (ii) a rise in the rate of interest will always raise λ, so that adjustment to K^{**} is slowed down, and (iii) the total effect of a change in the interest rate depends crucially on the sign of $(K_t^* - K^{**})$; if K^{**} exceeds K_t^*, a rise in r will reduce $\dot{K}_t^*$ through both effects, but if K_t^* exceeds K^{**}, the effect through λ is positive and it may well offset the negative K^{**}-effect. Thus a short-run 'perverse' effect of the rate of interest is possible: when the existing capital stock is already excessive, a rise in the rate of interest will make it more excessive but at the same time it will slow down the adjustment to K^{**} and the combined effect might lead to a rise in investment.

While the negative influence of r upon K^{**} is a well-established implication of classical theory, the positive influence of r upon λ has not been subjected to much analysis. Moreover, in empirical work the influence of r upon λ is generally ignored although r is usually introduced as one of the determinants of K^{**}. In order to be able to obtain some impression of the magnitude and nature of this relationship, Table IV.33 has been prepared. The annual rate of interest is allowed to vary between 2 per cent and 10 per cent and $p\gamma$ between $-0\cdot03$ and $-2\cdot0$. The resulting values for $|\lambda|$ in Table IV.33 are appropriate when $\dot{K}_t^*$ is measured at an annual rate. Most empirical estimates seem to suggest that $|\lambda|$ lies somewhere between $0\cdot2$ and $0\cdot5$. The following aspects of Table IV.33 are of interest: (i) over the relevant range, the influence of the rate of interest upon $|\lambda|$ does not seem to be very large, when they are compared with the differences in estimated values of $|\lambda|$. Suppose $K^{**} - K_t^* = £100$, then, with the lowest $|\lambda|$, net investment might vary between $£12$ and $£15$ and with the largest $|\lambda|$ between $£72\cdot8$ and $£71\cdot1$ for an $0\cdot08$ point difference in the rate of interest. In practice, changes in the rate of interest tend to be much smaller and, hence, its impact on $|\lambda|$ is correspondingly reduced. (ii) Over the relevant ranges the relationship between r and $|\lambda|$ seems to be approximately linear. Hence, it might be possible to estimate it linearly. (iii) $|\lambda|$ responds more strongly to changes in the rate of interest when $|p\gamma|$ is small than when it is large. The higher the adjustment cost coefficient (b) in relation to the price level (P) and the second derivative of the production function (γ) the more important is the rate of interest in the determination of the value of $|\lambda|$.

2. Empirical evidence on cost-of-adjustment models

Let us now turn to a discussion of the empirical work which has been undertaken on cost-of-adjustment models. Nadiri and Rosen [10], Schramm [11], and Coen and Hickman [3] have made contributions in this area, but in this paper attention will be confined to the work by Brechling and Mortensen [2]. This model is based on the following assumptions: first, firms are assumed to be cost-minimizers who take their output as predetermined, but are price takers in input markets. Second, the log-linear production function contains as arguments explicitly the utilization rates of capital and labour. These utilization rates may also be subject to adjustment costs but, for the purposes of the present paper, only the factor stocks have adjustment costs. Third, there may be some interdependence between the costs of adjustment and the arguments of the production function. This is Treadway's concept of 'internal'

TABLE IV.33

Values of |λ| for Various Assumed Values of r and py

r	py = −0·03	py = −0·10	py = −0·50	py = −0·80	py = −1·5	py = −2·0
0·02	0·150	0·262	0·493	0·574	0·681	0·728
0·03	0·146	0·258	0·490	0·571	0·679	0·726
0·04	0·142	0·254	0·487	0·568	0·677	0·724
0·05	0·138	0·250	0·484	0·565	0·674	0·722
0·06	0·134	0·246	0·481	0·562	0·672	0·720
0·07	0·130	0·242	0·477	0·560	0·670	0·718
0·08	0·127	0·239	0·474	0·557	0·667	0·715
0·09	0·123	0·235	0·471	0·554	0·665	0·713
0·10	0·120	0·232	0·468	0·551	0·663	0·711

costs of adjustment [13]. In the two-factor case, the production function can then be written as:

$$Q_t = A_t N_t^{a_1} U_{Nt}^{a_3} K_t^{a_2} U_{Kt}^{a_4} f\left(\frac{\dot{N}_t}{N_t}, \frac{\dot{K}}{K_t}\right) \tag{25}$$

where $f(\ )$ is the 'internal' adjustment cost function U_N and U_K stand for the utilization rates of labour and capital. The cost function contains the rentals (c_N and c_K) of both capital and labour as well as the costs of utilizing the stocks:

$$C_t = c_{Nt} N_t + c_{Kt} K_t + W_{Nt} U_{Nt} N_t + W_{Kt} U_{Kt} K_t. \tag{26}$$

The c's refer to the costs of the stocks of labour and capital which have to be met no matter whether or not they are used. In the case of labour, c_N measures the cost of fringe benefits, holidays, guaranteed wages, etc., while c_K has already been defined as $c_K = q(r + \delta)$ (without tax adjustments). By contrast, W_N and W_K measure the cost of using labour and capital: W_N should be the standard hourly wage rate and W_K the cost of using capital (e.g. costs of wear and tear due to utilization). The latter should clearly exclude pure time depreciation, which is measured by δ. The utilization rates U_N and U_K would, in general, be non-linear functions of some observable utilization rates, such as average hours worked. This non-linearity could accommodate overtime payments and similar increasing marginal utilization costs. For instance, as average hours rise by 10 per cent, U_N is assumed to rise by more than 10 per cent, and this catches the effect of increasing amounts of overtime pay.

The firm is assumed to minimize the sum of future discounted costs:

$$\bar{C} = \int_0^\infty C_t \, e^{-rt} \, dt \tag{27}$$

subject to the production function (25) and $Q_t = \bar{Q}$. If $a_1 > a_2$, $a_3 > a_4$, if all the a's are positive, if expectations are stationary, and if $f(0, 0) = 0$, then N_t and K_t approach N^* and K^* and in the neighbourhood or the steady state the following two relationships hold:

$$\dot{n} = m_{11}(n - n^*) + m_{12}(k - k^*) \tag{28a}$$

$$\dot{k} = m_{21}(n - n^*) + m_{22}(k - k^*) \tag{28b}$$

where $n = \ln N$ and $k = \ln K$. The n^* and k^* are the same as those resulting from the comparative static cost-minimization problem.

Since n^* and k^* contain the same parameters of the production function, the two equations were estimated jointly and the over-identifying restrictions were imposed. A large number of different specifications of the discrete versions of equations (28a) and (28b) have been estimated. It soon became apparent, however, that there was a persistently high level of autocorrelation in the residuals of the capital equation. Consequently, the two equations were subjected to a generalized rho-transformation. Let x_t, z_t, and u_t stand for the vectors of dependent variables, of independent variables, and of errors, respectively, and let R, M, and A be matrices of auto-correlation coefficients, of adjustment coefficients, and of combinations of structural parameters, respectively. Then the basic model, expressed in matrix notation, is:

$$x_t - x_{t-1} = M(x_{t-1} - x_t^*) + u_t = M(x_{t-1} - Az_t) + u_t \quad (29)$$

$$u_t = Ru_{t-1} + \varepsilon_t \quad (30)$$

where ε_t is a vector of randomly distributed errors. By lagging and pre-multiplying equation (29) by R, u_t can be eliminated and the following set of equations can be seen to hold:

$$x_t - x_{t-1} = (R + M)(x_{t-1} - x_{t-2})$$
$$+ (I - R)Mx_{t-2} - MAz_t + RNAz_{t-1} + \varepsilon_t \quad (31)$$

where, for purposes of estimation, the vectors and matrices had the following values:

(a) $x_t = \begin{bmatrix} \ln N_t \\ \ln K_t \end{bmatrix}$ (b) $R = \begin{bmatrix} \rho_{11} & \rho_{12} \\ \rho_{21} & \rho_{22} \end{bmatrix}$ (c) $M = \begin{bmatrix} m_{11} & m_{12} \\ m_{21} & m_{22} \end{bmatrix}$

(d) $A = \begin{bmatrix} \dfrac{a_1 - a_3}{s} - 1 & \dfrac{a_2 - a_4}{s} & \dfrac{1}{s} & \sigma_1 \\[3mm] \dfrac{a_1 - a_3}{s} & \dfrac{a_2 - a_4}{s} - 1 & \dfrac{1}{s} & \sigma_2 \end{bmatrix}$

$$(32)$$

(e) $z_t = \begin{bmatrix} \ln \dfrac{C_{Nt}}{W_{Nt}} \\[3mm] \ln \dfrac{C_{Kt}}{W_{Nt}} \\[3mm] \ln Q_t \\[2mm] t \end{bmatrix}$

where $s = a_1 + a_2$ and σ_1 and σ_2 are proportionate rates of change

TABLE IV.34

Parameter Estimates of Equation (31)

	All manufacturing industries	Durable goods industries	Non-durable goods industries
$a_1 - a_3$	2·0819 (0·1771)	1·7584 (0·2335)	3·1257 (0·3950)
$a_2 - a_4$	−0·0034 (0·0681)	−0·0475 (0·0920)	−0·2230 (0·1213)
s	1·0722 (0·0416)	1·2273 (0·0458)	0·9423 (0·1191)
σ_1	0·0050 (0·0066)	0·0002 (0·0043)	0·0373 (0·0839)
σ_2	0·0366 (0·0402)	0·0231 (0·0274)	0·1068 (0·2681)
m_{11}	−0·7729 (0·0542)	−0·8586 (0·0582)	−0·4629 (0·0642)
m_{12}	0·1208 (0·0234)	0·1221 (0·0294)	0·1449 (0·0270)
m_{21}	0·0621 (0·0585)	0·0512 (0·0613)	0·0586 (0·0559)
m_{22}	−0·0289 (0·0317)	−0·0340 (0·0365)	−0·0236 (0·0298)
ρ_{11}	−0·1090 (0·1034)	−0·0689 (0·1074)	0·0563 (0·1151)
ρ_{12}	0·0198 (0·2232)	0·0787 (0·2234)	−0·0924 (0·2014)
ρ_{21}	0·0337 (0·1005)	0·0590 (0·1034)	0·0236 (0·1027)
ρ_{22}	0·9076 (0·1576)	0·8835 (0·1872)	0·9094 (0·1221)
R^2(Lab)	0·8526	0·7747	0·9540
R^2(Cap)	0·9425	0·9271	0·9440
D–W(Lab)	2·0185	1·9556	1·9723
D–W(Cap)	1·3346	1·4780	1·3780
$a_3 + a_4$	−1·0063 (0·1902)	−0·4836 (0·2499)	−1·9604 (0·3506)

Asymptotic standard errors in parentheses.

attributable to productivity change as well as expected exponential growth in output and the price ratios.

The reduced forms which are appropriate for the stated assumptions should contain, as independent variables, the *three* price ratios C_{Nt}/W_{Nt}, C_{Kt}/W_{Nt}, W_{kt}/W_{Nt}, the level of output (Q_t), and a time trend. Information on C_{Nt} and W_{Kt} is unfortunately not available and, hence, either C_{Nt}/W_{Nt} or W_{kt}/W_{Nt} had to be approximated by $1/W_{Nt}$. It was decided rather arbitrarily that $C_{Nt}/W_{Nt} \simeq 1/W_{Nt}$ and that W_{Kt}/W_{Nt} could be assumed to be uncorrelated with the other explanatory variables. If this assumption is incorrect, well-known biases due to omitted variables will have arisen. As is shown by A and z, the omission of W_{Kt}/Q_{Nt} leads to impossibility of identifying a_1, a_2, a_3, and a_4, separately. It is, however, possible to identify $(a_1 - a_3)$, $(a_2 - a_4)$, and s. Since the latter is defined as $s = a_1 + a_2$, it is easy to construct the sum of a_3 and a_4 as $s - (a_1 - a_3) - (a_2 - a_4) = a_3 + a_4$. The second-order conditions for a maximum require that $a_1 > a_3$ and $a_2 > a_4$, and, to make economic sense, all a's should be positive. In other words, *the five estimated and constructed coefficients*, $(a_1 - a_3)$, $(a_2 - a_4)$, s, $(a_3 + a_4)$, *should all be positive* and strong negative values should be regarded as an indication of the inadequacy of the model.

Table IV.34 contains the estimates of the elements of the M, R, and A matrices. They were obtained by estimating the labour and investment equations jointly and by imposing the over-identifying restrictions.[14] The rental for capital was adjusted for tax changes. The output variable has already been described (see Section II.2). The labour series consists of production workers only. The sample period was 1954–69 (65 observations).

In the R matrix only ρ_{22} is consistently large and statistically significant. In the M matrix m_{11} is strong and has the expected negative sign. Moreover m_{12} is positive and also statistically strong; but neither m_{21} nor m_{22} is strong, though the latter has the expected negative sign. Neither σ_1 nor σ_2 is strong. The scale coefficients $s = a_1 + a_2$ are strong and have plausible values. All estimates of $(a_2 - a_4)$ are negatives but weak. The most implausible results refer to $(a_3 + a_4)$ all of which are negative and strong. Finally, all values of $(a_1 - a_3)$ are positive, very significant, and their absolute

---

[14] The criterion used for the selection of the parameters was the smallest trace of the variance–covariance matrix of the residuals of both equations. In other words, the program minimized $\sum_i \varepsilon_{1i} + \sum_i \varepsilon_{2i}$ where 1, 2 stand for equation and i for observations.

values tend to be large. These large values (which are responsible for the negative values of $(a_3 + a_4)$) may be due to biases arising from omitted variables. While these kinds of biases will have to be investigated further, the present results are not very encouraging.

Nor is the situation improved when no profits tax allowances are made in the rental of capital. Table IV.35 shows that while two

TABLE IV.35

Selected Parameter Values of Equation (31) without Tax Adjustments

	$a_1 - a_3$	$a_2 - a_4$	s	$a_3 + a_4$
All manufacturing industries	1·9067	0·1364	0·9323	−1·1108
	(0·1689)	(0·1057)	(0·0414)	(0·2233)
Durable goods industries	1·8715	0·5148	1·1625	−1·2238
	(0·1857)	(0·1411)	(0·0307)	(0·2700)
Non-durable goods industries	3·0818	−0·4465	0·8410	−1·7943
	(0·5096)	(0·1902)	(0·1645)	(0·4530)

values of $(a_2 - a_4)$ are now positive, the values of $(a_3 + a_4)$ are still strongly negative.

This concludes the analysis of the neo-classical model with adjustment costs. First, an attempt has been made to assess the influence of the rate of interest on the stock adjustment coefficient λ. In a simple one-equation model, this influence has been found to be small and, more importantly, approximately linear. Hence, there is some hope that future investigations might incorporate a linear influence of the rate of interest on the speed of adjustment. Moreover, there is a possibility that a rise in the rate of interest may affect current net investment 'perversely'. This may happen when net investment is already negative and a rise in the rate of interest slows down sufficiently the rate of adjustment of the actual to the desired capital stock. Second, a fairly elaborate cost-of-adjustment model of a cost-minimizing firm has been presented and the empirical results reported. Unfortunately these results are again predominantly negative: most of the parameters have implausible magnitudes or 'wrong' signs. Hence, the conclusions of Section II of this paper are reinforced: the reduced-form equation estimation used in this paper yields results which cast serious doubts on the adequacy of the neo-classical models of investment behaviour as a basis for the formulation of economic policy.

IV. Supply factors in the theory of investment

In view of the unsatisfactory conclusions which had to be drawn from the (admittedly imperfect) evidence at the end of Sections II and III, it is perhaps in order to point the way to an alternative approach in the theory of investment. One possibility would be to assume a different production function. However, in view of the frequency with which upward-sloping isoquants have been observed, this approach may not be too successful. In this part of the paper a different alternative will be explored very superficially. It will be supposed that in certain phases of the business cycle the observed level of gross investment is supply-determined because the capital goods industries are unable to meet the entire demand for new equipment. Moreover, the Keynesian assertion that the demand for capital is heavily influenced by expectations about future prosperity will be considered.[15] The procedure will consist of constructing simple plausible arithmetical examples and then of fitting neo-classical investment functions to the artificially generated data.

Since the present section contains only illustrative examples, let us omit labour and postulate a simple linear relationship between the desired steady-state level of the capital stock and the price of capital goods and an expectational variable Z_t:

$$K_t^{**} = Z_t - \beta q_t \tag{33}$$

where β is assumed to include the constant rate of depreciation and interest. Desired net investment is determined through a simple stock adjustment model:

$$\dot{K}^* = m_1(K_t - K^{**}) \tag{34}$$

where K_t, K_t^*, and K^{**} stand for the actual, the desired (short-run), and the steady-state levels of the capital stock.

Desired gross investment contains net and replacement investment:

$$I_t^* = \dot{K}_t^* + \delta K_t. \tag{35}$$

Equations (33) and (35) represent the demand side of the illustrative model. With the exception of the shift variable Z_t, they are

[15] In neo-classical terms, future expectations are probably best represented by autonomous changes in $\dot{q}_t/q_t$.

identical to a simple neo-classical model. On the supply side, let us postulate a linear upward-sloping curve of new capital goods:

$$I_t^s = \gamma + \eta q_t. \tag{36}$$

The market for new investment goods is not cleared instantaneously, but, instead, the price is assumed to rise in response to excess demand:

$$\dot{q}_t = m_2(I_t^s - I_t^*). \tag{37}$$

Finally, the actual gross investment and net capital accumulation are determined by I_t^s or by I_t^*, depending on which is the smaller:

$$I_t = \min(I_t^*, I_t^s) \tag{38}$$

and

$$\dot{K}_t = I_t - \delta K_t. \tag{39}$$

In equations (33) to (39) all coefficients, except m_1 and m_2, have been defined as positive.

The working of the above simple model can easily be illustrated in a simple demand-and-supply diagram which contains the flow demands and supplies of new investment goods. In times of excess demand, the price rises and actual gross investment is equal to the supply. By contrast, in times of excess supply, actual investment moves along the demand curve. The variable Z_t forces the demand curve to new positions and, hence, excess demand may be followed by excess supply and vice versa. Thus this illustrative model differs from the neo-classical approach in two crucial respects: first, there is an expectational variable Z_t in the demand for capital and, second, the realized investment is not necessarily equal to desired investment. Because of the discontinuity brought about by equation (38), we have two sets of two differential equations, one set describing the behaviour in conditions of excess demand and the other in conditions of excess supply.

In order to obtain an impression of the kind of biases that may arise if supply conditions are ignored, some simple arithmetical examples of the model of equations (33) and (39) were constructed on the following assumptions: for the 91 artificial observations, Z_t took on the values 150 ($t = 1, \ldots, 10$), 250 ($t = 11, \ldots, 20$), 300 ($t = 21, \ldots, 30$), 250 ($t = 31, \ldots, 40$), 50 ($t = 41, \ldots, 50$), 400

$(t = 51, \ldots, 70)$, and 100 $(t = 71, \ldots, 91)$. The parameters were assumed to be as follows

$$m_1 = -0\cdot75 \qquad \beta = 0\cdot50 \qquad \eta = 0\cdot40$$
$$m_2 = -0\cdot30 \qquad \gamma = 20 \qquad \delta = 0\cdot15$$

The initial capital price was $q_0 = 100$ and the initial capital stock $K_0 = 80$. As it happened, the system which resulted with these specific assumptions displayed excess supply conditions most of the time.

The next step in the analysis consisted of fitting a neo-classical investment demand function to the artificially generated data. The following equation was fitted:

$$\dot{K} = \hat{m}_1(K - K^*) \tag{40}$$

where

$$K^* = b_1 - \hat{\beta}q_t. \tag{41}$$

The relevant parameter estimates and their standard errors turned out as follows:

$$\hat{m}_1 = -0\cdot2285 \qquad \hat{\beta} = -2\cdot016$$
$$(0\cdot0377) \qquad\qquad (0\cdot264)$$

Thus the estimate of m_1 is biased strongly towards zero (i.e. towards slow adjustment) and $\hat{\beta}$ has the 'wrong' sign. In an attempt to ascertain the sensitivity of these biases to the parameter values, m_1 was allowed to vary between $-0\cdot15$ and $-0\cdot95$, and m_2 between $-0\cdot2$ and $-1\cdot2$. However, the resulting estimates of m_1 and β remained remarkably stable. It so happens that, in the empirical studies reported in the previous sections (especially under II.2 and III), the coefficients of the rental on capital are often badly determined or have the 'wrong' sign. Moreover, the adjustment coefficients of capital are usually very low. It is, therefore, interesting to observe that the above simple arithmetic example gives rise to biases which have the same sign as the suspected biases in the actual empirical estimates.

This concludes the brief discussion of supply factors in the analysis of investment. A simple but quite plausible model has been presented in which actual investment is sometimes demand-determined and sometimes supply-determined and in which expectations about the future shift the demand for capital (through Z_t). An arithmetic example was constructed and then a neo-classical investment demand function was fitted to it. The biases due to mis-specification turned out to be large and in the direction which we suspect in our actual empirical results. It seems desirable, therefore, that the neo-classical investment demand approach be complemented by the explicit recognition of supply factors.

V. Conclusions

In this paper an attempt has been made to assess the contribution which neo-classical models of investment behaviour might make to the formulation of a consistent and effective monetary policy.

In Section II profit maximization and cost minimization without adjustment costs were examined, while in Section III a two-equation cost-minimization model with adjustment costs was presented. Unfortunately the reduced-form estimation of the parameters of the underlying Cobb–Douglas production function yields unsatisfactory results. Implausible magnitudes, 'wrong' signs, large standard errors, and a high degree of sensitivity to minor changes in specification are the rule rather than the exception. In Section IV it has been suggested that the reasons for the relatively poor performance of the neo-classical demand for investment function may lie in the neglect of supply factors. If observed investment is, in fact, partially supply-determined, then serious biases may arise when a pure demand function is fitted to the data.

While the development of the neo-classical framework has raised the level of analytic rigour in investment analysis, these models appear to be still too simple to withstand severe testing. Hence, they ought to be refined and tested further in the hope that ultimately they will throw some light on the efficacy of monetary and fiscal policy.

REFERENCES

[1] BRECHLING, F., *Investment and Employment Decisions* (to be published by Manchester University Press).

[2] —— and MORTENSEN, D. T., 'Interrelated Investment and Employment Decisions', mimeo.

[3] COEN, R. M., and HICKMAN, B. G., 'Constrained Joint Estimation of Factor Demand and Production Functions', *Rev. Econ. Stats.*, Aug. 1970, pp. 287–300.

[4] EISNER, R., and STROTZ, R., 'Determinants of Business Investment', Research Study Two in *Impacts of Monetary Policy* (Englewood Cliffs, N.J.: Prentice-Hall, 1963).

[5] JORGENSON, D. W., 'Rational Distributed Lag Functions', *Econometrica*, vol. 34, Jan. 1966, pp. 135–49.

[6] —— 'The Theory of Investment Behavior', in R. Ferber (ed.), *The Determinants of Investment Behavior* (New York: N.B.E.R., 1967), pp. 129–55.

[7] ——, HUNTER, J., and NADIRI, M. I., 'A Comparison of Alternative Models of Quarterly Investment Behavior', *Econometrica*, vol. 38, Mar. 1970.

[8] —— and STEPHENSON, J. A., 'Investment Behavior in U.S. Manufacturing 1947–1960', *Econometrica*, vol. 35, Apr. 1967, pp. 169–220.

[9] LUCAS, R., 'Optimal Investment Policy and the Flexible Accelerator', *International Economic Review*, vol. 8, 1967, pp. 78–85.

[10] NADIRI, M. I., and ROSEN, S., 'Interrelated Factor Demand Functions', *American Economic Review*, Sept. 1969, Part I, 59(4), pp. 457–71.

[11] SCHRAMM, R., 'The Influence of Relative Prices, Production Conditions and Adjustment Costs on Investment Behavior', *Rev. Econ. Studs.*, vol. 37, 1970, pp. 361–73.

[12] SURVEY OF CURRENT BUSINESS, Apr. 1967, July 1968, July 1969, July 1970.

[13] TREADWAY, A. B., 'The Rational Multivariate Flexible Accelerator', *Econometrica*, vol. 39, Sept. 1971, pp. 845–55.

Discussion Papers

(a) ALAN WALTERS
(*London School of Economics*)

I HAVE found the study by Fisher and Sheppard a very valuable survey of the great quantity of paper—there are over 100 references —relating to the experience of the United States. The effort that has gone into the assimilation of the material is not small. Personally I find many of the published accounts of models and their many properties virtually unreadable; I begin wilting before I have got over the first hurdle, the notation, and then there is so much more to come. I suspect that many of us implicitly do a little calculation of marginal pay-off and marginal costs and come to the conclusion we want, put the pile of equations back in the bookshelf, and pray for a Sheppard and Fisher to come along and separate wheat from chaff, and to point out who has done what wrong or right, what results we should take seriously, and what we can safely ignore, and so on.

Ideally, the authors of a survey should be well-balanced individuals—free as far as one can ever be of doctrinal hang-ups. If they were extremists one would have to have an antidote and another survey, and I am sure that none of us here are extremists—we are all moderates. But Fisher and Sheppard manage to maintain their poise almost to the very end.

One of the least-publicized side effects of the monetarist counter-revolution was the self-conscious elaboration of econometric models to include a more sophisticated monetary sector (or financial sector). Only crude vestigial monetary sectors still appear in some well-known models, such as that of the Wharton school. But one can have little doubt that the resurgence of complex and sophisticated monetary sector models—culminating in the massive MIT–FRB effort—is a response to the Friedman–Meiselman attack on the Keynesian orthodoxy. Somehow, it was thought, if the comparison was done 'correctly' instead of through the 'crude reduced forms' of F–M one would get a different answer—money would not dominate and the lags would be shorter.

The survey surely firmly establishes one of Friedman's contentions: the fact that the lag is a long one. A lag averaging around 4 to 8 quarters is quite a common result both from the single-equation studies and from the model simulations. Although F–S cast some statistical haze around the results they do not discredit them. Indeed, if one considers the accumulation of other evidence on the length of the lag, the case seems as near conclusive as anything can be in economics. F–S conclude also that Friedman's contention that the lag is *variable* is largely untested.[1] For what it is worth, I would conjecture that the lag depends on the extent and suddenness of the monetary change—the larger the change the shorter the lag. Thus one would expect that a large change would make it worthwhile to bring forward normal adjustment dates, schedules, etc. But no work has been done on this.

A second feature of the results is the general, but not universal view, that indeed money does matter. The multiplier on *real* GNP of the reserve base is of the order of 10: a $1 billion increase in reserves ultimately increases real GNP by about $10 billion. But I would like to draw attention to a third feature of the results: the curious behaviour of the price level.

There is little doubt that one of the most unsatisfactory elements of the models is the explanation of price movements. Typically price is obtained by a mark-up equation on wage cost per unit of output. Wage rates are determined by a Phillips relationship. Thus an increase in the money supply (or reduction in discount rate) generates an expansion in real output greater than the increase in employment, thus *reducing* the wage cost per unit of output—and so we have the paradox that prices go down in response to an expansion in the money supply. (See especially the Brookings model which is one of the best-developed and most extensively tested of all the models used.) The change in unemployment takes a long time to affect the wage rates and so to affect wage cost per unit of output. One other model (FRB–MIT:D–8) shows the *opposite* path for prices, i.e. prices increase during the expansion (p. 227).

I think one can only conclude that the models have not yet got the price-fixing right. With their Keynesian heritage, of course, the emphasis has been on the real variables, and the price adjustment process has been much neglected.

---

[1] This is an odd way of putting it: a constant lag is more restrictive than a variable lag, so one would presumably test the hypothesis that it is constant.

But I suspect that we know really so little about the properties of the models because we have not 'leaned on them' sufficiently. Let there be a massive decrease of the money supply (or a massive increase) and explore the results. A simulation run by Zellner on the FRB–MIT model of a massive reduction of the money supply showed that there would be enormously high interest rates of 15 per cent or 16 per cent and prices would hardly fall—a far cry from 1929–31. Indeed this points out that one of the main objections to such large, complicated non-linear models is that one simply does not know what is going on, especially in the dynamic structure. The size and expense of running such models also serves as an insulation against criticism. Who has the $10,000 or so required for a set of computer runs?

F–S criticize such models, and particularly the final-form models of Anderson and Jordan, on grounds which have now become familiar in the last few years. First there is the usual complaint about serially correlated residuals and all the bad things that happen to those who let their residuals get serially entangled. I suppose this is largely due to the fact that econometrists have really refined ways of detecting such a thing and finding out the consequences. One would not mind so much if they paid *some* attention to the 'errors in variables' problem. We know it is enormously important in monetary economics—especially when we measure rates of returns on assets. Unfortunately, econometric theory has made little progress with the 'errors in variables' model, but this does not seem to be a good reason for neglecting it. It is well known that the empirical correlates rarely measure (even with jointly independent, normally distributed errors) the concept that the theory pursues. There are large biases. One is always afraid that the process by which models are constructed leads authors to filter out those series that give 'good results'.

The second major ground for criticism is that some models are 'wrongly specified' and many jibes of 'black boxes' (but not by F–S). I agree with F–S that the critical way of choosing between models should be a specific loss function. But rarely is it possible to spell out a loss function since the users of the model, including the degree of conviction it imparts, often cannot be even guessed *a priori*. How often do we hear the complaint that the model was not designed for *that* particular use? But I must seriously quarrel with the F–S criticism of the St. Louis group's approach. They ask (p. 239), 'Do the results emerge from a failure properly to specify a theoretical system or are they . . . plain spurious?' Although I cannot see how such results emerge from such a 'failure', I suspect that the final form of the St. Louis type can be obtained from a large number of models of conventional Keynesian forms. For example, one model with an explicit banking sector with the balance-sheet constraints carefully written in, but of course lacking the dynamic structure, was developed by Johanssen some twenty years ago; the reduced forms were Anderson–Jordan types.

F–S present us with presumably a properly specified model on pp. 239–240. But, alas, it is not even a starter. First, F–S define the variables in real terms, and the price level, and its rate of change, do not appear at all. Of course, Anderson and Jordan used nominal values, but F–S cannot do this and maintain the structure they have in mind, for had their model been in nominal values then it would have been (dare I risk the word?) mis-specified, since a doubling of the price level will halve the interest-rate effect both on the demand for money and on investment. Secondly, F–S have in mind a *fix-price* model of a Keynesian under-employment type—but this is a far cry both from the Anderson and Jordan neo-quantity side of their model and, more seriously, from the facts. In particular, I think Anderson and Jordan would have every reason to complain that F–S have assumed away the pure Fisherine expected-inflation effect. As I have argued elsewhere, I think the most interesting feature of modern monetary experience is the divergence between output and price effects; in the F–S version price effects are excluded *ab initio*, and no St. Louis fan could tolerate that.

Thirdly, not only Anderson and Jordan but, I suspect, everyone else would find the lag structure imposed by F–S quite inconsistent with the evidence. For example, in F–S investment fully responds to the rate of interest *in the current quarter*. Yet the evidence from the Keynesian investment functions of Jorgenson *et al.* is that there is a long distributed lag with a mean period of some 6 to 8 quarters! Similarly, I should have thought there is sufficient evidence on the permanent income hypothesis to suggest that a contemporaneous consumption function is rather *passé*. And one could go on. . . .

But I think one can use the F–S model to present a positive case for the St. Louis approach. The essence of the Keynesian model is to trace the effect of monetary variation on the interest rate and so on the level of investment. Thus the F–S structural equations

$$I_t = vr_t + I_0 + \varepsilon_{3t} \qquad\qquad (v \leq 0)$$
$$M_t = mr_t + kY_{t-1} + M_0 + \varepsilon_{4t} \quad (m \leq 0)$$

should be estimated to get $\hat{v}$ and $\hat{m}$. These are then entered as a *ratio* in the reduced form, i.e. $v/m\{1 - c(1 - x)\}$. Assume that the curly bracket term is about 0·95, and one can see that it is essentially the *ratio* v/m which plays the main role of the monetary multiplier.[3] Now in the above equations we know that substantial errors of measurement occur in all variables but particularly in r for the reasons sketched above. If we suppose that those errors are un-correlated with the true value and with ε_3 and ε_4 (and I suppose that is a doctrine of perfection) then a least squares estimate will produce a downward bias in both $|\hat{v}|$ and $|\hat{m}|$. The literature is littered with low, if not negative, estimates of the coefficients v and m, and I suspect this may be one of the main reasons.[4] Thus an estimate of the ratio v/m of the form $\hat{v}/\hat{m}$ will have a high likelihood of being most unstable with high standard errors. Now Anderson and Jordan avoid this statistical trap by estimating the ratio (v/m) as $\widehat{(v/m)}$ without using the treacherous measures of r (and indeed I) and the specified lag structure and form of the relationship. They avoid the silly results where $\hat{m} \simeq 0$ and $\hat{v}$ is finite and the monetary multiplier approaches infinity; and, after all, this is only the not un-common case where the demand for money is not affected by the nominal interest rate. I conclude therefore that (v/m) is best estimated by the St. Louis approach *and* that the attempt to trace the monetary effect through the investment and money-demand equations is doomed to fail. This does not mean that we should not attempt to measure investment and money-demand functions. It merely means that we should be careful in using the results.

I believe that there is a serious lacuna in this survey and it is the fault of the studies rather than that of F–S. This is the differential dynamic price and real output effects. This is the main under-researched area in the field.

Finally, may I congratulate the authors on the enormous amount of work that has gone into this survey. It is a difficult job to sum-

---

[3] In the final form we get powers of the ratio and the curly brackets.

[4] Incidentally, I suspect that these biases which are both small sample and asymptotic explain the low values of the monetary multiplier in Britain in 872–1914.

marize and distil the essence of these complex models. They have
done us well.

A note on the estimation of ratios

(1) If we write

$$\hat{v} = v + \varepsilon_v + B(v)$$

$$\hat{m} = m + \varepsilon_m + B(m)$$

where $\sum_v$ and $\sum_m$ are the random error term of the estimate with
zero mean and $B(v)$ and $B(m)$ represent the positive biases (note
that $m < 0$, $v < 0$) and we presume that $\hat{v}$, $\hat{m} < 0$.

(2) From the estimate v/m we get a small sample bias even if
$B(v) = B(m) = 0$.

(3) Define

$$x = \{\varepsilon_v + B(v)\}/v \qquad y = \{\varepsilon_m + B(m)\}/m$$

then the ratio estimate is only sensible if y is always less than unity in
absolute value. This can be seen as follows:

$$\frac{\hat{v}}{\hat{m}} = \frac{v}{m}\frac{(1 + x)}{(1 + y)} = \frac{v}{m}(1 + x)(1 - y + y^2 - y^3 + \cdots)$$

(4) There is evidence that it is wrong to assume that $|y| < 1$, but
even if one did accept that assumption we would still have an un-
manageable series. A further stringent assumption is required, i.e.
that y is so small that terms such as y^2, y^3 are trivial. Then

$$\frac{\hat{v}}{\hat{m}} = \frac{v}{m}(1 + x - y - xy) + 0(y^2).$$

With this formulation there is a chance of the biases offsetting one
another if

$$E(x) = E(y) + E(xy)$$

and we have argued that $B(v)$ and $B(m)$ are likely to be the same
sign.

(5) But this ratio method is likely to give rise to very large
sampling variances, as one can discover quite readily.

Discussion Papers

(b) MICHAEL J. HAMBURGER
(Federal Reserve Bank of New York)

THIS comment deals exclusively with Feige's very interesting and careful review of the empirical literature on the demand function for demand deposits derived from temporal cross-section data for the United States. The main objective of his paper is to determine the conclusions that can be drawn from the evidence concerning the degree of substitution between demand deposits and other liquid assets—the liabilities of financial intermediaries. Estimates of the substitutability of these assets are important for resolving many long-standing issues in monetary theory and policy.

Feige has done a thorough job in reviewing the results obtained from studies utilizing pooled temporal cross-section data, i.e. studies in which observations are taken both across states (or metropolitan areas) and over time. In addition, the restriction of the analysis to a single type of evidence has some expositional advantages. Where I think the analysis is deficient is that no attempt is made to compare the results obtained with those derived from other evidence. Moreover, it seems to me that a disproportionate amount of attention is devoted to questions raised by the specification of dummy variables.

On the basis of the time-series cross-section data, Feige concludes that at best the liabilities of financial intermediaries are very weak substitutes for demand deposits. The ranges of the cross-interest rate elasticities are: -0.20 to 0.0 for commercial bank time deposits; -0.05 to $+0.15$ for mutual savings bank deposits and -0.20 $+ 0.30$ for savings and loan shares. Since no other interest rates are included in these studies, the implication would seem to be that demand deposits are poor substitutes for other assets generally. Or to put it differently, that interest rates on alternative assets are not very important determinants of the demand for demand deposits.

This finding conflicts sharply with those obtained using aggregate time-series data and with the view held by most economists. As Friedman has stated, 'I know no empirical student of the demand for money who denies that interest rates affect the real quantity of money demanded—though others have misinterpreted me as so asserting' [2, p. 72]. According to Friedman, almost all elasticity estimates, including those he has obtained in subsequent work, are higher (in absolute values) than the one used by Anna Schwartz and himself in *A Monetary History of the United States* (−0·15).[1] Similar values for the lower bound of the interest-rate elasticity of the demand for money (from aggregate time-series data) are provided by Laidler [8] and by Goodhart and Crockett [5]. Moreover, as is shown by the latter authors, when money is defined as demand deposits plus currency and a long-term interest rate is used in the demand function the absolute value of the elasticity generally exceeds 0·50.

The differences between these estimates of the substitutability of money (or demand deposits) for other assets and those reported by Feige raise questions about the quality of the data and the empirical procedures that have been employed in time-series cross-section studies. The rest of this paper is devoted to a discussion of some of the problems encountered in conducting such studies, with particular emphasis on the factors that may introduce a downward bias in the estimates of the interest-rate elasticities.

First, the use of data arranged by state (or metropolitan area) almost seems to require one to assume some important imperfections in the markets for demand deposits and other liquid assets. In all the studies reviewed by Feige the quantity of an asset held in a particular area is treated as being totally independent of conditions in all other areas. Thus, it is assumed that investors in each state do not consider the liabilities of out-of-state intermediaries to be substitutes for the liabilities of in-state intermediaries. To the extent that there is some flow of funds across state lines—and there clearly was prior to the imposition of interest-rate ceilings on savings and loan shares and on mutual savings bank deposits in 1966—this assumption will produce a downward bias in the absolute values of the interest-rate elasticities.

A second problem involves the measurement of the negative rate of return on demand deposits (r_D) as the ratio of service charges to

---

[1] See [3, ch. 12]. The aggregate time-series estimates of the interest-rate elasticity of the demand for money are not strictly comparable to the time-series cross-section estimates of the elasticity of the demand for demand deposits. However, if currency is a poorer substitute for interest-bearing financial assets than demand deposits, the aggregate time-series estimates should, in fact, be lower (in absolute value) than the temporal cross-section estimates.

average deposit balances. This specification has been questioned before by Laidler [7] and is discussed at length by Feige. The problem is that, regardless of the effect of changes in bank charges on desired deposit balances, there is likely to be some negative correlation between the level of deposits and r_D simply because of the way the latter is measured. Thus, the inclusion of the ratio of service charges to average demand deposit balances on the right-hand side of the demand deposit equation could introduce some spurious correlation into the analysis. More important, though, and this is not mentioned by either Laidler or Feige, it may bias the coefficients of some of the other variables in the equation, i.e. changes in these variables which influence the level of deposits held are also likely to show up as changes in the ratio of service charges to deposits.

To test this hypothesis I estimated three demand deposit equations including and excluding the 'rate of return on demand deposits'.[2] The data are from Feige's original study [1] and are for the years 1949, 1959, and 1949 and 1959 combined. The only variable whose coefficient is significantly affected by whether the rate of return on demand deposits is included in the equation is the time deposit rate. The estimates of this coefficient (and its t-statistic) are shown below. In each case, exclusion of the ratio of service charges to average demand deposit balances substantially reduces the estimated value of the time deposit coefficient. In one case (1959) the sign changes from positive to negative and in another (1949–59 pooled) the absolute value of the coefficient rises by 95 per cent.

Estimates of the Time Deposit Rate Coefficient in Demand Deposit Equations Including and Excluding the Rate of Return on Demand Deposits
(t-statistic in parentheses)

	1949	1959	1949–59 (pooled)
Including the demand deposit rate	−151 (−1·75)	40 (0·54)	−71 (−2·25)
Excluding the demand deposit rate	−217 (−2·45)	−105 (−1·67)	−139 (−5·62)

[2] As may be easily verified, the regressions estimated here are not identical to those reported by Feige. The difference is that we did not include all of the dummy variables used by Feige. The data for these variables are not included in his study.

These results, although certainly not conclusive, raise serious questions about the use of the ratio of service charges to average demand deposit balances as a measure of the rate of return on demand deposits. In addition, they cast considerable doubt on Feige's finding of little, or no, substitution between time and demand deposits.

Finally, some downward bias in the interest-rate elasticities is to be expected because of the deposit and interest-rate data. In practically all of the studies reviewed by Feige, demand deposits include the holdings of both business firms and individuals, whereas the only interest rates included in the demand functions are those relevant for individuals. Prior to 1960 (the period used in most of the studies) business firms owned approximately one-half of the demand deposits, but practically no other intermediary claims. Hence, some understatement of the over-all interest-rate elasticity of the aggregate demand for demand deposits would seem certain.[3]

On the other hand, it may be argued that if movements in intermediary rates are positively correlated with movements in other rates, the exclusion of the latter from the regressions could introduce an upward bias in the absolute values of the intermediary-rate coefficients. Although this argument has some appeal, it is not consistent with the results obtained by Lee in the one time-series cross-section which uses data for individual households. (See study T1–9 in Feige's Table IV.7.) Lee finds that the elasticity of household demand deposits with respect to the savings and loan rate is $-1\cdot61$. Dividing this by 2 or 3, to obtain an estimate of the aggregate elasticity, yields a number which is considerably greater (in absolute value) than any of the other cross elasticities in the Table. Thus, once again there is reason to question the low estimates of the interest-rate elasticities reported by Feige.[4]

All things considered, I find the evidence for the conclusion that

[3] In fairness to Feige it should be noted that his main concern is the elasticity of the demand for demand deposits with respect to the interest rates on intermediary claims and not the over-all interest-rate elasticity of these deposits. However, considering the specification of demand deposits used in these studies, the failure to include *any* interest rate that might be relevant for the business sector strikes me as an important mis-specification and one that could account for a sizeable portion of the discrepancy between Feige's results and the aggregate time-series evidence.

[4] This is not to suggest that Lee's estimates should be taken at face value. Feige's reasons for not giving too much weight to Lee's results are discussed in his paper. In addition, see [4, pp. 183–4].

demand deposits are poor substitutes for other intermediary claims unpersuasive. Given the aggregate time-series evidence, this would imply that intermediary claims are poorer substitutes for demand deposits (or money) than are most other assets. This argument should not be taken as an acceptance of the Gurley–Shaw thesis. As I interpret the aggregate time-series evidence [6], it says that intermediary claims are neither significantly better nor significantly worse substitutes for money than are other assets.

REFERENCES

[1] FEIGE, E. L., *The Demand for Liquid Assets: A Temporal Cross-Section Analysis* (Englewood Cliffs, N.J.: Prentice Hall, 1964).

[2] FRIEDMAN, M., 'Interest Rates and the Demand for Money', *Journal of Law and Economics*, Oct. 1966, pp. 71–86.

[3] —— and SCHWARTZ, A. J., *A Monetary History of the United States* (New York: N.B.E.R., 1963).

[4] —— ——, *Monetary Statistics of the United States* (New York: N.B.E.R., 1970).

[5] GOODHART, C. A. E., and CROCKETT, A. D., 'The Importance of Money', *Bank of England Quarterly Bulletin*, June 1970, pp. 159–98.

[6] HAMBURGER, M. J., 'Household Demand for Financial Assets', *Econometrica*, Jan. 1968, pp. 97–118.

[7] LAIDLER, D. E. W., 'The Definition of Money: Theoretical and Empirical Problems', *Journal of Money, Credit and Banking*, Aug. 1969, pp. 508–25.

[8] ——, *The Demand for Money: Theory and Evidence* (Scranton, Pa.: International Textbook Co., 1969).

Discussion Papers

(c) DAVID LAIDLER
(University of Manchester)

BOTH of the papers that I am to discuss deal with work in progress and involve a mixture of economic analysis and econometrics. Inasmuch as the distinction can be made I will concern myself with their economic rather than their econometric content.

I found Nobay's paper extremely interesting, and it seems to me to represent a genuine step forward in the literature on the behaviour of the Monetary Authorities. Two innovations are particularly worth noting. First, instead of, as is too often done in such studies, deciding in a vacuum what the instruments of monetary policy probably are, and what the targets of such policy ought to be, and then stirring them together in a series of stepwise regressions, Nobay has taken careful note of what the authorities have actually said from time to time about their targets and instruments, and used this information in order to formulate hypotheses about their behaviour that may then be tested against quantitative evidence. The second innovation follows on directly from the first, for even a cursory inspection of the authorities' pronouncements makes it clear that policy instruments are used interdependently and not independently of one another. The hypothesis that it is vital to take account of simultaneity in the choice of policy instruments in studying the monetary authorities' behaviour is amply borne out by the evidence Nobay presents. The fact that Nobay's research strategy is so obviously sensible should not blind us to its novelty in this particular branch of literature.

This of course does not mean that Nobay has solved all the problems in the area, nor does he claim to have done so. I would offer three (I trust constructive) suggestions that might inform further work. First, Nobay lays heavy stress on the monetary authorities' responses to variables associated with the openness of the economy—the balance of payments, overseas interest rates, and so forth—and the underlying assumption of his analysis is that the authorities do have some freedom of choice over the policies they adopt. Yesterday we had a paper from Alexander Swoboda which argued persuasively that, in the long run, the monetary authorities of a small open economy with a fixed exchange rate have little if any control over their monetary policy. Now it may be that Nobay's work is concerned only with the short run, or it may be that Britain is neither small nor open enough, nor has an exchange rate that is fixed enough, for the full force of Swoboda's analysis to apply to it. Even so it does seem to me that there is scope for cross-fertilization between the two hitherto distinct branches of the literature that the two papers in question represent.

My second suggestion is more specific and concerns the use of the fiscal policy package variable called ITC. It may be, as Nobay asserts, that the use of this variable by-passes the problems associated with trying to assess what the authorities' implicit model of the economy is, but I would like to see a more explicitly analytic statement of the reasons for this assertion than I have found in his present paper before being completely convinced on this score. Moreover, I am not clear that Nobay's initial explanation of the role of ITC in his analysis is compatible with his suggestion that some odd signs that attach to it in certain regressions may be interpreted as reflecting the monetary authorities' response to fiscal policy. This latter suggestion points to the existence of simultaneity not only within the monetary instrument package but also between monetary and fiscal policy. I would like to see in Nobay's future work some explicit analysis of the problems this raises.

Finally, the underlying economic analysis of Nobay's paper is, like that of all its predecessors, static. The authorities have goals but do not appear to be particularly concerned with the time-paths by which those goals are achieved. This is certainly a simplification of reality, and the question as to whether it might not be an over-simplification is surely worth investigating. In short, it would probably be worthwhile to recast the problem in terms of an explicitly dynamic framework if only to see how robust are the results that emerge from the static analysis.

Let me now turn to the paper by Clayton, Dodds, Ford, and Ghosh. This is a very ambitious piece of work, but it does seem to me to be somewhat 'out of focus' at present. The main economic problem to which the paper is addressed is the extent to which the activities of non-bank financial intermediaries can offset the effects of monetary policy. It is now widely accepted that the problems for monetary control raised by the activities of these institutions may be investigated in terms of questions about the magnitude and stability of the elasticity of the demand for money with respect to the rates of return which their liabilities bear. It is far from clear that a multi-sector disaggregated portfolio choice model is the most appropriate analytic device with which to tackle these questions. If the important issues concern the non-bank public's demand function for money balances, then surely this function ought to be the centrepiece of the analysis.

However, there are several important questions in monetary economics which cannot be answered simply by looking at particular functions, but which require a portfolio approach. The relationship between the monetary variables which the authorities control and the supply of money depends, as is well known, upon the portfolio behaviour both of the commercial banks, and of the non-bank public.

Again, we have virtually no systematic knowledge about the extent to which monetary policy exerts differential effects on different sectors of the economy. Is it, for example, really the case that the building industry is particularly vulnerable to monetary stringency? It is hard to see how we could learn anything about such questions as this without investigating the portfolio behaviour of particular institutions.

The weakness of this paper, as it stands at the moment, is that the relationship between the questions to be asked and the analysis to be employed in answering them has not been fully thought through. Given the relative paucity of available data, and given the extreme complexity of the model as presented, there is surely a lot to be said for considerably simplifying the analysis, either by concentrating more on particular sectors, or by moving to a more aggregated type of analysis. A clear specification of the particular questions to be asked is surely the first, and vital, step to be taken in deciding upon the direction which such future work might take.

Discussion Papers

(d) P. K. TRIVEDI
(*University of Southampton*)

THE comments below concentrate on the econometric aspects of the paper by Professor Clayton and his team. One must accept that in many empirical situations where econometric methods are used there is a danger of over-emphasizing the technical aspects of work at the expense of those which have motivated the investigation in the first place. It appears to be a danger from which both researchers and discussants are likely to suffer. However, once a model is specified and the specification indicates a general approach to estimation, it seems reasonable to ask how well it has been done and what the estimates imply about the specification of the model.

The econometric model of the U.K. Financial Sector which Professor Clayton and his team are attempting to estimate is a large undertaking. The model as specified is linear, static, and interdependent; there are 67 stochastic equations, and 24 exogenous variables. Application of one of the simultaneous-equation estimation techniques is required. The equations are over-identified on order condition so the two-stage least squares estimator has been employed. The manner in which the equations of the model are derived implies certain across-equation linear restrictions which have had to be neglected since the estimation procedure used was of the single-equation type. Nevertheless, the task of estimating over 750 parameters using 28 quarterly observations is a formidable one, and one which raises many computational problems. The first problem, and a familiar one, is that of estimating the systematic components of the jointly determined variables from the unrestricted reduced form. Given the small number of observations, the chance of running into the singularity problem would seem high. If the matrix $(X'X)$ is singular, it is known that ordinary least squares and two-stage least squares estimates coincide. If the matrix is not singular, but merely badly conditioned, serious computational inaccuracies could arise in computing the reduced form. In the present case both are likely. It would seem advantageous, therefore, to work with a smaller set of predetermined variables in estimating the reduced form, although that in turn raises the related question of how such a reduced set must be obtained. There is a considerable literature which deals with this problem.

A second problem, and one of greater basic importance, posed by the results presented in the paper concerns the identifiability of the model. The fact that the system is identifiable on the basis of *a priori* information does not seem enough since such *a priori* restrictions, especially the zero restrictions, could be imposed arbitrarily. F. M. Fisher has emphasized that for an identifiability of an equation one requires a combination of *a priori* and sample information which enables one to distinguish its parameters from those of any other equation in the same form. As a logical consequence of this, once the model has been estimated, it should be 're-examined' to see if the zero-restrictions are correct. Basmann, amongst others, has developed test statistics for restrictions which are directly applicable in the present case. An examination of the coefficient estimates shows that a very large number of them are not significantly different from zero. Appendix Table 1 shows that $\bar{a}_{6.1}$ and $\bar{a}_{11.1}$ do not have coefficients significantly different from zero in any of the equations in which they are included; Appendix Table 7 shows virtually the same thing in respect of $\bar{a}_{11.7}$, Appendix Table 8 in respect of $\bar{a}_{11.8}$, and Appendix Table 9 in respect of $\bar{a}_{11.9}$. Is it the case then that these variables have virtually no role to play in the model? If so, any *a priori* restrictions on some equations in the model due to their inclusion in other equations are trivial and may not help to secure identification. These problems of identification also have a relevance to calculation of multipliers discussed in Section III of the paper. It is argued that the estimates of multipliers based on the computed (restricted) reduced form will be more efficient than those based on unrestricted reduced-form estimates. This is so, however, only if the restrictions are correct. Once again this emphasizes the need of a formal test of the restrictions.

A third point concerns not what has been done in terms of estimation but what is proposed for future work. In order to utilize the parametric restrictions on the model imposed by demand theory, it is proposed to estimate the entire system of equations 'by employing the technique of stacking equations developed by A. Zellner'. Although the authors do not refer to it so, the estimation procedure is similar to three-stage least squares modified to take account of side restrictions. Given a linear system, the application is not in principle a difficult one. But in the present case its implementation will lead to major problems unless a way can be found of estimating it in moderately small blocks without violating the spirit of the approach. No record seems to exist of work in which the three-stage least squares estimator has been applied in estimating *several hundred parameters*. It seems reasonable to ask how the authors intend to tackle what is by current standards an enormously large computational problem.

The authors also consider the possibility of utilizing inequality constraints in estimating the model. Quadratic programming-type techniques have been used by Zellner, Judge, and Lee in estimating single equations subject to inequality restrictions. But in the kind of model of this paper, estimation subject to such constraints does not seem at present feasible.

The authors remind us that 'a journey of even one thousand miles must begin with the first step'. This is rather modest because the first step represented by the paper is quite ambitious. But one wonders whether disaggregation has not been carried too far. There are fair arguments for advocating greater aggregation. To the reasons mentioned above one could also add the low explanatory power of a large proportion of equations—in case of some of the sectors, that of the majority of the equations. However, aggregation on grounds of econometric and computational convenience could lead to a loss of interesting detailed information about the working of the financial sector—a point which the authors themselves make with force. But detail is costly and there is the question of what the data will bear. It is admitted, however, that even if aggregation were acceptable in principle, to carry it out systematically, and in a way that leads to a non-negligible loss in the kind of information the data might yield, considerable thought would have to be given to the matter as there does not seem to be a straightforward way of aggregating.

REFERENCES

FISHER, F. M., *Identification Problem in Econometrics* (McGraw-Hill, 1966).
BASMANN, R. L., 'On Finite Sample Distributions of Generalised Classical Linear Identifiability Test Statistics', *Journal American Statistical Assoc.*, vol. 55, 1960, pp. 650–9.
LEE, T. C., JUDGE, G. G., and ZELLNER, A., *Estimating the Parameters of the Markov Probability Model From Aggregate Time Series Data* (North-Holland, 1969).

Discussion Papers

(e) R. J. O'BRIEN
(University of Southampton)

I PROPOSE to discuss only White's paper, and only the econometric aspects of that paper. I am conscious of considerable difficulty in criticizing this complex, thorough, and carefully considered piece of work. Having been associated with two of D. C. Rowan's papers in the same field, any criticism I make of White's assumption is *a fortiori* a self-criticism, as his assumptions are less restrictive than anyone else's, especially ours. Similarly, any failure of his model to fit is a failure with which I can commiserate, but not greatly deprecate.

So I must stress that I find this an impressive piece of work. It is conceived on a much larger scale and carried through with greater determination and resources than anyone else in the field has brought to bear.

This said, there are a number of detailed points in need of amendment. First, the paper is extremely difficult to follow. Poring over the equations (7) and (8) one finds the key in footnote 26 which then refers to Appendix B. Appendix B is in fact about something else, but helps with the equations. However, one must remember that these are not the ones actually used, but a continuous-time illustration of the discrete-time formulae employed in practice. However, if one then assembles the implicit function defining $\hat{y}_i$ in terms of the parameters in equations (7) and (8), then the next two sections reduce one's efforts to nought by changing the basis of the model: no final form is given.

This is purely a matter of presentation. Grossly oversimplifying the model, one can summarize as follows. If one assumes values for Y (a flat yield curve), at t_0 (end of decision period), given a certainty equivalence yield λ and a risk-aversion c, then for any B.G.S. one can compute a gross redemption yield $\hat{y}_i$ consistent with Y, t_0, c, and λ, which will differ from the observed redemption yield y_i.

[It is helpful to keep in mind current time, with price P_i and coupon rate r_i; the end of the decision period t_0, at which expected prices P_i^E and flat yield Y rule; and maturity t_i of the ith stock. Decision-period return x_i relates to the period up to $t_0 : y_i$ and $\hat{y}_i$ to the period up to t_i.]

One then chooses the parameters Y, t_0, λ, and c so that $\sum (\hat{y}_i - y_i)^2$ is minimized, which provides maximum likelihood estimates of the parameters, if each of the $\hat{y}_i - y_i$ are Normally and independently distributed with constant variance.

The introduction of the error term $(\hat{y}_i - y)$ is a little *ad hoc*, and perhaps needs justification. If attached to any other variable (e.g. P_i^E) as Normal, the errors in the $\hat{y}_i$ would not appear to be Normal owing to the non-linearity of the model.

White also manages to show empirically that the errors are not independent. He has succeeded in inventing a cross-section model with serial correlation, an achievement he would rather be without, no doubt.

The empirical results suggest rejection of the model. When one examines them: 32 cross-section studies, with 30 stocks in each, the natural conclusion is that we cannot ignore supply factors and the construction of rate curves in isolation is finally discredited. (However, White has further results, not in the paper, with better fit, using market segmentation.)

The fluctuations in t_0, and the low $\bar{R}^2$, indicate something seriously amiss. (It is possible to get such large negative $\bar{R}^2$ because there is no constant in this non-linear model.) t_0 still fluctuates even when $\bar{R}^2$ is not extremely low. One looks in vain for standard errors on Y, t_0, and λ: the Powell routine will provide the relevant second derivatives, as it perforce must numerically estimate them. These standard errors should be provided.

The low $\bar{R}^2$ is interesting. Other studies give high R^2 on, say, the long rate as explained by the short rate *over time*. This is really irrelevant to the fit of the rate curve. This study gives a very poor explanation in cross-section. White pays the penalty of being the first investigator to measure his fit properly!

One observes further that neither p (a tax parameter) or c enters explicitly into the maximization. This problem is commented on in the paper, but it must be pointed out that we thus have no maximum-likelihood estimates of c or p, and it is difficult to draw any inferences about them. In particular, one is told that $c = 0.01$ is better than $c = 0.00$, but one does not know whether one is already past the peak, or whether c should be much larger. The hypothesis of risk-aversion simply has not been tested.

In addition, the multi-collinearity involved suggests that the model may be very poorly identified. No test of non-linear identification has been carried out, and it would appear that a theoretical analysis would indeed be extremely complicated, if it went beyond the first approximation provided in the paper. Basically, one needs to look either at the matrix of second derivatives or at the contours in the $c-Y$ plane. One suspects that the concentrated likelihood surface over this plane is a long, nearly flat, ridge.

Examining diagrams provided for two of the badly fitting cases, one would imagine that quite a simple non-linear trend would produce a reasonable fit, and wonders whether the model incorporates volatility in the same way as the market.

Which considerations leads to a possible solution, suggested to me by Mr. White in private conversation. The market has become so sophisticated that everyone has his own yield curve. Any deviation of a B.G.S. from its customary position on, or in relation to, these 'crude', volatility-based, yield curves is rapidly corrected by market forces. (This is a remarkable example of nature imitating art, or, perhaps, 'econometric' technology influencing the evidence.) One has two possible courses of action. Either one fits a yield curve by the same 'crude' means as the market. *Or* one persuades the market that one's own yield curve is the right one. Because, if one is successful in persuasion, it will become the right one.

In view of the amount of good work in this paper, perhaps Mr. White ought to follow the second course.

Discussion Papers

(f) KARL BORCH
(*Norwegian School of Economics and Business Administration*)

FAIRLY early in Wood's paper, in Section II.1, the author states that he will 'abstract from all problems associated with risk and uncertainty'. This is dangerous since I consider these elements essential in any theory of investment behaviour. I found an explanation in Section II.3.

Equation (8) looks just like the definition of auto-regressive stochastic process, of the second order. The structure of the paper then became clear. The author first assumes away uncertainty, i.e. random fluctuations in the demand for loans. Since this, as one would suspect, makes the model trivial, he introduces deterministic fluctuations. In stochastic versions of Wood's model, the objective is usually taken to be to maximize the expected discounted sum of earnings, and this is also a way of getting rid of uncertainty—less obvious, and less honest than the way chosen by Mr. Wood.

Rejoinders by Authors of Survey Papers

(a) G. R. FISHER and D. K. SHEPPARD

SEVERAL criticisms of our paper have been made and a reply is called for; we hope this will clarify our position and carry the discussion forward.

In Section V of our paper we attempted to put forward a model from which equations similar to, but not identical with, those used by Anderson and Jordan could be derived. Our model is undoubtedly unrealistic. It was introduced merely to illustrate that Anderson–Jordan-type equations can be derived from a simple Keynesian model. Indeed, in selecting the model we were certainly guilty of failing to make use of an explicit loss function. However, the criticism that our model is excessively simplistic, or out of date, or just plain bad really serves to reinforce the strength of our argument about the need to know whence the Anderson–Jordan equations come. After all, our model does yield an Anderson–Jordan-type equation. Such an equation has the dubious merit that it could perhaps have been derived from one of a variety of possible models and hence it may be given a variety of interpretations. While this (or a similar) equation may be useful for some purposes, we should be clear that it does not by itself advance our knowledge of economic theory, unless its underlying structural form is also given. This was the first point we endeavoured to make.

Walters's criticism of the details of our illustrative model would also seem to support the main conclusion we draw, namely that a traditional Keynesian model would yield an interim form which included more terms than those used by Anderson and Jordan. A permanent income consumption function and/or an investment function with more realistic lags would serve to add to the terms included in the equation for ΔY. Thus a more realistic model would yield an equation *less*, not *more*, like an Anderson–Jordan form than ours. In respect of the derivation of the St. Louis equation, then, Walters's criticism leans in favour of the very point we make about the length of lags and the number of included variables. We accept the criticisms; our conclusions stand *a fortiori*.

Now why might this conclusion be important? The answer is that failure to include sufficiently long lags and/or all of the appropriate variables will bias the results as they stand in two respects. First, the coefficient estimates of the included terms will be biased, unless the exclusions are uncorrelated with any linear combination of the inclusions. Second, no account will be taken of effects which would have been significant had they been included. If any candidates for inclusion proved on hindsight to be insignificant, their initial inclusion would not have had such serious potential consequences as the *exclusion* of variables or lags which ought to have been included. The exclusion of variables and lags, then, will in general cause biases and hence will raise the probability of incorrect inferences and conclusions. Note carefully that we do not assert that Anderson's and Jordan's conclusions are wrong. We merely call these into question, on the ground that their methodological basis is not, in our view, entirely satisfactory.

With regard to Walters's remark that we introduce '. . . the usual complaint about serially correlated residuals and all the bad things that happen to those who let their residuals get serially entangled', we feel bound to say that we enjoyed the joke but not the implication that we were indulging in unnecessary pedantry. First, serially correlated residuals are likely to occur as a natural outcome of the well-known tendency of economic time-series to be autocorrelated. Therefore it is not in general a simple matter of letting your 'residuals get serially entangled'. Second, in dynamic systems, serially correlated residuals can lead to substantial biases in estimation. Third, whether or not the system is dynamic, failure to take serially correlated residuals into account will in general lead to misestimation of standard errors and hence to incorrect inferences. We make no excuse for introducing '. . . the usual complaint . . .', for it is a very important problem; indeed a problem which is not usefully tackled by assigning to it the role of an ancillary piece of econometric sophistication which does not substantially affect results and inferences.

We did not draw attention to errors in variables as an additional complication in structural estimation, perhaps because such complications are not readily amenable to solution. We accept that errors in variables may be an important problem, but we would add that there is nothing in our argument to preclude their playing a role.

An interim form or a reduced form may still be estimated when the structure is known. Indeed Walters's argument depends explicitly on a knowledge of the structure which, of course, is not given to us in the St. Louis work. The argument concerning which is the better of two procedures for estimating the ratio $v/[m\{1 - c(1 - x)\}]$ amounts to proposing a testable hypothesis about the influence of errors in variables; and such a hypothesis could not even be formulated, let alone tested, were the structure unknown.

Undoubtedly the '. . . treacherous measure of r and indeed I . . .' would cause problems with OLS estimation of the structural form, but the endogeneity of r would rule out the use of OLS in our illustrative model, even if errors in variables were not present. In contrast, suppose that a more appropriate structural estimation procedure were applied, such as 2SLS or 3SLS. In the first stage, the equations for r and I in the reduced form would be estimated. Then the least squares reduced-form predictions for r and I would be substituted into the structure in place of the original observations on r and I, and the structure estimated. Thus at the structural estimation stage, both r and I will have been 'purified' of jointly dependent residual variation, including that part of this variation derived from the sorts of errors in r and I that Walters introduces. We would not argue that 2SLS or 3SLS is necessarily the appropriate method of estimation in this case. Our point is that procedures which are appropriate to structural estimation go some way toward handling the additional complication that Walters introduces. In summary, while Walters's argument in defence of the reduced-form approach is accepted, it depends in part on knowing the structure and, once this is known, the problem he raises is much more amenable to detailed analysis than he states or implies. In particular, free estimation of the reduced form in ΔY (which Walters seems to recommend for the ratio $v/[m\{1 - c(1 - x)\}]$ when errors in variables are present) cannot be an efficient procedure, for it disregards the over-identifying restrictions. In our case these restrictions would be known, but in the St. Louis case they cannot be known, for there is no structure to begin with. Nevertheless, Walters is quite right in suggesting that the expected value of $\hat{v}/\hat{m}$ may not exist and, even if it does, that the sampling variance of this ratio is likely to be very large.

Walters argues that the properties of large models are not fully understood because '. . . we have not "leaned on them" sufficiently'. In replying to this suggestion, we think it is important to distinguish between 'leaning' on a model to detect its limitations and 'leaning' so much as to render it worthless for empirical analysis. We would certainly endorse the former, but we are doubtful about the latter.

As an analogy, suppose a shoe is designed for a size 5 foot and we attempt to understand its properties by trying to squeeze a size 10 foot into it. Given sufficient effort, resistance to pain, and perseverance, it seems that the shoe will need to burst before the foot can truly enter. Now what 'hidden' truths will this exercise reveal? Certainly that the shoe was not designed for a size 10 foot—but we knew this at the outset. Perhaps that leather has a limited elasticity—but there are better (certainly less painful) ways of measuring the elasticity of leather than the method used in the exercise.

Models of the economy are much like the shoe. Leaning on them too much will probably yield results which are not very helpful. This is because a model is known to be an imperfect representation of the real world which cannot in general cope with situations which are very much out of line with those on which estimation is based. To put the matter another way, models depend for their structure on a theory of what has taken place in the past, and hence they are limited in their ability to perform realistically in new maverick situations. Leaning too much on them is likely to produce 'peculiar' results because they have not been designed and have not been estimated to handle such leaning. Thus heavy leaning may point only to the difficulties of analysing very unlikely situations, and we are surely aware that this is a limitation of statistical analysis.

On the other hand, if the foot were a size 4 or a size 6, then, over a period, the effects of wearing, on the foot and on the shoe, might be quite interesting. Surely in practice, big shoes are bought for small feet to 'grow into' them. On the other side, it is often difficult to distinguish between a tight fit and the physiological need for a larger shoe. In much the same way, leaning on a model to detect the bounds within which it operates realistically seems to be sound research strategy; for when the bounds are exceeded it is time to cast the model aside in favour of another. This seems to us to be very useful information.

(b) EDGAR L. FEIGE*

HAMBURGER'S comment raises several points which leave him

* The author wishes to acknowledge the helpful comments from Robert Avery.

'unpersuaded' by the temporal cross-section evidence on liquid asset substitutability. The specific assertions he makes are as follows:

(1) The time-series evidence is not consistent with the temporal cross-section evidence.

(2) The omission of rates of return on liquid assets in other states involves a model mis-specification which results in an under-estimate of the true substitution elasticities.

(3) The inclusion of the rate of return on demand deposits pro-duces 'spurious correlation' which results in an underestimate of the true substitution elasticities.

(4) The inclusion of business holdings of demand deposits in the dependent variable involves a specification error which results in an underestimate of the true substitution elasticities.

I wish to argue that while a final evaluation of the empirical evidence on liquid asset substitutability must await a systematic analysis of the time-series studies, a cursory review of these studies supports the thrust of the temporal cross-section findings of limited substitutability. Moreover, Hamburger's conjectures concerning the probable consequences of model mis-specifications are faulty. A correct analysis of model mis-specifications suggests, that to the extent that such mis-specifications exist, their consequences are to overstate the true substitution relationships.

With respect to the time-series evidence, it is surprising that not one of the studies cited by Hamburger includes rates of return on non-bank financial intermediary liabilities in the demand function for demand deposits. The studies he cites include 'the rate of interest' (i.e. the rate on a government security) which reflects the combined substitution effects between demand deposits and all other financial assets. Since our intent was to examine the specific substitution relationships between demand deposits and other specific financial intermediary claims which are often asserted to be close substitution for demand deposits, the more aggregative studies shed no direct light on this issue. Furthermore, a preliminary investigation of sixteen time-series studies which do include specific returns on other liquid assets reveals that the cross elasticities between demand deposits and time deposits ranged from -0.56 to $+0.11$ with the average estimate in the neighbourhood of -0.10. Similarly the time-series evidence on substitution between demand deposits and savings and loan shares reveals a cross elasticity range from -0.52 to $+0.39$ with the average estimate falling in the neighbourhood of

-0.35. Thus the relevant time-series evidence is in fact broadly consistent with the temporal cross-section evidence.

Hamburger's contention that model mis-specification has given rise to a systematic *underestimate* of the 'true' cross elasticities is highly questionable. Hamburger's assertions can be examined within the framework of a simple model of mis-specification bias. Assume the true model is represented by:

$$Y = \beta_1 X_1 + \beta_2 X_2 + \varepsilon \tag{1}$$

but due to a mis-specification, $\hat{\beta}_1$ is estimated from a least squares regression of Y on X_1 alone, that is, from

$$Y = \beta_1 X_1 + \varepsilon. \tag{2}$$

If equation (2) had been estimated instead of equation (1), the bias in $\hat{\beta}_1$ introduced by omitting X_2 is simply

$$\text{Bias} = C\hat{\beta}_2 \tag{3}$$

since

$$E(\hat{\beta}_1) = \beta_1 + C\hat{\beta}_2, \tag{4}$$

where C is the coefficient of the auxiliary regression of X_2 on X_1 and $\hat{\beta}_2$ is the coefficient estimate of β_2 derived from the ordinary least squares estimate of the 'true' two-variable model.

Given the foregoing framework, consider Hamburger's first assertion that the omission of rates of return on out-of-state liabilities will 'produce a downward bias in the absolute values of the interest rate elasticities'. If X_1 represents the in-state rate of return on a money substitute, and X_2, the other-state rate of return, then since the rates of return on out-of-state liabilities are positively correlated with the in-state rates of return, the coefficient of the auxiliary regression will be positive. Moreover, if out-of-state liabilities are substitutes for in-state liabilities, $\hat{\beta}_2$ will be negative and thus the bias will add a negative component to the 'true' elasticity. Thus, to the extent that mis-specification exists, one must conclude that the estimated cross elasticities from the temporal cross-section models *overestimate* the true substitution relationships.

Hamburger's second point deals with the 'spurious correlation' which may be introduced by measuring the negative rate of return on demand deposits by the ratio of service charges to average demand deposits. First, it should be noted that since the time-dated demand deposit balances on the left-hand side of the equation are not the same as the average balances used to deflate service charges, the magnitude of the 'spurious correlation' is likely to be small. If such correlation does exist, the error term will be negatively correlated with the demand deposit rate and this in turn will give an upward bias to the own elasticity.

The bias that is introduced in the cross elasticities depends upon the correlation between the rates on money substitutes and the rate on demand deposits. For the period 1949–65 the rates on money substitutes increased while the rate of return on demand deposits became more negative. Thus the negative correlation between the demand deposit rate and the other rates implies that to the extent that the cross elasticities are biased, the bias will be negative, that is, the substitution effects will be *overstated*.

Hamburger suggests that dropping the demand deposit rate is a meaningful solution to the bias problem and he presents estimates based on regressions omitting the demand deposit rate. This procedure is, however, faulty as a test, since if the 'true' model suggests that the demand for demand deposits depends upon the rate of return on demand deposits, to omit the variable will also result in biased estimates of the remaining variables as shown in equation (3). In this case, if X_1 is assumed to be the time deposit rate and X_2 the demand deposit rate, then to estimate equation (2) (as Hamburger has done) instead of equation (1), will result in an *overestimate* of the cross elasticity between demand deposits and time deposits. Thus Hamburger's findings that the time elasticity is higher when the ratio of service charges to demand deposits is dropped is not surprising. It simply suggests that he has mis-specified the model and thus estimated the biased cross elasticity.

Hamburger's final assertion is that:

some downward bias in the interest-rate elasticities is to be expected because of the deposit and interest-rate data. In practically all of the studies reviewed by Feige, demand deposits include the holdings of both business firms and individuals, whereas the only interest rates included in the demand functions are those relevant for individuals. . . . Hence, some understatement of the over-all interest-rate elasticity of the aggregate demand for demand deposits would seem certain.

If we assume with Hamburger that the dependent variable does include business deposits and that these deposits are uncorrelated with the included interest rates, then while it is true that the explained variance in the dependent variable will be lower than if these deposits were excluded, the estimated coefficients are unbiased. The business deposits simply show up in the error term and, so long as they are uncorrelated with the other independent variables, none of the assumptions of the least squares model are violated.

If, alternatively, business deposits are sensitive to other rates of return which are positively correlated with the included intermediary rates, equation (3) suggests that the estimated cross elasticities are overestimates of the true rates.

Thus, having examined each of Hamburger's assertions of mis-specifications, we find that to the extent such mis-specifications exist, they always give an *upward* bias to the estimated cross elasticities. We can therefore view the temporal cross-section evidence as yielding upper bounds for the true elasticities. Since the estimated elasticities exhibit at best weak substitution, we must conclude that the temporal cross-section evidence is both broadly consistent and persuasive.

V

DOMESTIC MONETARY POLICY
Introduced by A. R. NOBAY

M. J. ARTIS
RICHARD L. HARRINGTON
D. F. LOMAX

Discussion Papers
(*a*) C. A. E. GOODHART
(*b*) BRIAN GRIFFITHS

DOMESTIC MONETARY POLICY

A. R. Nobay

(*University of Southampton*)

Introduction

POTENTIALLY far-reaching changes in British monetary policy followed the publication by the Bank of England in May 1971 of its proposals on competition and credit control. Initial reactions to these proposals were expressed at the Money Study Group seminar, held at the Bank, to discuss the then-consultative document.[1] This session provides a timely opportunity to consider in more detail some of the issues arising from the new measures.

The traditional concerns amongst monetary economists in the decade following the publication of the Radcliffe Report were dominated by two distinct though related issues—debt management and the control of deposits, and the effects of financial intermediation on the conduct of monetary policy. The latest changes mark a significant departure from the Radcliffe era in two respects. First, they adopt, as a matter of policy, developments in welfare analysis applied to monetary systems, and secondly, implicit in them is the recognition that the money supply has an important role to play in economic stabilization. Both these aspects of the new proposals were rejected by the Radcliffe Report, the former more by default than by any explicit consideration. Indeed, one may view a number of the Report's conclusions as arising from its acceptance of the clearing banks' cartel arrangements. Developments leading to the adoption of these two aspects have taken the form of the P.I.B. report on bank charges and the Monopolies Report on the proposed bank mergers, both of which were sharply critical of the then existing institutional arrangements,[2] together with the revival of monetarism and the

---

[1] 'Competition and Credit Control' and 'Key Issues in Monetary Policy' in *Bank of England Quarterly Bulletin*, June 1971. See also Harry G. Johnson, Artis and Parkin, and Gordon Pepper in *Bankers' Magazine*, Sept. 1971.

[2] See ch. IV in H. G. Johnson *et al.* (eds.), *Readings in British Monetary Economics* (O.U.P., 1972).

British government's I.M.F.-encouraged adoption of the money supply prescription.

The techniques and objectives of monetary policy clearly cannot be divorced from the prevailing institutions, and the new measures call for an examination of some of the issues involved, which the papers in this session attempt. Michael Artis examines the implications of the new measures for the targets and indicator issue. David Lomax analyses the implications of the increased competition for the clearing banks, whilst Richard Harrington stresses the necessity of competition for credit control.

MONETARY POLICY IN THE 1970s IN THE LIGHT OF RECENT DEVELOPMENTS*

M. J. ARTIS
(University of Wales, Swansea)

IT seems fair to accept that there has been a minor revolution in the monetary system recently, following the implementation of the proposals set out in the Bank of England's document 'Competition and Credit Control' [3], first published in May 1971. The broad intent and putative effect of this revolution is to give the forces of competition greater play in determining the over-all efficiency of the system, to which end changes in the basis of monetary control were made, so as to establish a basis of equity between competing institutions, freedom from interference in decisions about the allocation of resources, and a check on monopolistic devices.

But it would seem that progressive change in the conditions governing competition in the monetary system need not have entailed, or been accompanied by, the apparent shift in emphasis of monetary policy which took place at the same time. In the context of import controls, Meade [20] among others has shown that supply side competition could still be maintained by a system of auctioning; it does not seem impossible to imagine a similar device applied in the context of advances controls.[1] Equally, steps could have been taken to equalize the implicit taxation on members of the monetary system, and to abolish the cartel agreement, which did not involve the shift of emphasis in policy targets, and consequent change of instruments that appears to have taken place.

These changes in policy instruments and the shift of emphasis in policy targets were not simply rationalized on the basis of a trade-off

---

* This paper was written whilst the author was at the National Institute of Economic and Social Research, London.

[1] Lord Balogh proposed to the Radcliffe Committee [2] that control of advances should proceed through applying advances/deposits ratios, for example. Alternative schemes can easily be imagined.

of monetary control for system efficiency, however, but as independently justified. We now see the Bank of England saying that its past policy in the gilt-edged market had become its own worst enemy [5]; that the apparently clear-cut effects of control by bank advance 'ceilings' were not, in fact, so clear-cut; that more attention should be paid to the 'monetary aggregates'.

So the minor revolution has clearly not been confined to changes in the competitive structure of the banking system, but extends also to the conduct of monetary policy. But whilst the changes in the former respect are quite clear (at any rate in their formal aspects), the nature of the latter is not so clear. The document 'Competition and Credit Control' and a contemporary statement by the Governor of the Bank of England [4], though 'leaning' in the direction of the 'monetary aggregates', seemed to mention as targets of monetary policy pretty well every magnitude that anyone might care about. Was this a proper show of eclecticism or merely an exercise in public relations?

This paper is mainly addressed to the problem of Targets and Indicators in an effort to see whether this question can be answered. In the first part, the question of targets and indicators is considered in terms of the criteria appropriate to choosing any particular variable as an indicator; in the following section the recent record of various indicators is set out; and in the third, the changing views of the monetary authorities are recorded. The last section considers whether there is any persuasive evidence to be brought to bear in favour of one indicator or another in the context of current policy problems.

The indicator problem

In a fundamental way, the problem of indicators (or targets) appears to arise from a lack of knowledge. If we had complete knowledge of the behaviour of the economic system, and access to a well-defined social welfare function, we should be able to measure the effects of policy actions and assess their adequacy directly. There would not be any point in having some financial variable stand in as an indicator or, from the Central Bank's point of view, as the target of policy.[2]

[2] In such a situation it is possible to construct an 'ideal' indicator, of course, which Brunner and Meltzer [6] express as

$$I = \frac{du}{dy_1}\frac{dy_1}{dx_1}\,dx_1 + \frac{du}{dy_2}\frac{dy_2}{dx_1}\,dx_1$$

where I is the indicator, dx_1 stands for the changes in variables expressing

In the real world, where knowledge is seriously incomplete and the effects of policy on ultimate goal variables are not precisely known in advance, and cannot be continuously monitored owing to delays in the collection of data and lags in the effectiveness of policy, it is usually thought useful to have an indicator of policy, which will also serve as a target for policy.

Such an indicator is called upon to show the direction of policy, taking account of any relevant changes in the functioning of the economic system, and to provide some kind of scaling of the strength of policy, viewed from the standpoint of its ultimate effectiveness. Indicators, in themselves, appear to provide no presumption about the time-scale of effectiveness, which has to be judged as a separate issue; nor do they pre-empt the need for discussion of the adequacy of policy in any particular period, a subject which also has to be evaluated as a separate issue.[3]

A further point to be made about the scope of indicators is that they should describe more than the effect of actions explicitly taken. It is, after all, quite possible for lack of action to constitute a positive policy: for example, a Central Bank contemplating open-market sales could desist from taking this action if it perceived that an increase in liquidity preferences of economic units was about to arise, which would accomplish the increase in interest rates called for.[4] A change in economic behaviour may thus be acquiesced in by a monetary authority to achieve its ends, and it is desirable that an

---

monetary policy operations, y_1 and y_2 are endogenous variables like prices and output, and u is the social utility function. Inevitably, as will be seen, everything which is in practice regarded as an indicator is a long way from ideal in the sense of this expression.

[3] Appearances may sometimes run to the contrary of these two points, which nevertheless are implied by the construction of such indicators as are normally used. Thus, for example, observers do sometimes argue as if a rise in (say) the full-employment weighted budget surplus had the deflationary impact with which it is credited in the period within which it is measured; whereas the weights applied are in fact 'equilibrium' weights and the process of calculating the indicator does not allow for time lags in economic units' response to the fiscal change so measured. The implication is that observers must make some judgement about the time lags which actually are involved in deploying this kind of measurement. In the case of fiscal policy, of course, it may be that they would be justified in assuming the lags are very short, with instantaneous effect as a not too implausible extreme case.

[4] An analogue in the fiscal policy field is better known. In a system with a progressive tax structure cast in nominal terms, inflation will act as would a rise in scheduled rates in an inflation-free economy.

indicator should recognize this possibility and evaluate policy on the basis of any relevant changes in behaviour.[5]

An indicator of the kind described, if one can be found, cannot help but form an appropriate target variable for the monetary authorities. There is, apparently, no distinction between the two. This does not of course preclude the possibility that the authorities may choose to conduct policy on the basis of a target variable that is different from the indicator used by other people in assessing that policy. This would only show that the underlying model guiding the authorities' actions (or, their goals) differed from that employed by other people.

Criteria for choosing indicators

The problem of choosing an indicator, in a world of imperfect knowledge, may be viewed in terms of a number of determining factors, of which the following suggests itself as a useful taxonomy: the choice of economic model; the problem of measurement; the goals of policy; the extent of the monetary authorities' autonomy.

Clearly, the choice of a particular indicator must depend from a view that it lies within the monetary authorities' power to control it (the autonomy problem). Allied to this problem is that of the objective; although an ideal indicator would scale policy in terms of a social welfare function, at the practical level it is possible to think of a specialization of monetary instruments and indicators to particular goals, and the choice of indicator may reflect some priorities about goals. The problem of measurement arises both at the conceptual level (do the statistically observed figures form good correlates of theoretical variables?) and at the practical level (are the data speedily provided? Are they reliable?). Finally, the model of the economy which is employed, and in particular the specification of the link between monetary and real variables, is likely to exert influence in favour of one indicator rather than another. This presumption is the stronger to the extent that 'models', being partial accounts of reality, in effect sum up the subjective evaluations by their proponents of all manner of empirical propositions not only about signs, but about relative magnitudes and instabilities.

[5] The relevant changes here are those which could reasonably have been predicted. It would be going too far to admit just any change in behaviour, as this would ultimately entail the surrender of the evaluation of policy entirely to the *export* behaviour of the economy.

(i) Models

To illustrate the point about models, it is worth taking up some specific examples for discussion. The Hicksian IS–LM model provides the most suitable starting-point. In its deterministic form, this model allows one indifferently to regard 'the' interest rate or the money supply as the indicator variable, in the sense that the one implies the other. Thus it is clearly not enough to choose the interest rate as the indicator given by such a framework simply on the grounds that it is 'interest rates which do the work', for although this is true in the sense that changes in money supply do not affect the real magnitudes in the model unless they affect interest rates, the fact is that the deterministic system always provides this link.[6] What such a statement says, if it is a justification for using interest rates as an indicator, is (implicitly) that the LM schedule is regarded as unstable. In this event, changes in interest rates will be linked to changes in real expenditures and income, and not to money supply. And in such a case the monetary authorities will best stabilize the goal variable (real income) if they stabilize interest rates. Interest rates are a better indicator of the thrust of monetary policy (and they still remain so even if the monetary authorities have chosen, mistakenly, to stabilize money supply).

But it has been shown (by Poole [23]) that the opposite is true if the IS curve is regarded as the more unstable schedule: in that event, money supply forms a more appropriate target (and thus a better indicator of policy). Thus, adherence to what can perhaps be described as a standard (textbook) Keynesian[7] model of this kind does not commit one to a preference for one or other goal or indicator

---

[6] This has to be qualified for the *extreme* cases, of course, of the liquidity trap on the one hand (where changes in the money supply do not change the interest rate), and the interest-inelastic expenditure schedule, on the other (where changes in money supply, though causing changes in interest rates, do not affect expenditures).

[7] The issue of the *potency* of monetary policy has been debated in terms of the relative slopes of the schedules, and 'monetarist' and 'Keynesian' positions identified with opposing views on this question. Whilst illuminating and useful as a way of drawing attention to some of the central magnitudes in question, it is difficult to believe that this characterization of the 'Keynesian *versus* monetarist' debate can really be apt. It is difficult to see why the debate caused so much fuss if *that* was all it was about. (And, after all, a magnitude surely central to the debate—the absolute price level—is not determined in this model at all.) Some monetarists, at any rate, do appear to regard this way of putting the issue as inappropriate to their position (for example, Meiselman [21]).

of policy in the absence of an evaluation of the relative stabilities and slopes[8] of the schedules.

Given only a presumption about the relative instabilities of the IS and LM schedules, one or other target (or indicator) can be shown to be the best; with more precise knowledge a combined interest-rate/money-supply target can be shown to be optimal (Poole [23]). In practice, such knowledge is unlikely to be available, and the clues about instabilities will be derived from monitoring the economy's development; in a Hicksian IS–LM world it is easy to see that 'shifts' in the IS function will be associated with divergences of interest rates and income in similar directions, whilst shifts in the LM position will be associated with diverse movements, and the model suggests that policy could be readjusted on this basis.[9] It is worth noting, though, that in the (not unlikely) case that the IS curve slopes upwards, the same associated divergencies of income and interest rates will occur whatever the source of the shift.

An obvious presumption in favour of a money supply policy or indicator is provided by models which assert that $Y_t = (1/k)M_t$, or in more contemporary form $\Delta Y_t = f(\Delta M_t, \Delta M_{t-1}, \ldots, M_{t-1})$. Money multiplier relationships assert a stable relationship between money supply (changes in it) and nominal income (or changes in it), on the basis of an assumption about the exogeneity of money. They are, usually, described as 'reduced forms' of some structural system, though in the absence of an explicit specification of the latter 'pseudo-reduced forms' seems a better description.

One kind of structural system leading to this reduced form is, though, the Hicksian IS–LM framework,[10] and in this case the reduced form is evidently too ambitious a test. For the stability of 'money multipliers' depends not only on the stability of the demand for money (given the money supply, the LM curve) but also on the stability of expenditure schedules (the IS curve); whereas our previous discussion suggested only that a greater stability of the LM

[8] The slopes are important because they influence the cost (in terms of output) of the instabilities that arise.

[9] It is true that the debate over targets sometimes risks failing to emphasize the possibility of readjustment, giving the impression, rather, that a given target value must be pursued for all time. At the practical level, however, it has to be noted that there are considerable lags in the collection of data, and that these are subject to substantial revision. Within the present framework (where lags in the effect of policy are not at issue), this fact alone makes the question of targets an important one.

[10] Cf. Laidler [18].

schedule relative to that of the expenditure schedules would suffice to suggest a prima facie case for money supply control as the proximate target of policy. It is, though, not the case that all proponents of such an approach would accept that the implicit structural system can be expressed in terms of the IS–LM framework. Such a framework does not accommodate what may be implicit in at least some statements of the monetarist position,[11] the possibility of direct money/goods substitution; if this occurs, the result is that movements in the IS and LM schedules become interdependent. An increase in the money supply, for example, besides affecting interest rates, also increases aggregate consumption directly and so shifts the IS curve outward. The new equilibrium may then consistently involve increased interest rates as well as increased incomes, a result usually held to be counter-Keynesian.[12]

The Wicksellian view of the *modus operandi* of monetary policy also issues in a prescription of money supply in the indicator, although in detail it would justify an interest-rate target. The form of the latter, however, is such that it must be read in terms of its alignment with the 'natural' rate of interest, normally regarded as an unobservable. Harrington [16] in a recent paper, argues that in certain circumstances the Wicksellian system does not indicate the money supply as target. In particular, this is so when bank interest rates are constrained by monopolistic practices (or policy) to a sub-equilibrium position, with the result that non-bank financial intermediation in effect accomplishes some of the work that would otherwise be done by increases in the money supply. This suggests that the Radcliffe

---

[11] As is by now well known, the early (1963) statement by Friedman and Schwartz [11] about the transmission mechanism differed from standard 'Keynesian' accounts essentially only in the generalization of the standard interest/investment relationship to a wider definition of investment (as, for example, to include consumer durables). The idea of diffused and widespread effects of this kind, as opposed to the simple and confined effects of the 'standard' approach, served both to shield the monetarist position from exposure to the generally accepted belief that the investment/interest relationship was weak and to complicate further the practical issue of identifying 'relevant' interest rates.

[12] Although a 'Keynesian' might, of course, choose to write investment as a positive function of income in such a way as to yield an upward-sloping IS schedule, the system then yielding the same prediction about interest-rate and income movements (Smith [24]). Results have been derived suggesting that changes in money supply, though leading to reductions in interest rates in the short run, eventually produce increases (Gibson [12]), but these have been generally held to reflect the operation of a price expectations mechanism.

Report's emphasis on total credit flows was near the mark in the conditions of operation of the financial system in the 1950s and 1960s.

It is doubtful in fact whether the Radcliffe Report can be said to have had a view about an appropriate indicator of policy. Certainly, over any period of time, the views of the Report suggest that the flexibility of financial markets will provide alternative sources of credit flows to bank advances, and, as is well known, the Report refuses to suggest an indicator of its concept of 'general liquidity', drawing attention instead to a wide range of alternative assets and liabilities without stating a weighting scheme. In the short run, on the other hand, it is consistent with Radcliffe theory to propose bank advances as the implied indicator, for the Report explicitly noted that the banks were widespread and easily accessible lenders. A decline in their capacity to lend would therefore have clear short-run repercussions on total credit flows and activity. In a more general context, the view that monetary policy operates partly by playing on market imperfections and the creation of credit-rationing effects justifies regarding bank advances as an indicator of policy thrust. Within the rules of the money multiplier game, it is also arguable that the 'true' model should allow for variable lags of the effects of money supply increase on income wherein the variability of the lags depends on the composition of money supply increases (say, as between private sector and public sector lending).[13]

Some models of the monetary process, finally, stress that the importance of linkages between financial and real variables occur at the level of stock market prices, rather than in the market for government bonds, with unstable (or complicated) connections holding as between the financial markets directly affected by monetary operations and those where the significant link with real variables resides. Tobin's position [25] is of this kind; the obvious difficulty with it is the autonomy problem.[14]

Another model (or set of models), explicitly adapted to the open economy, suggests that policy indicators must be confined to domestic credit expansion (DCE). It is more convenient to draw on these models in the sections below dealing with objectives and

[13] Experiments of this kind would cast light on the question whether differences in the composition of money supply increases exert only 'first-round' effects or, on the other hand, exert long-run effects, on the ultimate change in income level.

[14] Consistently with his view, Tobin has elsewhere suggested that the monetary authorities should intervene directly in equity markets.

autonomy, as it is in these respects that the DCE indicator contains its novelty, rather than in any different view about the way in which monetary variables (whether under the control of the authorities or not) interact with other variables to influence the level of economic activity.

(ii) *The measurement problem*

Presumption about the 'relevance' of a particular model does not carry through to the choice of a particular indicator unless the measurement problem can be resolved. There are in principle two components to this problem: first of all, there is the question how far available data series provide information relevant to the theoretical variables; then there is the question of the speed of collection and reliability of the data themselves.

At the first level it is tempting to say that it is advocacy of interest-rate targets which encounters the most difficult measurement error. The interest rate relevant to expenditure decisions is generally supposed to be the real rate of interest, whereas the directly observable data refer to nominal rates. Where there is a presumption that price expectations are not changing it can be concluded that changes in nominal rates of interest are not a bad guide. But in the more general case it is apparent that nominal rates of interest may be a poor guide.[15] Nor is it clear which interest rates are the most relevant. Treasury bill rates in recent years, for example, surely come close to being nearly meaningless nominal numbers from the viewpoint of the economic effectiveness of monetary policy. At the same time, the suggestion that monetary policy influences the timing of expenditures by creating expectations about the durability of any given level of interest rates suggests that an additional requirement is some index of market beliefs about the future level of interest rates.

Money supply indicators are not short of similar criticism; there is no *a priori* presumption that one definition of the money supply must be superior to another. It would be comforting to know that it should make little material difference which series is used as an indicator or target of policy, at any rate on a short-term basis. It is a fact of recent U.K. experience, however, that growth rates of the 'wide' definition of money supply substantially outstrip that of the narrow series, a fact (presumably) not unconnected with the competitive

---

[15] Chart V.1, p. 531, shows the relationship between a nominal and an expected real rate of interest, on a certain assumption about the state of expectations with regard to the price level.

structure of the system and the type of policy pursued. Table V.1 tabulates the R^2 of quarterly first differences in the three official definitions of money supply,[16] and in the I.M.F. definition.[17] That these are not higher than shown may reflect, in part, the institutional considerations mentioned above.

TABLE V.1

Definitions of Money Supply

	Correlation matrix (first differences)[a]			
	ΔM_1	ΔM_2	ΔM_3	ΔM_{IFS}
ΔM_1	—	—	—	—
ΔM_2	0·753	—	—	—
ΔM_3	0·548	0·876	—	—
ΔM_{IFS}	0·392	0·570	0·648	—

DEFINITIONS: M_1, M_2, M_3 as officially defined in *Financial Statistics*, M_{IFS}, the money supply series derived from *International Financial Statistics* as employed by Laidler and Parkin [19].

[a] R^2; quarterly changes, 1963 II–1971 III, except for correlations involving M_{IFS}, when the period is 1963 II–1967 IV. All data seasonally adjusted.

The measurement of DCE raises a number of puzzles too numerous to illustrate here. Suffice to say that the official U.K. definition differs from the I.M.F. definition, and that current practice in the U.K. emphasizes its definition as a credit flow rather than as an adjusted money supply concept. This seemingly has the effect, for example, of treating an expansion of bank lending to private and public sectors, which is underpinned by an increase in banks' non-monetary liabilities (say, capital issues), as an increase in DCE, and no different from an increase financed by an expansion in deposits. Anyone working with these data will be struck by the enormous discrepancies between the two sides of the DCE equation partly accounted for by the complications this treatment introduces.

At the level of speed and reliability of collection and publication,

[16] One of these is given in seasonally adjusted form, and the same implicit (ratio) adjusters were applied to the remaining two series (M_1, M_2) to give the adjusted series used in the correlations. The problem of appropriate seasonal correction raised in this case reflects a practical problem of some difficulty from the viewpoint of control.

[17] This was the (uncentred) version of the series employed by Laidler and Parkin in their work on the demand for money [19].

interest rates are easy winners on current practice. These data are instantly available and (in their own terms) reliable. By contrast, money supply data are, so far, available only six months behind the event and quarterly. It is difficult to believe that the authorities work under these handicaps; they presumably obtain data faster and more frequently, though it may be less reliable in the sense of being more prone to revision.[18] Over and above these factors, there is the problem of allowing for seasonality and, in interpreting policy fairly, of allowing for 'noise' in the observed series. Comment reported in the Bank of England's *Quarterly Bulletin* suggests that these constitute serious difficulties for any policy instruction seeking to impose a short-period 'monetary rule'; but we know very little in detail about this problem.

(iii) *Objectives*

The choice of indicator reflects an assumption about the objectives or targets of policy. These need not be the targets of the authorities, clearly, since it may be that these are entirely misconceived or irrelevant, and the purpose of a good indicator is to comment on the important effects of their policy. Generally speaking, the implicit objectives have to do with stabilizing the level of economic activity (pressure of demand)—this is implicit in the IS/LM approach to the problem—or with the level of prices or the balance of payments.

It does seem that most people use indicators in a timeless fashion, though they have different time-scales in mind. For example, monetarists are generally credited with a belief in long lags, and with an additional belief that the long-run effect of money supply variations falls on prices rather than on real incomes. But the whole question of lags in the effectiveness of monetary policy still remains unclear: the early emphasis of the monetarists on 'long' lags was sharply reversed by the work of the St. Louis Federal Reserve Bank, for example, while Tucker [26] showed that it was possible for monetary policy to have quick effects despite evidence of long lags in investment functions.[19]

There is therefore considerable ambiguity in assertions drawn

[18] Even if so, it is difficult to see why these data should not be publicly released. The problem of revision has not inhibited faster release of national accounts data. (Since this passage was first written, money supply figures have become available on a monthly basis, and with only a short delay.)

[19] A recent consideration of the problem concludes that the measurement of policy lags depends a great deal on the choice of policy indicator (Hamburger [14]).

from inspection of indicators about the stance of policy, as to when the effects of the change in stance so described will become apparent. In addition, there is a distinction to be drawn between those who attribute to money supply a role in price formation distinct from anything connected with the pressure of demand and those who do not; the latter can be thought of as using indifferently a goal variable 'the pressure of demand', which embraces a description of both real economic activity and price pressures, while the former have something distinct in mind.

Balance-of-payments stabilization as a goal of policy is associated with the use of DCE as indicator. As practised in the U.K. in 1969 (and perhaps 1970) DCE targetry may well be presented as destabilizing for the level of economic activity. The policy pursued implied that control of DCE would be consistent with desired levels of economic activity only if the balance of payments turned out as desired. Errors in forecasting the latter would lead, given adherence to a fixed DCE target, to deviations in planned money supply growth and hence to deviations in the level of economic activity.[20]

(iv) *Autonomy*

Choice of policy indicator must, finally, be conditioned by a presumption about the autonomy, or area of discretion of the monetary authorities. What seems the necessary criterion for a variable to be an indicator in this case is that its value could, in principle,[21] be controlled by the monetary authorities. This means that it is no argument against (say) the choice of money supply as an indicator, that the authorities chose not to control it, but instead to control something else (say, interest rates).

There is sometimes a confusion between autonomy in this sense and exogeneity. The point is that autonomy over a variable in the sense just described does not guarantee that it may be taken as statistically exogeneous. Thus the argument that the money supply was what it was—and could have been otherwise—does not suffice for unbiased measurement of, say, the 'money multiplier' relationship $\Delta Y_t = f(\Delta M_t, \Delta M_{t-1}, \ldots, \Delta M_{t-i})$. A believer in this 'model'

---

[20] This assumes that it is money supply (or interest rates) and *not* DCE which is significant for planned expenditures and output; it seems incorrect to relate DCE and real expenditure (*pace* the suggestions given in the *Bank of England Quarterly Bulletin*, Sept. 1969, Suppt., p. 369).

[21] Although, in this context, it is customary to assume that the term 'in principle' is an expression of possibilities within a framework of law and conduct the same as, or very similar to, the one actually prevailing.

may still choose to use ΔM as an indicator, though his evidence for its relevance and scaling value will not necessarily be acceptable, if it appears that the policy rules governing the autonomous variable M were such as to render it endogenous.

Analogies with fiscal policy indicators lead to the suggestion that endogeneity problems require the normalization of monetary variables to neutralize the effects of the economy on them and so isolate the effects of policy: the standard fiscal policy analogue is the 'high employment budget surplus'. Attempts have been made to provide measures of the 'neutralized money stock' (Hendershott [17]) or potential money supply (Dewald [10]).

It is not so clear, though, that these analogies and the consequent neutralized measures, are necessarily well founded. The model of fiscal policy underlying the high employment surplus calculations, to begin with, rests on the assumption that it is changes in effective tax rates and rates of government spending which constitute fiscal policy; from this point of view, the actual surplus is irrelevant and the normalization process can be viewed as constituting a proximate means of isolating the changes in 'schedules' (of tax rates and government spending) from the changes in totals of tax revenues and expenditures.[22] The model of monetary policy, however, seems to imply that what is important is the *actual* change in money stock rather than a change in 'schedules'. This depends, though, on what view is taken about the stability of the demand for money. If there is stability in this function then fluctuations in income in an IS–LM framework stem from shifts in the IS curve, and stabilizing policy would call for increases in the supply of money to offset downward fluctuations and decreases to offset upward fluctuations. The change in money supply would appear to yield a reasonable reading of policy in both cases. If the monetary authorities choose to stabilize interest rates in the face of income fluctuations, money supply responses will be perverse, but again give a correct interpretation of policy. From this viewpoint, money supply seems a superior indicator in terms of possible income-endogeneity than interest rates; the latter would be most unreliable. On the whole, then, it does not seem that the fiscal policy analogue carries over strongly to money supply, actual changes in which (on the assumption of a stable demand function) should convey the correct reading of policy. Endogeneity problems do, however, become more important the further away from the centre of Central Bank intervention the indicator variable

[22] The process may not be efficient in doing this. (See Hansen [15].)

is; bank advances, for example (even under ceiling controls) cannot be held to reflect monetary policy all that strongly; still less, one would hazard, the level of stock market prices. On the grounds of proximity to the monetary authorities' direct control, the monetary base is sometimes advocated, though often enough this advocacy has continued to confuse autonomy with statistical exogeneity. In U.K. conditions it is doubtful whether the monetary base has any meaning.[23]

The criterion of autonomy is most forceful in its application to the (small) open economy, where it suggests that only DCE can be regarded as a monetary policy target or indicator. This follows from assumptions that interest rates and price levels are determined by the world, so that with free movement of securities and goods across frontiers an economy operating under a fixed-rate regime has no option for monetary policy other than to arbitrate the division of its money supply between domestically- and foreign-backed components. There is good evidence in the recent policy record of the extent to which controlled exchange rates issue in abdication of control of money supply or interest rates—or in the partial impairment of freedom to trade in securities across the frontier. This is some indication of the extent to which, in seeking to describe British monetary policy, what is actually being described is the reflection in the U.K. of world (or, specifically, U.S.) monetary policies.

On a day-to-day level, autonomy considerations lead us to notice that accurate control is probably not feasible; indicators are subject to large random fluctuations.

The record

(i) *Performance of alternative indicators 1963–71*

That there is an argument about indicators presupposes, among other things, that there actually are substantial differences in the readings given by alternative indicators.

Charts V.1–V.3 have been drawn up with a view to asking how far this is so.

Definitions of the series shown in the Charts is in order before

[23] At any rate under past regimes of policy (see Cramp [7]). Under the new regime there may be some chance of showing that the monetary base is a meaningful operational concept. Calculations of 'potential money' based on fitting multipliers to the total volume of reserve assets still seem infeasible in U.K. conditions, given the heterogeneous stock of eligible assets under the ruling definitions.

proceeding further. Chart V.1 shows the nominal rate of interest on one-year local authority bonds and the corresponding expected real rate of interest, the expected rate of inflation being identified with the forecast rate of rise of the consumer price index given in relevant issues of the *National Institute Economic Reviews*.[24] Obviously it is unclear either that this price index is the appropriate one or that the

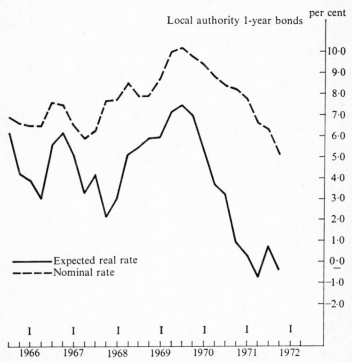

CHART V.1. *Monetary Policy Indicators: Nominal and 'expected real' rates of interest*

expectations about prices given in the *Review* reflected prevailing beliefs. However, the latter does not seem too implausible an assumption, and the series does have the merit of being a true ex-ante series

[24] The expected real rate of interest being defined, in percentage terms as $(r - p)/(100 + p)$ 100 where r is the nominal rate of interest, p the expected rate of inflation.

of expectations, reflecting estimates of, for example, the impact of incomes policy or devaluation. The observations are centred at mid-quarter. Chart V.2 gives the annual rate of change in money supply

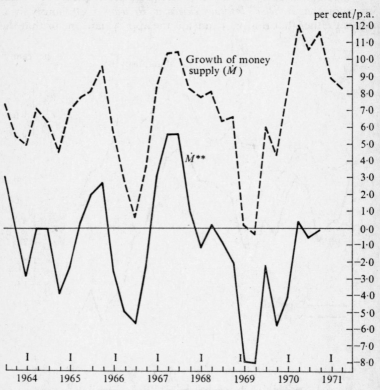

CHART V.2. *Monetary Policy Indicators: Growth of nominal money supply; growth in the 'normalized real money supply'*

(M_3, seasonally adjusted), centred at end-quarter,[25] and an interpretation of recent official doctrine as to the definition of a neutral money supply policy. This is that neutrality would consist in a growth of the money supply sufficient to 'finance' the underlying real

[25] End-quarter observations were centred by calculating (in annual percentage terms) the growth rate of money supply as $\dot{M} = (M_{t+1} - M_{t-1})/M_t$.

growth rate of the economy plus the 'going rate' of inflation. Accordingly, the observations designated $\dot{M}^{**}$ in the Chart were calculated by subtracting from the growth rate of real money supply[26]

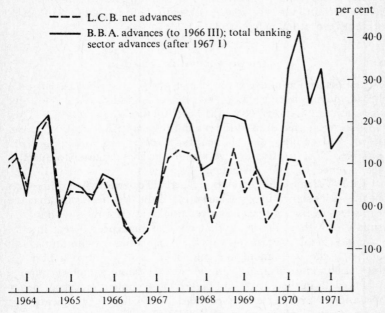

CHART V.3. *Monetary Policy Indicators: Growth in bank advances*

a 'standard rate' of 3 per cent representing the underlying growth potential of the economy. This was also centred at end-quarter.

Chart V.3 shows growth rates in narrow and broad definitions of bank advances. The former is identified with London Clearing Bank net advances (excluding nationalized industries), the latter with the British Bankers Association return and subsequently the figures of 'total banking sector' advances.[27]

[26] The implicit deflator of GDP was the price index used.

[27] The London Clearing Bank series are given in official sources in seasonally adjusted form. The latter series were adjusted by the method of ratio to moving average, presumptively a rather inadequate technique to apply in this case, especially over the short data run available for the second part of the (broken) series.

DCE was excluded from the coverage of the indicator charts partly because of failure to find a suitable means of expressing it in growth rate form, as seemed desirable. Attempts to estimate the 'stock' counterpart of the DCE flow foundered on an inability to obtain a convincing match of changes in the stock figures for net overseas claims on the public sector with the recorded flow of public sector external financing.[28]

Concurrence of indicators

Visual inspection and comparison of the Charts suggests that on a broad moving average basis the alternative indicators do not give very different impressions of the short-run movement of policy. They do, however, give quite different impressions of the scale of movement, and comparisons of their levels over long periods are unreliable. Nor, finally, are very short-period (quarter-to-quarter) movements very well correlated.

Table V.2 gives the correlation matrix of quarterly first differences in the series shown in the Charts. It will be seen from this that the expected inverse sign on the correlation of interest rates with money supply growth is obtained; that changes in expected real interest rates (as calculated) are not very well correlated with anything else; and that the new 'monetary rule' is little different as a basis for interpretation from changes in the growth of nominal money supply.

The data in the Charts can be used to comment on recent policy in various ways. For example, the data in Chart V.1 indicate that the relaxation of policy since 1969/70 has been very substantial indeed if the fall in the expected real rate of interest is used as the guide. Despite the indication given by the nominal rate of interest, policy should be interpreted as very much easier than in previous periods covered by the series.

Chart V.2 also confirms a strong relaxation of policy over the same period. The interpretation of the recent suggested definition of a passive policy, however, indicates that policy ought not to be thought of as so expansive as in 1967. Although nominal rates of money supply growth are as high or higher, they are doing no more

---

[28] This step should have identified R in the DCE equation $M = D + R$ where M is money supply, D domestic credit, and R is reserves or, more broadly, net claims of the public sector on the overseas sector. The latter are negative. Part of the reason for the failure to match the recorded flow against the corresponding change in stock is that the bases of valuation differ.

TABLE V.2

Concurrence of Indicators

Correlation matrix (r), quarterly first differences
$(1965\ \text{II}-1970\ \text{IV})^a$

	$\Delta\dot{A}$	$\Delta\dot{M}$	$\Delta\dot{M}$**	Δrn	Δrpe
$\Delta\dot{A}$	1·0	—	—	—	—
$\Delta\dot{M}$	+0·30	1·0	—	—	—
$\Delta\dot{M}$**	+0·04	0·93	1·0	—	—
Δrn	−0·49	−0·45	−0·41	1·0	—
Δrpe	−0·23	−0·22	−0·06	0·48	1·0

SOURCES: Bank of England *Statistical Abstract; Financial Statistics; National Institute Economic Review.*

NOTES: dotted variables indicate growth rates; $\dot{A}$ = bank advances (London Clearing Banks); $\dot{M}$ = money supply (M_3); $\dot{M}$** = normalized real money supply; rn = local authority one-year bond rate; rpe = real expected rate of interest.

^{a} Except for correlations involving Δrn, Δrpe, where the period was 1965 IV–1970 IV.

than stabilizing the growth of real money supply in line with underlying economic growth.[29]

The bank advance indicators suggest the problem of a choice between a narrow and a broad definition. On the latter basis the advances indicator has something in common with the nominal money supply, though the fall in the rate of increase from 1970 to 1971 is much sharper, indicative, no doubt, of the endogeneity problem in this instance.

It is apparent from the record, though, that despite some similarities in short-period movements, the alternative indicators are capable of giving significantly different readings of policy both in very short-run, quarter-by-quarter movements and in terms of comparisons across periods of years. One of the main problems, clearly, is the allowance to be made for inflation. The trend of expected real rates can, on this account, diverge significantly from that in nominal rates; and there are similar difficulties in using the rate of growth of money supply as an indicator. If, as in the interpretation given to the new 'monetary rule', it is accepted that current inflation is

[29] The suspicion would be, however, that the continued decline in interest rates in the second half of 1971 was associated with a more expansive phase of policy on this definition.

'given', then recent high rates of nominal money supply growth are doing no more than provide a steady growth of real money balances; this sounds like something that monetary policy might well aim to do. The comparisons, apart from drawing attention to such puzzles as this, do not provide a basis for choice. This rests with the judgements made on the criteria set out earlier, a subject which is rejoined in the last section of the paper.

Before broaching this issue, attention needs to be given to the shift of official opinion over monetary targets.

(ii) *Statements of policy*

There is clear evidence, from published statements, that official thinking has undergone considerable change in recent years, largely summarized as a movement 'away from interest rates' towards 'the monetary aggregates'. In fact, the record is more complicated than that, since the authorities have for a long time shown interest in one of the monetary aggregates—bank lending to the private sector—and have given expression of their policy in corresponding terms. With the help of ceilings, this target was kept under close supervision from the mid-sixties on. It was accompanied by a policy of stabilizing interest rates. It was the latter rather than the former policy which was modified in mid-1969, when various changes in dealing techniques in the gilt-edged market were undertaken.[30]

These modifications of interest-rate policy were confined to dealings in the 'medium' and 'long' end of the market. It seems that the interventionist 'smoothing' policy has, and will, continue at the short end of the market. Indeed the choice of designated reserve assets under the new regime of monetary control embarked upon last year was presumably enforced by this trading decision.[31] The new regime itself, however, was introduced by a further modification of the Bank's dealing arrangements in the gilt-edged market.

This distinction, in the change of interest-rate policy, between the 'short' and 'long' ends of the market is reflected in the figures given in Table V.3. These show the standard deviations of the monthly first differences of treasury bill and Consol yields in the periods 1963–5, 1965–8, and 1969–71. The substantial increase in the

[30] Actually, some mention is made in the Bank of England's *Quarterly Bulletin* for Mar. 1969 (p. 15) of a period in the previous year when dealing tactics were for a time modified.

[31] The reserve assets include, in addition to balances at the Bank of England, treasury bills and government bonds with up to one year to maturity, commercial bills, tax reserve certificates, and certain local authority bills.

TABLE V.3

Standard Deviations of the Monthly First Differences in Interest Rates

	Treasury bill rate	Consol rate
1963–5	0·384	0·122
1966–8	0·406	0·151
1969–71	0·323	0·284

SOURCE: C.S.O., *Financial Statistics*.

instability of the trend of Consol yields in the last period contrasts with the seeming reduction in instability of treasury bill yields.

The change of interest-rate policy reflects explicitly the Bank's conclusion that '[its] operations in the gilt-edged market should pay more regard to their quantitative effects on the monetary aggregates and less regard to the behaviour of interest rates'.[32] The decision also seems to have reflected the consideration, among others, that the Bank's interventions may have been responsible in themselves for stimulating large speculative transactions.[33]

The initial modifications were, it may be recalled, introduced at a time when monetary policy was reformulated round a target for domestic credit expansion. This particular monetary aggregate, however, seems subsequently to have been relegated to a subsidiary, perhaps even honorific, role. DCE 'targets' have been publicly set for two years—the financial years 1969/70 and 1970/1—and on both occasions the policy 'misses' were substantial, as might have been expected.[34] In contexts where the change in the public sector's net foreign indebtedness can undergo massive and unpredictable variation, adherence to an inflexible DCE target merely makes for massive instability in the money supply.[35] Apart from this, of course,

[32] 'Competition and Credit Control', extract from a lecture by the Chief Cashier of the Bank of England, *Bank of England Quarterly Bulletin*, Dec. 1971, p. 477.

[33] Ibid., p. 478. This possibility had earlier been suggested by W. E. Norton [22].

[34] The target DCEs for 1969/70 were, respectively, +£400m. and +£900m.; the outcome figures were −£540m.; and +£1,404m.

[35] Ignoring the rather extensive statistical complications of the measurement of DCE as it is done in the U.K., the change in the supply of money can be expressed as the sum of the reduction in the public sector's net indebtedness overseas and DCE.

the decline of interest in DCE is associated with a switch of objectives away from nearly exclusive concern with the balance of payments towards other goals. The associated change towards emphasis on money supply growth was evident towards the end of 1970 and has become clearer since.[36]

In the budget speech of 1971, the Chancellor referred explicitly to a money supply-oriented policy, one described in terms amounting to acceptance of the going rate of inflation and pursuance of a 'neutral' policy of seeing to it that the growth of real money balances approximated the growth of real incomes. There are signs that this policy was subsequently abandoned in favour of a more expansionary stance, associated with the desire to stimulate investment spending. However, the policy could still be described in terms of this modified 'monetary rule', though it seems more natural to see the proximate objective of the monetary authorities as having once more become interest rates.

Conclusions for policy

Does the foregoing allow us to say anything positive about where monetary policy should go in the 1970s?

Part of the answer to this question we should hope to find in an evaluation of such present evidence as we have about the stability and values of key relationships; but this evidence cannot be lightly used in a context where the operating conditions of policy have so recently been extensively altered, and it may be dangerous to recommend changes in policy on evidence drawn from another policy environment; finally, it is necessary to consider what the basic-policy problems are.

(i) *Evidence*

Foregoing discussion reveals as relevant evidence our knowledge about the stability of money demand functions, and aggregate expenditure functions; likewise, any knowledge we possess on the question of credit rationing effects, and the stability of money multipliers.

This is not the occasion to dwell at length on these points; and

---

[36] The assiduous reader of the *Bank of England Quarterly Bulletin* will notice how the sub-heads in the regular account of economic developments have progressed from 'domestic credit expansion' (in 1969) to 'domestic credit expansion and the money supply' (1970's style) to 'money supply and domestic credit expansion' (1971).

what follows is a very selective and partial view of the state of play. First of all, we can say that for post-war U.K. conditions and especially for recent periods,[37] the money multiplier approach fails to yield evidence that would convince even the converted. Relevant evidence, which I believe is representative, appears in Tables V.4 and V.5. Table V.4 gives material suitable to discussion of the view

TABLE V.4

The Monetary Equivalent of Changes in Velocity, 1963–71[a]

		ΔM	ΔV			ΔM	ΔV			ΔM	ΔV
1963	I	n.a.	n.a.	1966	I	+300	−160	1969	I	+190	−99
	II	+210	+358		II	+90	+216		II	−180	+530
	III	+200	−47		III	+100	+106		III	+150	+245
	IV	+210	+138		IV	−50	+215		IV	+330	−104
1964	I	+100	−37	1967	I	+290	−133	1970	I	+20	+30
	II	+180	+226		II	+290	−1		II	+640	+290
	III	+230	−126		III	+430	−362		III	+380	+31
	IV	+140	+115		IV	+320	−440		IV	+540	−95
1965	I	+130	+50	1968	I	+170	+507	1971	I	+500	−588
	II	+290	−102		II	+410	−319		II	+310	+540
	III	+190	+128		III	+210	+299				
	IV	+320	−145		IV	+290	−67				

SOURCE: *Financial Statistics, Economic Trends.*

[a] ΔM is the change in money supply (M_3, seasonally adjusted), ΔV, the monetary equivalent of the change in velocity defined for quarter t as $\Delta V = Y_t / V_{t-1} - M_t$, where Y is the seasonally adjusted level of GDP at current market prices.

that short-period velocity may be taken as a constant; although this view is not nowadays widely held, it seems it may have had some influence on policy at least as recently as 1969.[38] The Table shows, side by side, changes in the supply of money and the monetary equivalent of the accompanying change in (income) velocity. Of the 33 quarterly changes tabulated, there were 13 occasions when the velocity change was larger than the money supply change, 4 in the opposite direction, 9 in the same direction. In terms of scale, the variation in velocity was on average quite large enough in relation to

[37] I am not very impressed by the technique of giving great weight to the stability of key relationships by reference to their performance in earlier periods nor, come to that, by evidence derived from overseas experience. The British economy of today is sufficiently unique to demand that we seek to establish regularities on the basis of contemporary experience.

[38] Cf. the article 'Money Supply and Domestic Credit' in *Economic Trends*, May 1969.

actual changes in money stock to render the assumption of a constant velocity misleading for short-term policy purposes. Table V.5

TABLE V.5

Almon 'Reduced-form' Results Independent variable. Change in money supply; dependent variable, change in GDP or proxy measure

	Dependent variable				
Quarter	GDP		GDP proxy		
	'Compromise'	'Expenditure'	IPI × WPI	IPI × CPI	IPI × RPI
0	−0·027	−0·126	0·273*	0·165	0·189
1	0·004	−0·035	0·240*	0·194*	0·205*
2	0·025	0·028	0·202*	0·201*	0·202*
3	0·034	0·063	0·159*	0·185*	0·180*
4	0·034	0·070	0·111	0·146*	0·139*
5	0·022	0·049	0·058	0·084*	0·079
Coefficient sum	0·092	0·049	1·045	0·975	0·993
N	6	6	6	6	6
Q	2	2	2	2	2
R^2	0·016	0·059	0·457	0·439	0·412
D–W	2·863	3·132	1·836	1·810	1·994

NOTES: * indicates significant at 5 per cent level; equations were run over the period 1962 I–1970 I on quarterly, seasonally adjusted data and are excerpted from trials involving alternative lag lengths and higher orders of interpolation polynomials. The proxy variables are scaled products of the industrial production index (IPI), using alternative price indices—the wholesale price index (WPI), consumer price index (CPI), or retail price index (RPI).

gives some representative results for money multipliers of the form $\Delta Y_t = f(\Delta M_t, \Delta M_{t-1}, \ldots, \Delta M_{t-i})$ where ΔY_t is the change in GDP or substitute measures of economic activity rather misleadingly labelled 'proxies' in the Table heading.[39] Weak results of the kind shown in the Table have been established elsewhere (cf. Artis and Nobay [1], Goodhart and Crockett [13]). Money supply policies can hardly be supported on this basis.

In fact, the best case we have for regarding the control of money

[39] These proxy measures, which are based on the industrial production index scaled up by some price index, correlate only very weakly (in first difference terms) with changes in GDP. Industrial production constitutes less than one half of GDP.

supply as an important aim of monetary policy rests with the analysis of relative instabilities in IS and LM schedules. This case is very persuasive at the intuitive level: given the evidence in the stability of the demand for money, it seems reasonable to think of the LM curve being a good deal more stable than the IS curve. Even then, it is necessary to record that the evidence so far examined on the demand for money is unsatisfactory in numerous ways: for example, the influence of interest rates is not a very robust one.[40] The speculative demand for money has yet to be examined;[41] examination of lag structures is still incomplete and utilizes procedures which constrain the lag structures on alternative variables to be implausibly similar. Table V.6, again, gives some results which are representative of work so far completed suggesting 'long lags' (of adjustment and/or expectation)[42] and low interest elasticities.[43] The list of shortcomings could be extended; but all this is only to say that more evidence would be nice to have, and that the results so far obtained are really rather tentative—especially so, if they are to be used to recommend a change in policy operations. Even so, if one has to appraise the state of knowledge at the present stage it would be fair to say that the evidence in favour of a stable demand function for money is at least more favourable than was widely thought; certainly more so than was implied by, say, the Radcliffe Report.

It still needs to be shown, of course, that to control the money supply is to do something important. This means being able to show that interest rates are effective in influencing expenditure decisions; and here there is still a long way to go, although there is correspondingly much to hope for.

There is evidence, of a scattered kind, that bank advances are a highly significant quantity: there is the timing evidence established by Crockett [8], for example, and evidence that the consumption function is best specified to include advances (as well as the change

[40] Laidler and Parkin [19] failed to uncover a significant role for interest rates, though they feature significantly in the work reported by, e.g., Goodhart and Crockett [13] and in some of the equations reported in Table V.6.

[41] A recent article by Crouch [9], however, suggests that such a search may not prove fruitful.

[42] Laidler and Parkin's work [19] suggests that the 'long lags' picked up by using the procedure of including the lagged dependent term on the right-hand side of the equation should be explained by combining a short adjustment lag with a longer expectational lag; a result which seems intuitively very plausible.

[43] The most significant results are those obtained for the Consol rate, which indicate an equilibrium interest elasticity of demand (after taking account of the coefficient on the lagged dependent variable) of around -0.4.

TABLE V.6
Demand for Money Equations

Equation	Dependent variable	Constant	Income	Interest rates LAR	Interest rates COR	Lagged dependent variable	R^2	D-W
1.1	M	−0·09 (0·15)	0·17 (0·08)	−0·02 (0·01)		0·86 (0·09)	0·997	1·85
1.2	M	−0·49 (0·28)	0·26 (0·08)		−0·08 (0·03)	0·81 (0·08)	0·997	1·98
2.1	M/POP	0·14 (0·04)	0·17 (0·08)	−0·02 (0·01)		0·86 (0·09)	0·997	1·83
2.2	M/POP	0·36 (0·12)	0·27 (0·08)		−0·08 (0·03)	0·82 (0·08)	0·997	2·02
3.1	M/P	−0·72 (0·50)	0·15 (0·10)	−0·03 (0·01)		0·87 (0·11)	0·965	1·71
3.2	M/P	−2·24 (0·81)	0·36 (0·12)		−0·08 (0·03)	0·82 (0·10)	0·969	1·94
4.1	$M/P.POP$	−4·48 (0·98)	0·82 (0·28)	0·01 (0·02)		0·02 (0·11)	0·849	0·723
4.2	$M/P.POP$	−4·24 (0·84)	0·99 (0·24)		−0·06 (0·07)	−0·02 (0·13)	0·851	0·887

NOTES: M is money stock (M_3); POP is the (interpolated) adult population; P is the GNP deflator. The income variable is (expenditure-based) GNP at current market prices (equations 1.1 and 1.2), at 1963 market prices (equations 3.1 and 3.2), and in nominal and real *per capita* form (equations 2.1 and 2.2; 4.1 and 4.2). Interest-rate variables are: LAR, the local authority three-month rate; COR, the consol rate. All equations were run in logarithms, on seasonally adjusted quarterly data, for the period 1963 II–1971 II. Standard errors are shown in brackets.

in hire purchase outstanding).[44] It has not yet been formally demonstrated in published work, that money multipliers can be improved by incorporating advances, though this would seem to be one way of establishing whether the asset backing of a change in money supply has any enduring, or merely a 'first-round', effect (or none at all) on the multiplier.

On current evidence, the upshot is that the qualified move by the monetary authorities in the direction of control of the supply of money seems justified, both in itself and in its qualifications. That is, eclecticism has some valid claims on policy decisions.

(ii) *The new conditions*

Such a conclusion seems the better justified to the extent that the new operating decisions of financial markets ought to help remove the imperfections which were one of the proximate justifications for a policy of controlling advances. The new emphasis, too, serves to give monetary policy a greater degree of autonomy from fiscal policy than was possible under the influence of previous views about the need for 'orderly marketing' of gilt-edged securities, the effect of which was to render monetary policy little more than the validator of 'high multiplier' fiscal policy, exaggerating the mistakes of the latter as much as containing them. On the other hand, recent developments have demonstrated the limits set on domestic monetary policy by the openness of the economy, implying a diminution of autonomy. An important problem for empirical economics is to illuminate the extent of the autonomy which remains and to discover the dynamics which are finessed by the comparative statics of the modern theory of open-economy monetary economics.

(iii) *Policy problems*

With what policy problems can monetary policy be expected to deal in the 1970s?[45] Given sufficient autonomy to make it realistic to talk about a British monetary policy (rather than the effects in the U.K. of Federal Reserve policy), the short answer is that the unemployment/inflation problem is the leading issue. Problems of medium-term growth (i.e. whether the long-run growth rate is $2\frac{1}{2}$, 3,

---

[44] Consumption functions of this kind figure in standard national income forecasting procedures, where they appear to provide by far the strongest formal link between real and monetary variables.

[45] Problems associated with the transition to a Common Currency Area are not discussed here. They are the subject of other papers delivered to this conference.

or 4 per cent) are, as a matter of scale, completely dwarfed by the magnitude of current margins of slack (these amount to 5 per cent of GDP on reasonable definitions of 'full employment'); and they are in any case unlikely to be amenable to solution by monetary policy.

On this definition of 'the problem', the puzzles are: what contribution can monetary policy make to solving it; and is this in the nature of a fine-tuning recipe or is it in the form of a long-run objective?

We may start with the assertion that the Bank of England does not at the present time see itself as having a primary responsibility for the price level; its pronouncements indicate that the ruling belief is that inflation (the current inflation anyway) is a 'cost' inflation, unamenable to treatment by contractionary monetary policies except to the extent that these deflate real demand, raise unemployment, and so infringe the employment objective. The implication is that monetary policy's influence on prices is no different in kind from that of fiscal policy; and that the 'assignment' of price-level control belongs to incomes policy.[46] While my own view broadly coincides with this, it leaves open the question of the appropriate mix of fiscal and monetary policy; and, moreover, in view of the probable infeasibility of incomes policies, may invite a change of negativism.

The customary view of excess demand inflation suggests that because of the prevalence of mark-up practices in pricing policy, excess demand is reflected primarily in the labour market, and thence in prices. Assuming that unemployment is some measure of excess demand pressure, it is hard to see that those who assert that inflation would have been less had money supply, throughout the post-war period, grown more slowly (and had interest rates been higher) are saying more than that we could have less inflation with higher unemployment. Nor does this distinguish between inflation induced by fiscal or by monetary means. But there is clearly meant to be something more in assertions about the relationship between the money supply and prices, some dynamics which bridge the comparative statics gap. It is unclear what these are.

This leads me to make the suggestion that in the coming phase of

[46] This seems compatible with saying that cost inflation exists by virtue of its validation through accommodating monetary and fiscal policies; but this validation is necessitated by reason of the existence of an unemployment objective.

expansion there is an experiment which policy could make. This would be to combine expansionary fiscal policy with a relatively tight monetary policy. There are at least two separate reasons why such a policy mix might be recommended at the present time (early 1972). The first of these resides in the argument that monetary policy is characterized by longer lags in effectiveness than is fiscal policy. From this point of view, a posture of relative monetary restraint provides insurance against the risk of subsequent 'over-shooting'. The second reason is more speculative; but if there is anything in the view that monetary policy is more potent for price inflation than fiscal policy, then again circumstances point to the propriety of a policy mix in which monetary policy is relatively more restrained than fiscal policy.

It is of course true that there are some possible costs involved in such a policy emphasis, one of which is that fine-tuning of interest rates could not be undertaken: in particular, the current phase of policy which is (presumably) an attempt to encourage the bringing-forward of investment plans, would not be possible. It is very questionable, though, that this policy is having any present effect and whether, in any case, fiscal policy does not have—in the U.K.—a decisive comparative advantage in 'fine-tuning'. The suggested policy emphasis also assumes sufficient autonomy of monetary policy both from overseas influences and from fiscal policy to make it feasible.

REFERENCES

[1] ARTIS, M. J., and NOBAY, A. R. 'Two Aspects of the Monetary Debate', *National Institute Economic Review*, No. 49, Aug. 1969, pp. 33–51.

[2] BALOGH, T. Memorandum of Evidence to the Committee on the Working of the Monetary System, 1959.

[3] BANK OF ENGLAND. 'Competition and Credit Control', *Bank of England Quarterly Bulletin*, vol. 11, No. 2, 1971, pp. 189–93.

[4] —— Speech by the Governor at Munich; reprinted in *Bank of England Quarterly Bulletin*, vol. 11, No. 2, 1971.

[5] —— 'Competition and Credit Control': extract from a lecture by the Chief Cashier, reprinted in *Bank of England Quarterly Bulletin*, vol. 11, No. 4, 1971, pp. 477–81.

[6] BRUNNER, Karl, and MELTZER, Allan H. 'The Meaning of Monetary Indicators', in George Howick (ed.), *Monetary Process and Policy* (Homewood, Ill.: Irwin, 1967), pp. 187–217.

[7] CRAMP, A. B. 'Monetary Policy, Strong or Weak?', in N. Kaldor (ed.), *Conflicts in Policy Objectives* (Oxford: Basil Blackwell, 1971).

[8] CROCKETT, A. D. 'Timing Relationships between Movements of Monetary and National Income Variables', *Bank of England Quarterly Bulletin*, vol. 10, No. 4, 1970, pages 459–68.

[9] CROUCH, R. L. 'Tobin vs Keynes on Liquidity Preference', *Rev. Econ. Stats.*, Nov. 1971, pp. 368–71.

[10] DEWALD, William G. 'Indicators of Monetary Policy', *Economic Papers*, The Economic Society of Australia and New Zealand, New South Wales and Victorian Branches, No. 25, Aug. 1967, pp. 16–43.

[11] FRIEDMAN, M., and SCHWARTZ, A. J. 'Money and Business Cycles', *Rev. Econ. Stats.*, vol. 45, No. 1, part 2, Suppt., Feb. 1963.

[12] GIBSON, W. E. 'Interest Rates and Monetary Policy', *J.P.E.*, vol. 78, No. 3, May–June 1970, pp. 431–55.

[13] GOODHART, C. A. E., and CROCKETT, A. D. *et al.* 'The Importance of Money', *Bank of England Quarterly Bulletin*, vol. 10, No. 2, 1970, pp. 159–98.

[14] HAMBURGER, Michael J. 'The Lag in the Effect of Monetary Policy: A Survey of Recent Literature', F.R.B. New York, *Monthly Review*, Dec. 1971, pp. 289–98.

[15] HANSEN, A. *Fiscal Policy in Seven Countries, 1955–1969* (O.E.C.D., 1969).

[16] HARRINGTON, Richard. 'The Monetarist Controversy', *Manchester School*, Dec. 1971, pp. 269–92.

[17] HENDERSHOTT, P. *The Neutralised Money Stock* (Homewood, Ill.: Irwin, 1968).

[18] LAIDLER, D. E. W. 'The Influence of Money on Economic Activity—A Survey of Some Current Problems' in G. Clayton, J. C. Gilbert, R. Sedgwick (eds.), *Monetary Theory and Monetary Policy in the 1970s* (O.U.P., 1971), pp. 73–135.

[19] —— and PARKIN, J. M. 'The Demand for Money in the United Kingdom 1955–1967: Preliminary Estimates', *Manchester School*, Sept. 1970, pp. 187–208.

[20] MEADE, J. E. *The Theory of International Economic Policy* (London: O.U.P., vol. I, 1951; vol. II, 1955).

[21] MEISELMAN, David, in *Controlling money aggregates* (F.R.B. of Boston, 1969), pp. 145–51.

[22] NORTON, W. E. 'Debt Management and Monetary Policy in the United Kingdom', *Economic Journal*, vol. 79, No. 315, Sept. 1969, pp. 474–94.

[23] POOLE, W. 'Optimal Choice of Monetary Policy Instruments in a Simple Stochastic Macro Model', *Q.J.E.*, vol. 84, May 1970, pp. 197–216.

[24] SMITH, W. L. 'A Neo-Keynesian View of Monetary Policy', in *Controlling Monetary Aggregates* (F.R.B. of Boston, 1969), pp. 105–26.

[25] TOBIN, J. 'The Role of Money in National Economic Policy', and subsequent discussion, in *Controlling Monetary Aggregates* (F.R.B. of Boston, 1969), pp. 21–4; 78–82.

[26] TUCKER, D. 'Dynamic Income Adjustment to Money Supply Changes', *American Economic Review*, June 1966, pp. 433–49.

THE IMPORTANCE OF COMPETITION FOR CREDIT CONTROL*

RICHARD L. HARRINGTON
(*University of Manchester*)

1971 was a busy year for students of money. Internationally we had a long period of floating exchange rates followed by the devaluing of the dollar in terms of gold and the revaluing of many other currencies in terms of the dollar. Domestically, there was a sea change in monetary policy as run by the Bank of England and also a very forceful recommendation from a Royal Commission that the Treasury give up its main direct weapon of credit control: the ability to vary the permissible terms of hire-purchase contracts. This essay will look at the changes in British monetary policy, usually referred to under the heading Competition and Credit Control.

I shall not be concerned with the details of the new scheme but rather with explaining why the changes were necessary. The words competition and credit control are well chosen to describe the new measures for the two things are very closely linked, as I shall try to show. To do this, I must first look at some recent theoretical developments concerned with the issue of whether banks are or are not in any economically meaningful sense different from all other financial intermediaries. Recent work has stressed one notable difference between banks and other intermediaries, the importance of which has often been overlooked. When I have discussed this question I

* This paper, which is a revised version of the paper originally presented at the Bournemouth Conference, represents work in connection with an on-going study of British monetary policy being carried out as part of the Manchester University Inflation project, the whole of which project has been generously financed by a grant from the S.S.R.C.

The author would like to thank John Hacche, David Laidler, Victor Morgan, Michael Parkin, and Michael Sumner, and other members of the Manchester University Inflation Workshop for their comments on an earlier draft of this paper.

shall turn to its relevance for credit control and show why it is essential that the banking system should be competitive.

Commercial banks and financial intermediaries: the traditional and the new view

Traditional theory has always distinguished sharply between commercial banks and other financial intermediaries: banks can create credit, whereas the other financial intermediaries can only pass it on. This derives from the fact that bank deposits are money and therefore banks alone among financial intermediaries do not have to obtain money before making a loan—they can create it.

The position of the banks is usually described in the following way: a bank makes a loan by a book entry, simultaneously crediting the account of the borrower with the amount loaned (an addition to bank liabilities) and adding to bank assets the borrower's promise to repay. Loans and deposits rise by the same amount, and hence the maxim that every loan creates a deposit. Of course the borrower could demand to take his money in cash (bank-notes and/or coin) as could anyone subsequently receiving the money from him, but in practice cash is an inferior means of payment for all but small transactions and the amount of any newly created deposits that is encashed will be both small and predictable. Thus, given adequate reserves, banks will always be able to expand deposits, irrespective of any considerations of demand for these.

This is all very different from the traditional view of non-bank financial intermediaries (N.B.F.I.). Their liabilities are not means of payment and thus, it is argued, they cannot make loans by creating deposits; the position is rather that each intermediary must attract a deposit before it can make a loan. For example, a building society receives a deposit; a small part of this is put into reserves, the rest is lent, and there the matter ends. The loan is not made by creating a building society deposit, it is paid in money, and this is money lost to the building society, which must now await the next deposit before making any further loans.

This view for long accepted uncritically, received a strong challenge in the 1950s from the work of Gurley and Shaw ([2, 3, 4]), who, strongly supported by James Tobin [8] put forward a new view on commercial banks in which these latter were seen as being, in all important respects, similar to all other financial intermediaries. I shall summarize briefly the view of these writers.

All financial intermediaries sell deposits to (borrow from) some people in order to buy assets from (lend to) other people; that is to say, all financial intermediaries stand between ultimate lender and ultimate borrower. (This is, of course, the meaning of the word intermediate.) Financial intermediation is a form of specialization, the intermediary minimizing the cost of bringing together borrowers and lenders. In addition, financial intermediaries will usually be able to offer certain other services. For instance, an intermediary as a professional lender of money may be expected to be a better judge of risk than most individual lenders. Large intermediaries can take advantage of their size and of the law of averages and make their liabilities more liquid than their assets. Thus, banks borrow mostly at short or zero notice and lend for periods of several months or several years—building societies borrow at notice of a few months or zero notice and lend for periods of up to thirty years. Through the services of financial intermediaries, lenders gain convenience, liquidity, and a lower risk of loss. Borrowers gain convenience and a lower rate of interest than they would have to pay if dealing direct with individual lenders.

As well as providing these services which are directly related to the business of financial intermediation, intermediaries can, and do, provide other services incidental to the main business of transmitting funds from lender to borrower. Banks provide a money transfer service for their depositors, building societies give their depositors a prior claim on mortgage lending, life assurance companies combine an insurance service with financial intermediation. There is product differentiation, and this is not surprising, for all intermediaries have an incentive to try to attract deposits, all intermediaries can only lend to the extent to which people are prepared to make deposits[1] with them. Banks, according to this view, are no different, they cannot compel people to hold deposits with them, their growth like that of all other financial intermediaries depends upon the growth of demand for the assets that they sell. The conventional theory, it is argued, is deficient in that it ignores the demand for bank deposits. Banks were the earliest of the financial intermediaries to become established and this has led people into thinking that they are in some way different from the other intermediaries, whereas this is not so. In all important respects, in the matter of

---

[1] We shall refer to the liabilities of all financial intermediaries as deposits. It would be tiresome to have to point out continually that insurance companies sell policies, unit trusts sell units, etc.

making loans and of taking deposits banks are just one type of intermediary among others.

Tobin has summed up well this view with his statement that for all intermediaries, banks included, borrowing and lending *in a free market* will be pushed to the point where the marginal revenue gained by making one more loan is just equal to the cost of attracting one more deposit. The idea that banks can always expand loans, and hence deposits, subject only to the constraint of adequate reserves is thus contradicted.

Passing over many contributions to the subsequent debate on the new view, I would like now to consider two recent papers, both asserting the uniqueness of commercial banks. Gutentag and Lindsay [5] have argued that whilst N.B.F.I. may be able to bring about a multiple creation of credit in a fashion qualitatively similar to that of the banks, any such creation would be quantitatively much smaller than that of the banks. This result rests even if the total of commercial bank deposits is much less than the total of other financial intermediary liabilities. Expansion of bank credit, on plausible assumptions leads to an increase of financial intermediary credit—the reverse does not apply. Bank credit is high-powered credit.

The reason for this quantitative difference in the abilities of banks and other financial intermediaries to generate credit stems from the liabilities of commercial banks being a means of payment, or, to be more precise, it is due to the fact that the N.B.F.I. hold their reserves in the form of bank deposits. This results in the banks and the N.B.F.I. operating, so to speak, on different levels and has many important consequences.

It should be pointed out that the assumption made by Gutentag and Lindsay that N.B.F.I. reserves are composed solely of commercial bank deposits is not true for the United Kingdom. I shall consider the actual position later, for the moment let us remain with the thesis as put forward by Gutentag and Lindsay.

If the N.B.F.I. hold their reserves in the form of bank deposits it follows that the banks, when they expand both credit and their own deposits, cannot suffer any leakage of reserves to the N.B.F.I. If a bank makes a loan, which when used and put into circulation ends up by being deposited with an N.B.F.I., the N.B.F.I. will not ask the bank to pay to it the sum in cash—rather the N.B.F.I. will be quite content to receive payment in the form of an increase in its bank balance. Thus the banks if they have spare reserves can expand credit and their own deposits without fearing a drain on their reserves to any other financial institution,[2] the only important loss of reserves coming from the public's demand for cash.

On the other hand, if the N.B.F.I. extend credit they will lose reserves to the banks. When a financial intermediary makes a loan, that part of the loan which ends up in a bank deposit, either of the borrower or of someone who has obtained the money somewhere in the chain of transactions initiated by the borrower, is lost to the financial intermediary. It has drawn down its own bank account, which is to say it has reduced its reserves. Some of the money may be redeposited with the N.B.F.I., with the result that reserves are not reduced by the full amount of the loan. But the difference between banks and other financial intermediaries is still there: when a bank makes a loan the banks collectively will not lose reserves if the money so lent is redeposited with *either* a bank or an N.B.F.I; when a financial intermediary makes a loan the N.B.F.I. collectively will not permanently lose reserves if the money so lent is deposited with the same or another financial intermediary, but they will lose reserves if the money so lent is deposited with a bank.

This is not all. If, when a bank makes a loan, some of the proceeds are deposited with the N.B.F.I. this increases their reserves and they will be able to grant new loans. An increase in bank credit will beget N.B.F.I. credit. The converse does not hold: an increase in N.B.F.I. lending cannot beget an increase in bank lending. If an N.B.F.I. makes a loan and the borrower places the sum in a bank account there is a change of ownership of bank deposits—the banks debit the account of the N.B.F.I. and credit that of the borrower: there is no increase in bank deposits and no increase in bank reserves and thus no reason for the banks to expand new credit.

We have then this important difference between banks and N.B.F.I.: an expansion of credit (and deposits) by the banks cannot be curtailed through reserves being lost to the N.B.F.I., but will rather be reinforced by an expansion of credit (and deposits) by the N.B.F.I.; an expansion of credit and deposits by the N.B.F.I. will be limited through reserves being lost to the banks and will in no way be reinforced by an expansion of bank credit and deposits. This difference stems entirely from the fact that the intermediaries keep their reserves in the form of bank deposits—if they held reserves composed of the same assets as bank reserves then it would

[2] We are talking about the banks collectively. Obviously one bank can lose reserves to another.

cease to hold. Gutentag and Lindsay state that the N.B.F.I. hold their reserves in the form of bank deposits because these deposits serve as a convenient means of payment, and they therefore conclude that the difference between banks and N.B.F.I. does stem from the liabilities of the former being money. This conclusion can be questioned, and I shall return to it at the end of this essay.

The second paper I should like to look at is one by John Wood [11] in which he shows in a scholarly fashion that this issue is not a new one. The argument in the second half of the twentieth century as to whether the banks are different from the N.B.F.I. has a close parallel in the argument which took place in the second half of the nineteenth century as to whether the banking department of the Bank of England was different from the other commercial banks. Many people, including at least one director of the Bank of England, argued that it was not; Walter Bagehot asserted the contrary and pointed to the fact that the commercial banks held their reserves in the form of deposits with the Bank of England, which meant that there was a tiering of credit of precisely the same kind as we have today.

Wood goes on to point out that recognition of the tiered structure of credit does not negate completely the new view of banking, as Gutentag and Lindsay seemed to believe. One can still argue that banks, *in the absence of controls*, will be faced with profit-maximizing calculations identical to those of the other financial intermediaries. Each type of institution will, as Tobin [8] says, expand its assets and liabilities up to the point where the revenue gained from the marginal asset is just equal to the cost incurred in obtaining the marginal liability. It is a contingent point that the banks have to maintain the attractiveness of their deposits relative to cash, whereas other intermediaries have to make their deposits attractive relative to both cash and bank deposits.

It is the case that banks and N.B.F.I. still have many similarities; both, for instance, can engage in a multiple creation of credit. However, they do this on different levels, and the result is that the direct multiplier of the banks is larger than that of the N.B.F.I., and in addition credit creation by banks begets credit creation by other intermediaries, whereas the converse does not hold. Thus, the banks have a far greater potential for influencing credit conditions (and the supply of financial assets) in the economy than have the N.B.F.I.

Thus far I have talked in somewhat abstract terms and have

followed Gutentag and Lindsay in using the mechanical concept of the credit multiplier to illustrate the importance of the tiering of deposits. I would now like to go on to see if this concept is still valid given that the N.B.F.I. in the United Kingdom do not hold significant reserves in the form of bank deposits, and then to look at its relevance for banking competition.

The tiering of deposits and banking competition

It is not the case that in the United Kingdom bank reserves are composed wholly, or even primarily, of cash and balances with the Central bank; nor is it the case that the reserves of the N.B.F.I. are held to any important extent in the form of deposits with the commercial banks. Is the notion of a tiered structure of deposits as set out above applicable to the U.K.? The answer to this question is yes: we can relax the assumptions of Gutentag and Lindsay about reserve holdings without destroying the approach, what is important is that (a) bank deposits, and here we are talking about commercial bank deposits, should be used by both the N.B.F.I. and the public as a means of payment, (b) such reserves as the N.B.F.I. keep should not be in the same form as the reserves of the commercial banks. By and large these conditions were satisfied prior to the measures of 1971; condition (b) is no longer satisfied as far as some N.B.F.I. are concerned, and it is in this change that lies much of the interest of the recent reform.

I will take some examples of the consequences of attempts by the public to switch from bank deposits to N.B.F.I. deposits, taking conditions as they were prior to the 1971 changes. Let us take the case first of all of a person who wishes to swap his bank deposits for deposits with a building society. The person draws a cheque in favour of a building society, the initial effect of this is that the building society finds that both its deposits and its bank balance have risen—for the banks as a whole all that has happened is that the ownership of some deposits have been transferred from the account of the drawer of the cheque to that of the building society. This is not the end of the matter: sooner or later the building society will wish to lend most of the money newly acquired. But when the building society does this, it will again be by transfer of bank deposits— this time from the account of the building society to that of the borrower. The banks collectively will not lose deposits. Approximately 15 per cent of all new money accruing to building societies is put into reserves, the bulk of which are held in the form of government and local authority securities. A substantial part of the holding of government bonds are in assets with over five years to maturity; it is clear that there is very little overlap between the reserves of building societies and those of commercial banks. Building societies will purchase government bonds from members of the non-bank public, which purchases will again result in a transfer of bank deposits. The demand by building societies for government bonds may be expected to reduce the yield on such bonds—whether this will be significant for the commercial banks will be considered shortly.

Things will be similar if we consider other financial intermediaries. If a company decided to withdraw its bank deposits and place these on deposit with a finance house, the initial effect on the commercial banks would again be limited to a transfer of ownership of deposits. The finance houses used to keep very small reserves, almost all of their funds being on-lent in one form or another to the private sector. The banks could not lose reserves to the finance houses.

A switch by a company of its deposits from a commercial bank to a member of the secondary banking system would again have had an initial effect on the commercial banks limited to a transfer of ownership of deposits. The members of the secondary banking system for the most part also kept low reserves, most of their deposits being on-lent to other banks, to the local authorities, or to borrowers in the private sector. Of the reserves kept, some were in the form of short-term money market assets and so it was in principle possible that a rapid growth of the secondary banking system could have drawn reserve assets away from the primary banking system, but the amounts in question would have been very small.

Finally, we should look at the question of a switch of deposits from a commercial bank to a public-sector financial intermediary such as a trustee savings bank. These banks invest their funds in either government or local authority securities. If the investment was by purchase of an existing asset, then again the commercial banks could not lose deposits, they would just be transferred from the original depositor to the trustee savings bank and then to the seller of the asset—if the investment was by purchase of a new asset then it would transfer deposits either to a local authority or to the government. In the first case, this would again be a transfer of deposits within the banking system; in the second case, it would seem that the deposits would be transferred from the commercial banks to the account of the government at the Bank of England. However, it is the practice of the government never to build up its bank balances—all inflows of money are promptly disbursed. So once again we see that the commercial banks will not lose reserves or deposits if a person switches *his* deposits to an N.B.F.I.

This taxonomy is becoming tiresome—I will sum up. It has been the case that the commercial banks could not lose any appreciable quantity of reserves to the N.B.F.I. These latter kept their working balances in the form of bank deposits and they did not hold any important quantities of the short-term money market assets used as reserves by the banks. Purchases by the N.B.F.I. of government bonds would tend to lower yields on these bonds and it might be thought that such rate-of-interest changes would have affected the level of commercial bank deposits. Had we been dealing with unfettered banks which were equating the marginal cost of liabilities to the marginal revenue of assets then, indeed, a reduction in the yield on bonds would have forced the banks to sell bonds, thereby contracting their deposits. But this was not the position of the banks in the post-war period: for most of the time the government bond portfolios of the commercial banks has been a residual, being determined on the one hand by officially imposed reserve requirements and on the other by the possibilities of making advances given either the current official restrictions or the state of demand given the banks' predetermined rates of interest. Bond rates of interest have shown a tendency to rise during the period; the effect of a secular increase in N.B.F.I. demand for bonds would have been to moderate this rise. It would be very hard to imagine that in the circumstances prevailing this would have been sufficient to force the commercial banks to sell bonds and thereby reduce their total deposits.

The commercial banks could not lose deposits due to the activities of the N.B.F.I., and for the time being we shall use this term to include members of the secondary banking system, nor could they gain deposits by competing with the N.B.F.I. Thus the primary banking system as a whole appears to have stood to gain little by being competitive. This appears to have been the view taken by many bankers; they did not see how they could compete with the N.B.F.I., and in order to compete with the secondary banks they were obliged to establish subsidiary companies that were on the same deposit tier as both the N.B.F.I. and the secondary banks. It is arguable that in seeking to compete through subsidiary companies the banks were being very realistic, more so than their critics.

However, if the banks could not compete directly with the N.B.F.I., the consequences of their non-competition were nonetheless of great importance. Throughout the post-war period up until 1971, the banks were not competing on price: the rates of interest paid on deposits and charged on loans were agreed by the banks and were tied to Bank Rate. When the demand for loans rose to more than could be accommodated, the banks responded by rationing credit— either according to their own order of priorities or according to the priorities of the authorities.

By definition, rationing leaves a residue of unsatisfied demand. For much of the post-war period there would have been a number of people who would have wished to borrow from the banks at the rates being charged by the banks or at rates greater than these, but who were unable to do so. Such people provided a market for enter-prising financial intermediaries; which intermediaries, being able to charge rates of interest on loans above those being charged by the banks, were able to offer rates of interest on their liabilities in excess of those being offered by the banks. Thus there was an incentive to holders of bank deposits to switch out of bank deposits and into some other form of financial asset. As already seen, such switching would not cause any loss of deposits or reserves to the banks. There would be no decline in bank credit, but there would be an increase in N.B.F.I. credit. Switching deposits from banks to N.B.F.I., then, leads to an increase in credit and in consequence in aggregate demand.

This is not to say that every pound of credit granted affects im-mediately the level of demand for newly produced goods. Some credit may be used to buy existing assets, the most obvious example of which is credit granted by the building societies; but even if building society credit has its main effect in pushing up the price of housing, this must in time have wider effects on the economy, the demand for factors by the building industry being the most obvious example. In general we may say that the switching of deposits from banks to N.B.F.I. will always be inflationary. Conversely, the switch-ing of deposits from N.B.F.I. to banks will always be deflationary.

The non-bank financial intermediaries and the demand for money

We must be careful not to give the impression that the N.B.F.I. are inherently inflationary, that all growth in their deposits is only a consequence of the uncompetitive behaviour of the banks. This is not so. The N.B.F.I. can increase their deposits in three different ways, one of which has important effects on the level of aggregate demand, one of which has no such effect, and one of which has some, though probably small, effects on the level of aggregate demand.

The first way in which the N.B.F.I. can expand their deposits is the one discussed so far: they can induce holders of bank deposits to transfer their deposits to them. This is always inflationary, for there is a reduction in demand for nominal bank deposits while the nominal stock of bank deposits cannot fall, so the price level (and/or income) must rise to where the public and the N.B.F.I. (through their demand for working balances) are again willing to hold the original nominal stock of bank deposits.

The N.B.F.I. can also grow by making their deposits attractive to savers, the demand of whom for deposits does not represent a desire to switch from some other asset, but represents a demand for additional assets. In a growing economy there will always be this demand for additional financial assets; by meeting this demand the N.B.F.I. can expand their lending, but since what is lent is matched by new saving, such lending does not increase aggregate demand. Thirdly, the N.B.F.I. can also grow if they can persuade the holders of existing assets, such as bonds or shares, to exchange these for N.B.F.I. deposits. No new credit is granted; all that has happened is that the lender of money, instead of holding the liability of the ultimate borrower, now holds the liability of a N.B.F.I. which in turn holds the liability of the ultimate borrower. Transactions such as these, which alter the composition of existing portfolios, may be expected to have repercussions on the demand for money and hence on aggregate demand. I shall assume, however, that this effect is minor.

The only way, then, in which the N.B.F.I. can have an important inflationary impact on the economy is by their bringing about a reduction in the demand for bank deposits (or, for that matter for notes and coins). Since the nominal stock of bank deposits could not be reduced, a reduction in demand could only be given effect to by a reduction in the real value of a given nominal stock brought about by a rise in the price level.

The switching of deposits between banks and N.B.F.I. is, in principle, a stock adjustment effect; an improvement in the yield on N.B.F.I. liabilities should lead to a once-and-for-all shift of deposits leading to a once-and-for-all increase in prices. In practice, however, any such adjustment process is likely to be spread over a long period of time, with the result that instead of a once-and-for-all price movement there is a long period of inflation. One would expect there to be long lags in people becoming aware of the advantages of alternative assets to bank deposits, and especially would this be so before people had become accustomed to inflation and to discriminating between real and nominal yields. Further, the convenience yield on N.B.F.I. deposits would not be constant: as the N.B.F.I. grow, they may increase the number of their offices and the range of their services and in this way increase the attractiveness of their liabilities.

Considerations such as these may go some way to explaining why most of the statistical studies have been unable to find any evidence of a strong correlation between the demand for money and the yield on near-money assets. Certainly most such studies have come to the counter-intuitive conclusion that the demand for money is only influenced marginally by the returns available on the liabilities of N.B.F.I. Edgar Feige [1], in Part IV, pp. 260–89, above, discusses and adds to the various investigations with American data of the elasticity of demand for demand deposits with respect to the rate of interest on time deposits, savings and loan deposits, and mutual savings bank deposits. He concludes that, at most, the evidence is of weak substitutability.

These results should make us cautious, but they do not contradict directly the arguments here being advanced. I have argued that the growth of the N.B.F.I. in the post-war period in the United Kingdom has in part been the cause of a decline in the demand for money (appropriately defined), but have also argued that this would have been a slow continuing process. Regression analyses using annual data might very well not pick up such a secular trend.

The position we have now reached is as follows: owing to the tiered structure of deposits in the U.K., the commercial banks have been unable either to gain or to lose deposits to the N.B.F.I. At the same time, a reduction in demand for bank deposits would have been inflationary. We have a paradox, or seemingly so: banking competition is necessary for credit control, but the banks themselves do not appear to gain anything from competition. If the banks were to raise their rates of interest and in consequence some persons transferred deposits from the N.B.F.I. to the banks, this would not, as we have seen, raise the total of bank deposits, it would merely change the ownership of the deposits transferred.

Failure to compete on the part of the banks will not result in a reduction in the nominal value of bank deposits, but it will result in a reduction in the real value of these, and in the real value of all the financial assets held by the banks and in consequence of bank profits. The long-run health of the banking industry does, then, depend on its maintaining public demand for its deposits in the face of N.B.F.I. competition. The trouble is that very likely this will not be apparent. The banks will not see the N.B.F.I. as their competitors, and when inflation occurs and the real value of bank deposits falls, this will be regarded as something which is unfortunate but quite fortuitous as far as the banks are concerned.

There is more to this question of competition between the banks and the N.B.F.I. In a growing economy there will be a growth over time in the demand for financial assets. The N.B.F.I. will be able to cater to this demand and provide new deposits if they can get hold of extra bank deposits to serve as reserves. The banks will be able to cater to this demand and provide new deposits if they can get hold of extra liquid assets, but this depends upon the willingness of the authorities to supply these. Upon what will this depend? If the authorities are following a rule *à la* Friedman and increasing the stock of reserves by x per cent per annum, then the banks know in advance how much they will grow by and this is independent of whether they compete with the N.B.F.I. or not. If, however, the authorities are following a discretionary policy and are making available extra reserves depending on whether they feel a faster or slower rate of growth of the money stock is warranted, then how well the banks compete with the N.B.F.I. does matter. At one extreme, if the banks were very uncompetitive it could be that there was such an increase of N.B.F.I. deposits and credit that demand was high and prices were rising and the authorities would decide not to allow any growth in bank deposits. They might even introduce restrictive measures aimed at reducing bank deposits. At the other extreme, it could be that the banks competed so effectively with the N.B.F.I. that the latter lost deposits and there was a reduction in the total amount of credit granted in the economy. To prevent deflation, the authorities would be obliged to permit a large increase in bank deposits.

If the banks do not compete effectively with the N.B.F.I., then they will see the real value of their existing assets and liabilities reduced. Further, if the authorities are liable to vary the permitted growth of the money supply according to the current state of demand in the economy, then failure to compete on the part of the banks will affect the future growth of nominal assets and liabilities. It is still probable that this will not be clear to all concerned. Bankers will be more impressed by the realization that they cannot compete with the N.B.F.I. for nominal deposits directly and in the short term, than by any imprecise idea that by the taking up of a competitive stance today (which would not be without cost) they will, in some way, be affecting the value of their deposits tomorrow, both the real value and maybe the nominal value, depending on the good-will of the authorities. But the resolution of this problem is plain: the banks should compete amongst themselves, for in so doing they come naturally to be competitive with other financial intermediaries. It is only when there is an oligopolistic banking industry and/or one forced by government pressures to be uncompetitive that a problem arises.

In the end we find that it is necessary to the banks themselves to be competitive with the N.B.F.I. It is necessary, too, for credit control that they should be so. The absence of competition by the banks in the U.K. did not occur by chance, however; it was part and parcel of monetary policy as operated, and it is to this that I should now like to turn.

Monetary policy in the post-war era

Throughout the period, monetary policy focused primarily on rates of interest, leaving commercial bank deposits to be determined by market demand or, when the occasion demanded (and it often did), to be controlled by non-market methods such as the putting of a quantitative limit on bank advances. I have argued elsewhere [6] that, given this preoccupation of the authorities with interest rates, post-war monetary experience can usefully be interpreted in terms of the Wicksellian theory of natural and market rates of interest.[3]

Wicksell's natural rate of interest is the rate which would equate saving and investment at full employment; it is the rate which would prevail in an economy with complete and instantaneous price flexibility. If the banks, acting collectively, should peg the market rate of interest below the natural rate this would be inflationary: the desire to invest would exceed the desire to save; the supply of

[3] See Wicksell [9, 10].

bonds would exceed the demand for bonds; to prevent the rate of interest rising, the banks would have to buy up the excess.[4] By so doing they would convert potential excess demand into effective excess demand; the money supply would expand; there would be inflation. The real rate of interest would fall below the nominal rate and if the banks continued to hold the same nominal rate of interest then the rate of inflation would increase.

With this framework in mind let us consider post-war monetary policy in the U.K. The authorities sought to influence rates of interest and this influence took place at two levels. In the bond market the authorities were very active in buying and selling and at the level of bank deposits and advances, rates of interest were tied to the officially determined bank rate. In the bond market, policy was to prevent the rate of interest from rising too far and too fast and in order to do this it was often necessary for the authorities to buy quantities of bonds. This led to increased borrowing from the banks, which borrowing increased bank reserves and, in the absence of special requests or injunctions regarding bank advances, led to an increase in bank deposits. The Wicksellian theory is an appropriate description of what was going on, only it was the authorities who were seeking to hold down the rate of interest rather than the banks themselves.

It may be objected that the rate of interest has had an upward trend over the period with which we are concerned. This is true but it is unsurprising: in the early post-war years, real rates of interest were negative and it was to be expected that as people became accustomed to inflation the nominal rate of interest should rise. Real rates of interest have remained low throughout the post-war period.

If the authorities are not prepared to allow the bond rate of interest to be market-determined then they will inevitably find themselves buying bonds, and this will lead to an increasing money supply. There is no natural check to such a policy; it can continue indefinitely.

The U.K. authorities, however, frequently sought to offset the effects of their operations in the bond market by imposing non-market controls on the banks. Repeatedly the commercial banks were enjoined to limit their advances to the private sector; at times such requests were supplemented by the calling of special deposits.

[4] The word 'bond' is being used widely: all bank assets are bonds, advances are non-marketable bonds, bills are short-term bonds.

In short, the authorities created a situation in which the demand for funds exceeded the supply and then sought to escape from the inflationary consequences of this by imposing credit rationing on the banks. Nor was it always necessary for the authorities to impose rationing; the commercial banks tied their interest rates to Bank Rate; they did not compete on price and when faced with a high demand for loans did not consider raising their rates of interest. Credit rationing was virtually a permanent feature of banking in the U.K. during the post-war era.

It is in such a situation that the activities of the N.B.F.I. became very important. The many restraints on the commercial banks left great scope for the growth of other intermediaries; building societies, finance houses, life assurance companies, and the members of the secondary banking system all achieved rates of growth in their liabilities greatly in excess of the commercial banks. An unnamed commentator writing in a recent edition of the *Midland Bank Review* [7] was remarkably candid as to the reasons for the growth of the secondary banks when he wrote:

. . . when credit restrictions hampered other financial activities including those of the primary market, the new markets gained ground. *Above all, the maintenance in the primary market generally and by the clearing banks of long-established arrangements on interest rates, following a rigid pattern, left wide open opportunities* which the new markets with their uninhibited flexibility were not slow to fill [our italics].

Inflation has continued to be a problem, and it is hard not to think that the growth of the N.B.F.I. and the secondary banks has facilitated this.

The banks until recently did not see how they could compete with the N.B.F.I. and were in any case unsure as to whether they would be permitted so to do by the authorities. They sought to escape from the problem by acquiring or setting up subsidiary companies. In the late 1950s the larger clearing banks acquired finance-house subsidiaries and in the second half of the 1960s they established subsidiary banks to compete with the secondary banks. It should be clear that, whilst competition through subsidiaries might or might not safeguard the profits of the commercial banks, it would do nothing to solve the problem posed for credit control by the existence of a tiered structure of deposits and of credit.

At intervals during the post-war period, and usually when the balance of payments situation was difficult, the authorities introduced deflationary measures and the monetary side of these normally fell most heavily on the commercial banks, although the range of institutions receiving official requests or injunctions widened over the period. Putting it at its simplest, the commercial banks, and along with them British monetary policy, have been in a vicious circle: the banks were uncompetitive, other financial institutions were enabled to grow rapidly, their growth was partly through the switching of deposits, this was inflationary, the authorities reacted to inflation by controlling more tightly the banks, and this reduced still further their competitive ability.

What was required to break out of this vicious circle was that the banks should become price competitors. For this to be possible the authorities had to forswear certain forms of discriminatory control such as quantitative limits on bank advances. It was not necessary but was perhaps advisable that the tiering arrangement should be altered and that the secondary banks should be enjoined to hold reserves in the same form as the commercial banks and not in the form of deposits with the commercial banks. One could envisage competition between just the London clearing banks, but it is more likely that competition will be whole-hearted and that the rates of interest paid and charged by the clearing banks will be market-determined if these latter feel themselves not only to be in competition with each other but also with upwards of two hundred foreign banks, commonwealth banks, merchant banks, etc. Since the new arrangements now in force require the secondary banks to hold reserves composed of the same assets as the reserves of the commercial banks, competition between the two is now both immediate and evident. Commercial banks can lose deposits and reserves to secondary banks. As far as credit control goes, one no longer need worry about the switching of deposits from commercial banks to secondary banks. If a merchant bank, say, expands by attracting deposits from a commercial bank, then there will no longer be a net increase in deposits and credit, for the deposits of and the credit granted by the commercial bank will fall by the same amount as the deposits of and credit granted by the merchant bank rise.

There is still the possibility of the N.B.F.I., now excluding both the secondary banks and the finance houses, attracting deposits away from the banks (all the banks) and thereby expanding their own deposits and their own granting of credit in an inflationary manner; but given that the banks are competing amongst themselves they will be led automatically to become competitive with the N.B.F.I. Whilst it will still be possible for an enterprising financial intermediary or group of intermediaries to grow by inducing people to switch out of bank deposits and into its own deposits there is no longer any reason to expect this *a priori*. Or, to be more precise, there is no reason to expect this if the authorities stick to their guns. We have seen that much of the cause of the ineffectiveness of post-war monetary policy stemmed from official attempts to control rates of interest for reasons connected with what was thought to be a necessary strategy in the gilt-edged market. This strategy has now been abandoned and it is important that it should stay abandoned. Propping up the gilt-edged market leads the authorities to lean on the banks to get them to distort their preferred asset portfolio composition. Banks which are lent-on are uncompetitive banks and competition is very necessary for credit control.

A concluding note on banks and non-banks

The tiering of deposits is an important feature of financial markets and we are indebted to Gutentag and Lindsay [5] for having made clear its importance and also to Wood [11] for having shown the prevalence in time of this phenomenon. Wood, as noted, went on to argue that Gutentag and Lindsay had in no way discredited the new view of banks as put forward by Gurley and Shaw and by Tobin. We can go even further and ask if the existence of a tiering of deposits even establishes the uniqueness of commercial banks, as both Gutentag and Lindsay and Wood believe. We have seen how the secondary banks in the U.K. were up until recently on a different deposit tier from the commercial banks, but in other respects they were becoming more and more similar to the commercial banks with some of them even dabbling in retail banking. If we find two institutions doing the same business, but the first holds its reserves with the central bank and the second holds its reserves on deposit with the first institution, must we then necessarily declare the one a bank and the other a non-bank? If so, then we would have had long ago to differentiate from all the other secondary banks those few merchant banks which for historical reasons hold their money reserves on deposit with the Bank of England. Then, in America there is a tiering of deposits within the banking sector with many small banks holding their reserves not with the Federal Reserve Banks but with the large commercial banks such as the New York banks. Are we to regard the large city banks as banks and the small, often rural, banks as non-banks? The answer must surely be no.

We began this note by saying that the tiering of deposits was an important feature of financial markets. We need to recognize its consequence, but it is not clear that it alone provides a means of classifying institutions into banks and non-banks regardless of all other similarities and differences.

REFERENCES

[1] FEIGE, E., 'Alternative Temporal Cross-Section Specifications of the Demand for Demand Deposits', Part IV, pp. 260–89, above.

[2] GURLEY, J. G., and SHAW, E. S., 'Financial Aspects of Economic Development', *American Economic Review*, 1955.

[3] —— —— 'Financial Intermediaries and the Saving-Investment Process', *Journal of Finance*, 1956.

[4] —— —— *Money in a Theory of Finance* (Washington, D.C., 1960).

[5] GUTENTAG, J. H., and LINDSAY, R., 'The Uniqueness of Commercial Banks', *Journal of Political Economy*, 1968.

[6] HARRINGTON, R. L., 'The Monetarist Controversy', *Manchester School*, 1970.

[7] MIDLAND BANK, 'The Growth of the Secondary Money Market', *Midland Bank Review*, 1966.

[8] TOBIN, J., 'Commercial Banks as Creators of "Money"', in Deane Cason (ed.), *Banking and Monetary Studies* (Homewood, 1963).

[9] WICKSELL, K., 'The Influence of the Rate of Interest on Prices', *Economic Journal*, 1907.

[10] —— *Interest and Prices*, trans. R. F. Kahn (London, 1936).

[11] WOOD, J. H., 'Two Notes on The Uniqueness of Commercial Banks', *Journal of Finance*, 1970.

EFFICIENCY, COMPETITION, AND CREDIT CONTROL

D. F. LOMAX*
(*National Westminster Bank*)

I. Introduction

IN this paper I should like to concentrate on the micro-economics of the new system of credit control instituted last September. The macro-economics of credit control are the subject of other papers, and have been the focus of most of the public debate. The micro-economics have been explored less, and it is in this area that the new system is likely to reveal substantial unfinished business.

There is, however, one other major feature of the credit control system which merits brief mention. It seems that it will be very difficult to maintain entirely the liberal principles of the new system during a period of tight money. The system offers such scope for manufacturing reserves through the operations of the discount market that it would appear that the Bank of England will be forced in effect to 'administer' the activities of the discount houses in a restrictive period. That would in itself be illiberal but is not necessarily any specific concern of the clearing banks. However, if administration of such a focal area of the market led to direct intervention elsewhere, as seems quite possible, then the implications for the banks and for the economy would be much more severe. To the extent that weaknesses are apparent in the system, they could further the idea that a restrictive period must imply illiberal policies, which I do not believe to be true. The problems stemming from the discount houses' situation are especially unsatisfactory, since it would seem feasible to fit them into the system in such a way as not to lead to these difficulties.

In order to show that they have not been forgotten, I should like to mention various specific features of the new regulations which were raised with the authorities by the clearing banks. These included

---

* The views expressed are personal. The original paper has been amended slightly in the light of the discussion at the Bournemouth Conference.

the exclusion from reserve assets of cash in tills and the refinanceable portion of export and shipbuilding finance. Furthermore, only the clearing banks have to keep 1½ per cent of their eligible liabilities in cash at the Bank of England. Since this last requirement is related to the clearing banks' function in the transmission of money, it would seem more appropriate if this cash holding were linked to the banks' current accounts, rather than to their eligible liabilities. A change of this nature would remove the handicap the clearing banks face in undertaking wholesale business in their own name, since the cost of the 1½ per cent cash ratio is likely to represent a significant proportion of the wholesale margin.

The remainder of this paper will be concerned with the nature of financial markets and the competitive forces at work. The markets in which the major domestic banks operate can be divided into four main categories:

(a) wholesale deposits and lending;
(b) retail deposits, savings, and lending;
(c) money transmission, retail and wholesale;
(d) other markets, such as hire purchase, international business, computer services, registrars, insurance services, investment management, and many others.

These will be considered in turn.

II. The wholesale markets

The wholesale banking markets are most competitive, and competitive forces have been increasing in recent years. These markets have been characterized by substantial new entrants and by innovations in techniques and financial instruments. Sixty-seven new foreign banks opened offices in London between 1966 and 1971. A common feature intensifying competition in all wholesale markets has been the increasing sophistication of the corporate or other large customer. Multi-banking, for example, is now common among large companies.

On the deposits side, we have seen two major innovations. There has been the introduction of sterling certificates of deposit, with the total outstanding at end December 1971 amounting to £2,372 million. The second innovation is the system of making deposits or placings with major companies, in the form of unsecured loans of 3 months or so. This development was reported a few years ago, and has now become well established. With the abolition of ceiling control, banks are able to place money in this way. This form of borrowing is open only to the largest corporations, but for them it can represent a cheap means of raising money. A further wholesale market which has continued to show rapid growth is the sterling inter-bank market, which now amounts to about £2,000 million. The clearing banks participate in all these markets through subsidiaries, and, since September 1971, some have done so in their own name.

It is significant that the relatively fast growth of the wholesale deposit markets has meant that, as a proportion of total non-bank resident deposits with banks, the share of deposits with accepting houses, overseas and other banks (the wholesale banks) increased, between end-1966 and September 1971, from 11·4 per cent to 20·4 per cent. The retail market, which the clearing banks are obviously well placed because of their extensive branch networks, is a declining share of bank deposits. By June 1971, American banks, foreign banks and affiliates, and other overseas banks had non-bank resident deposits of £992·2 million, equivalent to 6·4 per cent of that market, indicating significant competitive pressure on the domestic banks from a policy of relatively easy entry to London in its broader interests as a financial centre.

As far as the lending side is concerned, a similar degree of innovation and greater competition has been shown. Three forms of borrowing which have developed strongly include term-lending, financing U.K. companies in non-sterling currencies, and the company placings mentioned above. Under the new regime for competition and credit control the discount houses are now better placed, because of their enhanced resources, to lend to corporations. As on the deposits side, the share of the lending from wholesale banks in total bank lending has increased significantly. In the case of lending to corporations it is now over a third—37·9 per cent in September 1971.

In considering banking competition one must also not forget more mundane physical matters, economic geography, including the small size of this country and the development of a better telephone system, good motorways and an inter-city train service. One American bank aims to service well over 1,000 companies in this country from one office. That is a large proportion of corporate business. In this situation having a retail network offers less and less advantage.

The key element in 'Competition and Credit Control' in unleashing competition in lending appears to have been the abolition of ceilings. Given that abolition it is indeed a moot point whether the traditional relationship between clearing-bank lending rates and Bank Rate could have been maintained as far as corporate lending is concerned, had Bank Rate followed the same course from September 1971 to February 1972, even had the 'cartel' been formally maintained. Experience over this period has shown the importance of market forces, rather than institutional arrangements, in furthering the cause of liberal economic policies.

Thus, in the wholesale sector competitive forces are becoming greater, while at the same time the wholesale sector is expanding relative to the retail.

III. The retail markets

On the retail side, the main competition for the clearing banks is not other private-sector banks, but other types of financial institutions, including hire-purchase companies (many of which are now becoming banks), Building Societies, the National Savings Bank (N.S.B.), the Trustee Savings Banks (T.S.B.s), and the National Giro, plus a number of smaller institutions offering various services. It is in this market that the clearing banks face heavy competition from institutions which possess various legal and other privileges. In the market for personal-sector deposits, the major developments over the past few years have been a significant increase in the share held by the Building Societies, a decline in the share of National Savings, and rough constancy in the banks' share. In the most recent period, there has been a spurt by the Building Societies and a recovery in National Savings.

The main ways in which the conditions of operation of the Building Societies and Trustee Savings Banks differ from those of any other private-sector institution operating in the same fields are well known, and may be summarized briefly as follows. Neither type of institution has an obligation to earn any particular return on the capital employed. Building Societies pay interest net of an average tax rate. No tax is payable on the first £21 interest on the ordinary accounts with the T.S.B.s. The legal status of T.S.B.s also enables them to offer a higher rate of interest on their special investment accounts than a private-sector savings bank investing in the same fixed-interest assets probably could. A private-sector bank would need to keep a larger liquid reserve to guard against withdrawals of funds, particularly at a time when the market value of its assets might have fallen. The T.S.B.s are, however, to some extent better placed because there are provisions in the relevant Act guaranteeing any deficiency.

These various features obviously enhance the terms which the Building Societies and savings banks can offer their depositors; and, particularly at a time of increasing financial sophistication and discrimination on the part of the consumer, can be expected to boost market shares in their direction. These privileges are given for various social objectives. However, in liberal theory, a subsidy should presumably be related to a *function*, and in equity should be given equally to all institutions performing the same function, whether mortgages or the provision of savings services.

It seems likely that over the next few years considerable attention will need to be paid to the relationship between subsidy and function, the degree of subsidy, the allocation of resources serving the personal deposit market, and the allocation of savings to their end uses, i.e. house-building, business credit, or other private credit. I should like to illustrate the difficulties in this area by considering the problems which arise in assessing the savings market, where the functions performed by the savings banks and the clearing banks overlap greatly.

Savings

The functions which are performed by public savings media, and which justify their special status, appear to be as follows:

(i) a social objective is performed, in providing a service to less well-off people who might have no effective alternative means of saving;

(ii) the total level of saving is increased, to the benefit of the individual and the economy as a whole;

(iii) they have a useful monetary effect in taking money out of circulation;

(iv) they may represent a relatively cheap form of government finance.

Information on the social profile of customers is given in the clearing bank's evidence to the Page Committee.[1] Market research comparing the characteristics of savers with Bank deposit accounts,

---

[1] Committee to Review National Savings: Chairman Sir Harry Page, until recently City Treasurer of Manchester.

T.S.B. ordinary accounts, and N.S.B. ordinary accounts shows that:

(i) All three types of institution have substantial numbers of customers from every socio-economic group.

(ii) The socio-economic groups D and E are under-represented (in comparison to the proportion of these groups in the population at large) at all three institutions. As a proportion of total customers they are highest at the N.S.B., and lowest at Banks. However, because of the greater number of Commercial Bank customers, the total *number* of D and E customers they cater for is very similar to those with accounts at the T.S.B.s.

(iii) The middle socio-economic groups (C1 and C2) are over-represented at all three institutions, but more so at T.S.B.s and the N.S.B.

(iv) The highest socio-economic groups (AB) are over-represented at Banks, and slightly so at the N.S.B. (which because of its greater total number of customers in fact has nearly as many AB customers as have Banks).

(v) Banks cater for a slightly higher proportion of young savers (under 35) than do the other two institutions.

(vi) The N.S.B. has the highest proportion of small savers (deposit of £100 or less)—over 70 per cent of all customers—but even for the Banks the proportion is about 45–50 per cent of all customers.

(vii) About 40–45 per cent of bank deposit account holders have no bank current account.

The faster growing part of national savings, the N.S.B. and T.S.B. special investment accounts, show, of course, a higher income group profile than do the ordinary accounts. There is unfortunately no precise profile of such customers, but the precondition that special account holders should have at least £50 in the ordinary accounts must shift the profile upwards.

Market research and other data show that these accounts are also all regarded similarly as savings accounts, behave similarly, and are augmented similarly, mainly by saving from earnings. Thus, to quote again from the evidence to the Page Committee, 80 per cent of new deposits at the above types of institutions are saved directly from income. None of the three is seen as principally either a long-term investment or a form of short-term saving; the most important characteristics from the customer's point of view seem to be convenience (and proximity of branch), ease of withdrawal in case of emergency, and rate of interest. Such figures as are available show average annual transactions per deposit account at about 4·6, with corresponding figures for active T.S.B. ordinary accounts of 9·5, and for all N.S.B. ordinary accounts of 3·25. In other words, within the inevitable margin of error of such data, all three types are relatively inactive accounts, where money lies, and in no way are used like current accounts. All this evidence shows that clearing bank deposit accounts fulfil the same economic and social functions for individuals as do deposits with the savings banks.

The second objective of public savings, increased over-all saving, may be a good thing, especially at certain phases of the economic cycle. It is, however, just as much saving, non-consumption, whether the accumulation of financial assets is in public- or private-sector institutions.

As far as the monetary policy aspects of national savings are concerned, one is, of course, not arguing in terms of any major transfer of deposits from public- to private-sector bodies or vice versa, which clearly would leave substantial funds to be mopped up or freed. National savings play, however, very little part in short-term monetary policy, and indeed their effect is likely to be contrary to the authorities' current aims. When the authorities wish to tighten credit, money is withdrawn from national savings (1969) —when they wish to ease credit, national savings increase (1971). One is therefore surprised that in peace-time conditions monetary policy appears as an important consideration.

It is difficult to be precise about the cost of government finance through national savings, because few figures are published and, indeed, there is no easy way to determine the most appropriate measure. For example, the ordinary accounts of the N.S.B. and T.S.B. are relatively cheap, and it would be expensive for the government if all this money were to leave. Much of this is sleepy money, however, and this is a declining source of funds. The most recently developed sources of savings and the most rapidly expanding ones are by no means cheap. S.A.Y.E. offers up to 12 per cent, while the latest figures show the N.S.B. and T.S.B. special accounts offering respectively 7·5 per cent and 6·9 per cent. To this has to be added the resource and administrative cost of running the accounts. Treasury bills now earn about 4½ per cent, and 5-year gilts have a redemption yield of less than 6 per cent. It seems difficult to argue that financing the government directly at the retail level is necessarily cheaper than using private-sector intermediation.

I would conclude from this section that there is a very substantial overlap between the functions performed by the clearing banks and by public savings institutions, and that in some cases private-sector intermediation is at least as effective and as efficient. This section has, however, been concerned to examine these matters in an academic light, rather than to argue a positive policy case, although it seems likely, particularly as competition for personal-sector deposits intensifies, such as in a period of tighter credit, that the issues considered here could come much more prominently into public discussion.

Lending

The retail lending market comprises lending to the personal sector and to the small businesses, partnerships, and institutions which are not large enough to be able to use the central markets. It is served mainly by the banks, hire-purchase companies, Building Societies, insurance companies, small financial institutions, and some public-sector bodies such as local authorities. It is a market which the clearing banks, because of the nature of their resources and their customers, are well placed to serve.

As discussed earlier, a large part of the financial market is becoming centralized, with the wholesale sector expanding faster than the retail. This leaves the clearing banks and Building Societies as the main private-sector financial institutions with large retail networks, and thus with a continuing and developing need to generate retail business to match their retail resources. The clearing banks are well placed to offer retail, including personal, credit, and that service is likely to be in increasing demand. In view of the past neglect of the personal borrower, and their need, because of the structure of their resources, to be on good terms with him or her, it was most necessary and desirable that the banks' personal lending increased as it did so sharply last year (by £332 million, 41 per cent, between January and December 1971).

This development is, however, under threat from the reimposition of qualitative control, the principle of which was specifically not excluded in the documents relating to the new system. The attitude of the clearing banks to qualitative control has been that, while not liking it, they accepted it when it was in the national interest, providing it was applied equitably over the whole financial system. The arguments for qualitative control will be examined further, but in the meantime it seems worthy of consideration whether equity is possible—if one group of institutions is essentially retail and another essentially wholesale, can it ever be fair if both are prevented from undertaking retail business? A further problem is that it is difficult to see how any future controls on personal borrowing could be evenly applied over the financial system. There is now much more personal credit about and a wide variety of sources. Suspicion was widespread in financial circles at the end of the last squeeze that the guidance was being flouted.

Given these problems in implementing fairly a policy of qualitative control, there is a need to re-examine the basic case for such controls. On the assumption that the over-all system of control can be run on liberal lines to provide a given total of credit, what is the justification for trying to restrict personal credit more than other credit?

Two arguments in favour of qualitative control appear to be, first, that in conjunction with H.P. terms control, it can be fairly quick acting, and second, that it can be used to guide or channel the growth of the economy. One cannot deny that it can be part of a quick-acting policy, although it is difficult to divide the credit for this between credit or terms control, and one would expect the latter to be the more powerful weapon. However, the speed of action is associated with a corresponding bias in the effects, with certain industries suffering badly—notably the car and the consumer durables industries. These adverse effects have been recognized generally, and are widely deplored. Now that more liberal ideas have been adopted in other areas, such as exchange-rate policy, and there is a general determination to avoid stop–go, one would have hoped that there would be a positive desire to discard in their entirety such disruptive policies as we have seen in the past two decades.

As for the second point, it seems very difficult to find evidence to support the view that, by restricting credit in some areas, such as personal credit, and letting it be freer in others, one can have a significantly easier or better over-all economic situation than would generally be associated with the main macro-economic policy. Clearly, by applying a very specific and intensive credit policy, such as, for example, the arrangements for credit to shipbuilding, one can have a considerable effect on the fortunes of a limited part of the economy. However, a broader policy, such as generally encouraging credit for production or investment and discouraging credit for consumption, is quite different in its nature and it seems difficult to determine what the *ultimate* effects are. How can one prove, or even have a clear indication, that the results are better than if one had not distorted markets in this way? The history of recent years shows that the market relationships between prices and exports, between growth, profits, and investment, and between production, stocks, and demand, are such that these fundamental relationships are likely to dominate the situation. This essential view was adopted in 1967, and the history of the past decades and in other countries would seem to confirm it amply.

There is, moreover, a positive argument against excessive controls on consumer credit. It would appear to slow down the possibilities for change. The offering of credit to the consumer enables him to express his preference through this discretionary buying power. This is especially of benefit when many of the new things which start as luxuries and become commonplace a few years later are bought on credit. In many cases it might simply not be possible to generate the scale of demand which enabled economies of scale to be obtained, if the debt were borne by the producer rather than the buyer. By offering producer credit, moreover, one is more likely to be merely maintaining the established firms and pattern of production.

Thus, given that controls on retail lending can never be fair, the wider adoption of liberal, market-related policies, the general disillusionment with stop–go, the realization that one cannot escape fundamental forces through minor modifications in the application of credit policy, and the innovatory benefit from freer consumer credit, one would hope that the authorities would take the step of formally discarding qualitative control.

IV. Transmission business

Money transmission is a substantial part of the clearing banks' business and it is indeed the facet of their activity which defines their name. It is also one area which has been under some criticism, on the alleged grounds that the ownership of the clearing is a restrictive practice. The oligopolistic element has been lessened by the foundation of the National Giro, which has, however, so far been unprofitable.

Reasonably compact management is necessary for efficient running of the clearings, and it is relevant here that the British bank system is an efficient one, better than any bank clearing system in the original E.E.C. countries, or that of the United States. Whatever happens to the formal structure of the clearings, the clearing banks will wish to continue to give their customers, retail and wholesale, an efficient service in the transmission of money.

V. Other markets

The various other markets in which the banks operate are very diverse, ranging from overseas branch banking to optical character recognition. These markets are probably regarded as growth points, even though some of them may be relatively small at the moment. There are various reasons for this diversification, such as the need to develop new services to attract customers, including multi-national companies, and the need to adapt to changing international factors such as the integration of Europe, or the Euro-dollar market. Some areas of diversification have been selected simply as profitable investments. Others are linked in some way to the banks' growing expertise, for example, computer services, while others have been developed as additional services suitable for existing customers, for example, insurance or registrars. The net effect of all this, however, is that a significant and probably growing part of resources is being devoted to areas of business well away from traditional retail banking.

VI. Conclusion

This paper has concentrated on the micro-economics of banking, as this has not been considered recently in as much detail as the macro-economics. The main patterns to emerge are the relative growth of the wholesale markets in relation to the retail, and the growing diversification of the clearing banks into other markets, such as international banking in various forms and new services. The traditional bastion of the clearing banks' business, domestic retail banking, is both declining in relative size and under heavy and, in effect, subsidized competition from other institutions offering retail savings deposits and money transmission services. At the same time, one of the natural markets for retail banking, personal lending, is on present policies under threat through administrative action by the authorities. There is potential inequity here, and it appears that the authorities have by no means adopted fully the logic of the convictions expressed in 'Competition and Credit

Control'. A degree of interference in financial markets is still contemplated which would be unthinkable in other areas.

Over the next few years the pressure of events is likely to lead to much greater emphasis on re-examining the competitive part of the new policy system. This will include further consideration of the use of resources, return on capital, and the appropriate degrees of subsidy, taking into account the substantial overlapping of public- and private-sector institutions in the retail financial markets. Various subsidies and legal privileges have been given to institutions operating in the retail markets, without these having been assessed against each other comprehensively. Similarly, institutions press for further advantages as the opportunity arises and not against the background of any over-all policy in this area. This situation could become increasingly unsatisfactory and is likely to require further study. I am not advocating any specific policy changes here, however, but it is perhaps preferable to raise these issues before they are urgent, rather than when they are.

Discussion Papers

(a) C. A. E. GOODHART
(Bank of England)

ONE of the pleasures involved in working in the Bank of England is that it gives a close view of the development and birth of long-standing traditions. You will, of course, recall the practice, observed by bankers since time immemorial, of keeping 12½ per cent of their funds in reserve assets. As a keen observer of newly developing traditions, I am particularly glad to be able to welcome a new entrant, the Wicksellian tradition at the University of Manchester. In honour of Professor Patinkin, I would like to start by sharing with you a fragment of what I imagine to be the oral tradition there, handed down over the years, roughly translated from the original German.

Imagine a venerable Professor of Money and Banking, whom we may, perhaps, call Victor Morgan, seated with his students, David Laidler and Richard Harrington, late in the evening of period $t - 1$, giving them the benefit of his accumulated wisdom. 'If you see the actual rate below the natural rate in the evening, there will be inflation before 11 a.m. in period t, after allowing for a variable lag.' Richard, being a bright lad, after a few hours' hard thought, then responds, 'I see the actual rate sinking in the West over Washington, but I cannot see the natural rate.' At this his mentor replies, 'No one can see the natural rate, but if there should be inflation any time tomorrow before 6 p.m., to allow for the variable lag, you will know that the actual rate was below the natural rate this evening.' David pondered all these things in his mind, and then asked what was the use of a concept such as the natural rate, as a guide to the state of the economy, if we could not observe it. At this his Professor stirred and said sharply, 'Of course it helps. Since the divergence between the actual and the natural rate is a monetary phenomenon, it pins the blame for bad economic weather on the Central Bank. Furthermore you may not be able to see the natural rate, but that does not mean that the Central Bankers cannot.

After all, they appear so confident on so many issues, where there is virtually no evidence, such as what would happen in a regime of floating exchange rates, that we must credit them with second sight.'

So much for the oral tradition. Even if the predictive power of the Wicksellian analytical approach is weak, because of the non-observable form of one of its key concepts, it does have the merits of making abundantly clear how the system works, what is the transmission mechanism involved. This is the interplay of relative yields, essentially between the yield on bonds, giving the actual rate, and the yield on real capital, affecting the natural rate. It follows that changes in the money supply may represent a good indicator of the effects of monetary policy under certain conditions, but that the changes in the money supply do *not* themselves embody any fundamental part of the transmission mechanism. The increase in the money stock is rather a contemporaneous result of the interplay of relative yields on desired asset portfolios.

This is a message that comes out of both Michael Artis's and Richard Harrington's papers. This message has, I would argue, two policy implications. First, it becomes quite clear that the attempt to ration credit, or to put ceilings on interest rates, or even to tax money holdings, is to confuse the indicator with the transmission process indicated. So long as relative yields are such as to allow for an excessive expansion, or deflation, of demand, direct non-market measures, rationing of one kind or another, to affect the growth rates of the monetary aggregates will mainly go to affect the symptoms, not the malaise. Indeed, they may allow the sickness to worsen, since the distortions to the indicators may help to relieve the anxiety of the authorities about the appropriate nature of their policy.

Take an extreme example. Suspending your practical doubts about the administrative feasibility of the scheme, suppose taxes were levied on people's money holdings so that they were virtually forced to increase them at a steady rate of, say, 4 per cent per annum, would this help to bring about a monetarist utopia? My answer is no: it would be a distortion of the system with very likely no economic benefit, and quite possibly significant losses. Movements in the monetary aggregates can only be useful indicators in an unconstrained, competitive system. Richard Harrington makes this point forcefully.

The second implication that comes from both papers is that monetary policy, acting primarily on relative assets yields, initially has its impact on expenditure decisions. It would seem to follow from this, and as Michael Artis rightly says the Bank believes, that inflation is not directly amenable to treatment by contractionary monetary policies except to the extent that these deflate real demand, raise unemployment, and so may infringe employment objectives. Monetary policy, like fiscal policy, is an instrument for macro-economic *demand* management.

Michael Artis is worried whether this conclusion really does justice to the gospel according to St. Louis, and I share these uncertainties. He ends rather plaintively, 'But there is clearly meant to be something more in assertions about the relationship between the money supply and prices, some dynamics which bridge the comparative statics gap. It is unclear what these are.' I second his plea for illumination.

On the basis of his analysis, which he says broadly coincides with that of the Bank, Michael Artis argues that the assignment of price-level control belongs to incomes policy. Now this does *not* follow from his previous argument, as he claims, unless it is shown that demand management is not an effective method of controlling wage settlements. In the light, or rather the shadow, of current events down at the mine face, do many here still want to dispute that judgement? Are there many here present who will seriously ascribe any resulting speed-up in the rates granted in this wage-round to the acceleration of monetary expansion in the U.K., or even more splendidly arcane to monetary developments in the U.S.A., during previous months?

If monetary policy is essentially just another tool, along with fiscal policy, of demand management, the relative use to be made of them depends on two main factors, the predictability of their effects and their allocative effects. If effects are predictable, they can in principle be made potent simply by scaling them up. As I understand it, much of the empirical work in the U.S. has been directed towards establishing the hypothesis that changes in monetary conditions have as predictable effects, or more predictable effects, on the economy as fiscal policy. This is not the case in the U.K., as Artis demonstrates. To the extent that monetary factors are included in structural models, their predicted effect in this country is often virtually zero. To the extent that quasi-reduced forms are run, the effect is extremely erratic, and frequently not statistically significant. No wonder that there is some tendency for monetary policy to be held neutral, or accommodating, or gently pushed into some far corner, so far as domestic policy is concerned. We do not understand enough about its working to use it effectively.

Why does there seem to be such a major divergence of experience between the U.S. and the U.K.? I do not know, and I wait eagerly for enlightenment, but I *suspect* that it is largely due to the relatively closed nature of the U.S. economy and the open nature of the U.K. economy.

In conclusion, I should like to turn quickly to David Lomax's paper, though much of it is concerned with arguments put to the Page Committee, which is currently sitting. He can, therefore, hardly contend that his arguments are not getting a full hearing, and indeed the subject is now *sub judice*. I cannot help noting, however, that, after the section dealing with the difficulties facing the banks in the market for retail savings, because of the 'protected' position of certain of their competitors, David Lomax goes on to take pleasure in 'the happy situation that the clearing banks are well placed to offer retail, including personal, credit'. As David well knows, the 'protected' position of certain other intermediaries, of which he complains on the savings side, goes hand in hand with certain restrictions on their use of funds to certain particular purposes. I have no doubt that there will be many who would abjure all such encouragements to specialization and compartmentalization among financial intermediaries, but I for one would be glad to be reassured about the impact of a complete free-for-all on the housing mortgage market.

Finally, I must express some disappointment to find David making the same old standard atavistic noises about the National Giro. It has long been my own contention that the development of the Giro will greatly benefit the efficiency and profits of our banking system by allowing the banks to bow gracefully out of a number of small branches maintained at a loss, in order to meet the local community's needs for a money transmission service.

Discussion Papers

(*b*) BRIAN GRIFFITHS
(*London School of Economics*)

IN 1971 there were three important changes in the U.K. banking system and in U.K. monetary policy: the application of a new set of reserve requirements to both clearing banks and certain near-banks; the termination of the clearing banks' cartel with respect to the rates paid on deposits, and a change of emphasis in monetary policy, away from control of bank lending to the private sector of the economy and toward control of a rather extended definition of the money supply. Both the latter were designed to increase the extent of interest-rate competition in the banking system. The three papers which are presented under this section each deal with separate aspects of these changes. I shall confine my remarks to the papers of Harrington and Lomax.

The paper by Harrington raises an interesting issue, namely, the relationship between the ease or difficulty of monetary control and the market structure of the banking system. Harrington states two propositions quite unequivocally. Firstly, that it is necessary for 'the long-run health of the banking industry' that the banks be competitive with non-bank financial intermediaries (N.B.F.I.), and, secondly, that a competitive banking system is necessary for credit control. Neither of these appears to me to be correct. In addition, both of these propositions are even more confused by introducing the Wicksellian process of inflation as illustrative of the possibilities of substitution between bank and N.B.F.I. deposits and by considering the difficulty of monetary control in the U.K. in the post-war period, when there has been not only a cartelized banking system but also, increasingly throughout the period, an attempt to control the level of bank lending to the private sector of the economy by direct rationing.

It is by no means clear why the long-run health of the banking industry depends on a particular market structure of banking. In comparative static terms, a change in the market structure of the banking system which was reflected in the rates paid on deposits relative to those paid on deposits at N.B.F.I., would result in a once-and-for-all change in the demand for bank deposits, a corresponding but opposite change in the demand for deposits at N.B.F.I., and a change in the level of money income. If such a change were from a competitive banking system to a monopoly, from the viewpoint of profit maximization, this would be in the interests of the banks. One cannot deduce that simply because the ratio of bank deposits to nominal income has fallen, this must be against the interests of the banks. Prior to the abolition of the clearing banks' cartel in 1971, the ratio of clearing current and small depositors' accounts to nominal income was particularly affected by the existence of the cartel, which paid a non-competitive rate on deposits.

The argument that a competitive banking system is necessary for credit control involves a similar confusion. The basis of Harrington's argument is that if, in a Wicksellian model, the banks fix the money rate of interest below the natural rate (as a result of lack of competition), this will be inflationary and will make monetary control more difficult. However, for a given natural rate of interest and expected rate of inflation, there will be a set of money rates of interest which will differ from each other depending on such factors as the degree of risk involved, the maturity structure of deposits, and the degree of monopoly of various financial sectors. The average of these money 'rates' will be below the natural rate only if the central bank is prepared to expand the rate of growth of the money supply. The effect of the banks as a whole setting a non-competitive rate on deposits will be a unique expansion in the velocity of circulation of deposits, but not a continuing cause of inflation. In order to examine the relationship between the market structure of banking and the difficulty of monetary control, it would be necessary to examine the extent to which the degree of monopoly of the banking system affected (i) the elasticity and (ii) the stability of both the demand for and the supply of bank deposits. While Harrington rightly raises this as an interesting question in the light of the market structure of U.K. banking, unfortunately his analysis sheds little light on the answer. Despite the weakness of the analysis in answering the key problem, on welfare grounds he is, in my judgement, nevertheless absolutely correct in arguing that the changes which were introduced in the U.K. in 1971 were a distinct improvement on the preceding system.

'Efficiency, Competition, and Control' by Lomax is a useful

analysis by a banker of the nature and extent of present competition in banking in the U.K. It points out very clearly some of the anomalies of the present system, which although specifically designed to create competition between financial institutions, nevertheless discriminates against the clearing banks by the non-inclusion of banks' holdings of note and coin, the minimum reserve requirement for bank cash, the exclusion of the refinanceable portion of export and shipbuilding finance from reserve assets, etc. Such irrational requirements need to be abolished. While the paper is useful in what it does, it is a pity it did not examine the extent to which competition in the U.K. banking system has been changed as a result of the structural reforms of 1971.

From the viewpoint of neo-classical price theory, the necessary condition for competition to exist in any industry is that there should be freedom of entry. This will ensure that banks pay a competitive rate of interest on deposits, earn a competitive rate on loans, that the price of financial services will be equal to the marginal costs of their provision, and that they will earn a rate of return on capital comparable to that of other competitive sectors of the economy. On this basis, simply instructing the banks to terminate their interest-rate cartel, as the monetary authorities have done, is neither a necessary nor a sufficient condition to establish a competitive banking system. By comparison, ensuring conditions of free entry is both necessary and sufficient. In particular, one barrier to entry still remains, the bankers' clearing house, which is jointly owned by the clearing banks. Along with the other changes mentioned above, the creation of a genuinely competitive banking system also requires that membership of the bankers' clearing house be open to all.

PARTICIPANTS IN THE
1972 MONEY STUDY GROUP
CONFERENCE

Organizing committee

CHAIRMEN—H. G. Johnson (L.S.E. and Chicago) and A. R. Nobay (Southampton); L. Dicks-Mireaux (Bank of England), J. Hopwood (National Westminster Bank), D. E. W. Laidler (Manchester), M. H. Miller (L.S.E.), J. M. Parkin (Manchester).

Professor S. Ahmed	University of Kent
Mr. R. G. Alford	L.S.E.
Professor M. J. Artis	University of Wales, Swansea
Mr. J. Aitkin	First National City Bank
Professor A. D. Bain	University of Stirling
Mr. R. Grant Baird	The Royal Bank of Scotland
Mr. C. R. Barrett	University of Birmingham
Professor R. J. Barro	University of Chicago
Professor K. Borch	The Norwegian School of Economics and Business Administration
Professor F. P. R. Brechling	University of Essex and Northwestern University
Mr. A. J. C. Britton	H.M. Treasury
Professor J. A. Carlson	University of Manchester
Mr. F. Cassell	H.M. Treasury
Miss V. Chick	University College, London
Professor E. Claassen	Université Paris Dauphine
Professor G. Clayton	University of Sheffield
Mr. A. S. Courakis	Merton College, Oxford
Mr. A. D. Crockett	Bank of England
Mr. D. Croome	Queen Mary College, London
Mrs. C. Cunningham	Social Science Research Council
Mr. J. C. Dodds	University of Sheffield
Mr. D. E. Fair	National & Commercial Banking Group Limited
Professor E. L. Feige	University of Wisconsin
Professor G. R. Fisher	University of Southampton
Professor M. Fleming	University of Bristol
Mr. J. S. Flemming	Nuffield College, Oxford

Mr. G. A. Fletcher	University of Liverpool
Mr. G. Forrest	Barclays Bank Limited
Dr. M. J. Fry	City University, London
Professor M. Gaskin	King's College, Aberdeen
Professor L. Gevers	Faculté des Sciences économiques et sociales, Namur
Mr. D. Ghosh	University of Sheffield
Professor N. J. Gibson	New University of Ulster
Professor J. C. Gilbert	University of Sheffield
Dr. C. A. E. Goodhart	Bank of England
Mr. M. Gray	University of Manchester
Mr. B. Griffiths	L.S.E.
Professor F. H. Hahn	Churchill College, Cambridge and L.S.E.
Dr. M. Hamburger	Federal Reserve Bank of New York
Mr. R. L. Harrington	University of Manchester
Mr. F. Hirsch	Nuffield College, Oxford
Dr. J. Jordan	Deutsche Bundesbank
Mr. P. N. Junankar	University of Essex
Professor N. Kaldor	King's College, Cambridge
Mr. J. T. Kneeshaw	Bank for International Settlements, Basle
Mr. D. F. Lomax	National Westminster Bank Limited
Mr. P. K. Marks	Midland Bank Limited
Dr. H. W. Mayer	Bank for International Settlements, Basle
Professor G. W. Maynard	University of Reading
Mr. T. C. Maynard	National Westminster Bank Limited
Mr. C. W. McMahon	Bank of England
Dr. A. J. Meigs	Argus Research Corporation, New York
Mr. A. Milton	Barclays Bank Limited
Dr. A. El Mockadam	University of Lancaster
Mr. A. Morgan	University of Southampton
Professor J. Myhrman	University of Stockholm
Professor M. Neumann	University of Konstanz
Professor W. T. Newlyn	University of Leeds
Mr. A. R. Nobay	University of Southampton
Mr. R. J. O'Brien	University of Southampton
Mr. O. J. Olcay	W. Greenwell & Company, London
Dr. J. M. Parly	Université Paris Dauphine
Professor D. Patinkin	The Hebrew University of Jerusalem
Mr. J. Pattison	University of Western Ontario
Professor I. F. Pearce	University of Southampton
Mr. G. T. Pepper	W. Greenwell & Company, London
Mr. D. L. C. Peretz	Inter-Bank Research Organisation

Dr. D. Pilisi	Université Paris Dauphine
Mr. L. D. D. Price	Bank of England
Professor G. L. Reuber	University of Western Ontario
Miss L. Rodgers	L.S.E.
Mr. A. R. Roe	University of Cambridge
Mr. T. M. Rybczynski	Lazard Bros. & Company
Dr. P. Salin	Université Paris Dauphine
Mr. P. B. Sedgwick	H.M. Treasury
Mr. R. Sedgwick	University of Sheffield
Mr. J. R. Shepherd	H.M. Treasury
Mr. D. Sheppard	Graduate Centre for Management Studies, Birmingham
Mr. K. Shigehara	O.E.C.D., Paris
Professor A. Swoboda	Graduate Institute of International Studies, Geneva
Mr. M. J. Thornton	Bank of England
Mr. N. Thygesen	O.E.C.D., Paris
Dr. P. K. Trivedi	University of Southampton
Mr. J. E. Wadsworth	Epsom, Surrey
Mr. J. Walmsley	Barclays Bank Limited
Professor A. A. Walters	L.S.E.
Mr. B. D. Wesson	Midland Bank Limited
Professor D. J. White	University of Manchester
Mr. W. R. White	Bank of England
Professor J. Williamson	University of Warwick
Professor M. Willms	University of Kiel
Professor J. S. G. Wilson	University of Hull
Mr. J. R. Winton	Lloyds Bank Limited
Mr. A. J. G. Wood	Bank of England
Professor J. Wood	University of Birmingham
Mr. K. M. Woodbridge	First National City Bank
Mr. J. J. H. Wormell	W. I. Carr, Sons & Company, London

INDEX